☆

Interpretations of American History

PATTERNS AND PERSPECTIVES

VOLUME I: TO 1877

SIXTH EDITION

EDITED BY

Gerald N. Grob
George Athan Billias

THE FREE PRESS
A Division of Macmillan, Inc.
NEW YORK

Maxwell Macmillan Publishers
LONDON

Maxwell Macmillan International
New York   Oxford   Singapore   Sydney

The Free Press
A Division of Macmillan, Inc.
866 Third Avenue, New York, N.Y. 10022

Maxwell Macmillan Canada, Inc.
1200 Eglinton Avenue East
Suite 200
Don Mills, Ontario M3C 3N1

Macmillan, Inc. is part of the Maxwell Communication
Group of Companies.

Printed in the United States of America

printing number

2 3 4 5 6 7 8 9 10

Library of Congress Cataloging-in-Publication Data

Interpretations of American history : patterns and perspectives /
edited by Gerald N. Grob, George Athan Billias.—6th ed.
    p. cm.
    Includes indexes.
    Contents: v. 1. To 1877—v. 2. Since 1877.
    ISBN 0–02–912685–1 (v. 1):
    ISBN 0–02–912686–X (v. 2)
    1. United States—History.   2. United States—Historiography.
I. Grob, Gerald N.   II. Billias, George Athan.
E178.6.I53   1992
973–dc20   91–22263
                                                              CIP

For Scott Athan Billias and Joshua David Grob

CONTENTS

PREFACE TO THE SIXTH EDITION

We designed this two-volume book of readings to accompany American history survey courses. Reflecting our philosophy of teaching history, the choice of readings is based on four main assumptions. First, that the approach to history should be broadly conceptual and not narrowly factual. Second, that students should read both the most recent scholarship and older and more traditional interpretations. Third, that students should have available historiographical introductions to shed light on the readings. And lastly, that the readings themselves should be intellectually stimulating, rich in interpretation, and attractive in style.

To meet the challenge posed by our first assumption, we chose selections that are conceptual in character. In each case these selections represent an interpretation that illuminates either a particular problem or period. Despite the different issues or eras presented, one theme emerges from all the selections: the view of American history is constantly changing.

Generally speaking, new interpretations appear for two reasons. First, the perspective of American historians of a given generation has been shaped in large measure by the sweep of events in the world outside the scholar's study. Scholars have tended to reflect in their writings, either explicitly or implicitly, the problems or predilections of the age in which they live. Each succeeding generation, therefore, has rewritten America's past, in part, to suit the felt needs of its own time. In our introductions we have sought to show how contemporary concerns of the age in which scholars wrote shaped their starting assumptions, gathering of evidence, and interpretation of events. From the 1960s to 1990, for example, the consciousness of many American historians was influenced by various social changes affecting racial minorities, women, ethnic groups, and social classes as well as by recent political, economic, and technological developments. It is not surprising, then, to find these same themes cropping up in the writings of recent scholars dealing with earlier periods of American history.

Secondly, the picture of America's past is constantly changing because of intellectual shifts within the historical profession itself. These changes have taken place inside the scholar's study, so to speak.

History, like most academic disciplines, has developed a built-in tendency toward self-generating change. When scholars sense they have reached the outermost limits in applying what has become an accepted interpretation, they do one of two things: they either introduce major revisions to correct the prevailing point of view, or they abandon it altogether and strike off in new directions. Some selections represent the writings of scholars seeking to revise existing interpretations. Other readings, however, reflect the work of a generation of younger scholars who wrote over the past three decades what has been called the "new history." The "new history" as will be shown in the text, differed from the "old," and superseded it.

To address ourselves to the third assumption and to answer the needs of students, we have written chapter-length introductions. These introductions will enable students to approach the selections with greater ease because they provide a historiographical background. In that historiography we have identified certain "schools" of historians, and in doing so have sometimes placed scholars within them in an admittedly arbitrary manner.

Finally, we sought historians who write with a distinctive literary flair. Much of the most exciting work in American history has been done by scholars who have a lively writing style and present their findings in spirited prose. Students will discover how stimulating history can be when they read in these pages the selections written by superb stylists like Perry Miller, Bernard Bailyn, Gordon S. Wood, Joyce Appleby, Arthur M. Schlesinger, Jr., John Hope Franklin, Gerda Lerner, Nathan I. Huggins, Eric Foner, and John A. Garraty, among others.

The preparation of a work of this kind becomes a cooperative enterprise. We are grateful to many who helped us in different ways during the quarter century this work has been in print.

First and foremost, we thank those scholars who granted permission to reprint the selections. Without their cooperation, the six editions we have prepared would not have been possible.

We also wish to thank fellow scholars who made helpful comments, suggestions, and criticisms in previous editions: my colleagues at Clark University, Paul Lucas and Daniel R. Borg; Ronald A. Petrin, Oklahoma State University; Milton M. Klein, professor emeritus, University of Tennessee; Francis G. Couvares, Amherst College; Ronald P. Formisano, University of Florida, Gainesville; Nancy Cott, Yale University; Peter S. Onuf, University of Virginia; the late Nathan I. Huggins of Harvard University; Robert Kolesar, John Carroll University; Sidney Hart, National Portrait Gallery; and Gordon Marshall, Library Company of Philadelphia.

Joyce Seltzer and the late Harry McConnell of The Free Press were helpful and encouraging editors over the years.

For this sixth edition we thank colleagues who read chapters in which they were experts and saved us from errors. At Clark University, Drew R. McCoy read the chapters on the Revolution, Constitution, and Federal Era; Jacqueline Goggin on Black History Since 1865; Sarah Deutsch and Deborah Gray on Women in History; and Douglas Little on the chapter on the 1980s. Colleagues at other institutions also contributed criticisms: Ronald A. Petrin, Milton M. Klein, Robert Kolesar, and Martin Ridge at the Huntington Library on the chapter on the 1980s; Barbara Lacey of St. Joseph College on Women in History; James Hoopes of Babson College on the Puritans; and Peter S. Onuf of the University of Virginia on the Introduction.

Members of the Clark community contributed greatly in preparing this sixth edition. Mary Hartman, Irene Walch, and Edward McDermott, reference librarians at the Robert Hutchings Goddard Library went beyond the bounds of professional duty in responding to calls for help. Susan Baughman, Librarian, kindly extended numerous courtesies. Rene Baril, once again, provided her accurate typing skills. Trudy Powers, secretary of the History Department, also assisted in many ways.

We owe a special debt of gratitude to our generous wives—Lila K. Grob and Margaret Rose Billias—whose love, cheerfulness, and moral support were so absolutely essential to this enterprise.

Last, but most importantly, we dedicate these volumes to our grandsons—Scott Athan Billias and Joshua David Grob—in the hope they will live in a better America, a more just society, and a safer world.

☆ 1 ☆

Introduction

"Every true history is contemporary history." Thus wrote Bene-detto Croce, the great Italian philosopher and historian, over a half century ago. By his remark Croce meant that history—as distinguished from mere chronicle—was meaningful only to the degree it struck a responsive chord in the minds of contemporaries who saw mirrored in the past the problems and issues of the present.

Croce's remark has special relevance to the writing of American history. Every generation of American scholars has reinterpreted the past in terms of its own age. Why is this so? One compelling reason, no doubt, has been the constant tendency of scholars to reexamine the past in light of the prevailing ideas, assumptions, and problems of their own day. Every age has developed its own climate of opinion—or par-ticular view of the world—which, in turn, has partially conditioned the way it looks upon its own past and present. Thus, each succeeding generation of Americans has rewritten the history of the country in such a way as to suit its own self-image. Although there were other reasons for this continual reinterpretation of American history, the changing climate of opinion more than any other single factor caused historians to recast periodically their view of the past.

Changing interpretations arose also from the changing nature of American historians and their approach to the discipline. The writing of history in America, broadly speaking, has gone through three dis-tinct stages. In the first stage—the era of Puritan historians during the seventeenth century—historical writing was dominated by ministers and political leaders of the Puritan colonies who sought to express the religious justification for their New World settlements. The second stage—the period of the patrician historians—saw the best history be-ing written by members of the patrician class from the early eight-eenth century to the late nineteenth century. Patrician historians—often gentlemen of leisure with private incomes—normally had little or no connection with the church or other formal institutions, as had the Puritan historians. They were stirred to write history by a strong sense of social responsibility that characterized the class from which they sprang, and by a personal conviction that each individual had a moral obligation to employ his best talents for the betterment of humankind. Their works, as a general rule, reflected the ideology and preconceptions of their class. Although they were amateur scholars for the most part, many patrician writers succeeded in reaching a high level of literary distinction and accuracy. The third stage—the period of the professional scholars—began during the 1870s and may properly be called "the age of the professional historians." These scholars qualified as professionals on several counts: they were specifically trained for their craft; they supported themselves by full-time careers of teaching, writing, and research at colleges and universities; and they looked to their professional group to set the standards of achievement by which historical studies were evaluated. Their work has been characterized by constant revisionism: they attempted to correct one another, to challenge traditional interpretations, and to approach old historical problems from new points of view.[1]

During each of these three stages of historical writing, the intellectual milieu in America was distinctly different. In the seventeenth century the best histories were written by Puritan ministers and magistrates who saw history as the working out of God's will. Theirs was a Christian interpretation of history—one in which events were seen as the unfolding of God's intention and design. Borrowing the concept of a Chosen People from the ancient Hebrews, they viewed the colonization of America in Biblical terms. They cast the Puritans in the same role as the Jews in the Old Testament—as a regenerate people who were destined to fulfill God's purpose. New England became for them New Canaan—the place God had set apart for man to achieve a better way of Christian living. Massachusetts, therefore, was more than simply another colony. In the words of John Winthrop, it was to be a "city upon a hill"—a model utopia to demonstrate to the rest of the world that the City of God could be established on earth along the lines set forth in the New Testament.

The major theme of most Puritan historians, whether they were ministers or lay leaders, was the same: to demonstrate God's special concern for His Chosen People in their efforts to build a New Canaan. New England's history served their purposes best because it was here that God's mercy could be seen more clearly than in any other part of the globe. To the Puritans, New England's history was one long record of the revelation of God's providence toward His people. Their disasters as well as their triumphs were seen only in relation to God, and

---

[1]John Higham *et al., History* (Englewood Cliffs, N.J., 1965), pp. 3–5.

the setbacks they suffered were viewed as evidence of God's wrath and displeasure.

Of all the Puritan histories, William Bradford's *Of Plimouth Plantation* was, perhaps, the preeminent work of art. Written in the 1630s and 1640s while Bradford was governor of the colony, this book recounted the tale of the tiny band of Pilgrims who fled first to Holland and then to the New World. No other narrative captured so perfectly the deep feeling of religious faith of New England's early settlers. None illustrated better the Puritan ideal of a plain and simple literary style, or mastered so well the rhythms of Biblical prose. Yet like most Puritan literature it was written during the few spare moments that Bradford could find from his more important activities as a governor of a new community in the wilderness.

The patrician historians of the eighteenth century replaced the Puritan historians when the church ceased to be the intellectual center of American life. The Christian theory of history with its emphasis on supernatural causes increasingly gave way to a more secular interpretation based upon the concepts of human progress, reason, and material well-being. Influenced by European Enlightenment thinkers, American historians came to believe that humans, by use of their reason, could control their destiny and determine their own material and intellectual progress in the world.

The patrician historians were profoundly influenced also by ideas derived from the writings of Sir Isaac Newton. This seventeenth-century English scientist, by applying a rational, mathematical method, had arrived at certain truths, or "natural laws," concerning the physical universe. Newton's systematization of scientific thought led many men to conclude that the same mathematical-scientific method could be employed to formulate similar natural laws in other fields. In order to develop a theory of history in keeping with Newtonian thought, writers began to postulate certain natural laws in the field of history. Thus, patrician historians abandoned the Christian theory in which God determined the events for a view of the universe in which natural laws were the motivating forces in history.

This shift from a Christian interpretation of history to a more secular approach was reflected in the change of leaders among American historians. Minister-historians were increasingly replaced by members of the patrician class—political leaders, planter-aristocrats, merchants, lawyers, and doctors.[2] In the eighteenth century, for example, America's outstanding historians included Thomas Hutchinson, member of the Massachusetts merchant aristocracy and royal governor of that colony; William Smith of New York, doctor, landowner, and lieutenant governor of that colony; and Robert Beverley and William Byrd of Vir-

---

[2]Harvey Wish, *The American Historian* (New York, 1960), p. 25.

ginia, who were planter-aristocrats, large landowners, and officehold-ers. Most of these men possessed a classical education, a fine private library, and the leisure time in which to write. With the growth of private wealth and the opening up of new economic opportunities, more members of the upper classes were in a position to take up the writing of history as an avocation.[3]

The reaction against the Christian interpretation of history was particularly evident in the writings of Thomas Jefferson. In his *Notes on the State of Virginia*, first published in 1785, Jefferson stressed rea-son and natural law instead of divine providence as the basis for histor-ical causation. Jefferson believed also that men were motivated by self-interest, and he employed this concept as one means of analyzing the course of historical events. As he wrote in his history of Virginia, "Mankind soon learn to make interested uses of every right and power which they possess, or may assume."

Jefferson's history showed the impact of yet another major influ-ence—nationalism—which affected historical writing after 1776. As author of the Declaration of Independence, Jefferson felt a fierce, patri-otic pride in the free institutions that emerged from the Revolution. He was convinced that America as a democratic nation was destined to pave the way for a new era in world history. A whole new generation of patrician historians sprang up after the Revolution, writing in a sim-ilar nationalistic vein—David Ramsay, Mercy Otis Warren, Jeremy Belknap, and Jared Sparks. They likewise contrasted America's free in-stitutions with what they considered to be Europe's corrupt and deca-dent institutions.

During the first three quarters of the nineteenth century, the writ-ing of history continued to be dominated by patrician historians. The influence of the romantic movement in the arts with its heightened appreciation of the past, emphasis upon pictorial descriptions, and stress upon the role of great men, caused history to be viewed increas-ingly as a branch of literature. Many outstanding literary figures—Washington Irving, Francis Parkman, Richard Hildreth, William H. Prescott, and John Lothrop Motley—wrote narrative histories about America, other lands, and other times, in a romantic style calculated to appeal to a wide reading public. Such authors were often part of an Anglo-American literary culture, for many English historians were writing in the same vein.

America's patrician historians, however, were not always content to provide only a colorful narrative. Writing within a developmental framework, they sought to reveal some of the underlying principles which they believed lay behind the rational evolution of historical events. For the most part, their writings reflected certain assumptions

---

[3]Higham, *History*, p. 3.

that were common to many historians on both sides of the Atlantic in the first half of the nineteenth century—the idea that history was essentially the story of liberty; that the record of the human race revealed a progressive advance toward greater human rights down through the ages; and that peoples of Anglo-Saxon origin had a special destiny to bring democracy to the rest of the world.

Many of these American historians, influenced by the pronounced nationalism of the period, used such broad assumptions within a chauvinistic framework. They felt a responsibility to help establish the national identity of the new United States. Thus, they employed history as a didactic tool to instruct their countrymen along patriotic lines and presented America's story in the best light possible. Running through their writings were three basic themes: the idea of progress—that the story of America was one of continuous progress onward and upward toward greatness; the idea of liberty—that American history, in essence, symbolized the trend toward greater liberty in world history; and the idea of mission—that the United States had a special destiny to serve as a model of a free people to the rest of humankind in leading the way to a more perfect life. The last theme, in effect, was nothing more than a restatement of the idea of mission first set forth by the Puritan historians.

George Bancroft, the most distinguished historian of the mid-nineteenth century, organized his history of the United States around these three themes. After studying in Germany in the 1820s, Bancroft returned to America determined to apply Teutonic ideas of history to the story of his own country. Bancroft believed in the progressive unfolding of all human history toward a future golden age in which all peoples would eventually achieve complete freedom and liberty. This march of all humankind toward a greater freedom was in accordance with a preordained plan conceived by God. One phase of God's master plan could be seen in the way that a superior Anglo-Saxon people developed a distinctive set of democratic institutions. The United States, according to Bancroft, represented the finest flowering of such democratic institutions. American democracy, then, was the fruition of God's plan, and the American people had a unique mission in history to spread democracy throughout the rest of the world. Such was the central theme of Bancroft's famous twelve-volume work, *History of the United States from the Discovery of the American Continent*, written between 1834 and 1882.

Francis Parkman, a patrician historian from New England, held many views similar to those of Bancroft. Writing about the intercolonial wars in his *France and England in North America*, Parkman portrayed the American colonists as democratic Anglo-Saxons of Protestant persuasion whose superior qualities enabled them to conquer authoritarian-minded French Catholics in Canada. But in many other

ways the two writers were quite different. Parkman was more representative of the gentlemen-historians of the nineteenth century who,
being drawn from the upper classes, usually reflected an aristocratic
bias in their writings, advocated a conservative Whig philosophy, and
were distrustful of the American masses. Bancroft, on the other hand,
eulogized the common man and was a Jacksonian in politics; his history was distinctly democratic in outlook.

By the 1870s two profound changes began to influence the writing
of American history. The first was the change in leadership from amateur patricians to professional historians. Until the last quarter of the
nineteenth century, American history had been written almost exclusively by men who had received no special training as historians—except, of course, for a few individuals like Bancroft. From this point on,
however, the writing of history was dominated by professionally
trained scholars educated in the universities of America and Europe.
Professionalization in the field was made possible by developments in
higher education as graduate schools appeared in increasing numbers
in America to train college history teachers. In the last three decades
of the century, this trend proceeded at a rapid rate: the Johns Hopkins
University, the first institution devoted to graduate study and research, began its activities in 1876; the American Historical Association was founded in 1884; and the *American Historical Review* made
its appearance in 1895.

The advent of professional historians brought about a marked
transformation in the field. No longer was historical writing to be
vested mainly in the hands of amateurs—though it should be emphasized that many patrician historians had been superb stylists, creative
scholars, and researchers who made judicious use of original sources.
Nor would historians be drawn almost exclusively from the patrician
class in the Northeast, particularly from New England. Professional
scholars came from all walks of life, represented a much broader range
of social interests than the patricians, and hailed from different geographic regions. Finally, instead of being free-lance writers, as many
patricians had been, professionals made their living as teachers in colleges and universities.

The second major development affecting the writing of American
history was the emergence of a new intellectual milieu that reflected
the growing dominance of novel scientific ideas and concepts. Influenced by Darwinian biology and its findings in the natural sciences,
historians began to think of history as a science rather than as a branch
of literature. Why couldn't the historian deal with the facts of history
in much the same way that the scientist did with elements in the labo-
ratory? If there were certain laws of organic development in the scientific field, might there not be certain laws of historical development?
What historian, wrote Henry Adams, with "an idea of scientific

method can have helped dreaming of the immortality that would be achieved by the man who should successfully apply Darwin's method to the facts of human history?"[4]

The first generation of professional historians—who held sway from about 1870 to 1910—was best exemplified by two outstanding scholars, Henry Adams and Frederick Jackson Turner. Henry Adams, a descendant of the famous Adams family that contributed American presidents, statesmen, and diplomats, turned to history and literature as his avocation after his hopes for high political office were dashed. In 1870 he was invited to Harvard and became the first teacher to introduce a history seminar at that institution. Adams pioneered in training his students in the meticulous critical methods of German scholarship, and searched for a time for a scientific philosophy of history based on the findings in the field of physics. His nine-volume history of the United States during the administrations of Jefferson and Madison was destined to become one of the classics of American historical literature. Although he left Harvard after a few years, his career symbolized the transformation from patrician to professional historian and the changing intellectual climate from romanticism to a more scientific approach in the writing of American history.

While Henry Adams was attempting to assimilate history and physics, Frederick Jackson Turner—perhaps the most famous and influential representative of the scientific school of historians in the first generation of professional historians—was applying evolutionary modes of thought to explain American history. Born and reared in a frontier community in Wisconsin, Turner attended the University of Wisconsin, received his Ph.D. from the Johns Hopkins University, and then went on to a teaching career first at Wisconsin and later at Harvard. Like Adams, Turner believed that it was possible to make a science out of history; he attempted, therefore, to apply the ideas of Darwinian evolution to the writing of history. Turner emphasized the concept of evolutionary stages of development as successive frontier environments in America wrought changes in the character of the people and their institutions. As one frontier in America succeeded another, each more remote from Europe than its predecessor, a social evolutionary process was at work creating a democratic American individualist. The unique characteristics of the American people—their rugged individualism, egalitarianism, practicality, and materialistic outlook on life—all resulted from the evolutionary process of adapting to successive frontier environments. Turner's famous essay, "The Significance of the Frontier in American History," written in 1893, re-

---

[4]Henry Adams, "The Tendency of History," *Annual Report of the American Historical Association for the Year 1894* (Washington, D.C., 1895), p. 19.

mains a superb statement of one approach that was employed by the scientific school of historians.

Between 1910 and 1945 a second generation of professional scholars—the Progressive historians—came to maturity and helped to transform the discipline by introducing new ideas and methodologies. Many of them were influenced by the Progressive movement of the early 1900s—a period when the future of American democracy appeared to be threatened by new economic and social forces arising from the rapid industrialization of American society. Rejecting the views of the older and more conservative patrician historians, the Progressive scholars viewed history as an ideological weapon that might explain the present and perhaps help to control the future. In sympathy with the aims and objectives of the Progressive movement between 1900 and 1920, these scholars continued to write history from a Progressive point of view even after the decline of the Progressive movement following World War I.

Unlike the New England patrician historians of the nineteenth century, the Progressive scholars tended to hail more from the Midwest and South. These Progressives complained that in the past American history had been presented mainly as an extension of the history of New England. American civilization, they argued, was more than a transplanted English and European civilization that had spread out from New England; it had unique characteristics and a mission all its own. But while the Progressive historians were as nationalistic as the patrician school, their nationalism was different in nature. The patricians had conceived of nationalism as a stabilizing force, preserving order and thus assuring the continued ascendancy of the aristocratic element in American life. The Progressives, on the other hand, considered nationalism a dynamic force. To them the fulfillment of democracy meant a continued and protracted struggle against those individuals, classes, and groups who had barred the way to the achievement of a more democratic society in the past.

In changing the direction of American historical writing, Progressive scholars drew upon the reform tradition that had grown out of the effort to adjust American society to the new demands of an urban-centered and industrialized age. This tradition had originated in the 1890s and reached maturity in the early part of the twentieth century with the Progressive movement. Drawing upon various sources, the adherents of the Progressive movement rejected the idea of a closed system of classical economic thought which assumed that certain natural laws governed human society. Society, these reformers maintained, was open-ended and dynamic; its development was determined not by immutable laws, but by economic and social forces that grew out of the interaction between individuals and their environment.

Reacting against the older emphasis upon logic, abstraction, and deduction, these reformers sought a meaningful explanation of human society that could account for its peculiar development. Instead of focusing upon immutable laws, they began viewing society and individuals as products of an evolutionary developmental process. This process could be understood only be reference to the past. The function of the historian, then, was to explain how the present had come to be, and then to try and set guidelines for future developments. As a result of this approach, history and the other social sciences drew together, seeking to explain the realities of social life by emphasizing the interplay of economic, technological, social, psychological, and political forces.

History, according to its Progressive practitioners, was not an abstract discipline whose truths could only be contemplated. On the contrary, historians had important activist roles to play in the construction of a better world. By explaining the historical roots of contemporary problems, historians could provide the knowledge and understanding necessary to make changes which would bring further progress. Like the Enlightenment *philosophes,* historians could reveal prior mistakes and errors and thus liberate men from the chains of tyranny and oppression of the past. When fused with the social sciences history could become a powerful tool for reform. "The present has hitherto been the willing victim of the past," wrote James Harvey Robinson, one of the greatest exponents of Progressive history; but "the time has now come when it should turn on the past and exploit it in the interests of advance."[5]

Clearly, the sympathy of this school lay with change and not with the preservation of the status quo. Committed to the idea of progress, they saw themselves as contributing to a better and more humane world for the future. Consequently they rejected the apparent moral neutrality and supposed objectivity of the scientific school in favor of a liberal philosophy of reform. In so doing they rewrote much of American history, greatly widening its scope and changing its emphasis. Instead of focusing on narrow institutional studies of traditional political, diplomatic, and military history, they sought to delineate those determinant forces that underlay human institutions. In their hands American history became a picture of conflict—conflict between polarities of American life: aristocracy versus democracy; economic "haves" versus "have-nots"; politically overprivileged groups versus those underprivileged; and between geographical sections, as the East versus West. In short, the divisions were between those dedicated to democratic and egalitarian ideals and those committed to a static conservatism.

---

[5]James Harvey Robinson, "The New History," *The New History: Essays Illustrating the Modern Historical Outlook* (New York, 1912), p. 24.

Believers in inevitable progress, the Progressive historians assumed that America was continually moving on an upward path toward an ideal social order. Not only was American society growing in affluence, but in freedom, opportunity, and happiness as well. The primary determinant of progress was the unending conflict between the forces of liberalism and those of conservatism. Thus all periods in American history could be divided into two clear and distinct phases: periods of active reform and periods of conservative reaction. As Arthur M. Schlesinger, Sr., wrote in 1939: "A period of concern for the rights of the few has been followed by one of concern for the wrongs of the many."[6]

Turner, a transitional figure between the scientific and Progressive historians, with Charles A. Beard and Vernon L. Parrington, best presented the Progressive point of view. After his epochal essay on the frontier in 1893—an essay that emphasized unity rather than conflict—Turner's interest turned elsewhere, particularly to the idea of sectional conflict. From the late 1890s until his death in 1932, he elaborated and refined his sectional conflict hypothesis. Turner and his students attempted to understand not only how a section came into being, but also the dynamics of conflict that pitted the East against West, North against South, labor against capital, and the many against the few. Under Turner's guiding hand American scholars wrote a series of brilliant monographs as well as broad interpretive studies that emphasized the class and sectional divisions in American society. Although a few favored the conservative side, the overwhelming majority of historians made clear their preference for democratic liberalism and progress.

While Turner was developing and elaborating his sectional approach, Charles A. Beard was applying the hypothesis of an overt class conflict to the study of American institutions. His *An Economic Interpretation of the Constitution,* written in 1913, was perhaps the most influential historical work of the twentieth century. Beard attempted to demonstrate that the Constitution, far from representing a judicious combination of wisdom and idealism, was actually the product of a small group of propertied individuals who were intent upon establishing a strong central government capable of protecting their interests against the encroachments of the American masses. In a series of books climaxed by *The Rise of American Civilization* in 1927, Beard argued that American history demonstrated the validity of the class conflict hypothesis between "haves" and "have-nots." Time and again, he showed the paramount role that economic factors played in determining human behavior. Fusing his ardent faith in progress with a

---

[6]Arthur M. Schlesinger, Sr., "Tides of American Politics," *Yale Review* 29 (December 1939):220.

qualified economic determinism, Beard made clear that his sympathies lay with the forces of democracy as opposed to those of reaction and privilege.

The culmination of the Progressive interpretation came with the publication of Vernon L. Parrington's *Main Currents in American Thought.* Using literature as his vehicle, Parrington portrayed American history in clear and unmistakable terms. The two central protagonists of Parrington's work were Jefferson and Hamilton. Jefferson stood for a decentralized agrarian democracy that drew its support from the great masses of people. Hamilton, on the other hand, represented a privileged and aristocratic minority seeking to maintain its dominant position. American history, according to Parrington, had witnessed a continual struggle between the liberal Jeffersonian tradition and the conservative Hamiltonian one. Underlying Parrington's approach was one major assumption that had also governed the thought of Turner and Beard: that ideology was determined by the materialistic forces in history. Like Turner and Beard, Parrington clearly preferred the forces of reform and democracy, but there were times when he was much less certain of their eventual triumph than his two intellectual companions.

The Progressive point of view generally dominated the field of American historical scholarship down to the end of World War II. Class and sectional conflict, Progressive historians implied, was a guarantor of progress. Even during those eras in American history when the forces of reaction triumphed—as in the post-Civil War period—their victory was only temporary; ultimately the forces of progress and good regrouped and thereby gained the initiative once again. Such an approach, of course, led to broad and sweeping interpretive syntheses of American history, for the basic framework or structure was clear and simple, and the faith of historians in the ultimate triumph of good over evil remained unquestioned.

Beginning in the 1930s, however, some American scholars began to question the idea of progress that was implicit in this view. The rise of Nazism in the 1930s and 1940s, and the menace of communism in the 1950s and 1960s, led to a questioning of older assumptions and generalities. How, some asked, could one subscribe to the optimistic tenets of liberalism after the horrors of Auschwitz, Buchenwald, Hiroshima, Nagasaki, and the threat of modern totalitarianism? Indeed, had not American historians, through their own optimistic view of history and their faith in progress, failed to prepare the American people for the challenges and trials that they would face during the middle of the twentieth century? Parrington himself had recognized as early as 1929 that the Progressive faith was under attack by those who did not subscribe to its basic tenets. "Liberals whose hair is growing thin and the lines of whose figures are no longer what they were," he wrote, "are likely to find themselves today in the unhappy predicament of being treated as mourners at their own funerals. When they pluck up heart to assert that they are not yet authentic corpses, but living men with brains in their heads, they are pretty certain to be gently chided and led back to the comfortable armchair that befits senility. Their counsel is smiled at as the chatter of a belated post-Victorian generation that knew not Freud, and if they must go abroad they are bidden take the air in the garden where other old-fashioned plants—mostly of the family *Democratici*—are still preserved."[7]

Following the end of World War II, a third generation of professional historians appeared on the scene to challenge the Progressive point of view. They were sometimes called neoconservatives because they seemed to hark back to the conservative historical position that had prevailed prior to Turner and Beard. Their rise was partly a result of pressures—both external and internal—upon the historical profession in the postwar era.

External pressures resulting from changing political conditions in the world at large brought about a major change in the mood of many Americans. Some neoconservative historians reflected, either consciously or unconsciously, an outlook that prevailed in the United States as the nation assumed the sober responsibility of defending the world against the threat of communism. During the Cold War era, when the country felt its security endangered from abroad, these scholars wanted, perhaps, to present an image to the rest of the world of an America that had been strong and united throughout most of its history. Hence, the neoconservative scholars pictured American history in terms of consensus rather than conflict.

Internal pressures within the profession itself likewise brought changes. Particular points of view expressed in any academic discipline seem to have an inner dynamism of their own. After subscribing to a given interpretation for a time, scholars often sense that they have pushed an idea to its outermost limits and can go no farther without risking major distortion. A reaction inevitably sets in, and revisionists begin working in a different direction. Such was the case of the Progressive interpretation of history. Having written about American history from the standpoint of conflict and discontinuity, scholars now began to approach the same subject from an opposite point of view—that of consensus and continuity.

One way this new group of scholars differed from the Progressives was in their inherent conservatism. Progressive historians had had a deep belief in the idea of progress. Neoconservative historians, on the

---

[7]Vernon L. Parrington, *Main Currents in American Thought*, 3 vols. (New York, 1927–1930), 3:401.

other hand, often rejected progress as an article of faith. Skeptical of the alleged beneficial results of rapid social change, they stressed instead the thesis of historical continuity.

Given their emphasis on continuity the neoconservatives were less prone to a periodized view of American history. Progressive scholars had seen American history in terms of class or sectional conflicts marked by clearly defined turning points—the Revolution, the Constitution, the Jeffersonian era, the Jacksonian period, the Civil War, and so forth. These periods represented breaks, or discontinuities, from what had gone on before. For the Progressives, American history was divided into two distinct phases that followed one another in a cyclical pattern: periods of reform or revolution when the popular and democratic forces in society gained the upper hand and forced social changes, and periods of reaction and counterrevolution, when vested interests resisted such changes. For the neoconservative scholars, however, the enduring and unifying themes on history were much more significant. To them the continuity of common principles in American culture, the stability and longevity of institutions, and the persistence of certain traits and traditions in the American national character represented the most powerful forces in history.

Consensus, as well as continuity, was a characteristic theme of the neoconservative historians. Unlike the Progressives, who wrote about the past in terms of polarities—class conflicts between rich and poor, sectional divisions between North and South or East and West, and ideological differences between liberals and conservatives—the neoconservatives abandoned the conflict interpretation of history and favored instead one that viewed American society as stable and homogeneous. The cement that bound American society together throughout most of its history was a widespread acceptance of certain principles and beliefs. Americans, despite their differences, had always agreed on the following propositions: the right of all persons in society to own private property; the theory that the power of government should always be limited; the concept that men possessed certain natural rights that could not be taken from them by government; and the idea of some form of natural law.

One of the foremost neoconservative historians writing in the 1950s was Louis Hartz. In *The Liberal Tradition in America*, Hartz took issue with those Progressive historians who had viewed the American Revolution as a radical movement that fundamentally transformed American society. America had come into being after the age of feudalism, Hartz claimed, and this condition had profoundly shaped its development. Lacking a feudal past, the country did not have to contend with the established feudal structure that characterized the *ancien régime* in Europe—a titled aristocracy, national church, national army, and the like. Hence, America was "born free" and did not require a radical social revolution to become a liberal society—it was one already. What emerged in America, according to Hartz, was a unique society characterized by a consensus upon a single tradition of thought—the liberal tradition. The absence of a feudal heritage enabled the liberal-bourgeois ideas embodied in the political principles derived from John Locke to flourish in America almost unchallenged. "The ironic flaw in American liberalism," wrote Hartz, "lies in the fact that we have never had a conservative tradition."[8]

What, then, of the "conservatives" in American history about whom the Progressive scholars had written? When viewed within the context of comparative history, Hartz said, American conservatives had much more in common with their fellow American liberals than with their European counterparts. Many of the presumed differences between so-called American conservatives and liberals was in the nature of shadowboxing rather than actual fighting, he concluded, because both groups agreed on a common body of liberal political principles. The Federalists, for example, were not aristocrats but whiggish liberals who misunderstood their society—they misread the Jeffersonian Democrats as being "radicals" rather than recognizing them as fellow liberals. What was true of the Federalists and Jeffersonians held for the other political confrontations in American history; if measured in terms of a spectrum of thought that included European ideologies, the American conflicts took place within the confines of a Lockean consensus.

Daniel J. Boorstin, another major neoconservative historian, also offered a grand theory which pictured American history in terms of continuity and consensus. Boorstin, like Hartz, stressed the uniqueness of American society, but he attributed this development to other causes. A neo-Turnerian, Boorstin postulated an environmental explanation of the American national character. To him the frontier experience was the source of America's conservatism.

In two books written in the 1950s—*The Genius of American Politics* and *The Americans: The Colonial Experience*—Boorstin denied the significance of European influences and ideas upon American life. Boorstin's premise was that the Americans were not an "idea-centered" people. From the very beginning Americans had abandoned European political theories, European blueprints for utopian societies, and European concepts of class distinctions. Americans concerned themselves instead with concrete situations and the practical problems experienced by their frontier communities. Thus they developed little knack for theorizing or any deep interest in theories as such. The "genius of American politics" lay in its emphasis on pragmatic mat-

---

[8]Louis Hartz, *The Liberal Tradition in America* (New York, 1955), p. 57.

ters—its very distrust of theories that had led to radical political changes and deep divisions within European societies.[9]

The American way of life which evolved during the colonial period, wrote Boorstin, set the pattern for the nation's later development. That pattern placed a premium on solutions to practical problems, adaptations to changing circumstances, and improvisations based upon pragmatic considerations. Lacking a learned class or professional traditions, the colonists were forced to create their own ways of doing things in the areas of education, law, medicine, science, diplomacy, and warfare. During this process the "doer" dominated over the "thinker" and the generalist over the specialist. Over the course of time this nontheoretical approach developed into a distinctive American life-style—one characterized by a naive practicality that enabled Americans to unite in a stable way of life and to become a homogeneous society made up of undifferentiated men sharing the same values.

The "cult of the 'American Consensus,'" as one scholar called it, made the nation's past appear tame and placid; it was no longer a history marked by extreme group conflicts or rigid class distinctions.[10] The heroes in America's past—Jefferson, Lincoln, Wilson, and Franklin D. Roosevelt—became less heroic because there occurred no head-on clash between individuals on the basis of ideology since all Americans shared the same middle-class Lockean values. Conversely, the old villains—Hamilton, Rockefeller, and Carnegie—became less evil and were portrayed as constructive figures who contributed much to their country. The achievements of the business community in particular were glorified. Without the material achievements of American entrepreneurs, according to some scholars, the United States could not have withstood the challenges to democracy during World War I and World War II. The underdogs in American history—the reformers, radicals, and working class—were presented as being less idealistic and more egocentric as neoconservative scholars sought to demonstrate that the ideology of these elements in society was no less narrow and self-centered than that of other elements. The "cult" of the neoconservatives continued into the 1960s—though "cult" was perhaps too strong a term, and implied a unanimity rarely found in the historical profession.

Besides Boorstin and Hartz, other neoconservative scholars published specialized studies which revised the Progressive point of view

---

[9]Daniel J. Boorstin, *The Genius of American Politics* (Chicago, 1953), and *The Americans: The Colonial Experience* (New York, 1958). Boorstin further elaborated on his views in two more volumes: *The Americans: the National Experience* (New York, 1965), and *The Americans: The Democratic Experience* (New York, 1973).

[10]John Higham, "The Cult of the 'American Consensus': Homogenizing Our History," *Commentary* 27 (February 1959): 93–100.

in virtually every period of American history. The neoconservative
trend, marked by a new respect for tradition and a de-emphasis on class
conflict, brought many changes in American historiography: the revival of a sympathetic approach to the Puritans; the treatment of the
American Revolution as a conservative movement of less significance;
the conclusion that the Constitution was a document faithfully reflecting a middle-class consensus; the favorable, if not uncritical, attitude toward the founding fathers of the new republic; the diminution
of the traditional ideological differences between Hamiltonianism and
Jeffersonianism; the consensus interpretation of the Jacksonian era;
the enhanced reputation of America's business tycoons; a renewed appreciation of such controversial political leaders as Theodore Roosevelt; the inclination to play down the more radical aspects of the Progressive and New Deal periods; the predisposition to support the
correctness of America's recent foreign policy; and the tendency to
view American society as being satisfied, unified, and stable throughout most of the nation's history. Implicit in the neoconservative approach was a fear of extremism, a yearning to prove that national unity
had almost always existed, and a longing for the security and way of
life America presumably had enjoyed before becoming a superpower
and leader of the free world.

   During the decades of the 1960s and 1970s the assumptions and
conclusions of the neoconservative historians were rudely overturned
by two major developments. First, the mood of the American people
shifted markedly as the seemingly placid decade of the 1950s was succeeded by tumultuous events in America's foreign and domestic affairs. Second, within the historical profession itself a reaction to the
neoconservative point of view led to the rise of many revisionist interpretations. The result was a pronounced fragmentation in the field of
American historiography.

   The prevailing mood among the American people shifted dramatically in the 1960s and 1970s because of a series of shattering events
on the domestic scene. Gone were the complacency, national self-
confidence, optimism, and moral composure that seemed to have characterized the 1950s. Many historians were stirred by the great social
upheavals that undermined previously held assumptions. A marked
trend toward racial divisions within American society appeared with
the newfound militancy among blacks during the civil rights movement. The resulting hostility to integration among many whites
showed that American society was hardly as homogeneous as had been
previously believed. At the same time, an increased tendency toward
violence during the urban riots in the 1960s indicated that Americans
were not always committed to the idea of peaceful compromise. President Kennedy's assassination in 1963 followed by that of Martin Lu-
ther King and Robert Kennedy revealed that the United States was as

vulnerable to political terrorism as other societies. There was also a renewed awareness of poverty with the economic downturn in the 1970s, and some scholars began voicing doubts about the supposed social mobility within American society, the virtues of technological change, and the benefits of economic growth.

The appearance of numerous social-protest movements during those two decades also made many American historians more conscious of the importance of minority groups in the nation's past. Having witnessed protest movements by the blacks, the poor, and the women's liberation movement, some scholars took a greater interest in black history, women's history, and in protest groups like the Populists and IWW. Generally speaking, historians became more sympathetic to the role of the underdog in American history.

Changes in America's foreign affairs during these decades similarly had a profound effect on the writing of history. The Vietnam War, above all, divided the American people. Students participated in large-scale antiwar demonstrations, and college campuses were transformed into centers of political protest and activism. Many intellectuals grew disenchanted with the government's military policy and became increasingly suspicious of the political establishment in general. The Vietnam War also exposed the dangers of what one historian termed "the imperial presidency." President Nixon and the Watergate scandal revealed further the threat posed to constitutional government by this concept of the presidency. As some historians grew more critical of America's foreign policy, they began to question the credibility of the government both in the present and past.

During the course of the 1960s and 1970s scholars were affected also by sweeping intellectual changes within the historical profession itself. Some began by challenging the traditional approach to history—one that assumed the discipline was separate and self-contained. Acting on the premise that the other social sciences—psychology, sociology, anthropology, and political science—could contribute to the study of history, they turned more to an interdisciplinary approach. In doing so, these historians applied concepts, laws, and models from other social sciences in order to understand the conduct of individuals and social groups in the past. This interdisciplinary approach could hardly be called new for it had been employed during the first half of the twentieth century. Still, there was a stronger tendency among scholars to apply social science techniques during these two decades.

A second major development was the use of new methodological approaches to the study of history. Some historians began relying more on quantitative techniques in their efforts to derive scientifically measurable historical data to document their studies. Other scholars turned to a comparative history approach—comparing entire societies or segments of societies—to illuminate the American past. Quantitative and comparative history were but two of a number of methodological approaches which were employed with greater frequency in the 1960s and 1970s.

It was within this general context that there arose a significant challenge to the neoconservative historians in the 1960s from a group of younger radical scholars known as the New Left. Like the older Progressives, these historians sought to fuse historical scholarship with political activism, and might be called neo-Progressives. Unlike the neoconservatives who emphasized consensus, continuity, and stability, the New Left saw social and economic conflict as the major theme in American history. Of all historians, the individuals identified with the New Left were the most disenchanted with the course of events in recent American history. As a result they presented a radical critique of American society and took a more jaundiced view of the American past.

These scholars reinterpreted American history along more radical lines and insisted that their colleagues pay far greater attention to the lower classes and minority groups of all kinds. Members of the New Left were exceedingly critical in particular of those neoconservative scholars who tended to celebrate the virtues and achievements of the American people. Because the neoconservatives had excluded conflict in their interpretation, the New Left argued, the American people were unprepared to cope with the social upheavals that occurred in the 1960s. These younger historians declared that the resort to violence by social groups to achieve their goals was a theme that had deep roots in the American past. The New Left historians sought to create a "usable past"—a history that would account for the country's social problems, such as racism, militarism, economic exploitation, and imperialism, and would serve as the basis for reforming American society. American history had too often been written from "the top down"—that is, from the point of view of elites and the articulate like Washington, Lincoln, and Franklin D. Roosevelt. History, they argued, should be written "from the bottom up," a perspective which would reflect the concerns of the common people, the inarticulate masses, and nonelites. Viewing history in this way, scholars would discover the radicalism inherent in the American past.

In their treatment of America's foreign policy, for example, the New Left developed a much more critical interpretation than previous historians. America from its beginnings, they argued, had been an aggressive, expansionist, and imperialist nation. It expanded first at the expense of the Indians, and then later at the expense of its weaker neighbors like Mexico. The United States turned subsequently to an overseas imperialist foreign policy based on its need for foreign markets, raw materials, and investment opportunities. This expansionist foreign policy had global ramifications, the New Left claimed. America had played a major role in precipitating two world wars and was primarily responsible for bringing about the Cold War. The Vietnam War, according to the New Left, was simply a logical extension of America's aggressive and expansionist foreign policy.

The New Left view of American history never attained the importance or cohesion of either the Progressive or the neoconservative interpretation. One reason was that few Americans were prepared to accept either the analyses or the solutions proposed by these radical historians. Another was that the American withdrawal from Vietnam and the economic downturn of the 1970s brought a halt to most radical protest movements. Although New Left scholarship failed to develop the potential many had expected of it, some of its insights and concerns were absorbed by nonradical historians seeking to break out of the mold and limitations of the neoconservative approach of the 1950s.

A more significant challenge to both the older school of Progressive historians and the neoconservatives came from the "new social historians," who transformed the writing of American history between the 1960s and 1990s. Generally speaking, the main focus of these scholars was on the American social structure and the changes this structure underwent over the course of time. The "new social historians" claimed they differed from more traditional historians in four ways: their approach to history; their subject matter; the nature of their evidence; and the methodologies and philosophies of history they employed.[11]

The "new social historians" claimed that their approach to history was more analytical. Traditional historians, they argued, had written descriptive, narrative history in narrow terms, and depicted historical events in isolation from broad conceptual considerations. The "new social historians" declared that social, political, and economic events were inevitably related to changes in America's social structure, and that such events could be traced back to that structure in an analytical way.

Regarding the subject matter treated, the "new social historians" charged that traditional historians had focused on political events, diplomacy, revolutions, and wars. The new scholars insisted that they studied a much broader spectrum of human affairs. Thus, they focused more on social groups rather than on individuals, on the masses rather than on elites, and on ordinary folk rather than on prominent people. They were interested in exploring the consciousness and actions of various groups—women, races, workers, ethnics, immigrants and na-

---

[11]The term "new social historians" was used to distinguish these scholars from an older generation of social historians—scholars who wrote descriptive and narrative history dealing with the manners and lifestyle of the common people that was sometimes termed "pots and pans history."

tional minorities. They concentrated more on the activities of ordinary people and sought to present events "from the bottom up." By doing so, they could view the masses not as inarticulate and impotent with no control over events and constantly at the whim of impersonal forces, but rather as actors in their own right, building a culture or subcultures, creating strategies of survival, and influencing events as much as they were influenced by them.

The "new social historians" argued also that the traditional historians had made generalizations based on vague and fuzzy evidence. Historical evidence, they said, should be more precise and approached in a scientific manner. Numerical evaluations expressed in such vague terms as "some," "few," and "many," were unacceptable. Such evidence, where possible, should be set forth in quantitatively verifiable terms to provide greater precision. Moreover, evidence of this sort should be employed to test in a systematic way broad conceptual hypotheses about human behavior advanced by other social science disciplines.

The "new social historians" focused more on material matters. They were more interested in material considerations such as geography, demography, economics, and technology, and somewhat less in ideology. Institutions concerned with the socialization of individuals—the family, schools, factories, prisons and asylums—were also apt to draw their attention. Their greatest interest perhaps, was in the processes affecting social change—sexism, racism, classism—and in social and geographical mobility. A more materialistic approach, they declared, would lead to a richer synthesis of American history.

The "new social historians" also applied new methodologies in their studies. To reconstruct meaningful patterns of behavior about the so-called inarticulate masses, they borrowed methods from the other social and behavioral sciences—psychology, sociology, and anthropology. At the same time they resorted to different methodological techniques, including model-building and the use of paradigms, and also were prone to analyze large data sets and to use computers.

Finally, some "new social historians" raised anew the question of epistemology: How do historians know what they know? There was disagreement about how objective historians could be; whether objectivity was possible at all; what the relationship between historians and their subject matter should be; and what interpretive strategies should be employed in research.[12]

Several important influences affected the rise of the "new social history" in America. First, French scholars since the 1930s had been moving away from narrow political and institutional studies, and

---

[12]With regard to the issue of objectivity, see Peter Novick, *That Noble Dream* (Cambridge, 1988).

raised new questions or resorted to novel methodologies. The most significant outlet for the work of these European scholars was the *Annales*, a French journal. The aim of this distinguished publication was to break down traditional disciplinary barriers and to create a new and more unified approach to understanding the totality of human experience. Under the editorship of Lucien Febvre and Marc Bloch, the *Annales* became the leading journal in creating the new field of social history. Continuing such innovative studies after World War II, the *Annales* increasingly served scholars who used quantitative techniques or multidisciplinary approaches. Slowly but surely, the influence of this French scholarship made itself felt in England and the United States.

A second influence on history was work in the behavioral and social sciences on history after World War II. Behavioral and social science methodologies were applied increasingly in other fields to attack certain contemporary social problems. Such issues included race relations, sexism, family problems, child-rearing, patterns of social and geographical mobility, crime, and the improvement of educational and employment opportunities. American historians inevitably began to examine the historical roots of such problems and to study them with the aid of insights derived from other disciplines.

A third influence came from the powerful protest movements that swept through American society during the troubled decades of the 1960s through the 1980s. Scholars shifted their focus to the history of social groups that heretofore had been largely "invisible" in American history—women, blacks, Indians and the poor, among many others. By becoming visible in the public eye, such social groups became more visible to historians. Scholars responded by writing history that was directly relevant to the expressed needs of these social movements. Thus, the women's liberation movement stimulated interest in women's history, and the civil rights movement spurred black history.

The fourth and final major influence on the "new social historians" was the use of new quantification techniques and computer analysis. These methods permitted the "new social historians" to analyze historical evidence from previously unusable sources. Before the advent of computers, scholars found it almost impossible to analyze massive amounts of data. Historians, for example, had been unable to make much use of manuscript census schedules that formed the basis for published federal and state censuses. These census schedules, which furnished information about individuals, families, and households in the past, had remained untouched because of problems encountered in reducing the mass of discrete information to usable data. Computers made it possible to collect and manipulate these data, while new quantitative techniques enabled researchers to analyze the information in more meaningful ways. New quantification techniques that made use of computers also made it possible to pose and answer historical questions in new and different ways.

Although the "new social historians" were loosely united in their efforts to examine the American social structure, they did not constitute a coherent coalition of scholars. They were fragmented instead into separate groups and divided along different lines in terms of subject matter. As Thomas Bender pointed out, the groups were assumed to be autonomous, and there was no organizing synthesis to show how the various parts might be related to some whole.[13]

The "new social history" was only one part of a totality that came to be called "the new history." American history as a whole was splintered into different specialties: the "new political history," "new economic history," "new intellectual history," "new women's history," "new labor history," and "new urban history," among others. Some disciplines, like the "new women's history," in turn, split into subfields like "family history." This bewildering array of specialties and subdisciplines was identified under the general broad heading of the "new history."

The "old history," by way of contrast, differed somewhat from the "new history." It was concerned with politics—administrations, regimes, and legislation—diplomacy and foreign policy, wars, revolutions, and intellectual movements in a more traditional way. Its method was usually narrative in form. Its cast of characters often hailed from elite groups: presidents, politicians, and important leaders in public life. It was sometimes described as elitist history written "from the top down." It tended to place greater emphasis on the role of individuals in history rather than on the workings of impersonal forces. And it often stressed the idealist rather than the materialist approach to history.

The "new history" began initially as a revolt against the "old." But as is so often the case, what started as rebellion ended up as orthodoxy. Within the historical profession, the "new history" soon triumphed over the "old." The "old history," once at the center of the profession, was relegated to the periphery.

Despite the differences, the "old" and "new" histories did not constitute mutually exclusive categories. Some eminent senior historians writing so-called "old history" used methodologies and approaches usually associated with "new history." By the same token, some enterprising younger scholars simply applied new methodologies to old and more traditional topics. Nevertheless, the degree of emphasis and in-

---

[13]Thomas Bender, "Wholes and Parts: The Need for Synthesis in American History," *Journal of American History* 73 (June 1986):127.

tent was sufficiently different to justify making the distinction between "old" and "new" history.[14]

An example of how the "old history" was transformed to the
"new" could be seen in intellectual history. Older intellectual historians, like Perry Miller, had been interested in ideas, but ideas largely
disembodied from their social and economic origins. The "new intellectual historians" took a different approach. Many of them employed
a new concept of ideology advanced by Clifford Geertz, a cultural anthropologist. Geertz insisted upon viewing ideology in a new way, as
a cultural system—a set of symbols, values, and beliefs that enabled
members of a society to give meaning to and find order in their political and social lives. Ideology, in Geertz's terms, reflected the way of
life of an entire society, not just the status and thought of a particular
group. Puritanism, for example, was viewed in such terms by recent
scholars like Kenneth Lockridge, who published a study of society in
Dedham, Massachusetts. The "republican synthesis" postulated by
J.G.A. Pocock, discussed later in this volume, was also in this mode.
Eugene Genovese's work on the plantation ideology in the slave South,
however, cited the Italian theorist Gramsci. These new approaches to
ideology changed the older tradition by insisting more on the primacy
of the social structure when dealing with ideas.[15]

Another example of the "new intellectual history" was what one
historian termed the "emerging organizational synthesis." This hypothesis presupposed the triumph of a new bureaucratic ideology
based on the needs and values of large-scale management in the American economy. In some accounts this ideology arose as an inevitable
response to the modernization and centralization of American society
in the nineteenth century. It provided a framework of belief appropriate for living in a mature industrial state where business, labor, and
government were all organized on a national scale. Its practitioners
were scholars such as Robert Wiebe, Alfred Chandler, Louis Galambos,
and Samuel P. Hays. These scholars emphasized that the behavior of
individuals might be better understood when seen within such an organizational context.[16]

But the dominance of the "new history" did not eliminate older
and more traditional approaches that were continued. First, as previously mentioned, the old Progressive tradition was carried on after
World War II by a group of scholars known as the neo-Progressives.
These historians, who included among them the populist-oriented

---

[14]Much of this discussion is drawn from Gertrude Himmelfarb, *The New History
and the Old* (New York, 1987).

[15]Daniel J. Singal, "Beyond Consensus: Richard Hofstadter and American Historiography," *American Historical Review* 89 (October 1986):998–1001.

[16]*Ibid.*, 1001.

New Left, continued to interpret American history in ways similar to those of their Progressive predecessors.

A second development, comparative history, likewise represented an extension of an older tradition that was continued. Comparative historians usually studied the histories of two or more countries in search of similarities and differences in national experiences. Their approach was often transnational in character; this goal was to shed light on the origins and destiny of the modern world. At other times they compared ideas and concepts like democracy, nationalism, and imperialism to discover what effect these concepts had and whether they operated the same or differently within diverse historical settings.

A third development—the Marxist or neo-Marxist tradition—was also continued among some American historians. Many of them were influenced by the writings of two English radical historians, Eric Hobsbawm and Edward P. Thompson. But the collapse of communist ideology worldwide during the 1980s decade dealt a severe setback to this tradition.

The result of all this intermingling of "new" and "old" history led to intellectual confusion, particularly when dealing with subjects and methodologies. Some approached the discipline of history differently in terms of subject matter and studied a major specialty such as the "new economic history" or "new political history." Others studied an older subfield (community studies), or new subfields (women's or black history). Scholars also resorted to different new methodologies, including quantitative techniques and linguistic theories to tackle historical problems. Such eclecticism led to the charge that history had become so fragmented as to be incoherent as a separate discipline. History, it was said, was "a discipline in crisis."

What is the status of American history, and just where does the field stand at the beginning of the 1990s? Fragmentation is its hallmark; any unifying or synthesizing theme is lacking. There is a diversity and disparity of both subjects and methods. Part of the problem arises from the intense specialization within the field. The "new social history" in particular has given rise to a loose coalition of scholars in subdisciplines or subfields analyzing a variety of discrete problems, rather than a community of scholars—a community which can agree on what is worth investigating and how the results of research should be evaluated.

First, there is fragmentation in the subjects studied. Greater specialization, to be sure, has opened up new areas of research, led to new methodologies, and produced more sophisticated interpretations. But at the same time, overspecialization posed difficulties for scholars seeking to maintain some coherence within the discipline as a whole.

Secondly, fragmentation arises from the application of new and different methodologies. Quantification is a case in point. The issue was not over quantification as a technique; it raised instead a profound epistemological question regarding the meaning of reality itself. On one side were the materialists, who sought to prove their theories by statistical exactness, replicable precision, and generalized knowledge. On the other, were historians seeking to restore the role of the individual in history, or to discover meaning through an intuitive personal study of *mentalités*—that is, the study of popular beliefs, customs, sentiments and modes of behavior within society.[17]

Another cause of fragmentation was the presence of two other broad competing sets of historians in certain areas—those committed to radical change, and those who believed in the use of concepts and methods drawn from the social and behavioral sciences. They overlapped and often could be identified with the groups of scholars already discussed. At issue between them were two competing paradigms of historical understanding. The radicals—social democrats of different persuasions—were highly critical of American society and skeptical of its presumed liberalism. They also distrusted the use of computers. They saw them as conservative instruments created by what they called America's ruling class. Those drawn toward the social sciences, on the other hand, relied more heavily on statistical methods, serial data, and computer analysis. What was significant in separating these two groups were four main issues: the character of American society regarding its liberalism or conservatism; the source and scope of theories of history to be applied; the proper methods of evaluating data and drawing conclusions; and the role that moral judgments should play in the writing of history.[18] When writing on a given subject, the two groups often came to opposite conclusions because of divergent starting assumptions.

The attempts by certain scholars to turn history more in the direction of the social sciences likewise led to greater fragmentation. Traditional-minded scholars successfully resisted such efforts for the most part. Many rejected these moves on the grounds that a dangerous reductivism was inherent in the social science approach.

The process of fragmentation was exacerbated, moreover, by the tendency of historians to apply methodologies borrowed from the other behavioral sciences. Social theories from other disciplines—psychology, sociology, and increasingly of late, anthropology—often enabled historians to develop new insights. At the same time, however, these methodologies were derived from certain behavioral sciences that were themselves in intellectual disarray. Thus, fragmentation in

---

[17]Robert Swierenga, "Historians and Computers: Has the Love Affair Gone Sour?" *O.A.H. Newsletter* (November 1984).

[18]Robert Berkhofer, "Two Histories: Competing Paradigms for Interpreting the American Past," *O.A.H. Newsletter* (May 1982).

the other disciplines sometimes compounded the problems historians were encountering in their own profession.

The result of all this fragmentation led to a loss of direction and any sense of coherence. As John Higham has argued, somewhere in the late 1960s the ruling paradigms of homogeneity and consensus were replaced by the paradigms of fragmentation and heterogeneity. He described historians, perhaps too harshly, as a field of solitary gophers, each digging its own hole.[19]

Despite the diversity and confusion within the historical profession, there were some signs that suggested a more fruitful reconceptualization may be in the offing. One sign was the greater emphasis the "new social history" placed on various so-called minority groups—women, blacks, Indians and immigrants—and less stress laid on more elite groups—mostly whites, males, and prominent persons. This change of focus brought about a better balance in American history; it incorporated into the story social groups that had been neglected before. It also emphasized the ties, values, and experiences of family, sisterhood, fraternity, and sense of community that bound together these subordinate social groups and gave them a sense of group consciousness. What needs to be explored now is a new agenda: the relationship of these groups to public life and to society as a whole.[20]

A second sign has been the call for a return to narrative history voiced by two leading historians in America—Bernard Bailyn and Lawrence Stone—among others. Both called on scholars to emphasize more narrative effects, readability, and human interest aspects in their writings. Such a narrative approach would arouse and hold reader interest and recapture the wider audience once held.[21]

A third sign might be seen in Carl Degler's presidential address to the American Historical Association in 1987, when he called upon historians to rediscover our national unity and national identity. This could be done, he suggested, by using as a framework the following broad question: "What does it mean to be an American, that is, a citizen of the United States?" By framing this question, Degler hoped to integrate traditional emphases with findings in the "new history."[22]

To return, then, to the main issue: What is the status of American history?[23] The first answer is that with fragmentation has come re-

---

[19]John Higham, cited in Lawrence W. Levine, "The Unpredictable Past: Reflections on Recent American Historiography," *American Historical Review* 94 (June 1989):672.

[20]Thomas Bender, "Making History Whole Again," *New York Times Book Review* (October 6, 1985).

[21]Bernard Bailyn, "The Challenge of Modern Historiography," *American Historical Review* 87 (February 1982):1–24; and Lawrence Stone, *The Past and the Present* (Boston, 1981).

[22]Carl N. Degler, "In Pursuit of the American Dream," *American Historical Review* 92 (February 1987):1–2.

[23]A recent development in historiography worth mentioning, perhaps, was the notion of the "end of history" suggested by Francis Fukuyama, a State Department policy

form. Scholars, instead of worrying about the "crisis" in the discipline, should take some solace in how far they have come. At the end of the nineteenth and beginning of the twentieth centuries, scholars were writing a narrowly conceived history. This history was conceptualized mostly as the history of liberty on an onward and upward course, its concern was mainly with high politics, wars, and diplomacy, and its actors were mostly white, males, and prominent persons. Since the end of World War II, however, scholars have broadened the field both in terms of subjects and methodologies. They have been more creative, perhaps, than at any other time in American history. This exciting change, to be sure, was achieved at some cost—the loss of hegemony, diminution of the narrative form, and decline in a wide reading public. But as Joan W. Scott has observed, history has always been a changing field, and she concluded that "those who expect moments of change to be comfortable and free of conflict have not learned their history."[24]

A second answer is the possible effect that the collapse of socialist and communist movements throughout the world in the 1980s will have upon American scholars. The shattering events of the revolutions in Europe in 1989 and the break-up of the Soviet empire in 1990 will, no doubt, affect the views of American scholars. We have seen that American historians in the past have been influenced in their writings by developments taking place outside their library studies; we may safely assume that in this instance history will repeat itself.

In conclusion, it may be said that two provocative questions will continue to pose challenges to American historians in future years: Who has the right to write about whom in American history? Is it possible to write a history of our country which is convincing, or at least plausible, to us all?

---

planner. In the summer of 1989, he proclaimed that America and the world at large had arrived at a different crucial point in time that had never been achieved before—namely, the end of history. Fukuyama argued that the two challenges to Western liberalism— fascism and communism—had been defeated, and therefore the ultimate triumph or millennium was near at hand in the form of the universal homogeneous liberal state. The West had essentially achieved the classless society Karl Marx had envisioned, and modern America was the very model of such a society. The other two potential obstacles to the "end of history" were religion and nationalism, but these were troublesome only in the Third World and trouble spots in Europe like Northern Ireland. Thus, the Western world—and the United States in particular—had nothing to fear from communism, so- cialism, and nationalism, racism, or religious fundamentalism, and history would end as the consciousness of Western liberalism ultimately spread and remade the material world in its own image.

This post-historicism had little to recommend it, and is not to be taken seriously. The United States, with its homeless roaming the streets, was hardly the picture of a model classless society. Fukuyama overlooked the fervent nationalism America itself reflects. He disregarded the racism and sexism still prevalent in advanced Western socie- ties, including the United States. Moreover, he greatly underestimated the power of reli- gious fundamentalism—for example, in Islamic countries—which motivated many parts of the world.

[24]Joan W. Scott, "History in Crisis: The Other Side of the Story," *American Histor- ical Review* 94 (February 1989):692.

☆ 2 ☆

The Puritans

BIGOTS OR BUILDERS?

Puritanism occupies a crucial position in the mainstream of American thought. The term "Puritanism" is normally used to identify the religious philosophy and intellectual outlook which characterized New England's first settlers. But as the descendants of New Englanders migrated from the Northeast to pioneer in the West, they carried with them traits of the Puritan mind clear across the continent. Many historians, therefore, have postulated a direct connection between Puritanism and the subsequent development of American civilization. Indeed, one colonial scholar has gone so far as to remark, "Without some understanding of Puritanism . . . there is no understanding of America."[1]

Just what that understanding of Puritanism should be, however, is a matter of dispute. To one group of historians the Puritans were reactionary bigots—people opposed to freedom of thought, religious liberty, and the idea of democratic government. For these historians Massachusetts represents a perfect case study of the kind of undemocratic colony the Puritans founded. Massachusetts was a theocracy—a state in which the civil government was under the control of the ministers or churches. The colony was dominated by a Puritan oligarchy of ministers and religious-minded lay leaders who worked hand-in-hand to maintain a rigid religious orthodoxy and to keep themselves in political power. Resisting change and repressing all dissenting views, these Puritan oligarchs banished independent-minded persons like Anne Hutchinson and Roger Williams whose radical religious ideas represented a threat to the more orthodox views in the colony. The Puritan clergy in particular were intolerant and narrow in their viewpoint. By rejecting the new ideas of Newtonian science and remaining indifferent to cultural matters, the ministers froze all freedom of thought in Massachusetts; they imposed a "glacial period" on the

---

[1]Perry Miller, *The American Puritans* (New York, 1956), p. ix.

28

intellectual life of the colony from the 1630s to the outbreak of the American Revolution.

A second group of historians, however, took a much more sympathetic view of the Puritans and developments in Massachusetts. To them the Puritans represented the torchbearers of religious liberty and political freedom—brave pioneers who contributed significantly to the formation of American democracy. The strict discipline and control exercised by the Puritan oligarchy in Massachusetts was necessitated by the rigors and demands of a frontier environment. Rather than being hostile to science and indifferent to culture, the Puritan clergy did everything possible to stimulate intellectual activity. In fact, it was largely through the efforts of their ministers that the Puritans founded the first college and public school system in the American colonies. These conflicting interpretations of the Puritans and the question of the influence of Puritanism on American life began with the founding of New England and are with us still.

The image of the Puritans down through American history has been a favorable one for the most part. One need not look far for the reasons behind this pro-Puritan attitude. Until well into the nineteenth century the writing of American history and literature was dominated by New Englanders who were themselves the descendants of Puritans. The so-called filiopietist school of historians, reflecting both ancestor worship and provincial pride, identified the Puritans as the source of all virtues attributed to the American people—thrift, hard work, moral earnestness, and a sense of social responsibility. The accepted view among these historians was that America's political and religious liberty of the nineteenth century sprang from the seventeenth-century Puritan tradition.

John Gorham Palfrey, a leader of the filiopietist school, took this typical approach in his five-volume *History of New England* (1858–1890). A descendant of early seventeenth-century New England stock, Harvard graduate, and Unitarian clergyman from Boston, Palfrey deeply admired his ancestors and his work was one long paean of praise in their behalf. "In the colonial history of New England," he wrote, "we follow the strenuous action of intelligent and honest men in building up a free, strong, enlightened, and happy state."[2] John Winthrop emerged as one of Palfrey's heroes, because in his eyes this builder of the Bay Colony had helped to establish the idea of self-government in America. "The influence of his genius and character," said Palfrey, "have been felt through seven generations of a rapidly multiplying people."[3] Biased in favor of the Puritan oligarchy, Palfrey could see few flaws in the Massachusetts clergy and defended the ac-

---

[2]John Gorham Palfrey, *History of New England*, 5 vols. (Boston, 1875), 4:x.
[3]*Ibid.* (Boston, 1860), 2:266.

tions of the ministers against such disruptive religious radicals as Anne Hutchinson.

A few New England historians, like Charles Francis Adams and Brooks Adams, managed to shake off their chauvinism in looking back at their forebears. Although the two brothers were members of the famous Adams family, Harvard graduates, and eminent New Englanders, they took a dim view of the interpretations that pictured their Puritan ancestors as the founders of America's religious and political liberty. Both men considered the Puritan clergy in Massachusetts a tyrannical force—one which fostered religious intolerance, political oligarchy, and intellectual apathy. But the Adams brothers represented very much of a minority view among American historians near the turn of the century.

As early as the 1920s there was a marked change in attitude toward New England Puritanism as historians and commentators began to reexamine different aspects of American culture. The shift in emphasis to a large degree arose from the intellectual currents at work during that period. Disillusioned by the bickering that broke out among the Allies at the close of World War I and longing to return to the supposed isolationist ways of the prewar days, America turned her back on Europe and underwent a wave of cultural nationalism. Some writers began to disparage or minimize the influence of Europe upon American society and institutions in the past. They turned instead to a reexamination of the nation's history with the hope of discovering what was unique and indigenous in the American tradition. It was in this spirit that many writers took a second look at Puritanism.

In certain literary circles the reexamination of Puritanism in these terms led to the conclusion that the Puritan heritage was *not* an integral part of America's true tradition. H. L. Mencken, the social satirist, typified many of the alienated intellectuals who took a debunking attitude toward the Puritans in the 1920s. Defining Puritanism as "the haunting fear that someone, somewhere, may be happy," Mencken equated the Puritan heritage of the 1600s with the narrow-minded bigots of his own day who wanted to censor books, to continue Prohibition, and to perpetuate an inhibited way of life. Mencken attacked the Puritan heritage primarily because he believed it had held back the growth of realism in American literature.[4]

In historical circles the burst of cultural nationalism manifested itself in a reaction against the imperial school of colonial historians led by Herbert L. Osgood and Charles M. Andrews. The imperial school of historians viewed the American colonies as a natural outgrowth and extension of British culture. Influenced by the disenchantment with

---

[4]Richard Schlatter, "The Puritan Strain," in *The Reconstruction of American History*, John Higham, ed. (New York, 1962), p. 30.

Europe, however, scholars began searching for uniquely American traditions—such as Puritanism—that might have developed differently
and apart from our British heritage. Thus many historians writing
about Puritanism in the 1920s did so with the hope of relating the
Puritan heritage to the development of certain peculiar national characteristics of the American people as a whole.

The rise of intellectual history in the post-World War I period was,
perhaps, an even more important force than cultural nationalism in
directing attention of scholars to the study of Puritanism. Throughout
the nineteenth and early twentieth centuries, historians who wrote
about Puritanism dealt almost exclusively with its political and institutional aspects. Relatively little attention was paid to Puritan ideas
and culture. In the 1920s, however, American historians began to question whether they could properly assess the function of Puritan governments, churches, and schools without understanding the history of
ideas behind such institutions. Throwing off the old distrust of the
study of ideas that had characterized much of nineteenth-century
scholarship, historians now forged ahead on the assumption that the
study of Puritan thought was crucial to any examination of Puritanism.

One final development during the 1920s which also affected the
approach to Puritanism was the influence of the Progressive school of
historians. This school had arisen during the Populist and Progressive
era, and, in many instances, its adherents were strongly committed to
reform endeavors. Viewing the contemporary social problems which
they felt had resulted from the inequities in the distribution of wealth
and power in modern industrialized America, the Progressive historians tended to read the social conflicts of their own day back into the
nation's past. Hence they began to rewrite American history in terms
of conflict—as a continuous struggle between the forces of liberalism
and conservatism, aristocracy and democracy, and the rich and the
poor. Many of these scholars also adopted an economic interpretation
of history which colored their view of movements and men in America's past. Some of the proponents of the Progressive school who took
up the topic of Puritanism, therefore, were destined to arrive at strikingly different conclusions than earlier historians.

Influenced by these forces, a triumvirate of scholars—James Truslow Adams, Vernon L. Parrington, and Thomas J. Wertenbaker—
founded an anti-Puritan school of historians in the 1920s which rejected the findings of the filiopietists. Adopting a more critical attitude, these historians pictured the Puritans as reactionary rather than
progressive, authoritarian rather than democratic, bigoted rather than
broad-minded, and pious hypocrites rather than sincere and devoted
believers. These scholars prided themselves on being "realists" and in
the debunking era of the postwar period they found a receptive audi-

ence when they attacked the myth that the Puritans had founded American democracy.

James Truslow Adams inaugurated this cult of anti-Puritanism with his book *The Founding of New England*, published in 1921. Viewing the Puritans largely in political terms, Adams came to the conclusion that their leaders were totally undemocratic. In Massachusetts, he observed, the ministers and magistrates worked together to regulate the public lives of the inhabitants in order to bring them into harmony with the expressed will of God, as it was interpreted by these self-appointed rulers. "In such a church-state, no civil question could be considered aside from its possible religious bearings; no religious opinion could be discussed apart from its political implications. It was a system which could be maintained permanently only by the most rigid denial of political free speech and religious toleration."[5]

Puritanism repressed not only the public life of the individual, Adams claimed, but his private behavior as well. With the ministers and magistrates interpreting the will of God, the Puritan was left with no "free spaces in life." No detail of the Puritan's personal conduct was too small to escape a ruling by the oligarchy. "The cut of clothes, the names he bore, the most ordinary social usages, could all be regulated in accordance with the will of God," concluded Adams.[6] As a historian with a libertarian outlook, Adams resented the conformity he felt had been forced upon Massachusetts colonists.

Adams reflected also the economic interpretation of history which influenced the thinking of many historians in the 1920s. He interpreted the Puritan creed as being primarily an economic ideology fashioned by the middle class to rationalize its dominance over the lower classes. In his opinion the Puritan leaders of Massachusetts had been motivated mainly by economic rather than religious considerations in moving to the New World. Once in America, "they looked with fear, as well as jealousy, upon any possibility of allowing control of policy of law and order, and of legislation concerning persons and property, to pass to others."[7] To Adams the ministers, together with many of the lay leaders, formed an elite class that perpetuated an oligarchical form of government in order to protect their socioeconomic interests.

Vernon L. Parrington's stand on the Puritans was similar to that of Adams, but Parrington approached the problem from a different viewpoint. The first volume of his *Main Currents in American Thought*, published in 1927—*The Colonial Mind*—was intellectualized literary history. Viewing literature as a body of ideas, Parrington read the leading authors, intellectuals, and politicians with the hope of writing a

---

[5]James T. Adams, *The Founding of New England* (Boston, 1921), p. 143.
[6]*Ibid.*, p. 79.
[7]*Ibid.*, p. 143.

general history of American thought. Parrington symbolized the stimulus toward American intellectual history and helped to redefine the meaning of Puritanism in terms of the history of ideas.

Parrington's interpretation, however, was conditioned by the reformist spirit of the Populist-Progressive era through which he lived. Born in Kansas in 1871, he had grown up in the Populist period of rebellious agrarian radicalism. Although his work was not published until some years later, Parrington began writing in 1913—a peak year in the Progressive movement when reformers were fighting to achieve certain goals of social justice within American society. Observing these social struggles about him, Parrington tended to interpret all of American history in terms of continuous conflict. Broadly speaking, he saw the American past as a clash of ideologies between liberals and conservatives running from the colonial period to his own time.

Liberalism was America's true tradition, Parrington concluded, and Puritanism had contributed little to this heritage. Parrington frankly admitted in his preface to *The Colonial Mind* that his viewpoint was "liberal rather than conservative, Jeffersonian rather than Federalistic." In his opinion the history of American thought in the colonial and early national period could best be seen in the figure of Thomas Jefferson and within the ideological framework of Jeffersonian liberalism. Seeing much of American history as Jeffersonianism versus Hamiltonianism writ large, Parrington proceeded to push this dichotomy backwards into the colonial period. To his satisfaction, at least, there emerged a consistent pattern in colonial thought. There was a line of liberalism running from Roger Williams to Benjamin Franklin and down to Jefferson. The line of conservatism could be traced through John Cotton and Jonathan Edwards to Hamilton.

To Parrington, orthodox Puritanism was a reactionary theology. In New England the "absolutist theology . . . conceived of human nature as inherently evil . . . postulated a divine sovereignty absolute and arbitrary, and projected caste divisions into eternity."[8] A succession of liberal heroes, like Roger Williams and Anne Hutchinson, rose up to oppose such reactionary views. These religious liberals and heretics, Parrington wrote, represented the liberal tradition that America was destined to follow. "In banishing the Antinomians and Separatists and Quakers, the Massachusetts magistrates cast out the spirit of liberalism."[9] For Parrington, then, Puritanism played no part in the native tradition of American liberalism.

Thomas J. Wertenbaker, the third member of the anti-Puritan school, agreed with Parrington that the Massachusetts oligarchy was

---

[8]Vernon L. Parrington, *Main Currents in American Thought*, 3 vols. (New York, 1927–1930), 1:iv.

[9]*Ibid.*, 1:15.

illiberal and intolerant. "The sermons and published writings of the founders of Massachusetts, "Wertenbaker wrote in 1927," make it clear that they never entertained the thought of opening the doors of their new Zion to those who differed from them. So far from being champions of toleration, they opposed it bitterly."[10] Two decades later Wertenbaker, in *The Puritan Oligarchy*, claimed that the Puritan leaders had held Massachusetts back and that New England failed to make any contribution to the mainstream of American life until the power of the ministers and magistrates was broken. His work strikes a note similar to that of Parrington: "Most of the contributions were made after the fall of the Puritan oligarchy, and the men to whom the chief credit is due were not its supporters, but, on the contrary, those who rebelled against it."[11] To Wertenbaker, then, the Puritans were bigots who blocked the path of progress in the development of a better America.

The anti-Puritan writers of the 1920s were followed in the 1930s by a host of historians at Harvard University who were more sympathetic and understanding in their study of seventeenth-century Puritanism. Three of these scholars—Samuel Eliot Morison, Clifford K. Shipton, and Perry Miller—proceeded to rehabilitate the somewhat battered reputation of the early Puritan leaders. Less imbued with the idea of progress than their predecessors, these historians did not view the Puritan oligarchy as a barrier blocking the irresistible march of events toward a better world in which freedom of thought and the idea of representative government would inevitably triumph. Rather than judging the Puritans in terms of twentieth-century liberalism, the Harvard historians studied these early pioneers in terms of their own age and background.

The work of these three scholars also showed an increasing awareness of the role of ideas in history. All of them devoted more time to reconstructing the circumstances surrounding Puritan thought and culture. Unlike Parrington, they evaluated Puritan ideas on their own merit rather than trying to fit them into a rigidly deterministic framework. One result of their efforts was that the study of the colonial period showed more emphasis upon intellectual history than works written in the 1930s about other eras in American history.

Samuel Eliot Morison, then a professor at Harvard, published in 1930 his *Builders of the Bay Colony*, a book which proved to be the turning point in this fresh appraisal of the Puritans. Writing in a brilliant literary style, Morison transformed the rigidly stereotyped Puritans presented by Adams, Parrington, and Wertenbaker into living,

---

[10]Thomas J. Wertenbaker, *The First Americans, 1607–1690* (New York, 1927), pp. 90–91.

[11]Thomas J. Wertenbaker, *The Puritan Oligarchy* (New York, 1947), p. 345.

breathing human beings. As he recalled two decades later, his was a lonely voice at the time "crying in the wilderness against the common notion of the grim Puritan ... the steeple-hatted, long-faced Puritan living in a log cabin and planning a witch-hunt or a battue of Quakers as a holiday diversion."[12] Morison humanized many of the major Puritan figures by showing that they were not averse to the simple pleasures of life—sex, strong drink, and colorful clothes—but that their dedication and unswerving zeal to serve God provided them with even greater satisfaction.

In a second work, *The Puritan Pronaos* published in 1936, Morison emphasized the intellectual content of Puritanism. Morison described the Puritans as humanists—intellectual heirs of the Renaissance as well as of the Reformation and medieval Christianity. They preserved in their culture certain aspects of the Renaissance humanist tradition—especially the study of classical literature—far better than the non-Puritan settlers in other English colonies. From the Reformation, the Puritans had gained such a zeal for education and love of learning that they insisted upon founding elementary and grammar schools and setting up a university even while they were still clearing the forests in the hostile frontier environment in Massachusetts. Morison noted that the Puritans were not only vitally interested in schools, printing presses, and libraries, but also in contemporary English literature and the latest scientific theories of their day. The Puritan creed, he concluded, was "an intellectualized form of Christianity that steered a middle course between a passive acceptance of ecclesiastical authority on the one hand and ignorant emotionalism on the other, [and] stimulated mental activity on the part of those who professed it."[13]

Morison's books helped to establish the changed view of the Puritans which was basically sympathetic in outlook. To Morison the Puritans' greatest contribution was their success in transmitting the intellectual and cultural heritage of Western civilization to the New World. While the struggle with frontier conditions in other colonies led to intellectual degeneracy and, in some instances to spiritual decay, the Puritans at great sacrifice managed to transplant those features of civilized life and learning which have characterized the finer aspects of American civilization. The primitive ideas and beliefs of the Puritans, Morison maintained, represented the first, faint stirrings of the American mind that emerged in full bloom in the nineteenth and twentieth centuries.

---

[12]Samuel Eliot Morison, "Faith of a Historian," *American Historical Review* 56 (January 1951):272.

[13]Samuel Eliot Morison, *The Puritan Pronaos* (New York, 1936), p. 264. This work was reissued under the title *The Intellectual Life of Colonial New England* (New York, 1956).

Clifford K. Shipton, the second of the Harvard historians, produced a series of articles in the 1930s whose general theme was expressed in the title of one of them—"A Plea for Puritanism." One of the most militant defenders of the Puritan contribution to American democratic thought, Shipton was particularly concerned about what he felt was an unfair portrayal of the Puritan clergy as undemocratic and bigoted leaders. He rejected the thesis of James Truslow Adams, who claimed that an unpopular clergy had tyrannized Massachusetts in the early years and had maintained an undemocratic hold over the people by means of a religious requirement for suffrage exercised under the old Bay Colony charter. Once the oppressed masses gained the franchise under the new charter of 1691, Adams had suggested, they had promptly used the ballot to overthrow the unpopular theocracy made up of clergy-dominated magistrates. Shipton pointed out, however, that there was no widespread anticlerical feeling in the Puritan colonies. Moreover, once the religious requirement for the franchise was removed, there was no great turnover in political leaders.

Shipton likewise attacked the stereotyped picture of a bigoted clergy that prohibited freedom of thought and stifled intellectual inquiry. The clergy were the most learned class in the Puritan colonies, according to Shipton; they were always open-minded and receptive to new ideas. "Far from being narrow bigots, the ministers were the leaders in every field of intellectual advance in New England."[14] They were tolerant in religious matters, leading their congregations in the changes that Puritanism was undergoing, and making allowances for the theological differences with other sects.

Three decades later, in the 1960s, Shipton was still challenging those historians who claimed Massachusetts was a theocracy. The sources of both civil and religious authority in the colony, he noted, were located on the local level. In the political sphere, authority tended to devolve upon the town governments rather than to remain at the provincial level. In the area of religion, the churches evolved along congregational lines, each church developing its own doctrine from a consensus of the religious views of the congregation or town inhabitants. If political power rested for the most part in the towns, and if the magistrates had to look to the local level for approval of their actions, how, asked Shipton, could an oligarchy of Puritan ministers control the government of Massachusetts as a theocracy? If each church developed its own doctrine from a consensus of the congregation or inhabitants of individual communities, how could historians

---

[14]Clifford K. Shipton, "A Plea for Puritanism," *American Historical Review* 40 (April 1935):467.

speak of the "Puritan orthodoxy" or an "established church" in describing the religious situation in Massachusetts?[15]

The work of Perry Miller, the third of the Harvard historians, constituted an important landmark in American intellectual history. In the 1930s Miller published two works, *Orthodoxy in Massachusetts* and *The New England Mind: The Seventeenth Century*, which dissected the principal ideas in Puritan thought. Miller argued that reason had played a major role in Puritan theology; that the Puritans looked upon man as an essentially rational and responsible being despite their belief that he was tainted by original sin. By holding such views the Puritans were taking part in the great intellectual revolution that was being fought all over Europe—the revolt against scholasticism. "Puritanism," according to Miller, "was one of the major expressions of the Western intellect, [in] that it [had] achieved an organized synthesis of concepts which are fundamental to our culture."[16]

In *Orthodoxy in Massachusetts*, published in 1933, Miller showed the seriousness with which people in the early 1600s took their religious ideas and their willingness to act upon them. He held there was a continuous line of thought stretching from the early stages of Puritanism in old England to the founding of the political, religious, and social institutions of early New England. The founders of the Bay Colony, while still in England, believed in a congregational form of church government, he noted, and had opposed the hierarchical structure of the Church of England. As nonseparating Congregationalists they remained within the fold of the church, however, hoping to persuade others to their point of view. After moving to the New World, they could claim that any church founded in Massachusetts was an integral part of the Church of England—since they still considered themselves nonseparatists. With such a claim to legitimacy they could set up a church and state, define heresy, and maintain religious orthodoxy without fear of British reprisal. The problems the Puritans encountered in putting their ideas of church government into practice in Massachusetts, Miller observed, arose more from their experiences in New England than opposition from old England. Much of what Miller had to say in this work was not new, but he demonstrated as never before that the history of the Bay Colony during its first two decades could be "strung on the thread of an idea."[17]

Six years after the publication of his first work, Miller produced

---

[15]Clifford K. Shipton, "The Locus of Authority in Colonial Massachusetts," in *Law and Authority in Colonial America*, George A. Billias, ed. (Barre, Mass., 1965), pp. 136–148.

[16]Perry Miller, *The New England Mind: The Seventeenth Century* (New York, 1939), p. viii.

[17]Perry Miller, *Orthodoxy in Massachusetts 1630–1650* (Cambridge, Mass., 1933), p. xii.

The New England Mind: The Seventeenth Century, a more detailed analysis of the ideas of New England Puritanism. Viewing Puritanism as a coherent intellectual system, Miller took up its principal concepts and showed how each was related to the whole and to the Puritan view of human beings. He described the interlocking system of covenants— the covenant of grace, social covenant, and church covenant—which formed the core of Puritan theology. Miller demonstrated more conclusively than earlier scholars that the doctrine of the covenant was the keystone to Puritan thought. He argued that this covenant theology made allowances for man's activity in the process of his own salvation; thus Puritanism, rather than being fatalistic in outlook, was a stimulus to action. Some of these ideas he traced back to their origins in Renaissance humanism, scholasticism, and the writings of the French philosopher Petrus Ramus. Running throughout this work was the major theme that Miller had introduced in his earlier book: the transformation of Puritan thought as New World experiences and the passage of time made an impact upon the ideas the settlers had originally brought over with them.[18]

In the second volume of *The New England Mind*, published in 1953 and subtitled *From Colony to Province*, Miller explored his main theme more fully. The first generation of Puritans, he noted, was imbued with a deep sense of mission and viewed themselves as Europeans participating in a worldwide struggle which pitted Protestantism against all its enemies. During the second and third generations, however, much of this zeal was lost, and the Puritans became more provincial as they began grappling with the day-to-day problems in the New World. The original Puritan idea of society broke down, or, at any rate, underwent a profound alteration. Material success within the colony undermined spiritual life; Christian brotherhood and Puritan consensus gave way to personal squabbles; theological conflicts were replaced by political struggles; and secular values triumphed over religious aims. Miller's description of the metamorphosis of the Puritan mind from the arrival of the first settlers in the 1620s to the beginnings of Enlightenment thought in the 1720s thereby became a tale of irony as well as change.

Miller's works succeeded in lifting the study of New England Puritanism out of the narrow framework of national history and placed it within the much broader context of world history. He was able to discover hitherto unsuspected connections between the ideas in America and those in the rest of the world—between New England Puritanism and Renaissance humanism, the Reformation, and scholasticism. In his hands the study of Puritanism became more than a history of the ideas of the New England founders; it became instead a study of an

---

[18]Miller, *The New England Mind*, passim.

important epoch in the intellectual history of the Western world. The first selection presents Miller's point of view and is drawn from a book of readings he coauthored with Thomas H. Johnson.

In the decades since the 1960s, the direction of the study of American Puritanism entered upon an entirely new phase marked by four different lines of approach. The first were the direct revisionist critiques of Miller's monumental work, often by intellectual historians. The second were studies by literary historians of the 1970s, who brought literary analysis to bear on Puritan texts and sometimes expanded upon or attacked Miller's hypothesis. The third were the insights of seminary scholars, who studied in seminaries or departments of religion in graduate schools and approached Puritanism from a different angle of vision. Finally, there were the contributions of the "new social historians," who began in the 1960s writing, among other works, New England community studies to examine Puritanism within a microcosm. This mounting scholarship was not only diversified but massive: between 1960 and 1987 it was estimated that more than 1,000 books, articles, and dissertations were written on the subject.[19]

Generally speaking, Perry Miller's interpretation of Puritanism in particular and his view of American history in general was the main focus of this new phase. The controversy surrounding Miller centered upon his standing as an American historian. By some he was acknowledged to be not only the most important Puritan scholar but also the greatest American historian of the twentieth century. His reconstruction of the Puritan intellectual world was considered by his proponents to be the towering achievement of American scholarship in our time. But in these and his other writings, his stress on American exceptionalism, efforts to provide a usable past for his countrymen, and attempts to link Puritanism to subsequent developments in the nation's history marked him as unique and unusual. According to other scholars, however—especially the "new social historians" of the 1960s with whom Miller disagreed at the time of his death in 1963—he did not deserve such a ranking. Although many critics admired his work, they thought his perspective flawed, his conclusions unsound, and his writings too highly praised.

Miller's opponents were critical of his work on several counts. First, he was criticized for focusing on elites and giving little attention to the thinking, beliefs, and behavior of the common people. His view of Puritanism, it was argued, was unrepresentative: it was reconstructed from the writings of well-educated Puritan clergymen rather

---

[19]David D. Hall, "On Common Ground: The Coherence of American Puritan Studies," *William and Mary Quarterly*, 3d Ser. 44 (1987):193. The four categories listed above are drawn from Hall's article.

than from those of the average laymen. Second, Miller had a reputation for abstract intellectualism. He concentrated on the inner life of abstract ideas and disregarded the social and economic forces from which such ideas sprang. Third, he purportedly stressed the Puritan mind at the expense of the heart, emotions, and feelings. Fourth, he held that the New England Puritans had formulated their covenant theology to free themselves from the strictures of Calvinism. Finally, he pictured Puritanism as being in a process of gradual spiritual decline; he postulated a "declension" of the New England mind and a trend toward secularism and materialism as religious orthodoxy weakened during the seventeenth century.

Intellectual historians in the 1950s and 1960s began challenging Miller's conclusions on all these points. Alan Simpson in a work in the mid-1950s comparing Puritanism in England and New England stressed the emotional and experiential side of Puritanism and argued Miller had overintellectualized the Puritans. Norman Pettit's *The Heart Prepared,* written in the 1960s, took issue with Miller's perspective on the origins and significance of the act of preparing for salvation. Robert Pope, who combined intellectual history and social history in *Half-Way Covenant,* took the position that religious fervor had not declined in the seventeenth century and resorted to a quantitative approach to support his findings. Michael Walzer, a political scientist, used an interdisciplinary approach and employed theories of twentieth-century political behavior to study the attitude of the Puritan "saints" of seventeenth-century England to show that theirs was a revolutionary attempt to change society and politics as well as religion.[20]

David D. Hall, an intellectual historian, emerged as one of the sharpest critics of Miller in the 1970s and approached Puritanism in a different way by examining the relationship between Puritan ideas and the New England social and economic environment. Miller was charged with ignoring the social environment from which ideas sprang. Hall's study of the Puritan ministry in *The Faithful Shepherd* was aimed at correcting this flaw. He maintained that the migration from England posed new problems for ministers and forced many of them to rethink the older teachings inherited from English Puritanism. But, Hall concluded, the ideas and values derived from the mother country were probably more influential in shaping the New England ministers than the New World frontier environment. Hall, in a separate historiographical article written in 1970, summarized some of the critical reaction to Miller—focusing on a different aspect—the rela-

---

[20]Alan Simpson, *Puritanism in Old and New England* (Chicago, 1955); Norman Pettit, *The Heart Prepared* (New Haven, 1966); Robert G. Pope, *The Half-Way Covenant* (Princeton, 1969); and Michael Walzer, *Revolution of the Saints* (Cambridge, 1965).

tionship between Puritanism and Calvinism which Miller had portrayed.[21]

Many other intellectual historians challenged Miller's interpretation on different grounds in the 1970s. Robert Middlekauff, for example, in a thoughtful multiple biography of members of the Mather family disagreed with Miller's depiction of a "declension" in the Puritan sense of mission. Examining three generations of Mathers—Richard, Increase, and Cotton—Middlekauff found a different pattern, one which showed a spiritual strengthening and growing piety over time.[22]

The decade of the 1980s brought to a climax the work of intellectual historians on Miller's structure of interpretation. These scholars centered their attention on two features in particular: the idea of "declension" and an examination of lay or "popular" religious beliefs of the people in New England. Some of these themes, among others, were taken up in a symposium on Miller held in 1982 by James Hoopes of Babson College.

Hoopes, a supporter of Miller, sought to show that the corpus of Miller's work had an internal coherence that had not been grasped completely by the critics. *The New England Mind*, organized topically, had been scored for the supposed two-way tension existing between piety and intellect and between intellectual history and social analysis. But Hoopes pointed out there was a continuity between this volume and *From Colony to Province*, which was organized chronologically and published some fourteen years later. The two books had to be read all of a piece, Hoopes maintained. In *From Colony to Province* Miller explored the transformation of ideas that resulted in changes in seventeenth-century Massachusetts society and demonstrated that the early Puritan belief system was ill-suited to serve the needs of new social patterns.[23]

Hoopes's symposium included such scholars as David D. Hall, Joyce Appleby, P. M. G. Harris, and Margaret Sobczak, many of whom attacked Miller's idea of "declension." Although it settled nothing, this discussion made it clear that the dispute over Miller and his scholarly achievement, though not as secure as it once had been, would continue for the foreseeable future.[24]

---

[21]David D. Hall, *The Faithful Shepherd* (Chapel Hill, 1972); and Hall's essay "Understanding the Puritans," in Herbert J. Bass, ed., *The State of American History* (Chicago, 1970), pp. 330–349.

[22]Robert Middlekauff, *The Mathers* (New York, 1972).

[23]James Hoopes, "Art as History: Perry Miller's *New England Mind*," *American Quarterly* 34 (1982):3–25.

[24]Joyce Appleby, "History as Art: Another View"; David D. Hall, "A Reader's Guide to the New England Mind: The Seventeenth Century"; P. M. G. Harris, "Of Two Minds, Falsely Sundered: Faith and Reason, Duality and Complexity, Art and Science in Perry Miller and in Puritan New England"; and Margaret Sobczak, "Hoopes' Symposium on Perry Miller"; *ibid.*, pp. 25–48.

This conclusion became more evident when another scholar, Francis T. Butts, came to Miller's defense in 1982. Butts in an article claimed that much of the revisionist criticism of Miller was based on a caricature rather than on a true understanding of Miller's philosophical assumptions and his perspective of the monumental meaning of Puritanism in American history. This stereotyped view of Miller had become the conventional wisdom among historians, Butts maintained, and was based on a misunderstanding of the master's work.[25]

Miller, in his *New England Mind*, in particular, had treated Puritan literature as though it were the product of a single homogeneous group. Philip Gura, like others before him, noted the well-known presence of prominent dissenters from the tradition. Such persons as Roger Williams and Anne Hutchinson and such groups as Quakers, certain Baptist sects, and some millenarians constituted a long line of radicals who were just as Puritan as John Winthrop's mainstream orthodox establishment. The second selection in this chapter is from Gura's book, *A Glimpse of Sion's Glory*.[26]

Other intellectual historians attacked the Miller thesis from a different point of view. Theodore D. Bozeman in *To Live Ancient Lives* provided an important corrective to Miller's "errand" hypothesis. Miller had argued in his influential essay "Errand into the Wilderness" that the Massachusetts Bay Colony was to be a shining example by the Puritans to save England from its excesses by providing a more perfect model society. A careful reading of the primary sources, taking seriously the Puritans' own words, and appreciating their Biblical primitivism, Bozeman held, failed to justify such a conclusion.[27]

Some intellectual historians, like David D. Hall, focused upon the lay or popular beliefs of New Englanders and thereby indirectly attacked Miller's more formal, organized cosmology of Puritanism. In *Worlds of Wonder, Days of Judgment*, Hall studied the English popular culture of the day to arrive at a wider understanding of the religious culture of New England. He analyzed such matters as folk beliefs, the appeal of "magic," the popular "wonder" books of the era, rates of literacy, and common rituals of the conversion process to show how their role in shaping the religious beliefs in America was much broader than the definition of Puritanism Miller had employed. By revealing the impact of such matters on New England culture, Hall showed that orga-

[25]Francis T. Butts, "The Myth of Perry Miller," *American Historical Review* 87 (1982): 665–694. For a penetrating critique of Miller which points out some fundamental flaws in his work, see Arihu Zakai, "'Epiphany in Matadi': Perry Miller's *Orthodoxy in Massachusetts* and The Meaning of American History," *Reviews in American History* 13 (1985):627–640.

[26]Philip Gura, *A Glimpse of Sion's Glory* (Middletown, Conn., 1984).

[27]Theodore D. Bozeman, *To Live Ancient Lives* (Chapel Hill, 1988).

nized religion was only one way in which the Puritans viewed their place in the cosmos.[28]

By introducing popular culture into the religious perspective, Hall completely changed the parameters of the debate about Puritanism. The corpus of Miller's work was defended, extended, and criticized by other intellectual historians too numerous to mention except for a few. Harry S. Stout read several thousand sermons in manuscript and showed that Miller's picture of the pervasiveness of Puritanism in New England society and culture held up, though he disagreed with many of Miller's assumptions. Norman Fiering suggested that the inner life of New Englanders developed over a long time, and that new theories of the mind led to a more subjective life which subsequently gave rise to more complicated theories. James Hoopes, though not addressing Miller directly, formulated a view of conversion (the crucial event in Puritan life as self-interpretation), and sought to connect Puritanism with some of the more modern notions of self. Charles L. Cohen likewise analyzed the conversion experience along the lines of self-interpretation. His work, like that of Stout, Fiering, Hoopes, Bozeman, and others showed that the intellectual history approach which had generally fallen into disrepute proved to be one of the most fruitful perspectives employed in the study of Puritanism throughout the 1980s.[29]

A second line of approach was taken by the so-called seminary scholars who were better versed in Biblical scripture and Christian doctrine. Many of them focused more on the relationship between Puritanism and Calvinism and looked more carefully at the doctrinal history that served as a background for Puritan thought. Generally speaking, these seminary scholars reconstructed the history of doctrine along lines quite different from those of Miller. Miller's view of Calvinism was more static in conception; the seminary scholars, on the other hand, saw Calvinism as more ambivalent, derived from far more sources, and capable of changing and growing.[30]

Miller viewed Puritanism as a compromise with Calvinism, and a tradition that steadily deteriorated through internal decay during the seventeenth century. Many seminary scholars—several working at Yale in the 1970s—saw ambivalence rather than compromise and continuity rather than change. William Stoever in the 1970s pointed out that this meant, among other things, a different view of covenant the-

---

[28]David D. Hall, *Worlds of Wonder, Days of Judgment* (Knopf, 1989).

[29]Harry S. Stout, *The New England Soul* (New York, 1986); Norman Fiering, *Moral Philosophy at Seventeenth-Century Harvard* (Chapel Hill, 1981); James Hoopes, *Consciousness in New England* (Baltimore, 1989); and Charles L. Cohen, *God's Caress* (New York, 1986).

[30]David D. Hall, "Religion and Society: Problems and Reconsiderations," in Jack P. Greene and J.R. Pole, eds., *Colonial British America* (Baltimore, 1984), p. 325.

ology than the one Miller had postulated. E. Brooks Holifield was even more convinced about change within Calvinism. His description of the doctrine of baptism showed a persistent ambivalence rather than compromise. Holifield, in discovering a sacramental renaissance among ministers in the late seventeenth century, likewise challenged Miller's idea of "declension."[31]

Michael McGiffert, a knowledgeable historian of religion, took a different tack. His interpretation harked back to the English origins of covenant theology. He showed in two key articles how preachers in Elizabethan England groped their way to new concepts of the covenant of grace and the covenant of works in the late seventeenth century.[32]

The third line of approach was much more novel in terms of its methodology; it involved the work of literary historians who took a predominantly literary approach to religious and social phenomena. These scholars brought about a dramatic change in the understanding of the Puritan imagination and the relationship between literature and ideas by resorting to developments in theory such as deconstruction and semiotics. They tended to view New England in holistic terms, and they suggested that the ideas developed in the region paralleled the development of society itself. In this regard, they postulated the hypothesis that Puritanism had given rise to a powerful myth: the myth of New England as the place God had chosen to create His millennial kingdom on earth as the New Jerusalem. The self-identity of New England as a separate and exceptional place, in other words, was derived from the American Puritan vision. This regional self-identity gave way to the national myth—the concept of American exceptionalism: the idea that America was unique and fundamentally different from Europe and the rest of the world. Perry Miller himself, of course, had been an exemplar of American exceptionalism, and many literary scholars drew their inspiration from him.

Sacvan Bercovitch, perhaps better than any other literary scholar, expanded upon Miller's notion of a Puritan mission and the concept of American identity. In his *Puritan Origins of the American Self,* Bercovitch explored the essence of Puritan rhetoric through literary analysis of the language, symbolism, and myth. He viewed Cotton Mather's method in *Magnalia Christi Americana* as being symptomatic of the movement from colonial to national identity. To Bercovitch the early

---

[31]William Stoever, *'A Faire and Easie Way to Heaven'* (Middletown, Conn., 1978); and E. Brooks Holifield, *The Covenant Sealed* (New Haven, 1974).

[32]Michael McGiffert, "Grace and Works: The Rise and Division of Covenant Theology in Elizabethan Puritanism," *Harvard Theological Review* 75 (1982):463–502; and "Tyndale's Conception of Covenant," *Journal of Ecclesiastical History* 32 (1981):167–184.

See also the important work of another historian of religion, Charles Hambrick-Stowe, *The Practice of Piety* (Chapel Hill, 1980)

New England rhetoric provided the framework for the inversion of subsequent secular values with which America later became identified—human perfectibility, technological progress, and democracy—and the writings of American literary giants like Ralph Waldo Emerson.[33]

Bercovitch in *The American Jeremiad* revised Miller's somewhat pessimistic view of the jeremiad, or political sermon, to explain how the Puritans saw their place in God's design of the world. Where Miller stressed the darker side of the jeremiad, Bercovitch concluded that the Puritan cry of "declension" was part of a strategy designed to revitalize the idea of an "errand into the wilderness." Where Miller saw decline in the seventeenth century, Bercovitch argued that Puritanism succeeded in giving rise to a "myth" of an American mission that gave meaning not only to New England in the eighteenth century but to the entire nation in the nineteenth and twentieth centuries.

The concept of a chosen people with a national mission, manifest destiny, and promise of a redemptive future which in the eyes of many historians has characterized American middle-class culture was derived in large part from Puritan jeremiads, according to Bercovitch. Even more than Miller, Bercovitch found modernity and the meaning of America rooted in the Puritan past. Some scholars, however, felt that Bercovitch's strong emphasis on the jeremiad went too far and was not always convincing.[34] Bozeman's book, *To Live Ancient Lives*, for example, sided more closely with Miller's view of the jeremiad than Bercovitch's interpretation which suggested that Puritan millennialism was "there at the creation," so to speak.

Patricia Caldwell, a literary scholar and student of Miller's disciple Alan Heimert, used the tools of her discipline in the 1980s to reinforce the Miller thesis concerning the importance of the Puritan conversion experience. She, too, supported the concept of a Puritan literary tradition that served as the foundation for a distinctly American literature. Her thesis in this regard was reflected in the subtitle of her book *The Beginnings of American Expression.*[35]

Literary scholars did not always agree with Miller. Andrew Delbanco, for example, denied that there was any grand "errand" or journey toward the millennium in the minds of the Puritans when they came to America. The Puritans, according to him, were fleeing the chaos they found in England and in themselves.[36] Although literary

---

[33]Sacvan Bercovitch, *Puritan Origins of the American Self* (New Haven, 1975).

[34]Sacvan Bercovitch, *The American Jeremiad* (Madison, 1978). For a searching review essay from which much of this discussion is drawn, see Gordon S. Wood, "Struggle Over the Puritans," *New York Review of Books,* Nov. 8, 1989.

[35]Patricia Caldwell, *The Puritan Conversion Narrative: The Beginnings of American Expression* (New York, 1983).

[36]Andrew Delbanco, *Puritan Ordeal* (Cambridge, 1989).

scholars like Lazar Ziff, Emory Elliott, and Everett Emerson, often disagreed among themselves in their approach to Miller, they did succeed in casting a new light on Puritanism from a different perspective.

The fourth and final major development in Puritan studies was the appearance of the "new social historians" from the 1960s on. They rejected Miller's intellectual history approach that claimed the early history of New England could be strung "on the thread of an idea." These scholars often resorted instead to the study of secular records— wills, deeds, tax lists, town records, and registers of births, marriages, and deaths—to reconstruct the building of Puritan communities or to arrive at communitarian values. They were more interested in re-creating the lives of the common people who rarely left behind written records.

By subjecting secular, nontraditional sources to statistical analyses, interdisciplinary approaches, and different paradigms, the "new social historians" proceeded to write New England's local history of Puritanism along different lines. Taking their lead from the French *Annales* scholars, they were convinced history should be written more from the bottom up, be more precise in its conclusions, and resort to insights from other disciplines such as social psychology, historical demography, and cultural anthropology. Many shared a common approach: they explored the structure and character of New England society by a close examination of the experiences of persons, families, and groups within particular communities, localities, or regions.

A whole host of community studies of New England written between the 1960s and the end of the 1980s analyzed the impact of Puritanism on the everyday life of the early settlers. Sumner Chilton Powell's *Puritan Village*, for instance, demonstrated that local English institutions were transformed by the Puritans to produce a new kind of community in Sudbury, Massachusetts. What was transplanted was transformed. David Grayson Allen took a different point of view and showed the persistence of English laws and customs in the New World in his *In English Ways*.[37]

Kenneth Lockridge traced the evolution of local institutions in Dedham, Massachusetts over a one-hundred-year period. He concluded that the town during its first fifty years was a "Christian Utopian Closed Corporate community." But in the second fifty years, conflicts

---

[37]Sumner Chilton Powell, *Puritan Village* (Middletown, Conn., 1963) and David Grayson Allen, *In English Ways* (Chapel Hill, 1981). The literature on Puritan community studies is voluminous, and the studies cited are merely representative of certain theses or generalizations. Among the first of the community studies to challenge Miller's findings directly was Darrett Rutman, *Winthrop's Boston* (Chapel Hill, 1965). See also his *American Puritanism: Faith and Practice* (Philadelphia, 1970).

eroded the prevailing consensus, shattered the Puritan vision of a perfect society, and gave rise to a modern provincial town.[38]

In their study of witchcraft in seventeenth-century Massachusetts, *Salem Possessed*, Paul Boyer and Stephen Nissenbaum investigated the tensions that arose as the result of the growing gap between Puritan ideals and social realities. Major problems developed in Salem because of the emerging merchant capitalism resulting from rising commercialism, the explosive rate of population growth, and the decreasing availability of land. All these material developments coupled with the prevailing traditional peasant world outlook conflicted with accepted Puritan values. The outbreak of witchcraft hysteria, according to Boyer and Nissenbaum, was caused by these conflicts rather than by the Puritan dogmatism and bigotry stressed in the older and more traditional interpretations.[39]

Some "new social historians" employed a larger-sized model than a small town when analyzing the impact of Puritanism. Gregory H. Nobles in his study of Hampshire County, Massachusetts, synthesized his findings of the individual towns on the county level to analyze changes in the social structures of this frontier region from 1740 to 1775. Among other things, he discovered a desire by the populace to recreate the accepted patterns of English society—including the formal institutions and restraining forces of Puritanism. Both the elites—rulers of the towns—and the ruled, or common people, shared a belief in a hierarchical social order. The county oligarchy that developed, therefore, rested upon popular support. Although the Great Awakening of the 1740s and the "population explosion" of the 1760s shook the county hierarchy—the ministers and magistrates—this political structure, albeit reshaped, remained fundamentally unaltered. David T. Konig's study of Essex County, Massachusetts, in the seventeenth century, presented a similar microstudy on the regional level, emphasizing the relationship between the law and Puritan society.[40]

But there was increasing disenchantment with the large number of community studies that had appeared by the end of the 1980s. Although the studies were interesting individually, there was growing skepticism about their offering collectively much in the way of new generalizations about Puritanism, or about anything else for that matter. No community could be taken as being typical of a region or colony or as representative of the American colonies as a whole. As Darrett Rutman pointed out, moreover, American colonial historians

---

[38]Kenneth Lockridge, *A New England Town* (New York, 1970).

[39]Paul Boyer and Stephen Nissenbaum, *Salem Possessed* (Cambridge, 1979).

[40]Gregory H. Nobles, *Divisions throughout the Whole* (Cambridge, 1983), and David T. Konig, *Law and Society in Puritan Massachusetts, Essex County, 1629–1692* (Chapel Hill, 1982).

assumed that Puritanism led to communal cohesiveness, while English historians saw Puritans as being a divisive force in the villages of the mother country. Thus, the definition of the term "Puritan" itself came under question. To use community studies to discover more about Puritanism, Rutman concluded, "new social historians" would have to explore outward linkages—economic, governmental, political, religious and intellectual—between individual communities and surrounding places.[41]

Studies of the colonial family by the "new social historians" also provided important insights into the Puritan value system and behavior. John Demos in his study of the Plymouth colony in the seventeenth century, *A Little Commonwealth*, pioneered an exploration of Puritan child-rearing practices, and resorted to the techniques of demography, social psychology, and archeology to arrive at his conclusions. Philip Greven in *Four Generations* argued, as did Demos, that the family was the key institution in socializing the individual within the Puritan community. Greven studied changes within the family household and community structure in Andover, Massachusetts over four generations, and concluded that landholding practices, geographic mobility, birth-and-death rates, marriage customs, and intergenerational relationships all helped to shape the outlines of this Puritan town in new ways.[42]

Other "new social historians" employed interdisciplinary approaches to show how the Puritans stressed consensus and conformity to build communities on the basis of such values. Kai T. Erikson, for example, used sociological and psychological theories to analyze Puritan values. Erikson studied those groups that Puritans defined as deviants, and then sought to establish the social norms that constituted the "boundaries" of acceptable behavior within Puritan society. Michael Zuckerman, on the other hand, applied the conceptual tools of cultural anthropology. He concluded that a kind of communal consensus created peace, order, and harmony within a number of eighteenth-century towns based in part on a carry-over of Puritan cultural ideals. These communities remained "peaceable kingdoms" until the eve of the Revolution, according to Zuckerman, despite underlying social tensions.[43]

---

[41]Darrett Rutman, "Assessing the Communities of Early America." *William and Mary Quarterly*, 3rd ser. (1986): pp. 163–178.

[42]John Demos, *A Little Commonwealth* (New York, 1970), and Philip Greven, *Four Generations* (Ithaca, 1970).

The work on this subject by the "new social historians" was preceded by Edmund S. Morgan's insightful *Puritan Family* (Boston, 1944). Morgan wrote brilliantly on many aspects of Puritanism and generally was sympathetic to Miller's point of view.

[43]Kai T. Erikson, *Wayward Puritans* (New York, 1966), and Michael Zuckerman, *Peaceable Kingdoms* (New York, 1970).

All four of these different lines of approach to Puritanism resulted in shattering or questioning the Miller synthesis, but they gave rise to problems of their own. Intellectual historians who dismantled much or parts of Miller's synthesis failed to replace it with a convincing overarching interpretation. Seminary scholars traced the roots of Puritanism to other places and other times than previous generations of historians had done, but came to question the definition of the term "Puritanism" itself. Literary historians with their new perspective tried to provide a new synthesis, but they did not succeed in persuading most traditional historians. Social historians, particularly those involved in community studies to explore Puritanism, appeared to have foundered on the problem of representativeness.

In view of the fragmentation in the field of Puritan studies, how can the student of history arrive at any proper evaluation of these early settlers and their subsequent impact on America? To do so the student must first ask the following questions. Were the Puritans primarily religious bigots or consensus-minded community-builders? Were the Puritans pious idealists concerned mainly with maintaining their special Protestant way of life? Or were they practical-minded pioneers simply seeking to establish settlements in the hostile New World environment? Were they the avant-garde of the movement that flowered into the evangelical Pietism of the eighteenth century? Or were they part of a reactionary movement that helped to extend the sixteenth-century medieval world of Calvin into seventeenth-century America? Was Puritanism mainly a theology dedicated to a search for individual salvation? Or was it a way of life that called for the regeneration of an entire society and thereby inspired the creation of new kinds of communities? Was Puritanism as a cultural movement restricted to its own time in terms of its influence? Or did it give rise to a New England myth that was regional in character in the colonial period and then became national in nature in the late eighteenth and nineteenth centuries? Only by wrestling with such crucial questions can the student come to any meaningful conclusion about the precise role of the Puritans and their proper place in American history.

Perry Miller and
Thomas H. Johnson

PERRY MILLER (1905–1963) *was professor of American literature at Harvard University until his death. He was the author of numerous articles and books, including* The New England Mind, 2 vols. *(1939–1953),* Errand into the Wilderness *(1956),* Jonathan Edwards *(1949), and* The Life of the Mind in America: From the Revolution to the Civil War *(1965).* THOMAS H. JOHNSON *(1902–1986) taught for many years at the Lawrenceville School in New Jersey as well as at a number of universities. He was the author of* Emily Dickinson: An Interpretive Biography *(1955) and* The Oxford Companion to American History *(1966).*

Puritanism may perhaps be described as that point of view, that philosophy of life, that code of values, which was carried to New England by the first settlers in the early seventeenth century. Beginning thus, it has become one of the continuous factors in American life and American thought. Any inventory of the elements that have gone into the making of the "American mind" would have to commence with Puritanism. It is, indeed, only one among many: if we should attempt to enumerate these traditions, we should certainly have to mention such philosophies, such "isms," as the rational liberalism of Jeffersonian democracy, the Hamiltonian conception of conservatism and government, the Southern theory of racial aristocracy, the Transcendentalism of nineteenth-century New England, and what is generally spoken of as frontier individualism. Among these factors Puritanism has been perhaps the most conspicuous, the most sustained, and the most fecund. Its role in American thought has been almost the dominant one, for the descendants of Puritans have carried at least some habits of the Puritan mind into a variety of pursuits, have spread across the country, and in many fields of activity have played a leading part. The force of Puritanism, furthermore, has been accentuated because it was the first of these traditions to be fully articulated, and because it has inspired certain traits which have persisted long after the vanish-

---

Perry Miller and Thomas H. Johnson, eds., *The Puritans* (New York: American Book Company, 1938), pp. 1–19. Reprinted with omissions by permission of the American Book Company.

ing of the original creed. Without some understanding of Puritanism, it may safely be said, there is no understanding of America.

Yet important as Puritanism has undoubtedly been in shaping the nation, it is more easily described than defined. It figures frequently in controversy of the last decade, very seldom twice with exactly the same connotation. Particularly of recent years has it become a hazardous feat to run down its meaning. In the mood of revolt against the ideals of previous generations which has swept over our period, Puritanism has become a shining target for many sorts of marksmen. Confusion becomes worse confounded if we attempt to correlate modern usages with anything that can be proved pertinent to the original Puritans themselves. To seek no further, it was the habit of proponents for the repeal of the Eighteenth Amendment during the 1920s to dub Prohibitionists "Puritans," and cartoonists made the nation familiar with an image of the Puritan: a gaunt, lank-haired killjoy, wearing a black steeple hat and compounding for sins he was inclined to by damning those to which he had no mind. Yet any acquaintance with the Puritans of the seventeenth century will reveal at once, not only that they did not wear such hats but also that they attired themselves in all the hues of the rainbow, and furthermore that in their daily life they imbibed what seem to us prodigious quantities of alcoholic beverages, with never the slightest inkling that they were doing anything sinful. True, they opposed drinking to excess, and ministers preached lengthy sermons condemning intoxication, but at such pious ceremonies as the ordination of new ministers the bill for rum, wine, and beer consumed by the congregation was often staggering. Increase Mather himself—who in popular imagination is apt to figure along with his son Cotton as the archembodiment of the Puritan—said in one of his sermons:

> Drink is in it self a good creature of God, and to be received with thankfulness, but the abuse of drink is from Satan; the wine is from God, but the Drunkard is from the Devil.

Or again, the Puritan has acquired the reputation of having been blind to all aesthetic enjoyment and starved of beauty; yet the architecture of the Puritan age grows in the esteem of critics and the household objects of Puritan manufacture, pewter and furniture, achieve prohibitive prices by their appeal to discriminating collectors. Examples of such discrepancies between the modern usage of the word and the historical fact could be multiplied indefinitely. It is not the purpose of this volume to engage in controversy, nor does it intend particularly to defend the Puritan against the bewildering variety of critics who on every side today find him an object of scorn or pity. In his life he neither asked nor gave mercy to his foes; he demanded only that conflicts be joined on real and explicit issues. By examining his own words it may become possible to establish, for better or for worse, the meaning of Puritanism as the Puritan himself believed and practiced it.

Just as soon as we endeavor to free ourselves from prevailing conceptions or misconceptions, and to ascertain the historical facts about seventeenth-century New Englanders, we become aware that we face still another difficulty: not only must we extricate ourselves from interpretations that have been read into Puritanism by the twentieth century, but still more from those that have been attached to it by the eighteenth and nineteenth. The Puritan philosophy, brought to New England highly elaborated and codified, remained a fairly rigid orthodoxy during the seventeenth century. In the next age, however, it proved to be anything but static; by the middle of the eighteenth century there had proceeded from it two distinct schools of thought, almost unalterably opposed to each other. Certain elements were carried into the creeds and practices of the evangelical religious revivals, but others were perpetuated by the rationalists and the forerunners of Unitarianism. Consequently our conception of Puritanism is all too apt to be colored by subsequent happenings; we read ideas into the seventeenth century which belong to the eighteenth, and the real nature of Puritanism can hardly be discovered at all, because Puritanism itself became two distinct and contending things to two sorts of men. The most prevalent error arising from this fact has been the identification of Puritanism with evangelicalism in many accounts, though in histories written by Unitarian scholars the original doctrine has been almost as much distorted in the opposite direction.

Among the evangelicals the original doctrines were transformed or twisted into the new versions of Protestantism that spawned in the Great Awakening of the 1740s, in the succeeding revivals along the frontier and through the back country, in the centrifugal speculations of enraptured prophets and rabid sects in the nineteenth century. All these movements retained something of the theology or revived something of the intensity of spirit, but at the same time they threw aside so much of authentic Puritanism that there can be no doubt the founding fathers would vigorously have repudiated such progeny. They would have had no use, for instance, for the camp meeting and the revivalist orgy; "hitting the sawdust trail" would have been an action exceedingly distasteful to the most ardent among them. What we know as "fundamentalism" would have been completely antipathetic to them, for they never for one moment dreamed that the truth of scripture was to be maintained in spite of or against the evidences of reason, science, and learning. The sects that have arisen out of Puritanism have most strikingly betrayed their rebellion against the true spirit of their source by their attack upon the ideal of a learned ministry; Puritans considered religion a very complex, subtle, and highly intellectualized affair, and they trained their experts in theology with all the care we would lavish upon preparing men to be engineers or chemists. For the same reasons, Puritans would object strenuously to almost all recent attempts to "humanize" religion, to smooth over hard doctrines, to introduce sweetness and light at the cost of hardheaded realism and invincible logic. From their point of view, to bring Christ down to earth in such a fashion as is implied in statements we sometimes encounter—that He was the "first humanitarian" or that He would certainly endorse this or that political party—would seem to them frightful blasphemy. Puritanism was not only a religious creed, it was a philosophy and a metaphysic; it was an organization of man's whole life, emotional and intellectual, to a degree which has not been sustained by any denomination stemming from it. Yet because such creeds have sprung from Puritanism, the Puritans are frequently praised or blamed for qualities which never belonged to them or for ideas which originated only among their successors and which they themselves would have disowned.

On the other hand, if the line of development from Puritanism tends in one direction to frontier revivalism and evangelicalism, another line leads as directly to a more philosophical, critical, and even skeptical point of view. Unitarianism is as much the child of Puritanism as Methodism. And if the one accretion has colored or distorted our conception of the original doctrine, the other has done so no less. Descendants of the Puritans who revolted against what they considered the tyranny and cruelty of Puritan theology, who substituted taste and reason for dogma and authority and found the emotional fervor of the evangelicals so much sound and fury, have been prone to idealize their ancestors into their own image. A few decades ago it had become very much the mode to praise the Puritans for virtues which they did not possess and which they would not have considered virtues at all. In the pages of liberal historians, and above all in the speeches of Fourth of July orators, the Puritans have been hymned as the pioneers of religious liberty, though nothing was ever farther from their designs; they have been hailed as the forerunners of democracy, though if they were, it was quite beside their intention; they have been invoked in justification for an economic philosophy of free competition and laissez-faire, though they themselves believed in government regulation of business, the fixing of just prices, and the curtailing of individual profits in the interests of the welfare of the whole.

The moral of these reflections may very well be that it is dangerous to read history backwards, to interpret something that was by what it ultimately became, particularly when it became several things. . . . The Puritans were not a bashful race, they could speak out and did; in their own words they have painted their own portraits, their majestic strength and their dignity, their humanity and solidity, more accurately than any admirer had been able to do; and also they have betrayed the motes and beams in their own eyes more clearly than any enemy has been able to point them out.

Puritanism began as an agitation within the Church of England in the latter half of the sixteenth century. It was a movement for reform of that institution, and at the time no more constituted a distinct sect or denomination than the advocates of an amendment to the Constitution of the United States constitute a separate nation. In the 1530s the Church of England broke with the pope of Rome. By the beginning of Elizabeth's reign it had proceeded a certain distance in this revolt, had become Protestant, had disestablished the monasteries and corrected many abuses. Puritanism was the belief that the reform should be continued, that more abuses remained to be corrected, that practices still survived from the days of popery which should be renounced, that the Church of England should be restored to the "purity" of the first-century church as established by Christ Himself. In the 1560s, when the advocates of purification first acquired the name of Puritans, no one, not even the most radical, knew exactly how far the process was to go or just what the ultimate goal would be; down to the days of Cromwell there was never any agreement on this point, and in the end this failure of unanimity proved the undoing of English Puritanism. Many Puritans desired only that certain ceremonies be abolished or changed. Others wanted ministers to preach more sermons, make up their own prayers on the inspiration of the moment rather than read set forms out of a book. Others went further and proposed a revision of the whole form of ecclesiastical government. But whatever the shade or complexion of their Puritanism, Puritans were those who wanted to continue a movement which was already under way. Their opponents, whom we shall speak of as the Anglicans—though only for the sake of convenience, because there was at that time not the remotest thought on either side of an ultimate separation into distinct churches, and Puritans insisted they were as stoutly loyal to the established institution as any men in England—the Anglicans were those who felt that with the enthronement of Elizabeth and with the "Elizabethan Settlement" of the church, things had gone far enough. They wanted to call a halt, just where they were, and stabilize at that point.

Thus the issue between the two views, though large enough, still involved only a limited number of questions. On everything except matters upon which the Puritans wanted further reformation, there was essential agreement. The Puritans who settled New England were among the more radical—though by no means the most radical that the movement produced—and even before their migration in 1630 had gone to the lengths of formulating a concrete platform of church organization which they wished to see instituted in England in place of the episcopal system. Joining battle on this front gave a sufficiently extended line and provided a vast number of salients to fight over; the gulf between the belief of these Puritans and the majority in the Church of England grew so wide that at last there was no bridging it at all. But notwithstanding the depth of this divergence, the fact still remains that only certain specific questions were raised. If we take a comprehensive survey of the whole body of Puritan thought and belief as it existed in 1630 or 1640, if we make an exhaustive enumeration of ideas held by New England Puritans, we shall find that the vast majority of them were precisely those of their opponents. In other words, Puritanism was a movement toward certain ends within the culture and state of England in the late sixteenth and early seventeenth centuries; it centered about a number of concrete problems and advocated a particular program. Outside of that, it was part and parcel of the times, and its culture was simply the culture of England at that moment. It is necessary to belabor the point, because most accounts of Puritanism, emphasizing the controversial tenets, attribute everything that Puritans said or did to the fact that they were Puritans; their attitudes toward all sorts of things are pounced upon and exhibited as peculiarities of their sect, when as a matter of fact they were normal attitudes for the time. Of course, the Puritans acquired their special quality and their essential individuality from their stand on the points actually at issue, and our final conception of Puritanism must give these concerns all due importance. Yet if first of all we wish to take Puritan culture as a whole, we shall find, let us say, that about 90 percent of the intellectual life, scientific knowledge, morality, manners and customs, notions and prejudices, was that of all Englishmen. The other 10 percent, the relatively small number of ideas upon which there was dispute, made all the difference between the Puritan and his fellow Englishmen, made for him so much difference that he pulled up stakes in England, which he loved, and migrated to a wilderness rather than submit them to apparent defeat. Nevertheless, when we come to trace developments and influences on subsequent American history and thought, we shall find that the starting point of many ideas and practices is as apt to be found among the 90 percent as among the 10. The task of defining Puritanism and giving an account of its culture resolves itself, therefore, into isolating first of all the larger features which were not particularly or necessarily Puritan at all, the elements in the life and society which were products of the time and place, of the background of English life and society rather than of the individual belief or peculiar creed of Puritanism.

Many of the major interests and preoccupations of the New England Puritans belong to this list. They were just as patriotic as Englishmen who remained at home. They hated Spain like poison, and France only a little less. In their eyes, as in those of Anglicans, the most important issue in the Western world was the struggle between Catholicism and Protestantism. They were not unique or extreme in thinking that religion was the primary and all-engrossing business of man, or that all human thought and action should tend to the glory of God. . . .

In its major aspects the religious creed of Puritanism was neither peculiar to the Puritans nor different from that of the Anglicans. Both were essentially Protestant; both asserted that men were saved by their faith, not by their deeds. The two sides could agree on the general statement that Christians are bound to believe nothing but what the Gospel teaches, that all traditions of men "contrary to the Word of God" are to be renounced and abhorred. They both believed that the marks of a true church were profession of the creed, use of Christ's sacraments, preaching of the word—Anglican sermons being as long and often as dull as the Puritan—and the union of men in profession and practice under regularly constituted pastors. The Puritans always said that they could subscribe to the doctrinal articles of the Church of England; even at the height of the controversy, even after they had left England rather than put up with what they considered its abominations, they always took care to insist that the Church of England was a "true" church, not Anti-Christ as was the Church of Rome, that it contained many saints, and that men might find salvation within it. Throughout the seventeenth century they read Anglican authors, quoted them in their sermons, and even reprinted some of them in Boston.

The vast substratum of agreement which actually underlay the disagreement between Puritans and Anglicans is explained by the fact that they were both the heirs of the Middle Ages. They still believed that all knowledge was one, that life was unified, that science, economics, political theory, aesthetic standards, rhetoric and art, all were organized in a hierarchical scale of values that tended upward to the end-all and be-all of creation, the glory of God. They both insisted that all human activity be regulated by that purpose. Consequently, even while fighting bitterly against each other, the Puritans and Anglicans stood shoulder to shoulder against what they called "enthusiasm." The leaders of the Puritan movement were trained at the universities, they were men of learning and scholars; no less than the Anglicans did they demand that religion be interpreted by study and logical exposition; they were both resolute against all pretenses to immediate revelation, against all ignorant men who claimed to receive personal instructions from God. They agreed on the essential Christian contention that though God may govern the world, He is not the world itself, and that though He instills His grace into men, He does not deify them or unite them to Himself in one personality. He converses with men only through His revealed word, the Bible. His will is to be studied in the operation of His providence as exhibited in the workings of the natural world, but He delivers no new commands or special revelations to the inward consciousness of men. The larger unanimity of the Puritans and the Anglicans reveals itself whenever either of them was called upon to confront enthusiasm [as seen in] . . . Governor John Winthrop's account of the so-called Antinomian affair, the crisis produced in the little colony by the teachings of Mistress Anne Hutchinson in 1636 and 1637. . . . Beneath the theological jargon in which the opinions of this lady appear we can see the substance of her contention, which was that she was in direct communication with the Godhead, and that she therefore was prepared to follow the promptings of the voice within against all the precepts of the Bible, the churches, reason, or the government of Massachusetts Bay. Winthrop relates how the magistrates and the ministers defended the community against this perversion of the doctrine of regeneration, but the tenor of his condemnation would have been duplicated practically word for word had Anne Hutchinson broached her theories in an Anglican community. The Anglicans fell in completely with the Puritans when both of them were confronted in the 1650s by the Quakers. All New England leaders saw in the Quaker doctrine of an inner light, accessible to all men and giving a perfect communication from God to their inmost spirits, just another form of Anne Hutchinson's blasphemy. John Norton declared that the "light of nature" itself taught us that "madmen acting according to their frantick passions are to be restrained with chaines, when they can not be restrained otherwise. . . ."Enthusiasts, whether Antinomian or Quaker, were proposing doctrines that threatened the unity of life by subduing the reason and the intellect to the passions and the emotions. Whatever their differences, Puritans and Anglicans were struggling to maintain a complete harmony of reason and faith, science and religion, earthly dominion and the government of God. When we immerse ourselves in the actual struggle, the difference between the Puritan and the Anglican may seem to us immense; but when we take the vantage point of subsequent history, and survey religious thought as a whole over the last three centuries, the two come very close together on essentials. Against all forms of chaotic emotionalism, against all oversimplifications of theology, learning, philosophy, and science, against all materialism, positivism or mechanism, both were endeavoring to uphold a symmetrical union of heart and head without impairment of either. By the beginning or middle of the next century their successors, both in England and America, found themselves no longer capable of sustaining this unity, and it has yet to be reachieved today, if achieved again it ever can be. The greatness of the Puritans is not so much that they conquered a wilderness, or that they carried a religion into it, but that they carried a religion which, narrow and starved though it may have been in some respects, deficient in sensuous richness or brilliant color, was nevertheless indissolubly bound up with an ideal of culture and learning. In contrast to all other pioneers, they made no concessions to the forest, but in the midst of frontier conditions, in the very throes of clearing the land and erecting shelters, they maintained schools and a college, a standard of scholarship and of competent writing, a class of men devoted entirely to the life of the mind and of the soul.

Because the conflict between the Puritans and the Churchmen was as much an intellectual and scholarly issue as it was emotional, it was in great part a debate among pundits. This is not to say that passions were not involved; certainly men took sides because of prejudice, interest, irrational conviction, or for any of the motives that may incite the human race to conflict. The disagreement finally was carried from the field of learned controversy to the field of battle. There can be no doubt that many of the people in England, or even in New England, became rabid partisans and yet never acquired the erudition necessary to understand the intricate and subtle arguments of their leaders. A great number, perhaps even a majority, in both camps were probably not intelligent or learned enough to see clearly the reasons for the cause they supported. . . .

The wonder is that by and large the populace did yield their judgments to those who were supposed to know, respected learning and supported it, sat patiently during two- and three-hour sermons while ministers expounded the knottiest and most recondite of metaphysical texts. The testimony of visitors, travelers, and memoirs agrees that during the Puritan age in New England the common man, the farmer and merchant, was amazingly versed in systematic divinity. A gathering of yeomen and "hired help" around the kitchen fire of an evening produced long and unbelievably technical discussions of predestination, infant damnation, and the distinctions between faith and works. In the first half of the seventeenth century the people had not yet questioned the conception of religion as a difficult art in which the authority of the skilled dialectician should prevail over the inclinations of the merely devout. This ideal of subjection to qualified leadership was social as well as intellectual. Very few Englishmen had yet broached the notion that a lackey was as good as a lord, or that any Tom, Dick, or Harry, simply because he was a good, honest man, could understand the Sermon on the Mount as well as a master of arts from Oxford, Cambridge, or Harvard. Professor Morison has shown that the life of the college in New England was saved by the sacrifice of the yeomen farmers, who contributed their pecks of wheat, wrung from a stony soil, taken from their none too opulent stores, to support teaching fellows and to assist poor scholars at Harvard College, in order that they and their children might still sit under a literate ministry "when our present Ministers shall lie in the Dust."

When we say the the majority of the people in the early seventeenth century still acceded to the dictation of the learned in religion and the superior in society, we must also remark that the Puritan leaders were in grave danger of arousing a revolt against themselves by their very own doctrines. Puritans were attacking the sacerdotal and institutional bias which had survived in the Church of England; they were maintaining a theology that brought every man to a direct experience of the spirit and removed intermediaries between himself and the deity. Yet the authority of the infallible church and the power of the bishops had for centuries served to keep the people docile. Consequently when the Puritan leaders endeavored to remove the bishops and to deny that the church should stand between God and man, they ran the hazard of starting something among the people that might get out of hand. Just as the Puritan doctrine that men were saved by the infusion of God's grace could lead to the Antinomianism of Mrs. Hutchinson, and often did warrant the simple in concluding that if they had God's grace in them they needed to pay no heed to what a minister told them, so the Puritan contention that regenerate men were illuminated with divine truth might lead to the belief that true religion did not need the assistance of learning, books, arguments, logical demonstrations, or classical languages. There was always a possibility that Puritanism would raise up a fanatical anti-intellectualism, and against such a threat the Puritan ministers constantly braced themselves. It was no accident that the followers of Mrs. Hutchinson, who believed that men could receive all the necessary instructions from within, also attacked learning and education, and came near to wrecking not only the colony but the college as well. . . .

[T]he New England leaders were face to face with a problem as old as the history of the Christian church. Throughout the Middle Ages there had been such stirrings among the people as those to which Mrs. Hutchinson or the Fifth Monarchy Men gave voice. The great scholastic synthesis always remained incomprehensible to the vulgar, who demanded to be fed again and again with the sort of religious sustenance they craved. The Reformation drew upon these suppressed desires. Common men turned Protestant primarily because Protestantism offered them a religion which more effectively satisfied their spiritual hunger. Yet in Europe theologians and metaphysicians retained the leadership and kept Protestantism from becoming merely an emotional outburst. They supplied it with a theology which, though not so sophisticated as scholastic dogma, was still equipped with a logic and organon of rational demonstration. Though Protestantism can be viewed as a "liberation" of the common man, it was far from being a complete emancipation of the individual. It freed him from many intellectual restraints that had been imposed by the church, but it did not give him full liberty to think anything he pleased; socially it freed him from many exactions, but it did not permit him to abandon his traditional subjection to his social and ecclesiastical superiors. The original settlers of New England carried this Protestantism intact from Europe to America. Except for the small band that was driven into exile with Anne Hutchinson, and one or two other groups of visionaries who also were hustled across the borders into Rhode Island, the rank and file did follow their leaders, meekly and reverently. Captain Johnson probably represents the average layman's loyalty to the clergy. the New England "theocracy" was simply a Protestant version of the European social ideal, and except for its Protestantism was thoroughly medieval in character.

It was only as the seventeenth century came to a close that the imported structure began to show the strain. In Europe social tradition had conspired with the ministers to check enthusiasts in religion and "levellers" in society; in England the authorities, whether Anglican or Puritan, royal or Cromwellian, were able to suppress the assault upon the scholarly and aristocratic ideal. In America the character of the people underwent a change; they moved further into the frontier, they became more absorbed in business and profits than in religion and salvation, their memories of English social stratification grew dim. A preacher before the General Court in 1705 bewailed the effects of the frontier in terms that have been echoed by "Easterners" for two hundred years and more; men were no longer living together, he said, in compact communities, under the tutelage of educated clergymen and under the discipline of an ordered society, but were taking themselves into remote corners "for worldly conveniences." "By that means [they] have seemed to bid defiance, not only to Religion, but to Civility it self: and such places thereby have become Nurseries of Ignorance, Profaneness and Atheism." In America the frontier conspired with the popular disposition to lessen the prestige of the cultured classes and to enhance the social power of those who wanted their religion in a more simple, downright and "democratic" form, who cared nothing for the refinements and subtleties of historic theology. Not until the decade of the Great Awakening did the popular tendency receive distinct articulation through leaders who openly renounced the older conception, but for half a century or more before 1740 its obstinate persistence can be traced in the condemnations of the ministers.

The Puritan leaders could withstand this rising tide of democracy only by such support as the government would give them—which became increasingly less after the new charter of 1692 took away from the saints all power to select their own governors and divorced the state and church—or else by the sheer force of their personalities. As early as the 1660s and '70s we can see them beginning to shift their attentions from mere exposition of the creed to greater and greater insistence upon committing power only to men of wisdom and knowledge. . . . By the beginning of the eighteenth century the task of buttressing the classified society, maintaining the rule of the well-trained and the culturally superior both in church and society seems to have become the predominant concern of the clergy. Sermon after sermon reveals that in their eyes the cause of learning and the cause of a hierarchical, differentiated social order were one and the same. . . . Leadership by the learned and dutiful subordination of the un-learned—as long as the original religious creed retained its hold upon the people these exhortations were heeded; in the eighteenth century, as it ceased to arouse their loyalties, they went seeking after gods that were utterly strange to Puritanism. They demanded fervent rather than learned ministers and asserted the equality of all men.

Thus Puritanism appears, from the social and economic point of view, to have been a philosophy of social stratification, placing the command in the hands of the properly qualified and demanding implicit obedience from the uneducated; from the religious point of view it was the dogged assertion of the unity of intellect and spirit in the face of a rising tide of democratic sentiment suspicious of the intellect and intoxicated with the spirit. It was autocratic, hierarchical, and authoritarian. It held that in the intellectual realm holy writ was to be expounded by right reason, that in the social realm the expounders of holy writ were to be the mentors of farmers and merchants. Yet in so far as Puritanism involved such ideals it was simply adapting to its own purposes and ideals of the age. Catholics in Spain and in Spanish America pursued the same objectives, and the Puritans were no more rigorous in their application of an autocratic standard than King Charles himself endeavored to be—and would have been had he not been balked in the attempt.

Philip F. Gura

PHILIP F. GURA (1950–   ) *is professor of English at the University of North Carolina. His books include* The Wisdom of Words: Language, Theology and Literature in the New England Renaissance *(1981) and* A Glimpse of Sion's Glory: Puritan Radicalism in New England 1620–1660 *(1984).*

Between 1630 and 1660, among the approximately twenty thousand colonists who settled in New England were many individuals,

ministers as well as laymen, whose Puritanism was not consonant
with the official ideology of the Bay Colony. . . . The Massachusetts
Puritans attempted to limit the colony's population to those whose
religious views were compatible to their own, and as the decade of the
1630s wore on, compatibility more and more meant agreement with
the principles of nonseparating congregationalism. Nevertheless, the
great Puritan migration that, beginning in 1629, brought to New England a cross section of old England's population, included many who
had been influenced by theological views more radical than those officially sanctioned in Massachusetts and who subsequently sought to
promulgate them in the communities where they settled. By the 1640s
New England's congregationalists (as well as their conservative English critics) complained that the colonies harbored self-declared (or
scarcely disguised) separatists, antinomians, familists, Seekers, ana-
baptists, Ranters, Adamites, and Quakers, all implicitly aligned
against the established church system because of their insistence that
an individual's personal religious experience supersede the demands of
ecclesiastical tradition and civil law. In many cases, theirs were the
same Protestant principles Winthrop and others earlier had defended
in England yet, under pressure to settle a wilderness and codify their
ecclesiology, soon enough condemned as seditious or heretical.

The experiences of the Husbandmen and other radical Puritans in
seventeenth-century New England have not been studied with any
completeness because of a prevailing disposition among historians of
colonial America to regard American Puritanism as relatively homogeneous and the American sectarians only as weak, if prophetic, advocates of religious toleration. To be sure, accounts of early New England
history invariably mention such prominent dissenters as Roger Williams, Anne Hutchinson, and the Quakers; still, no historian has attempted to document either the widespread presence of radical Puritans in New England or their complex and extended relationship to
their English counterparts. A number of studies—most notably those
of Christopher Hill and Keith Thomas—do describe the radical Protestant sects that flourished in England between the death of Queen Elizabeth and the Restoration, but historians of American Puritanism have
insistently portrayed it as but one branch of an English plant and not
itself a vigorous if slender rootstock that brought forth the same exotic
varietals as its English counterpart. Williams, Hutchinson, and the
Quakers, as significant as were their challenges to the New England
Way, offer only the most memorable examples of an inescapable fact:
between 1630 and 1660 the doctrinal and ecclesiastical, as well as the
imaginative, development of American Puritanism was nurtured in
soil thoroughly turned by radical elements in the New Englanders'
midst.

This resistance to an acknowledgment of the radicals' effect upon

New England Puritanism can be traced to the still-pervasive influence of Perry Miller, who in his magisterial account of "the New England mind"—what he termed his "map of the intellectual terrain of the seventeenth century"—continually emphasized what he considered the New England Puritans' supreme achievement. To him this achievement was the theological and ecclesiastical synthesis known as nonseparating congregationalism, an ecclesiastical system under which individual congregations maintained their autonomy while at the same time claiming their continued allegiance to the hierarchy of the Church of England. But in his desire to illustrate the extent to which the American Puritans were successful in promulgating and defending this world-view, Miller was too willing to believe that "after the New England divines had weathered the storm of 1637–1638 they were never seriously threatened by any form of Antinomianism, though they were horrified by the sectarian outbursts in England . . . and magnified the few Quakers who ventured within their jurisdiction." He sketched the contours of his "map" of New England's intellectual development under the assumption, too readily accepted by other scholars, that "the first three generations in New England paid almost unbroken allegiance to a unified body of thought, and that individual differences among particular writers or theorists were merely minor variations within a general frame." In the two decades since Miller's death, it has become all too clear that the "liberty" he took of "treating the whole literature as though it were the product of a single intelligence" reveals more about his own desire for order than it does of the full complexity of the New England mind in the seventeenth century.

Miller's eagerness to identify those characteristics that distinguished American Puritanism from its English and Continental counterparts and his insistence that the American wilderness guaranteed such distinctions, led him to claim that through the early eighteenth century the "official cosmology" of the Bay Colony remained unmarked by any challenge to its legitimacy. Even in *From Colony to Province* (1953), a study devoted to the institutional development of New England Puritanism, he maintained that "such developments as took place [in the colonists' ideology]" only affected "lesser areas of church polity, political relations, or the contests of groups and interests." Miller admitted that some of these developments had been "intense and shattering experiences" for those who were involved in them, yet, he believed, these events did not cause "any significant alterations" in the "doctrinal frame of reference" within the colony. But the sheer intellectual vigor of Miller's narrative in this work (and in other works of his that deal with seventeenth-century New England) undercuts his assumption: the intensity of the conflicts over matters of church polity and colonial politics, as well as over theological doctrine, indicates that, no matter how decidedly the Puritan authorities "triumphed" in these "contests of groups and interests," the various challenges to the magistrates' authority initiated by dissenting colonists had an undeniable effect upon the future course of New England's history. Miller viewed New England dissent as a sideshow to the events on the main stage of New England's intellectual and social history.

I will argue, in contrast, that in large measure New England Puritanism developed as it did because of, and not in spite of, the criticism of the colony from those in the population whose vision of the kingdom of God in America differed significantly from John Winthrop's. . . .

A perusal of church, town, and colony records of seventeenth-century New England reveals . . . a surprisingly wide range of theological opinion in the colonies before the Restoration and a complex relation of such diversity to the internal development of American Puritan doctrine. *Heterogeneity,* not unanimity, actually characterized the colony's religious life. Darrett Rutman, who has gone as far as anyone to challenge Miller's conclusions about the existence of a unified body of thought called "American Puritanism," noted that, contrary to the observations of Miller and other historians, "orthodox New England possessed the semblance but not the substance of unity." In such works as *Winthrop's Boston: Portrait of a Puritan Town* and *American Puritanism: Faith and Practice,* Rutman argues that, even among the ministers in the colony, "disparity of doctrine and even practice was the rule, not the exception." For him, American Puritanism can best be explained as chance confluence of diverse cultural and religious forces; "if what eventually emerged was uniquely American," he writes, "it was only because one found here a continuing juxtaposition of varied elements which could not be duplicated anywhere." In New England "there was no Puritan way, no constant to be injected" by the settlers into the waiting body of the new continent. There were merely the "actions, reactions, interactions" of the heterogeneous population themselves.

Rutman's astute assessment addresses itself specifically to the range of theological opinion in colonial New England; his conclusions are derived from detailed demographic analyses. If he fails finally to explore the significance of the dialectic between the dissenters and more moderate Puritans in New England for the development of Puritan doctrine, or the dissenters' role in what in effect was a transatlantic debate about the nature and extent of the Puritan renovation of society, Rutman at least calls attention to the ideological blinders that narrowed Miller's delineation of the intellectual contours of the New England mind. As one recent student has said of the Antinomian Controversy—in seventeenth-century New England the most important radical challenge to the ideology of nonseparating congregationalism: "it was apparent from the outset that not all who came to the Bay Colony had been listening to the same spirit or brought the same notions about the nature of the New England enterprise." Here, in the very complexity of English Puritanism on the eve of the colonization of New England, we must seek an understanding of the true import of what Miller and others hitherto have dismissed as "minor" events in the development of American Puritanism.

In 1936 Charles M. Andrews noted that the large influx of settlers to New England between 1630 and 1640 had "brought an unusual number of ministers . . . whose interpretations of scripture and the purpose of God in his relations with men . . . represented many shades of opinion." It is also important to recognize that the New England mind was formed as much, if not more, by the laity, by what another historian has called "the spontaneous, irrepressible aggregation of like-minded saints in shifting voluntary groups . . . seeking comfort and enlightenment for themselves from the Gospel." A full understanding of seventeenth-century New England Puritanism depends on an acknowledgment that many of those who migrated to America did not share a fixed ideology or commitment to an agreed-upon ecclesiastical program as much as a common spiritual hunger and a disenchantment with the Church of England's refusal to address the nation's spiritual famine. Further, English Puritans—including those who later emigrated to the New World—had not tempered their intellectual and social bonds at any single ideological forge but over the spiritual flames of countless private devotional meetings or "conventicles" throughout England. From these private meetings, which perhaps more than any institution or idea provided Puritans with a group identity, sprang not only the likes of John Winthrop, Thomas Hooker, Thomas Shepard, and others who became staunch supporters of nonseparating congregationalism, but also those individuals who by the mid-1640s had helped to generate a myriad of radical Puritan sects that threatened to fulfill the prophecy of Acts 17:6 and turn the known world upside down. In England the soon-to-be settlers' experience as "Puritans" had been as varied as the regions from which they came. This fact must inform any examination of the variety of American Puritanism.

From what we know of the persistence of English local institutions in the various New England towns that have been examined by such historians as T. H. Breen and David Grayson Allen, it should come as no surprise that once in the New World many Puritans sought to replicate the form and quality of their previous religious experience. They replicated precisely what one would expect from English Puritanism between 1630 and 1660: everything from the most structured presbyterianism to the religious and social radicalism of antinomians, Seekers, and Ranters. Moreover, in the free air of the New World, English Puritans had every right to anticipate that what they had learned in the privacy of their conventicles would form the basis of a new social order. History would prove their dreams illusory. Many individuals, once as powerless before the bishops as other of their brethren, who had justified their resistance to the Church of England through appeals to individual religious experience similar to those that led others to more radical positions, in the New World assumed a more conservative posture. They came to believe that, no matter what their experience with more radical forms of Puritan thought in England, they must establish and maintain strict doctrinal orthodoxy to achieve civil order in a new society. Most historians have minimized the resistance to the institution of such a unified body of doctrine in New England. It is clear, nevertheless, that the experience of English Puritanism was too varied to have been so easily transformed without serious challenge by those whose understanding of the logic of the Gospel plan differed at many points from that of the leaders of the more conservative colonies. Miller would have us marvel at how compelling the colonists found the New England Way. Rather, we should ask why anyone who had experienced the range of English Puritan thought, and the spiritual and social liberation it offered, would accept the ideological limitations of New England congregationalism.

Consider Samuel Gorton, founder of Warwick, Rhode Island, a radical spiritist with many connections to the sectarian underground in England, particularly to the General Baptist groups. Frequently linked to such prominent English radicals as John Saltmarsh and William Dell, Gorton was instrumental in preparing the way for the reception of the Quakers in his colony. Or John Clarke, of Newport, also in the Rhode Island colonies, a Particular Baptist who, along with Obadiah Holmes and John Crandall, openly challenged the relationship of church and state in Massachusetts. He maintained close contact with his doctrinal counterparts in London, particularly Henry Jessey and John Tombes, two of the signers of the famous Baptist Confession of 1644. Then, too, there was William Pynchon, first settler of Springfield in the Connecticut Valley of Massachusetts, who took his inspiration from such English latitudinarians or "Socinians" as Anthony Wotton and John Goodwin. Pynchon's tracts published in the 1650s display his advocacy of an enlightened rationalism in religion, particularly as a basis for toleration of diverse Christian opinions; his settlement in the Valley initiated that region's long-standing challenge to the supremacy, religious and otherwise, of the clergy of eastern Massachusetts. William Aspinwall, one of the antinomians disarmed in 1637, later returned to England to become a prolific pamphleteer for the cause of the Fifth Monarchy; his conception of a divinely instituted church state was reviewed and accepted by some of the most advanced radicals of the 1650s. One of his followers, Thomas Venner, left his trade as a wine cooper in Boston to lead the major Fifth Monarchy uprising in London in 1661; he was hanged, drawn, and quartered, and his head was placed on a pike atop one of the city gates. These are but a few of the more prominent spokesmen for Puritan radicalism in New England. Many have received insufficient attention.

The response of the Bay Colony and of Connecticut to the presence of such radicals was complicated by the fact that some of the points of doctrine which from the outset of the migration had been central to the evolution of the New England Way encouraged the same radical conclusions about church and society advanced by the sectarians, both at home and in England. Note, in particular, the colonists' fervent millennialism and their belief in both a gathered church of Christian saints and, more important, the animating power of the Holy Spirit. These emphases within New England Puritanism, especially the Puritans' stress on the witness of the Spirit in each saint and on the saint's obligation to bring Christ's kingdom to earth, were irreducible elements of the religious culture within which the colonists had lived in old England. It was by fully addressing the ideological implications of such beliefs that the leaders of Massachusetts and Connecticut could implement their own more conservative plans for the renovation of the English church. The nature and extent of the dialogue between representatives of nonseparating congregationalism and those among the settlers who, at least initially, refused to relinquish their own very different plans for the establishment of a Christian commonwealth lies at the center of any appreciation of the complexity of New England's religious culture in the mid-seventeenth century.

The radicals' ideas, in addition to affecting the officially sanctioned theology of New England Puritanism, contributed significantly to the social and political development of the New England colonies. This was particularly so in the ways in which Massachusetts and Connecticut congregationalists protected themselves against the further spread of radical ideas, and in their response to the increasing criticism of their repressive policies levelled at them by their English brethren. Further, the radicals' various challenges to the New England Way also had profound effect on the Puritans' imaginative conception of themselves and their social experiment. It is the underlying premise of Sacvan Bercovitch's *The American Jeremiad* that since their earliest days in the New World the Puritans had adhered to a "myth of America" that involved the creation and maintenance of an ideological community most clearly defined not by its territorial or political integrity but by its members' incessant rhetorical self-justification of a divinely ordained purpose. Scholars of American Puritanism, including Miller and Bercovitch himself, have described the development of this myth of American exceptionalism in terms of the colonists' adoption and subtle modification of the principles of nonseparating congregationalism, particularly in light of an increasing awareness of their physical and ideological distance from old England. But what is apparent in the colonists' elaborate definitions and justifications of their ecclesiastical polity and evident in their polemics against dissenters is that the New Englander's ideological self-image was shaped less by any set of ecclesiastical principles than by an unyielding effort to neutralize the influence of those who argued for a much more radical reorganization of the society. The "middle-class culture" that defined New England from its earliest days was the result not merely, as Bercovitch suggests, of the New Englanders' freedom from the feudal restrictions of Europe, of a corrupt opportunism in the face of New World opportunity, or of an antipathy to the Arminian tendencies of the Church of England, but also of a sharp and continual debate with those who from their English Puritan experience had formed a particularly democratic notion of their errand into America's wilderness.

I am concerned with the social and political, as well as with the religious, implications of the radical Puritans' presence in New England. Like Miller . . . and Bercovitch, I recognize the importance for American history of the ideological consensus that later generations of Americans discerned in the first decades of New England's settlement. But, once aware of the nature and extent of the radical challenges to this consensus, we have every right to ask why seventeenth-century New England did not become *more* radicalized and *more* democratic than it did. Such scholars of English Puritanism as William Haller and Christopher Hill have taught us that the Puritan sectarians fundamentally challenged many of the traditional assumptions on which their society was based. In the religious sphere they raised searching questions about the proper relationship of church and state, the minister and his congregation, the word of the Bible and the witness of the Spirit. They also reexamined the moral bases of society: they challenged the established relationship of the sexes in both the religious and domestic spheres; they questioned the very existence of heaven and hell, and of sin, and wondered aloud if in an age of impending apocalypse an educated ministry was at all necessary. As Haller himself noted many years ago, to attempt to reform the Church of England in the seventeenth century was quite simply "to attempt the reorganization of society." Why, then, did the New England Puritans, three thousands miles away from the iron grasp of the bishops, refuse to incorporate into their society more of the ideas the radicals advocated? If, as the Woburn, Massachusetts, militia-captain Edward Johnson wrote, New England was "the place where the Lord will create a new Heaven, and a new Earth in, new Churches and a new Commonwealth together," what prevented the colony from being modeled after the spiritual utopia of a John Saltmarsh, or the political democracy of a John Lilburne?

Such speculation is not out of line, for a large number of those who came to New England in the 1630s and 1640s, before the advent of the English civil wars had shifted the Puritans' focus back to England, clearly believed that their transatlantic voyage had been undertaken for much more than an escape from ecclesiastical persecution. Since the 1620s they had heard countless Puritan preachers remind them of the Books of Daniel and Revelation, in which it was apparent that "there be many Prophesies and Promises . . . that are not yet fulfilled; and the fulfilling whereof will bring the *Church* into a more glorious condition than ever it was yet in the World." For many who came to America in those two decades it seemed perfectly plausible that in their new home such prophecy would be fulfilled. From New England one could view not only the return of Christ, but the staging of his triumph over Satan's legions. New Englanders were not hesitant to raise Christ's standard and march in the vanguard of his armies, for they believed that they were a chosen people. As Edward Johnson put it, "God hath . . . caused the dazeling brightnesse of his presence to be contracted in the burning-Glasse of [their] zeal." New England was destined to be more than a shining beacon upon a hill. Its spiritual ardor would set Christ's fire to the whole world, its flames never quenched "till it hath burnt up Babilon Root and Branch."

Thomas Tillam, who later returned to England a fervent Fifth Monarchist, in a poem written "Upon the first sight of New-England, June 29, 1638," hailed a "holy-land wherein our holy lord/Hath planted his most true and holy word" for the sake of a society in which he and his fellow colonists, "free from all annoye," could "Injoye" Christ's presence in every aspect of their lives. A similar eschatological hope compelled Ezekiel Rogers of Rowley to remind Governor Winthrop in 1639 that the "worke of the Lorde in bringing so many pretious ones to this place is not for nothing." Like Boston's minister, the renowned John Cotton, who that same year began to preach the sermons that would comprise *An Exposition upon the Twelfth Chapter of the Revelation,* Rogers looked forward to the reappearance of Christ on earth and the bestowal of his blessing on "none but [the] downright godly ones" who had prayed for his reappearance; Rogers was sure that the Saviour first would be seen in New England. By 1647 Samuel Symonds of Ipswich knew enough of New England to proclaim that the days of the New Jerusalem had indeed commenced: "Is not government in church and Common weale (according to gods own rules) that new heaven and earth promised, in the fullnes accomplished when the Jewes come in; and the first fruites begun in this poore of New Engl[and] . . . ?" Similarly, Sir Symonds D'Ewes, writing in his autobiography in 1638 from the perspective of England, believed the New England experiment of paramount importance, "a true type of heaven itself" in which the colonists, "in the main, aim simply at God's glory, and to reduce the public service of God to that power and purity which it enjoyed in primitive times." In 1651 his sentiment was echoed by none other than Oliver Cromwell, who begged John Cotton to write

to tell him "What is the Lord a-doing? What prophecies are now fulfilling?"

New England, then, was settled in the belief that it was to become
nothing less than a fulfillment of biblical prophecy, a land in which
the life of the spirit informed all behavior and so would mark the spot
of the New Jerusalem. Within such a context of millennial expectation
the Puritan radicals presented plans, which they believed to be as
firmly grounded in Scripture as the more conservative Puritans did
theirs, for the religious and social reformation that would initiate
Christ's holy commonwealth.

The radicals' challenge to the church and state in England was effectively defused by the political and religious settlement of the Restoration. By the 1660s in the New World, however, compromise had
taken a different form: the dissenters seemingly had become *bona fide*
members of the congregational order on which Winthrop, Hooker,
Shepard, and others had expended so much intellectual effort. In New
England, where the Church of England never had been institutionalized, one found instead the gradual evolution of an ideological system
that, while it could not fully satisfy the spiritist longings of the radicals, harnessed enough of the potential energy of their ideas to garner
the support of the majority of the settlers. Only at the fringes of Massachusetts and Connecticut—in the Rhode Island communities (which
one observer called "the receptacle of all sorts of riff-raff people, and
. . . the sewer of New England") and to the north in what eventually
became New Hampshire and Maine—did the inhabitants continue to
press for a different social order from that overseen by Winthrop or
Thomas Dudley. At the meetings of the Synod of 1662, which set the
direction of the New England Way for the next fifty years, those who
represented congregationalism—"a speaking *Aristocracy* in the face of
a silent Democracy," in the words of the Hartford minister Samuel
Stone—emerged with enough power to end the plans of more radical
Puritans for the establishment of a New Canaan.

The manner in which the supporters of both the Synods of 1648
and 1662 gathered such power to themselves of course is of great interest, for the compromises over polity and doctrine to which the colonies' leaders were forced by their more radical brethren also led to the
American Puritans' most impressive achievement, the sublimation of
radical ideology into the emerging "myth of America" described by
scholars like Bercovitch and Robert Middlekauff in their accounts of
the New England mind. Through the rhetorical power of the ministers'
jeremiads and the subtle redefinition of New England's errand within
the terms of scriptural typology, much of the original force of the radicals' criticism of seventeenth-century society was subsumed into the
millennial component of Puritan thought that always had formed a
significant part of the Puritans' understanding of their position in the
New World.

The full co-optation of the radicals' program into what Bercovitch elsewhere calls "the American self" had to await the second generation of American Puritans, who had missed both the excitement of life in outlawed conventicles and the heady delight of viewing the New World as "a new Indes of heavenly treasure" where "yet more . . . may be." But even as the foundation of the New England Way was being laid in the years before 1660, Puritans in both old and New England had begun to worry whether the colony was fulfilling the divine destiny to which it was called. In 1644, for example, Roger Williams thought it a "monstrous Paradox" that within the Bay Colony "Gods children should persecute Gods children" and reported "the Speech of an honourable Knight of the Parliament" who, on hearing of the intolerance of the Massachusetts leaders, exclaimed: "What, Christ persecute Christ in New England?" Isaac Penington, arguing against John Norton's defense of the colony's persecution of the Quakers in the 1650s, asked New Englanders to consider whether they really had felt themselves "to grow in the inward life, upon [their] coming into *New-England*, or did that [life] begin to flag and wither, and [their] growth chiefly consist in form and outward order?" Even Peter Bulkeley, minister to the frontier outpost of Concord and a strong supporter of Shepard, warned that unless the colonists rearranged their priorities "God [may] remove thy Candlesticke out of the midst of thee" and change Massachusetts from "a Citie upon an hill, which many seek unto," to "a Beacon upon the top of a mountaine, desolate and forsaken." Though John Cotton, as his grandson Cotton Mather reported, may indeed have written to John Davenport that in New England *"the order of the churches and commonwealth . . . brought to his mind the new heaven and the new earth,"* it is essential to realize that his sentiment simply was not shared by all the population. Some had very different expectations for the future of the colony.

In the place of the spiritual and, by implication, political democracy the radicals demanded, the New Englanders erected only a half-way house on the road to a more democratic society—the congregationalism that played so large a part in the liberation of radical ideology in England but which, when institutionalized as it was in New England, more often than not produced supporters as harsh and intolerant as the English prelates. But some historians—Stephen Foster, for example—argue that the colonists "actually put into practice the Independents' most visionary and apparently unachievable goals," specifically, an "insistence on the rule of the saints, on government of and by the regenerate." More important, for the first four decades of New England's history individuals and groups who represented the full range of English Puritan thought fertilized the New England mind with much more novel, and sometimes downright startling, ideas carried with them from their English experience.

☆ 3 ☆

British Mercantilism and the American Colonies

HELP OR HINDRANCE?

Historians have often employed British mercantilism as a yard-stick by which to measure the fairness of the mother country toward her American colonies. British mercantilist policies, after all, provided the impetus for much of the imperial legislation passed in the seventeenth and eighteenth centuries. The question historians traditionally have asked was this: To what degree did these policies subordinate the interests of the American colonies to those of Britain? Implicit in this question was a second of far greater importance: Was British mercantilism so unfair and one-sided that it helped bring on the American Revolution?

In answering these questions, historians disagreed widely. Some argued that Britain's mercantilism was a selfish system which deprived American colonists of the fruits of their labors and stifled their economic growth by repressive measures. Others stressed the economic advantages inherent in the mother country's mercantilist system and noted that prior to 1763 American colonists rarely protested against Britain's policies. Still another group of historians concluded that British mercantilism did not have the great impact usually ascribed to it because the colonists evaded or ignored Britain's economic regulations and resorted to smuggling. These opposing points of view, as we shall see, often reflected the political, economic, and social climate of the era in which a given historian was writing.

Before tracing the impact of mercantilism on the American colonies, it is necessary to understand the British background of mercantilist theory and practice. The term "mercantilism" itself did not come into general use until the eighteenth century, and even then was used to bring together a number of disparate ideas that were never clearly defined. Although mercantilism was never the coherent system pictured in most textbooks, some generalizations may be made about this complex concept.

When the first colonies were being settled, one assumption of English mercantilist thinkers was that nation-states should regulate their economic life so as to strengthen themselves for competition with other nation-states. As far back as the fifteenth century the English government had adopted policies on a nationwide basis regulating the buying and selling of goods in order to encourage trade which was good for England and to discourage that which was bad. England was not alone in accepting the concept of mercantilism; the same economic philosophy was being practiced by all major countries of western Europe. Each nation, however, tended to stress those distinctive features of mercantilism which would produce for it the greatest prosperity and national strength. Spain, for example, stressed the amassing of precious metals, Holland the control of external trade, and France the regulation of internal trade.

England, on the other hand, appeared to emphasize four major aims in her mercantilism: (1) to encourage the growth of a native merchant marine fleet so that England might control the shipping of her own goods; (2) to provide protection for England's manufactures; (3) to protect England's agriculture, especially her grain farmers; and (4) to accumulate as much hard money as possible. The ultimate goal of these mercantilist measures invariably was the same: to make England self-sufficient, rich, and strong as a military power.

Beginning in the seventeenth century these mercantilist principles were expanded to include the idea of colonies. Mercantilist thinkers began emphasizing that no nation could achieve greatness without colonies, and Britain rather belatedly embarked upon her career as a colonizing power. Colonies presumably were to supplement the economy of the mother country in three ways: by supplying the mother country with raw materials; serving as markets for English manufactures; and conducting their trade in such a way as to benefit Britain. In order that various segments of the British Empire might fit within this mercantilist framework, Parliament passed laws which regulated, in part, the economic life of all her colonies.

Parliament's program for the American colonies in this regard during the century between the 1650s and 1750s was called the Old Colonial System. The emphasis in this chapter, for the most part, will be on this program and period. One of the main features of this system was a series of navigation acts designed to channel colonial commerce into paths profitable for the mother country. To assure the dominance of Britain's merchant marine fleet over the lucrative carrying trade between England and America, Parliament passed the Navigation Act of 1651. This act required all goods traded within the empire to be carried in British or American ships, or in the ships of the country of manufac-

ture. To make certain that the mother country would receive the benefit of valuable raw materials produced in the colonies, the Enumerated
Commodities Act of 1660 was passed. This law specified that certain
colonial products, such as tobacco, sugar, and indigo, could be shipped
only to England or to other English colonies. The mother country exercised control over colonial imports as well as exports. Under the Staples Act of 1663 Parliament ruled that some goods shipped from Europe to the American colonies had to pass through English ports first.
Thus duties could be placed on European goods before they were
shipped to America, thereby protecting British merchants from foreign
competition in the colonial market.

A second aim of the Old Colonial System was to make it possible
for England to continue to accumulate hard money. The balance of
trade between Britain and the American colonies favored the mother
country and, whenever possible, it insisted on being paid in specie.
Consequently, whatever hard money the colonies obtained in their
trade with the West Indies or other parts of the world was drained off
to Britain. English merchants refused for the most part to accept colonial paper money in payment for debts, and Parliament backed them
by ruling that colonial notes were not legal tender for such transactions. British merchants also made it a general rule never to send bul-
lion or gold or silver coins to America, and eventually Parliament
passed a law to that effect. Statutes regulating the flow of hard money,
then, were designed to protect the mother country.

Certain American industries were also subjected to regulation under the system to prevent them from competing with Britain. The
woolen industry was restricted to some degree by the Woolens Act of
1699, which prohibited the export of wool, yarn, or woolen cloth in
foreign or intercolonial trade. In 1732 the Hat Act prohibited the sale
of hats abroad or to any other colonies. Under the Iron Act of 1750
steps were taken to prohibit the making of many finished iron products. American attempts at manufacturing were also discouraged to
some degree by British laws which made it a crime to lure skilled
workers or import textile machinery from England.

Although historians agreed on the essential features of the Old Colonial System, they disagreed about its effects on the American economy. The idea that the navigation acts were so oppressive as to constitute a primary cause of the American Revolution was first given
prominence by George Bancroft in his multivolume *History of the
United States.* Writing in the late 1830s Bancroft, in his second volume, portrayed the acts as a prime example of British selfishness. Colonial trade was confined so strictly by regulations, according to Bancroft, that Americans were allowed to sell to foreign nations only those
goods in which England had no interest. When it came to buying goods
the colonies were restricted to so few markets that they could not com-

pete on a fair basis. "The commercial liberties of rising states were shackled by paper chains, and the principles of natural justice subjected to the fears and covetousness of English shopkeepers." Prepared to believe the worst about Britain, Bancroft misunderstood the provisions of the Navigation Act of 1660 and wrote mistakenly that under this law the carrying trade within the British Empire was open only to those merchants residing in England. Such economic exploitation ruined the relations between Britain and her colonies, said Bancroft, and helped to bring about the Revolution. "It converted commerce, which should be the bond of peace, into a source of rankling hostility, and scattered the certain seeds of a civil war. The navigation act contained a pledge of the ultimate independence of America."[1]

Bancroft believed that Britain's restrictions on American manufacturing were equally burdensome. Carelessly reading the laws that prohibited the production of hats, woolens, and finished iron goods under certain circumstances, he jumped to the conclusion that the mother country had stifled *all* manufacturing. "America was forbidden, by act of parliament, not merely to manufacture those articles which might compete with the English in foreign markets," wrote Bancroft, "but even to supply herself, by her own industry, with those articles which her position enabled her to manufacture with success for her own wants."[2] Once again he was in error. The three industries noted above were the only ones upon which Britain had imposed any major limitations. But right or wrong, Bancroft was convinced that British restrictions of any kind on colonial trade and manufacturing were mischievous, wicked and hopelessly one-sided.

Bancroft's sharp condemnation of Britain's regulatory measures becomes more understandable when one recalls the economic theories current in the 1830s and 1840s—the decades in which he wrote his volumes on the prerevolutionary period. The older concept of mercantilism was giving way by this time to the ideas of laissez-faire capitalism, which sought to minimize the role of government in economic affairs. Many of the theories current in the 1830s and 1840s harked back to the teachings of Adam Smith, who had favored free trade and opposed government controls which might affect the laws of supply and demand. Both Britain and the United States were moving in the direction of free trade and more modern laissez-faire practices. Bancroft was injecting the economic doctrines of his day into the past when he criticized the navigation acts and other mercantilist restrictions over the American colonies.

An entire generation of Americans formed their ideas of the British

---

[1]George Bancroft, *History of the United States* (1st ed., Boston, 1837), 2:42–47, 122, 157–158, and 198–199.

[2]*Ibid.*, p. 44.

mercantilist system on the basis of Bancroft's writings. Before Bancroft wrote, few textbooks had mentioned the navigation acts in connection with the Revolution. But Bancroft kept insisting that British economic restrictions had caused the break between the colonies and mother country. In his fifth volume Bancroft stated unequivocally: "American independence, like the great rivers of the country, had many sources; but the head-spring which colored all the stream was the Navigation Act."[3] Most schoolbooks in the 1850s, as a result, listed the acts as one of the chief causes of the American Revolution.

In the 1880s and 1890s, fifty years after Bancroft had published his first volumes, a new group of scholars—the imperial school of historians—appeared to challenge his findings. The imperial school reacted against Bancroft's intensely nationalistic approach, which viewed the colonies solely within the narrow context of American history. These scholars proposed to look at the American colonies within a much broader framework—as parts of the British Empire as a whole. Many of the members of the imperial school had a pro-British bias. Hence they looked upon the British policies and actions in the colonial period in a much different light than Bancroft. Two members of the imperial school in particular—George L. Beer and Charles M. Andrews—studied the way in which the British had regulated the economic life of the American colonies in accordance with certain mercantilist ideas.

Beer began his first work, *The Commercial Policy of England toward the American Colonies*, published in 1893, by criticizing Bancroft and other nineteenth-century nationalist historians for writing with an ultrapatriotic point of view. "They start," he wrote, "with the idea that England consciously pursued an egotistic and tyrannical policy. By making the facts conform to this preconception, they have produced books that are notably unjust to England."[4] Freed from such a patriotic bias, Beer said he was able to study his subject in a more objective light. But Beer was to err in the opposite direction; he exhibited a pro-British bias in his writings. Indeed, in his work as a publicist and propagandist during World War I Beer went so far as to call for a reunion of the English-speaking peoples in Britain and America to help maintain world peace.

Beer was likewise critical of the present-minded approach of Bancroft and other historians who had evaluated Britain's mercantilist policy from the point of view of nineteenth-century ideas of free trade and laissez-faire doctrine. In his own work Beer examined mercantilism within the context of seventeenth- and eighteenth-century economic

---

[3] *Ibid.*, 5:159. This volume appeared in 1852.

[4] George L. Beer, *The Commercial Policy of England toward the American Colonies, Columbia College Studies in History, Economics, and Public Law*, vol. 3, pt. 2 (New York, 1893), pp. 7–8.

ideas. "No institution can be condemned from the historical stand-point," he wrote, "if it is really in advance of that which preceded."[5] Viewing the mercantilist system in this light, Beer concluded that mercantilism represented a marked advance over the economic theories upon which Britain had been relying.

In his overall evaluation of the British mercantilist system, Beer saw benefits as well as burdens for America. He stressed the constructive side of mercantilism by showing that the navigation acts were actually responsible in large measure for the commercial prosperity of British North America. After all, he noted, colonial goods were guaranteed markets within the British Empire—one of the major trading blocs of the Western world. Moreover, American ships were permitted to participate in Britain's lucrative carrying trade on a favorable basis. Beer discussed certain disadvantages such as restrictions on colonial trade and manufacturing, but he felt that these regulations were a fair exchange for the protection provided to the colonists by the British army and navy, and the monopoly granted to certain American goods on the English market. After comparing the mother country's mercantilist policy with that of other nations, Beer declared that Britain's was "much more liberal."[6] The system as a whole, he concluded, "was thus based on the idea of the mutual reciprocity of the economic interests of the mother country and colony."[7]

Contrary to Bancroft's findings Beer believed that the economic restrictions imposed by Britain's colonial policy had little to do with the coming of the Revolution. Beer's work dealt primarily with the Old Colonial System and he concluded: "The colonial system, as it was administered before 1763, contributed but slightly in bringing about the revolution of 1776."[8] It was only after 1763, when economic principles were subordinated to political considerations in Britain's colonial policy, Beer declared, that relations between the mother country and colonies deteriorated rapidly.

Beer published three more works between 1907 and 1912 dealing with various aspects of Britain's mercantilist policy. In *The Origins of the British Colonial System, 1578–1660* and *The Old Colonial System, 1660–1754* he showed how the British gradually evolved what he considered to be an efficient administrative machinery for running the empire. These two works broadened the investigation of Britain's colonial policy by describing the workings of mercantilism not only in the thirteen American colonies but in Newfoundland and the West Indies as well. Beer's most brilliant book, *British Colonial Policy, 1754–1765,*

---

[5]*Ibid.*, p. 8.

[6]*Ibid.*, p. 9.

[7]George L. Beer, *British Colonial Policy, 1754–1765* (New York, 1907), p. 195.

[8]Beer, *Commercial Policy of England toward the American Colonies*, p. 157.

carried the story forward to the period during and after the French and Indian War. In this work Beer argued that the mother country had to make sacrifices equally as great as those of the colonies in order to maintain a self-sufficient empire. The picture that emerged from Beer's works was that of a well-regulated and reasonable mercantilist system in which the economic benefits and burdens were neatly balanced between the colonies and mother country.

Charles M. Andrews, a second member of the imperial school, took a sympathetic view of Britain's mercantilist policy, similar to that of Beer, when he wrote his four-volume _magnum opus_ in the 1930s—_The Colonial Period of American History_. To Andrews the navigation acts did not represent a policy of economic oppression but rather a sincere attempt by Britain to organize the administration of the empire. In his fourth volume Andrews described in detail the various agencies such as the vice-admiralty courts, the Board of Trade, and customs service which Britain employed to administer colonial trade and commerce. Andrews came to the conclusion that Britain's mercantilist regulations in the main proved ineffectual because the imperial policy of supervision and administration was weak and defective. American colonists, Andrews claimed, were restrained very little in their economic activities by the regulations of British mercantilism.

While the imperial school of historians was proclaiming Britain's mercantilist policies as being eminently fair, another group of American scholars was taking issue with this point of view. The reaction against Bancroft's highly nationalistic interpretation of the colonial period was in full swing by the turn of the twentieth century, and certain scholars, influenced by the Populist and Progressive movements, were digging beneath the surface of events to discover what to them appeared to be the true underlying forces which shaped the course of history. Many became convinced that economic forces were the single most important factor in history, and an economic interpretation of history grew increasingly popular during the first three decades of the century. Charles and Mary Beard wrote their _Rise of American Civilization_ in the late 1920s in this vein and were critical of the sympathetic view taken by the imperial school of historians toward the British mercantilist system. "Modern calculators," they wrote, "have gone to some pains to show that on the whole American colonists derived benefits from English policy which greatly outweighed their losses from the restraints laid on them. For the sake of argument the case may be conceded; it is simply irrelevant to the uses of history. The origins of the legislation are clear; and the fact that it restricted American economic enterprise in many respects is indisputable."[9]

---

[9]Charles and Mary Beard, _The Rise of American Civilization_, 2 vols. (New York, 1927), 1:196.

But the most rigid application of an economic interpretation of the British mercantilist system came during the Great Depression of the 1930s in the Marxist point of view of Louis M. Hacker. A professor at Columbia University, Hacker set forth his thesis in three works: a sketch of American economic history entitled *The United States: A Graphic History;* an article in the 1937 *Marxist Quarterly;* and a fully documented work, *The Triumph of American Capitalism,* in 1940. In both books Hacker pictured Britain and the American colonies as two rival capitalisms, or competing economic systems. British mercantile capitalism, Hacker wrote, sought constantly to keep the American colonies in a subordinate relationship within the empire. The whole aim of the mercantilist system was to force the colonists to conduct their economic life in such a way as to enrich the English capitalist class. In America two sets of capitalists, merchants in the northern colonies and planters in the South, consistently resisted such efforts. As the colonies grew in wealth, power, and maturity, clashes between the British and American economic systems grew more intense and led ultimately to the break with Britain. "In its fullest historical meaning . . . [the American Revolution] had as its function the release of American merchant and planting capitalism from the fetters of the English Mercantile System," Hacker concluded.[10]

To Hacker British mercantilist policies represented "prison walls" from which there was no escape by American capitalists as long as they remained within the empire. English capitalists deliberately choked off any areas of economic growth in America by passing imperial legislation that denied colonial capitalists opportunities for investments in profitable trade outside the empire, native manufacturing, or speculation in western lands. Few benefits were to be derived by Americans in the British mercantilist system, he wrote, and a clash between the two competing systems became inevitable.

Hacker's books were, in fact, not so much an attack upon British mercantile capitalism in colonial times as a full-scale assault upon the capitalist system itself as a way of life. As the depression deepened in the 1930s many Americans questioned the effectiveness of laissez-faire capitalism. Disillusioned by the economic disintegration that seemed to be taking place in many parts of the Western world, Hacker became a formidable critic of the capitalist system. It seemed to him that capitalism was incapable of providing abundance, work, and security for vast numbers of people. With the economic crises uppermost in his mind, Hacker examined the American past and rewrote the nation's

---

[10]Louis M. Hacker *et al., The United States: A Graphic History* (New York, 1936), p. 28. Although two other coauthors were listed for this work, Rudolf Modley and George R. Taylor, Hacker himself was solely responsible for the written text. See also *The Triumph of American Capitalism* (New York, 1940).

history along bold new lines. Hacker's analysis of the British mercantilist system, then, was set within the framework of a Marxist interpretation of American history. For Hacker, freedom from the British merchant capitalists prepared the way for the native industrial capitalists
to dominate society in America; the American people merely exchanged one capitalist master for another. Hacker's article from the
Marxist Quarterly is reprinted as the first selection in this chapter.

Although Beer, Andrews, and Hacker shed new light upon the imperial regulations and possible motives behind the mercantilist system, much research remained to be done on the laws themselves.
What were the specific provisions of the navigation acts, for example,
and how well had these measures been administered? What was the
effect of the navigation laws upon England's economy? To what degree
had these laws achieved the purpose for which they had been passed?
Such specific questions were raised and answered in the works of Lawrence A. Harper.

Harper's *The English Navigation Laws: A Seventeenth Century
Experiment in Social Engineering*, published in 1939, viewed this legislation primarily from the point of view of English administration and
policy. In dealing with the navigation acts of the 1600s Harper attempted to put these laws in proper historical context by showing that
they were the culmination of a three-century-long program to build up
England's shipping fleet. By examining the period both before and after
the passage of these acts Harper was able to ascertain that they had
a decidedly beneficial effect upon England's economy. The laws, he
concluded, had stimulated England's shipbuilding industry, provided
employment for England's shipwrights, and enabled England's sailors
to receive training in the merchant marine that stood them in good
stead when called to serve in the Royal Navy. Some historians had assumed the navigation acts were ineffective in America because the colonists had evaded them, but Harper's study showed that in the 1600s, at
least, there was very little smuggling in the trade across the Atlantic.
Although Harper's conclusions were based only upon estimates of English shipping (because complete statistics were unavailable), his book
remains the most thoroughgoing evaluation of the navigation acts in
the seventeenth century.

Harper, as his subtitle indicates, approached the navigation acts as
an experiment in the idea of a planned economy. That is, he looked
upon the acts as a deliberate attempt by the English government to
regulate the economic conduct of the state along predetermined lines
by means of social planning. His work appeared at precisely the time
that similar efforts were being made in America under the New Deal.
Indeed, Harper confessed at the beginning of his book that he was interested in analyzing the process of social engineering "in the hope

that it may throw some light upon the problems involved in our present social experiments."[11]

In a penetrating essay written in the same year as his book, Harper turned his attention to the effect of the navigation acts upon the economic life of the American colonies. Harper took exception to the conclusions of Beer that the Old Colonial System was so fair that economic benefits and burdens were neatly balanced between Britain and the American colonies. In his statistical analysis Harper found that the burdens of the navigation acts outweighed the benefits received and that such legislation had actually retarded the economic growth of the mainland colonies. But, Harper quickly added, this did not mean that British mercantilism was bad or that the navigation acts had caused the Revolution; the American colonies received many advantages from the imperial tie—such as military and naval protection—which he admittedly did not take up in his essay.[12]

Harper discussed the broader question of British mercantilism and the American Revolution in another article published in 1942. In this piece Harper sought to measure in quantitative terms the burdens imposed by British mercantilist policies on various segments of the American economy. So far as commerce across the Atlantic was concerned, he estimated that it cost the Americans between $2 million and $7 million each year to trade within the framework laid down in the regulations of the mother country. The picture was less clear, however, when it came to British regulations on American manufacturing. The Woolens Act of 1699 probably had little impact on the woolen industry, and opportunities for exporting woolen goods from one colony to another were limited. The Hat Act of 1732 had restricted the colonial hat industry, but, Harper added, this type of manufacturing played only a minor part in the American economy. As for the Iron Act of 1750, Harper was dubious whether the legislation had had much influence upon the iron industry. In his overall evaluation Harper concluded that "an analysis of the economic effects of British mercantilism fails to establish its exploitative features as the proximate cause of the Revolution."[13]

The study of history reveals that it is not events as they actually are, but as people think that they are, which often determines the course of history. Although it was true that many historians concluded

---

[11]Lawrence A. Harper, *The English Navigation Laws: A Seventeenth Century Experiment in Social Engineering* (New York, 1939), p. viii.

[12]Lawrence A. Harper, "The Effect of the Navigation Acts on the Thirteen Colonies," in *Era of the American Revolution*, Richard B. Morris, ed. (New York, 1939), pp. 3–39.

[13]Lawrence A. Harper, "Mercantilism and the American Revolution," *Canadian Historical Review* 23 (March 1942):12.

that the Old Colonial System did not exploit the colonists, it was conceivable that many Americans *thought* the British mercantilist system was taking advantage of them, and upon the basis of supposed economic grievances, embarked upon the Revolution. It was left to Oliver M. Dickerson to investigate just what the American reaction was to one aspect of British mercantilism—the navigation acts.

Dickerson's *The Navigation Acts and the American Revolution*, published in the 1950s, dealt a severe blow to those who still clung to a strict economic interpretation on the coming of the Revolution and to the acts as one of the important long-range causes for the separation from Britain. The colonists, Dickerson concluded, did not object to the navigation acts as such nor to the mercantilist policies of the Old Colonial System. Searching through much of the contemporary literature—newspapers, pamphlets, broadsides, and writings of leading political figures—Dickerson discovered that the colonists rarely raised the British mercantile system as an issue before 1763. Instead of driving the colonies and mother country apart, Britain's trade and navigation laws, according to Dickerson, provided "the most important cement of empire."[14]

It was only after 1763, Dickerson went on, when the British altered their mercantilist system to raise revenue rather than to control trade within the empire, that the colonists began protesting. In the period after the French and Indian War, the dominant motive of British mercantilism changed from the regulation of trade and commerce to regulation for the sake of revenue and political exploitation. George III and his corrupt faction sought to shift part of the burden of defending British North America to the colonies by levying a series of new taxes and to use the taxing power to create jobs as customs officials in America for their political henchmen. America was exploited by these newly appointed officials who resorted to "customs racketeering" to victimize wealthy colonial merchants under the technicalities of the law. Within a decade, the loyalty and mutual interest that bound the colonies and mother country together in a "cement of empire" had dissolved. "The hostility was not [due] to the old navigation and trade system," concluded Dickerson, "but to a new policy contrary to that system."[15] Dickerson's book attempted to demonstrate that the colonies were not only prosperous under the old navigation laws, but loyal and satisfied as well.

One of the most ardent defenders of the British mercantilist system in the mid-twentieth century was Lawrence H. Gipson, a prolific scholar who continued to uphold the tradition of the imperial school

---

[14]Oliver M. Dickerson, *The Navigation Acts and the American Revolution* (Philadelphia, 1951), p. 157.

[15]*Ibid.*, p. xiv.

of historians. Unlike Harper and Dickerson, who were openly critical of the change in mercantilist policy after 1763, Gipson took the position that the mother country was perfectly justified in levying taxes to pay part of the costs of administering the empire in America. Gipson viewed the mercantilist system in the broadest possible context and wrote a multivolume work on the British Empire in the period prior to the Revolution which placed the development of the American colonies in a world setting. The wars Britain waged against France in America were not motivated by a lust for empire, Gipson claimed, but rather by an ardent desire to protect her colonies from being conquered by the French. Gipson felt it only fair that the Americans, having been the beneficiaries of Britain's military might from 1754 to 1763, should pay part of the bill for such protection. Gipson also took up the question of oppressive taxation as a cause of the Revolution and concluded that in view of the protection Britain had provided, the taxes imposed upon the American colonists after 1763 were neither excessive nor oppressive.[16]

Gipson's works were as important for their pro-British interpretation as for their presentation of the mercantilist system from an imperial point of view. During the war with France the Americans were pictured as being shortsighted and selfish by their unwillingness to accept their responsibilities as members of the British Empire. Britain, on the other hand, was presented in very favorable terms. The mother country spent enormous sums of money in defending America, subsidized colonial defense efforts, and sent over large numbers of redcoats to fight the French. Gipson stated in a one-volume work published in the 1950s that the Americans continued their selfish ways once the war was over. With the threat of the French removed from Canada, the Americans felt less of a need for the mother country. They began demanding more autonomy, resisted the payment of taxes, and refused to accede to Parliamentary laws passed to bring greater order and organization to Britain's enlarged empire in North America. According to Gipson, then, the Americans were lacking in that loyalty that might reasonably have been expected of them after they had received the benefits of a mercantilist system that had provided both military protection and profitable commerce.[17]

Thus the changing view of the mercantilist system had moved from a pro-American position of George Bancroft in the 1850s to a pro-British interpretation by Lawrence Gipson in the 1950s. Gipson's work had demonstrated one thing: that in the past century American histo-

---

[16]Lawrence H. Gipson, *The British Empire before the American Revolution*, 15 vols. (Caldwell, Idaho, and New York, 1936–1970).

[17]Lawrence H. Gipson, *The Coming of the Revolution, 1763–1775* (New York, 1954), pp. xi–xiv, 26–27, and 230–234.

rians had found it possible at long last to break free from the bonds of the narrow, nationalist bias in evaluating the mercantilist system.

From the 1960s to the mid-1980s, two new approaches to the study of imperial relations emerged. One group of scholars might be termed the neoimperialists to distinguish them from the more traditional school. The second group—the self-styled "new economic historians"—revolutionized the study of economic history, employing research strategies that involved quantitative techniques and the use of economic model-building.

These two groups of scholars were less concerned with determining the benefits or burdens of the Old Colonial system than in raising different questions regarding the political and economic life of the British Empire. The neoimperialists focused more upon the informal structures within the political and administrative institutions of the Old Colonial System. The "new economic historians"—who were a fragment group within the "new social history"—on the other hand, concentrated on two other issues. First, they described the workings of the North Atlantic economic community as a whole. Second, they sought to explain America's economic growth within the broad context of the Anglo-American commercial world. The contributions of the two groups illuminated not only some hitherto unknown forces at work within the empire but also introduced new methodologies in doing research on economic developments in the mother country as well as in the colonies.

Many of the historians of the traditional imperial school—such as Gipson—were favorably inclined toward Britain and pictured America as being too selfish, self-centered, and shortsighted. The neoimperial historians were less interested in taking sides and concerned more with analyzing the complexities of the relationships between mother country and colony. In writing about British politics they focused more upon the informal structure of authority—the attitudes, goals, and rivalries of the groups and individuals running the machinery of the empire—than upon the formal structure of public institutions, officials, and agencies. When dealing with the perpetual struggle for power within the British bureaucracy, they wrote about the colonial agent-lobbyists, interest groups, and social groupings within Parliament who contributed to the decision-making process on imperial policies. And in discussing ideology they were more cognizant of the central role that ideas played in precipitating the Revolution—the conspiracy theory held by many British officials that the colonists were determined to throw off their dependence upon the Crown; the conspiracy theory among Americans that the mother country was aiming to deprive them of their rights and liberties under the British constitution; and the colonists' attitudes toward their status as subordinates within the British Empire.

The neoimperialist scholars partly reflected both external and internal pressures upon the historical profession. In the world at large the collapse of the old European empires in Asia and Africa after World War II resulted in a reexamination of the effects of imperialism. With many former colonies emerging into nationhood, some American historians felt there were parallels between the American colonial experience in the seventeenth and eighteenth centuries and the experiences of other colonial peoples who gained their independence in the mid-twentieth century.

Some neoimperial scholars revised an earlier school of historians who had followed the lead of Lewis B. Namier, a distinguished British scholar who had destroyed the old idea of the existence of Whig and Tory parties in England during the reign of George III. Namier substituted instead an atomistic picture of British politics with a fragmented Parliament made up of competing factions and family groupings whose members were concerned solely with securing political offices for themselves, their kin, or local constituents. Thus Parliament's outlook was narrow-minded, factious, and provincial, and its workings were organized around material interests, family connections, and patronage. This situation made it impossible for Parliament to achieve the kind of broad-minded, imperial view required for sound policies of empire. Because of this grasping, circumscribed, and nonideological approach to politics, Namier concluded, Britain could not have produced a viable imperial policy, resolved her quarrel with the colonies, or prevented the loss of her empire.

Certain neoimperial scholars, however, were prone to see the ideology of interest groups at work within the Parliament in the formulation of imperial policy. A leading representative of the neoimperial approach, Michael Kammen, studied the workings of such interest groups in British politics from the mid-1600s to 1800 in his *Empire and Interest,* published in 1970. He claimed that British mercantilism gave rise to a host of interest groups—men bound together by special interests who united their efforts to advance, maintain, and defend those interests. Kammen examined the total environment of each of these groups—the concepts, assumptions, and attitudes as well as the material motivation of its members—and used the history of such interest groups to analyze and explain changes in domestic and imperial politics. Such an approach, among other things, enabled him to place the coming of the American Revolution within the broader context of interest-group politics inside the British Empire.

Thomas C. Barrow, another scholar identified with the neoimperial approach, sought to examine the inner workings of the formal institution he was studying in his *Trade and Empire: The British Customs Service in Colonial America, 1600–1775.* In this work Barrow inquired into the motivation and ideology of the men who ran this part of the imperial machinery. Rather than concentrating only on the operation of the customs service, Barrow analyzed the experiences and reactions of the British bureaucrats in London who were administering that agency. Barrow concluded that these administrators were mainly concerned with the domestic affairs of the mother country and paid only casual attention to American problems. When they did interest themselves in colonial affairs, these men revealed that they were operating on one underlying assumption: that the interests of the mother country were in conflict and inherently incompatible with those of the colonies, and that the Americans—aware of this fact—were looking forward to the day when they would be free from Britain. In contrast to the older school of imperial historians who sometimes suggested that Anglo-American relations prior to 1760 were essentially harmonious, Barrow concluded that the relationship engendered hostility among British administrators; they were haunted continually by the fear of eventual American independence.

In an article published after his book, Barrow carried this last neo-imperialist argument one step further. After analyzing reports of British governors, agents, and bureaucrats, Barrow argued that they had grown increasingly impatient both with the colonists' recalcitrant attitude as well as with the ineffectiveness of the Old Colonial System itself. Viewing the situation from the vantage point of the British, he concluded that many British officials before 1763 had decided there was great need for a more effective exercise of authority on the part of the mother country. This need led George Grenville and others within the British government to launch a program of reform that led to the new taxation policies and other programs after 1763. Thus it was the need for imperial reform—and not necessarily the demands of the French and Indian War—which brought about the changes in policies that resulted in the constitutional crisis that ended in revolution.[18]

The "new economic historians," like the neoimperialists, moved in quite a different direction from the scholars who had preceded them. Prior to the 1960s American economic historians tended to be primarily descriptive in their writings. They focused largely on studies of individual businessmen, institutional changes, and separate sectors of the economy. Some of the problems with which they dealt concerned the nature of economic institutions and the impact of social and political factors upon economic development or stagnation. To support their conclusions they tended to rely upon traditional literary sources, impressionistic information, and scattered statistical evidence. The new generation of economic historians were skeptical of both the problems

---

[18]Thomas C. Barrow, "The Old Colonial System from an English Point of View," in *Anglo-American Political Relations, 1675–1775*, Alison Olson and Richard Maxwell Brown, eds. (New Brunswick, 1970), pp. 125–139.

posed and the evidence presented by these older scholars. They insisted that the study of economic history be analytical rather than descriptive, systematic instead of fragmentary, and that it focus on economic growth rather than on piecemeal economic developments. The study of economic history, they believed, should be firmly grounded in statistical information—hard quantitative data capable of empirical verification. With the help of high-speed computers such data could be interpreted in the light of models derived from contemporary economic theory. Their emphasis on these new research techniques led them to study long-term trends and more sweeping economic developments.

Applying the techniques of quantification and model-building the "new economic historians" raised once again the question of how severely the navigation acts had affected America's economy. Harper had attempted earlier to quantify the burdens resulting from British regulations which compelled colonial merchants to reroute their trade. Robert Paul Thomas, using more sophisticated quantitative techniques, wrote an article in the 1960s that confirmed Harper's findings. Thomas estimated that between 1763 and 1772 the annual per capita loss to the American colonies from Britain's mercantile system averaged only about twenty-six cents per person, or about 0.5 percent of the estimated per capita income. On this basis, he argued, neither the navigation acts nor the new British imperial regulations applied after 1763 imposed any significant economic burden upon Americans.[19]

The overall result of these recent findings has been to deemphasize the impact of the navigation acts on the colonial economy. Stuart Bruchey in his book, however, argued that Britain's mercantilist policies probably hindered America's economic growth prior to the Revolution. But he went on to caution that this generalization was by no means conclusive, for the problem required further study. The second selection in this chapter is from Bruchey's book.

George R. Taylor, in an essay on America's economic growth from its founding in the early 1600s to 1840, produced evidence that suggested the rate of growth from 1710 to 1775 was almost as high as it had been from 1775 to 1840. Besides de-emphasizing the effect of the navigation acts, Taylor's essay demonstrated the virtue of looking at the process of economic development over long periods of time.[20]

Other scholars have examined America's colonial economic growth in a similar light. James F. Shepherd and Gary M. Walton, in

---

[19]Robert Paul Thomas, "A Quantitative Approach to the Study of the Effects of British Imperial Policy upon Colonial Welfare: Some Preliminary Findings," *Journal of Economic History* 25 (1965):615–638. See also, Peter McClelland. "The Cost to America of British Imperial Policy," *American Economic Review Proceedings* 59 (1969):370–381.

[20]George R. Taylor, "Economic Growth Before 1840: An Exploratory Essay," *Journal of Economic History* 24 (1964): 427–444.

one of their books, examined the long-range economic development of the colonies within the context of the Anglo-American commercial community. Their conclusion was that though the balance of trade may have been against the colonies, the balance of payments was not. The sale of ships made in America to Britain, purchases by the British army in America, and insurance and freight charges all contributed to make up the deficit. The balance of payments between Britain and America from 1768 to 1772, in fact, was even.[21]

Marc Egnal approached the problem of America's economic growth in the colonial period from a somewhat different perspective. Like most "new economic historians" Egnal turned away from the questions raised by Harper and Hacker; he did not focus his attention either on the navigation acts or upon the structure of the Old Colonial System. Concerned primarily with explaining America's economic growth, Egnal concentrated instead upon certain key determinants during the early colonial period: the dynamics of population increase; the rising prices of products; and the increasing availability of capital within the international Atlantic economy.

Egnal argued that much of the economic development of the colonies was affected by conditions outside of America. It was the fluctuations within the British economy between 1720 and 1775 that helped determine to a large degree the pace at which both the colonial population and the American standard of living grew. The increase in new settlers and per capita income in the colonies was characterized by two long waves of expansion—from 1720 to 1745 and from 1745 to 1775—though there were patterns of acceleration and retardation within these long swings. Thus by noting that colonial economic development was largely dependent upon incoming immigrants (as well as on the rise in population by natural means, of course) and upon the influx of British funds, Egnal succeeded in placing America's economic growth within an international rather than an a narrow, nationalistic context.[22]

Walton and Shepherd, in another of their coauthored books, likewise dealt with the problem of the economic growth of colonial America from a broad perspective. First, they treated the subject within the context of Britain's overall overseas trade as well as that of colonial

---

[21]James F. Shepherd and Gary M. Walton, *Shipping, Maritime Trade, and the Economic Development of Colonial America* (Cambridge, Eng., 1973). Two studies that dealt with America's economic growth after the Revolution but which discussed briefly the situation in the colonial period were Douglass C. North's *The Economic Growth of the United States 1790–1860* (rev. ed., New York, 1966), and Gordon Bjork, "The Weaning of the American Economy: Independence, Market Changes, and Economic Development," *Journal of Economic History* 24 (1964):541–560.

[22]Marc Egnal, "The Economic Development of the Thirteen Continental Colonies, 1720 to 1775," *William and Mary Quarterly*, 3d ser. 32 (April 1975):191–222.

America's total trade. Second, they noted that there was often lax enforcement of the navigation acts since the colonists frequently resorted to smuggling to evade them. Third, they observed that the burden of the navigation acts was unevenly distributed because of the economic regionalism present in colonial America. And finally, they pointed out that the statistical information available on trade was sometimes sketchy, and implied that definitive conclusions on the subject were difficult, if not impossible, to draw.[23]

Summarizing the findings of several quantitative scholars Walton and Shepherd came to similar conclusions regarding the possible costs to colonial America of Britain's navigation acts. They all concurred that any exploitation resulting from such legislation ranged "between 1 to 3 percent of the colonial national income, with 1 percent or less being the more acceptable estimate." Although the 1 to 3 percent figure was not trivial, it was by no means intolerable.[24]

But because of the regional structure of the colonial economy this figure by no means told the whole story. The burden fell more on one region—the South—than on the northern or middle colonies. By far the greatest portion of colonial exports to Britain—tobacco, rice, and indigo—came from the southern colonies. All these crops were eventually listed as enumerated commodities, and that meant that they could be sold only to the mother country or other parts of the empire, and not on a free market. Therefore, if any section suffered under the navigation acts, it was the South.[25]

In reviewing the question of whether or not British mercantilism was a help or hindrance to the American colonies, students must draw a balance sheet of the relative benefits and burdens resulting from the imperial system. Were the blessings provided by the British—military and naval defenses, protected markets for many colonial products, and commercial credit—offset by the burdens imposed by the imperial system? Or did the colonists pay too dearly for such benefits by the burdens they had to bear as members of the British Empire? Does the absence of much opposition to the Old Colonial System before 1763 indicate that Americans did not object seriously to the system? Or were the Americans content to leave well enough alone because the system was so ineffective and left them virtually free to do as they pleased? Was the older school of imperial historians correct in assuming that the Americans were selfish and shortsighted because they refused to pay taxes and to accept the other responsibilities required of them as members of the British Empire? Or were the historians of the

---

[23]Gary M. Walton and James F. Shepherd, *The Economic Rise of Early America* (Cambridge, Mass., 1979), pp. 70–79, 79–90, and 158.

[24]*Ibid.*, p. 174.

[25]*Ibid.*, pp. 80–81.

1960s, 1970s, and 1980s more correct in taking a neutral position on this matter when they analyzed the complex imperial relationship from different perspectives and with new research techniques? Were the "new economic historians" on the right track when they insisted upon viewing colonial economic development within the broad framework of the North Atlantic commercial community rather than within a more narrow American context? In answering such questions students are apt to come to some conclusions not only about the British mercantilist system but about some of the possible causes of the American Revolution itself.

Louis M. Hacker

LOUIS M. HACKER (1899–1987) *taught at Columbia University and other American and English universities. Among his many books are* The Triumph of American Capitalism *(1940),* Alexander Hamilton in the American Tradition *(1957), and* The World of Andrew Carnegie: 1865–1901 *(1968).*

At the outbreak of the American Revolution the great majority of the American population—perhaps nine-tenths of it—was engaged on the land. The owning farmers, whether they were planter lords or modest family farmers, were commercial agriculturists: for either they produced cash crops for sale in a market or they developed subsidiary activities to net them a money return. Self-sufficiency, even on the frontier, is impossible under capitalist organization. Cash is needed everywhere, whether it is to pay taxes or for harvesting the crop or to buy salt, iron, and a squirrel gun. Hence, the colonial farmer either produced a cash crop or he tried to find employment among a number of occupations that did not interfere with his agricultural activities. He either trapped or hunted; or worked in logging operations; or shipped with a fishing fleet. Often he really obtained his cash from land speculation: that is to say, as the result of constantly mounting land values, the farmer was in a position to sell his improved land and buy a cheaper farm in the frontier areas. Thus, the American farmer was a dealer in land from the very dawn of settlement until 1920, a period of three centuries. When land values began to decline after 1921, the basis of American agricultural well-being was shaken to its foundations.

This need to develop a cash crop made for the production of staples everywhere. By the eighteenth century New England was producing and sending to market beef, cattle and hogs, work animals and corn to be used for stall feeding. The Middle Colonies had become the great granary of the English settlements, and on the big farms of New York and Pennsylvania, where tenants and indentured servants were being employed, wheat was being grown, processed into flour and sold in the towns and the faraway West Indies. In the Southern Colonies agriculture was the keystone of the whole economic structure: Virginia and

---

Louis M. Hacker, "The American Revolution: Economic Aspects," *Marxist Quarterly* 1 (January–March 1937):46–67. Reprinted with omissions by permission of Louis M. Hacker.

Maryland planters grew tobacco for sale in England; interior farmers grew grains and raised cattle to be used in the West Indian trade; the tidewater planters of the Carolinas and Georgia cultivated and harvested rice, indigo and some cotton. These crops were sent to seaports, put on ships and carried to distant places to furnish those funds which were the basis of the commercial enterprise of the day. . . .

The plantation economy sprang up in colonial Virginia and Maryland, notably, for obvious reasons. The cultivation of a staple like tobacco served excellently the purposes of the Mercantilist System: it did not compete with an important English crop and hence might be grown on a grand scale; it produced a colonial return on the basis of which large English exports might be sent to the Southern Colonies; it furnished opportunities for the investment of English capital—short-term funds for the financing of the crops and long-term funds for the hypothecation of plantation properties; and it created an outlet for England's surplus populations. Thus tobacco cultivation was closely bound to English mercantilist policy. . . .

There was no question that the tobacco market kept on expanding: at the end of the seventeenth century Maryland and Virginia were exporting 35 million pounds to the mother country; by 1763 the quantity had trebled. On the other hand, the industry was at the mercy of the imperial system. Tobacco was on the enumerated list and could be sent, therefore, only to England; high sumptuary taxes were placed on it; prices were controlled in London and tended to drop periodically below the cost of production. In addition, capital costs of plantation operation continued to mount, due to the high cost of labor (the price of indentured servants and, more particularly, that of slaves went up while their productivity remained constant), the exhaustion of the soil in the older regions, and the necessity on the part of the planters to buy new lands to which they could be ready to transfer their activities. The other charges against operations—of freight costs, insurance, merchants' commissions and profits, interest on borrowings—hung like millstones about the necks of the encumbered planters.

The plantation system was particularly dependent upon credit. The tobacco grower required credit to assist in the acquisition of the labor force; to market his cash crop; to furnish his equipment; and to finance his purchase of consumer goods. The only source of funds was the English merchant capitalist: and to him the southern planter was compelled to pay high interest rates, mortgage his land and slaves and turn for the supplying of those necessaries without which his home and plantation could not continue. Constantly weighed down by debt, it was small wonder that the planters of colonial America ever sought to expand their activities, by extending their tobacco lands and engaging in the more speculative aspects of land dealing; and that they turned to thoughts of inflation as relief from debt oppression was also to be expected.

Because the wild lands of the frontier areas were so important to the maintenance of the stability of the southern planting economy, southern capitalists were constantly preoccupied with them. The West was not opened up by the hardy frontiersman; it was opened up by the land speculator who preceded even the Daniel Boones into the wilderness. But the English (and also the Scotch) had also learned to regard with more than a curious interest these wild lands of the West: they saw in them profits from the fur trade and from the speculative exploitation of the region by their own capitalist enterprise. It was at this point that English and southern merchant capital came into conflict; and when, as a result of the promulgation of the Proclamation Line of 1763 and the Quebec Act of 1774, the western lands were virtually closed to colonial enterprising, the southern planting economy began to totter. Without the subsidiary activity of land speculation, planters could not continue solvent; there is no cause for wonder, therefore, that the owners of great plantation properties should be among the first to swell the ranks of the colonial revolutionary host in 1775.

Colonial producers and enterprisers engaged in all those other activities that are associated with a newly settled region. The trapping and slaying of the wild animals of the forests early attracted pioneers and promoters; and the prevalence of the beaver, otter, mink, bear, raccoon and fox in the New England and Middle Colonies and of the deer, raccoon, fox and beaver in the Southern Colonies led to the creation of a thriving peltry and hide industry and trade. The English demand for furs and skins was constant, profits were great, and quickly capitalism became interested and sought to monopolize the field. This it was not difficult to do, particularly when the lines of the traffic lengthened as the wild lands kept on receding beyond the tidewater settlements. English merchants and the great southern and northern landlords financed the individual hunters, trappers and traders, or employed them as their agents, and furnished the truck and firearms which served as the basis for the Indian barter. As the extermination of wildlife went on, the keeping open of an ever-extending frontier zone became one of the necessities of the colonial economy: the struggle over the fur trade had involved England and France in the long series of colonial wars in America; and the desire to continue the fur traffic was one of the reasons for colonial interest in the wild lands beyond the crest of the Appalachians—and, hence, collision with the mother country. . . .

There existed no manufacturing, in the commercial or industrial sense, in colonial America: and in this fact we are to find one of the important keys to the outbreak of the American Revolution. Household manufacturing there was: the colonial farming households, partic-

ularly of the more modest sort and where the necessaries of indentured
servants and Negro slaves were concerned, supplied many of their own
needs. Food was prepared for home consumption: bread was baked,
butter was churned, shoulders and hams were salted and smoked,
fruits were dried, beer was brewed. Wool, flax, hemp and, in the South,
cotton for clothing and home uses were carded, spun, woven and sometimes even rudely dyed. Leather was tanned and made into shoes, caps,
gloves and rough workclothes. The woodlot furnished the timber for
house and barn, shingles, furniture, carts, implement handles, casks
and staves. Ashes were leached, soap was boiled, candles were molded
and kitchen utensils of wood, horn and gourd were devised. Sometimes
working with his family, sometimes assisted by traveling artisans, the
colonial farmer was able to fabricate many crude articles for his daily
needs out of those raw materials that he had at hand. Occasionally a
surplus of cloth, linen, butter or honey was taken to the local village
and sold or exchanged for the salt, iron, paint and tools that were essential to the conduct of the household; for self-sufficiency, of course, was
never fully attained.

This was not manufacturing in the capitalist sense. The conversion of raw materials into finished goods and their sale in large and
distant markets, in modern times, has been under the supervision of
two different types of organization. Sometimes found side by side but
in the broad and abstract sense existing in a sequential relationship,
these have been domestic manufacturing, or the putting-out system,
and industrial manufacturing, or the factory system. . . .

Neither of this type of manufacturing organization was to be found
in colonial America. Why was this? Colonial America did not want for
liquid capital: witness the extraordinary extension of capitalist enterprise, the work of both English and American capitalists, in trade, shipbuilding, land speculation, the financing of the plantation system and
crude iron production. Colonial America had its fair share of wealthy
men: as early as 1680 there were said to be at least thirty merchants in
Massachusetts alone who were worth between $50,000 and $100,000.
Thomas Amory, one of the greatest early colonial merchants, left an
estate worth $100,000; Peter Faneuil, who died a generation later, left
many times that amount. Every colony could boast of its big merchants, who were, in fact, capitalists; indeed, George Washington, the
greatest of these, in the 1770s was calling himself not "planter" but
"merchant." It did not want for the means of creating a free labor supply: the engrossing, or monopolization, of the lands in the settled areas
had compelled small farmers either to become tenants or to move
westward where they squatted on the wild lands held by absentee landlords. The frontier had not been made secure against the Indians because of the fur trade, and the necessity for maintaining tidewater land
values; but had the owners of the wild lands so desired it, the pacifica-

tion of the western areas would have driven the landless into domestic manufacturing or workshops. It did not want for a market: by 1770, concentrated in a relatively small area and excellently served by harbors and rivers, lived a population one-third as great as England's; too, the very rich market for finished goods of the sugar islands easily was capable of exploitation. It did not want for raw materials: for never was a land endowed with richer natural resources. Manufacturing did not appear in colonial America because the very nature of the Mercantilist System prohibited it.

The English Mercantilist System, in its imperial-colonial relations, following the triumph of English merchant capital in the Puritan Revolution, was based on the economic subservience of the colonies. Indeed, every imperial and administrative agency had this end constantly in view: and most significant among these was the Board of Trade. The Board of Trade, in its final form, had been established in 1696, and among its various instruments for control over the colonies, these three were notable: it had the right to deny charters or patents to English-financed companies seeking to engage in enterprises in the colonies which were inimical to the interests of home merchant capitalists; it had the power to review colonial legislation and recommend to the Privy Council the disallowance of such colonial enactments as ran counter to the welfare of the mother country; and it prepared specific instructions for the deportment of the royal governors in the colonies, in particular indicating where the veto power was to be used to prevent colonial encroachments on the privileges and prerogatives of English citizens.

Ever vigilant, the Board of Trade proceeded against the colonies when they threatened to impinge on the interests of Englishmen: it refused to tolerate colonial interference with the mother country's hold on foreign trade and shipping; it checked colonial attempts to control the traffic in convicts and slaves; it prevented colonies from lowering interest rates, easing the judicial burden on debtors, and seeking to monopolize the Indian trade. Most significant were the stern checks imposed on attempts by the colonial assemblies to encourage native manufacturing and to relieve the oppression of debts by the increase of the money supply of the colonies.

Following in the footsteps of the English themselves, colonials looked to public authority to aid in the development of native industries. In the best mercantilist tradition, therefore, colonial statute books came to be filled with legislation which offered bounties to enterprisers, extended public credit to them, exempted them from taxation, gave them easy access to raw materials, and in their behalf encouraged the location of new towns.

Against such legislation the Board of Trade regularly moved. On important matters, appeal was had to Parliament and general statutes were passed, notably the Woolens Act of 1699, which barred colonial wool, woolen yarn and woolen manufactures from intercolonial and foreign commerce; the Hat Act of 1732, which prevented the exportation of hats out of the separate colonies and restricted colonial hatmakers to two apprentices; and the Iron Act of 1750. In addition, the axe of disallowance descended regularly. As early as 1705, a Pennsylvania law for building up the shoemaking industry was disallowed; in 1706, a New York law designed to develop a sailcloth industry was disallowed; in 1706, 1707 and 1708, laws of Virginia and Maryland, providing for the establishment of new towns, were disallowed on the grounds that such new communities must invariably lead to a desire to found manufacturing industries and that their existence would draw off persons from the countryside where they were engaged in the production of tobacco. Indeed, in 1756, when the Board of Trade recommended disallowance of a Massachusetts law for aiding the production of linen, it could say flatly: "the passing of laws in the plantations for encouraging manufactures, which in any ways interfere with the manufacture of this kingdom, has always been thought improper, and has ever been discouraged."

Also, the royal governors were closely instructed to veto all legislation designed to assist the development of such manufactures as might compete with those of England. This had its effect, so that E. A. Russell, an outstanding American authority upon the subject, has been led to conclude: "Largely as a result of the government's determined attitude in the matter, comparatively few laws for this purpose were enacted in the plantations." In no small measure the general result was heightened by the limitations imposed on English capital seeking investments in the colonies. English balances in the colonies and English new capital were kept away from manufactures; and they might be placed only in land and land operations. The overextension of sugar planting, in the West Indies, and of tobacco planting, in the mainland colonies, undoubtedly was due to this restriction and therefore helped in the shaping of the crisis in the imperial-colonial relations which set in the 1760s.

Thus, at the very time in England when the domestic system was rapidly being converted into the factory system and great advances were being made in the perfection of machinery exactly because the existence of a growing market was demanding more efficient methods of production, in the colonies methods of production remained at a hopelessly backward level because English and colonial capital could not enter manufacturing. An important outlet for accumulated funds was barred. The colonial capitalist economy, therefore, was narrowly restricted largely to land speculation, the dealing in furs and the carrying trade. When English mercantilism, for the protection of its home merchant capital, began to narrow these spheres than catastrophe threatened. The American Revolution can be understood only in terms of the necessity for colonial merchant capital to escape from the contracting prison walls of the English Mercantilist System.

In an imperial economy the capitalist relationships between mother country and colonies as a rule lead to a colonial unfavorable balance of trade. The colonies buy the goods and services of the mother country and are encouraged to develop those raw materials the home capitalists require. In this they are aided by the investment of the mother country's balances and by new capital. Thus, in the Southern Colonies, tobacco largely was being produced to furnish returns for the English goods and services the plantation lords required; but, because the exchange left England with a favorable balance, by the 1770s its capitalists had more than £4 million invested in southern planting operations. To meet the charges on this debt, Southern planters were compelled constantly to expand their agricultural operations and to engage in the subsidiary activities of land speculation and the fur trade.

The Northern Colonies were less fortunately placed. The Northern Colonies directly produced little of those staples necessary to the maintenance of the English economy: the grains, provisions and work animals of New England, New York and Pennsylvania could not be permitted to enter England lest they disorganize the home commercial agricultural industry; and the same was true of the New England fishing catches. The Northern Colonies, of course, were a source for lumber, naval stores, furs, whale products and iron, and these England sorely needed to maintain her independence of European supplies. England sought to encourage these industries by bounties and other favored positions; but in vain. Notably unsuccessful was the effort to divert northern colonial capital from shipbuilding and shipping into the production of naval stores by the Bounty Act of 1706.

The Northern Colonies, therefore, produced little for direct export to England to permit them to pay their balances, that is to say, for the increasing quantities of English drygoods, hardware and house furnishings they were taking. In view of the fact, too, that the Northern Colonies presented slight opportunities for the investment of English capital, it was incumbent upon the merchants of the region to develop returns elsewhere in order to obtain specie and bills of exchange with which to balance payments in England.

Out of this necessity arose the economic significance of the various triangular trading operations (and the subsidiary industries growing out of trade) the northern merchants organized. Northern merchants and shipowners opened up regular markets in Newfoundland and Nova Scotia for their fishing tackle, salt, provisions and rum; they established an evergrowing commercial intercourse with the wine islands of the Canaries and Madeira, from which they bought wines direct and to which they sold barrel staves, foodstuffs and live animals;

they sold fish to Spain, Portugal and Italy; their ports acted as entrepots for the transshipment of southern staples to England and southern Europe.

The trade with the West Indian sugar islands—as well as the traffic in Negro slaves and the manufacture of rum, which grew out of it—became the cornerstone of the northern colonial capitalist economy. Northern merchants loaded their ships with all those necessaries the sugar planters were unable to produce—work animals for their mills; lumber for houses and outbuildings; staves, heads and hoops for barrels; flour and salted provisions for their tables; and refuse fish for their slaves—and made regular runs to the British islands of Barbados, the Leeward Islands and Jamaica, and then increasingly to the French, Spanish, Dutch and Danish islands and settlements dotting the Caribbean. Here they acquired in return specie with which to pay their English balances, indigo, cotton, ginger, allspice and dyewoods for transshipment to England, and, above all, sugar and molasses for conversion into rum in the distilleries of Massachusetts and Rhode Island. It was rum that served as the basis of the intercourse between the Northern Colonies and the African Coast: rum paid for ivory, gums, beeswax and gold dust; and rum paid for Negroes who were carried to the sugar islands on that famous Middle Passage to furnish the labor supply without which the sugar plantation economy could not survive.

Such commercial transactions—in addition, of course, to the profits derived from the fisheries, whaling and shipbuilding—furnished the needed sources of return and their conduct [furnished] the outlets for northern merchant capitalist accumulations. But they were not enough with which to pay all the English bills and to absorb all the mounting funds of the Amorys, Faneuils, Hancocks and Boylstons of Boston; the Whartons, Willings and Morrises of Philadelphia; the Livingstons, Lows and Crugers of New York; the Wantons and Lopezes of Newport; and the Browns of Providence. In three illegal forms of enterprises—in piracy, smuggling generally and the illicit sugar and molasses trade with the foreign West Indian islands—northern merchants found opportunities for the necessary expansion.

Piracy—at least up to the end of the seventeenth century, when England was able to exterminate it—played a significant part in maintaining the merchant capital of the Northern Colonies. English and colonial pirates, fitted out in northern ports and backed financially by reputable merchants, preyed on the Spanish fleets of the Caribbean and even boldly fared out into the Red Sea and the Indian Ocean to terrorize ships engaged in the East Indies trade; and with their ships heavily laden with plate, drygoods and spices, put back into colonial ports where they sold their loot and divided their profits with the merchants who had financed them.

Smuggling contributed its share to the swelling of merchant fortunes. In the first place, there was the illegal direct intercourse between the colonies and European countries in the expanding list of enumerated articles; and, in the second place, ships on the homebound voyages from Europe or the West Indies brought large supplies of drygoods, silk, cocoa and brandies into the American colonies without having declared these articles at English ports and paid the duties. Most important of all was the trade with the foreign West Indian sugar islands, which was rendered illegal, after 1733, as a result of the imposition by the Molasses Act of prohibitive duties on the importation into the colonies of foreign sugar, molasses and rum.

In this West Indian trade was to found the strength and the weakness of colonial merchant capital. The English sugar interest was the darling of the Mercantilist System. Sugar, more so even than tobacco, was the great oversea staple of the eighteenth-century world; and not only to it was bound a ramified English commercial industry made up of carriers, commission men, factors, financiers, processors and distributors: but sugar was converted into molasses and in turn distilled into rum to support the unholy slave traffic and the unsavory Indian trade. The sugar cultivation therefore had the constant solicitude of English imperial officialdom and a sugar bloc, made up of absentee landlords, exerted a powerful influence in Parliament. Indeed, so significant a role did sugar play in the imperial economy that in the 1770s the capital worth of West Indian sugar properties stood at £60 million: of which at least one-half was the stake of home English investors. When it is noted that in the whole of the northern American mainland colonies the English capitalist stake at most was only one-sixth as great, then the reason for the favoring of the sugar colonies as against the northern commercial colonies, after 1763, is revealed in a single illuminating flash.

The feud had long been smoldering. With the third decade of the eighteenth century, northern merchants increasingly had taken to buying their sugar and molasses from the foreign sugar islands. Prices were cheaper by from 25 percent to 40 percent: due largely to the fact that the English planters were engaged in a single-crop exploitative agriculture in the interests of an absentee landlordism, while the French, Spanish, Dutch and Danish planters were owner-operators who cultivated directly their small holdings and diversified their crops; too, the foreign sugar was not encumbered by imposts and mercantilist marketing restrictions. In the foreign sugar islands, as well, northern ship captains and owners found it possible to develop new markets for their flour, provisions, lumber, work animals and fish, thus obtaining another source from which specie and bills of exchange could be derived.

So heavy had this traffic become that the alarmed British sugar interest in Parliament succeeded in having passed the Molasses Act of

1733, which was designed virtually to outlaw the colonial-foreign island trade. But the act did not have the desired effect because it could not be adequately enforced: the British customs machinery in the colonies was weak and venal and the naval patrols that could be allocated to this duty were inadequate because of England's engagement in foreign wars from 1740 almost continuously for twenty years. . . .

It is not to be wondered that British planters, threatened with bankruptcy, kept up a constant clamor for the enforcement of the laws and the total stoppage of the foreign island trade. Beginning with 1760, imperial England began to tighten the screws with the stricter enforcement of the Acts of Trade and Navigation; from thence on, particularly after France had been compelled to sue for peace in 1763, England embarked on a systematic campaign to wipe out the trade between the Northern Colonies and the foreign West Indies. Northern merchant capital, its most important lifeline cut off, was being strangulated; it is not difficult to see why wealthy merchants of Philadelphia, New York, Boston, Newport and Providence should be converted into revolutionists. . . .

Such were the objective economic factors which resulted in making the position of the colonies, within the framework of the imperial-colonial relations, intolerable. The period of 1763–1775 was one of crisis, economically and politically: for in that decade it was demonstrated that English and colonial merchant capital both could not operate within a contracting sphere in which clashes of interest were becoming sharper and sharper. From 1760 on, pushed by those various groups whose well-being had been neglected during the years England was engaged in foreign wars, the rulers of the empire labored mightily to repair the rents that had appeared in the Mercantilist System.

The northern "smuggling interest" was hunted down vigorously. The admiralty courts and their procedure were augmented and strengthened; placemen in the customs service who were living in England were ordered to their colonial posts; in 1763 the navy was converted into a patrol fleet with power of search even on the high seas; informers were encouraged; and suits involving the seizure of cargoes and the payment of revenues were taken out of the hands of the local courts.

Utilizing the tax measures of 1764 and later (presumably designed to raise a revenue for the defense of the colonies) as a screen, Parliament imposed limitation after limitation upon the activities of the merchants. The Act of 1764 and the Stamp Act of 1765 called for the payment of duties and taxes in specie, thus further draining the colonies of currency and contracting the credit base. To divert colonial capital into raw materials, the first measure increased the bounties paid for the colonial production of hemp and flax, placed high duties on the colonial importation of foreign indigo, and removed the British import duties on colonial whale fins. To cripple the trade with the foreign West Indies a high duty was placed on refined sugar; while the importation of foreign rum was forbidden altogether and lumber was placed on the enumerated list. To give English manufacturers a firmer grip on their raw materials, hides and skins, pig and bar iron, and potash and pearl ashes were also included among the enumerated articles. To maintain the English monopoly of the colonial-finished goods market the entrance into the colonies of certain kinds of French and Oriental drygoods was taxed for the first time.

In 1764, to weaken further colonial merchant activity, high duties were imposed on wine from the wine islands and wine, fruits and oil from Spain and Portugal brought directly to America (in American ships, as a rule), while such articles brought over from England were to pay only nominal duties. And in 1766, in order to extend the market of English merchants in Europe, Parliament ordered that all remaining nonenumerated articles (largely flour, provisions and fish) bound for European ports north of Cape Finisterre be landed first in England.

It is significant to note that the revenue features of these acts were quickly abandoned: the Stamp Tax was repealed in 1766; and, in 1770, three years after their passage, the Townshend duties on paper, paint and glass were lifted. Only the slight tax on tea remained: and even this was used as an instrument to bludgeon the aggressive northern merchant class into helplessness.

In order to save the East India Company from collapse, in 1773 that powerful financial organization was given permission to ship in its own vessels and dispose of, through its own merchandising agencies, a surplus stock of 17 million pounds of tea in America: and, in this way, drive out of business those Americans who carried, imported and sold in retail channels British tea (and, indeed, foreign tea, for the British tea under the new dispensation could be sold cheaper even than the smuggled Holland article). The merchants all over America were not slow to read the correct significance of this measure. As the distinguished historian Arthur M. Schlesinger has put it, pamphleteers set out to show "that the present project of the East India Company was the entering wedge for larger and more ambitious undertakings calculated to undermine the colonial mercantile world. Their opinion was based on the fact that, in addition to the article of tea, the East India Company imported into England vast quantities of silks, calico and other fabrics, spices, drugs, and chinaware, all commodities of staple demand; and on their fear that the success of the present venture would result in an extension of the same principle to the sale of the other articles."

The southern landlords did not escape. The Proclamation Line of 1763, for the purpose of setting up temporary governments in the far western lands wrested from France after the Seven Years' War, in effect shut off the whole area beyond the crest of the Appalachians to colonial fur traders and land dealers. By taking control of the region out of the hands of the colonial governors, putting it in charge of imperial agents and ordering the abandonment of the settlements already planted, the British looked forward to the maintenance of a great Indian reservation in which the fur trade—in the interests of British concessionaires—would continue to flourish. A few years later these rigorous regulations were relaxed somewhat: but the designs of English land speculators on the area, the prohibition of free land grants, the ordering of land sales at auctions only and the imposition of high quitrents, hardly improved matters. The planters were lost to the English cause. Their situation, already made perilous by the Currency Act of 1764, was now hopeless.

Thus, merchant capitalists—whether land speculators or traders—were converted from contented and loyal subjects into rebellious enemies of the Crown. Tea was destroyed in Boston harbor, turned back unloaded from New York and Philadelphia, and landed but not sold in Charleston. In 1774 the First Continental Congress, to which came delegates from all the colonies, met and wrote the Continental Association, an embargo agreement, which was so successfully enforced that imports from England virtually disappeared in 1775.

The discontents of planters and merchants, in themselves, were not enough to hasten the releasing process. To be successful, assistance was required from the ranks of the more numerous lower-middle-class small farmers, traders, artisans and mechanics, and the working-class seamen, fishermen and laborers. This was not difficult: for the material well-being of the lower classes was tied to the successful enterprising of the upper.

The colonies had enjoyed a period of unprecedented prosperity during the years of the war with France. The expanding market in the West Indies, the great expenditures of the British quartermasters, the illegal and contraband trade with the enemy forces, all had furnished steady employment for workers on the fleets and in the shipyards and ports and lucrative outlets for the produce of small farmers. But with the end of the war and the passage of the restrictive legislation of 1763 and after, depression had set in to last until 1770. Stringency and bankruptcy everywhere confronted the merchants and big farmers; seamen and laborers were thrown out of work, small tradesmen were compelled to close their shops and small farmers were faced by ruin because of their expanded acreage, a diminished market and heavy fixed charges made particularly onerous as a result of currency contraction. Into the bargain, escape into the frontier zones—always the last refuge of the dispossessed—was shut off as a result of the Proclamation of 1763.

In addition, the colonial petty bourgeoisie groaned under specific class political and economic disabilities. Politically, almost universal disfranchisement, unequal legislative representation for the newer areas and the wide absence of local government placed state power in the hands of a small group of big propertied interests closely identified with the Crown. In colonial America only men of sizable properties could vote and hold office; indeed, before the Revolution, the proportion of potential voters varied from one-sixth to one-fiftieth of the male population in the different colonies. In the economic sphere, the constricting hand of monopoly everywhere was to be found. On the land, the legal institutions of entail and primogeniture checked opportunity for younger sons; engrossing landlords and land speculators (whether they were the Crown, the proprietaries, absentee owners or the New England "common" land proprietors) prevented the settlement and improvement of small properties; in the South, the tidewater lords would not erect warehouses to encourage tobacco cultivation among the farmers of the up-country; and in New York, inadequate boundary surveys furnished the big manor lords with an easy instrument of oppression over their smaller neighbors. Everywhere, the threat of Indian uprisings, in the interests of the fur trade and the maintenance of land values in the settled regions, filled the days and nights of frontiersmen with dread.

In the towns, small tradesmen and mechanics and artisans were compelled to struggle unequally against the great merchant interests. Peddlers were submitted to close regulation and forced to pay high license fees. It was impossible to maintain city markets for long, because small merchants here tended to compete successfully with the big ones. In New England, a small company of candlers had got the whole whaling industry in its grip and not only choked off the competition of the lesser manufacturers but fixed the prices for the basic raw material. In New York, and undoubtedly in the other urban communities as well, opportunities to obtain the freedom of the city—which meant the right to engage in certain occupations, whether as tradesmen or artisans—were very severely restricted.

Men of little property were weighed down by debts and oppressed by an inadequate currency; they were forced to support, in many of the colonies, an established church; and they were at the mercy of arbitrary executive and judicial authority. On many sides, too, they saw looming larger and larger the threat of a slave economy to the free institutions of small properties and independent craftsmen. These were the persons who constituted the left-wing of the colonial revolutionary host.

Such was the concentration of colonial forces that made possible the challenging of the power of Great Britain; and the American Revolution proceeded inexorably through the preliminary stages of discussion and illegal organization into the revolutionary one of armed resistance.

Stuart Bruchey

STUART BRUCHEY (1917–   ) *is professor emeritus of history at Columbia University. He has written widely in American economic history, and his books include* Robert Oliver: Merchant of Baltimore 1783–1819 *(1956) and* The Roots of American Economic Growth 1607–1861 *(1965).*

It remains to discuss the difficult question of the impact of government on the colonial economy. Did the British Acts of Trade and Navigation encourage or restrain economic development? Among modern scholars Oliver M. Dickerson and Lawrence A. Harper would presumably range themselves on opposite sides of the issue. While the thrust of Dickerson's work is forcefully against the thesis that the Navigation Acts belong among the causes of the American Revolution, he goes beyond this to present the pre-1764 development of the policies underlying the Acts as a positive contribution to growth in colonial prosperity and population. Harper, on the other hand, maintains that "the colonists were exploited by English mercantilism: and presents quantitative estimates of the costs to Americans of the Navigation Acts, which range from a low of approximately $2,500,000 to a high of about $7,000,000 a year. Relatively small as are these sums, he points out that the annual burden per capita represented by the smaller figure comes within sixteen cents per person of meeting all the expenses of operating the national government during the last six years of Washington's administration. A brief description of the familiar Acts must precede our examination of the issue.

Enacted from time to time after the mid-seventeenth century, the laws contained shipping, commodity, and restraining clauses. The purpose of the shipping clauses was to confine the trade of the empire to English (including colonial) vessels and seamen. The commodity clauses affected both colonial exports and imports. Export regulations were designed to direct to the mother country the important staples of the southern colonies and British West Indies. While tobacco and other "enumerated" articles might also be shipped to another English colony, the so-called "plantation duties," imposed by the Act of 1673, had the intent, at least, of virtually eliminating the development of New England as a distribution center for staples shipped directly to the continent in New England vessels. The objective of the import provisions was to induce the colonists to buy British-made goods in preference to those manufactured elsewhere, and to this end all European and East Indian commodities were required to pass first through an English port before being sent to the colonies. The purpose of the restraining Acts was to discourage the growth within America of industries the output of which might narrow the colonial market for British-made goods, and to this end the Woolens, Hat, and Iron Acts were passed. Other laws regulated the value of foreign coins in the colonies and limited the issuance of paper money at the behest of British creditor interests. In addition to the foregoing, British law also provided for the payment of bounties to encourage the production of such items as indigo and naval stores and for preferential tariff treatment within the British market. Informing this body of legislation was the mercantilist conception of colonies as sources of raw materials and as markets for the manufactures of the mother country. The American colonies were thus envisaged as subservient to the growth of English commerce and industry.

That some of these provisions stimulated the colonial economy seems incontrovertible. Indigo provides an excellent example: the post-Revolution loss of the bounty previously paid on it, together with the increased profitableness of cotton, caused its cultivation to be virtually abandoned. The case of tobacco is more difficult and well illustrates some of the complexities of the subjunctive mood in historiography. Harper argues that Britain was not the natural market for the crop, which only went there under the compulsion of law. Its ultimate destination was the Continent. In 1773 official British consumption amounted to 3,747,979 pounds, with the remainder of the 100,482,007 pounds imported being transshipped, mainly to Holland and Germany. After the Revolution, despite strenuous efforts on the part of the British government to retain control of the trade, British importations steadily declined from 99.8 per cent in 1773 to 62.2 per cent in 1790, 45.5 per cent in 1799, 31.7 per cent in 1821, and 22.7 per cent in 1840. Would not colonial Americans have gained more by direct shipments to the Continent?

In all probability they would have, although not by as much as might appear. Not all of the English middleman's profits, together with extra freights, handling and insurance charges, would have gone to them. Dickerson points out that the English merchants did far more than merely transship the tobacco in the form in which they had received it from America. They graded, sorted, and repacked it, and they used their superior sources of market information to send the right amounts at the right times to the right places for sale. Had Americans shipped their tobacco directly to the Continent, they rather than the British would have had to perform these middleman services. Dickerson implies that they would not have performed them as well. In the decades following the Revolution, he points out, *total* tobacco exports fell off sharply, and he attributes the decline to the loss of the superior British marketing services.

Other considerations complicate even more an effort at quantitative precision in the estimation of colonial loss from tobacco. Had New England rather than British vessels been free to carry the Southern staple to Continental markets, those vessels would probably have had to be large ones. But the heavier operating costs of larger vessels would have lessened the ability of New Englanders to engage profitably in the coasting trade by which they assembled cargoes for West Indian markets. And if the latter trade be assumed under these changed conditions to be of lesser importance as a means of paying for British imports, the cost of West Indian molasses would have risen by at least the amount of freights paid on some non-New England ships employed to import it, with cost-consequences to the rum distilling business of that section. In sum, a judgment that one of the clauses of the Navigation Acts lessened returns to Americans requires an estimate of what the returns would have been in the absence of the clause. But the very absence of the clause implies change in one or more elements of the historical situation so that the values of the changes must also be brought into account.

Similar considerations must be brought to bear in any assessment of the extra costs borne by Americans because of the requirement that European and East Indian goods be transshipped via England. As Harper notes, the requirements entailed the imposition upon colonial trade of extra mercantile profits, taxes, fees, cooperage, porterage, brokerage, warehouse rent, and commissions, costs which would not have been incurred by direct shipments. But had America-bound cargoes been assembled bit by bit in a number or ports instead of being gathered from a single British depot, additional operating costs (including interest) would almost certainly have had to be met. So far as the colonial shipbuilding industry was concerned, Harper makes the telling point that after the Revolution American ships found foreign markets without the protection afforded by the shipping clauses. How little the industry depended upon the British market may be seen in construction statistics. On the eve of the Revolution the thirteen colonies are said to have been building 28,747 tons per year; by 1790 tonnage built amounted to at least 29,606 tons, and in 1815 the total reached 154,624 tons.

It is evident that an assessment of the economic impact of the Navigation Acts must take into account considerations which preclude the facile firmness of a conclusion, quantitative or otherwise. Indeed, the question ought not be separated from the larger one of the savings afforded Americans by the military and naval protection of the British. Nothing less than a full-scale effort at social cost-accounting will do, and, needless to say, one has not yet been undertaken. Until it is, until the probable ramifications of each subjunctive hypothesis are carefully weighed, historical judgment must be tentative. If and when the returns are finally in, however, I believe they will tend to support Harper's judgment that the earnings of Americans were less than they would have been in the absence of the British connection. But whatever the amount of the "loss," previously noted propensities to consume warn against any easy assumption that the whole of it would have been converted into capital.

So far as colonial manufacturing is concerned, the restraining clauses appear to have exerted far less influence than natural conditions. The administration of the restrictive policy was often less than rigorous, depending as it did largely upon the ability and willingness of governors to enforce it. Some governors were colonials in sympathy with the commercial and manufacturing ambitions of the colonists, and some formed profitable business connections in America. Even governors from England sometimes preferred easy duties and local popularity to a tumultuous and embarrassed administration. Weeden's shrewd observation concerning colonial New Englanders probably applies more widely: "They had grown up doing things they found profitable, whatever the British laws had been." More important than the laws were the underlying economic conditions. The shortage of skilled labor and both the scarcity and preferred allocations of capital funds gave to a country in possession of abundant resources an absolute advantage in the production of raw materials and semiprocessed goods. "Balancing advantage against disadvantage," says the historian of American manufactures, Victor S. Clark, "their manufactures seem not to have been retarded or furthered decidedly by subordination to the British government."

Nevertheless, it seems clear that changes in this underlying situation, especially in the advancing eighteenth century, were creating a progressively sharper division between the interests of mother country and colonists. The proportionality of the factors of production was changing as available supplies of capital and skilled labor increased. In this situation, governmental policies that sought to promote rather than to curb industrialization might well have helped set America on

an earlier path to more rapid growth. Instead, policies that had sometimes been indifferently enforced were defined and applied with new
vigor in the general tightening of the administrative machinery of empire following the Seven Years' War.

Alarmed lest the promise of more rapid Western settlement after
1763 lead to renewed Indian wars and to a situation wherein, because
of the distance from the Atlantic seaboard, inland communities would
manufacture for themselves, the British government took measures to
check or prohibit Western settlements. Manufacturing, noted a paper
relating to Indian affairs laid before the Board of Trade in 1768, was "a
consequence which, experience shows, has constantly attended, in a
greater or less degree, every inland settlement." On the eve of the Revolution Benjamin Franklin learned at first hand how adamant British
policy had become on this point. Just before leaving England in 1775,
Franklin was drawn into informal negotiations with men closely connected with the ministry and asked to write out a set of propositions
he believed would lead to permanent union. One of his propositions
was that all acts restraining manufactures be repealed. This proposition, Franklin relates, "they apprehended would meet with difficulty.
They said, that restraining manufacturers in the colonies was a favorite here; and therefore they wish'd that article to be omitted, as the
proposing it would alarm and hinder perhaps the considering and granting others of more importance."

It may be wondered why the colonial governments did not themselves enact legislation to encourage the development of manufactures. The answer, of course, is that they did. Especially before 1750
provincial legislatures often gave monopoly rights to individuals in order to encourage the regular and reliable supply of some article of large
consumption, such as salt, refined sugar, pitch, paper, or stoneware.
Sometimes, too, they enacted tariff laws, as, for example, South Carolina did in 1716, when that province laid a duty on all imports except
salt. But in 1724 an order-in-council prohibited any colony from imposing duties on British goods. Laws seeking to encourage specific industries were sometimes disallowed by the British government, as, for example, was an attempt by Virginia in 1680 to aid shipbuilding, and one
in 1682 to promote the manufacturing of cloth. Vetoing a Pennsylvania
statute of 1706, the Board of Trade remarked: "It cannot be expected
that encouragement should be given by law to the making any manufactures made in England in the plantations, it being against the advantage of England." Nevertheless, both provincial and town governments
on numerous occasions granted bounties, loans, land grants, tax
exemptions, and other aids in efforts to encourage the provision of
some facility or service—for example, grist mills, deemed essential to
community welfare—and such legislation was seldom disallowed.

Similarly, not British opposition but the relatively undeveloped nature of the economy principally explains the paucity of business corporations in the colonial period. As Joseph S. Davis has emphasized, businesses were generally small-scale and local in character. No large supplies of capital or labor were seeking employment, at least before approximately the mid-eighteenth century. Those which were found outlets in unincorporated joint stock companies, legally partnerships, which sometimes reached surprising size in mining, land speculation, and other areas of late colonial enterprise. Had capitalists sought incorporation they would generally have found few legal obstacles in the way. Not only Parliament and Crown, but colonial proprietors, governors, and legislatures as well, possessed, "within limits which were not always clear but which were for the most part wide, the right to erect corporations for operation in America."

While it must be concluded that neither interference by the Crown nor Parliamentary restrictions, not even the extension of the Bubble Act to America in 1741, appreciably hampered the development of corporations in the colonies, it does not follow that the mushroom growth of corporations in the early national period was unrelated to political change. During the entire colonial period only a half-dozen business corporations have been traced, two in the seventeenth century and four in the eighteenth. In contrast, more than 300 business corporations received charters from state governments during the eleven-year period between 1789 and 1800. To ascribe this startling growth, as Davis does, to a greater degree of economic and social maturity in the post-Revolutionary period, seems insufficient. A distinct political element is present and deserves recognition.

Most colonial corporations were erected by charters granted by royal governors in the name of the Crown, although usually with the consent of the provincial councils. That is to say, the sovereign was recognized as the source of legal authority, with Parliamentary approval required after 1688 in the case of a grant of exclusive or monopoly privilege. In both royal and proprietary colonies the legal right of the assembly to incorporate was subject to the negative of the governor or of higher English authority. The Revolution brought an important change in this situation. Because of the fiction that the Revolution was fought to free the colonists from the exactions of the Crown, a revulsion against executive authority became manifest in the early state constitutions, as well as in the Articles of Confederation. The power to incorporate, in a word, shifted from the executive to the legislative arm, where it was more sensitively responsive to community pressures upon government to aid in the provision of community services. . . . [M]ost of the corporations erected before 1800 were quasi-public in nature, and the community purposes they served continued to dominate the objectives of incorporation well into the nineteenth century.

In the growth of the American economy the Revolution forms a watershed. . . . As Alexander Hamilton remarked in 1781, it had been a "narrow colonial sphere" in which Americans "had been accustomed to move" rather than "that enlarged kind suited to the government of an independent nation." But prominent among the contributions of the Revolution is the one we have just discussed. The transfer of full political authority to the legislative arm of governments close to hand and more amenable to popular pressures made it far easier for communities to use the device of the business corporation to obtain the roads, bridges, and other "social overhead capital" necessary to growth.

☆ 4 ☆

The American Revolution

REVOLUTIONARY OR NONREVOLUTIONARY?

The American Revolution is the single most significant event in this country's history. Within twenty years—1763 to 1783—Americans declared their independence, waged a war of liberation, transformed colonies into states, and created a new nation. These changes occurred with such remarkable rapidity that their speed was truly revolutionary. But scholars disagree about using the term "revolutionary" to describe how new or different these developments were. Some historians argue that the Revolution was solely a colonial rebellion aimed at achieving only the limited goal of independence from Britain. Colonial society, they say, was a democratic society and there was a consensus among Americans about keeping things as they were once the break with Britain had been accomplished. Others claim that the Revolution was accompanied by a violent social upheaval—a class conflict—as the radical lower classes sought to gain a greater degree of democracy in what had been a basically undemocratic society in the colonial era. The question is, then, was the Revolution revolutionary, or was it not?

American historians for the most part did not probe very deeply into the revolutionary nature of the Revolution in the first century after the event. Throughout most of the nineteenth century scholars reflected one of the underlying assumptions of that era—that the main theme of American history was the quest for liberty. Within this context the Revolution was inevitably viewed in black and white terms as a struggle of liberty versus tyranny between America and Britain.

George Bancroft, one of the outstanding exponents of this point of view, set forth his thesis in his ten-volume *History of the United States*, published between the 1830s and 1870s. To Bancroft the Revolution represented one phase of a master plan by God for the march of all mankind toward a golden age of greater human freedom. America, in his eyes, symbolized the forces of liberty and progress; Britain those of tyranny and reaction. The Revolution was "radical in its character," according to Bancroft, because it hastened the advance of human beings toward a millennium of "everlasting peace" and "universal brotherhood." He went on to add that the Revolution was achieved within the colonies in "benign tranquility" because the American people were united in their determination to fight for freedom.[1]

With the spirit of nationalism prevalent in nineteenth-century America it is not too difficult to understand why Bancroft wrote as he did. There was an intense desire among the American people for a national historian who would tell the epic story of the Revolution in patriotic terms, and Bancroft fulfilled this longing. More important, Bancroft intuitively wrote the kind of history that could meet the needs of Americans in yet another way. Throughout much of the period between the 1830s and 1870s, the country was split; it was divided by the bitter political battles of the Jacksonian era and the brutal military conflict of the Civil War. Bancroft painted a picture of the Revolution as a great national struggle, reminding Americans that they had once fought as a united people for many beliefs they held in common.[2]

Around the turn of the twentieth century a reaction set in against Bancroft's ultrapatriotic interpretation. With the growing rapprochement between Britain and America after the signing of the Treaty of Washington in 1870, there was a tendency to view past relations between the two countries in a more favorable light. Developments on the domestic scene such as the Populist and Progressive movements also affected the outlook of some scholars. Influenced by these reform movements, which appeared to constitute a popular reaction against the concentration of power and wealth in the hands of a relatively small number of financial and business leaders in modern industrialized America, some historians began viewing the Revolution in a somewhat similar light as an uprising by the lower classes against the control of the upper classes. Finally, the rising class of professional academic historians who appeared on the scene about the 1880s also began to explore the Revolution from a different perspective than had Bancroft.

The scholars who revised Bancroft's interpretation between the 1890s and 1940s fell into two broad schools. One group—the imperial school of historians—believed that political and constitutional issues brought on the Revolution. The other—the Progressive historians—held that the primary causes were social and economic in nature. While these two groups of historians disagreed with Bancroft on the

---

[1] George Bancroft, *History of the United States of America,* 10 vols. (Boston, 1852), 4:12–13.

[2] Wesley F. Craven, "The Revolutionary Era," in *The Reconstruction of American History,* John Higham, ed., (New York, 1962), pp. 46–47.

precise causes and nature of the Revolution, they were often in agreement with his conclusion that the movement was, indeed, a revolutionary one.

The imperial school of historians headed by George L. Beer, Charles M. Andrews, and Lawrence H. Gipson took the position that the Revolution was not to be viewed solely within the narrow confines of national history. To be properly understood, the Revolution had to be set in a broader context and considered as an integral part of the history of the British Empire as a whole. Hence they directed their attention to the empire, emphasizing in particular the political and constitutional relationship between the colonies and the mother country. Since Anglo-American relations were improving around the turn of the twentieth century, these scholars were inclined to be less harsh on the former mother country than Bancroft had been.

After examining the operations of the empire, the imperial historians concluded that Britain's colonial policies were not as unjust as Bancroft had declared. Beer wrote four monographs between the years 1893 and 1912 on Britain's commercial policies in the seventeenth and eighteenth centuries and claimed that the colonists prospered under a system that was both liberal and enlightened. Andrews, writing a four-volume work in the 1930s, saw benefits as well as burdens in Britain's Navigation Acts because of the protection provided for America's goods and ships. Gipson, who was a student of Andrews's, took an even more favorable view of imperial policies in his multivolume work *The British Empire before the American Revolution*, published between the 1930s and 1960s. The British were justified in taxing the Americans and tightening the navigation acts after 1763, claimed Gipson, because it had been largely British blood and money that was expended in defending the North American colonies in the "Great War for Empire," 1754–1763.

All three historians believed that constitutional issues lay at the bottom of the dispute between the colonies and mother country. Andrews, for example, argued that the British Empire in North America from its beginnings down to the Revolution had been characterized by two movements working at cross purposes. The colonies kept moving steadily in the direction of greater self-government; the mother country toward greater control over the empire. By the eve of the Revolution, the colonists had arrived at a new concept of empire—colonies as self-governing units within an empire held together only by a common allegiance to the king. But the British, clinging to their traditional ideas of dependent colonies, considered this idea both radical and dangerous. "On the one side was the immutable, stereotyped system of the mother country, based on precedent and tradition and designed to keep things comfortably as they were," wrote Andrews, "on the other, a vital, dynamic organism, containing the seeds of a great nation, its forces untried, still to be proved."[3] The dispute, while constitutional in nature, was the very essence of revolution for Andrews; it represented a deep-seated conflict between two incompatible societies.

The Progressive historians took quite a different point of view from the imperial school. They were firmly convinced that social and economic issues constituted the main causes of the Revolution. On the one hand, they tended to emphasize the growing economic split caused by the competition between the colonies and mother country. On the other, they placed great stress upon class conflict between the lower and upper classes in colonial America.

That the Progressive historians saw the Revolution in terms of an internal class conflict was hardly surprising. Many of these scholars were themselves committed to the reform movements of the early 1900s and tended to see their own era in terms of an unending struggle by the people to free themselves from the shackles of the large corporate monopolies and trusts that constituted the plutocracy of modern America. Consequently they tended to read back into the Revolution the same conflict between the masses and the upper classes that seemed to be taking place before their eyes in the Progressive period from 1900 to 1920.

The emergence of such Progressive historians as Carl L. Becker, Charles A. Beard, Arthur M. Schlesinger, Sr., and J. Franklin Jameson during this period marked also a sharp shift toward an economic interpretation of history. Such scholars believed that materialistic forces—not ideological factors—were the major determinants in history. Some of these historians, therefore, were economic determinists who felt that humans were motivated mainly by their economic self-interest. They insisted that any political or constitutional ideas that persons might possess would be dictated by economic considerations. To their way of thinking pocketbook interests, not ideas of patriotism, had motivated the leaders that Bancroft had pictured as heroes.

Carl L. Becker, one of the first and most effective of the Progressive historians, took the position that the American Revolution should be considered not as one revolution but two. The first was an external revolution—the colonial rebellion against Britain—caused by a clash of economic interests between the colonies and mother country. The second was an internal revolution—a conflict between America's social classes—to determine whether the upper or lower classes would rule once the British departed. In his first major study of the Revolution, *The History of Political Parties in the Province of New York, 1760–1776*, published in 1909, Becker summed up his thesis of a dual revolution in a striking phrase. New York politics prior to the Revolu-

---

[3]Charles M. Andrews, "The American Revolution: An Interpretation," *American Historical Review* 31 (January 1926):231.

tion, he wrote, revolved around two questions—the "question of home rule" and the "question . . . of who should rule at home."[4]

Although Charles A. Beard's *An Economic Interpretation of the Constitution*, which was published in 1913, did not deal directly with the Revolution, it became a landmark for scholars writing about this era of American history. After an examination of the economic holdings of the framers of the Constitution, Beard advanced his now-famous hypothesis that the events leading to the convention of 1787 mirrored a split in American society—a conflict between the rich and the poor, farmers and merchants, debtors and creditors, and holders of real wealth and paper wealth. More than any other single work written in the Populist-Progressive era, Beard's book caused Progressive historians to view the period between the 1760s and the 1780s as one of continuous conflict between social classes in America over economic matters.

The conclusion that the Revolution might be seen in terms of a class struggle over economic issues was further spelled out in Arthur M. Schlesinger's *The Colonial Merchants and the American Revolution*, published in 1918. Schlesinger studied the merchant class in all the colonies during the period 1763–1776 and noted that this usually conservative group played a leading role in bringing on the Revolution. Why had they done so? Disenchantment of the merchants with British rule, said Schlesinger, arose from the economic reverses they suffered as a result of the strict policy of imperial control enacted by the mother country after the French and Indian War. But resistance by the merchants against the mother country grew less intense after 1770, he noted, for fear of what might happen to their position and property if the more radical lower classes—"their natural enemies in society"—should gain the upper hand.

Schlesinger's book dealt mainly with the period prior to 1776, but the author went on to comment about the increasing dread of class conflict once independence was declared. The merchant class split and many men refused to participate enthusiastically in the struggle against the British lest the lower classes seize control and rule at home. Biding their time during the troubled years of the Confederation period, the merchants drew together again in the late 1780s to found a new government that would safeguard their class interests. Once united, the merchant class became, in Schlesinger's words, "a potent factor in the conservative counterrevolution that led to the establishment of the United States Constitution."[5] To Schlesinger the Constitu-

---

[4]Carl L. Becker, *The History of Political Parties in the Province of New York, 1760–1776* (Madison, Wis., 1909), p. 22.

[5]Arthur M. Schlesinger, *The Colonial Merchants and the American Revolution, 1763–1776* (New York, 1918), p. 606.

tion was the antithesis of the Revolution; the same classes and men who were pitted against one another in the 1770s continued to contend for control of the government in the 1780s.

J. Franklin Jameson, another historian writing within the Progressive tradition, likewise viewed the Revolution as a class conflict—a social movement by the lower classes to achieve a greater degree of democracy within American society. His book *The American Revolution Considered as a Social Movement*, published in 1926, described the sweeping social and economic reforms that took place during the war; reforms that reduced the power of the prewar aristocracy and improved the lot of the common man. Economic democracy advanced, Jameson claimed, as a result of the redistribution of landed property. Large Loyalist estates were confiscated and broken up into lots for sale to small farmers; vast domains controlled by the Crown and proprietors passed into the hands of state legislatures, which threw open these lands for settlement; and new state laws put an end to the old aristocratic practices of primogeniture and entail. Social democracy made similar strides as property qualifications for voting and officeholding were lowered, slavery and the slave trade were abolished in some states, and the Anglican church was disestablished in many parts of the country. Jameson's book summed up the point of view of the Progressive historians who exercised such a profound influence over the interpretation of the Revolution during the first part of the twentieth century. The Progressive approach to the Revolution was maintained by the late Merrill Jensen, a distinguished scholar, and by numerous other historians active from 1945 to the present.

After World War II, however, a new group of scholars—the neoconservative school of historians—emerged to challenge the interpretation set forth by the Progressive historians. The fundamental disagreement between these two groups derived from the different way that each viewed the colonial period as a whole. To the Progressive historians, American society in the colonial era was undemocratic, giving rise to class conflicts throughout the entire period. The lower classes being poor, underprivileged, and deprived of the right to vote, kept up a constant class struggle to improve their lot in society. In the eyes of these historians, then, the Revolution represented the climax of a movement by the masses to advance their economic well-being and to wrest greater political rights from the upper classes.

The neoconservative historians, on the other hand, believed that American society was essentially a democratic society in the colonial period. Most colonists, rather than being poor, these scholars claimed, could qualify as members of the middle class by virtue of the property they owned. Political democracy was the order of the day because the majority of colonists were small farmers who possessed enough land to meet the necessary qualifications for voting. Colonial society was an open, not a closed society, and characterized by a high degree of social mobility. Thus the common man in the colonial era was satisfied with his lot in society and felt no urge to participate in class conflict in order to achieve a greater degree of democracy.

As a corollary to this second point of view, neoconservative scholars argued that the Revolution was basically a conservative movement. Americans fought the Revolution, according to these historians, in order to preserve a social order that was already democratic in colonial days. When British reforms after 1763 threatened to upset the existing democratic social order in America, the colonists rose up in rebellion. In the struggle between the colonies and mother country the Americans emerged as the "conservatives" because they were trying to keep matters as they were before 1763. It was the British who were the "radicals" because they kept insisting upon making changes and innovations in the colonial system after the French and Indian War.

Scholars of the neoconservative school rejected the idea of class struggle and stressed instead the concept of a general consensus among the American people in the Revolutionary War era. Most Americans held certain ideas in common, they argued, and these views united the colonists to the degree which made it possible for them to act in concert against Great Britain. One important element in this American consensus was the widespread belief among all social classes that the liberties of the people were based upon certain fundamental principles of self-government which could not be changed without their consent. Led by such scholars as Robert E. Brown and Daniel J. Boorstin, the neoconservative school saw consensus and continuity rather than class conflict and disunity as the main themes in this period of American history.

Robert E. Brown, in *Middle-Class Democracy and the Revolution in Massachusetts*, set out specifically to challenge the thesis of the Progressive school of historians that the Revolution was, in part, a class conflict over the question of who should rule at home. One of the starting assumptions of the Progressive scholars, Brown noted, was that the structure of American society in the colonial period was undemocratic because property qualifications for suffrage prevented many persons in the lower classes from voting. After studying the structure of society in prewar Massachusetts, Brown concluded that the vast majority of adult males in that colony were farmers whose real estate holdings were sufficient to meet the necessary property qualifications for voting. Middle-class democracy in Massachusetts before the war was an established fact, Brown maintained, and the purpose of the Revolution was to preserve the existing democratic social order on the local level—not to change it.

In a similar vein Daniel J. Boorstin argued that the Revolution was a conservative movement on the imperial as well as the local level because Americans were fighting to retain traditional rights and liberties granted to them under the British constitution. The colonists rebelled against Great Britain to maintain the status quo, Boorstin insisted in *The Genius of American Politics*, not to initiate a new order. When the British introduced changes in the government of the empire after the French and Indian War, the Americans kept resisting these disturbing innovations on the grounds that they were contrary to the British constitution. In refusing to accept the principle of no taxation without representation, Boorstin wrote, the patriots were insisting upon an old liberty and not a new right.

The leaders of the Revolution, in Boorstin's view, were reluctant rebels. American patriots thought of themselves as Englishmen who were more true to the tenets of the British constitution than the British themselves. Resistance to imperial authority began when the Americans felt that they were being denied their rights as Englishmen by a misguided Parliament. After taking the drastic step of declaring their independence with considerable reluctance, Americans did not turn their backs upon their British heritage. Instead they carried over into the new nation many of the traditional rights of Englishmen that they had prized so highly: trial by jury, due process of law, the concept of no taxation without representation, and the rights of free speech, free petition, and free assembly. Thus, in Boorstin's view, the American Revolution was regarded as an act of faith in favor of the British constitution. The patriots were defending ancient British traditions and institutions when they waged the American Revolution.

Edmund S. Morgan, the distinguished colonial historian, stressed two themes—the consensus among Americans on principles, and the continuity of ideas—in his *Birth of the Republic 1763–1789*. Certain principles and ideas unified most Americans from the time of the Stamp Act in 1765 to the writing of the Constitution in 1787, according to Morgan. Throughout this period the majority of Americans consistently sought to realize three principles: the protection of property and liberty; the achievement of human equality; and, after the break from Britain, a form of American nationalism that would embrace the ideas of both liberty and equality. Morgan concluded that the Progressive historians had grossly exaggerated the divisions among the American people during the revolutionary era, and that the "most remarkable and exciting fact was union."[6]

In many respects the neoconservative interpretation of the Revolution that arose after 1945 seemed to mirror the conservative climate of opinion that pervaded the United States after World War II. In the area of foreign affairs the Cold War era profoundly affected American

---

[6]Edmund S. Morgan, *The Birth of the Republic 1763–1789* (Chicago, 1956), p. 163.

thought. With the United States acting as the leader of the free world and facing the threat of communist totalitarianism, Americans became increasingly preoccupied with the problem of national security. Historians sometimes reflected this concern, either consciously or unconsciously, by playing down any past differences among the American people in order to present an image of a nation that was strong and united throughout most of its history. Thus the picture of the Revolution as a period of disorder and disunity gave way to one that emphasized a consensus among the American people and stressed the continuity between our colonial past and our beginnings as a nation.

Developments on the domestic front during the 1940s and 1950s likewise caused historians to recast the Revolution along more conservative lines. Prosperity in the post-World War II period and the concomitant rise in affluence in American society, coupled with the rise of the social welfare state which sought to improve the living conditions among lower-income groups, tended to blur the lines of rigid class distinctions within the country. Living in an era in which class distinctions presumably played a less important role, neoconservative historians were less prone to see the element of class conflict in the Revolution. In short, the neoconservative school of historians seemed to be reflecting the dominant ideas of their own time in treating the Revolution as they did.

Although neoconservative historians continued to publish during the 1960s, they found their position subjected to attack from several quarters. One challenge came from the writings of certain intellectual historians who saw the Revolution as a radical rather than a conservative movement. Another came from a group of scholars—who might be termed "neo-Progressive historians"—using different approaches or orientations in searching for the social and economic origins of the revolutionary movement. Yet a third challenge came from the revived interest in studies of the Loyalists—a group to whom the neoconservative historians had paid little or no attention.

The trend toward greater emphasis upon intellectual history resulted in part as a reaction against the Progressive scholars who had generally shown a profound distrust of ideas as determining forces in history. Strongly influenced by the thought of Freud and Marx the Progressive historians looked upon ideas as mere rationalizations designed to mask the deep-seated self-interests that motivated human behavior. They insisted that the upper classes in colonial America had manipulated ideas solely to suit the interests of their class. When members of the merchant class employed a slogan such as "No taxation without representation," their aim was basically to stir up support among the lower classes; they were not genuinely concerned about an abstract principle. Colonial merchants turned the Stamp Act into a propaganda campaign over the issues of constitutionalism and natural rights, argued Progressive historians, in order to conceal their true class interests.

Rejecting this view of the role of ideas in history, certain historians writing after World War II emphasized the primacy of ideas in bringing on the Revolution. Some scholars who viewed the Revolution from the standpoint of intellectual history, including certain neoconservatives, came to the conclusion that conservative ideas had prevailed and that the movement was a conservative one. Other historians, however, came to exactly the opposite conclusion.

Bernard Bailyn was the foremost scholar to view the Revolution as a radical intellectual movement. In *The Ideological Origins of the American Revolution,* Bailyn took the position that ideas themselves constituted the major determinants in history.[7] After analyzing the pamphlet literature written in the period just prior to the Revolution, Bailyn concluded that ideas had played a dual role in bringing about the break with Britain. First, he noted that the thought expressed in the pamphlets was *explanatory* in nature. The ideas taken up, in other words, not only revealed the position taken by the colonists but also gave the reasons *why* such a stand had been adopted. Second, the ideas themselves acted as determinants during the period by causing changes in the beliefs, attitudes, and assumptions of the colonists.

Bailyn argued that an elaborate theory of politics lay at the heart of the American revolutionary ideology—an ideology whose roots could be traced back to the antiauthoritarian tradition in England. This theory was based on an unflattering view of human nature, a belief in the innate selfishness of man. Man had a natural lust for power, this theory held, and power by its very nature was a corrupting force and could be attained only by depriving others of their liberty. To protect liberty against the corrupting force of power, all elements of the body politic had to be balanced off against each other in order to prevent one from gaining dominance over the others. The best solution, of course, was a balanced constitution, but the malignant influence of power was such that no system of government whatsoever could be safe or stable for very long.

Bailyn's thesis was that this theory of politics shaped the course of America's revolutionary thought from the 1730s through the constitutional crisis of the 1760s and 1770s. Viewed within the context of this theory the arguments expressed in the pamphlets could be interpreted in a different light. The colonists, it seemed, were convinced that there was a sinister plot against liberty in both England and America. In England it was the king's ministers who were conspiring against liberty. They usurped the prerogatives of the Crown, systematically

---

[7]Bernard Bailyn, *The Ideological Origins of the American Revolution* (Cambridge, Mass., 1967).

encroached upon the independence of the Commons, and upset the balance of the British constitution in their corrupt drive for power. In America the king's ministers were assisted in their conspiratorial designs by royal officials who likewise aimed at destroying the balance of the constitution and seizing as much power and authority as possible.

From the American point of view, then, the British measures after 1763 were nothing less than a widespread plot to rob all Englishmen of their liberties at home and abroad. Believing that the conspiracy had succeeded in England, the colonists came to feel that America represented the last bastion for the defense of English liberties and the freedom of all mankind. These ideas and this interpretation of British behavior, Bailyn believed, finally led the colonists in desperation to resort to armed rebellion.

Bailyn thus took issue with the Progressive historians who declared that the patriot leaders were indulging in mere rhetoric and propaganda when they employed such words as "conspiracy," "corruption," and "slavery." Bailyn concluded that the colonists meant what they said; that the fear of conspiracy against constitutional authority was built into the very structure of politics, and that these words represented "real fears, real anxieties, [and] a sense of real danger."[8] These assumptions, beliefs, and attitudes had fashioned the world view of the American Whigs and caused them to reinterpret British behavior in the manner that they did.

To Bailyn the Revolution represented, above all, an intellectual revolution—a radical change in the way most Americans looked upon themselves and their institutions. The true revolution, he suggested, took place inside men's minds more than out in the political or social arena. This "ideological" revolution constituted a complete transformation in the image that the colonists had of themselves. Before the Revolution the Americans saw their divergences from the norms of European society as shortcomings; they felt a sense of inferiority because they lacked a titled aristocracy, cosmopolitan culture, stratified society, and established church along national lines. After the Revolution, on the other hand, they came to look upon these differences as good, not bad; as virtues, not vices; and as advantages rather than defects. These differences, Americans felt, would enable them to establish a republican government which would correspond with their republican society. This change in perspective, in Bailyn's eyes, was *the* American Revolution, and a section of his book is included as the first selection in this chapter.

The argument in Bailyn's book was extended in Gordon S. Wood's *Creation of the American Republic, 1776–1787,* which explained how the colonists' antiauthoritarian tradition was transformed after inde-

---

[8]*Ibid.,* p. ix.

pendence into a distinctive American republican ideology. These two
works written in the 1960s gave rise to what came to be called the
"republican synthesis" and coupled with J. G. A. Pocock's *Machiavellian Moment*, published in the 1970s claimed that this republican ideology dominated the political culture throughout the whole sweep of
American history from the 1760s to the Civil War. The republican synthesis contained in these three books constituted a major historiographical breakthrough: it proved to be the most widely accepted interpretation in the voluminous literature written from the mid-1960s to
the mid-1980s.[9]

But as supporters of the republican synthesis pushed the implications of the thesis too far, a reaction set in during the late 1980s and
even earlier. Bailyn, who had revised the neoconservatives by making
the Revolution seem radical again, was subjected to revisionist assaults as were Wood and Pocock. Other interpretations of the Revolution were offered either by intellectual historians or by scholars employing different methodologies.

Adherents of the republican synthesis were scored for errors of
both commission and omission. Bailyn was criticized, for example, because he seemed to suggest that there was an ideological consensus
among American Whigs, and that they all held the same republican
ideas in common. Other scholars quickly pointed out there were other
ideologies at work—evangelical Protestantism, class-based perspectives, or different political orientations—and that America's political
culture was more diversified and less homogeneous. Those upholding
the republican synthesis also relied heavily on the classical republican
tradition—which emphasized citizenship and public participation—
and had roots stretching back to antiquity and the Renaissance. Pocock, in fact, declared the Revolution to be "the last great act of the
Renaissance." Other scholars, however, supported the liberal tradition—which stressed individualism and private rights—and had more
recent antecedents that could be found readily in the Anglo-American
world of the seventeenth and eighteenth centuries. Supporters of the
republican synthesis were criticized, moreover, for omitting a discussion of the various theories of political economy that were so important to those of the Revolutionary generation.[10]

---

[9]Gordon S. Wood, *Creation of the American Republic, 1776–1787* (Chapel Hill,
1969), and J. G. A. Pocock, *The Machiavellian Moment* (Princeton, 1975).

[10]For an attack on the idea of an ideological consensus, see some of the essays in
Alfred A. Young. ed., *The American Revolution: Explorations in the History of American Radicalism* (Dekalb, 1976). For two books that take up the issue of whether liberalism or republicanism was dominant in the Revolutionary era, see Joyce Appleby, *Capitalism and A New Social Order* (New York, 1984), and Lance Banning, *The Jeffersonian
Persuasion* (Ithaca, 1978). See the Appleby book cited above and Drew R. McCoy, *The
Elusive Republic* (Chapel Hill, 1980) for discussions of the important role of political
economy in the Revolutionary and post-Revolutionary period. For the Pocock quotation,

One scholar—Rhys Isaac—analyzed different religious ideologies at work before, during, and after the Revolution, and by implication undermined the idea of any ideological consensus. Focusing on pre-revolutionary Virginia as a case study, Isaac showed that deep ideological differences existed between two groups—the Anglicans and Baptists. Resorting to imaginative techniques employed by cultural anthropologists like Clifford Geertz to study oral and nonliterary cultures in different parts of the world, Isaac analyzed these two religious subcultures. What he found was evidence of two contrasting world views: the tradition-oriented Anglican gentry who represented the established order; and the humble evangelical Baptists who challenged the ruling Anglican establishment. To demonstrate the differences in lifestyle between the two, Isaac examined gestures and behavior in religious meetings, personal demeanor and dress, militia musters, and even the way homes were built. Isaac also analyzed existing literary sources to show not only religious differences but changes in the social structure from the 1740s to the 1790s. His work did more than destroy the idea of a possible ideological consensus: it showed that by omitting much serious discussion of religious beliefs, Bailyn and Wood had overlooked the important role religion played in the formation of political beliefs during the Revolution.[11]

Gary B. Nash in his book *Urban Crucible* discussed a different ideology—one found among laboring class and artisan groups on the eve of the Revolution—that had not been treated by either Bailyn or Wood. Viewing the lives of urban dwellers in three cities—Boston, New York, and Philadelphia—from the 1680s to the Revolution, Nash concluded that social changes had turned these seaport communities into "crucibles of revolutionary agitation." He noted the increasing poverty, narrowing of economic opportunities, as well as the resulting resentment and rise of class consciousness among segments of the artisan class. A section from Nash's book is the source for the second selection in this chapter.[12]

The second trend from the mid-1960s to 1990 that contradicted the neoconservative view of the Revolution was contained in the writings of a group called the neo-Progressives. These scholars resembled the older Progressive historians in several ways. They believed, for example, that the Revolution could best be studied from the perspective of average citizens—the inarticulate masses, and sometimes the disadvantaged, or downtrodden. The chief sources of the Revolutionary movement, they argued, were to be found in the profound economic

---

see "Virtue and Commerce in the Eighteenth Century," *Journal of Interdisciplinary History* 3 (1972):120.

[11]Rhys Isaac, *Transformation of Virginia, 1740–1790* (Chapel Hill, 1982).

[12]Gary B. Nash, *Urban Crucible* (Cambridge, 1979).

and social dislocations within eighteenth-century America. The tensions generated by such changes led to social unrest and protest on the part of the lower social orders during the Revolution. The neo-Progressive historians portrayed the Revolution as a democratic movement stimulated in part by these growing social inequalities. In their view, the Revolution was a popular upsurge which aimed to broaden participation in American political life by breaking down the structures of authority by which local elites had ruled the colonies.

The leading neo-Progressive historian to inherit the mantle of Beard was Merrill Jensen who continued to view the Revolution in terms of conflict—particularly political and economic clashes both between the colonies and mother country and within the colonies themselves. Jensen's *The Founding of a Nation*, published in the late 1960s, focused on the political instability in Britain and the American provinces and the tensions that arose as a result of these differences. In a work published on the eve of the Bicentennial, Jensen's *The American Revolution within America* continued the conflict interpretation of the Revolution stressing the economic causes as did many of his students such as Jackson Turner Main at Wisconsin. On the whole, the neo-Progressives were not successful in linking the widening economic inequalities directly to the causes of the Revolution itself.[13]

One of the main themes pressed by the neo-Progressives was that there were severe limitations in the socioeconomic opportunities prior to the Revolution and that with the unfolding of that event the rising masses were able to take advantage of new opportunities generated. James Kirby Martin, a Jensen student, concluded in his fine study that the transfer of political power occurred mainly among elites, and that this process from which the people ultimately benefited came about through chance rather than through the actions of revolutionary leaders.[14]

The neo-Progressives were not only influenced by the writings of the earlier Progressive historians, Beard and Becker, but in large measure by the social and political concerns of the times in which they lived. These scholars brought to the study of the Revolution a renewed awareness of the existence of minority groups and disadvantaged groups in American history.

Similar concerns and attitudes were most evident in the work of the New Left historians—the most extreme proponents of the neo-Progressive point of view. The protest movements in the 1960s, 1970s,

---

[13]Merrill Jensen, *The Founding of a Nation* (New York, 1968) and *The American Revolution within America* (New York, 1974). For Jensen's students, see Jackson Turner Main, *The Sovereign States, 1775–1783* (New York, 1973), as but one example among many.

[14]James Kirby Martin, *Men In Rebellion* (New Brunswick, 1973).

and 1980s on behalf of specific groups in the population—the poor, blacks, ethnic minorities, and women—made these scholars more sensitive to the claims of these and other social groups who had been oppressed in the past. Having become more visible in the present, these groups drew the attention of more historians writing about the past. The work of the New Left then, reflected in many instances the intense interest in social justice so evident during the decades in which these historians wrote.

Among the most aggressive spokesmen of the New Left was Jesse Lemisch, who was one of the first to argue that the history of the Revolution had been written too much "from the top down"—that is, from the viewpoint of the elites—the Washingtons, Jeffersons, and Adamses. Such a historical perspective, by its nature remained blind to the concerns of the common man and the inarticulate masses. History, according to Lemisch, should be written "from the bottom up." If viewed in this way, the Revolution might be shown to be more radical and characterized by greater class conflict than the neoconservatives realized. To make this point, Lemisch wrote an article singling out the omission of any mention of British impressment of American sailors in works on the Revolution. Lowly American seamen, he argued, were deeply distressed by this pernicious practice of the Royal Navy. Yet scholars all but ignored this issue because it was seldom protested by members of the middle and upper classes. Lemisch concluded that other ordinary citizens, like these seamen, might have supported the Revolution for other reasons historians had failed to investigate. By doing so, he opened the possibility of viewing the Revolution as a radical movement undertaken by lower social groups in the society to remedy specific grievances they suffered under British rule. Lemisch went on to suggest that more research done from the perspective of the common people might reveal other instances of a similar nature, and result in a view of the Revolution written along different lines.[15]

One of the most important books written by members of the New Left to challenge the neoconservative historians and adherents of the "republican synthesis" was a collection of essays edited by Alfred E. Young entitled *The American Revolution: Explorations in the History of American Radicalism*, published in 1976. Many scholars in this volume took issue with Bailyn's interpretation in particular. They rejected the idea of an ideological consensus among the American people, or that the Revolution was mainly an ideological revolution. Some pictured the Revolution as a social movement—an internal struggle within the colonies—caused in part by class antagonisms. Others, however, held that the Revolution was ideological in nature,

---

[15]Jesse Lemisch, "The American Revolution Seen from the Bottom Up," in *Towards a New Past*, Barton J. Bernstein, ed. (New York, 1968), pp. 3–45.

but on a different basis than that presented by Bailyn. They saw serious differences in ideology between local leaders who shared a Whig view and the middle and lower orders of society who held different political beliefs.[16]

Edward Countryman, another New Left historian, continued this tradition into the 1980s. His study of New York went much farther than Jensen in tracing the Revolution to a distinct drive for democracy. Countryman concluded that the radical leaders carried through a revolutionary redefinition of New York politics and society in the late 1770s that transformed the state temporarily. Using a sophisticated quantitative analysis, he revealed how the unruly crowds of the pre-Revolutionary period evolved into the popularly-based committees of correspondence of the independence movement. His study showed also how closely economic issues—taxes, price controls, and monetary policies—were linked not only to clashing interest groups but to conflicting visions of what republican society and government ought to be. Countryman's depiction of the collapse of the old elite order in New York after the war began undermined any idea of continuing the old consensus approach for that state.[17]

A third distinct challenge to the neoconservative interpretation came from the historians who studied the Loyalists. The neoconservatives had pictured the Revolution as a conservative movement aimed at preserving constitutional and political principles and undertaken to defend traditional American liberties. To the neoconservatives the Revolutionary period represented no break with the colonial past. They traced a line of continuity in political and constitutional principles from the late colonial era through the writing of state constitutions to the Constitution in 1787. To them the Constitution represented the culmination of the Revolution, not a rejection of that event. The Constitution was not a counterrevolution, as the old Progressive historians had maintained. Given the premise of a conservative Revolution, the neoconservatives could not fit the Loyalists comfortably within their interpretation. How could conservatives like the Loyalists oppose a conservative Revolution? For this reason, the neoconservatives either failed to mention the Loyalists, or made only superficial references to them.[18]

---

[16]Young, ed., *The American Revolution, passim*

[17]Edward Countryman, *A People in Revolution* (Baltimore, 1981).

[18]Daniel J. Boorstin in *The Americans: The Colonial Experience* (New York, 1958), *The Americans: The National Experience* (New York, 1965), and "The American Revolution: Revolution Without Dogma," in *The Genius of American Politics* (Chicago, 1953), pp. 66–98, do not discuss the Loyalists. Louis Hartz, *The Liberal Tradition in America* (New York, 1955), p. 58, and Clinton Rossiter, *Seedtime of the Republic* (New York, 1953), pp. 3, 155, 319, 322, 340, and 349 say very little. Edmund S. Morgan in *Birth of the Republic, 1763–1789* (Chicago, 1977 edition), pp. 99 and 119–120 made only a slight

During the decades from the 1960s to 1990, however, there was a revival of interest in the Loyalists. The most important work to appear during the 1960s was William H. Nelson's *The American Tory*. Although Nelson's book was a form of intellectual history, it reflected the trends current among more recent scholars: the tendency to concentrate more on social history; and the inclination to resort to concepts drawn from other academic disciplines. Nelson presented the arresting hypothesis that the Loyalists constituted a collection of isolated "cultural minorities"—certain social groups who were acutely aware of the fact that they had never been assimilated into American society. These cultural enclaves, therefore, looked to Britain for protection against the threatening Whig majorities that surrounded them. Included in these social groups were: ethnic minorities such as the Scots, recent British immigrants, and Germans in the South; religious minorities like the Anglicans in the North, Presbyterians in the South, and Quakers and German Pietists in the middle colonies; and certain racial minorities—many black slaves and certain Indian tribes. In defining these minorities in terms of their sense of group consciousness and their feelings of alienation from the prevailing Whig majority, Nelson applied to history the negative reference group theory often employed by sociologists.[19]

Efforts to analyze the social origins of the Loyalists were continued by Wallace Brown, who inquired into their socioeconomic and geographic backgrounds. Contrary to the findings of earlier historians, Brown argued that the Loyalists were not primarily members of the upper class; they came mainly from the lower and middle classes. Loyalism, moreover, was "a distinctly urban and seaboard phenomenon"—except in New York and North Carolina where there existed "major rural inland pockets." Despite John Adams's frequently misquoted estimate that the Loyalists constituted one-third of the population, Brown's statistics showed that they composed somewhere between 7.6 to 18 percent of the white population.[20]

Mary Beth Norton treated the Loyalists from a different perspective: comparative history. She followed the fortunes of the Loyalists after their exile in England. Loyalists came to recognize how "American" they were when they felt ill at ease and out of place in English

---

mention, but Benjamin F. Wright, *Consensus and Continuity* (Boston, 1958), hardly accounted for the Loyalists at all.

[19]William H. Nelson, *The American Tory* (New York, 1961).

[20]Wallace Brown, *The King's Friends* (Providence, 1965), pp. v, 250, 257–258, and 261–267. Another work that treated the Loyalists throughout the original thirteen states was Robert Calhoon, *The Loyalists of Revolutionary America, 1760–1781* (New York, 1973). One especially insightful biography of a Loyalist among many was Bernard Bailyn, *The Ordeal of Thomas Hutchinson* (Cambridge, 1974).

society. Once again the negative reference group theory proved useful.[21]

Before, during, and after the decade in which the American Revolution Bicentennial was celebrated, at least four major trends were noticeable in the staggering amount of literature that poured forth. One was the use of a comparative history methodology and a tendency to view the Revolution within a broader context rather than a narrowly nationalistic framework. The second was the appearance of the "new social historians" who saw the Revolution in different terms. The third was a group of scholars who explored the Revolution from a psychological point of view. The fourth was the group of "new military historians" who discussed the Revolution as an armed conflict.

The outstanding comparative historian was Robert R. Palmer, who concluded that the period from the American Revolution in 1776 to the European revolutions in 1848 constituted a series of democratic revolutions. He saw the American Revolution, then, as part of the process of democratization that was taking place throughout the entire Western world at that time. In his magisterial two-volume work, *The Age of the Democratic Revolution*, published in the late 1950s and early 1960s, Palmer was able to gain new insights into the process of revolution by resorting to the method of comparative history.[22]

Richard B. Morris carried the comparative method even farther in terms of time in this regard. He found that the American Revolution served as a model for many of the new emerging nations that came into being in the 1950s and 1960s. During the great age of decolonization that took place after World War II, Morris saw some analogies between the Revolution and the modern anticolonial movements.[23]

A second major trend during the period from the 1960s to 1990 was the rise of the "new social historians" who devoted their attention to the Revolution. These scholars were united loosely by their desire to examine America's social structure and changes within that social structure over time. Their work in many instances was characterized by methodological innovations, quantitative techniques, and research in nontraditional sources like wills, deeds and tax lists to get at the inner lives of the inarticulate masses who left few personal memoirs. By resorting to such records they hoped to re-create the universe in which ordinary citizens lived. They often directed their attention to small communities as a means of tracing changes over time and saw such villages and towns as microcosms of the entire American society.

---

[21]Mary Beth Norton, *The British Americans* (Boston, 1972).

[22]Robert R. Palmer, *The Age of the Democratic Revolution*, 2 vols. (Princeton, 1959 and 1964).

[23]Richard B. Morris, *The Emerging Nations and the American Revolution* (New York, 1970).

Like the New Left historians, they sometimes were interested in specific socially or politically disadvantaged groups: the poor, blacks, and women. And like the "new intellectual historians" they followed changes in the attitudes and behavior of groups over long periods of time.

One community case study by a "new social historian" was Robert Gross's *The Minutemen and Their World*, which analyzed Concord, Massachusetts. Much of Gross's work was quantitative in nature; he reconstructed the life of the community not only from traditional literary sources but from church records, wills, deeds, petitions, tax lists, and minutes of town meetings. Rather than making sweeping statements about the Revolution as a broad social movement, Gross demonstrated how the events affected the lives of individuals within a single town. His conclusion was that the townspeople had gone to war not to promote social change, but to stop it. Concord's Minutemen were driven to rebellion by a desire to defend their traditional way of life from encroachment by the British and other outside forces. Ironically enough, the results of the Revolution opened the way to unintended innovations that profoundly altered Concord's way of life.[24]

The term "community" was often defined in different ways. Sometimes it was used to refer to a particular colony, describing its transformation from a "gemeinschaft" community—harmonious, stable, and well-ordered, and bound together by certain traditional values—to a "gesellschaft" community—chaotic, unstable, and disorderly, and torn apart by a sense of alienation caused by conflicting forces. Richard L. Bushman in *From Puritan to Yankee* described Connecticut in such terms as a result of changes taking place from 1690 to 1765. Connecticut was transformed from a homogeneous Puritan community held together by religious values to a secular society torn by various competing groups. His was but one of a number of "gemeinschaft to gesellschaft" community studies along such lines.[25]

The "new social historians," among many others, paid more attention to certain social and racial groups such as blacks, women, and Indians to examine how they were affected by the Revolution. Donald L. Robinson in *Slavery in the Structure of American Politics, 1765–1820* dealt with the institution of slavery over a long period of time. Edmund S. Morgan, more than a "new social historian," produced the most searching study, *American Slavery—American Freedom*, dealing with the paradox of how slavery and freedom developed side-by-side

---

[24]Robert Gross, *The Minutemen and Their World* (New York, 1976).

[25]Richard L. Bushman, *From Puritan to Yankee* (New York, 1967). See also Bushman's *King and People in Provincial Massachusetts* (Chapel Hill, 1985) for an insightful study of how both the country and prerogative traditions helped to shape American resistance in that colony.

in the colonies. Two splendid books—Mary Beth Norton's *Liberty's Daughters* and Linda K. Kerber's *Women of the Republic*—covered the role of women in the Revolution and post-Revolutionary period. The part that one Indian tribe played was portrayed in Barbara Graymount's *The Iroquois in the American Revolution*—the first full-scale ethnohistory of Indian participation in the war. With the "new social history" in full swing by the time of the American Revolutionary Bicentennial, many works on the subject were written in that mode.[26]

A third trend took place in the 1970s to 1990 as scholars explored the nature of the Revolution in psychological terms. Historians resorted to classical psychological theories, including those of Freud, to come up with social science concepts that might prove useful. Several scholars made use of psychohistory—a subdiscipline that had recently come into prominence. They suggested the Americans may have been caught up in a serious identity crisis as a people on the eve of the Revolution. This attitude, they concluded, might explain the colonists' rebellious behavior.

Viewed in psychological terms, Americans were said to be involved in an identity crisis that resulted in a love/hate relationship toward the mother country. Colonial society underwent a process of "Anglicization" in the eighteenth century, and according to this hypothesis, Americans became more self-consciously English as they copied British ways. In becoming Anglicized, however, Americans turned their backs on certain indigenous native styles, habits, and traditions they had developed earlier. Hence, the colonists were torn. On the one hand, they admired the mother country so much that they imitated British ways. On the other, they resented the idea of emulating the British because they were seeking to establish a separate sense of American identity. Jack P. Greene, John M. Murrin, and Robert M. Weir, among others, treated the theme of an identity crisis in several essays.[27]

---

[26]Donald L. Robinson, *Slavery in the Structure of American Politics, 1765–1820* (New York, 1971); Edmund S. Morgan, *American Slavery—American Freedom* (New York, 1975); Mary Beth Norton, *Liberty's Daughters* (Boston, 1980); Linda K. Kerber, *Women of the Republic* (Chapel Hill, 1980); and Barbara Graymount, *The Iroquois in the American Revolution* (Syracuse, 1972).

[27]Jack P. Greene, "Search for Identity: An Interpretation of the Meaning of Selected Patterns of Social Response in Eighteenth-Century America," *Journal of Social History* 3 (1980):189–220; John M. Murrin, "The Legal Transformation: The Bench and Bar of Eighteenth-Century Massachusetts," in *Essays in Politics and Development: Colonial America*, Stanley N. Katz, ed. (Boston, 1971); Jack P. Greene, "An Uneasy Connection: An Analysis of the Pre-Conditions of the American Revolution," in *Essays on the American Revolution*, Stephen G. Kurtz and James H. Hutson, eds. (Chapel Hill, 1973); Rowland Berthoff and John M. Murrin, "Feudalism, Communalism, and the Yeoman Freeholder: The American Revolution Considered as a Social Accident," *ibid.*, pp. 256–288; and Robert M. Weir, "Who Shall Rule at Home: The American Revolution as a Crisis of Legitimacy for the Colonial Elite," *Journal of Interdisciplinary History* 6 (1976):679–700.

Other attempts at psychohistory explored the colonial relationship within a more Freudian framework. This hypothesis employed connotations with familiar sex role models—Britain as a mother country, the English king as a father figure, and the colonists as rebellious adolescents—and suggested they were all locked in an oedipal conflict. That contemporaries viewed the Revolution in such terms was clear. John Adams explained in 1765 that the colonists indeed might be children, but "have not children a right to complain when their parents are attempting to break their limbs . . . ?" Thomas Paine put it more eloquently in 1777 when he wrote "To know whether it be the interest of the continent to be independent, we need only ask this simple question 'Is it the interest of a man to be a boy all his life'?" Such scholars as Winthrop D. Jordan, Edwin G. Burrows, Michael Wallace, and Bruce Mazlish all explored the psychological dimensions of the Revolution along such lines.[28]

One of the most interesting attempts at psychohistory was Jay Fliegelman's *Prodigals and Pilgrims*, published in the early 1980s. Fliegelman postulated the rise of an antipatriarchal movement in both Britain and America during the Revolutionary era. Involved in this movement were new antipatriarchal assumptions regarding the respective rights and duties of children and those of parents toward children. The aim of the movement was to try to perfect and improve the purely voluntary contractual relationship existing between the two generations. The old fidelity to rigid parental precepts and prolonged submission to parental rule was to give way. In the new age dawning, the young were to be properly prepared to take their place in the world—a world assumed to be filled with great temptations and corruption—and to be released freely, without rancor, and with no expectations of continuing gratitude. It was within this frame of reference, Fliegelman argued, that the dispute between Britain and America should be cast. This struggle for filial revolution and independence underlay many of the important disputes over the nature and limits of authority and obedience between the mother country and colonies. By discussing political issues in such terms, Fliegelman related the public discourse to private attitudes regarding patriarchy, authority, and child-rearing, and uncovered an important strain of thought which illuminated the imperial crisis in a strikingly different way.[29]

Psychobiography along with psychohistory attracted historians of

---

[28]Winthrop D. Jordan, "Familial Politics: Thomas Paine and the Killing of the King, 1776," *Journal of American History* 60 (1973):249–308; Edwin G. Burrows and Michael Wallace, "The American Revolution: The Ideology and Psychology of National Liberation," *Perspectives in American History* 6 (1972):167–306; and Bruce Mazlish, "Leadership in the American Revolution: The Psychological Dimension," in *Leadership in the American Revolution*, Elizabeth H. Kagan, comp. (Washington, D.C., 1974).

[29]Jay Fliegelman, *Prodigals and Pilgrims* (Cambridge, Mass., 1982).

the Revolution. Some scholars examined the lives of individuals seeking to make a connection between child-rearing practices and adult behavior. They were hoping to determine whether there were any patterns in child-rearing that might explain why persons from the same socioeconomic backgrounds became patriots while others remained Loyalists. Other biographers, Fawn M. Brodie, Kenneth S. Lynn and William B. Willcox, for example, relied on theories of individual psychology to explain the behavior of their subjects. These writings employing theories of social and individual psychology to explain the coming of the Revolution showed the tendency of scholars to resort more to the use of other social sciences in the discipline of history.[30]

A fourth and final trend in historiography of the Revolution was the interest in military history. It was, after all, a military conflict and this side of the story has been well told by a group of scholars known as the "new military historians." They represent an offshoot of the "new social historians," for they broke away from the old-fashioned drum-and-trumpet narrative approach to war, and wedded military and social history. They removed military history from the narrow confines of the battlefield and placed it within a much broader context— that of the relationship between warfare and society as a whole.

The "new military historians" believed that military history could be illuminated by sophisticated conceptualization and analyses rather than resorting to simple narrative. Among other things, they felt that they could apply to military history insights derived from other disciplines—psychology, sociology, and anthropology. These scholars analyzed the military behavior of men and armies in light of theories drawn from the fields of individual and social psychology. They evaluated tensions between the military and nonmilitary segments of society as well as groups within the military itself from a sociological perspective. Employing the tools of anthropology they studied the interaction between the various armed forces engaged in the Revolutionary War: the American, British, French, and German. Some of these scholars viewed military actions from the point of view of the private on the battlefield rather than from that of the generals back at headquarters.

Many "new military historians" believed that the way a nation waged war shed important light on the values held by its people. John Shy, in a book of brilliant essays, maintained that the pattern of military events during the Revolutionary War helped to shape the way the American people came to view themselves and their relationship to

---

[30]Philip Greven, *The Protestant Temperament: Patterns of Child-Rearing, Religious Experience, and the Self in Early America* (New York, 1977); Kenneth S. Lynn, *A Divided People* (Westport, Conn., 1977); Fawn M. Brodie, *Thomas Jefferson* (New York, 1974); and William B. Willcox, *Portrait of a General* (New York, 1964).

the rest of the world. To Shy the war was not an instrument of policy or a sequence of military operations solely, but rather a social process of education. The actions of the British army in certain colonies, New Jersey in 1776, for example, politicized the populace and galvanized heretofore apathetic neutrals into fierce fighting men.[31]

Another leader in the field, Don Higginbotham, analyzed the ideas, attitudes, and traditions that helped determine how the war was fought. He showed how the armies were projections of the societies from which they sprang: the Continental army beginning as citizen-soldier amateurs, while the British forces were composed of professional fighting men led by aristocratic officers. Higginbotham was especially insightful in showing the interaction between war and society that resulted in significant changes within both American civil and military institutions.[32]

Charles Royster's *A Revolutionary People at War* probed the American character and employed the Continental army as a touchstone to reveal the complex views that the army and society had of each other. He dismissed the materialistic interpretation of many recent studies that concluded men were motivated to enter the service for reasons of self-interest. These studies claimed that those who went to war were primarily the poor who were anxious to escape a desperate or near-desperate situation. In a subtle and imaginative analysis, Royster showed that after the *rage militaire* of 1775 in which men enlisted with great fervor, the people's army gave way increasingly to a more European-style professional army—though one which never lost the force of revolutionary ideals. Once independence was achieved, the belief grew that victory had been won by a virtuous people, and not simply by the army. To make certain that the future security of American independence would rest on public virtue and not on a military establishment, that virtue had to be strengthened by claiming that the people, and not the army, had won the war. The American people thus reclaimed the war from the army, and ungratefully shunted the army aside, leaving behind an ambiguous military legacy.[33]

E. Wayne Carp took a different approach in his *To Starve the Army at Pleasure*, published in 1984. His book had two aims: to describe

---

[31]John Shy, *A People Numerous and Armed* (New York, 1976), p. 224. For the British army in America before the Revolution and the colonists' reaction to its presence, see Shy's *Toward Lexington* (Princeton, 1965).

[32]Don Higginbotham, *War of American Independence* (New York, 1971). For a fine set of selected essays, see also Don Higginbotham, ed., *Reconsideration of the Revolutionary War* (Westport, Conn., 1978), one of which deals with the issue of the militia's use in conventional warfare.

[33]Charles Royster, *A Revolutionary People at War* (Chapel Hill, 1979). See also Royster's *Light-Horse Harry Lee and the Legacy of the American Revolution* (New York, 1981).

the difficulties of supplying the Continental army; and to analyze the symbiotic relationship between the administration of the army and eighteenth-century American political culture. What Carp concluded is that the experience of the war changed the attitudes of many Americans toward the two institutions they had opposed prior to the conflict—professional armies and a strong central government. The near fatal consequences of waging war under a weak central government and the difficulties of securing supplies from the thirteen sovereign states convinced many people of the limitations of eighteenth-century American political culture and eventually set the stage for a more powerful central government under the Constitution.[34]

In summary it should be noted that historians who have addressed themselves to the question of whether the Revolution was revolutionary or not must answer a number of related questions. Was American society democratic during the colonial period so that the Revolution became nothing more than a colonial rebellion? Or was American society undemocratic during the colonial era, thus resulting in a dual revolution: a struggle to see who would rule at home as well as a fight for home rule? Were the reforms that accompanied the Revolution the result of a gradual evolution, and carried out with the blessings of a basic consensus among the American people? Or were such reforms the product of a radical revolution that resulted in class conflict between America's upper and lower classes? What was the true nature of the Revolution? Was there a radical ideological change in the ideas that most Americans held regarding their image of themselves and of their institutions? Or did most of the changes take place within the political and social sphere rather than in the world of ideas? Was the "republican synthesis," with its emphasis on republican ideology a convincing interpretation of this cataclysmic event? Were the Loyalists disloyal Americans because they did not share the Whig consensus on constitutional and political principles? Or were they instead "cultural minorities" fearful of surrounding majorities they regarded as hostile? What motivated men to go off to fight in the Revolutionary War—was it materialistic self-interest or revolutionary idealism? Was the Revolution a unique event and therefore one to be examined within the context of American history and in terms of its own time?

---

[34]E. Wayne Carp, *To Starve the Army at Pleasure* (Chapel Hill, 1984). For writings by other "new military historians" see Richard Kohn, *Eagle and Sword* (New York, 1975) and his "The Social History of the American Soldier: A Review and Prospectus for Research," *American Historical Review* 86 (1981):533–567, as well as the two books of collected essays edited by George Athan Billias, *George Washington's Generals* (New York, 1964), and *George Washington's Opponents* (New York, 1969).

For a "new military historian" writing from a Marxist perspective, see Steven Russwurm, *Arms, Country, and Class* (New Brunswick, 1987), which shows how the Philadelphia militia composed of the "lower sort" transformed the laboring poor in that city and provided them with an opportunity to express their class consciousness.

Or did it bear some relationship to revolutions that took place in other parts of the Western world at a later time? The answers to these questions, in the final analysis, will determine the answer to the broader question of whether the American Revolution was revolutionary or nonrevolutionary.

Bernard Bailyn

BERNARD BAILYN (1922–   ) *is Adams University Professor of History at Harvard University. He has written numerous books on American colonial history, including* The New England Merchants in the Seventeenth Century *(1955),* Education in the Forming of American Society *(1960),* The Origins of American Politics *(1968),* The Ordeal of Thomas Hutchinson *(1974),* The Peopling of British North America *(1986), and* Voyages to the West *(1986).*

What was essentially involved in the American Revolution was not the disruption of society, with all the fear, despair, and hatred that that entails, but the realization, the comprehension and fulfillment, of the inheritance of liberty and of what was taken to be America's destiny in the context of world history. The great social shocks that in the French and Russian revolutions sent the foundations of thousands of individual lives crashing into ruins had taken place in America in the course of the previous century, slowly, silently, almost imperceptibly, not as a sudden avalanche but as myriads of individual changes and adjustments which had gradually transformed the order of society. By 1763 the great landmarks of European life—the church and the idea of orthodoxy, the state and the idea of authority: much of the array of institutions and ideas that buttressed the society of the *ancien régime*—had faded in their exposure to the open, wilderness environment of America. But until the disturbances of the 1760s these changes had not been seized upon as grounds for reconsideration of society and politics. Often they had been condemned as deviations, as retrogressions back toward a more primitive condition of life. Then, after 1760—and especially in the decade after 1765—they were brought into open discussion as the colonists sought to apply advanced principles of society and politics to their own immediate problems.

The original issue of the Anglo-American conflict was, of course, the question of the extent of Parliament's jurisdiction in the colonies. But that could not be discussed in isolation. The debate involved eventually a wide range of social and political problems, and it ended by 1776 in what may be called the conceptualization of American life. By then Americans had come to think of themselves as in a special cate-

---

gory, uniquely placed by history to capitalize on, to complete and fulfill, the promise of man's existence. The changes that had overtaken their provincial societies, they saw, had been good: elements not of deviance and retrogression but of betterment and progress; not a lapse into primitivism, but an elevation to a higher plane of political and social life than had ever been reached before. Their rustic blemishes had become the marks of a chosen people. "The liberties of mankind and the glory of human nature is in their keeping," John Adams wrote in the year of the Stamp Act. "America was designed by Providence for the theatre on which man was to make his true figure, on which science, virtue, liberty, happiness, and glory were to exist in peace."

The effort to comprehend, to communicate, and to fulfill this destiny was continuous through the entire revolutionary generation—it did not cease, in fact, until in the nineteenth century its creative achievements became dogma. But there were three phases of particular concentration: the period up to and including 1776, centering on the discussion of Anglo-American differences; the devising of the first state governments, mainly in the years from 1776 to 1780; and the reconsideration of the state constitutions and the reconstruction of the national government in the last half of the eighties and in the early nineties. In each of these phases important contributions were made not only to the skeletal structure of constitutional theory but to the surrounding areas of social thought as well. But in none was the creativity as great, the results as radical and as fundamental, as in the period before Independence. It was then that the premises were defined and the assumptions set. It was then that explorations were made in new territories of thought, the first comprehensive maps sketched, and routes marked out. Thereafter the psychological as well as intellectual barriers were down. It was the most creative period in the history of American political thought. Everything that followed assumed and built upon its results. . . .

It was an elevating, transforming vision: a new, fresh, vigorous, and above all morally regenerate people rising from obscurity to defend the battlements of liberty and then in triumph standing forth, heartening and sustaining the cause of freedom everywhere. In the light of such a conception everything about the colonies and their controversy with the mother country took on a new appearance. Provincialism was gone: Americans stood side by side with the heroes of historic battles for freedom and with the few remaining champions of liberty in the present. What were once felt to be defects—isolation, institutional simplicity, primitiveness of manners, multiplicity of religions, weakness in the authority of the state—could now be seen as virtues, not only by Americans themselves but by enlightened spokesmen of reform, renewal, and hope wherever they might be—in London coffeehouses, in Parisian *salons*, in the courts of German princes. The mere

existence of the colonists suddenly became philosophy teaching by example. Their manners, their morals, their way of life, their physical,
social, and political condition were seen to vindicate eternal truths
and to demonstrate, as ideas and words never could, the virtues of the
heavenly city of the eighteenth-century philosophers.

But the colonists' ideas and words counted too, and not merely
because they repeated as ideology the familiar utopian phrases of the
Enlightenment and of English libertarianism. What they were saying
by 1776 was familiar in a general way to reformers and illuminati
everywhere in the Western world; yet it was different. Words and concepts had been reshaped in the colonists' minds in the course of a decade of pounding controversy—strangely reshaped, turned in unfamiliar
directions, toward conclusions they could not themselves clearly perceive. They found a new world of political thought as they struggled
to work out the implications of their beliefs in the years before independence. It was a world not easily possessed; often they withdrew in
some confusion to more familiar ground. But they touched its boundaries, and, at certain points, probed its interior. Others, later—writing
and revising the first state constitutions, drafting and ratifying the federal Constitution, and debating in detail, exhaustively, the merits of
these efforts—would resume the search for resolutions of the problems
the colonists had broached before 1776.

This critical probing of traditional concepts—part of the colonists'
effort to express reality as they knew it and to shape it to ideal ends—
became the basis for all further discussions of enlightened reform, in
Europe as well as in America. The radicalism the Americans conveyed
to the world in 1776 was a transformed as well as a transforming force.
. . .

In no obvious sense was the American Revolution undertaken as
a social revolution. No one, that is, deliberately worked for the destruction or even the substantial alteration of the order of society as it
had been known. Yet it was transformed as a result of the Revolution,
and not merely because Loyalist property was confiscated and redis-
tributed, or because the resulting war destroyed the economic bases of
some people's lives and created opportunities for others that would not
otherwise have existed. Seizure of Loyalist property and displacements
in the economy did in fact take place, and the latter if not the former
does account for a spurt in social mobility that led earlier *arrivés* to
remark, "When the pot boils, the scum will rise." Yet these were superficial changes; they affected a small part of the population only, and
they did not alter the organization of society.

What did now affect the essentials of social organization—what in
time would help permanently to transform them—were changes in the
realm of belief and attitude. The views men held toward the relation-

ships that bound them to each other—the discipline and pattern of society—moved in a new direction in the decade before Independence.

Americans of 1760 continued to assume, as had their predecessors for generations before, that a healthy society was a hierarchical society, in which it was natural for some to be rich and some poor, some honored and some obscure, some powerful and some weak. And it was believed that superiority was unitary, that the attributes of the favored—wealth, wisdom, power—had a natural affinity to each other, and hence that political leadership would naturally rest in the hands of the social leaders. Movement, of course, there would be: some would fall and some would rise; but manifest, external differences among men, reflecting the principle of hierarchical order, were necessary and proper, and would remain; they were intrinsic to the nature of things.

Circumstances had pressed harshly against such assumptions. The wilderness environment from the beginning had threatened the maintenance of elaborate social distinctions; many of them in the passage of time had in fact been worn away. Puritanism, in addition, and the epidemic evangelicalism of the mid-eighteenth century, had created challenges to the traditional notions of social stratification by generating the conviction that the ultimate quality of men was to be found elsewhere than in their external condition, and that a cosmic achievement lay within each man's grasp. And the peculiar configuration of colonial politics—a constant broil of petty factions struggling almost formlessly, with little discipline or control, for the benefits of public authority—had tended to erode the respect traditionally accorded the institutions and officers of the state.

Yet nowhere, at any time in the colonial years, were the implications of these circumstances articulated or justified. The assumption remained that society, in its maturity if not in its confused infancy, would conform to the pattern of the past; that authority would continue to exist without challenge, and that those in superior positions would be responsible and wise, and those beneath them respectful and content. These premises and expectations were deeply lodged; they were not easily or quickly displaced. But the Revolution brought with it arguments and attitudes bred of arguments endlessly repeated, that undermined these premises of the *ancien régime.*

For a decade or more defiance to the highest constituted powers poured from the colonial presses and was hurled from half the pulpits of the land. The right, the need, the absolute obligation to disobey legally constituted authority had become the universal cry. Cautions and qualifications became ritualistic: formal exercises in ancient pieties. One might preface one's charge to disobedience with homilies on the inevitable imperfections of all governments and the necessity to

bear "some injuries" patiently and peaceably. But what needed and received demonstration and defense was not the caution, but the injunction: the argument that when injuries touched on "fundamental
rights" (and who could say when they did not?) then nothing less than
"duty to God and religion, to themselves, to the community, and to
unborn posterity require such to assert and defend their rights by all
lawful, most prudent, and effectual means in their power." Obedience
as a principle was only too well known; disobedience as a doctrine
was not. It was therefore asserted again and again that resistance to
constituted authority was "a doctrine according to godliness—the doctrine of the English nation . . . by which our rights and constitution
have often been defended and repeatedly rescued out of the hands of
encroaching tyranny. . . . This is the doctrine and grand pillar of the
ever memorable and glorious Revolution, and upon which our gracious
sovereign George III holds the crown of the British empire." What better credentials could there be? How lame to add that obedience too "is
an eminent part of Christian duty without which government must
disband and dreadful anarchy and confusion (with all it horrors) take
place and reign without control"—how lame, especially in view of the
fact that one could easily mistake this "Christian obedience" for that
"blind, enslaving obedience which is no part of the Christian institution but is highly injurious to religion, to every free government, and
to the good of mankind, and is the stirrup of tyranny, and grand engine
of slavery."

Defiance to constituted authority leaped like a spark from one
flammable area to another, growing in heat as it went. Its greatest in-
tensification took place in the explosive atmosphere of local religious
dissent. Isaac Backus spoke only for certain of the Baptists and Congregational Separates and against the presumptive authority of ministers,
when, in the course of an attack on the religious establishment in Massachusetts, he warned that

> we are not to obey and follow [ministers] in an implicit or customary
> way, but each one must consider and follow others no further than
> they see that the end of their conversation is Jesus Christ the same
> yesterday, and today, and forever more. . . . People are so far from
> being under obligation to follow teachers who don't lead in this way
> they incur guilt by such a following of them.

It took little imagination on the part of Backus's readers and lis-
teners to find in this a general injunction against uncritical obedience
to authority in any form. Others were even more explicit. The Baptist
preacher who questioned not merely the authority of the local orthodox church but the very "etymology of the word [orthodoxy]" assured
the world that the colonists

> have as just a right, before GOD and man, to oppose King, ministry,
> Lords, and Commons of England when they violate their rights as

Americans as they have to oppose any foreign enemy; and that this is no more, according to the law of nature, to be deemed rebellion than it would be to oppose the King of France, supposing him now present invading the land.

But what to the Baptists was the establishment, to Anglicans was dissent. From the establishment in New England, ever fearful of ecclesiastical impositions from without, came a strong current of antiauthoritarianism as from the farthest left-wing sect. It was a pillar of the temple, a scion of the church, and an apologist for New England's standing order who sweepingly disclaimed "all human authority in matters of faith and worship. We regard neither pope nor prince as head of the church, nor acknowledge that any Parliaments have power to enact articles of doctrine or forms of discipline or modes of worship or terms of church communion," and, declaring that "we are accountable to none but *Christ*"—words that had struck at the heart of every establishment, civil and religious, since the fall of Rome—concluded with the apparent paradox that *"liberty* is the *fundamental* principle of our establishment."

In such declarations a political argument became a moral imperative. The principle of justifiable disobedience and the instinct to question public authority before accepting it acquired a new sanction and a new vigor. Originally, of course, the doctrine of resistance was applied to Parliament, a nonrepresentative assembly three thousand miles away. But the composition and location of the institution had not been as crucial in creating opposition as had the character of the actions Parliament had taken. Were provincial assemblies, simply because they were local and representative, exempt from scrutiny and resistance? Were they any less susceptible than Parliament to the rule that when their authority is extended beyond "the bounds of the law of God and the free constitution . . . 'their acts are, *ipso facto,* void, and cannot oblige any to obedience'"? There could be no doubt of the answer. Any legislature, wherever located or however composed, deserved only the obedience it could command by the justice and wisdom of its proceedings. Representative or not, local or not, any agency of the state could be defied. The freeholders of Augusta, Virginia, could not have been more explicit in applying to local government in 1776 the defiance learned in the struggle with Parliament. They wrote their delegates to Virginia's Provincial Congress that

should the future conduct of our legislative body prove to you that our opinion of their wisdom and justice is ill-grounded, then tell them that your constituents are neither guided nor will ever be influenced by that slavish maxim in politics, "that whatever is enacted by that body of men in whom the supreme power of the state is vested must in all cases be obeyed," and that they firmly believe at-

tempts to repeal an unjust law can be vindicated beyond a simple remonstrance addressed to the legislators.

But such threats as these were only the most obvious ways in which traditional notions of authority came into question. Others were more subtly subversive, silently sapping the traditional foundations of social orders and discipline.

"Rights" obviously lay at the heart of the Anglo-American controversy: the rights of Englishmen, the rights of mankind, chartered rights. But *"rights,"* wrote Richard Bland—that least egalitarian of revolutionary leaders—"imply *equality* in the instances to which they belong and must be treated without respect to the dignity of the persons concerned in them." This was by no means simply a worn cliché, for while "equality before the law" was a commonplace of the time "equality without respect to the dignity of the persons concerned" was not; its emphasis on social equivalence was significant, and though in its immediate context the remark was directed to the invidious distinctions believed to have been drawn between Englishmen and Americans its broader applicability was apparent. Others seized upon it, and developed it, especially in the fluid years of transition when new forms of government were being sought to replace those believed to have proved fatal to liberty. "An affectation of rank" and "the assumed distinction of 'men of consequence'" had been the blight of the Proprietary party, a Pennsylvania pamphleteer wrote in 1776. Riches in a new country like America signified nothing more than the accident of prior settlement. The accumulation of wealth had been "unavoidable to the descendants of the early settlers" since the land, originally cheap, had appreciated naturally with the growth of settlement.

> *Perhaps it is owing to this accidental manner of becoming rich that wealth does not obtain the same degree of influence here which it does in old countries. Rank, at present, in America is derived more from qualification than property; a sound moral character, amiable manners, and firmness in principle constitute the first class, and will continue to do so till the origin of families be forgotten, and the proud follies of the old world overrun the simplicity of the new.*

Therefore, under the new dispensation, "no reflection ought to be made on any man account of birth, provided that his manners rise decently with his circumstances, and that he affects not to forget the level he came from."

The idea was, in its very nature, corrosive to the traditional authority of magistrates and of established institutions. And it activated other, similar thoughts whose potential threat to stability lay till then inert. There was no more familiar notion in eighteenth-century political thought—it was propounded in every tract on government and every ministerial exhortation to the civil magistracy—than that those who wield power were "servants of society" as well as "ministers of God," and as such had to be specially qualified: they must be acquainted with the affairs of men; they must have wisdom, knowledge, prudence; and they must be men of virtue and true religion. But how far should one go with this idea? The doctrine that the qualifications for magistracy were moral, spiritual, and intellectual could lead to conflict with the expectation that public leaders would be people of external dignity and social superiority; it could be dangerous to the establishment in any settled society. For the ancient notion that leadership must devolve on men whose "personal authority and greatness," whose "eminence or nobility," were such that "every man subordinate is ready to yield a willing submission without contempt or repining"—ordinary people not easily conceding to an authority "conferred upon a mean man . . . no better than selected out of their own rank"—this traditional notion had never been repudiated, was still honored and repeated. But now, in the heated atmosphere of incipient rebellion, the idea of leaders as servants of the people was pushed to its logical extreme, and its subversive potentialities revealed. By 1774 it followed from the belief that "lawful rulers are the servants of the people" that they were "exalted above their brethren not for their own sakes, but for the benefit of the people; and submission is yielded, not on account of their persons considered exclusively on the authority they are clothed with, but of those laws which in the exercise of this authority are made by them conformably to the laws of nature and equity." In the distribution of offices, it was said in 1770, "merit only in the candidate" should count—not birth, or wealth, or loyalty to the great; but merit only. Even a deliberately judicious statement of this theme rang with defiance to traditional forms of authority: "It is not wealth—it is not family—it is not either of these alone, nor both of them together, though I readily allow neither is to be disregarded, that will qualify men for important seats in government, unless they are rich and honorable in other and more important respects." Indeed, one could make a complete inversion and claim that, properly, the external affluence of magistrates should be the consequence of, not the prior qualification for, the judicious exercise of public authority over others.

Where would it end? Two generations earlier, in the fertile seed-time of what would become the revolutionary ideology, the ultimate subversiveness of the arguments advanced by "the men of the rights" had already been glimpsed. "The sum of the matter betwixt Mr. Hoadly and me," the Jacobite, High Church polemicist Charles Leslie had written in 1711, is this:

> I think it most natural that authority should descend, that is, be derived from a superior to an inferior, from God to fathers and kings, and from kings and fathers to sons and servants. But Mr. Hoadly

would have it ascend *from* sons *to* fathers *and from* subjects *to* sovereigns, *nay to* God himself, *whose* kingship *the men of the* rights *say is* derived *to* Him *from the* people! *And the* argument *does naturally carry it all that way. For if* authority *does* ascend, *it must* ascend *to the* height.

By 1774 it seemed undeniable to many, uninvolved in or hostile to the revolutionary effort, that declarations "before GOD . . . that it is no rebellion to oppose any king, ministry, or governor [who] destroys by any violence or authority whatever the rights of the people" threatened the most elemental principles of order and discipline in society. A group of writers, opposed not merely to the politics of resistance but to the effect it would have on the primary linkages of society—on that patterning of human relations that distinguishes a civilized community from a primitive mob—attempted to recall to the colonists the lessons of the past, the wisdom, as they thought of it, of the ages. Citing adages and principles that once had guided men's thoughts on the structure of society; equating all communities, and England's empire in particular with families; quoting generously from Filmer if not from Leslie; and explaining that anarchy results when social inferiors claim political authority, they argued, with increasing anxiety, that the essence of social stability was being threatened by the political agitation of the time. Their warnings, full of nostalgia for ancient certainties, were largely ignored. But in the very extremism of their reaction to the events of the time there lies a measure of the distance revolutionary thought had moved from an old to a very new world.

One of the earliest such warnings was written by a young Barbadian, Isaac Hunt, only recently graduated from the College of Philadelphia but already an expert in scurrilous pamphleteering. Opening his *Political Family,* an essay published in 1775 though written for a prize competition in 1766, with a discourse on the necessary reciprocity of parts in the body politic he developed as his central point the idea that "in the *body politic* all inferior jurisdictions should flow from *one superior fountain* . . . a due subordination of the less parts to the greater is . . . necessary to the *existence* of BOTH." Colonies were the children and inferiors of the mother country; let them show the gratitude and obedience due to parents, and so let the principle of order through subordination prevail in the greater as in the lesser spheres of life.

This, in the context of the widespread belief in equal rights and the compact theory of government, was anachronistic. But it expressed the fears of many as political opposition turned into revolutionary fervor. Arguments such as Hunt's were enlarged and progressively dramatized, gaining in vituperation with successive publications until by 1774 they were bitter, shrill, and full of despair. Three Anglican clergymen wrote wrathful epitaphs to this ancient, honorable, and moribund philosophy.

Samuel Seabury—Hamilton's anonymous opponent in the pamphlet wars and the future first bishop of the Episcopal church in America—wrote desperately of the larger, permanent dangers of civil disobedience. The legal, established authorities in New York—the courts of justice, above all—have been overthrown, he wrote, and in their places there were now "delegates, congresses, committees, riots, mobs, insurrections, associations." Who comprised the self-constituted Committee of Safety of New York that had the power to brand innocent people outlaws and deliver them over "to the vengeance of a lawless, outrageous mob to be *tarred, feathered, hanged, drawn, quartered, and burnt*"? A parcel of upstarts "chosen by the weak, foolish, turbulent part of the country people"—"half a dozen fools in your neighborhood." Was the slavery imposed by their riotous wills to be preferred to the tyranny of a king? No: "If I must be devoured, let me be devoured by the jaws of a lion, and not *gnawed* to death by rats and vermin." If the upstart, pretentious committeemen triumph, order and peace will be at an end, and anarchy will result.

> *Government was intended for the security of those who live under it—to protect the weak against the strong—the good against the bad—to preserve order and decency among men, preventing every one from injuring his neighbor. Every person, then, owes obedience to the laws of the government under which he lives, and is obliged in honor and duty to support them. Because if one has a right to disregard the laws of the society to which he belongs, all have the same right; and then government is at an end.*

His colleague, the elegant, scholarly Thomas Bradbury Chandler, was at once cleverer, more thoughtful, and, for those who heeded arguments, more likely to have been convincing. Two of his pamphlets published in 1774 stated with peculiar force the traditional case for authority in the state, in society, and in the ultimate source and ancient archetype of all authority, the family. His *American Querist*, that extraordinary list of one hundred rhetorical questions, put the point obliquely. It asked:

> *Whether some degree of respect be not always due from inferiors to superiors, and especially from children to parents; and whether the refusal of this on any occasion be not a violation of the general laws of society, to say nothing here of the obligations of religion and morality?*

And is not Great Britain in the same relation to the colonies as a parent to children? If so, how can such "disrespectful and abusive treatment from children" be tolerated? God has given no dispensation to people under any government "to refuse *honor* or custom or *tribute* to whom they are *due;* to contract habits of thinking and *speaking evil of dignities,* and to weaken the natural principle of respect for those in authority." God's command is clear: his will is that we *"submit to every ordinance of man for the Lord's sake;* and require[s] us on pain of *damnation* to be duly *subject to the higher powers,* and *not to resist* their lawful authority."

Chandler's *Friendly Address to All Reasonable Americans* was more direct. It touched the central theme of authority at the start, and immediately spelled out the implications of resistance. The effort "to disturb or threaten an established government by popular insurrections and tumults has always been considered and treated, in every age and nation of the world, as an unpardonable crime." Did not an apostle, "who had a due regard for the rights and liberties of mankind," order submission even to the cruelest of all despots, Nero? And properly so: "The bands of society would be dissolved, the harmony of the world confounded, and the order of nature subverted, if reverence, respect, and obedience might be refused to those whom the constitution has vested with the highest authority."

The insistence, the violence of language, increased in the heightening crisis. "Rebellion," Daniel Leonard wrote flatly in 1775, "is the most atrocious offense that can be perpetrated by man," except those committed directly against God. "It dissolves the social band, annihilates the security resulting from law and government; introduces fraud, violence, rapine, murder, sacrilege, and the long train of evils that riot uncontrolled in a state of nature." But the end was near. By the spring of 1775 such sentiments, fulminous and despairing, were being driven underground.

Jonathan Boucher's sermon "On Civil Liberty, Passive Obedience, and Nonresistance" had been written in 1775 "with a view to publication," and though it had been delivered publicly enough in Queen Anne's Parish, Maryland, it was promptly thereafter suppressed; "the press," Boucher later wrote, "was shut to every publication of the kind." Its publication twenty-two years afterward in a volume of Boucher's sermons entitled *A View of the Causes and Consequences of the American Revolution* was the result of the French Revolution's reawakening in the author, long since safely established in England, the fears of incipient anarchy and social incoherence that had agitated him two decades before. It was a fortunate result, for the sermon is a classic of its kind. It sums up, as no other essay of the period, the threat to the traditional ordering of human relations implicit in revolutionary thought.

Boucher sought, first and foremost, to establish the divine origins of the doctrine of obedience to constituted authority—a necessity, he felt, not merely in view of the arguments of the Reverend Jacob Duché whom he was ostensibly refuting, but, more important, in view of the gross misinterpretation rebellious Americans had for years been making of that suggestive verse of Galatians 5:1: "Stand fast, therefore, in the liberty wherewith Christ hath made us free." What had been meant by "liberty" in that passage, he said, was simply and unambiguously freedom from sin, for "every sinner is, literally, a slave . . . the only true liberty is the liberty of being the servants of God." Yet the Gospel does speak to the question of public obligations, and its command could hardly be more unmistakable: its orders, always, "obedience to the laws of every country, in every kind or form of government." The rumor promoted in the infancy of Christianity "that the Gospel was designed to undermine kingdoms and commonwealths" had probably been the work of Judas, and patently mixed up the purpose of the First Coming with that of the Second. Submission to the higher powers is what the Gospel intends for man: "obedience to government is every man's duty because it is every man's interest; but it is particularly incumbent on Christians, because . . . it is enjoined by the positive commands of God."

So much was scriptural, and could be buttressed by such authorities as Edmund Burke, Bishop Butler, "the learned Mr. Selden," and Lancelot Andrewes, whose biblical exegesis of 1650 was quoted to the effect that "princes receive their power only from God, and are by him constituted and entrusted with government of others chiefly for his own glory and honor, as his deputies and viceregents upon earth." More complicated was the application of this central thesis to the associated questions of the origins and aims of government and of the equality of men. As for the former, the idea that the aim of government is "the common good of mankind" is in itself questionable; but even if it were correct, it would not follow that government should rest on consent, for common consent can only mean common feeling, and this a "vague and loose" thing not susceptible to proof. Mankind has never yet agreed on what the common good is, and so, there being no "common feeling" that can clearly designate the "common good," one can scarcely argue that government is, or should be, instituted by "common consent."

Similarly popular, dangerous, and fallacious to Boucher was the notion "that the whole human race is born equal; and that no man is naturally inferior, or in any respect subjected to another, and that he can be made subject to another only by his own consent." This argument, he wrote, is "ill-founded and false both in its premises and conclusions." It is hard to see how it could conceivably be true in any sense. "Man differs from man in everything that can be supposed to lead to supremacy and subjection, *as one star differs from another star in glory."* God intended man to be a social animal; but society requires government, and "without some relative inferiority and superiority" there can be no government.

> *A musical instrument composed of chords, keys, or pipes all perfectly equal in size and power might as well be expected to produce harmony as a society composed of members all perfectly equal to be productive of order and peace.... On the principle of equality, neither his parents nor even the vote of a majority of the society ... can have ... authority over any man.... Even an implicit consent can bind a man no longer than he chooses to be bound. The same principle of equality ... clearly entitles him to recall and resume that consent whenever he sees fit, and he alone has a right to judge when and for what reasons it may be resumed.*

A social and political system based on the principles of consent and equality would be "fantastic"; it would result in "the whole business of social life" being reduced to confusion and futility. People would first express and then withdraw their consent to an endless succession of schemes of government. "Governments, though always forming, would never be completely formed, for the majority today might be the minority tomorrow, and, of course, that which is now fixed might and would be soon unfixed."

Consent, equality—these were "particularly loose and dangerous" ideas, Boucher wrote; illogical, unrealistic, and lacking in scriptural sanction. There need be no mystery about the origins of government. Government was created by God. "As soon as there were some to be governed, there were also some to govern; and the first man, by virtue of that paternal claim on which all subsequent governments have been founded, was first invested with the power of government.... The first father was the first king: and ... it was thus that all government originated; and monarchy is its most ancient form." From this origin it follows directly that resistance to constituted authority is a sin, and that mankind is "commanded to *be subject to the higher powers.*" True, "kings and princes ... were doubtless created and appointed not so much for their own sakes as for the sake of the people committed to their charge: yet they are not, therefore, the creatures of the people. So far from deriving their authority from any supposed consent or suffrage of men, they receive their commission from Heaven; they receive it from God, the source and original of all power." The judgment of Jesus Christ is evident: the most essential duty of subjects with respect to government is simply "(in the phraseology of a prophet) *to be quiet, and to sit still.*"

How simple but yet how demanding an injunction, for men are ever "*prone* to be presumptuous and self-willed, always disposed and ready to despise *dominion,* and to *speak evil of dignities.*" And how necessary to be obeyed in the present circumstance. Sedition has already penetrated deeply; it tears at the vitals of social order. It threatens far more than "the persons invested with the supreme power either legislative or executive"; "the resistance which your political counselors urge you to practice [is exerted] clearly and literally against *authority* . . . you are encouraged to resist not only all authority over us as it now exists, but any and all that it is possible to constitute."

This was the ultimate concern. What Boucher, Leonard, Chandler, and other articulate defenders of the status quo saw as the final threat was not so much the replacement of one set of rulers by another as the triumph of ideas and attitudes incompatible with the stability of any standing order, any establishment—incompatible with society itself, as it had been traditionally known. Their fears were in a sense justified, for in the context of eighteenth-century social thought it was difficult to see how any harmonious, stable social order could be constructed from such materials. To argue that all men were equal would not make them so; it would only help justify and perpetuate that spirit of defiance, that refusal to concede to authority whose ultimate resolution could only be anarchy, demagoguery, and tyranny. If such ideas prevailed year after year, generation after generation, the "latent spark" in the breasts of even the most humble of men would be kindled again and again by entrepreneurs of discontent who would remind the people "of the elevated rank they hold in the universe, as men; that all men by nature are equal; that kings are but the ministers of the people; that their authority is delegated to them by the people for their good, and they have a right to resume it, and place it in other hands, or keep it themselves, whenever it is made use of to oppress them." Seeds of sedition would thus constantly be sown, and harvests of licentiousness reaped.

How else could it end? What reasonable social and political order could conceivably be built and maintained where authority was questioned before it was obeyed, where social differences were considered to be incidental rather than essential to community order, and where superiority, suspect in principle, was not allowed to concentrate in the hands of a few but was scattered broadly through the populace? No one could clearly say. but some, caught up in a vision of the future in which the peculiarities of American life became the marks of a chosen people, found in the defiance of traditional order the firmest of all grounds for their hope for a freer life. The details of this new world were not as yet clearly depicted; but faith ran high that a better world than any that had ever been known could be built where authority was distrusted and held in constant scrutiny; where the status of men flowed from their achievements and from their personal qualities, not from distinctions ascribed to them at birth; and where the use of power over the lives of men was jealously guarded and severely restricted. It was only where there was this defiance, this refusal to truckle, this

distrust of all authority, political or social, that institutions would express human aspirations, not crush them.

Gary B. Nash

GARY B. NASH (1933–   ) *is professor of history at the Univer-*
sity of California, Los Angeles. He is the author of Quakers and Politics *(1968),* Red, White, and Black *(1974),* The Urban Crucible *(1979),*
and Race, Class and Politics *(1986).*

Although eighteenth-century America was predominantly a rural,
agricultural society, its seaboard commercial cities were the cutting
edge of economic, social, and political change. Almost all the alterations that are associated with the advent of capitalist society happened first in the cities and radiated outward to the smaller towns,
villages, and farms of the hinterland. In America, it was in the colonial
cities that the transition first occurred from a barter to a commercial
economy; where a competitive social order replaced an ascriptive one;
where a hierarchical and deferential polity yielded to participatory and
contentious civic life; where factory production began to replace small-
scale artisanal production; where the first steps were taken to organize
work by clock time rather than by sidereal cycles. The cities predicted
the future, even though under one in twenty colonists lived in them
in 1700 or 1775 and even though they were but overgrown villages
compared to the great urban centers of Europe, the Middle East, and
China.

Considering the importance of the cities as dynamic loci of change,
it is surprising that historians have studied them so little. Even the
fascination with urban history in the last few decades has done little
to remedy this. We have at our disposal a shelfful of books on the early
American inland villages, whose households numbered only in the
hundreds, but have comparatively little to inform us about the colonial urban centers. . . .

This book proceeds from a different conception of how urban societies changed in the eighteenth century and is based largely on different

sources. It stems from my interest in the social morphology of America's colonial cities and how it was that urban people, at a certain point in the preindustrial era, upset the equilibrium of an older system of social relations and turned the seaport towns into crucibles of revolutionary agitation. More particularly, I have tried to discover how people worked, lived, and perceived the changes going on about them, how class relationships shifted, and how political consciousness grew, especially among the laboring classes.

What has led early American historians to avoid questions about class formation and the development of lower-class political consciousness is not only an aversion to Marxist conceptualizations of history but also the persistent myth that class relations did not matter in early America because there were no classes. Land, it is widely held, was abundant and wages were high because labor was always in great demand. Therefore, opportunity was widespread and material well-being attainable by nearly everybody. If being at the bottom or in the middle was only a way station on a heavily traveled road to the top, then the composition of the various ranks and orders must have been constantly shifting and class consciousness could be only an evanescent and unimportant phenomenon. Thus, our understanding of the social history of the colonial cities has been mired in the general idea that progress was almost automatic in the commercial centers of a thriving New World society.

Only recently has the notion of extraordinary elasticity within classes and mobility between them begun to yield to a more complex analysis of how demographic trends, economic development, the spread of a market economy, and a series of costly wars produced a social, political, and ideological transformation. Historians have begun to create a far more intricate picture of social change by studying the extent of vertical and horizontal mobility, the degree of stratification, the accumulation and distribution of wealth, the social origins of the elite, the changing nature of economic and political power, and the shaping of class, ethnic, and religious consciousness. Historians are also coming to understand the need to retreat from discussing how *the* community was affected and to consider instead how different groups within the community were affected. Armies were supplied by some urban dwellers and manned by others, and those who gained or lost were not randomly selected. Price inflation and monetary devaluation caused problems for the whole society but the burdens were not distributed evenly. A sharp rise in overseas demand for American grain might increase the profits of inland farmers and seaboard merchants but could undercut the household budget of urban laborers and artisans.

Much of this book is about those who occupied the lower levels of urban society, the people who frequently suffered the unequal effects

of eighteenth-century change. This is no mere quest for aesthetic balance or for simple justice in recreating the past. Examination of the
circumstances of life for the great mass of common people in every
period and place and inquiry into their ways of thinking and acting are
essential if we are ever to test and correct the hallowed generalizations
made from the study of the select few upon which our understanding
of history is primarily based. What is more, I proceed from the conviction that the success of any society is best measured not by examining
the attainments and accumulations of those at the top but by assaying
the quality of life for those at the bottom. if this be thought the maxim
of a utopian socialist, it was also the notion of an eighteenth-century
English aristocrat whose writings circulated in Boston. "Every Nation," wrote Sir Richard Cox, "has the Reputation of being rich or poor
from the Condition of the lowest Class of its Inhabitants."

In examining the lives of the lower classes in the eighteenth-
century American cities I have repeatedly encountered evidence of social situations for which there is no accounting in the standard scholarship. Boston, I have found, was not only the commercial and intellectual center of New England Puritanism, as we have been taught, but
also, by the 1740s, the New England center of mass indebtedness,
widowhood, and poverty. By the end of the Seven Years War in 1763
poverty on a scale that urban leaders found appalling had also appeared
in New York and Philadelphia. The narrowing of opportunities and the
rise of poverty are two of the subthemes of this book. This is not to
deny that compared with most places from which the colonists
came—at least those who were white and free—the material circumstances of life were far more favorable than they had previously
known. Comparisons between life in the colonial cities and life in Europe, however, like comparisons today between the plight of the urban
poor in Chicago and Calcutta, miss the mark. An indebted shoemaker
in Boston in 1760 took little satisfaction that for many of those who
worked with hammer and awl life was worse and the future even
bleaker in Dublin or London. People's sense of deprivation is not as-
suaged by referring them to distant places or ancient times. Like those
above them, they measure the quality of their lives within their own
locales and make comparisons primarily with the world of their parents.

To study those who resided at the bottom of the seaport societies
it is also necessary to study those in the middle and at the top.
Whether it is the reaction of the poor to the new formulae for dealing
with urban poverty or the role of the crowd in the Stamp Act demonstrations of 1765, nothing is explicable without understanding the ideology and conduct of men at the higher levels. It was, after all, with
those who possessed economic, political, and social power that the
lower orders ultimately had to resolve matters. All urban people were

linked together in a social network where power was unevenly distributed, and one part of this social organism cannot be understood in isolation from the others. Above all, this book is about the relationships among urban people who occupied different rungs of the social ladder.

The concept of class is central to this book. Therefore, it is important to specify that the term has a different meaning for the preindustrial period than for a later epoch. I employ it as both a heuristic and a historical category. It is a term which enables us to perceive that urban people gradually came to think of themselves as belonging to economic groups that did not share common goals, began to behave in class-specific ways in response to events that impinged upon their well-being, and manifested ideological points of view and cultural characteristics peculiar to their rank. This is not to say that all carpenters or all shopkeepers occupied the same position along the spectrum of wealth or that all ship captains or all caulkers thought alike or that merchants and shoemakers consistently opposed each other because they occupied different social strata. Nor can class be determined simply by notations on a tax assessor's list or by occupations given in inventories of estate. Moreover, evidence is abundant that vertical consciousness was always present in a society where movement up and down the social ladder never stopped and where the natural tendency of economic networks was to create a common interest among, for example, the merchant, shipbuilder, and mariner.

Thus, we must recognize the problems in employing the concept of class in eighteenth-century society, for the historical stage of a mature class formation had not yet been reached. To ignore class relations, however, is a greater problem. The movement between ranks and the vertical linkages that were a part of a system of economic clientage did not foreclose the possibility that horizontal bonds would grow in strength. People who had always thought of themselves as belonging to the lower, middling, or upper ranks, but saw no reason that this implied social conflict, would gradually associate these rough identifiers of social standing with antagonistic interests and make them the basis for political contention. One of the main tasks of this book is to show that many urban Americans, living amidst historical forces that were transforming the social landscape, came to perceive antagonistic divisions based on economic and social position; that they began to struggle around these conflicting interests; and that through these struggles they developed a consciousness of class. This is quite different, as E. P. Thompson points out, than arguing "that classes exist, independent of historical relationship and struggle, and that they struggle *because* they exist, rather than coming into existence out of that struggle."

Hence, I am concerned with the evolving relations among different groups of urban people who were subject to historically rooted changes that may have been as perplexingly intricate to them as they have been to historians since. It is not my argument that by the end of the colonial period class formation and class consciousness were fully developed, but only that we can gain greater insight into the urban social process between 1690 and 1776 and can understand more fully the origins and meaning of the American Revolution if we analyze the changing relations among people of different ranks and examine the emergence of new modes of thought based on horizontal rather than vertical divisions in society. The shift in social alignments would continue after the Revolution, not moving with telic force toward some rendezvous with destiny in the industrial period but shaped by historical forces that were largely unpredictable in 1776.

This book is also comparative in its approach. Examining concurrently the process of change in Boston, New York, and Philadelphia has enabled me to comprehend how particular factors intertwined in each city to hasten or retard the formation of class consciousness and to give a particular texture to social discourse and political behavior. I have chosen these three cities not only because they were the largest northern maritime centers, as well as the seats of provincial government, but also because their populations differed significantly in racial and ethnic origins, in religious composition, and in the legacies of their founding generations. It should be apparent in what follows that class consciousness developed according to no even-paced or linear formula. It emerged and receded depending upon conditions, leadership at both the top and bottom, cultural traditions, and other factors. The comparative approach has also convinced me that the Marxist maxim that the mode of production dictates the nature of class relations has only limited analytic potential for explaining changes during some historical eras. It is not different modes of production that account for the striking differences among the three port towns in the historical development of class consciousness but the different experiences of people who lived within three urban societies that shared a common mode of production. Thus, it is necessary to go beyond determining objective class structures and objective productive relations to examining "the specific activities of men [and women] in real social and economic relationships, containing fundamental contradictions and variations and therefore always in a state of dynamic process." Bostonians, New Yorkers, and Philadelphians experienced their situations differently between 1690 and 1776 because discrete factors impinged upon them, ranging from their proximity to Anglo-French theaters of war to the development of their hinterlands to their cultural heritage.

In inquiring into the history of the common people of the northern port towns I have adopted the term "laboring classes." I do so in order to take account of the fact that before the American Revolution—in fact, for more than half a century after the Revolution—there was no industrial working *class* composed of a mass of wage laborers who toiled in factories where a capitalist class wholly owned and controlled the productive machinery. My concern is with broad groupings of people who worked with their hands but were differentiated by skills and status. Thus, the laboring *classes* included slaves, whose bondage was perpetual, indentured servants, whose unfree status was temporary, and free persons, whose independence could be altered only in unusual circumstances. The laboring ranks also ascended from apprentice to journeyman to master craftsman. Likewise, there were gradations among ill-paid merchant seamen, laborers, and porters at the bottom; struggling shoemakers, tailors, coopers, and weavers who were a step higher; more prosperous cabinetmakers, silversmiths, instrument-makers, and housewrights; and entrepreneurial bakers, distillers, rope-walk operators, and tallow chandlers. There was, in short, no unified laboring class at any point in the period under study. That does not mean that class formation and the shaping of class consciousness was not happening in the era culminating with the American Revolution.

Despite the importance attached to economic and social change, this book argues that ideology in many instances was far more than a reflection of economic interests and acted as a motive force among urban people of all ranks. But it needs to be emphasized at the outset that ideology is not the exclusive possession of educated individuals and established groups. Nor do I believe that those at the top established an ideology that was then obligingly adopted by those below them. Slaves, indentured servants, the laboring poor, women, and the illiterate also had an ideology, although many of these people did not express ideas systematically in forms that are easily recoverable by historians two hundred years later. What I mean by ideology is awareness of the surrounding world, penetration of it through thought, and reasoned reactions to the forces impinging upon one's life. People living in communities as small as the prerevolutionary port towns, linked together as they were by church, tavern, workplace, and family, exchanged views, compared insights, and through the face-to-face nature of their associations, arrived at certain common understandings of their social situations. The world for them may have always been half-seen and imperfectly comprehended, but, as is universally true, they acted upon reality as they understood it, whether they were university trained and rich or could barely keep their shop books by crooked hand in a rented room.

It is not possible to fathom the subterranean social changes that transformed the urban centers of colonial America or to peer into the minds of the mass of urban dwellers who have been obscured from historical sight by consulting only the sources that are most accessible to the historian—newspapers, municipal records, business accounts, diaries and correspondence, and published sermons, political tracts, and legislative proceedings. As vital as these sources are, they are insufficient to the task, for they most often came from the hands of upper-class merchants, lawyers, clergymen, and politicians, who, though they tell us much, do not tell all. These sources are particularly silent on the lives of those in the lower reaches of the urban hierarchy and they are only occasionally helpful in revealing the subsurface social processes at work. This is not surprising, for on the one hand the gentry was not interested in illuminating the lives of laboring-class city dwellers and on the other hand they were often unaware of, mystified by, or eager to obscure the changing social, economic, and political relationships in their cities. Buried in less familiar documents, virtually all of them unpublished and many of them fragmentary and difficult to use, are glimpses of the lives of ordinary people. The story of how life was lived and conditions changed in the colonial cities can be discerned, not with mathematical precision or perfect clarity but in general form, from tax lists, poor relief records, wills, inventories of estate, deed books, mortgages, court documents, and portledge bills and wage records. This book draws extensively upon such sources as well as upon more traditional forms of evidence. It also infers lower-class thought from lower-class action, which is justifiable when the action is adequately recorded and is repetitive. . . .

IT IS NOT within the compass of this book to analyze the revolutionary process that occurred after the outbreak of fighting in eastern Massachusetts in the spring of 1775. It is enough to note that the work of a new generation of historians has begun to demonstrate that much of the complexity and significance of the American Revolution is missed by portraying it primarily as a movement for independence and the creation of republican institutions. It was certainly that, but it was also a social upheaval involving "the rapid and often violent mobilization into public life of many different groups," the challenging of gentry control of public affairs, and the proposing of remedies for the social ills that many believed had beset American society.

The burden of this book has been to show how the growth and commercial development of the northern seaport towns brought about multifaceted change involving the restructuring of social groups, the redistribution of wealth, the alteration of labor relations, the emergence of states of consciousness that cut horizontally through society, and the mobilization into political life of the lower ranks of laboring people. Haltingly it was recognized by many in the cities that the ligaments of the corporate society of the past had been torn in ways that struck at their opportunities, well-being, and sense that equity prevailed. In this century-long process there emerged no perfect crystallization of classes or class consciousness. But both master craftsmen and small retailers in the middle ranks and lesser artisans, merchant seamen, and laborers below them learned to define their interests and identify the self-interested behavior of those they had been taught to believe acted for the good of the whole. We have seen them beginning to struggle around the issues that were most palpable in terms of their daily existence and, in the process of struggling, developing a consciousness about their separate roles and their antagonistic interests with others in their communities.

Liberal theory, as imbibed by historians, recognizes tension and conflict only in terms of the "explicit and unwarranted intrusion of authority upon individual [political] freedom." But on a wide ensemble of issues—including political rights, but extending beyond them to wages and prices, charity, taxes, market and labor relations, and evangelical religion—the urban lower orders formulated distinctly different points of view from the ones held by those above them. It is necessary to reiterate that there was no unified ideology among those who worked with their hands or among those who did not. Urban society was much too fluid for that. Nor can it be said that there were no important areas where interclass agreement prevailed. Nevertheless, within their own cognitive structures, merchant seamen, artisans, and the poor, as well as merchants, shopkeepers, and professional men, saw their world changing. This led, as the Revolution approached, to the rise of a radical consciousness among many and to an interplay between calls for internal reform and insurgency against external forces that adversely affected the lives of city people. Challenges to the concentration of economic, political, and cultural authority ultimately shattered the equilibrium of the old system of social relations.

Although no social revolution occured in America in the 1770s, the American Revolution could not have unfolded when or in the manner it did without the self-conscious action of urban laboring people—both those at the bottom and those in the middle—who became convinced that they must create power where none had existed before or else watch their position deteriorate, both in absolute terms and relative to that of others. Thus, the history of the Revolution is in part the history of popular collective action and the puncturing of the gentry's claim that their rule was legitimized by custom, law, and divine will. Ordinary people, sometimes violently, took over the power and the procedures of the constituted authorities. With wealth becoming far more concentrated at the top of urban society, plebeian urban dwellers forced their way into the political arena, not so much through the formal mechanisms of electoral politics as through street demonstrations, mass meetings, extralegal committees that assumed governmental powers, the intimidation of their enemies, and, in some cases, spirited defenses of traditional norms. This reordering of political power required a mental breakthrough, for it had to be accomplished in the face of a model of social relations, set by the elite, which claimed the superior wisdom and public mindedness of the educated and wealthy and prescribed deference as the customary and proper role of "inferior" people.

This shattering of the habit of obedience, advanced by the Great Awakening, proceeded far more rapidly in Boston in the second third of the century than in the other towns. Yet it relapsed after 1765, as traditional leaders, aided by the descent of a red-coated enemy on the community, reasserted themselves and as the people closed ranks in a reaffirmation of the spirit of covenant. In New York and Philadelphia the political leadership of the elite was challenged only sporadically until the end of the Seven Years War, when economic derangements and internal factionalism set the stage for the rise of laboring men to political power. But in all the cities those who labored with their hands, especially those who found it most difficult to weather the changes that had overcome their society, formed a picture of the social arrangements by which they lived. It was a picture that was political in its composition and increasingly vivid in its portrayal of the port towns as places where men struggled against each other rather than working harmoniously for the mutual good of the whole society.

☆5☆

The Constitution

CONFLICT OR CONSENSUS?

The Constitution remains one of the most controversial documents in all of American history. Generations of Supreme Court justices have reinterpreted the document according to their own predilections when handing down constitutional decisions bearing upon the problems of American society. Presidents and political parties in power traditionally have viewed the Constitution in the light of their own interests, pursuits, and philosophies of government. Historians, too, have presented conflicting interpretations of the Constitution in different periods of American history. But to a large degree such scholars have confined their controversies to the writing and ratification of the Constitution. They have usually disagreed about the intent of the founding fathers in framing parts of the Constitution and the motives of the men involved. The changing outlook of historians toward the Constitution, moreover, has often tended to coincide with changes in the intellectual climate of opinion within America itself.

From the Convention of 1787 to the close of the Civil War the Constitution was considered a controversial document by historians because of the questions it raised regarding the nature of the federal union. Politicians in both North and South were fond of citing the Constitution in support of their arguments concerning the relationship between the states and central government, and the respective rights of majorities and minorities under the federal form of government. Since the overwhelming preoccupation of American historians during this period was with politics, scholars tended to reflect this point of view in their writings about the Constitution. They usually interpreted the document in terms of two opposing doctrines: states' rights versus national sovereignty, or a strict versus a loose construction of the Constitution. The outcome of the Civil War seemed to settle the issue in favor of the national theory of the Constitution by force of arms.

In the century since the Civil War, however, five distinct groups

of historians have arisen to offer differing interpretations of the constitutional period. The first, the nationalist school, emerged in the 1870s
and 1880s; its approach to the Constitution was conditioned by the
intense nationalism that marked American society in the decades following the Civil War. Around the turn of the century there appeared
the Progressive school, which viewed the document and its framing in
light of the Populist-Progressive reform movements of the 1890s and
early 1900s. Charles A. Beard, the outstanding scholar in the Progressive school, saw the Constitution as a document that was intended to
protect private property and one that reflected the interests of privileged groups in the American society of the 1780s. The Beardian interpretation remained the dominant view of the Constitution for more
than four decades. Since World War II three groups of historians—the
neoconservatives, the "new intellectual historians," and the so-called
neo-Progressives—arose either to revise or to refine the Beardian interpretation.

The nationalist school, which developed in the decades after the
Civil War, was best represented by George Bancroft and John Fiske.
Both their histories were written in highly nationalistic terms. Within
a broader context both believed also in the racial superiority of white
Anglo-Saxon Protestant peoples. They subscribed to the idea that the
orderly progress of mankind in modern times toward greater personal
liberty was due largely to the preeminent political ability of Anglo-
Saxon peoples to build strong and stable national states. According to
these two writers America's democratic institutions could be traced
all the way back to the ancient political practices of Teutonic tribes in
the forests of Germany. The Constitution, in their eyes, represented
the high point in world history in the efforts of human beings to civi-
lize and govern themselves. Thus they dealt with it not only as a democratic document for America but also as a possible model instrument
of government for the rest of mankind.

For Bancroft the Constitution symbolized the capstone of the
American Revolution. In his two volumes on the constitutional era,
published in the 1880s, he visualized the years 1782 to 1788 as a single
period with the ratification of the Constitution coming as a climax of
the Revolution itself.[1] The Articles of Confederation, ratified in 1781,
in his opinion, represented a false start on the road to self-government.
Faced with a need for a more coercive central government because of
external threats from Britain and Spain and internal problems such as
Shays's Rebellion, the American people demanded a new and better
instrument of government. Since America was divinely ordained to
create the first perfect republic on earth—according to Bancroft—the

---

[1]George Bancroft, *History of the Formation of the Constitution of the United States
of America*, 2 vols. (New York, 1882).

Constitution symbolized the crowning success of the movement for a more popular government that had started with the Revolution.

Bancroft's work deified the Constitution and contributed to the growing reverence with which the document was viewed in the post-Civil War era. Indeed the last paragraph in his *History* ended with a stirring peroration on the Constitution:

> *In America a new people had risen up without king, or princes, or nobles, knowing nothing of tithes and little of landlords, the plough being for the most part in the hands of free holders of the soil. They were more sincerely religious, better educated, of serener minds, and of purer morals than the men of any former republic. By calm medita-tion and friendly councils they had prepared a constitution which . . . excelled every one known before; and which secured itself against violence and revolution by providing a peaceful method for every needed reform.* [2]

Bancroft conveniently overlooked the bloody Civil War that had just been fought.

Fiske's *The Critical Period of American History, 1783–1789* pre-sented a dramatic story of the change in the state of the nation before and after the writing of the Constitution. In Fiske's view the five-year period after the peace of 1783 represented "the most critical move-ment in all the history of the American people." [3] Under the Articles of Confederation the nation was on the verge of collapse: the weak central government could not cope with the problems of diplomacy, quarrels between the states, the postwar economic depression, and the near anarchy of domestic disturbances like Shays's Rebellion. Once the Constitution was written, however, the situation changed dramati-cally. Most of these issues disappeared when they were dealt with by the new strong central government, and the country was saved from disaster.

Fiske's book, published one year after the centennial celebration of the Constitution, reflected the great awe in which the document was held. The British statesman Gladstone had called the Constitution "the most wonderful work ever struck off at a given time by the brain and purpose of man." Not to be outdone, Fiske called it "this wonder-ful work—this Iliad, or Parthenon, or Fifth Symphony, of statesman-ship." [4] His glowing praise was typical of the generation of historians who sought to canonize the Constitution in the post-Civil War years.

---

[2] *Ibid.*, 2:366–67.

[3] John Fiske, *The Critical Period of American History, 1783–1789* (New York, 1888), p. 55.

[4] *Ibid.*, p. 223. One exception to the almost universal chorus of praise showered on the Constitution was the multivolume work of the German-born historian Hermann

The nationalist school of historians, then, was uncritical in its approach to the Constitution and viewed the document in terms of pious patriotism. In the eyes of these historians, the founding fathers were great men motivated mainly by the principles of right and justice and whose only concern was the welfare of the nation. The American people, they insisted, were united in their common devotion to these same principles of a democratic society, and the Constitution was the embodiment of the nation's dreams. Those opposed to the Constitution were dismissed lightly as men who lacked the faith and breadth of vision of the founding fathers.

Around the turn of the twentieth century the rise of the Populist and Progressive reform movements brought about a marked change in attitude toward the Constitution. Progressive reformers, concerned with the problems that had arisen from the nation's increasing industrialization, became convinced that unless the imbalance in wealth and political power in American society could be redressed, democracy in the United States was doomed. Only by passing legislation which would regulate industry and improve the lot of the common people could democracy be saved. In response to such demands, state governments in the 1890s and early 1900s began extending their laws regulating various aspects of the economy under their jurisdiction. Congress at the same time was making serious efforts to regulate certain industries like the railroads and to break up business enterprises such as the trusts. Labor legislation was introduced to protect workers and to improve working conditions of both men and women. To check the growing maldistribution of wealth, income tax measures were passed by both the state and federal governments. When the Supreme Court declared much of this state and national legislation unconstitutional, however, many persons began to view the Constitution in a new light. To them the Constitution now seemed to be an undemocratic document whose express purpose was to protect the rich and powerful interests in society and to frustrate the fulfillment of the democratic aspirations of the American people.

The Progressive school of historians which arose at this time was greatly influenced by this growing disillusionment with the Constitution. These scholars proceeded, therefore, to read this hostile view of the Constitution of the early 1900s back into the motives of the men who framed the document in the 1780s. The Constitution, according to these scholars, was a reactionary rather than a democratic document. Just as the Constitution was being used in the Progressive period to protect the interests of the rich and powerful against the encroach-

von Holst in his *Constitutional History of the United States,* 8 vols. (Chicago, 1876–1892). Von Holst criticized American historians for viewing the document as a divine product of the unique wisdom of the founding fathers, but his was very much of a minority view among scholars of the period.

ments of the common man, they said, so the founding fathers in their day had written the document to defend their property rights and to protect themselves against the social reforms that were under way.

To Progressive historians, then, the Constitution represented a reactionary document—one written by the conservatives at the convention to thwart the radicals who held more liberal views and had visions of completely reforming American society. In support of their thesis these scholars pointed to the undemocratic features of the Constitution—the system of checks and balances, the difficult procedure for adopting amendments, and the idea of judicial veto—which made majority rule all but impossible. Unlike the nationalist historians who had seen the Constitution as a forward step in the development of democracy, the Progressive historians considered the document a serious setback to the movement for popular government during the Revolutionary era.

Besides being influenced by the general current of reform, Progressive scholars were affected also by certain developments within the historical profession itself. One of these was the emergence of what came to be known as the "new history." In the past, advocates of the "new history" claimed, history had been written by conservatives who used their findings to buttress the status quo. The "new historians" now wished to rewrite history along liberal lines and to use the lessons of the past as a means of bringing about progress and reform. Many of these scholars were personally involved in the reform movements of the Progressive era and wrote from a historical viewpoint in support of the idea of governmental intervention and regulation in the public interest. Thus advocates of the "new history" such as Charles A. Beard looked at the Constitution in a completely different light from earlier conservative historians.

Many writers of the Progressive school reflected another major trend in historical circles at the time—the tendency toward an economic interpretation of history. Such scholars were convinced that human beings were motivated mainly by economic self-interest and that economic factors were the major determinants in shaping the course of history. People's political views and actions in particular, they charged, were determined primarily by economic considerations. Many Progressive historians, therefore, advanced the idea that the Constitution had been framed by persons with certain economic interests in such a way as to protect their property rights.

The Progressive interpretation of the Constitution, then, was based upon class conflict along economic lines—a point of view that had grown out of the interpretation of the American Revolution as a dual revolution. They began with the premise of Carl L. Becker that the Revolution had been a twofold struggle—a question of home rule and a question of who should rule at home once the British departed.

In the internal class struggle that took place, the lower classes—made up of small farmers in the interior and workingmen along the eastern seaboard towns—gained dominance over the upper classes—composed of merchants, financiers, and manufacturers. Once the lower classes were in control, the Progressive version continued, they proceeded to democratize American society by writing radical state constitutions and the Articles of Confederation. Being almost propertyless the lower classes set up democratic governments which passed cheap paper money legislation, debtor laws, and measures that favored the small farmers whose interests lay in land and real estate.

Members of the upper classes who survived the war, according to the Progressive interpretation, became increasingly disenchanted with the political and economic state of affairs. Those whose economic stake was in personal property—holdings in money and public securities or investments in manufacturing, shipping, and commerce—became particularly alarmed because the democratic governments seemed to be discriminating against their kind of property and in favor of those who owned land and real estate. Failing to amend the Articles of Confederation in such a way as to protect their property interests, the conservative upper class carried out what was, in effect, a counter-revolution. They conspired to undermine the democratic Articles of Confederation and instituted instead the more conservative Constitution.

The Progressive point of view was most ably expressed in Charles A. Beard's *An Economic Interpretation of the Constitution*, published in 1913. Although other scholars—historians like Richard Hildreth and John Marshall and political scientists like J. Allen Smith—had taken an economic approach to the Constitution, none had been able to demonstrate as convincingly as Beard that the document might be best interpreted in economic terms. The key to Beard's path-breaking study was a person-by-person examination of the economic holdings and status of the framers of the Constitution. Using the Treasury records Beard was able to show that most of these men held public securities—a form of personal property which would obviously increase in value if a new Constitution were written to strengthen the government and improve the credit standing of the country. His research showed also that these men had heavy investments in three other kinds of personal property. Beard's findings led him to conclude, "The movement for the Constitution of the United States was originated and carried through principally by four groups of personalty interests which had been adversely affected under the Articles of Confederation: money, public securities, manufactures, and trade and shipping."[5] His

---

[5]Charles A. Beard, *An Economic Interpretation of the Constitution of the United States* (rev. ed., New York, 1935), p. 324.

implication was clear: the framers had designed the Constitution to safeguard the kind of property in which they had a pocketbook interest.

If the lower classes represented a majority of the population, how could personal property holders who were a minority control the Constitutional Convention? Beard's answer to this question rested mainly upon his interpretation of the property qualifications for voting. Most small farmers and workingmen, according to him, were in debt or owned so little property that they could not qualify for voting rights. "A large propertyless mass was, under the prevailing suffrage qualifications, excluded at the outset from participation . . . in the work of framing the Constitution."[6] Thus Beard viewed the Constitution as an undemocratic document foisted upon the majority of the American people by a propertied minority.

When it came to ratifying the Constitution, the "propertyless masses," according to Beard, were excluded once again from political participation. Only one-fourth of adult white men in the nation voted on the question of ratification because the rest were either disfranchised or disinterested. The total number voting in favor of the Constitution came to no more than one-sixth of the adult white males. Those who supported ratification on the state level, Beard wrote, had precisely the same economic interests as the framers of the document. In his eyes the voting on ratification, like the framing of the Constitution itself, gave clear evidence of a class conflict: the struggle pitted men with substantial personal property on the one hand against small farmers and debtors on the other.

Beard's book exercised a profound influence upon the historical profession. A whole generation of American historians became convinced that the Constitution could be understood only in terms of class conflict. Vernon L. Parrington's *Main Currents in American Thought,* published in 1927, and Louis M. Hacker's *Triumph of American Capitalism,* which appeared in 1940, expressed the Beardian point of view. Textbooks in history and political science repeated the Beard thesis in their pages verbatim. *An Economic Interpretation of the Constitution,* without doubt, was one of the most influential books on American history published in the twentieth century. Almost all interpretations of the Constitution written since its publication in 1913 have taken either a pro- or anti-Beard position. It is safe to say that down to World War II the dominant position taken by the historical profession on the Constitution was a pro-Beardian one.

Since World War II three groups of historians arose either to challenge or to extend the Beardian interpretation. Although these scholars often disagreed in their interpretations of the Constitution, they all

---

[6]*Ibid.*

agreed that Beard's study did not offer a satisfactory explanation of the document. These three groups may be identified in broad terms as the neoconservatives, the "new intellectual historians," and the neo-Progressives.

The neoconservative historians were the first to challenge the Beardian interpretation. Their tendency was to reject two of Beard's basic assumptions. First, they viewed the Constitution as evidence of a consensus rather than a class conflict among the American people. Second, they believed that the Revolution and Constitution periods represented a line of continuous growth; they dismissed Beard's idea of a period of radical revolution followed by one of conservative reaction.

These two themes were reflected in the suggestive title—*Consensus and Continuity, 1776–1787*—of a book written by Benjamin F. Wright in 1958. Wright, a political scientist, viewed the Constitution as a political, not an economic document. The most striking characteristic among the delegates at the Constitutional Convention, he claimed, was the broad area of agreement among them regarding what they considered to be the essentials of good government:

> *The most fundamental political or constitutional issues were taken for granted without debate, or they were only briefly discussed. These include such basic issues as representative government, elections at fixed intervals, a written constitution which is a supreme law and which contains an amendment clause, separation of powers and checks and balances, a bicameral legislature, a single executive, and a separate court system. These principles could have been taken for granted in no other country in the eighteenth century, nor could they in combination have been accepted in any other country even after discussion and vote. The nature and extent of this basic agreement throws far more light upon the political and constitutional thought of Americans in 1787 than do the disputes over questions which were nearly always matters of detail, or which were based largely upon sectional disagreement, or upon the size of the several states.[7]*

Thus Wright viewed the writing of the Constitution as evidence of the basic consensus that existed among the American people.

Wright showed also an essential continuity between the Revolution and the Constitution periods so far as men and ideas were concerned. The very same men held responsible public offices in 1787 as had in 1776, he wrote. Other scholars who did research on this same point estimated that 89 percent of those who held office before the Revolution also occupied a public position under one of the new state governments. Wright noted, moreover, that the political ideas of the Revolution were expressed best in the state constitutions, which were,

---

[7]Benjamin F. Wright, *Consensus and Continuity, 1776–1787* (Boston, 1958), p. 36.

in many instances, framed by the very same men who had written and signed the Declaration of Independence. In view of this evidence how could the constitutional period be considered a reaction to the Revolution? he asked. For Wright, as for most neoconservative historians, the Constitution was seen as the fulfillment of the Revolution.

A second line of attack on the Beardian thesis was taken by the neoconservative historian Robert E. Brown in his study *Charles Beard and the Constitution*, published in 1956. Brown challenged the evidence that Beard had used in making his case for an economic interpretation of the Constitution. He showed, first of all, that Beard had resorted to Treasury records dated several years after the Constitutional Convention in order to substantiate the point that the founding fathers had held public securities at the time they framed the document. After studying the property holdings of the signers, moreover, Brown came to the conclusion that the framers had more capital invested in land and real estate than in securities. This evidence dealt a blow to Beard's idea that the framers had written the document in order to protect their personal property in securities from those who held land and real estate.

Brown's study went one step further, however, and challenged one of Beard's underlying assumptions that the Constitution was an undemocratic document because the "propertyless masses" made up of small farmers and workingmen were unable to participate in the political process. American society in the 1780s, according to Brown, represented a "middle-class democracy." Most Americans were members of the middle class because they owned and operated their own small farms. American society was basically democratic, he claimed, because the majority of the population were small farmers who owned enough land to qualify for the right to vote. To Brown, then, the Constitution represented the wishes of a democratically minded middle class rather than the wishes of an aristocratically minded upper class. By viewing American society in terms of a broad middle class, Brown took a position completely opposite to that of the class-conflict interpretation of the Beardian school of historians.

The neoconservative school of writing resulted in a general reaction against the Beardian interpretation of the Constitution in the post-World War II period. There was an increasing emphasis placed upon the Constitution as a "consensus" document and less written about it as an undemocratic document. The attitude toward the framers of the Constitution was far more favorable than it had been a generation earlier, when many of them had been denounced by debunkers for taking political positions in order to protect their pocketbook interests. College textbooks stressed the areas of agreement between men at the Constitutional Convention and de-emphasized the areas of disagreement. Constitutional historians such as Henry Steele Commager declared that the Constitution was primarily a political document, focusing mainly on the problem of federalism, and not an economic document. Many historians praised the constitutional period as a constructive era rather than describing it as a destructive age in which the majority of the American people were robbed of their rights and liberties by a propertied minority.

In reevaluating the constitutional period in such laudatory terms many neoconservative historians in the 1950s were reflecting a response to the challenges of communism abroad. To bolster America's position as preeminent leader of the free world, a great many historians became Cold War warriors and sought to show that the United States had always been a strong and united country throughout its history. Hence they rewrote much of American history in terms of a basic consensus among the American people. Within this context, the consensus thesis of the Constitution increasingly replaced the Beardian idea of the Constitution as a document of dissent that emerged from a clash of economic interests among various elements of American society.

The second challenge to the Beardian interpretation came from the rise of a generation of "new intellectual historians" whose work first appeared in the mid-1950s. Their approach was to take the ideas of the founding fathers seriously and to accept their rhetoric as reflecting more their view of reality. They rejected Beard's emphasis on economic considerations and the Progressives' assumption that ideas were mere rhetoric used to mask the desire for materialistic self-interests. Instead of the Progressive materialistic view of history, they proposed an ideological interpretation. This renewed interest in ideas as an explanation of the Revolutionary era led scholars like Bernard Bailyn, Gordon Wood, Douglass Adair, and Cecelia Kenyon to view the confederation period and the writing of the Constitution in a completely different light.

Many of these intellectual historians cast such ideas within a much broader framework and stressed America's intellectual inheritance from Europe. Scholars like Caroline Robbins and Bernard Bailyn, writing in the 1960s, demonstrated the importance of British antiauthoritarian thought and how it influenced the formulation of America's republican ideology. Hence the coming of the Revolution and writing of the Constitution were placed within an Anglo-American framework. American ideas regarding the role of representatives in government, the relationship of the rulers and ruled, the nature of human rights, the notion of a written constitution, and the concept of divided sovereignty were traced in many instances back to British traditions in seventeenth- and eighteenth-century republicanism.

One major problem facing the founding fathers was how to erect a republic whose representatives were elected by the people and, at the same time, to prevent the formation of a majority faction which might undermine the government. Republican governments in the past had inevitably succumbed to the tyranny of a majority faction. James Madison used an idea derived from his reading of David Hume, a Scottish philosopher, to propose a republican remedy. America's enormous size and the multiplicity of factions and interests arising from that size, Madison argued, would make it less likely that this country would suffer the fate of earlier republics. The existence of so many diverse interests would make it difficult, if not impossible, for factions to reconcile their differences and to come together to form a majority faction. In a large republic, as Hume had suggested, the clash among more competing factions would provide greater safety and stability for society. Douglass Adair, one of the "new intellectual historians," wrote an article pointing out that Madison's thoughts on the subject—contrary to Beard's presentist interpretation—could be traced back to Hume.[8]

Cecelia Kenyon took issue with Beard's view of the debate between the Federalists, who supported the Constitution, and the Antifederalists, who opposed it. In an essay published in the mid-1950s, she examined the differences between the two groups in terms of their ideas. Beard had portrayed the Antifederalists as democrats and majority-minded men who opposed such antidemocratic devices in the Constitution as the separation of powers and checks and balances. The Federalists, Beard said, supported these same devices to protect their property interests from the threats posed by state legislatures dominated by democratic small farmers. Kenyon argued that the Antifederalists were as much antimajoritarians as the Federalists, and shared a common Whig mistrust of governmental power—legislative as well as executive. The Antifederalists believed, however, that a successful republic must be geographically small and composed of a homogeneous population. In support of their position the Antifederalists often cited the writings of Montesquieu, the French philosophical historian. What ultimately distinguished the Antifederalists from the Federalists, Kenyon concluded, was their lack of faith in the ability of Americans to create and sustain a republic continental in size.[9]

The single most important work representing the point of view of these intellectual historians was *The Creation of the American Republic, 1776–1787* by Gordon S. Wood, published in 1969. A student of Bailyn, Wood explicitly connected the conceptual scheme of the American patriots to the classical republican tradition that existed in England. Wood portrayed American leaders as idealists at the start of the Revolution—men who dreamed of setting up a utopian common-

---

[8]Douglass Adair, "'That Politics May be Reduced to a Science': David Hume, James Madison, and the Tenth *Federalist*," *Huntington Library Quarterly* 20 (1957):343–360.

[9]Cecelia M. Kenyon, "Men of Little Faith: The Antifederalists on the Nature of Representative Government," *William and Mary Quarterly*, 3d ser. 12 (1955):3–43.

wealth along lines English thinkers had earlier set forth. The patriots hoped to create a classical republic based upon a virtuous people and rulers, a society which would set America apart from the materialism and monarchy of England. Republicanism was a radical ideology with moral implications according to Wood. Revolutionary leaders, believing there was a direct relationship between the type of government a nation had and the character of its people, hoped that a republican government would morally regenerate the American people and thereby enable them to sustain a republic that would rest ultimately upon the people's virtue.

Events of the late 1770s and early 1780s dashed these high hopes. The Revolution unleashed democratic forces that accelerated the breakdown of the existing organic hierarchical society. What emerged in the 1780s was a society characterized by excessive egalitarianism, a contempt for the law by state legislatures bent on abusing their supremacy, oppression of minorities by the majority, and an increasing love of luxury that undermined the people's virtue. The 1780s was a "critical period" in moral terms, Wood said, because it shattered the dreams American leaders had in 1776 of creating a republican government along traditional lines.

The writing of the Constitution, then, was an attempt to save the Revolution from possible failure by restraining some of its democratic excesses. To Wood the Constitution developed into a struggle between forward-looking Federalists and old-fashioned Antifederalists. The Federalists wrought a revolution by introducing an American science of politics based upon a new notion of sovereignty. Instead of the old idea of mixed government, in which the Antifederalists believed, the Federalists proposed a new concept: that sovereignty resided in the people rather than in any single branch of government. Hence government should be divided into separate parts not because each part represented a different social constituency, as the Antifederalists supposed, but simply because it would serve as a check upon the other branches of government. Every branch of government, in effect, represented the people. The Federalists at the same time created a national republican government with other mechanical devices and institutional contrivances—mechanisms that were not necessarily dependent upon the virtue of the people and which could contain the excesses of state legislatures. The result was the creation of a governmental system more modern, more realistic about political behavior, and marked, according to Wood the "end of classical politics in America."[10]

To Wood the conflict between the two groups was a dispute between the Federalists' conception of politics which was more aristo-

---

[10]Gordon S. Wood, *Creation of the American Republic, 1776–1787* (Chapel Hill, 1969), p. 606.

cratic, and that of the Antifederalists which was more democratic. The Federalists, troubled by the need to slow disorder in America during the Confederation period, clung to a notion of political representation that emphasized deference and an elitist conception of republicanism. The Antifederalists, fearing the aristocratic tendencies, were more prepared to engage in popular styles of political practices, and followed a definition of republicanism that gave ordinary citizens greater direct power. Wood's book was destined to achieve the status of a classic; it dominated much of the profession for a decade and a half after its publication in 1969. The first selection in this chapter is from Wood's volume.

It remained for J. G. A. Pocock in 1975 to round out what came to be called "the republican synthesis." This synthesis incorporating the writings of Bernard Bailyn, Gordon Wood, and Pocock involved an increased appreciation of the role republican ideology played in shaping the world view of America's founding fathers. Pocock demonstrated how republican ideas instilled from the philosophers of ancient Greece and Rome, Renaissance Italian writers like Machiavelli, seventeenth-century republicans such as Harrington, and eighteenth-century English "country party" authors contributed to the American intellectual outlook.[11]

The republican synthesis held that this republican ideology dominated America's political culture over a long span of time—during the Revolutionary era, constitutional period, and, according to Pocock, down to the Civil War. Embodied in this ideology was a constellation of ideas: the view of an inherent republican character in the American people; their desire for virtue; their fear of tyranny, corruption, and luxury; and particularly their dread of power. Changing views on these ideas, it was said, helped to bring on the Revolution, led to the writing of the Constitution, and influenced political leaders and the people alike throughout the early national period. This idealist approach was obviously at odds with the old Progressive interpretation that had downplayed the role of ideas.[12]

From the mid-1960s beginning with the publication of Bailyn's book until about the mid-1980s, the slowly emerging republican synthesis exercised a strong sway over the profession. But before, during,

---

[11]Robert Shalhope, "Toward a Republican Synthesis: The Emergence of an Understanding of Republicanism in American Historiography," *William and Mary Quarterly*, 3d ser. 29 (1972):49–80; and Shalhope, "Republicanism and Early American Historiography," *ibid.*, 39 (1982):334–356. For Pocock's works see *The Machiavellian Moment* (Princeton, 1975); *Politics, Language, and Time* (New York, 1960); and *The Ancient Constitutions and Feudal Law* (Cambridge, 1957).

[12]Gordon Wood in a penetrating essay in the mid-1960s himself called for a synthesis of the two historiographical traditions—the idealist and Progressive—but they continued on their separate paths. See Wood, "Rhetoric and Reality in the American Revolution," *William and Mary Quarterly*, 3d ser. 23 (1966):3–32.

and after the Bicentennial of the Constitution, the synthesis came under increasing criticism. The synthesis from the mid-1980s to 1990 was the subject of intense historiographical controversy, underwent some changes, and its hold over the profession became less strong and persuasive.

It is impossible to summarize the vast literature appearing during the Bicentennial, but at least three major trends were discernible. First, there were the battles over the republican synthesis and its alleged shortcomings: its overemphasis of ideology and its de-emphasis of interests; its slighting of other important intellectual influences besides classical republicanism, including classical liberalism, Scottish common sense philosophy, and English common law; its failure to address ideas and practices regarding the political economy; and its omission of religion as a meaningful force in shaping political ideology. Second, there appeared a discernible trend away from the preoccupation with ideology that had dominated the entire field for more than two decades. There was a move toward a more integrative approach in the study of the late eighteenth century, one that incorporated institutional, intellectual, political and economic history as well as ideology. Third, there was a considerable amount of writing about the framing of the Constitution by scholars in other disciplines—political scientists, law professors, and legal theorists.[13]

Many of the criticisms of the republican synthesis were highlighted in a symposium held on Wood's book in 1987. Ruth Bloch was critical of Wood's contention that classical republicanism had ended by 1790; she noted that Pocock, Lance Banning, John Murrin, and Drew McCoy had all demonstrated that this concept had continuing vitality beyond that decade. Edward Countryman criticized Wood for writing his book too much as though a single intelligence lay behind the quotations he employed to draw a composite portrait of the Federalists and Antifederalists rather than focusing on single individuals for the intellectual positions taken. John Patrick Diggins took exception to the picture of consensus politics he felt was portrayed in Wood's description of the period. John Howe concluded that Wood had not emphasized enough the role of America's religious beliefs in forming political convictions or the views on political economy that had played such an important part. Howe's article is the second selection in this chapter.

---

[13]The best historiographical essay on writings in the Bicentennial was Peter Onuf's "Reflections on the Founding: Constitutional Historiography in Bicentennial Perspective," *William and Mary Quarterly*, 3d ser. 46 (1989):341–375—a piece that not only reviews the literature but contains many original insights. See also Richard Bernstein, "Charting the Bicentennial," *Columbia Law Review* 87 (1987):1565–1624, and Jack P. Greene, *A Bicentennial Bookshelf* (Philadelphia, 1986).

For a work that shows the popular neglect of the Constitution and its meaning, see Michael Kammen, *A Machine That Would Go of Itself* (New York, 1986).

Other members of the symposium disagreed with Wood on different grounds. Ralph Ketcham and Pauline Maier took exception to Wood's interpretation of the Constitution as a counterrevolutionary document and to his view of the Federalists. Jackson Turner Main took a staunchly neo-Progressive position indicating that ideas were only one of many factors motivating men when framing the Constitution. Jack Rakove adopted a Namierist position and wanted political behavior introduced as a motivating force as well as political ideology. John Murrin wanted the paradigm of liberalism to be viewed within a broader context—that of comparative history. Gary Nash, as a "new social historian" and member of the New Left, wanted more of a discussion of social groups left out of Wood's discussion—urban artisans, women, and blacks—people who were outside the formal arena of politics but not outside the political culture itself. Peter Onuf felt Wood was not interested enough in the forces making for an American union and a strong central government. On a different basis Gary Wills shared many of the same concerns.[14]

Wood responded with a spirited reply to his critics and defended his position on two grounds. First, he claimed that many of his critics had assumed a different role of ideas in human experience than he had intended. Their assumptions were that there is "a sharp separation between beliefs and behavior, between ideas and actions, [and] between culture and society." Wood, on the other hand, believed that "all human behavior can only be understood and explained, indeed can only exist, in terms of the meanings it has. Ideology creates behavior." The dispute, in other words, was largely over epistemology. Second, the issue was raised as to whether classical republicanism or liberalism was the dominant position in the late eighteenth century. Wood responded that republicanism and liberalism were historical constructs created by scholars and when treated as such gave rise to questions other than which was the dominant tradition. Despite Wood's defense it was clear that in the future the republican synthesis would have to address itself to certain issues he had either omitted or de-emphasized: the political economy, religion, and interests such as sectionalism, among other matters.[15]

One other major debate sparked by Wood's book during the Bicentennial was whether the Constitution had indeed marked "the end of classical politics in America." Some scholars held that classical republicanism was supplanted by another tradition—liberalism—either before, during, or after the adoption of the Constitution. This shift was said to signal the transition from premodern to modern America. Un-

---

[14]"The Creation of the American Republic, 1776–1787: A Symposium of Views and Reviews," *William and Mary Quarterly* 3d ser., 44 (1987):550–657.

[15]*Ibid.*, 628, 631, and 634. Quotation from p. 631.

der classical republicanism citizens presumably had followed the precepts of civic humanism within a premodern society—the pursuit of the public good, the upholding of virtue, and the hatred of luxury and corruption. With classical liberalism there appeared instead the pursuit of self-interest, a sense of personal acquisitiveness, and greater individual striving and competitiveness. In short, the attributes of modern America—an emphasis on materialism and money-making, the open promotion of interests in politics and economics, and crass commercialism—had all appeared. The debate focused on the relative importance of these two traditions in America as well as on the question of which became dominant and at what time. By the end of the 1980s, it was generally agreed that both were present in the new republic, that both were very influential, and that neither tradition appeared to have had undisputed primacy during the decades of the 1780s or 1790s.[16]

Another major controversy over Wood's book arose over what intellectual traditions besides republicanism and liberalism had influenced America during the constitutional period. Gary Wills in *Explaining America: The Federalist* made a case for Scottish moral philosophy. The writings of Sacvan Bercovitch and others on Puritanism, and Alan Heimert and Rhys Isaac on evangelical Protestantism demonstrated the importance of religion to America's political culture in that period. Forrest McDonald showed in an insightful way the bearing that certain English and European traditions had upon the framing of the Constitution. Isaac Kramnick from a political science point of view pointed to still other intellectual influences and traditions. Wood, to be sure, had acknowledged certain of these intellectual traditions, as well as the role of religion, but it was felt that his thesis regarding the framing of the Constitution would be incomplete unless such emphases were addressed more forcefully.[17]

The fact that historians were moving "beyond" the republican synthesis in these and other studies was seen in a second important symposium whose results were published in a volume entitled *Beyond Confederation* which appeared in the year of the Bicentennial. The theme of most essays, either expressed or implied, was to show omissions or shortcomings of the revisionist interpretation of the Constitution set forth by Wood and others. Instead of a preoccupation with

---

[16]Lance Banning, "Quid Transit? Paradigms and Process in the Transformation of Republican Ideas," *Reviews in American History* 17 (1989):199.

[17]Gary Wills, *Explaining America: The Federalist* (New York, 1981); Sacvan Bercovitch, *American Jeremiad* (Madison, 1978); Alan Heimert, *Religion and the American Mind* (Cambridge, 1966); Rhys Isaac, *Transformation of Virginia, 1740–1790* (Chapel Hill, 1982); Forrest McDonald, *Novus Ordo Seclorum* (Lawrence, 1985); and Isaac Kramnick, "The 'Great National Discussion': The Discourse of Politics in 1787," *William and Mary Quarterly*, 3d. ser., 45 (1988):3–22.

ideology that had characterized the studies of the constitutional period for over two decades, the thirteen scholars who contributed essays emphasized more the role of interests, institutions, and political behavior. This signaled a trend toward a more balanced and integrated approach and away from a single-minded focus. There were essays, for example, devoted to regionalism, constitutional structures, and church-state relationships. Wood himself contributed an essay which revised the view of the Antifederalists. He argued that the Antifederalists and not the Federalists were the "real prophets" of the period. They understood and accepted changes that were taking place in politics, the economy, and society, and therefore should be seen as farsighted modern men who had glimpsed the future of America more clearly that their opponents.[18]

Historians had to contend also with controversies from scholars in other disciplines who were writing about the Constitution. One such challenge came from political scientists or legal theorists who did not agree with the methodologies employed by historians. This was particularly true of the followers of the political theorist, Leo Strauss. The Straussians, as they were called, condemned historicism and resorted to a conservative interpretation that was historical in nature, based on timeless truths, and hostile to what they considered to be the historians' preoccupation with contextual problems on a relativistic basis. Historians, despite their disagreements with Straussians, found them useful for making all scholars much more aware of the intellectual complexities involved in evaluating the constitutional period.[19]

Yet another challenge to historians came from present-minded members of the Reagan administration—such as Edwin Meese, the United States Attorney General—who claimed that the Supreme Court should show greater respect for the "original intent" of the framers. Meese and other conservative public officials argued that if judges could freely ignore both the intentions of the framers and later legislators, they could substitute their own preferences of values for the decisions of popularly-elected officials. Jack Rakove in an article written in 1986 replied that the relationship between the meaning of the Constitution and the actual intentions of its framers could never be taken for granted; it was often too difficult to discern or pinpoint.[20]

As a result of these developments—the writings of the "new intellectual historians" and other scholars during the Bicentennial, the re-

---

[18]Richard Beeman, et al., eds., Beyond Confederation (Chapel Hill, 1987). The thirteen scholars were: Richard Beeman, Stanley N. Katz, Ralph Lerner, Gordon S. Wood, Richard D. Brown, Janet A. Riesman, Lance Banning, Paul Finkelman, Drew R. McCoy, Jack N. Rakove, Richard E. Ellis, Stephen Botein, and John M. Murrin.

[19]See Gordon S. Wood, "The Fundamentalists and the Constitution," New York Review of Books, 35 (Feb. 18, 1988):33–40.

[20]Jack Rakove, "Mr. Meese, Meet Mr. Madison," Atlantic 258(Dec., 1986):77–86.

vision of the republican synthesis, and the definition of the political culture in eighteenth-century America—the constitutional period and early national era both became exciting and creative areas of American historical scholarship. Having come at the American Revolution from a fresh and new perspective arising from the works of Bailyn and Wood, scholars were able to push their research forward into the early national period, and with the help of Pocock's overarching hypothesis, to create a new periodization that revolutionized American historiography. Although they disagreed on just when the transition from premodern to modern America took place, the "new intellectual historians" and others had raised and tried to answer one of the most pressing questions in our nation's history: just when did modern America emerge, and what were the forces that led to that emergence?[21]

The neo-Progressive scholars, the third group writing since World War II, presented an alternative viewpoint to the republican synthesis. The aim of the neo-Progressives was to continue to refine the old Progressive interpretation. This group of scholars was a loose one; it lumped together historians who often disagreed as much with one another as they did with certain findings of the older Progressive school. The one characteristic they held in common was the belief that economic and social forces were the crucial determinants in the positions men took for or against the Constitution. Some neo-Progressives, moreover, agreed with Beard in viewing American society in terms of polarized groups, while others pictured divisions along more pluralistic lines.

The main heir of the Beardian tradition was the neo-Progressive scholar Merrill Jensen, who taught at the University of Wisconsin. In two major works—*The Articles of Confederation* (1940) and *The New Nation* (1950)—Jensen singlehandedly rewrote the history of the period from 1774 to 1789 in terms of a socioeconomic division between two well-defined groups. The "nationalists" composed of conservative creditors and merchant interests favored strengthening the central government. They were opposed by those whom Jensen called the "federalists"—the radical agrarian democrats who controlled the state legislatures. The latter supported state sovereignty, of course, and for the most part favored rural and debtor interests.

The struggle between these two groups was the major theme running through the entire Revolutionary era, according to Jensen. During

---

[21]In tracing the evolution of republican ideology, several biographical studies showed that republicanism meant different things to different men. See, for example, Gerald Stourzh, *Alexander Hamilton and the Idea of Government* (Stanford, 1970); John Howe, *The Changing Thought of John Adams* (Princeton, 1966); George Athan Billias, *Elbridge Gerry: Founding Father and Republican Statesman* (New York, 1976); and Pauline Maier, *The Old Revolutionaries* (New York, 1980).

the early 1770s the radical agrarian democrats led the fight against both Britain and the entrenched colonial commercial aristocrats in order to achieve local self-government and to pass legislation in keeping with their interests. While leading the Revolution, they created the Articles of Confederation—a document embodying the idea of state sovereignty. Their dominance enabled them to pass laws favoring agrarian democratic ideas. But in the 1780s the agrarian democrats became apathetic, lost interest, and failed to maintain those political organizations they had formed to help them wage the Revolution. The commercial aristocrats, many of whom had withdrawn from politics, used this opportunity to move back into power. They mounted an aristocratic conservative counterrevolution, overthrew the Articles of Confederation, and wrote the Constitution in order to create a strong central government that would protect their political and commercial interests.

Jensen's thesis was similar to Beard's in many ways. Like Beard, he pictured American society as split into polarized groups throughout the period. Jensen was also like Beard in viewing the Constitution as a repudiation rather than a fulfillment of the Revolution. He argued that the Articles of Confederation represented an expression of faith in the principles of the Declaration of Independence. The Constitution, on the other hand, was a determined political effort by the nationalists to overthrow the localist forces that had formed the Articles in order to set up a decentralized form of government. Jensen, in fact, resorted to a conspiracy theory, charging the nationalists had deliberately undermined the Articles—a document that created a government that might have served the United States well.[22]

The leading neo-Progressive scholars of the 1960s and 1970s—Jackson Turner Main and E. James Ferguson—were both Jensen students and part of the so-called Wisconsin school. Although they carried on the tradition of their mentor, they made original contributions of their own. Main, in many books and articles, sketched out the broad outlines of a neo-Progressive political dichotomy existing in the 1780s. He pictured the struggle over the Constitution as a fight within each state between two fairly cohesive "parties" divided along socioeconomic and geographical lines. The parties were made up of "commercial cosmopolitans," on the one hand, and "agrarian localists," on the other. Main reaffirmed the older Progressive view of the Antifederalists as democrats and small farmers, but he revised Beard's term "realty" by describing the farming population not as subsistence farmers

---

[22]Jensen continued the neo-Progressive tradition in the documentary history of the ratification of the Constitution, which he was in charge of editing until his death in 1980. Merrill Jensen, et al., eds., The Documentary History of the Ratification of the Constitution, 15 vols. to date (Madison, 1976–   ).

but as noncommercial elements of the population. Ferguson also reinforced the idea of social cleavages between mercantile capitalists and
agrarians, but showed that they split over such issues as public finance
and the movement for constitutional reform. He went on to show the
connection that existed between those individuals holding certain
kinds of securities and paper money and their political stand on the
Constitution. At the same time, however, Ferguson's careful research
cast doubt upon Beard's clear-cut distinction between personalty and
realty interests.[23]

The neo-Progressive scholar who dealt most directly with Beard's
thesis was Forrest McDonald. In two books McDonald tested Beard's
major hypotheses regarding the origins and ratification of the Constitution by subjecting to a close analysis the economic interests of the
delegates in both the federal and state constitutional conventions. His
conclusion was that Beard's use of polarized categories—lower classes
versus upper classes, real property versus personalty, creditors versus
debtors, and commercial versus agricultural interests—to explain the
framing and ratification of the Constitution simply did not work. Such
categories were too simplistic and the situation far more complicated
and atomized than Beard had imagined. McDonald found pluralistic
rather than polarized political and economic interests at work on the
local, state, and regional levels. The Antifederalists, he found, for example, held much more in the way of personalty interests than Beard
realized. Beard's explanation of a more uniform economic motivation
was wrong, McDonald concluded, because so many different kinds of
property were held by the Philadelphia delegates and members of the
state ratifying conventions as to make Beard's simplistic dichotomies
of little use.[24]

Certainly by the end of the 1980s, most scholars found the debate
over economic interests and the Constitution along Beardian lines to
be neither helpful nor rewarding. Scholarly interests had shifted to an
analysis of the American political economy as a whole, or to the links
between society, economics, and politics. With the appearance of the
"new social historians," more attention was being paid to the social
bases of the Federalists and Antifederalists and somewhat less to their
economic holdings in securities.

This discussion of the three major post–World War II approaches
to the study of the Constitution by no means exhausts the many hist-

---

[23]Jackson Turner Main, *The Antifederalists* (Chapel Hill, 1961), and *Political Parties Before the Constitution* (Chapel Hill, 1973), among many other works. See E. James
Ferguson, *Power of the Purse* (Chapel Hill, 1961) and "The Nationalists of 1781–1783
and the Economic Interpretation of the Constitution," *Journal of American History* 56
(1969):241–261.

[24]Forrest McDonald, *We the People* (Chicago, 1958), and *E Pluribus Unum* (Boston,
1965).

oriographical approaches to this subject. During the post–World War II era the controversy over the Constitution went off in a number of different directions. On the one hand, historians increasingly applied social science concepts in their efforts to understand men's behavior during the period. Older scholars like Oscar and Mary Handlin, Lee Benson, Stanley Elkins and Eric McKitrick had resorted to concepts from sociology and psychology to revise the findings of the Progressive historians. But more recent scholars like Bailyn and Wood tended to rely more on the insights of Clifford Geertz's cultural anthropology and Thomas Kuhn's conceptualization of the history of science. Older political scientists had formerly been interested in analyzing documents like *The Federalist* in terms of general ideas, whereas many more recent scholars explored conceptual changes in the political language of such documents within more specific contexts. At the same time, some political scientists in departments of government continued the older tradition of analyzing certain constitutional ideas—federalism, sovereignty, separation of powers, and judicial review—though they often failed to connect these ideas with specific historical events.[25]

Two major historiographical controversies about the constitutional period emerged more prominently during the post–World War II era. One was the question on which scholars remained divided: just how critical was the so-called critical period? John Fiske back in the 1880s had labeled the period "critical," but over the years historians kept disagreeing about how bad conditions really had been. Merrill Jensen, writing in the 1950s, concluded that the picture was a mixed one—progress in certain areas and backsliding in others. Forrest McDonald, writing in the 1960s, ridiculed the idea of a critical period; he felt Americans did well during the era. But Michael Lienesch in an article in 1980 charged that the critical period was simply a myth created by Federalist propagandists to make certain the Constitution would be written and ratified. Herbert Storing, who published in 1981

---

[25]Oscar and Mary Handlin, "Radicals and Conservatives in Massachusetts after Independence," *New England Quarterly* 17 (1944):343–355; Lee Benson, *Turner and Beard* (Glencoe, Ill., 1960); Stanley Elkins and Eric McKitrick, "The Founding Fathers: Young Men of the Revolution," *Political Science Quarterly* 76 (1961):181–216; Martin Diamond, "Democracy and *The Federalist:* A Reconsideration of the Framers' Intent," *American Political Science Review* 53 (1959):53–61; Terence Ball and J.G.A. Pocock, eds., *Conceptual Change and the Constitution* (Lawrence, 1988). For the older tradition of scholars in departments of government and law schools interested mainly in constitutional ideas in terms of political theory, see Andrew C. McLaughlin, *A Constitutional History of the United States* (New York, 1955); Edwin Corwin, "Progress of Constitutional Theory Between the Declaration of Independence and the Meeting of the Philadelphia Convention," *American Historical Review* 30 (1925):511–536. For a work by a historian who posits the continuing constitutional dilemma of reconciling the claims of "center" and "periphery" within an extended imperial model and the independent American polity, see Jack P. Greene, *Peripheries and Center* (Athens, Ga., 1986).

his superb edition of Antifederalist writings, arrived at a different conclusion. The crisis was real and acute, Storing said, and the Antifederalists conceded that conditions were bad. Richard B. Morris, writing in 1987, argued that the postwar years were very critical indeed. To Gordon Wood in his magisterial work, the critical period was mainly a moral crisis, rather than a political and economic one: American elites faced a moral dilemma in trying to create a republican government— one premised on the notion of a virtuous people—with an American public that these leaders considered not virtuous. In short, the historiographical controversy had yet to be settled satisfactorily.[26]

A second theme that became more pronounced during the period was the sectional basis of politics—a development that influenced the creation of the Constitution. H. James Henderson in the mid-1970s produced the most exhaustive account of politics during the Confederation to appear since Jensen's work in the 1950s. Employing a voting-bloc analysis of the members of the Continental Congress, Henderson described the parties within that body as sectional in nature and with various sections becoming dominant at different times. New England radicals controlled the Congress from 1776 to 1779, but from 1780 to 1783 the middle-state nationalists prevailed. After 1783 there existed a period of three-way sectional tension—among the New England, middle, and southern states—that was partly alleviated by the adoption of the Constitution. Although the three sections pulled and tugged in different directions they were united in their belief in a republican ideology. Henderson's ideological-sectional interpretation was distinctly at odds with Jensen's neo-Progressive interpretation.[27]

Sectionalism likewise played an important part in Peter Onuf's important work, *Origins of the Federal Republic,* published in 1983. Onuf demonstrated that the thinking of the founders about an American union was profoundly shaped by the experience of interstate conflict, the difficulties of defining congressional authority, and the promotion of national interests under the Confederation. New York's northeastern counties, Pennsylvania's Wyoming Valley, and the trans-Ohio re-

---

[26]Merrill Jensen, *The New Nation* (New York, 1950), *passim;* Forrest McDonald, *E Pluribus Unum,* p. 154; Michael Lienesch, "The Constitutional Tradition: History, Political Action, and Progress in American Political Thought, 1787–1793," *Journal of Politics* 42 (1980):13; and Herbert Storing, ed., *The Complete Anti-Federalist* 7 vols. (Chicago, 1981), 1:26; Richard B. Morris, *Forging of the Union* (New York, 1987); Gordon S. Wood, *Creation of the American Republic, 1776–1787,* pp. 393–429.

[27]H. James Henderson, *Party Politics in the Continental Congress* (New York, 1974). For sectional tensions during the period, see also William Crosskey and William Jeffrey, Jr., *Politics and the Constitution in the History of the United States,* 3 vols. (Chicago, 1953–1980) which argues that Madison and some of the other principal framers deliberately sought to create a government with a broad grant of power under the commerce clause. See also Jack N. Rakove's brilliant, *The Beginnings of National Politics* (New York, 1979).

gion all either sought to become separate states (as in the case of the New York counties that became Vermont) or were the source of a quarrel over conflicting western land claims (as, for example, Connecticut's invasion of Pennsylvanias's Wyoming Valley). Only the newly formed Congress, Onuf argued, could settle such overriding issues. The states had come to recognize that a central authority was needed to resolve these problems. Thus, instead of the orthodox story which pictured the new federal government and the states locked in a power struggle over sovereignty, Onuf showed there was an expansion of central authority and reinforcement of state sovereignty at one and the same time. Simultaneously, as a result of these jurisdictional disputes, there emerged a sectional view of politics that superseded the large-versus-small states distinction which presumably had prevailed since the start of the Revolution. Sectionalism as an interpretive principle in the writing of the Constitution had come into its own after some years of relative neglect.[28]

History students coming to grips with the problem of evaluating the Constitution and the developments that led to its writing and ratification must address a series of complex questions. Was the Constitution a fulfillment or a repudiation of the ideals of the Revolution expressed in the Declaration of Independence? What was the nature of the Constitution, and in what ways did its framing reflect the developments in political thought during the 1780s? Were the differences that divided those who favored and those who opposed the Constitution based more on ideology or interests? Was the Constitution, as Beard and some neo-Progressive historians argued, an undemocratic document—the work of a political and propertied minority who drafted an instrument of government to suit their own purposes and thereby limited the liberties of the people? Were the proponents of the republican synthesis persuasive in their conviction that Americans shared a common republican ideology that formed a basic consensus among the American people? Or did the incompleteness of the republican synthesis render it unsatisfactory as a viable interpretation? Were the Antifederalists tradition-minded classical republicans or enterprising proto-liberals who glimpsed the future of America as Wood suggested? Only by raising such questions can the student decide whether the Constitution was a document that reflected conflict or consensus, and, in the case of some kind of conflict interpretation, to determine what the basis of that conflict was.

---

[28]Peter Onuf, *Origins of the Federal Republic* (Philadelphia, 1983). See also his *Statehood and Union* (Bloomington, 1987); Joseph Davis, *Sectionalism in American Politics* (Madison, 1977); and Drew R. McCoy, "James Madison and Visions of American Nationality in the Confederation Period: A Regional Perspective," in Beeman, *et al.*, eds. *Beyond Confederation*, pp. 226–258.

Gordon S. Wood

GORDON S. WOOD (1933–   ) *is professor of history at Brown University. His book,* The Creation of the American Republic, 1776–1787, *received the John H. Dunning Prize of the American Historical Association in 1970.*

The division over the Constitution in 1787–1788 is not easily analyzed. It is difficult, as historians have recently demonstrated, to equate the supporters or opponents of the Constitution with particular economic groupings. The Antifederalist politicians in the ratifying conventions often possessed wealth, including public securities, equal to that of the Federalists. While the relative youth of the Federalist leaders, compared to the ages of the prominent Antifederalists, was important, especially in accounting for the Federalists' ability to think freshly and creatively about politics, it can hardly be used to explain the division throughout the country. Moreover, the concern of the 1780s with America's moral character was not confined to the proponents of the Constitution. That rabid republican and Antifederalist, Benjamin Austin, was as convinced as any Federalist that "the luxurious living of all ranks and degrees" was "the principal cause of all the evils we now experience." Some leading Antifederalist intellectuals expressed as much fear of "the injustice, folly, and wickedness of the State Legislatures" and of "the usurpation and tyranny of the majority" against the minority as did Madison. In the Philadelphia Convention both Mason and Elbridge Gerry, later prominent Antifederalists, admitted "the danger of the levelling spirit": flowing from "the excess of democracy" in the American republic. There were many diverse reasons in each state why men supported or opposed the Constitution that cut through any sort of class division. The Constitution was a single issue in a complicated situation, and its acceptance or rejection in many states was often dictated by peculiar circumstances—the prevalence of Indians, the desire for western lands, the special interests of commerce—that defy generalization. Nevertheless, despite all of this confusion and complexity, the struggle over the Constitution, as the debate if nothing else makes clear, can best be understood as a

---

Gordon S. Wood, *The Creation of the American Republic, 1776–1787* (Chapel Hill: University of North Carolina Press, 1969) pp. 485–492, 494–499, 506–508, and 513–518. Reprinted with omissions by permission of the University of North Carolina Press and the Institute of Early American History and Culture.

social one. Whatever the particular constituency of the antagonists may have been, men in 1787–1788 talked as if they were representing distinct and opposing social elements. Both the proponents and opponents of the Constitution focused throughout the debates on an essential point of political sociology that ultimately must be used to distinguish a Federalist from an Antifederalist. The quarrel was fundamentally one between aristocracy and democracy. . . .

The disorganization and inertia of the Antifederalists, especially in contrast with the energy and effectiveness of the Federalists, has been repeatedly emphasized. The opponents of the Constitution lacked both coordination and unified leadership; "their principles," wrote Oliver Ellsworth, "are totally opposite to each other, and their objections discordant and irreconcilable." The Federalist victory, it appears, was actually more of an Antifederalist default. . . .

But the Antifederalists were not simply poorer politicians than the Federalists; they were actually different kinds of politicians. Too many of them were state-centered men with local interests and loyalties only, politicians without influence and connections, and ultimately politicians without social and intellectual confidence. In South Carolina the up-country opponents of the Constitution shied from debate and when they did occasionally rise to speak apologized effusively for their inability to say what they felt had to be said, thus leaving most of the opposition to the Constitution to be voiced by Rawlins Lowndes, a low-country planter who scarcely represented their interests and soon retired from the struggle. Elsewhere, in New Hampshire, Connecticut, Massachusetts, Pennsylvania, and North Carolina, the situation was similar: the Federalists had the bulk of talent and influence on their side "together with all the Speakers in the State great and small." In convention after convention the Antifederalists, as in Connecticut, tried to speak but "they were browbeaten by many of those Cicero'es as they think themselves and others of Superior rank." "The presses are in a great measure secured to *their* side," the Antifederalists complained with justice: out of a hundred or more newspapers printed in the late eighties only a dozen supported the Antifederalists, as editors, "afraid to offend the great men, or Merchants, who could work their ruin," closed their columns to the opposition. The Antifederalists were not so much beaten as overawed. . . .

[F]ear of a plot by men who "talk so finely and gloss over matters so smoothly" ran through the Antifederalist mind. Because the many "new men" of the 1780s, men like Melancthon Smith and Abraham Yates of New York or John Smilie and William Findley of Pennsylvania, had bypassed the social hierarchy in their rise to political leadership, they lacked those attributes of social distinction and dignity that went beyond mere wealth. Since these kinds of men were never assimilated to the gentlemanly cast of the Livingstons or the Morrises, they, like

Americans earlier in confrontation with the British court, tended to view with suspicion and hostility the high-flying world of style and connections that they were barred by their language and tastes, if by nothing else, from sharing in. In the minds of these socially inferior politicians the movement for the strengthening of the central government could only be a "conspiracy" "planned and set to work" by a few aristocrats, who were at first, said Abraham Yates, no larger in number in any one state than the cabal which sought to undermine English liberty at the beginning of the eighteenth century. Since men like Yates could not quite comprehend what they were sure were the inner maneuverings of the elite, they were convinced that in the aristocrats' program, "what was their view in the beginning" or how "far it was Intended to be carried Must be Collected from facts that Afterwards have happened." Like American Whigs in the sixties and seventies forced to delve into the dark and complicated workings of English court politics, they could judge motives and plans "but by the Event." And they could only conclude that the events of the eighties, "the treasury, the Cincinnati, and other public creditors, with all their concomitants," were "somehow or other, . . . inseparably connected," were all parts of a grand design "concerted by a few *tyrants*" to undo the Revolution and to establish an aristocracy in order "to lord it over the rest of their fellow citizens, to trample the poorer part of the people under their feet, that they may be rendered their servants and slaves." In this climate all the major issues of the Confederation period—the impost, commutation, and the return of the Loyalists—possessed a political and social significance that transcended economic concerns. All seemed to be devices by which a ruling few, like the ministers of the English Crown, would attach a corps of pensioners and dependents to the government and spread their influence and connections throughout the states in order "to dissolve our present Happy and Benevolent Constitution and to erect on the Ruins, a proper Aristocracy."

Nothing was more characteristic of Antifederalist thinking than this obsession with aristocracy. Although to a European, American society may have appeared remarkably egalitarian, to many Americans, especially to those who aspired to places of consequence but were made to feel their inferiority in innumerable, often subtle, ways, American society was distinguished by its inequality. . . . In all communities, "even in those of the most democratic kind," wrote George Clinton (whose "family and connections" in the minds of those like Philip Schuyler did not "entitle him to so distinguished a predominance" as the governorship of New York), there were pressures—"superior talents, fortunes and public employments"—demarcating an aristocracy whose influence was difficult to resist.

Such influence was difficult to resist because, to the continual annoyance of the Antifederalists, the great body of the people willingly submitted to it. The "authority of names" and "the influence of the great" among ordinary people were too evident to be denied. "Will any one say that there does not exist in this country the pride of family, of wealth, of talents, and that they do not command influence and respect among the common people?" "The people are too apt to yield an implicit assent to the opinions of those characters whose abilities are held in the highest esteem, and to those in whose integrity and patriotism they can confide; not considering that the love of domination is generally in proportion to talents, abilities and superior requirements." Because of this habit of deference in the people, it was "in the power of the enlightened and aspiring few, if they should combine, at any time to destroy the best establishments, and even make the people the instruments of their own subjugation." Hence, the Antifederalist-minded declared, the people must be awakened to the consequences of their self-ensnarement; they must be warned over and over by the popular tribunes, by "those who are competent to the task of developing the principles of government," of the dangers involved in paying obeisance to those who they thought were their superiors. The people must "not be permitted to consider themselves as a grovelling, distinct species, uninterested in the general welfare."

Such constant admonitions to the people of the perils flowing from their too easy deference to the *"natural aristocracy"* were necessary because the Antifederalists were convinced that these "men that had been delicately bred, and who were in affluent circumstances," these "men of the most exalted rank in life," were by their very conspicuousness irreparably cut off from the great body of the people and hence could never share in its concerns nor look after its interests. It was not that these "certain men exalted above the rest" were necessarily "destitute of morality or virtue" or that they were inherently different from other men. "The same passions and prejudices govern all men." It was only that circumstances in their particular environment had made them different. There was "a charm in politicks"; men in high office become habituated with power, "grow fond of it, and are loath to resign it"; "they feel themselves flattered and elevated," enthralled by the attractions of high living, and thus they easily forget the interests of the common people, from which many of them once sprang. By dwelling so vividly on the allurements of prestige and power, by emphasizing again and again how the "human soul is affected by wealth, in all its faculties, . . . by its present interest, by its expectations, and by its fears," these ambitious Antifederalist politicians may have revealed as much about themselves as they did about the "aristocratic" elite they sought to displace. Yet at the same time by such language they contributed to a new appreciation of the nature of society.

In these repeated attacks on deference and the capacity of a conspicuous few to speak for the whole society—which was to become in time the distinguishing feature of American democratic politics—the Antifederalists struck at the roots of the traditional conception of political society. If the natural elite, whether its distinctions were ascribed or acquired, was not in any organic way connected to the "feelings, circumstances, and interests" of the people and was incapable of feeling "sympathetically the wants of the people," then it followed that only ordinary men, men not distinguished by the characteristics of aristocratic wealth and taste, men "in middling circumstances" untempted by the attractions of a cosmopolitan world and thus "more temperate, of better morals, and less ambitious, than the great," could be trusted to speak for the great body of the people, for those who were coming more and more to be referred to as "the middling and lower classes of people." The differentiating influence of the environment was such that men in various ranks and classes now seemed to be broken apart from one another, separated by their peculiar circumstances into distinct, unconnected, and often incompatible interests. With their indictment of aristocracy the Antifederalists were saying, whether they realized it or not, that the people of America even in their several states were not homogeneous entities each with a basic similarity of interest for which an empathic elite could speak. Society was not an organic hierarchy composed of ranks and degrees indissolubly linked one to another; rather it was a heterogeneous mixture of "many different classes or orders of people, Merchants, Farmers, Planter Mechanics and Gentry or wealthy Men." In such a society men from one class or group, however educated and respectable they may have been, could never be acquainted with the "*Situation* and Wants" of those of another class or group. Lawyers and planters could never be "adequate judges of tradesmen concerns." If men were truly to represent the people in government, it was not enough for them to be for the people; they had to be actually of the people. "Farmers, traders and mechanics . . . all ought to have a competent number of their best informed members in the legislature."

Thus the Antifederalists were not only directly challenging the conventional belief that only a gentlemanly few, even though now in America naturally and not artificially qualified, were best equipped through learning and experience to represent and to govern the society, but they were as well indirectly denying the assumption of organic social homogeneity on which republicanism rested. Without fully comprehending the consequences of their arguments the Antifederalists were destroying the great chain of being, thus undermining the social basis of republicanism and shattering that unity and harmony of social and political authority which the eighteenth century generally and indeed most revolutionary leaders had considered essential to the maintenance of order.

Confronted with such a fundamental challenge the Federalists initially backed away. They had no desire to argue the merits of the Constitution in terms of social implications and were understandably reluctant to open up the character of American society as the central issue of the debate. But in the end they could not resist defending those beliefs in elitism that lay at the heart of their conception of politics and of their constitutional program. All of the Federalists' desires to establish a strong and respectable nation in the world, all of their plans to create a flourishing commercial economy, in short, all of what the Federalists wanted out of the new central government seemed in the final analysis dependent upon the prerequisite maintenance of aristocratic politics. . . .

The course of the debates over the Constitution seemed to confirm what the Federalists had believed all along. Antifederalism represented the climax of a "war" that was, in the words of Theodore Sedgwick, being "levied on the virtue, property, and distinctions in the community." The opponents of the Constitution, despite some, "particularly in Virginia," who were operating "from the most honorable and patriotic motives," were essentially identical with those who were responsible for the evils the states were suffering from in the eighties—"narrowminded politicians . . . under the influence of local views." "Whilst many *ostensible* reasons are assigned" for the Antifederalists' opposition, charged Washington, "the real ones are concealed behind the Curtains, because they are not of a nature to appear in open day." "The real object of all their zeal in opposing the system." agreed Madison, was to maintain "the supremacy of the State Legislatures," with all that meant in the printing of money and the violation of contracts. The Antifederalists or those for whom the Antifederalists spoke, whether their spokesmen realized it or not, were "none but the horse-jockey, the mushroom merchant, the running and dishonest speculator," those "who owe the most and have the least to pay," those "whose dependence and expectations are upon changes in government, and distracted times," men of "desperate Circumstances," those "in Every State" who "have Debts to pay, Interests to support or Fortunes to make," those, in short, who "wish for scrambling Times." Apart from a few of their intellectual leaders the Antifederalists were thought to be an ill-bred lot: "Their education has been rather indifferent—they have been accustomed to think on the small scale." They were often blustering demagogues trying to push their way into office—"men of much self-importance and supposed skill in politics, who are not of sufficient consequence to obtain public employment." Hence they were considered to be jealous and mistrustful of "every one in the higher offices of society," unable to bear to see others possessing "that fancied blessing, to which, alas! they must themselves aspire in vain." In the Federalist mind therefore the struggle over the Constitution was not one between kinds of wealth or property, or one between commercial or noncommercial elements of the population, but rather represented a broad social division between those who believed in the right of a natural aristocracy to speak for the people and those who did not.

Against this threat from the licentious the Federalists pictured themselves as the defenders of the worthy, of those whom they called "the better sort of people," those, said John Jay, "who are orderly and industrious, who are content with their situations and not uneasy in their circumstances." Because the Federalists were fearful that republican equality was becoming "that *perfect equality* which deadens the motives of industry, and places Demerit on a Footing with Virtue," they were obsessed with the need to insure that the proper amount of inequality and natural distinctions be recognized. . . . Robert Morris, for example, was convinced there were social differences—even in Pennsylvania. "What!" he explained in scornful amazement at John Smilie's argument that a republic admitted of no social superiorities. "Is it insisted that there is no distinction of character?" Respectability, said Morris with conviction, was not confined to property. "Surely persons possessed of knowledge, judgment, information, integrity, and having extensive connections, are not to be classed with persons void of reputation or character."

In refuting the Antifederalists' contention "that all classes of citizens should have some of their own number in the representative body, in order that their feelings and interests may be the better understood and attended to," Hamilton in *The Federalist*, Number 35, put into words the Federalists' often unspoken and vaguely held assumption about the organic and the hierarchical nature of society. Such explicit class or occupational representation as the Antifederalists advocated, wrote Hamilton, was not only impractical but unnecessary, since the society was not as fragmented or heterogeneous as the Antifederalists implied. The various groups in the landed interest, for example, were "perfectly united, from the wealthiest landlord down to the poorest tenant," and this "common interest may always be reckoned upon as the surest bond of sympathy" linking the landed representative, however rich, to his constituents. In a like way, the members of the commercial community were "immediately connected" and most naturally represented by the merchants. "Mechanics and manufacturers will always be inclined, with few exceptions, to give their votes to merchants, in preference to persons of their own professions or trades. . . . They know that the merchant is their natural patron and friend; and . . . they are sensible that their habits in life have not been such as to give them those acquired endowments, without which in a deliberative assembly, the greatest natural abilities, are for the most part useless." However much many Federalists may have doubted the substance of Hamilton's analysis of American society, they could not doubt the truth of his conclusion. That the people were represented better by one of the natural aristocracy "whose situation leads to extensive inquiry and information" than by one "whose observation does not travel beyond the circle of his neighbors and acquaintances" was the defining element of the Federalist philosophy.

It was not simply the number of public securities, or credit outstanding, or the number of ships, or the amount of money possessed that made a man think of himself as one of the natural elite. It was much more subtle than the mere possession of wealth: it was a deeper social feeling, a sense of being socially established, of possessing attributes—family, education, and refinement—that others lacked, above all, of being accepted by and being able to move easily among those who considered themselves to be the respectable and cultivated. It is perhaps anachronistic to describe this social sense as a class interest, for it often transcended immediate political or economic concerns, and, as Hamilton's argument indicates, was designed to cut through narrow occupational categories. The Republicans of Philadelphia, for example, repeatedly denied that they represented an aristocracy with a united class interest. "We are of different occupations; of different sects of religion; and have different views of life. No factions or private system can comprehend us all." Yet with all their assertions of diversified interests the Republicans were not without a social consciousness in their quarrel with the supporters of the Pennsylvania Constitution. If there were any of us ambitious for power, their apology continued, then there would be no need to change the Constitution, for we surely could attain power under the present Constitution. "We have already seen how easy the task is for *any character* to rise into power and consequence under it. And there are some of us, who think not so meanly of ourselves, as to dread any rivalship from those who are now in office."

In 1787 this kind of elitist social consciousness was brought into play as perhaps never before in eighteenth-century America, as gentlemen up an down the continent submerged their sectional and economic differences in the face of what seemed to be a threat to the very foundations of society. Despite his earlier opposition to the Order of the Cincinnati, Theodore Sedgwick, like other frightened New Englanders, now welcomed the organization as a source of strength in the battle for the Constitution. The fear of social disruption that had run through much of the writing of the eighties was brought to a head to eclipse all other fears. Although state politics in the eighties remains to be analyzed, the evidence from Federalist correspondence indicates clearly a belief that never had there occurred "so great a change in the opinion of the best people" as was occurring in the last few years of the decade. The Federalists were astonished at the outpouring in 1787 of influential and respectable people who had earlier remained quiescent. Too many of "the better sort of people," it was repeatedly said, had withdrawn at the end of the war "from the theatre of public action, to scenes of retirement and ease," and thus "demagogues of desperate fortunes, mere adventurers in fraud, were left to act unopposed." After all, it was explained, "when the wicked rise, men hide themselves." Even the problems of Massachusetts in 1786, noted General Benjamin Lincoln, the repressor of the Shaysites, were not caused by the rebels, but by the laxity of "the good people of the state." But the lesson of this laxity was rapidly being learned. Everywhere, it seemed, men of virtue, good sense, and property, "almost the whole body of our enlighten'd and leading characters in every state," were awakened in support of stronger government. "The scum which was thrown upon the surface by the fermentation of the war is daily sinking," Benjamin Rush told Richard Price in 1786, "while a pure spirit is occupying its place." "Men are brought into action who had consigned themselves to an eve of rest," Edward Carrington wrote to Jefferson in June 1787, "and the Convention, as a Beacon, is rousing the attention of the Empire." The Antifederalists could only stand amazed at this "weight of talents" being gathered in support of the Constitution. "What must the individual be who could thus oppose them united?"

Still, in the face of this preponderance of wealth and respectability in support of the Constitution, what remains extraordinary about 1787–1788 is not the weakness and disunity but the political strength of Antifederalism. That large numbers of Americans could actually reject a plan of government created by a body "composed of the first characters in the Continent" and backed by Washington and nearly the whole of the natural aristocracy of the country said more about the changing character of American politics and society in the eighties than did the Constitution's eventual acceptance. It was indeed a portent of what was to come. . . .

If the new national government was to promote the common good as forcefully as any state government, and if, as the Federalists believed, a major source of the vices of the eighties lay in the abuse of state power, then there was something apparently contradictory about the new federal Constitution, which after all represented not a weakening of the dangerous power of republican government but rather a strengthening of it. "The complaints against the separate governments, even by the friends of the new plan," remarked the Antifederalist James Winthrop, "are not that they have not power enough, but that they are disposed to make a bad use of what power they have." Surely, concluded Winthrop, the Federalists were reasoning badly "when they purpose to set up a government possess'd of much more extensive powers . . . and subject to much smaller checks" than the existing state governments possessed and were subject to. Madison for one was quite aware of the pointedness of this objection. "It may be asked," he said, "how private rights will be more secure under the Guardianship of the General Government than under the State Governments, since they are both founded in the republican principle which refers the ultimate decision to the will of the majority." What, in other words, was different about the new federal Constitution that would enable it to mitigate the effects of tyrannical majorities? What would keep the new federal government from succumbing to the same pressures that had beset the state governments? The answer the Federalists gave to these questions unmistakably reveals the social bias underlying both their fears of the unrestrained state legislatures and their expectations for their federal remedy. For all of their desires to avoid intricate examination of a delicate social structure, the Federalists' program itself demanded that the discussion of the Constitution would be in essentially social terms.

The Federalists were not as much opposed to the governmental power of the states as to the character of the people who were wielding it. The constitutions of most of the states were not really at fault. Massachusetts after all possessed a nearly perfect constitution. What actually bothered the Federalists was the sort of people who had been able to gain positions of authority in the state governments, particularly in the state legislatures. Much of the quarrel with the viciousness, instability, and injustice of the various state governments was at bottom social. "For," as John Dickinson emphasized, *the government will partake of the qualities of those whose authority is prevalent.*" The political and social structures were intimately related. "People once respected their governors, their senators, their judges and their clergy; they reposed confidence in them; their laws were obeyed, and the states were happy in tranquility." But in the eighties the authority of government had drastically declined because "men of sense and property have lost much of their influence by the popular spirit of the war." "That exact order, and due subordination, that is essentially necessary in all well appointed governments, and which constitutes the real happiness and well being of society" had been deranged by "men of no genius or abilities" who had tried to run "the machine of government." Since "it cannot be expected that things will go well, when persons of vicious principles, and loose morals are in authority," it was the large number of obscure, ignorant, and unruly men occupying the state legislatures, and not the structure of the governments, that was the real cause of the evils so much complained of.

The Federalist image of the Constitution as a sort of "philosopher's stone" was indeed appropriate: it was a device intended to transmute base materials into gold and thereby prolong the life of the republic. Patrick Henry acutely perceived what the Federalists were driving at. "The Constitution," he said in the Virginia Convention, "reflects in the most degrading and mortifying manner on the virtue, integrity, and wisdom of the state legislatures; it presupposes that the chosen few who go to Congress will have more upright hearts, and more enlightened minds, than those who are members of the individual legislatures." The new Constitution was structurally no different from the constitutions of some of states. Yet the powers of the new central government were not as threatening as the powers of the state governments precisely because the Federalists believed different kinds of persons would hold them. They anticipated that somehow the new government would be staffed largely by "the worthy," the natural social aristocracy of the country. "After all," said Pelatiah Webster, putting his finger on the crux of the Federalists argument, "the grand secret of forming a good government, is , to put good men into the administration: for wild, vicious, or idle men, will ever make a bad government, let its principles be ever so good. . . .

In short, through the artificial contrivance of the Constitution overlying an expanded society, the Federalists meant to restore and to prolong the traditional kind of elitist influence in politics that social developments, especially since the Revolution, were undermining. As the defenders if not always the perpetrators of these developments—the "disorder" of the 1780s—the Antifederalists could scarcely have missed the social implications of the Federalist program. The Constitution was intrinsically an aristocratic document designed to check the democratic tendencies of the period, and as such it dictated the character of the Antifederalist response. It was therefore inevitable that the Antifederalists should have charged that the new government was "dangerously adapted to the purposes of an immediate *aristocratic tyranny.*" In state after state the Antifederalists reduced the issue to those social terms predetermined by the Federalists themselves: the Constitution was a plan intended to "raise the fortunes and respectability of the *well-born few,* and oppress the plebians"; it was "a continental exertion of the *well-born* of America to obtain that darling domination, which they have not been able to accomplish in their respective states"; it "will lead to an aristocratical government, and establish tyranny over us." Whatever their own particular social standing, the Antifederalist spokesmen spread the warning that the new government either would be "in practice a *permanent* ARISTOCRACY" or would soon "degenerate to a compleat Aristocracy." . . .

Aristocratic principles were in fact "interwoven" in the very fabric of the proposed government. If a government was "so constituted as to admit but few to exercise the powers of it," then it would "according to the natural course of things" end up in the hands of "the natural aristocracy." It went almost without saying that the awesome president and the exalted Senate, "a compound of *monarchy* and *aristocracy,*" would be dangerously far removed from the people. But even the House of Representatives, the very body that "should be a true picture of the people, possess a knowledge of their circumstances and their wants, sympathize in all their distresses, and disposed to seek their true interest," was without "a tincture of democracy." Since it could never collect "the interests, feelings, and opinions of three or four millions of people," it was better understood as "an Assistant Aristocratical Branch" to the Senate than as a real representation of the people. When the number of representatives was "so small, the office will be highly elevated and distinguished; the style in which the members live will probably be high; circumstances of this kind will render the place of a representative not a desirable one to sensible, substantial men, who have been used to walk in the plain and frugal paths of life." While the ordinary people in extensive electoral districts of thirty thousand inhabitants would remain "divided," those few extraordinary men with "conspicuous military, popular, civil or legal talents" could more easily form broader associations to dominate elections; they had family and other connections to "unite their interests." If only a half-dozen congressmen were to be selected to represent a large state, then rarely, argued the Antifederalists in terms that were essentially no different from those used by the Federalists in the Constitution's defense, would persons from "the great body of the people, the middle and lower classes," be elected to the House of Representatives. "The Station is too high and exalted to be filled but [by] the *first Men* in the State in point of Fortune and Influence. In fact no order or class of the people will be represented in the House of Representatives called the Democratic Branch but the rich and wealthy." The Antifederalists thus came to oppose the new national government for the same reason the Federalists favored it: because its very structure and detachment from the people would work to exclude any kind of actual and local interest representation and prevent those who were not rich, well born, or prominent from exercising political power. Both sides fully appreciated the central issue the Constitution posed and grappled with it throughout the debates: Whether a professedly popular government should actually be in the hands of, rather than simply derived from, common ordinary people.

Out of the division in 1787–1788 over this issue, an issue which was as conspicuously social as any in American history, the Antifederalists emerged as the spokesmen for the growing American antagonism to aristocracy and as the defenders of the most intimate participation in politics of the widest variety of people possible. It was not from lack of vision that the Antifederalists feared the new government. Although their viewpoint was intensely localist, it was grounded in as perceptive an understanding of the social basis of American politics as that of the Federalists. Most of the Antifederalists were majoritarians with respect to the state legislatures but not with respect to the national legislature, because they presumed as well as the Federalists did that different sorts of people from those who sat in the state assemblies would occupy the Congress. Whatever else may be said about the Antifederalists, their populism cannot be impugned. They were true champions of the most extreme kind of democratic and egalitarian politics expressed in the revolutionary era. Convinced that "it has been the principal care of free governments to guard against the encroachments of the great," the Antifederalists believed that popular government itself, as defined by the principles of 1776, was endangered by the new national government. If the Revolution had been a transfer of power from the few to the many, then the federal Constitution clearly represented an abnegation of the Revolution. For, as Richard Henry Lee wrote in his *Letters from the Federal Farmer,* "every man of reflection must see, that the change now proposed, is a transfer of power from the many to the few."

Although Lee's analysis contained the essential truth, the Federalist program was not quite so simply summed up. It was true that through the new Constitution the Federalists hoped to resist and eventually to avert what they saw to be the rapid decline of the influence and authority of the natural aristocracy in America. At the very time that the organic conception of society that made elite rule comprehensible was finally and avowedly dissolving, and the members of the elite were developing distinct professional, social, or economic interests, the Federalists found elite rule more imperative than ever before. To the Federalists the greatest dangers to republicanism were flowing not, as the old Whigs had thought, from the rulers or from any distinctive minority in the community, but from the widespread participation of the people in the government. It now seemed increasingly evident that if the public good not only of the United States as a whole but even of the separate states were to be truly perceived and promoted, the American people must abandon their revolutionary reliance on their representative state legislatures and place their confidence in the highmindedness of the natural leaders of the society, which ideally everyone had the opportunity of becoming. Since the Federalists presumed that only such a self-conscious elite could transcend the many narrow and contradictory interests inevitable in any society, however small, the measure of a good government became its capacity for insuring the predominance of these kinds of natural leaders who knew better than the people as a whole what was good for the society.

The result was an amazing display of confidence in constitutionalism, in the efficacy of institutional devices for solving social and political problems. Through the proper arrangement of new institutional structures the Federalists aimed to turn the political and social developments that were weakening the place of "the better sort of people" in government back upon themselves and to make these developments the very source of the perpetuation of the natural aristocracy's dom-

inance of politics. Thus the Federalists did not directly reject democratic politics as it had manifested itself in the 1780s; rather they attempted to adjust to this politics in order to control and mitigate its
effects. In short they offered the country an elitist theory of democracy.
They did not see themselves as repudiating either the Revolution or
popular government, but saw themselves as saving both from their excesses. If the Constitution were not established, they told themselves
and the country over and over, then republicanism was doomed, the
grand experiment was over, and a division of the confederacy, mon-
arch, or worse would result.

Despite all the examples of popular vice in the eighties, the Federalist confidence in the people remained strong. The letters of "Caesar,"
with their frank and violent denigration of the people, were anomalies
in the Federalist literature. The Federalists had by no means lost faith
in the people, at least in the people's ability to discern their true leaders. In fact many of the social elite who comprised the Federalist leadership were confident of popular election if the constituency could be
made broad enough, and crass electioneering be curbed, so that the
people's choice would be undisturbed by ambitious demagogues. "For
if not blind to their own interest, they choose men of the first character
for wisdom and integrity." Despite prodding by so-called designing and
unprincipled men, the bulk of the people remained deferential to the
established social leadership—for some aspiring politicians frustrat-
ingly so. Even if they had wanted to, the Federalists could not turn
their backs on republicanism. For it was evident to even the most pessimistic "that no other form would be reconcilable with the genius of
the people of America; with the fundamental principles of the Revolution; or with that honorable determination which animates every vo-
tary of freedom, to rest all our political experiments on the capacity of
mankind for self-government." Whatever government the Federalists
established had to be "strictly republican" and "deducible from the
only source of just authority—the People."

John Howe

JOHN HOWE (1935–   ) *is professor of history at the University
of Minnesota. He is the author of* The Changing Political Thought of

John Howe, "Gordon S. Wood and the Analysis of Political Culture in the American
Revolutionary Era," *William and Mary Quarterly* 44 (1987):569–575. Reprinted with the
permission of John Howe.

John Adams *(1966) and* From the Revolution Through the Age of Jackson *(1973).*

Seldom has a book exerted such powerful and lasting influence on the interpretation of early American history as Gordon S. Wood's *The Creation of the American Republic.* Probably no other single work has so dominated the political and constitutional historiography of the American Revolutionary and constitutional eras during the past two decades. Why has the book had such a profound effect, and how is it to be regarded, nearly twenty years after its publication, in the historiographical context of 1987?

Part of the explanation for the book's initial impact lies in the timing of its publication and its association with the work of Wood's mentor, Bernard Bailyn. In the early 1960s Bailyn published two major works that dramatically altered historians' interpretations of the Revolution. In the introduction to his volume of Revolutionary pamphlets, and then at greater length in *The Ideological Origins of the American Revolution,* Bailyn argued, eloquently and persuasively, that the key to an understanding of American Revolutionary behavior lay in the controlling influence of a powerful political culture centered in the English dissenting or country tradition. Neither conflicts within colonial society nor British efforts at imperial reform, Bailyn argued, fully explain the onset of the Revolution. Rather, one must look to distinctive colonial habits of mind, assumptions about history and human nature, notions of power and liberty, and theories of conspiracy to understand why the colonists broke with England.[1]

In conceptualization as well as content, *Creation of the American Republic* can be seen as an extension, elaborate and creative in its own right, of Bailyn's work, for in it Wood explains how that dissenting tradition was transformed during the years following Independence into a distinctive American republican ideology and how, under the forcing pressure of Revolutionary events, that ideology evolved from its original, utopian formulation of 1776–1778 into the quite different federalist republicanism of the late 1780s. Taken together, Wood's and Bailyn's work, mutually reinforcing though not always in detailed agreement with each other, offered a compelling, encompassing interpretation of the nation's founding and the beginning of a distinctive national politics.

Wood's work found a congenial historiographical environment in another way as well. At the time of *Creation's* publication in 1969,

---

[1]Bailyn, ed., *Pamphlets of the American Revolution, 1750–1776* (Cambridge, Mass., 1965), and *The Ideological Origins of the American Revolution* (Cambridge, Mass., 1967). Page references to Gordon S. Wood, *The Creation of the American Republic, 1776–1787* (Chapel Hill, N.C. 1969), are incorporated into the text.

Revolutionary historiography was at something of a standstill. The once-dominant Progressive interpretation of the Revolution was under siege, its dichotomous, class-based view of Revolutionary politics attacked as oversimplified and inconsistent with historical evidence. In place of the Progressives' conflict-based model of politics, the so-called neo-whig historians substituted a model that emphasized political consensus based on a broadly participatory politics and a shared commitment to political liberty. Wood extended that neo-whig argument by offering an interpretation that downplayed social conflict, stressed the causal importance of ideas, and emphasized the predominantly ideological character of Revolutionary change, while at the same time deepening the analysis of connections between ideas and behavior, and locating the main theme of Revolutionary politics in a continuing tension between the advocates of egalitarian and hierarchical politics. In the process, he fashioned a dramatic interpretation of the nation's origins and explored in remarkable detail the central course of political/constitutional development during the Revolutionary era.

Historiographical breakthroughs, of course, are not fundamentally a matter of fortuitous timing, for countless historiographical opportunities go unexploited. Ultimately, *Creation* succeeded so handsomely because of its remarkable qualities: its erudition; its comprehensiveness of theme and chronology; its interpretive control over a sprawling, volatile period of history; the complexity and yet organizational clarity of its argument; the far-reaching importance of its subject matter to an understanding of the nation's history; and the provocative interpretation it offers of the central role of political culture in the nation's founding. It is this last point, the book's analysis of political culture—its content, connections with its historical environment, and relationships to political behavior—that I wish to examine in this essay.

In an important article entitled "Rhetoric and Reality in the American Revolution," published in 1966 in the *William and Mary Quarterly*, Wood criticized what he called the traditional "idealist" interpretation of Revolutionary thought for its failure to go beyond the analysis of formal, rational bodies of theory—doctrines of liberty and natural rights, of mixed and balanced government—to examine the underlying, often implicit, but nevertheless powerful cultural values that informed them. This call for enlarging the agenda of intellectual history—for dealing with the full range of subconscious as well as conscious, affective as well as rational modes of understanding—was closely connected with Wood's search for a more subtle interpretation of connections between belief and behavior—that is, of human motivation.

If we are to understand the Revolution, Wood explained, we must transcend the colonists' stated intentions and recognize that "the purposes of men, especially in a revolution, are so numerous, so varied, and so contradictory that their complex interaction produces results that no one intended or could even foresee." Historical explanation that "relies simply on understanding the conscious intentions of the actors," he argued, is severely limited. Instead, historians must recognize that "men act not simply in response to some kind of objective reality but to the meaning they give to that reality," a meaning that is shaped by a wide range of beliefs, values, fears, and predispositions—exactly the stuff of which political cultures are made.

Finally, Wood argued that in order to understand the language of a political culture and grasp its meaning, the analyst must locate the culture in its social, economic, and political environment, for culture is shaped by, as well as gives shape to, human experience. Thus the "frenzied rhetoric" of Revolutionary political culture "reveals as nothing else apparently can the American Revolution as a true revolution with its sources lying deep in the social structure." It was "the natural, even the inevitable, expression of a people caught up in a revolutionary situation . . . and . . . involved in a basic reconstruction of their political and social order."[2]

Wood took his own invocations seriously in the major work upon which he was already well embarked. One of *Creation's* most impressive strengths is the skill with which it weaves together themes of Anglo-American constitutionalism and the powerful, emotive assumptions about power, equality, virtue, and historical change that derived from the English dissenting tradition and fed directly into Revolutionary republicanism. Wood proved sensitive as well to the indeterminacy of political and constitutional debate, to inconsistencies of thought, confusions of intention, and the difficult, drawn-out processes of intellectual clarification. While tracing the evolving complexities of constitutional argumentation, Wood made wonderfully clear the ways in which constitutionalism was grounded in and shaped by political culture.

As rich as his conception of political culture is, however, it can be seen, when viewed from the historiographical perspective of our own time, as lacking two essential components. The first is American religious belief. The connections between religion and politics in Revolutionary America are difficult to unravel, as a sizable and disputatious body of scholarship reveals. Yet taken together, the works of Sacvan Bercovitch and Rhys Isaac, Alan Heimert and William G. McLoughlin, Harry S. Stout and Catherine L. Albanese, among others, make clear the intimate and powerful connections between religious and political belief. One cannot, for example, fully grasp the Revolutionary genera-

---

[2]Gordon S. Wood, "Rhetoric and Reality in the American Revolution," *William and Mary Quarterly*, 3d Ser., XXIII (1966), 16, 19, 26–27.

tion's understanding of equality, human liberty, or America's historic mission without taking religious beliefs into account, whether they were expressed within the covenant structure or by Baptists and other dissenting enthusiasts. Nor can one adequately explain the spread of Revolutionary doctrine or the force of political commitment among the American people without considering the mobilizing power of religion.[3]

At several points Wood acknowledges the place of religion (he terms it scripture) along with history and Enlightenment rationalism in "the Whig science of politics" (p.3). But the Revolutionary generation, he asserts, turned above all to secular rationalism and its promise of access to the "scientific" principles of social and political behavior. Perhaps so; no doubt Wood's preoccupation with constitutional debate encouraged that conclusion. Yet his broader concern with political culture, it now seems clear, should have generated a more careful examination of the connections between religious and political/constitutional thought.

Recent work by Joyce Appleby and Drew R. McCoy calls attention to another important dimension of Revolutionary political culture— what Appleby and McCoy refer to as political economy—that is largely missing from Wood's analysis.[4] Wood discusses at length the Revolutionary generation's fascination with the interdependence of the economic, social, moral, and political orders. He understates, however, the importance to eighteenth-century Americans of economic arrangements in shaping the essential character of a republic, as well as the extent to which government was viewed as an instrument for fashioning a republican socioeconomic order.

This is especially surprising because Wood is fully aware of how large the linked themes of commercialism, wealth, debt, dependence, luxury, and political corruption loomed in the dissenting tradition's critique of England. When he turns to the analysis of Revolutionary republicanism, however, he focuses attention on constitutional issues and loses sight of the fact that conflicting responses to the accelerating commercialism of the American economy shaped much of the argu-

---

[3]Bercovitch, *The American Jeremiad* (Madison, Wis., 1978); Isaac, *The Transformation of Virginia, 1740–1790* (Chapel Hill, N.C., 1982); Heimert, *Religion and the American Mind: From the Great Awakening to the Revolution* (Cambridge, Mass., 1966); McLoughlin, *New England Dissent, 1630–1833: The Baptists and the Separation of Church and State* (Cambridge, Mass., 1971); Stout, "Religion, Communications, and the Ideological Origins of the American Revolution." *WMQ.* 3d Ser., XXXIV (1977), 519–541; Albanese, *Sons of the Founders: The Civil Religion of the American Revolution* (Philadelphia, 1976).

[4]Appleby, "The Social Origins of American Revolutionary Ideology," *Journal of American History,* LXIV (1978), 935–958, and *Capitalism and a New Social Order: The Republican Vision of the 1790s* (New York, 1984); McCoy, *The Elusive Republic: Political Economy in Jeffersonian America* (Chapel Hill, N.C., 1980).

ment over constitutional structures, governmental power, and the meaning of republican liberty.

This becomes most evident in Wood's discussion of the political crisis of the 1780s, the drive for a stronger national government, and the Constitution. Though one learns in part four that issues such as debt relief, paper money, tax policy, and commercial development kept state politics in an uproar during the 1780s, Wood fails to explain that those issues were so volatile, first, because of the economic and social turmoil generated by revolution and war, and, second, because they brought to a focus sharply conflicting social visions and theories of political economy. Recent works such as David P. Szatmary's study of Shays's Rebellion, Ronald Hoffman's book on Revolutionary politics in Maryland, and Edward Countryman's study of New York reveal how closely tax, price control, and monetary policies were tied not only to clashing economic interests but to different visions of what republican society and government should be.[5]

In part five Wood offers a vivid comparison of the contrasting political philosophies of Federalists and Antifederalists—the Antifederalists harkening back to a locally based, democratic polity guided by the principles of 1776; the Federalists reaching forward to a new, energetic, elite-led national government capable of fashioning an expanding republican empire. In reading Wood's analysis, however, one is struck again by how little attention he gives to Federalists' and Antifederalists' notions of political economy, their sharply conflicting attitudes toward manufacturing and commerce, credit and wealth, and their views of the government's role in national development.

A careful rereading of *Creation* raises questions as well about Wood's handling of two other thorny and closely related problems of historical interpretation: the connections between political culture and its socioeconomic context, and the sources of cultural change.

One of the book's major strengths is its remarkably effective rhetorical structure. Part one offers a clear point of departure via a description of "The Ideology of Revolution," a body of thought fixed in colonial minds well before 1776 and ultimately responsible for persuading Americans that England was bent on enslaving them and that Independence was their only recourse. Parts two through four, which form the heart of the book, deal with the processes of historical change that transformed this ideology into republican utopianism, which, during the decade following Independence, was in turn debated, clarified, applied to the tasks of constitution making, evaluated against the chang-

---

[5]Szatmary, *Shays' Rebellion: The Making of an Agrarian Insurrection* (Amherst, Mass., 1980); Hoffman, *A Spirit of Dissension: Economics, Politics, and the Revolution in Maryland* (Baltimore, 1973); Countryman, *A People in Revolution: The American Revolution and Political Society in New York, 1760–1790* (Baltimore, 1981).

ing realities of Revolutionary life, and ultimately transmuted into the distinctive federalist republicanism of 1786–1787. That "fundamental transformation of political culture" into an "entirely new conception of politics" that took the American people "out of an essentially classical and medieval world of political discussion into one that was recognizably modern" constitutes Wood's main story (p. viii). In parts five and six these processes of historical change find resolution in a new cultural paradigm that Wood titles the "federalist persuasion," an ideology once again fixed and stable, ready to guide national development.

The book's design is rhetorically effective because it provides both dramatic tension and cathartic resolution. At the same time, it gives an exaggerated impression of ideological fixedness at both ends of the Revolution, as if at these two moments consensus had been reached and all essential questions answered. One need only consider the violent philosophical debates of the 1790s to realize that such was not the case. Of greater concern is Wood's treatment of the process of cultural change between 1776 and 1787, for his explanation of that fundamental transformation remains unclear.

Wood addresses the issue head on, explaining in the preface that the transformation of republican ideology resulted from "the strongest kinds of polemical and experiential pressures" (p. viii). By that he means both the relentless, clarifying logic of constitutional debate and the reciprocal encounter between political culture and its rapidly changing environment. Fair enough, for surely both were at work. The problem is that by book's end Wood has told us a great deal about constitutional argumentation but surprisingly little about the interactions between republican political culture and its socioeconomic and political contexts. In a sense, the book's greatest strength, its interior analysis of republican political culture, is also its greatest liability, for Wood ties his discussion of that culture only loosely to the economic, social, and political revolutions of which it was a part.

We are told in part one, for example, that the "opposition" or "country" view of politics exerted such a powerful influence in late colonial America because of "widespread anger and frustration with the way the relationships of power and esteem seemed to be crystallizing" (p. 79), yet the sources and extent of those social and political tensions are not explored. At one point, Wood acknowledges his lack of clarity on the matter with the blunt statement: "Whatever the social reality prior to the Revolution may have been . . ." (ibid.).

Again, we read in chapters two and six about the explosive debates between Republicans and Constitutionalists in Pennsylvania over political equality and the appropriate design of state government, and Wood tells us that those debates reflected deep-seated social conflict. "Nowhere else," he writes, "was there more social antagonism expressed during the Revolution" (p. 84). He offers little more by way of explanation, however, than a vague reference to "the new men . . . socially outside the establishment" who now challenged the old whig elite for control (p. 85). Nowhere does he undertake the kind of social and economic analysis of political divisions that, for example, Eric Foner offers in his book on *Tom Paine and Revolutionary America*.[6]

Even more jarring is Wood's treatment of Federalist and Antifederalist politics in *Creation's* closing chapters, for though he develops a surprisingly Progressive-like interpretation of the Constitution, he offers only the most rudimentary explanation of the socioeconomic bases of Federalist and Antifederalist political support. Federalism, he explains, represented "the profoundest disillusionment with the great hopes of . . . 1776," a "conservative" movement mounted, in Federalist minds, to protect "the worthy against the licentious" (pp. 472, 475). Which elements of American political society responded to this conservative agenda, or to the other agendas addressed by the Constitution (for example, commercial expansion), is never made clear.

One can hardly fault Wood, of course, for not having written comprehensive social and political histories of the Revolution before undertaking his own work. As *Creation* stands, it is herculean enough! At the same time, it is important to note the difficulties Wood has in unraveling the ties between culture and its environment, explaining the causes of cultural change, and detailing the role of culture in guiding political behavior, because those are the analytical problems he set out to explore. Nor can Wood be held accountable for work produced after his own. Such work, however, provides the essential perspective by which we can judge the continuing importance of what he has done.

Where then does *Creation of the American Republic* stand today in the historiography of the Revolution? Though less dominant than before, its place remains secure as one of a handful of works demanding the attention of anyone seeking to know what the American Revolution was about. To have survived the shifting historiographical tides so long—and serve as the focus of a symposium such as the one in which this essay appears—attests to its remarkable strength. Every historian dreams of someday producing her or his "great book." Gordon Wood is one of the precious few who has turned that dream into reality.

----

[6]Foner, *Tom Paine* (New York, 1976).

☆6☆

The Federal Era

HAMILTONIAN OR JEFFERSONIAN?

The federal era—1789 to 1829—forms a distinct period in American history. It is preceded and followed by periods that are strikingly different: the period prior to the introduction of the federal Constitution in 1789 has a coherence all of its own; the years after 1829 mark the emergence of the Jacksonian movement. In the four decades after the framing of the new Constitution Americans set up a functioning federal system, organized their first political parties, and laid the foundations of their foreign policy for years to come. The federal era thus represents one of the most important periods in our nation's history.

Historians have been so impressed by these formative influences that some of them in the first half of the twentieth century attributed to the federal era an even greater significance by viewing it as a microcosm for all of American history. To certain historians the political battle between Hamilton and Jefferson in the 1790s marked the beginning of an ideological and political split that shaped the entire future course of the country. These scholars tended to view the rest of American history in terms of a Hamiltonian-Jeffersonian dichotomy and went to the federal era to discover the origins of America's development as a nation.

To those who saw American history in this context, Hamilton and Jefferson symbolized a clash of conflicting principles at work in the country during this era. These historians interpreted the period as a struggle between aristocracy and democracy, industrialism versus agrarianism, and the supremacy of the national government as opposed to the ideas of states' rights. In the area of foreign policy they saw a similar polarity. There was general agreement among the parties and men of the period that America's foreign policy should result in a free and independent nation isolated in so far as possible from the affairs of Europe. The two protagonists were pictured as advocating different means of reaching the same ends—Hamilton being pro-British and Jefferson pro-French.

In this kind of interpretation the Federalist party of Hamilton was presented as being the party of the aristocratic and conservative forces in American society. Composed of the rich and well-born it was headed by men of property who had no wish to yield political power to the lower classes. During the administrations of Washington and of John Adams the Federalists set up a strong, centralized government which favored their own economic interests in commerce, finance, and industry and attempted to perpetuate a social and political system that was fundamentally undemocratic. The Federalists supposedly took a pro-British stand in foreign policy because they were in sympathy with Britain's ideas about class distinctions and her system of government. Although the Federalists were defeated in 1800, according to this interpretation, their influence continued well beyond this date. Federalist ideas were enacted into legislation by Jeffersonian Republican presidents who changed their point of view and endorsed programs for a protective tariff, a Bank of the United States, and American manufactures. Federalist doctrines were espoused in the Supreme Court by John Marshall, who presided over that body until the 1830s.

Conversely, the Jeffersonian Republican party was represented as being the party of the common people and of democracy. Made up of small farmers and led by Thomas Jefferson and James Madison the party presumably was devoted to keeping America an agrarian paradise. Being suspicious of big government and big business it stood for states' rights and the interests of the farming class. Since party members favored the idea of an egalitarian society they were sympathetic to the French Revolution and generally pro-French in foreign policy. When the Federalists pressed their antidemocratic tendencies too far in the Alien and Sedition Acts of 1798, this interpretation continued, the small farmer class rose up in wrath and voted them out of office in what has been called the "Revolution of 1800."

Thus this early twentieth-century interpretation viewed all American history as a continuous struggle between the democratic aspirations of the common people and the despotism of the upper classes. The Hamiltonian-Jeffersonian dichotomy was projected down through the rest of the nation's history. The Jeffersonian Republicans were looked upon as being the forebears of the democratic spirit—giving rise to the Jacksonian Democrats, Populists, Progressives, and New Dealers of a later day. The Federalists, on the other hand, were considered to be the progenitors of the antidemocratic forces—making way for the Whig party of the pre–Civil War period and the Republican party of the post–Civil War era.

This interpretation of the federal era, however, has not always been accepted. Other interpretations were also advanced at various times

as historians continued their never-ending evaluation of the course of American history. Generally speaking, historians have tended to view the federal era in terms of their own time and to reflect their personal beliefs when writing about the parties and personalities of the period. Despite their claims to the contrary scholars have not always been impartial in their evaluations of the era; if they took a pro-Hamiltonian position they were usually hostile to Jefferson; if, on the other hand, they favored a Jeffersonian stand they characteristically were antagonistic to Hamilton.

Throughout most of the nineteenth century the majority of American historians who wrote about the federal era did so within the context of a Hamiltonian-Jeffersonian split. Most of the historical writing in that century, indeed, was overwhelmingly political in tone. Scholars paid particular attention to national politics and political parties as a means of explaining the major trends in American life. It is safe to say that a far greater number of American historians took what might be described as a Federalist-Whig-Republican point of view toward the federal era than did those who took a Jeffersonian-Jacksonian-Democratic outlook.

The predominantly Federalist-Whig interpretation, for example, was readily evident in the work of Richard Hildreth—a Massachusetts Whig, historian, and journalist. In his six-volume *History of the United States*, published between 1849 and 1852, Hildreth dealt with American history down to the conclusion of the Missouri Compromise crisis in 1821. His work was friendly toward the Federalists, and he had high praise for Hamilton as the leader of the party and a man "possessed of practical talents of the highest orders."[1] Hamilton's wisdom, wrote Hildreth, resulted from his recognition that the greatest threat to the republic lay in the resistance of the state governments to federal power. Much of Hamilton's program, therefore, was directed toward strengthening the central government. Support for Hamilton's measures came from America's "natural aristocracy" comprised of judges, lawyers, clergymen, large landowners, merchants, and manufacturers. In the area of foreign affairs, as might be expected, Hildreth's sympathies lay with the Federalists and a pro-English policy.

Hildreth's history was anti-Jeffersonian in its outlook, but probably more for philosophical reasons than for narrowly partisan ones. A believer in the ideas of Jeremy Bentham—the English philosopher who propounded the concept of utilitarianism—Hildreth sought to apply such ideas in the writing of his history. Jefferson's predilection for theories did not fit into Hildreth's preconceived liberal utilitarian point of view and for this reason the historian was critical of him. As one

---

[1]Richard Hildreth, *The History of the United States of America . . . 1788-1821,* 6 vols. (rev. ed., New York, 1875), 4:296.

recent scholar has observed, Hildreth's "temperamental preference for experience over theory," his New England background and training, and his utilitarianism, caused him to prefer Hamilton's practical achievements to Jefferson's theories.[2]

The coming of the Civil War simply reinforced the prevailing Hamiltonian point of view. Hamilton's place in history was made more secure by the outcome of events. To many historians the war appeared to vindicate Hamilton's position as an exemplar of national power. If Hamilton's plan for an even stronger central government had not been rejected in the federal Constitutional Convention of 1787, some scholars insisted, the Union might have been spared the bloody ordeal of civil strife in the 1860s. Jefferson's reputation, on the other hand, declined sharply because his advocacy of states' rights seemed to place him in the same camp as the defeated South. Moreover, the Democratic party was in disrepute in this period because of its close identification with the Southern cause; as one of the founders of that party, Jefferson's position in American history suffered accordingly.

Hamilton's reputation was raised still higher in the postwar period as the emerging Republican party proclaimed him one of its prophets. Devoted to the idea of building an industrial America, many Republicans maintained that Hamilton had anticipated the economic principles to which they were dedicated. Was it not Hamilton, they asked, who was the sole statesman of his time to prophesy the future destiny of America as a great industrial nation? Republicans advocating a sound money system and a high protective tariff as necessary attributes for industrial growth pointed to Hamilton's program as their model. From the end of the Civil War to the close of the nineteenth century the Hamiltonian tradition supplied the rhetoric and arguments employed by the Republican party and the rising industrial order. Generally speaking, historians tended to reflect this same point of view in their writings.

Jefferson's reputation by way of contrast continued to decline during the post–Civil War period. The majority of American historians of the time took an anti-Jeffersonian stand when writing about the federal era. Hermann E. Von Holst, a German-trained scholar who came to America to write his multivolume *Constitutional and Political History of the United States*, published between 1876 and 1892, took a hostile view of Jefferson. John T. Morse, a Boston lawyer who wrote and edited biographical sketches known as the American Statesmen series, showed a similar bias in his writing and choice of authors. His two-volume biography of Hamilton published in 1876 was highly critical of Jefferson and lauded Hamilton. In categorizing the American his-

---

[2]Arthur M. Schlesinger, Jr., "The Problem of Richard Hildreth," *New England Quarterly* 13 (June 1940):233–245.

torians who dealt with Jefferson during the last quarter of the nineteenth century one recent scholar has remarked: "The dominant theme of these historians was the *Union*. Most of them were New Englanders, may were influenced by Germans such as Holst, nearly all were Republicans. With marked exceptions such as Henry Adams and the lesser known James Schouler, whose seven-volume political history was nationalistic without enmity to Jefferson, their works were vehemently antiJeffersonian."[3]

The outstanding exception to this hostile trend in Jeffersonian historiography was the brilliant study of the great American historian Henry Adams. His nine-volume *The History of the United States during the Administrations of Jefferson and Madison*, published between 1889 and 1891, remains one of the masterpieces of American historical literature. What Adams did was to shift his focus from the period when the Federalist party was in power to a point in time—1800—when the Jeffersonians were in control. Since the Federalists were on the decline from that date on, Adams was able to pay less attention to the conflict between political parties and to concentrate instead upon other important developments. To Adams two main themes dominated the sixteen-year span when Jefferson and Madison were in office: the rise of nationalism, and the development of American democracy.

Even Adams's *History*, however, did not make Jefferson a heroic figure. The work established beyond any doubt the crucial contribution of Jefferson and his administration in developing an American national consciousness and in fixing the direction that American democracy was to take. But at the same time Adams made it clear that the course of events during the administration was not due to any philosophical design on the part of Jefferson. Time and again, Adams demonstrated, Jefferson was forced to deviate from his theories and to temper his doctrines when faced with the realities of governmental power. Adams delighted in showing the inconsistencies between Jefferson the theorist and Jefferson the pragmatist. In the final analysis, however, he failed to solve the enigma of Jefferson; scholars argue to this day whether Adams's *History* is pro- or anti-Jeffersonian.[4]

In many ways Adams was a transitional figure among the American historians who wrote about the federal era. Instead of approaching his subject in the traditional nineteenth-century manner of narrative history, Adams was impressed with the idea of a scientific philosophy of history and sought to apply concepts borrowed from physics and biology as the key to historical developments. Unlike many earlier writers who were amateur gentlemen-historians, he was a professional

---

[3]Merrill D. Peterson, *The Jeffersonian Image in the American Mind* (New York, 1962), p. 279.

[4]*Ibid.*, pp. 281–291.

scholar who taught medieval and American history at Harvard for a number of years. Contrary to the prevailing view among historians which favored the Federalists, Adams was openly hostile to that party; he considered the Federalist leaders to be conservative and decadent figures in an American society that was essentially dynamic and democratic.

The real turning point in the treatment of the federal era, however, came just after Adams had completed his magnum opus at the close of the nineteenth century. With the rise of the Populist and Progressive movements in the 1890s and early 1900s the whole climate of opinion in America underwent a dramatic change. The currents of reform sweeping the country affected America's social and political thought and historians suddenly became more sympathetic to Jefferson's liberal ideas. Scholars increasingly began to pay more attention to the democratic tradition in American history and Jefferson came into his own. For the first time the majority of historians began writing about the American past from a Jeffersonian-Jacksonian-Democratic rather than a Federalist-Whig-Republican point of view.

During the first three decades of the twentieth century a trio of writers from the Progressive school of historians—Charles A. Beard, Claude G. Bowers, and Vernon L. Parrington—showed a keen interest in Jefferson and his place in American history. All three proceeded to rewrite the history of the federal era from the vantage point of Jeffersonian democracy. Viewed in broad terms this triumvirate had certain distinguishing characteristics. They all hailed from the Middle West and believed in the Progressive ideas prevalent in that part of the country. Between them they helped to break the hold of New Englanders over Jeffersonian historiography. They were influenced also by the new intellectual orientation sweeping scholarly circles called the "new history." Advocates of the "new history" were arguing that in the past history had been used by conservative elements in the United States to provide a rationale for maintaining the status quo. The Progressive scholars wanted to use history instead as an instrument of progress to recast the future of the country along more liberal lines. In short, the proponents of the "new history" wanted to employ history as a kind of intellectual weapon to bring about political changes and reforms. Finally, both Beard and Parrington were greatly influenced by the ideas of economic determinism that were becoming increasingly popular in the historical profession at this time.

Charles A. Beard's *Economic Origins of Jeffersonian Democracy*, the first work of these three men on the subject to appear, was published in 1915 and applied an economic interpretation of history to the federal era. Starting with his well-known hypothesis that the Constitution represented the work of a small group of capitalists who were intent upon establishing a strong central government to protect their property against the encroachments of the agrarian masses, Beard argued that the capitalist-agrarian split of the 1780s continued and was institutionalized by the formation of political parties in the 1790s. Those favoring the Constitution formed the agrarian base of the Republican party founded by Jefferson and other planter-aristocrats. Economic forces, in short, were the basis of party divisions in the period. Beard then went on to point out that, contrary to popular belief, the movement called Jeffersonian Democracy did not constitute an assault upon property or political privilege as such. It merely transferred political power from one socioeconomic group to another—the power shifted from the capitalist class to the agrarian masses. "Jeffersonian Democracy," wrote Beard, "simply meant the possession of the federal government by the agrarian masses led by an aristocracy of slave-owning planters, and the theoretical repudiation of the right to use the Government for the benefit of any capitalistic groups, fiscal, banking, or manufacturing."[5]

What were the consequences of this shift in political power, according to Beard? They were not as great, he claimed, as many Americans assumed. Beard, surprisingly enough, considered Jefferson something of a failure in this book. He noted that Jefferson as president made many concessions to the Federalists in his policies by perpetuating a number of aspects of the Hamiltonian economic system. Jefferson's mistrust of the "mobs of great cities" also resulted in a limitation of his democratic doctrine, Beard believed, because his plans failed to include the urban working classes. Moreover, Beard observed, Jefferson's ideas of political democracy did not differ greatly from those of the Federalists because he was just as anxious as they to guard against the "tyranny of majorities." Beard's book was actually something of a polemic addressed to his fellow Progressives and intended as a lesson in history from which they might draw a moral for their own day. He wanted to show them that Jefferson had not understood clearly the economic bases of politics and therefore had not gone far enough in supporting the forces of democracy against those of reaction and privilege.

Claude G. Bowers, whose *Jefferson and Hamilton: The Struggle for Democracy in America* was published a decade after Beard's book, took a much more positive approach to Jeffersonian Democracy. To Bowers the conflict between Jefferson and Hamilton symbolized a clear-cut fight between the forces of democracy and aristocracy to determine nothing less than the future destiny of the nation. Viewing the protagonists in this light, Bowers portrayed the fierce struggle waged by the two men during the first crucial decade under the new

---

[5]Charles A. Beard, *Economic Origins of Jeffersonian Democracy* (New York, 1915), p. 467

Constitution. In Bower's eyes Jefferson was not a theoretician but a master politician who succeeded in marshaling the popular forces in America against the entrenched Federalist opposition. America, as the result of Jefferson's triumph, escaped the terrible fate that lay in store had the aristocratic forces under Hamilton maintained their power.

Bowers, a journalist for a Democratic newspaper at the time, wrote his biography in a popular style and from a present-minded point of view. From a literary perspective the publication of his work was timely because it came on the eve of the centennial of Jefferson's death and the sesquicentennial of America's independence. But from a political viewpoint his work was even more appropriate. The Democratic party was in the doldrums after the Wilsonian era and had split into warring factions. By reviving the image of Jefferson as the founder of the party and presenting a Democratic interpretation of the federal era, Bowers provided the politicians of his own day with a rallying point. In 1928 Bowers was named as keynote speaker of the Democratic National Convention, and in eloquent phrases called upon his fellow Democrats to return to the principles of Jefferson. His writings and speeches on Jefferson helped to spark a revival of the Jeffersonian tradition in the popular imagination during the 1920s.

The climax in writing about Jefferson by the Progressive historians in the 1920s came with the publication of Vernon L. Parrington's three-volume *Main Currents in American Thought*. Parrington approached the nation's past in terms of intellectual history and looked upon American literature as the main form of expression employed by the nation's social and political thinkers. To Parrington the major current in American thought was the enduring dichotomy throughout the country's history between two rival political philosophies—the liberal and idealistic tradition of Jefferson and the conservative and materialistic one personified by Hamilton. Viewing all of American history in terms of a Jefferson-Hamilton dichotomy, Parrington proceeded to push his analogy backward into the colonial period and forward to the twentieth century. His overall view was that America's liberal tradition had been declining since Jefferson's day. But there was no question on which side his sympathies lay, for he admitted that his bias was "liberal rather than conservative, Jeffersonian rather than Federalistic."

Parrington believed that Jefferson symbolized a native American brand of liberalism that had arisen in the New World. American liberalism, as he saw it, was influenced by three separate strands of thought—French liberalism, English liberalism, and the democratizing influence of the frontier. French liberalism, or romantic and idealistic thought, resulted in egalitarianism; it rejected the Puritan idea of a degraded human nature and substituted instead the concept of man as a potentially perfectible being. English liberalism, or realistic and materialistic thought, looked upon human nature as being acquisitive; it called for a social and political philosophy to conform with capitalism rather than the rights of man. The American frontier, on the other hand, provided a free environment in which these often contradictory Old World philosophies could develop in a different way.

With the coming of the New Deal the Jeffersonian tradition had an even greater appeal to the popular imagination. The Democratic party made a conscious effort during the Great Depression of the 1930s to revive Jeffersonian slogans and symbols to show that the proposed programs for the New Deal were in the American tradition. Among other things the New Deal was pictured as a modern adaptation of long-standing Jeffersonian principles rather than any radical revision of the American system. Paradoxically, the opponents of the New Deal resorted to the same tradition for their arguments. They sought to show that Jeffersonianism in the past had defended liberty largely by abstaining from governmental restrictions and restraints.

The outbreak of World War II likewise proved a boon to the Jeffersonian tradition. In the struggle against totalitarianism there was a fight for men's minds, and democracy as a way of life became a faith to disseminate and defend. No other major American figure was better equipped to serve as a symbol of the democratic tradition than Jefferson, author of the Declaration of Independence. His ringing phrases were particularly relevant in the fight against totalitarianism being waged by the free world. Jefferson came into his own as never before as historians, journalists, and politicians sought to give renewed meaning to the liberal Jeffersonian tradition within an international as well as a national context.

In the immediate post–World War II era the Jeffersonian tradition continued its popularity, but unlike earlier periods in American history the trend this time did not result in a decline of the Hamiltonian tradition. The Hamiltonian revival in the post–Civil War period had ground to a halt with the coming of the Progressive era. Although it was true that a small segment of Progressive historians praised Hamilton for his bold use of powers of the central government to achieve constructive national goals, the predominant view among scholars in the first three decades of the twentieth century favored the Jeffersonian tradition. Hamilton's reputation sank to its lowest point during the depression of the 1930s as the Republican party fell into disfavor. But from the late 1930s on, Hamilton's reputation was on the rise.

One of the first signs of the shift in Hamilton's favor was the publication of two perceptive articles on him by Rexford Guy Tugwell and Joseph Dorfman in the *Columbia University Quarterly* of 1937 and 1938. Tugwell, a member of Roosevelt's "brain trust" in the early days of the New Deal, was a vigorous advocate of government planning for bringing about reforms in the economic and social sphere. After leaving his government post Tugwell coauthored two articles on Hamilton with Dorfman, a former colleague and professor of economics at Columbia University. In view of his recent experiences Tugwell showed an increased appreciation of Hamilton's unprecedented use of strong national governmental powers to build up the new nation in its early years.

Developments during the decade of the 1940s continued the trend of a more favorable attitude toward Hamilton by historians. The booming American economy during the wartime and postwar period, no doubt, helped to enhance Hamilton's reputation. With the mounting affluence of American society there was less tendency on the part of many historians to read an economic class conflict back into the American past, and Hamilton's economic program for shoring up the nation's economy in the 1790s and early 1800s came in for considerable praise in the immediate post–World War II period.

At the same time another side of Hamilton's career—his role as nation-maker—was being stressed anew. The decline of imperialism and the post–World War II settlement gave birth to a whole host of newly independent countries, and American historians came to view the problems involved in nation-building in a different perspective. There was a growing awareness of the great debt owed to Hamilton for helping to mold the foundations for a strong nation-state. Historians like Charles A. Beard, Louis M. Hacker, and Leonard D. White all touched upon Hamilton's contribution to statecraft in their writings in the 1940s.

The most important new tendency in the 1940s, however, was not the presentation of Hamilton in a more favorable light but rather the emergence of a more evenly balanced evaluation of the Hamiltonian-Jeffersonian dichotomy. This trend began with the approach taken by Richard Hofstadter in his book of essays entitled *The American Political Tradition and the Men Who Made It*, published in 1948. Hofstadter's essay on Jefferson deemphasized the differences between the two men and stressed instead the continuance of Hamilton's system under Jefferson as president. The beliefs that Hamiltonians and Jeffersonians had in common, concluded Hofstadter, proved to be a more powerful bond in uniting them than the specific political issues that were dividing the two groups.

Hofstadter's thesis was that much of America's political past had to be viewed in terms of consensus rather than conflict. In studying the ideology of leading American statesmen such as Jefferson and Hamilton, he became convinced that there was a pressing need for reinterpreting our political traditions within a new framework—one that emphasized a common climate of opinion in America. The tendency of earlier historians to place political conflict in the foreground of American history, he claimed, had obscured the common areas of

agreement among political leaders who were often pictured as antagonists. "However much at odds on specific issues," Hofstadter wrote,
"the major political traditions have shared a belief in the rights of property, the philosophy of economic individualism, the value of competition; they have accepted the economic virtues of capitalist culture as
necessary qualities of man."[6] The main theme of the federal era, according to Hofstadter, was the essential agreement between Jefferson and
Hamilton on these fundamental political traditions. This common
area of agreement set the stage for the assimilation of Jeffersonian Democracy into Hamiltonian capitalism that took place after the election
of 1800.

The consensus thesis characterized much of the writing on the federal era in the 1950s and 1960s. Louis Hartz, during the mid-1950s,
for example, identified the liberal tradition as being the one tradition
forming the common climate of opinion in America.[7] The clash of
principles attributed to Hamilton and Jefferson represented nothing
more than a sham battle, Hartz said, because such controversy took
place within the confines of a liberal society whose values were already agreed upon. There was no deep ideological split between the
two men, and the differences between them occurred within the Lockean liberal tradition which all Americans accepted.

Although a conscious "school" of consensus historians writing
about the federal era cannot be identified as such, there was a noticeable trend toward a more balanced assessment of the Hamiltonian-
Jeffersonian dichotomy among scholars in the post–World War II period. This tendency was evident in many general studies on the era.
Marcus Cunliffe, covering the years 1789–1837, warned readers not to
view the period solely in terms of a struggle between Hamiltonianism
and Jeffersonianism and stressed instead a number of other forces in
conflict—urban versus rural areas, nationalism versus sectionalism,
and conservatism versus experimentalism. A second general study, by
John C. Miller, dealing only with the period when the Federalist party
was in power—1789 to 1801—argued that out of the two extreme positions held by Hamiltonians and Jeffersonians there had emerged a
middle-of-the-road approach that served the nation well in future
years.[8]

This more balanced view was apparent also in many of the biographies written after World War II. Dumas Malone's multivolume work
on Jefferson, begun in the late 1940s, presented him in a more impar-

---

[6]Richard Hofstadter, *The American Political Tradition and the Men Who Made It*
(New York, 1948), p. viii.

[7]Louis Hartz, *The Liberal Tradition in America* (New York, 1955).

[8]Marcus F. Cunliffe, *The Nation Takes Shape, 1789–1837* (Chicago, 1959), and John
C. Miller, *The Federalist Era, 1789–1801* (New York, 1960).

tial light than earlier works and stressed the consistency of his thought. John Dos Passos and Nathan Schachner, who wrote studies and sketches of Jefferson in the 1950s, likewise avoided the pitfalls of violent partisanship in their writings.[9] Such portrayals led one Jeffersonian scholar, Merrill Peterson, to remark in the early 1960s that "Jefferson . . . appears less radical and more conservative, less theoretical and more practical, less universal and more national."[10] The one-volume biography of Hamilton by John C. Miller written in the late 1950s showed the same influence. Miller maintained that Hamilton's political thought was a curious blend of contradictions that made him more moderate than he was usually pictured.[11]

College textbooks published in the immediate post–World War II period reflected this same shift in emphasis. Some saw a line of continuity from Federalist to Jeffersonian presidents—there was no "Revolution of 1800" and the election represented a change of men, not measures. Other texts treated the federal era in terms of intellectual history, claiming that the ideas of Hamilton, Jefferson, Adams, and Madison were all derived from the same source: the Enlightenment. Hence these founding fathers were pictured as sharing almost the same political philosophy and differing only in particulars. Still others de-emphasized the Hamilton-Jefferson split by arguing that the clash of political extremes in the 1790s quickly gave way to a more moderate and middle-of-the-road approach. At any rate the trend was unmistakably moving away from the Hamiltonian-Jeffersonian dichotomy as an explanation of all American history.

During the three decades from the 1960s to 1990, however, the federal era was destined to undergo massive historiographical changes when the profession as a whole experienced a great age of reinterpretation. The "new social history" that appeared in the 1960s, for one thing, introduced significant changes. It turned attention away from great men like Hamilton and Jefferson and the practice of studying presidential administrations; it analyzed instead American society and culture as a whole or else examined the lives or ordinary citizens. The "new social historians" challenged the assumptions and conclusions of both the Progressives and neoconservatives. They did so by addressing totally different questions or by resorting to new research strategies and techniques. One category of "new social historians"—the "new political historians"—focused upon the bases of political parties and social origins of those who joined them. Another, the "new intel-

---

[9]Dumas Malone, *Jefferson and His Time*, 6 vols. (Boston, 1948–1981); John Dos Passos, *The Men Who Made the Nation* (New York, 1957); and Nathan Schachner, *Thomas Jefferson: A Biography*, 2 vols. (New York, 1951).

[10]Peterson, *Jeffersonian Image in the American Mind*, p. 450.

[11]John C. Miller, *Alexander Hamilton: Portrait in Paradox* (New York, 1959).

lectual historians" examined the ideas related to the political culture of the new republic, many of them doing so within the framework of the republican synthesis discussed in earlier chapters. A third, the "new cultural historians," took up cultural changes in the mores, attitudes, and behavior of Americans living through the federal era. At the same time, scholars employing more traditional approaches, like comparative history, continued to write about the period.

The older Progressive interpretation, it will be recalled, tended to picture the origins and development of political parties in polarized terms. Parties presumably waged intense battles which pitted antithetical forces in society against one another. Within this oversimplified dichotomous view the following forces were seen as arrayed against one another: upper versus lower classes; fluid capital versus landed agrarian interests; urban versus rural groups; creditors versus debtors; aristocrats versus democrats; and Westerners versus Easterners. Charles Beard, for example, had pictured the struggle of the 1790s as being between two interest groups; fluid capital and agrarian interests. These two groups, according to Beard, had clashed in the Constitutional Convention in the 1780s and continued to struggle in the party battles in the decade that followed. The overall tendency of the new approaches used from the 1960s to the 1990s was to demonstrate that American political parties did not represent such polarities; they reflected instead pluralistic interests of a broad cross section of society. Older generalizations based upon class, sectional, and ideological differences were showed to be inaccurate in numerous revisionist studies.

The most important challenge to the older interpretation came from the "new political historians." Like many contemporary scholars, the "new political historians" drew heavily upon the social sciences for both their methods and theories. They were prepared to introduce more quantification and greater methodological rigor in their work. Certain "new political historians" made a great effort, for example, to formulate more precise definitions of such terms as "political party" and "party system." In general their work tended to be more empirical in nature; and they often utilized case studies to examine in detail the workings of a political party within a state, country, or community. The perspective of these scholars reflected the influence of the behavioral approach to politics—an approach begun by political scientists like Charles Merriam in the pre-World War II period—which gained favor among historians as a result of more interdisciplinary studies done in the late 1940s and the decades beyond.

To achieve greater precision in their findings, some of these historians resorted to new quantitative techniques. Noble Cunningham used roll-call analyses, for example, to pinpoint the time when political parties first appeared within the Congress. Two articles—one by H.

James Henderson and the other by Mary P. Ryan—employed even more sophisticated quantitative methods to identify voting blocs in the first Congresses. They concluded that it was probably in the third Congress that sectional voting blocs were transformed into a two-bloc system covering a broad spectrum of issues. Rudolph M. Bell also made great use of computers to write the most comprehensive study of voting patterns within the congresses of the 1790s.[12]

The "new political historians," for the most part, rejected the consensus interpretation of the neoconservatives; they held that the early national period was characterized by conflict. At the same time, however, they disagreed with the older Progressive interpretation over the bases of that conflict. They took issue with the Beardian view that the politics of the era was a clear-cut struggle between agrarian Antifederalists, who had opposed the Constitution, and a coalition of merchants, planters, and security-holders, who had favored it. In their search for the causes of conflict the "new political historians" examined numerous economic and political groups on the local level and concluded that existing differences were based not on narrow economic grounds but rather upon broad symbolic social issues. They deemphasized sectional and economic sources of conflict and stressed instead ethnocultural considerations—racial, ethnic, and religious ties—as well as ideological commitments and localized concerns.

Some "new political historians" held that many conflicts arose from underlying ethnocultural antagonisms between social groups. Ethnic groups were aligned against each other, members of one religion were opposed to those of a different faith, and even groups with differing cultural traditions—in terms of their attitudes toward the Sabbath, drinking, and marriage customs—were pitted against one another. Such hatreds and feuds persisted over time, aroused group consciousness, and often determined the way people voted. Lee Benson, one of the early advocates of this behavioral approach to political history, for example, reexamined some of Beard's conclusions in such terms. He analyzed voting patterns in New York and offered as a possible alternative explanation a kind of localist-cosmopolitan interpretation based on ethnic and religious differences. Benson's conclusions suggested that ethnocultural considerations were probably more important than the economic forces Beard had stressed. Generally speaking the most

---

[12]Noble Cunningham, Jr., *The Jeffersonian Republicans: The Formation of Party Organization, 1789–1801* (Chapel Hill, 1957), and *The Jeffersonians in Power, 1801-1809* (Chapel Hill, 1963). H. James Henderson, "Quantitative Approaches to Party Formation in the United States Congress," *William and Mary Quarterly*, 3d ser. 30 (1973):307–324; Mary P. Ryan, "Party Formation in the United States Congress 1789 to 1796: A Quantitative Analysis," *ibid.*, 28 (1971):523–542; and Rudolph M. Bell, *Party Faction in American Politics* (Westport, Conn., 1973). See also John F. Hoadley, *Origins of American Political Parties, 1789–1803* (Lexington, Ky., 1986).

important conclusion of the "new political historians" was that conflict in the early national period reflected a more complex set of issues that precluded Beard's simplistic polarities.[13]

One major question addressed by the "new political historians" concerned the origin and development of political parties. Beard's *Economic Origins of Jeffersonian Democracy* had set the stage for such a debate; he claimed that the battle between Federalists and Republicans in the 1800 election was nothing more than a continuation of the alignment of Federalist and Antifederalist forces that had appeared during the struggle over the Constitution in 1787. Joseph Charles, in a book published in the 1950s, challenged the idea of party continuity. He concluded that parties had not originated in the fight over Hamilton's financial program, as many Beardian scholars had supposed, but in differences over foreign policy such as the Jay treaty of 1795. Other historians, such as Noble Cunningham and Paul Goodman, also claimed that there was a break in continuity because political groups were realigned in the 1790s as new issues arose. In doing so, they dismantled much of the Beardian interpretation.[14]

Another question these scholars argued was whether political parties had been formed from the bottom up or the top down. Noble Cunningham advanced the hypothesis that factions—a more primitive form of political organization—had developed into parties within the Congress and inside Washington's cabinet. Then, like a stone thrown into a pool, these parties radiated outward in waves from the capital into the states in 1794–1795. Leaders in the nation's capital, through the use of party organization and machinery, were able to link up with local elites and to create parties that eventually became truly national in scope.[15]

---

[13]Lee Benson, *Turner and Beard: American Historical Writing Reconsidered* (Glencoe, Ill., 1960). For a sweeping interpretation of American political history from an important ethnocultural perspective, which touches upon this period, see Robert Kelley, "Ideology and Political Culture from Jefferson to Nixon," *American Historical Review* 82 (1977):531–582.

[14]Beard, *Economic Origins of Jeffersonian Democracy*, and Joseph Charles, *Origins of the American Party System* (Williamsburg, Va., 1956). Alfred Young, *Democratic Republicans of New York* (Chapel Hill, 1967); and Norman K. Risjord, "The Evolution of Political Parties in Virginia, 1782–1800," *Journal of American History* 60 (1974):961–984, agree with Beard that there was continuity in the groups who lined up for and against the Constitution and those who became Federalists and Jeffersonians. Noble Cunningham, in his *Jeffersonian Republicans: The Formation of Party Organization, 1789–1801*, and Paul Goodman, *Democratic-Republicans of Massachusetts* (Cambridge, Mass., 1964) argue that there was a break in continuity because political groups realigned themselves in the 1790s as new sets of issues appeared on the scene. This discussion of party development which follows draws heavily on the article by Ronald P. Formisano, "Differential-Participant Politics: The Early Republic's Political Culture, 1789–1840," *American Political Science Review* 68 (1974):473–487.

[15]Cunningham, *The Jeffersonian Republicans: The Formation of Party Organization, 1789–1801*. See also, Manning Dauer, *The Adams Federalists* (2d ed., Baltimore, 1953).

Even as Cunningham's interpretation was being accepted in many quarters, two case studies appeared that showed localism was a very powerful determinant in political party development in Massachusetts and New York. Both studies underscored the fact that parties had arisen in response to local conditions and concerns. Implicit in these works was the assumption that the parties in these states had been formed from the bottom up rather than the top down.[16]

The two case studies—written by Paul Goodman and Alfred Young on the Democratic Republicans of Massachusetts and New York respectively—inquired also into the social backgrounds of party members. Goodman took issue with the Progressive view of polarized parties and concluded that "the social sources of parties were far more complex and less homogeneous than Beard suggested."[17] Massachusetts Republicans, he found, represented a heterogeneous coalition of far-flung interests that cut across the more conventional lines of sectional, economic, and occupational groupings. Included among the Republicans were rich and poor, land speculators and squatters, professional persons and artisans, and Deists and Calvinists. The one bond that united these diverse groups, however, was the widespread belief that persons long entrenched in positions of authority were blocking the advance of more capable people who were out of power. Thus the Massachusetts Republicans tended to attract newcomers, men on-the-make, and outsiders.

Young's book also inquired into the social sources of the Republican party in New York, and likewise discovered complex pluralistic forces at work. Young agreed with Beard, however, on one crucial point: there was considerable continuity between the New York Antifederalists and those who subsequently became Republicans in the 1790s, and that both reflected mainly the agrarian interests. Young proved, moreover, that there was an important urban wing to the Republican party located in New York City—one based primarily upon mechanics, or skilled workers. He went on to show that the Republicans succeeded precisely because they were the first to recognize the power of the common people and to take steps to mobilize that segment of the electorate.

David Hackett Fischer, another "new political historian," challenged the Beardian interpretation of politics in the early national period from a different perspective. Fischer produced the most important book on the Federalists in the 1960s. Focusing on Federalists in the years 1800 to 1816 he concluded that these conservatives had undergone a great generational change during the period. Conservative Fed-

---

[16]Goodman, *Democratic-Republicans of Massachusetts,* and Young, *Democratic Republicans of New York.*

[17]Goodman, *Democratic-Republicans of Massachusetts,* p. xi.

eralist leaders experienced a revolution in attitudes and beliefs before and after the election of 1800. Before 1800 Federalist leaders had been members of the "Old School"—those who had supported the movement for American independence, subscribed firmly to the idea of deference, and insisted upon "standing" for office. After the defeat of 1800 these leaders were replaced by "young Federalists" who revolutionized the party. The younger Federalists proved to be more flexible in their political principles. They were willing to suppress their preference for a deferential society, to "run" for office, and to borrow the political tactics of their Jeffersonian opponents in organizing and seeking votes from the masses. Fischer's study, like those of Goodman and Young, sought also to identify the social sources that affected the composition of the political parties in the new nation.[18]

One "new political historian" presented a broad-ranging synthesis in 1983 that broke through the traditional chronological boundaries of the federal era and linked this period to political party developments later in the nineteenth century. Ronald P. Formisano's *The Transformation of Political Culture* dealt with the history of the political culture of Massachusetts from the 1790s to the 1840s. His case study evaluated the degree to which the nation's early parties contributed to democracy in the Bay State and by implication to other parts of the country.

Formisano's work presented three important and provocative contributions to the historiography of politics in antebellum America. He rejected, first of all, the first party system thesis held by many scholars. Formisano argued that the Federalists and Republicans in the 1790s and early 1800s were too rudimentary and immature to constitute a full-fledged party system. It was not until the 1830s, with the emergence of mass parties—the Whigs and Democrats with their more professional politicians and permanent party institutions—that America had a genuine two-party system. Second, Formisano found that traditional forms of political influence persisted well into the period of Whig and Democratic party formation, thereby casting doubt on hypotheses which asserted that political modernization had taken place during the early years of the republic. Third, Formisano pointed to the importance of what he called "the Politics of the Revolutionary Center." This was the practice among many political figures who had played a role in the Revolution to appeal to the myths and principles of that event as a touchstone of unity—a practice which helped to keep politics on a centrist course and to sustain antiparty attitudes.

To evaluate the degree to which America's early parties contributed to democracy in Massachusetts and elsewhere, Formisano re-

[18]David Hackett Fischer, *The Revolution of American Conservatism* (New York, 1965).

sorted also to comparative history. Compared with parties in other countries, he argued, Massachusetts parties were open, kept close ties with the electorate, and provided the public with a strong sense of political involvement. But judged on their own terms, Formisano concluded, Massachusetts parties failed to offer meaningful policy choices to the electorate. Formisano believed that it was through third parties or populist movements—the Anti-Masons, Workingmen's parties, and Know-Nothings who brought up controversial issues like slavery and labor's working hours—that the cause of democracy was best sustained and invigorated during the 1830s, 1840s, and 1850s. Formisano's study constituted an important landmark: his challenge to the first party synthesis of the 1790s, emphasis on the continuing role the Revolution played in early national politics, and stress on the concept of political culture all broke new ground in the historiography of the federal era.

Ralph Ketcham, like Formisano, presented a broad synthesis and rejected the concept of a first party system in the 1790s. His *Presidents above Party* (1984) dealt with the first six men who held that office during the federal era—Washington, John Adams, Jefferson, Madison, Monroe, and John Quincy Adams. All six took a nonpartisan view of the presidency, Ketcham claimed. They believed in a strong activist executive, but one who would hold a vision of the common good and would remain above partisan factionalism. Despite the divisive issues, partisan struggles, and primitive political party formations facing them, they succeeded in keeping faith with their philosophy while in office. They were able to do so, Ketcham argued, because their ideas of leadership were all influenced by the precepts laid down by Lord Bolingbroke, the eighteenth-century British politician, in his *Idea of a Patriot King*. Bolingbroke called for a ruler to be a person noted for his virtue, independence, and personal responsibility, and who would rise above faction and represent the public good. These ideas were transplanted to this country, transformed to fit republican needs, and grafted onto certain indigenous American beliefs on what constituted a wise magistrate. But these basic assumptions of American political leadership underwent a transition as the social realities of Jacksonian America forced changes, Ketcham concluded, and considerations of party and interest became more important instead.

A second challenge to the older interpretations of politics came from the "new intellectual historians." These scholars concentrated on the ideas influencing the development of political parties, the thinking of contemporaries as well as that of later historians regarding the American political party system, and the intellectual framework within which party developments took place. One of the "new intellectual historians" went so far as to relate to the federal era the "republican synthesis" posited by Bernard Bailyn and Gordon Wood in explaining the political ideology of the revolutionary and constitutional periods.

Such was the case of J. G. A. Pocock's *Machiavellian Moment*, published in 1975. His brilliant overarching synthesis traced America's ideology back to much earlier periods in world history—the ancient days of Greece and Rome, the age of the Renaissance, and to seventeenth- and eighteenth-century England. What Pocock suggested was that the political struggles in the 1790s between the Federalists and Jeffersonians might best be understood within the context of a republican ideology that stretched back centuries. Pocock, along with Bernard Bailyn and Gordon Wood, emerged as the leading proponents of the "republican synthesis," a major interpretation mentioned in earlier chapters that had dominated the field much of the time from the mid-1960s to the mid-1980s.

There was a long-standing body of political thought, Pocock argued, called civic humanism or classical republicanism whose roots could be traced to the golden age of Greece and Rome. This tradition held that men were by nature citizens who reached the greatest flowering of their humanity by being members of a self-governing republic. Only within a republican government—one which balanced the one, the few, and the many—could men achieve their greatest measure of moral fulfillment. A republic could be maintained, however, only as long as its citizens were virtuous—that is, were willing to sacrifice and subordinate their self-interest to the public good. To remain virtuous men had to stay independent and not be influenced by the petty interests of the marketplace. Such interests could corrupt them by interfering with their functions as free and autonomous individuals. Citizens could prevent any danger of an expanding government or governmental power as long as they remained propertied, independent persons. History had shown that a republic was a very fragile form of government, and that republics invariably succumbed either to change or corruption on the part of the people.

This classical republican tradition, according to Pocock, was periodically rediscovered down through the ages. During the Renaissance Machiavelli, in fifteenth-century Florence, involved many of these ideas—hence the title of Pocock's book. The tradition was revived again in the seventeenth century, by such political philosophers as James Harrington and poets like John Milton who believed that an ideal republic could be established in England. In eighteenth-century England the tradition was refined further by "country party" thinkers—men ranging from John Trenchard and Thomas Gordon among the radical Whigs to a Tory, Lord Bolingbroke. These men believed that the virtue of the English people and the English constitution itself were being corrupted by the unprecedented growth in commerce and finance taking place. Such marketplace developments brought with them, they said, luxury, selfishness, and a dependence on "connections," or nepotism. The "country party" dissenters were opposed by the "court party," which represented the establishment—men who looked upon this rise of commerce as a sign of progress. The "court party" was willing to tolerate corruption in the interests of prosperity, to enjoy the wealth and national power arising from commerce, and to put off to another day any possible constitutional consequences.

The republican tradition crossed the Atlantic, Pocock said, and became the basis for the revolutionary ideology in America during the 1760s and 1770s. In embracing republicanism Pocock suggested, like Bailyn before him, that Americans adopted English "country party" attitudes: a fear of corruption; an emphasis on virtue; and a belief that the English constitution was being undermined by arbitrary power. Pocock went further, however. He identified the republicanism that the Jeffersonians used in their conflicts with the Federalists in the 1790s with the English "country party" ideology. Pushing his paradigm still further, Pocock argued that the survival of a virtuous republic was the dominant theme in American political culture from the triumph of the Jeffersonians in 1800 down to the Civil War.[19]

Pocock's paradigm represented a historiographical shift of enormous proportions—especially as it related to the Revolution and post-Revolutionary eras. To Pocock the Revolution was not a forward-looking event that propelled America into a brave new liberal, capitalistic world. Rather, the Revolution was a backward-looking movement—one concerned with a dread of modernity, obsessed with the dialectic between virtue and commerce, and which harked back to the classical republicanism of the Renaissance and of ancient times.

Pocock's paradigm was contrary to the neoconservative interpretation of Louis Hartz's *Liberal Tradition in America,* which still proved persuasive to many scholars. For Hartz America had a modern liberal ideology—one preoccupied with individual private rights, emphasizing a bourgeois consensus on capitalism, and having as its seminal thinker John Locke, who espoused many of these ideas. Pocock, however, pictured a different America. Pocock's America was concerned more with a continuation of the classical republican tradition—a tradition that stressed communitarian values, had a fear of commerce, and whose central figure was Machiavelli. In short Pocock was proposing that this

---

[19]Dorothy Ross, another scholar, found traces of the classical republican tradition still in evidence as late as the 1880s. See her article, "The Liberal Tradition Revisited and the Republican Tradition Addressed," in *New Directions in American Intellectual History,* John Higham and Paul Conklin, eds. (Baltimore, 1979), pp. 116–131. For a special issue devoted to the ramifications of the classical republican tradition in American history throughout most of the nineteenth century, see the *American Quarterly* 37 (Fall 1985).

Machiavellian interpretation be substituted for Hartz's Lockean interpretation.[20]

The Pocock paradigm precipitated a controversy among the "new intellectual historians" who focused specifically on the federal era. Lance Banning, agreeing with Pocock, traced the antecedents of what he called "the Jeffersonian persuasion" back to British roots. Jeffersonian thought, Banning argued, represented an Americanization of the "country party" ideology developed by British politicians earlier in the eighteenth century. Involved in this creed were certain specific ideas— the separation of powers, the balancing of social interests, and the principle of a stake-in-society—all of which the Jeffersonians transformed to fit the needs of the new republic. On the American scene this ideology called for a strict construction of the Constitution and thereby helped to check the danger of too much government and governmental power. During the 1790s followers of the Jeffersonian persuasion warned that freedom and the fruits of the Revolution were under constant danger from conspiratorial designs by the Federalists who aimed to undermine the Constitution and to destroy American liberties. After Jefferson came to power in 1800 this "country" ideology continued to play an important role in shaping the policies of Republican administrations, according to Banning. Thus, for Banning, republicanism became the dominant ideology in the 1790s, and the first selection

---

[20]Gordon Wood, review of John Patrick Diggins's *The Lost Soul of American Politics* in the *New York Review of Books* (February 28, 1985). For an impassioned critique of Pocock's paradigm, see Diggins's *The Lost Soul of American Politics* (New York, 1984). Diggins did not accept the "republican synthesis" or the Pocock paradigm that ideas distilled from classical republicans in Greece and Rome, Renaissance Italy, and England's "country party" thinkers dominated America's political culture from the Revolutionary era, through the Jeffersonian and Jacksonian eras, and down to the Civil War. Nor did Diggins believe that civic humanism or virtue formed the basis of the ideology of America's founding fathers. He insisted instead, like Louis Hartz, that a Lockean liberalism was America's main tradition. This liberalism stressed the pursuit of individual rights, property rights, and happiness. But America's liberal ideology had a religious dimension to it in the eighteenth century, Diggins argued. There was an interrelated tradition of Lockeanism and Calvinism. Calvinism created a tension between sinful self-interest and the demands of Christian morality. Diggins suggested that what had characterized American political thought and culture since the Revolutionary era was not the absence of civic virtues but the absence of Christian values. Hence, he rejected the Pocock paradigm not only for the federal era but for the periods beyond. By the middle of the nineteenth century, Diggins continued, America's liberal political culture had completely abandoned its Calvinist strain and degenerated into unrestrained, self-indulgent capitalism. Two major figures—Abraham Lincoln and Herman Melville—struggled to reintroduce the sacred element to political thought. Rediscovering "the lost soul of American politics," they tried to restore a sense of Calvinist conscience to restless, capitalist-minded, liberal Americans. Although they failed, Diggins concluded, Lincoln and Melville remain to remind today's Americans that liberal virtue lies in love and forgiveness and the self-restraint that comes from those qualities. In a modern-day jeremiad Diggins calls for current American narcissists and followers of the consumer culture to reunite religious sentiment and the sense of political obligation in order to save America's true liberal heritage.

in this chapter is from his book, *The Jeffersonian Persuasion*, published in 1978.[21]

Joyce Appleby in her *Capitalism and a New Social Order* disagreed with the Pocock paradigm and Banning, holding that liberalism was the dominant tradition in the 1790s. To her the Jeffersonians were champions of capitalism and commercialism. The Republican vision of the 1790s linked capitalistic individualism to the hopes that some kind of a new social order would emerge in the future. Jeffersonians sought American commercial prosperity at the same time they were echoing the "country" rhetoric of eighteenth-century English politicians. The second selection in this chapter is drawn from Appleby's book, published in 1984.

The debate whether republicanism or liberalism was the dominant ideology during the 1780s and 1790s was continued by other scholars in the late 1980s. Steven Watts, a historian, argued that the liberal tradition achieved hegemony within the republic between the early 1790s and the end of the War of 1812 in his *The Republic Reborn* (1987). But Michael Lienesch, a political scientist, in *New Order of the Ages* (1988) took a different view. Although he agreed that the thinking of Americans had been transformed by 1800, what emerged was a hybrid—a mixture that combined republican and liberal themes. Indeed, Lienesch went on, the most significant feature of modern American political thought may be that it is not completely modern: it has always carried with it much of the baggage of the classical past. By the end of the 1980s almost all scholars agreed that America had undergone some kind of great transformation in political beliefs and behavior between the Revolution and the age of Jackson—though they disagreed on the exact nature of that change.

One historian, John M. Murrin, labelled this change "the Great Transition"—that is, the movement from a premodern to a modern society—and concluded that it was "the most important controversy taking shape in years about early American history."[22] The idea of "the Great Transition" arose from the fact that much of the exciting scholarship in social and intellectual history had demonstrated how very different late eighteenth-century life and values in America were from developments which emerged later in the nineteenth century. For

---

[21]For an important qualification of Banning's ideas on this issue at a later date, see Lance Banning, "Jeffersonian Ideology Revisited: Liberal and Classical Ideas in the New Republic," *William and Mary Quarterly* 3d ser. 43 (1986):3–19. Appleby's rejoinder is in "Republicanism in Old and New Contexts," *ibid.*, 20–34.

[22]John M. Murrin, "Self-Interest Conquers Patriotism: Republicans, Liberals and Individuals Reshape the Nation," in Jack P. Greene, ed., *The American Revolution: Its Character and Limits* (New York, 1987), p. 225. David H. Fischer had argued a decade earlier that the period 1780 to 1820 was one of deep change in many areas—demographic, economic, and cultural; see *Growing Old in America* (New York, 1977).

those scholars who thought in terms of more precise periodization, "the Great Transition" appeared to have taken place somewhere between the mid-1790s and the mid-1820s.

Drew R. McCoy in his *Elusive Republic* (1980) remained deliberately vague about periodization when he explored what was called "political economy" in Jefferson's lifetime, that is, the modern combined disciplines of political science, sociology, and economics. Earlier scholars had described the Jeffersonians as agrarians who had built a national following by appealing to subsistence farmers. McCoy, in his original and impressive book, among other things, destroyed the whole concept of subsistence farmers by showing that the agrarians he studied were market-oriented. The purpose of Jeffersonian politics, according to McCoy, was to sustain territorial expansion and to protect markets in Europe and the Caribbean for Americans raising agricultural surpluses. Republican values were premised on the idea of independent voters as free men, beholden to no one, and hence being virtuous individuals. By the time America went to war in 1812, however, the definition of virtue had changed; it had given way to greater emphasis on individual assertiveness in the marketplace. Free trade now meant that the state relied on the market to provide the social stability previously thought achievable by virtuous citizens. The Jeffersonian republic, despite its victories over the Federalists and Britain, McCoy concluded, was becoming more elusive.

Certain "new intellectual historians" approached the problems of political parties in other ways. Some were interested in the reaction of American leaders to the appearance of parties—a totally unexpected development. Others discussed the idea of a loyal opposition, and precisely when this political tradition took hold in the United States. Still others were intrigued by the role public opinion played in the formulation of policies as Federalists and Republicans faced important political issues.

One theme that constantly intrigued scholars was the seeming paradox between the thought and practice of the founding fathers regarding the rise of political parties. On the one hand, Federalists and Jeffersonians alike took a public stance in the crisis-ridden 1790s that opposed the formation of any political parties since they seemed to pose a threat to the body politic. On the other, politicians went to work furiously to establish party organizations almost as soon as the new national government was founded.

In *The Idea of a Party System* (1969) Richard Hofstadter dealt with the shift in attitude toward political parties on the part of both Federalist and Jeffersonian leaders. Although strong antiparty feelings prevailed during the time of the Constitution, many men who had previously resisted the idea of parties participated in the formation of America's first party system. In Hofstadter's phrase these men became "antiparty party builders." After the election of 1800 the American party system presented to the world a shining example of the peaceful transfer of governmental power from one popularly elected party to another. Even after the election, however, the concept of a legitimate political opposition failed to take hold in the United States. General acceptance of the idea of a legitimate loyal opposition, Hofstadter argued, did not occur until much later—in the period of Andrew Jackson.

Other "new intellectual historians" tackled the problem from a different vantage point by seeking to show how public opinion and attitudes influenced the shaping of America's first parties. Richard Buel, in *Securing the Revolution* (1972), demonstrated that different attitudes toward the role of public opinion in formulating government policy had separated Federalists from Republicans. He argued, moreover, that the success of the Republicans was rooted in their acceptance of the role of public opinion in the decision-making process.

Lastly, some "new intellectual historians" focused on the ideology of only a single party. Federalist ideology was analyzed in a state study by James M. Banner, Jr., who traced the sources of Massachusetts Federalist thought back to the late eighteenth century. Banner concluded in *To the Hartford Convention* (1970) that this ideology arose in the Bay State after the Revolution in response to new disruptive forces set loose by that cataclysmic event. Massachusetts Federalists continued to share these same concerns down to the Hartford Convention of 1814. Frustrated by a series of setbacks—the declining influence of New England, the embargo acts which ruined commerce, the political success of the Jeffersonians, and the badly managed War of 1812—the Federalists called the Hartford Convention. Fortunately, the more moderate elements of the party in the state dominated the convention, thereby preventing the more extremist wing from following a course of secession.

A third challenge to the older interpretations of the federal era arose from what might loosely be called the "new cultural historians" writing in the last decade or so. Generally speaking they dealt with specific developments in society and culture rather than with prominent men. Many studies were broad-ranging social histories of groups or issues previously neglected—the emerging professions, creation of common schools, rise in liquor consumption, transformation of the artisan class, and the changing nature of urban mobs—to mention only a few.[23]

---

[23]Donald M. Scott, *From Office to Profession: The New England Ministry, 1750–1850* (Philadelphia, 1978); Gerard W. Gawalt, *The Promise of Power: The Emergence of the Legal Profession in Massachusetts, 1760–1840* (Westport, 1979); Carl F. Kaestle, *Pillars of the Republic: Common Schools and American Society, 1780–1860* (New York, 1983); W. J. Rorabaugh, *The Alcoholic Republic: An American Tradition* (New York, 1979); Paul G. Faler, *Mechanics and Manufacturers in the Early Industrial Revolution, Lynn, Massachusetts, 1780–1860* (Albany, 1981); Sean Wilentz, *Chants Democratic:*

What was significant about these studies, Gordon Wood noted in an article, was the different periodization they employed. Instead of observing the traditional distinction between colonial and national history, these scholars followed their topics through time and in the process of doing so created new periodizations. These cultural studies often began in the 1760s or 1780s and ran through the 1830s, 1840s, and 1850s. Within these new contexts, the Revolution and writing of the Constitution appeared as mere political events within the working out of broader cultural changes and themes. The concept of "the Great Transition" coupled with the new periodizations created by the "new cultural historians" brought about a virtual revolution in American historiography whose implications remain unexplored.[24]

A fourth challenge to older interpretations of the federal era came from the comparative history approach employed by some scholars to place the development of the American party system within an international perspective. The studies of Seymour M. Lipset and William N. Chambers, for example, compared the political experiences of the infant American republic in the late eighteenth century with those of the newly emerging nations in Africa and Asia during the mid-twentieth century. Lipset, a political sociologist using a multidisciplinary approach, pointed out certain important parallel developments. He compared the turbulent 1790s, when the Federalist party was in office and seeking to legitimize the new national system of authority through the charismatic person of George Washington, with the turmoil experienced by the newly independent African country of Ghana in the 1950s. Like the United States, Ghana sought to achieve some semblance of legitimacy for the new regime through the person of a charismatic leader—Kwame Nkrumah.[25]

Scholars such as Chambers dealt with the issue of political party development within an implicit comparative perspective by introducing what was at the time a new concept—the idea of a "party system." This concept presupposed the existence of a competitive two-party system in America and assumed that political developments arose from the pattern of rivalry between competing groups. It was, in short, the symbiotic relationship between the two parties rather than the parties themselves that determined political events. This concept of a party system was developed best in *Political Parties in a New Nation*, in which Chambers concluded that Americans had invented the first modern political parties in world history. He went on to suggest that

---

New York City and the Rise of the American Working Class, 1788–1850 (New York, 1984).

[24]For a brilliant reconceptualization of the period from which much of this account is drawn, save for the designation of the "new cultural historians," see Gordon S. Wood, "The Significance of the Early Republic," *Journal of the Early Republic* 8 (1988):1–20.

[25]Seymour M. Lipset, *The First New Nation* (New York, 1963).

this American "invention" of the late eighteenth century provided a useful model for the new nations that had come into being in Africa and Asia during the 1960s. This book, besides its important thesis, was significant for its methodology, which resorted to a social science approach and employed concepts used by political scientists.[26] The idea of a first party system in the 1790s, as noted previously, was later challenged by Ronald P. Formisano and other scholars.

Robert R. Palmer, on the other hand, set the process of America's party development within an explicit comparative history context: in an "age of the democratic revolution" that affected much of Western civilization at the close of the eighteenth century. Americans, it should be remembered, had created their republic at a time when nearly all countries in Europe were ruled by monarchs. When the French, following the American example, overthrew their king and established a republic, everyone in the United States rejoiced. But for many Americans that joy was short-lived when the French Revolution entered upon a reign of terror where persons were killed and property confiscated. America was soon divided into two camps: those who favored the French Revolution because France represented a sister republic, and those who opposed it for fear that foreign terrorism might spread to the United States. When France and England went to war in 1793 the cleavage within the United States widened. The Federalists in power sympathized with England, and their Jeffersonian opponents sided with France. Party lines became even sharper after Washington signed Jay's treaty—a move that was viewed as bring pro-British. Palmer's work assessed the impact of the French Revolution on American politics, evaluated its effect of party development, and viewed the process of democratization from a comparative perspective that covered both sides of the Atlantic.[27]

All four major challenges to the older interpretations were revisionist in nature. Some were characterized by the increased use of social science concepts such as intergroup conflict, status anxiety, reference group theory, the part played by the subconscious, social mobility, the roles of leaders and followers in the political process, microanalysis, and macroanalysis. Others resorted to quantitative techniques to measure in a more precise manner the group behavior of various elements in society. In the questions they raised and the conclusions they reached, recent scholars had moved away from the Hamiltonian-Jeffersonian polarity that had dominated the field for so long.

A whole host of new questions have been raised, then, regarding the historiography of the federal era. Was the older Progressive view of

---

[26]William N. Chambers, *Political Parties in a New Nation* (New York, 1963).

[27]Robert R. Palmer, *Age of the Democratic Revolution*, 2 vols. (Princeton, 1959 and 1964).

a polarized society completely discredited? To what degree were the neoconservative scholars correct in their assumptions that the Federalists and Republicans had a great deal in common and were close to a consensus? Were the "new political historians" nearer the truth when some of them suggested that the conflicts between social groups were more over ethnocultural issues—ethnic, racial, and religious—rather than economic matters? When did a full-fledged first party system arise in America: during the Federalist-Jeffersonian era of the 1790s, or in the Whig-Democratic period of the 1840s? Does the republican synthesis provide a more meaningful framework within which to view the differences between Federalists and Republicans in the 1790s and early 1800s? Was the Pocock paradigm of a republican ideology stretching all the way from ancient times in Greece and Rome to America's federal era and beyond a persuasive interpretation of events? Or was it more proper to view the era from the perspective of a Lockean liberal tradition as Hartz suggested? Did the concept of "the Great Transition" or the new periodizations suggested by some "new cultural historians" mean that the federal era as a distinctive period in American history was destined to disappear? These are some of the new questions that must be addressed before one accepts the older explanation that the federal era represented a Hamiltonian-Jeffersonian dichotomy writ large on the later period of American history.

Lance Banning

LANCE BANNING (1942–   ) *is professor of history at the University of Kentucky. He is the author of* The Jeffersonian Persuasion: Evolution of a Party Ideology *(1978).*

The final proof of principle is conduct. Accordingly, no study of the origins and nature of Republican convictions can avoid the question whether the persuasion that developed in the years of opposition exercised a central influence when the party came to power. The years of the Republican ascendency are properly the subject for another work. The present one, however, would be incomplete without some effort to address at least two crucial questions.

Were Republicans in power faithful to the principles they urged in opposition? As much so, I will argue, as almost any party we could name. Enough so that historians have made a strong beginning toward an understanding of the Jeffersonian ascendency that has, as one of its essential themes, a recognition of the lasting influence of the principles of 1798. In 1801, if my analysis is right, the "Country" came to power. A party that defined its character in terms derived from eighteenth-century British oppositions was entrusted, for the first time, with the guidance of affairs. Without insisting that Republicans were of a single mind, without suggesting that the most important leaders of the party were the helpless captives of their thought, it still seems possible to argue that the party's triumphs and its failures were the products, in large part, of its attempt to govern in accordance with an ideology that taught that power was a monster and governing was wrong.

If this is so, however, then a second question must be raised. If the party conflict of the 1790s was so largely a derivative of British arguments between the Country and the Court—if, in addition, we can see the history of the United States between 1800 and 1815 as the story of a party's effort to apply its Country principles to the direction of affairs—then when will it be possible to mark an "end of classical politics" and the emergence of a more genuinely indigenous mode of thought? At no point, I would think, before the finish of the War of 1812. Although the years in opposition had already carried the Republicans some distance from the British sources of their thought, there was no point before the months surrounding the conclusion of that war when it is possible to say that the ideas received by revolutionary thinkers from the English eighteenth century had ceased to exercise a guiding influence on American affairs.

Thomas Jefferson wrote proudly of "the revolution of 1800," calling it "as real a revolution in the principles of our government as that of 1776 was in its form." Many of his followers agreed. Today, however, most historians would probably prefer a different phrase. Too little changed—and that too slowly—to justify the connotations present in that loaded word. There were no radicals among the great triumvirate who guided the Republicans in power, as they had led them through the years of opposition. The President was bent on reconciliation with the body of his former foes. "We are all Republicans, all Federalists," he said. He wanted to detach the mass of Federalists from their former leaders, and he knew that this was incompatible with an abrupt reversal of the policies that had been followed for a dozen years. He had, in any case, no notion that his predecessors' work could be dismantled all at once. The Hamiltonian system might be hateful, but it had bound the nation to a contract it had no alternative except to honor. Madison and Gallatin, who were by instinct more conservative than Jefferson himself, were not disposed to disagree.

From the beginning of the new administration, nonetheless, Republicans insisted that a change of policies, not just of men, was necessary to return the state to its republican foundations. In his inaugural address, Jefferson announced commitment to "a wise and frugal government which shall restrain men from injuring one another, shall leave them otherwise free to regulate their own pursuits of industry and improvement, and shall not take from the mouth of labor the bread it has earned." This kind of government, he hinted, would be guided by a set of principles that could be readily distinguished from the policies of years before. Among them were

> Peace, commerce, and honest friendship with all nations; entangling alliances with none.
> The support of the state governments in all their rights as the most competent administrations for our domestic concerns and the surest bulwarks against anti-republican tendencies. . . .
> A well disciplined militia, our best reliance in peace and for the first moments of war, till regulars may relieve them. . . .
> Economy in public expense, that labor may be lightly burdened.
> The honest payment of our debts and sacred preservation of the public faith.

Reform began while Jefferson awaited the assembly of the first Republican Congress. Pardons were issued to the few men still affected by sedition prosecutions. The diplomatic corps, a target for its costs and for the influence it was thought to give to the executive, was cut to barest bones. A few of the most active Federalists were purged from office, while the President withheld commissions signed by Adams after his defeat was known. The evolution of a partisan appointments policy was too slow for some members of the party, who argued that "no enemy to democratic government will be provided with the means to sap and destroy any of its principles nor to profit by a government to which they are hostile in theory and practice." But even the most radical were satisfied with the administration's purpose when the President announced his program to the Seventh Congress.

Jefferson's first annual message was "an epitome of republican principles applied to practical purposes." After a review of foreign policy and Indian affairs, the President suggested abolition of all internal taxes. "The remaining sources of revenue will be sufficient," he believed, "to provide for the support of government, to pay the interest on the public debts, and to discharge the principals in shorter periods than the laws or the general expectations had contemplated. . . . Sound principles will not justify our taxing the industry of our fellow citizens to accumulate treasure for wars to happen we know not when, and which might not perhaps happen but from the temptations offered by that treasure." Burdens, he admitted, could only be reduced if expenditures fell too. But there was room to wonder "whether offices of officers have not been multiplied unnecessarily." The military, for example, was larger than required to garrison the posts, and there was no use for the surplus. "For defence against invasion, their number is as nothing; nor is it conceived needful or safe that a standing army should be kept up in time of peace." The judiciary system, packed and altered by the Federalists at the close of their regime, would naturally "present itself to the contemplation of Congress." And the laws concerning naturalization might again be liberalized.

The Seventh Congress, voting usually on party lines, did everything that Jefferson had recommended. It also gave approval to a plan prepared by Gallatin, the Secretary of the Treasury, for the complete retirement of the public debt before the end of 1817. Along with its repeal of the Judiciary Act of 1800, it reduced the army to three thousand officers and men, while lowering appropriations for the navy in the face of war with Tripoli. Of all its measures, though, the abolition of internal taxes (and four hundred revenue positions) called forth the most eloquent enunciation of the principles on which the new majority thought it should act. . . . Before the session ended, Jefferson could tell a friend that "some things may perhaps be left undone from motives of compromise for a time and not to alarm by too sudden a reformation," but the proceedings of the Congress gave every ground for hope that "we shall be able by degrees to introduce sound principles and make them habitual." Indeed, the session was so good a start that there was little left to recommend in 1802. The effort of the next few years would be to keep the course already set.

"Revolution" may not be the proper word to characterize the changes introduced in 1801 and early 1802. "Apostasy," however, would be worse. Yet every study of the Jeffersonian ascendency must come to terms with the magnificent and multivolumed work of Henry Adams. Though now almost a century old, the scope and literary power of this classic give it influence that has lasted to the present day. And one of Adams' major themes was the abnegation of the principles of 1798 by the Republican regime. Jefferson had hoped to put an end to parties by detaching the great body of Federalists from their irreconcilable leaders. By 1804 he seemed to have approached this end. To Adams, though, his great successes were a consequence of Jefferson's abandonment of principle and single-minded quest for popularity. If party lines were melting, it had been the Jeffersonians who had compromised their principles the most. . . . It was the Federalists, not the Republicans, who now upheld the states' rights principles of 1798.

Every part of Adams' powerful indictment could be contradicted or excused. Thus, Jefferson abandoned scruple in the case of the Louisiana Purchase with reluctance and because there seemed some danger that the Emperor of France might change his mind about a bargain that could guarantee the nation's peace while promising indefinite postponement of the day when overcrowding and development might put an end to its capacity for freedom. Jefferson continued to distrust the national bank, but would not break the public's pledge by moving to revoke its charter. The party *had* repudiated the Sedition Law, explicitly refusing to renew it in the session that had also seen a relaxation of the naturalization law. The national debt *had* been considerably reduced before the purchase of Louisiana raised it once again, and it would fall much further in the years to come.

It is necessary to admit, however, that the list of Adams' charges also could be lengthened. While Jefferson himself was never reconciled, Gallatin and Madison eventually supported the Bank of the United States. While Jefferson preferred to lead by indirection, he was in fact a stronger President than either of his predecessors ever tried to be. His public messages *suggested* measures, but his hints were often taken as commands by party members in the Congress. Informally or through floor leaders in the House, the administration made its wishes known and drafted most of the important legislation. Finally, in 1808, in its progressively more stringent efforts to enforce the embargo, Jefferson's administration wielded powers over the daily life of Americans that far exceeded anything its predecessors ever sought, even using regulars to help enforce the law.

There were, without a doubt, occasions after 1801 when the warring parties came so close to switching sides that one might doubt that principle meant much to either group. The Federalists stood forth, when they could hope to profit, as defenders of states' rights. They shamelessly employed old opposition rhetoric to criticize the massive force of party loyalty and the influence of the President on Congress. Nor was Henry Adams first to charge the Jeffersonians with a surrender to the principles of their opponents. Jefferson and his successor faced a swelling discontent from a minority of purists among Republicans themselves. . . .

Strongest in Virginia and including several of the most important party writers of the 1790s—George Logan and John Taylor as well as Pendleton himself—this band of "Old Republicans" soon found an eloquent, if vitriolic and eccentric, spokesman in the Congress. In 1806, John Randolph, who had led the party's forces in the Seventh Congress, broke with the administration and commenced a systematic opposition to the moral bankruptcy and "backstairs influence" of the government. As Jefferson and Madison began to face the gravest crisis of their leadership, they were persistently annoyed by a minority of vocal critics from within their former ranks. In 1808, Monroe became the unsuccessful candidate for those expressing this variety of discontent.

The Old Republicans—in name as well as principle—should bring to mind the English faction to which revolutionary thinkers were indebted for so many patterns in their thought. In eighteenth-century England, too, Old Whigs insisted that they were the remnant of the larger party who had not abandoned principle for power. In the same vein, John Taylor warned Monroe that if the latter ever won the presidential office, "it would probably be an irreparable breach with the republican minority . . . because you must in some measure suffer yourself to be taken in tow by an administration party, and I do not recollect in the history of mankind a single instance of such a party being republican." Taylor would himself do everything to aid in the election of Monroe, then join immediately with the minority who voted independently by conscience. "This is the sum total of what I understand by minority republicanism. Majority republicanism is inevitably, widely (but not thoroughly) corrupted with ministerial republicanism."

The ideology of opposition days had undeniably considered party loyalty as one of several agencies that might corrupt the independence of the people's representatives and undermine the necessary separation of the branches of a balanced government. Each of Pendleton's proposals also had firm roots in neo-opposition thought. Still, we need not follow the minority or Henry Adams in concluding that abandonment of principle—or compromise, at least—should be a major theme for histories of the new regime. We need not grant the Old Republicans' contention that they were the sole legitimate defenders of the principles of '98.

Both Adams and the Old Republicans identified the principles of '98 with the Virginia and Kentucky Resolutions of that year. To both, the party's creed in years of opposition centered on allegiance to states' rights. But I have tried to show that such an understanding is too narrow. Even in the crisis introduced by the repressive laws, states' rights and strict construction of the Constitution were among the means to more essential ends. The means were taken seriously, indeed, but they were never held among the absolutes. The body of the party and its most important leaders never sought, as their essential end, to hold the federal government within the narrowest of bounds. They sought, instead, a federal government that would preserve the virtues necessary to a special way of life. Their most important goal had been to check a set of policies—among them loose interpretation of the Constitution—that Republicans had seen as fundamentally destructive of the kind of government and social habits without which liberty could not survive. To judge them only on the basis of their loyalty to strict construction and states' rights is to apply a standard they had never held.

Minds changed when party leaders were confronted with responsibility. But they did not change thoroughly enough to justify the charge that they adopted principles of their opponents. The principles of the Republicans had not been Antifederalist. Republicans had traced the evils of the 1790s to the motives of the governors, not to the government itself. With few and brief exceptions, most had thought a change of policy, without a change of structure, would effect a cure. Moreover, in the last years of the decade, the development of party thought had probably persuaded many members to believe that a simple change of men might cure more evils than they once had thought.

The Republican persuasion rose, in the beginning, under circumstances that conjoined to make a reconstruction of an ideology developed in a different time and place seem relevant for the United States. The revolutionary debt to eighteenth-century opposition thought was certainly sufficient, by itself, to have assured loud echoes of the old ideas in the first years of the new republic. But this is not the lesson of this work. Republican convictions were not simply reminiscent of the old ideas. Republicans revived the eighteenth-century ideology as a coherent structure, reconstructed it so thoroughly that the persistence of an English style of argument is easily as striking as the changes we might trace to revolutionary alterations of the American polity. At least three circumstances of the 1790s had to join with expectations prompted by the heritage of revolutionary thought to generate a reconstruction so complete. None of these circumstances persisted to the decade's end. First, popular respect for Washington and ambiguity about the nature of the new executive directed discontent at the first minister. Second, Hamiltonian finance was modeled on an English prototype. And finally, an opposition first appeared in the House of Representatives.

The Republican persuasion, in its early years, attempted to alert the nation to a ministerial conspiracy that was operating through corruption to secure the revival of a British kind of constitution. Ministerial influence would subvert the independence of the Congress, which would acquiesce in constitutional constructions leading to consolidation of the states and thence to monarchy. Meanwhile, a decay of public virtue, spread by the example of the lackeys of administration and encouraged by the shift of wealth resulting from the funding plan, would ease the way for a transition to hereditary forms. With relatively minor changes, this was just the accusation that the eighteenth-century English opposition had traditionally directed at governments in power, and, like its prototype, it was, in the beginning, the weapon of a legislative group that had to reconcile its status as minority with its commitment to majority control. Legislative blocs were fluid, and the minority could understand its own position and appeal for popular support with the assistance of traditional assumptions that the influence of the Treasury, when added to an honest difference of opinion, was sufficient to account for policies with which they disagreed.

Images of conspiracy and accusations of corruption continued to provide the starting point for Republican analyses of Federalist policies, but it was not so many years before events and circumstances pushed Republican opinion away from its original foundations. First, circumstances undermined a logical necessity of neo-opposition arguments by making the Republicans a majority in the House. Then, Hamilton resigned. Concurrently, however, Jay's Treaty and the foreign war became the major issues for dispute. In other words, just when the opposition might have savored the retirement of the arch-conspirator, just when their logic was endangered by their own success, events conjoined to redirect attention to the powers of the Senate and the actions of the President himself. British influence and affection for the cause of monarchy displaced attachment to the funding system as the leading explanation for administration policies. But the Republicans could see that the financial structure was dependent on the British trade, and thus the Federalists' foreign policy appeared to be a new means to old ends. In this way, the Republicans continued their conspiratorial analysis into the Adams years.

Only in the last years of the decade can we see a clearer movement of Republican concerns away from the inherited foundations of their thought and toward a style of argument that seems more native. The alteration might be traced to 1794, when the Republicans began to count on a majority of Representatives. From that point forward, we have seen, party writers focused somewhat less on the corruption of the lower house and somewhat more on dangers posed by enemies of the Republic in the several branches of the government and in the country as a whole. During the first years under Adams, critics concentrated their denunciations less on the "funding and banking gentry" or the Hamiltonian "phalanx" than on the "anglo-federal," "anglo-monarchial," or simply "tory" party. The crisis of 1798—the popular hysteria, the Quasi-War, and the Sedition Law—strengthened this trend. Such a crisis in a polity that rested on a large electorate made the administration's influence on the legislature seem less important than the efforts of a ruling party to mislead the people and destroy effective checks on Federalist abuses. Finally, the split among the Federalists confirmed the inclination to direct attacks, not at the link between the government and its dependents in the Congress—the characteristic target of the British critics of administration—but at a party that depended on its influence with the voters. During the last two years of the decade, Republican newspapers gave less space to criticism of the Congress or administration than they did to mockery of their Federalist competitors or efforts to assassinate the reputations of the leaders of the other party. The scurrility of party sheets reflected their recognition that the enemy, in the United States, was not a governmental faction of the British type, but a party with its base among the people.

When Jefferson assumed the presidential office, he and the body of his party were prepared to believe that they had wakened a majority of voters and thereby put an end to the most immediate danger to the American Republic. Removal of the enemy from power and from public trust had come to seem sufficient, by itself, to safeguard liberty while friends of freedom worked toward gradual replacement of the Hamiltonian system with one better suited to republican ways. With the conspirators deposed, the country could afford to *ease* toward change—and change would come more certainly that way. Still, change it must—change as rapidly as possible according to a very different vision of the good society. Republicans were still persuaded that the debt must be retired as rapidly as preexisting contracts would permit, without internal taxes. It should not be clung to for its broader economic uses. It would not be used as an excuse to push the federal government into revenue resources better left to separate states. Even here, fanaticism was eschewed by a majority. Jefferson's administration did not hesitate to borrow more for the Louisiana Purchase. But the Republicans were willing to subordinate almost all else to the reduction of the debt. Every year the debt existed meant, to them, another year that taxes would inflate the rich, another year of the increasing gap between the rich and poor, which was potentially destructive to free states. By 1812, Republican administrations had reduced the debt from $83 million, where it had climbed under the Federalists, to $27.5 million. They would have retired it completely in a few more years if war had not gotten in the way.

Reform did not go far enough to satisfy the Old Republicans. Change was incomplete enough—and leaders compromised enough— to make it possible for Henry Adams to support his accusation that the Jeffersonians surrendered to the principles of their opponents. Yet even Adams tried to have it several ways. Sometimes he condemned the Jeffersonians for lack of principle. Sometimes he accused them of a change of mind. At other times, however, he switched ground to level his attacks on their adherence to a set of principles that were ill-suited to the country's needs. The effort to retire the debt, he pointed out, committed the first $7.3 million of yearly revenues to payment of principal and interest. The remainder was too small to run the government and meet the costs of national defense. . . .

If we would choose among the different condemnations Adams made of the Republican regime, it would be better to prefer the last. Adherence to the principles of ninety-eight—a strikingly consistent effort to adopt and maintain policies implicit in the ideology of opposition days—is a better explanation for Republican actions during their years in power than any emphasis upon hypocrisy or change. The Old Republicans were worrisome beyond their numbers for no other reason than that they appealed to principles that still had the allegiance of large portions of the party. And, as Adams saw, it was the party's loyalty to old ideas that brought the country to the edge of ruin in 1812.

The first years of the new republic were a time of unexampled prosperity and growth. The most important reason was the European war, which continued with few interruptions from 1790 to 1815. With France and Britain both preoccupied with warfare, a portion of the trade that they would normally have carried fell by default to neutrals. As the greatest trading neutral of the age, America had much to gain. It also risked involvement in the war, since both the European powers periodically attempted to deny the other neutral help.

During the 1790s, America's attempt to carry on a thriving commerce had nearly brought a war with Britain. The effort in fact resulted in a limited conflict with France. Thomas Jefferson came to the Presidency near the beginning of a brief respite in the European struggle, and the interlude of peace gave the Republicans a chance to apply their principles of governmental economy. In 1803, however, France and Britain resumed their titanic war. With Napoleon in power, Republicans had long since dropped their admiration of the French. But the commercial problems of the 1790s now returned with doubled force. After 1805, when Admiral Lord Nelson destroyed most of the French fleet in the Battle of Trafalgar, Britain was unchallengeable at sea, while Bonaparte was temporarily supreme on land. Both powers turned to economic warfare, catching the United States between.

For America the situation reached its worst in 1807. In that year Napoleon's Milan Decree completed a "continental system" under which the Emperor threatened to seize any neutral ship that had submitted to a British search or paid a duty in a British port. Britain replied with Orders-in-Council that promised to seize any neutral trading with the continent *unless* that ship had paid a British fee. The combined effect of French and British measures was to threaten any vessel engaged in the continental trade. To make the situation worse, in the summer of 1807, near the mouth of Chesapeake Bay, the British frigate "Leopard" fired upon the American warship "Chesapeake," forced it to submit to search, and impressed four sailors into British service. By any standard, "Leopard's" action was a cause for war.

War might have been an easy choice. There was a storm of patriotic outrage possibly a match for that following the revelation of the XYZ Affair ten years before. Particularly in the Old Northwest, where British officials in Canada soon began to give assistance and encouragement to Tecumseh and his efforts to unite the western tribes against the progress of new settlement, demands for war rose steadily from that point on. But the Republicans did not want war. They were determined to face the present troubles in the way that they believed the Federalists should have responded to similar problems in the 1790s.

Since the beginning of the party quarrel, Republicans had consistently expressed a fear of war and a profound distrust of normal preparations for defense. They were afraid of war's effects on civil liberties. They clung to the traditional distrust of standing armies. They had consistently opposed the frightful cost of navies. Their ideology identified high taxes, large armed forces, and the increase in executive authority that seemed inseparable from war as mortal dangers to republican society and government. Even preparations for hostilities would require abandonment of all the most important policies that they had followed since the triumph seven years before: low taxes, small armed forces, little governmental guidance of the nation's life, and quick retirement of the public debt.

In any case, Republicans had always argued that America possessed a weapon that provided an alternative to war, a weapon that had proved its effectiveness during the long struggle preceding independence. This weapon was its trade. Since opposition days, the party's leaders had maintained that the things America exported—mostly food and other raw materials—were necessities of life. The things America imported, on the other hand, were mostly manufactured goods and other "luxuries." In case of trouble, then, America could refuse to trade. Healthier than Europe, because it was not bound to large-scale manufacturing, America would win a test of wills, creating potent discontent and dislocation in the feebler state. Trade restrictions could secure the national interest as effectively as war and without the dangers to free government and social health that war would necessarily incur. Trade was the weapon that the Madisonians had wanted to employ against the British back in 1794. It was the weapon that Republicans preferred when difficulties once again arose. Indeed, the party held to economic warfare, to its antiwar and antipreparation ideology, so long and so stubbornly that the result was nearly a disaster for the United States. . . .

To anyone inclined to balance gain with loss, the War of 1812 must seem a masterpiece of folly. The god who ruled its fortunes was decidedly perverse. Two days before the Senate completed a declaration of war, though not in time for news to cross the sea, the British government announced that the Orders-in-Council would be repealed. The battle at New Orleans was planned by generals who had not learned that peace had been agreed upon at Ghent on December 24, 1814, two weeks before. The slaughter on the Mississippi—nineteen months of warfare—ultimately went for naught. The Treaty of Ghent simply restored the situation that had existed before the war. Boundaries were unaltered. Disputes over neutral rights and impressment were left unresolved.

Contemporaries, however, were not disposed to make a practical calculation of this sort. After all, the war had not been fought for rational reasons alone. National honor, the reputation of republican government, and the continuing supremacy of the Republican party had seemed to be at stake.

National honor had been satisfied. Jackson's stunning victory at New Orleans more than redeemed earlier reverses in the field. And news of his triumph arrived in the East just before the news of peace. Americans celebrated the end of the struggle with a brilliant burst of national pride. They felt that they had fought a second war for independence, and had won. If little had been gained, nothing had been lost in a contest with the greatest imperial power on the earth. . . .

Survival in the War of 1812 had nonetheless required an ample portion of good luck. Republican principles had combined with a lack of planning, poor management, and the alienation of New England to brew a bitter soup. For years, the principles and beliefs that recommended commercial coercion as an alternative to war had also bolstered many members of the party in their inclination to refuse requests for normal preparations for defense. Similar motives had encouraged Jefferson's first Congress to repeal internal taxes, and, in 1811, they had entered into the refusal to renew the charter of the Bank of the United States.

In 1812, America challenged a great empire with sixteen warships and a regular army of less than seven thousand well-trained men. Congress provided for larger forces once it was clear that war could not be escaped, but ships could not be built in time to have an effect. Enlistment in the army was painfully slow, so that regulars carried the largest part of the burden only in the northern campaign of 1814. Meanwhile, the British fleet drove the American from the ocean, the finest American militia sat home in New England, and Western soldiers enjoyed a very mixed success. Meanwhile, too, the government showed itself a financial cripple. When war became inevitable, Congress approved new taxes. But revenues were slow in coming in. Until they did, funds were difficult to find. Without a national bank, the Treasury had no dependable source of ready loans, no easy way to transfer the monies it had from one part of the country to another. Against a less distracted, more determined foe, complete humiliation might well have been the result.

The administration learned its lessons. Early in 1815, President Madison recommended a peacetime army of twenty thousand men. In his annual message of December 5, 1815, the great architect of the old Republicanism called upon Congress to consider federal support for certain internal improvements, tariff protection for new industries which had been encouraged by the argument with England, and creation of a new national bank. The implications of this message were profound. It might be said they mark the advent of a very different age.

In the first years of the new federal government, Alexander Hamilton had grounded his great plans on the assumption that the world was not the kind of place where republican purists could pursue their schemes in peace. Republicans had insisted that there was an alternative to the Secretary's system, one which could secure national respectability without the unacceptable risks to revolutionary accomplishments that Hamilton's seemed to entail. In the years after 1800, they had gradually dismantled much of the foundation on which the Federalists had meant to build an America that could compete with empires such as England's on English terms. They had substituted a different vision, [one] in which a society of independent men of virtue would appear in arms when necessary to defend America's shores, but trust their influence on the course of history, more generally, to the moral force of republican example and the necessary demand for the raw materials they would produce for trade. Jefferson and Madison had also tried a different course in foreign policy. Under the pressure of Napoleonic wars, the Republican alternative had failed.

Hamilton had been right, at least in significant part. America did not have the capacity to force the great states of Europe to accept the kind of international order within which the new nation could pursue the Republican ideal, a society in which the virtue of independent farmers and craftsmen would not be threatened by great cities, large-scale industry, professional armed forces, and a polity committed to the mysteries and dangers of English-style finance. The choice did seem to lie between greater self-sufficiency and national humiliation or war. Now, implicitly, a Republican President admitted this truth.

It was not an unconditional surrender to Hamilton's ideas. Madison could hope that vast expanses of western land and the continued leadership of genuine republicans would postpone to an indefinite future the debilitating corruption that Republicans had always feared. He still had no desire to see the land become a democratic England. Yet he did suggest that old Jeffersonian principles might be tempered with a program that would resurrect an essential portion of the Hamiltonian state. In doing so, he legitimized the other side of a debate that had held the nation's attention since 1789. He hinted that America could build on an amalgam of Republican and Federalist ideas, and the majority of his party agreed. If we must mark a single point at which to write an end to the debate that traced back to the eighteenth-century argument between the English Country and the Court, we might select the second session of the Fourteenth Congress, which adopted all of Madison's proposals.

The ancient argument did not abruptly stop. The old ideas did not abruptly lose their influence. The United States has seldom had a less effective government than in the years between 1817 and 1829, not least because its chief executives did not believe in leading Congress and Republicans in Congress did not believe in being led. Presidential leadership and the effective use of patronage still smelled of influence and a danger to the public good. Allegiance to a party still seemed too much like corruption. As the "American System" of Henry Clay, the Hamiltonian vision of a self-sufficient republic, where industrial development would provide a domestic market for agricultural goods and federal programs would tie diverse sections into an imperial whole, remained a central topic for political division and dispute. Jacksonians attacked "aristocracy" and "corruption." Whigs condemned "King Andrew." John C. Calhoun was intensely concerned with something strongly reminiscent of corrupting influence. The new Republicans who followed Lincoln celebrated virtue and the independent man. As a consequence of revolutionary hopes and thought, proponents of American grandeur have always had to answer those who worry about a loss of innocence at home. In the years around 1815, however, the context of these controversies underwent a fundamental change. Experiments with economic coercion, followed by the War of 1812, had exposed an undeniable weakness in the principles on which the Republican party had based its rule. But the war had also made it easier to contemplate a change of course. Events destroyed one of the two great parties to the long dispute over the shaping of a society and government that could make republicanism lasting and complete. Doing this, they freed the other party to turn its attention to the needs of the future. Leadership passed increasingly to younger men, whose lives had not been molded by the great Revolution that had shaped the experience of the generation before. Arguments among the younger men would still be fierce, but the edges of hysteria grew blunt. For it was now the most appropriate means of national development that seemed to be at stake, not the very meaning of America itself.

Joyce Appleby

JOYCE APPLEBY (1929–   ) *is professor of history at the University of California in Los Angeles. She has written several books, including* Economic Thought and Ideology in Seventeenth-Century England *(1978) and* Capitalism and a New Social Order: The Republican Vision of the 1790s *(1984).*

My intellectual debts to those with whom I disagree are large. Having studied Thomas Jefferson before the publication of the works that have depicted him as a nostalgic defender of country party values, I was resistant to this view, but the recovery of the role of classical republican thought in revolutionary America has made it possible to appreciate why the Jeffersonians construed the Federalists as a threat. Similarly, the older scholarly tradition that presented the Jeffersonians as a Southern-based party with lineal connections to the Antifederalists made clear that it took the radical propensities and Enlightenment enthusiasms of the political newcomers in the middle states to recast American politics in the 1790s.

Despite the persistent appeal of Jeffersonian idealism in the United States, the material and moral underpinnings for the vision of a free society of independent men prospering through an expansive commerce in farm commodities proved short-lived. The second great awakening undermined the secular faith in a natural social order and the growth of industry strengthened the tendency of capitalism to divide workers and employers. Both developments compromised the Jeffersonians' commitment to equality of opportunity and esteem. By emphasizing the democratic faith that the Jeffersonians infused into their version of a capitalistic society, I hope to make more salient the contradictions that lie at the heart of the American self-image. . . .

The last time a group of politicians in the United States publicly defended the traditional concept of society . . . was in the 1790s. The defeat of the Federalists at the end of the decade signalled the defeat of the concept as well. Never again would any group of Americans seriously seeking power in a national election champion hierarchical values or deferential political practices. Men might continue to espouse the rule of the rich, well-born, and the able but they would have to do it privately at their clubs, or . . . withdraw from public life in order to preserve their purity. . . .

I shall look at the demise of the venerable political tradition which the Federalists defended or, to put it more positively, I shall examine the elements that went into the triumph of the first truly American political movement, that of the Jeffersonian Republicans who swept into power in 1800. The Jeffersonians coalesced around a set of ideas—radical notions about how society should be reorganized. These ideas were propagated less by a class of men—that is, persons tied together by common economic interests—than by a kind of man—men attracted by certain beliefs. Their common vision about the reform of politics and the liberation of the human spirit made a national democratic party possible in the 1790s because that vision alone had the power to hold together otherwise quite disparate individuals and groups. Ideas—not interests or old loyalties or institutional identities—supplied the unity needed for success. Ideas joined a group of established elite reformers to a network of political interlopers; ideas attached the voters of the middle states to those of the south, confounding all expectations about regional coalitions. A distinctly secular conception of politics drew together in one voting bloc rationalists, free thinkers, and ardent members of a variety of evangelical sects. All of these alignments were necessary for the Republican victory in 1800.

American political culture changed decisively in that election. Men who believed in democracy found a national voice where in the past their strength had been local. The idea of limiting government because firmly associated with egalitarian goals. Popular sovereignty was reinterpreted to justify active, intrusive participation from the body of voters. Ordinary citizens formed voluntary political clubs, and newspaper editors took it upon themselves to report congressional debates and to publish highly critical evaluations of public officials and presidential policies. Election campaigns lost their genteel rhetoric about disinterested service, and candidates appealed openly to voters with their position on specific issues. These activities have so exactly characterized American politics ever since 1800 that historians have had some difficulty coming to terms with what was novel—even revolutionary—about them at the time. There is nothing so hard to discover in the past as that which has subsequently become familiar. Yet in the 1790s there was something frightening about the rambunctious politicking that gave birth to the Jeffersonian Republican party. The success of this broadly based opposition to the Federalists—one bent on reforming political practices—meant, moreover, that instead of a gradual modification of American institutions and values there was an explicit reworking of them.

Drawing upon the radical implications in the American Revolution, the Jeffersonians overpowered the conservative elements that had survived the Independence movement. Their triumph at the level of ideology was so enduring that no politician would again think of defending the old order of an elite leadership and passive citizenry. Indeed, when an opposition to the triumphant Jeffersonians finally did form in the 1830s, it grew from the Jeffersonian ranks and constituted a variant of those same American principles. . . .

The main reason the 1790s witnessed a decisive change in American political culture is that there was something fundamental to decide. We can detect this in the behavior of the Federalists. They exuded the confidence of men whose views reflected deeply ingrained ways of thinking about politics. When public discourse turned polemical their voices became shrill, but they never lost their posture of protecting known truths about civil society. They knew that it was their opponents who were treading unfamiliar paths and they appealed to history and common sense to prove them wild visionaries. The Jeffersonians for their part took on the task of uncovering the propositions about human nature and society that underlay the Federalists' goals. They deliberately set up venerable ideas as the targets for their shafts of rhetoric. Pushed to expose the assumptions in each other's positions, the Federalists and the Jeffersonians made brilliantly clear that the character of America's future was at issue. By 1800 two coherent but opposing conceptions of society had emerged to polarize the voters' sympathies. This ideological cohesion ran well ahead of any economic or social integration within the United States.

The basis for the political divisions in the early national period has only become apparent during the past two decades since research on the character and structure of colonial society has revealed how deeply conservative many colonial communities were and hence how much was at stake when accepted ways of thinking and acting were challenged after the Revolution. Not too long ago historians were quite sure that the English had traveled very lightly to the New World. In fact the authority, faith, submission, and reverence . . . were among those things scholars thought the colonists had left at the dock when they set sail for America. It was so easy to imagine those intrepid men and women—the ones with enough get up and go to leave Europe— landing in the proverbial wilderness and setting to work immediately to clear the fields, build homes, and convert the natural abundance around them into vendible commodities, somehow knowing that they were working to bring forth a new nation with a government of the people, by the people, and for the people. Implicit in this description is a view of European culture—the one the colonists brought with them—as a set of arbitrary restraints that held in check men's natural ability to take care of themselves. Without the restrictions of old world institutions, it was suggested, latent human tendencies could manifest themselves and each individual's natural propensity to seek self-improvement would come to the fore. . . .

In intellectual history too, recent scholarship has challenged the old notion that the colonists were either Lockean liberals or Enlightenment men. Instead we have been taught through the work of Bernard Bailyn and Gordon Wood that the ideas that animated colonial leaders were ancient ones, going back to classical texts of politics rendered accessible to eighteenth-century readers by the English Commonwealthmen or Country party writers. These classical views that we now see as shaping the colonial consciousness involved assumptions very much at odds with a progressive conception of history. Classical theory emphasized that civil society was fragile, that men lusted after power, that stability required a carefully constructed constitution. It also taught that there were two orders of men—the talented few and the ordinary many—and because there were inevitable social divisions, a properly balanced constitution would balance the powers of these two groups. But constitutional stability rested ultimately in this classical paradigm upon the exercise of civic virtue—upon the capacity of some men to rise above private interests and devote themselves to the public good. Men deeply involved in their own business, in getting ahead, and seizing opportunities for gain were not proper candidates for public office. Commerce which prompted private interests therefore threatened civil order. Ideally property should not serve as a way of making money, but rather, as J. G. A. Pocock has said, as a means of anchoring the individual in the structure of power and virtue and liberating him to practice these activities. In this classical political tradition men realized their fullest potential in politics, in serving the public good, and protecting the constitution.

What we have learned about the social structure and the exercise of authority in colonial America is congruent with the central propositions of classical republican thought. Compatible too was the concept of human nature in Protestant theology. Men and women were prone to sin, and civil order was hard to maintain. Liberty depended upon the solution to difficult political problems. The values associated with free enterprise and greater productivity—what we would call capitalism—did not inspire confidence, but rather provoked anxiety. Like so many elements of English thinking that found their way into the colo-

nial consciousness, the concepts of balanced government and of political participation based upon secure property embodied the ideals of an
upper class that had arrogated to itself the unique qualifications for
assuming power. They also reflected the yearning for tranquility in an
age newly introduced to the disruptive force of an expanding economy.
Far from colonial society diverging steadily from English ways, what
we actually find in eighteenth-century America is a pervasive Anglicization that can be traced to several mutually reinforcing developments.

After three—sometimes four—generations many colonial towns
had acquired a settled look. Strong community ties had finally materi-
alized in the networks of families that only time can create. The fathers' authority at home and in town meetings assured stability and
continuity. Fathers often arranged marriages, controlled inheritance,
and used both law and custom to subordinate individual desires to the
goals of the group. The economic development promoted by the flourishing Atlantic trade had brought new concentrations of wealth to the
older colonies. Translated into cultural terms this meant that moneyed families could build handsome town houses and country estates.
They imported carriages, put their servants into livery, and reared their
children for genteel living. Imitating European tastes, they created the
visible signs for the theoretical distinction between the few and the
many.

Although material abundance was widely diffused in the colonies,
commercial growth increased the number of landless and decreased
the holdings of land of those in the bottom ranks. In part this was
because a more complex economy called into being more tradesmen
whose wealth was in tools and skills, but it also reflected the relentless
dynamic of market growth to consolidate disadvantages as well as advantages. To lose one's access to property at a time of rising land prices
is to alter fundamentally one's long-term prospects. Historians have
named this process one of Europeanization because the division between rich and poor, which had been modified during the initial period
of settlement, reappeared. Ordinary colonists frequently expressed
great bitterness at the ostentatious displays of wealth and the first evidence of real poverty in America. What was a traditional class structure in the old world appeared as an ugly novelty in the new. To be
sure, in mid–eighteenth-century America there was a large bulge in
the center of the social pyramid and still no apex of enormous wealth.
People in the middling ranks predominated; those propertyless poor at
the bottom represented a minority of white men, distinguished as
often by age as any other factor. But the abrupt swings in the trade
cycles—the ups and downs occasioned by an international market still
in the making—led to uncertainty. Americans even then depended
upon credit. The very promise of their wealth-producing capacity facil-

itated borrowing and exposed them to the temptations and punishments of social mobility. . . .

With this new understanding of the colonial era, it is easy to accept the Federalists' presumption that they and not their opponents were speaking for a conception of civil order deeply rooted in American values. What now needs to be explored are the origins of those Jeffersonian values that appear to us so quintessentially American. Like the classical version espoused by the Federalists, Jeffersonian republicanism began in an English frame of reference. . . . Voltaire once described history as a pack of tricks that the present plays on the past. He failed to mention that the people of the past have their own dissembling pranks. The most troublesome for historians is the tendency to change without notice the meaning of words. Whole new concepts can take shape behind an unvarying set of terms. Virtue is such a one. In the context of classical republican thought virtue meant civic virtue, the quality that enabled men to rise above private interests in order to act for the good of the whole. By the 1780s this meaning is less clear. . . . [B]y the end of the century virtue more often referred to a private quality, a man's capacity to look out for himself and his dependents— almost the opposite of classical virtue. . . .

Probably the least familiar concept of liberty used then was that most common to us—that is, liberty as personal freedom bounded only by such limits as are necessary if others are to enjoy the same extensive personal freedom. Before the Revolution liberty more often referred to a corporate body's right of self-determination. Within countless communities the ambit of freedom might well be circumscribed, yet men would speak of sacrificing their lives for liberty—the liberty of the group to have local control. In the classical republican tradition discussed earlier—that ornate theory about the constitutional balance between the one, the few, and the many—liberty was a cherished goal and its essence was political. To be a free man (and they always were men) was to participate in the life of the polis or community. To have liberty was to share in the power of the state, to be actively involved in making and executing decisions. Thus liberty in this sense was associated with a republic—the rule of law—and could not exist in a monarchy where the will of the king or queen was supreme. Liberty in the classical republican tradition pertained to the public realm and not the private. Indeed, it was the capacity of men to rise above personal interest that made republics and therefore liberty possible. Virtue and liberty were indissolubly linked in classical republican theory. From the time of the Glorious Revolution, Englishmen in the ruling class could feel themselves in possession of this classical liberty because their mixed, constitutional monarchy had created a new sovereign, that of the King in Parliament. Colonists considering their own legislatures to be copies of the British Parliament responded equally warmly to the ancient ideal of free men realizing their human potential in service to the commonwealth.

The classical republican definition of liberty appealed especially to men whose talents and superior position in society encouraged them to identify strongly with the group as a whole. For this reason the liberty of classical republicanism bears careful examination. For instance, the assertion that society is divided between the few and the many—the elite and the common people—is an assertion of human inequality presumed to be rooted in nature and therefore unavoidable in social practice. It is because of this inequality that the few, defined either as an hereditary nobility or those who held property, were given a separate house in the legislature. The disproportionate amount of power given to the few was in turn justified, because without their check upon popular power liberty itself would be lost to everyone as one or the other group gained ascendency and ruled in its own interest. Writers in the classical republican tradition—James Harrington, John Trenchard, and Thomas Gordon—illustrated these principles with references to the civil wars, tyrannies, and usurpations so replete in the histories of Greece and Rome. Although classical republicanism offered the possibility of establishing an enduring republic where men might enjoy the liberty of civic participation, the theory itself was grounded in an historical realism that cautioned against having too high hopes, given the fickle, power-lusting nature of men.

Equally rooted in history was another concept of liberty familiar to Englishmen on both sides of the Atlantic. This was the liberty of secure possession—the enjoyment of legal title to a piece of property or the privilege of doing a particular thing without fear of arrest or punishment. Unlike classical republican liberty, this kind of liberty was negative, private, and limited. When people talked about these liberties, they referred to promises between the ruler and the ruled that carried no implications about the kind of rule that prevailed. Preserved in custom and the common law, specified by documents, interpreted through formal procedures, such promises formed the ligaments of the body politic. While law courts were developed to implement these promises, the liberty of secure possession could be enjoyed under a monarchy or aristocracy or in a democracy. Nor need the liberties be spread throughout the populace. The ancient distinctions between freemen and denizens or freemen and villeins reminds us of this. These liberties did not flow from a theory of government, but rather from specific arrangements that in time became institutionalized. They were concrete and verifiable. When colonists in the 1760s spoke of the rights and privileges of Englishmen, they had in mind this meaning of liberty. Their outrage at the stamp tax, the Quartering Act, and the various reforms of the American customs fed on the sense of betrayal implicit in a broken promise. In the ensuing debates about the status of the charters and precedents which the colonists thought guaranteed their liberties, this outrage turned to despair, for they heard Parliament make claim to a sovereign authority totally incompatible with their concept of liberty.

Liberty in the classical republican paradigm and liberty in the historic rights tradition are distinct and potentially contradictory concepts. The classical liberty of freemen to participate in political decisions celebrates the public arena and the disinterestedness of civic virtue. The liberty of secure possession protects private, personal enjoyments—liberties that become vested interests. There is no suggestion of limiting the power of government in the classical tradition as long as that power serves the common good, whereas the particular liberties of citizens or subjects secured by law limits the scope of public authority. Classical republican liberty is a lofty ideal; the liberty of legal rights pertains to the mundane and everyday aspects of living. Despite these dissimilarities, these two meanings could and did merge with one another, particularly in those moments when men feared the loss of their liberty, however defined. The classical republican theory was after all a particular solution to the enduring political predicament: how to secure liberty when its enjoyment required order and order was most efficiently achieved through the imposition of the ruler's will. History was a record of usurpations as kings, nobles, and popular assemblies vaulted over the limits of law. Monarchies become tyrannies, aristocracies oligarchies, while democracies dissolved into chaos as ruling groups forsook the good of the whole. Subject to attack from without and corruption from within, civil society indeed seemed imperilled, and the source of the peril was human nature itself. England's mixed constitution, with its balance of monarchical, aristocratic, and democratic elements, held out hope, but wise men read their histories and kept a careful watch.

A third meaning of liberty one could encounter in the public discourses in the Anglo-American world of the eighteenth century entered the political lexicon in the mid-seventeenth century. Often called Lockean in reference to the great political philosopher, John Locke, its distinctive characteristics actually came from Thomas Hobbes, and I shall talk about it as the liberal concept of liberty. It is a tribute to the scholarly virtuosity of Bernard Bailyn and J. G. A. Pocock that we no longer believe, as generations of historians before us have, that America's revolutionary leaders were simple Lockean liberals, though it would be a mistake to underestimate the early influence of the social contract theorists. Unlike the classical and legal meanings of liberty, the liberal conception ignores history as a source of guidance. Hobbes and Locke and the succession of writers who followed them reasoned from an imaginary account of man in the state of nature to an abstract definition of liberty. More analytical than didactic, the liberal theory rationalized government by deriving its function from general propositions about human nature and the formation of civil society. Twentieth-century readers are struck by Hobbes's description in the *Leviathan* of life in the state of nature as "solitary, poor, nasty, brutish and short." But Hobbes's contemporaries in mid–seventeenth-century England found little startling in this. After all, they heard about the fallen state of man in much more graphic terms almost every Sunday. Neither poets nor dramatists—certainly not historians—offered a prettier picture of human nature. What shocked contemporaries about Hobbes was his insistence that men were naturally equal. . . .

It was men's equal ability to achieve their own ends that created the brutish state of nature, according to Hobbes, and explained why men consented to put themselves under the rule of an absolute sovereign who could produce order so that they might enjoy peace and commodious living. Writing a generation after Hobbes, Locke accepted his method of starting with an abstract model of the state of nature—or the absence of civil society—in order to determine what civil society contributed. Unlike Hobbes, Locke gave all men a conscience and a specific injunction—the law of nature—which taught them that since all mankind are "equal and independent, no one ought to harm another in his life, health, liberty or possessions." With these premises Locke put together his famous explanation for the origin of government. Living free and equal in a state of nature with the protection of natural law, men formed civil society only for convenience. By giving up their private right to execute the law of nature they created government to do the policing, but civil society added nothing to their rights nor to the content of natural law; it existed only to implement what was already a part of God's creation. Its power, most importantly, was limited to those measures necessary to protect the life, liberty, and property of the members of society. So fundamental were they to civil society that revolution itself was justified when it became abundantly clear that a particular government no longer served those ends.

To recapitulate the argument alone fails to do justice to the effect of Hobbes's and Locke's reasoning, for to follow their logic in the seventeenth century was to be liberated from the awe and reverence—at a minimum the didacticism—that accompanied discussions of sovereign authority. Nothing turned out to be more subversive than the analytical spirit that the liberal approach encouraged. Instrumental, utilitarian, individualistic, egalitarian, abstract, and rational, the liberal concept of liberty was everything that the classical republican concept was not. So at odds were these two liberties that it is hard to understand how they could have coexisted in the same political discourse. That is a puzzle yet to be solved. A clue to it lies in the use put to the various theories. Locke offered a rationale and a justification for bringing an autocratic ruler to heel. His theories took shape and circulated when England's Parliamentary leaders sought to displace James II in the 1680s. Classical republicanism flourished during those periods when the English upper class either anticipated or enjoyed political power. Its civic humanism offered a concept of public life that served the moral and intellectual needs of the ruling English gentry. By emphasizing the organic nature of human society, classical republicanism gave the talented few a critical function as the brains of the body politic, just as the Lockean appeal to individual rights encouraged the exertions of all in a revolutionary situation. Well known to the colonists, Locke's lucid explanation of the origins of government was pushed to the fore during the crisis over Parliamentary taxation in the 1760s.

Initially the colonists had insisted that they were protecting the rights of Englishmen. Only when it became clear that their interpretation of the imperial crisis was not shared in the mother country did colonial rebels shift ground from the historic rights of English subjects to the abstract rights of all men. Then, as with an earlier high-minded group of English leaders, Locke's right to revolution offered a justification for opposing one's sovereign, a heinous crime in a world still knit together by loyalty. After the Revolution, both Lockean liberal and classical republican liberty figured in American political discourse. We might say that the several meanings of liberty were like elements suspended in a solution, awaiting the catalyst that would crystalize them. It was not long in coming for the gentlemen constitution-drafters who had spent the summer of 1787 together in Philadelphia. In the very months that many of them were settling into their new offices under that constitution in New York, the catalytic agent appeared in the form of the French Revolution. In the ensuing decade the full implications of the liberal concept of liberty were clarified and its fundamental incompatibility with the venerable classical tradition made starkly apparent.

It is the modern notion of liberty that undergirds the free enterprise system which received its political framework in America with the adoption of the constitution. This liberal definition of liberty, I will argue, also gave shape and direction to "the Republican Vision of the 1790s" which forms the subject of this volume. The capitalism in my title of course refers to a way of organizing the economy—a particular system for producing and distributing the material goods that sustain and embellish life. The word has acquired as well the protean characteristics of an ideal, a symbol, a myth, and a shibboleth which also figure in its history. In the eighteenth century two features of the market economy fascinated contemporaries: the reliance upon individual initiative and the absence of authoritarian direction. Increasingly private arrangements were counted upon to supply the public's material needs. At the same time the productive goal of making wealth to produce wealth supplanted the older notion of wealth as the maintainer of status. In these transformations we come close to the conceptual heart of capitalism, for money becomes capital through the changed intentions of those with the money—that is, with the decision to invest rather than spend or hoard wealth. We need to keep in mind the novelty of all these elements when we assess how men and women in the 1790s responded to the elaboration of the market economy.

The "new social order and Republican vision" in my title points to a change in thinking about human association in the late eighteenth century. A hundred years earlier, as we have seen, people spoke of the state of nature, a predicament, and civil society, a solution. A century and a quarter of economic development had dramatically enhanced public opinion about voluntary human actions, and society was the word that emerged to represent the uncoerced relations of people living under the same authority. "Society," Paine wrote in *Common Sense*, "is produced by our wants and government by our wickedness; the former promotes our happiness positively by uniting our affections, the latter negatively by restraining our vices." It is this vision which animated the Jeffersonians and draws our attention to the role of ideas in their history, particularly those ideas that formed their imaginative construction of reality. By looking at the dramatic events of the 1790s in the United States, I hope also to say something in general about how economic activities, social movements, political institutions, and the ways men and women think about them impinge on each other. The particular ideas the Republicans and Federalists thought and fought with came from an English frame of reference, but it was only a frame of reference. They gave the ideas their operative meaning, working within their own situation in the polemics of the early national period. In the case of the Republicans and participants produced what Jefferson called Americanism, a political brew so heady that Cambridge undergraduates were not allowed to drink it until our century.

☆ 7 ☆

Jacksonian Democracy

FACT OR FICTION?

To many historians the election of Andrew Jackson as president in 1828 represents a pivotal turning point in American history. Prior to Jackson's election the men who occupied the presidency had come from either Virginia or Massachusetts; they were closely identified with an aristocratic elite which seemed far removed from the great mass of Americans. Andrew Jackson, on the other hand, seemed to symbolize the common man rather than the aristocrat. Being a self-made man and military hero—characteristics which made him a somewhat charismatic figure—Jackson's election was viewed by many as representing the ultimate triumph of democracy in American society.

Although historians for many years accepted the relationship between Jackson and political democracy, they disagreed sharply over the precise nature of what came to be known as Jacksonian Democracy. Indeed, the period from 1828 to 1840 became one of the most controversial eras in American history insofar as scholars were concerned. This was hardly surprising. Americans traditionally had attempted to define the unique characteristics that separated them from the rest of the world—a quest that inevitably led to an extended discussion of democracy and its meaning. Historians were no exception to this rule and much of their writing revolved around a historical examination of the nature and development of democracy in America. Because Andrew Jackson and democratic politics seemed so closely related, both topics became the subject of innumerable books and articles.[1]

Like that of Jefferson before him and other political leaders after him, Jackson's historical reputation has changed markedly from time to time. The earliest evaluations of his presidential career tended to be highly critical and hostile in tone. James Parton, Jackson's first serious

---

[1] For a significant analysis of the historiography of Jacksonian Democracy, see Charles G. Sellers, Jr., "Andrew Jackson versus the Historians," *Mississippi Valley Historical Review* 44 (March 1958):615–634.

biographer, freely admitted that Old Hickory was indeed the idol of the American people. Yet his portrait of Jackson was anything but flattering. Recognizing the complex nature of his subject, Parton concluded that "his elevation to power was a mistake on the part of the people of the United States. The good which he effected has not continued; while the evil which he began [the spoils system] remains, has grown more formidable, has now attained such dimensions that the prevailing feeling of the country, with regard to the corruptions and inefficiency of the government, is despair."[2]

Parton's criticisms were echoed even more strongly by other nineteenth-century writers, including Hermann E. von Holst, William Graham Sumner, and James Schouler. These writers agreed that Jackson was illiterate, uneducated, uninformed, emotional, and that his actions were motivated by a desire to dominate merely for the sake of power. In short, his election as president in 1828 was considered to be a mortal blow to cherished American ideals. "His ignorance," wrote Parton, "was as a wall around him—high, impenetrable. He was imprisoned in his ignorance, and sometimes raged round his little, dim enclosure like a tiger in his den."[3]

The hostility of these historians toward Jackson, oddly enough, did not arise from the fact that their own political ideology and preferences differed sharply from those held by Old Hickory. Indeed, most of these scholars were all nineteenth-century economic liberals who staunchly championed laissez-faire principles, condemned governmental intervention in the economy, and supported a sound currency. In this respect they were in general agreement with many of Jackson's policies, including his attack on the Second Bank of the United States and his hard-money views. Moreover, they approved of his forceful and assertive nationalism—particularly his bold stand during the South Carolina nullification controversy.

What these nineteenth-century scholars found most deplorable about Jackson's presidency, however, was the fact that the democratization of American politics had resulted in the exclusion from high public office of those individuals and groups that had been traditionally accustomed to hold the reins of power. The older political leaders were being replaced by the wrong sort of men—men who pandered to the desires and wishes of the mob and acted according to the dictates of political expediency rather than to the principles of right and justice. "The undeniable and sadly plain fact," wrote von Holst, "is that since that time the people have begun to exchange the leadership of a small number of statesmen and politicians of a higher order for the rule of an ever increasing crowd of politicians of high and low degree, down

---

[2]James Parton, *Life of Andrew Jackson*, 3 vols. (New York, 1861), 3:694.
[3]*Ibid.*, p. 699.

even to the pot-house politician and the common thief, in the protecting mantle of demagogism . . . politics became a profession in which mediocrity—on an ever descending scale—dominated, and moral laxity became the rule, if not a requisite."[4] Von Holst's words were echoed by other writers. Since Jackson, Parton charged, "the public affairs of the United States have been conducted with a stupidity which has excited the wonder of mankind."[5]

The antipathy of these nineteenth-century scholars toward Jackson is not difficult to understand. Most of them had come from eastern, middle-class, patrician families that had enjoyed social and political leadership for well over a century. Viewing themselves as an aristocratic elite that held a monopoly of the ability to govern wisely and effectively, they were especially resentful of the democratization and seeming debasement of American politics. In their eyes Jacksonian Democracy was the movement that had resulted in their own loss of status and power. Believing that the affairs of the state should be conducted by the "right" sort of people, they condemned Jackson for supposedly beginning the process of corrupting an ideal state of affairs. The masses of people, these patrician aristocrats believed, were incapable of self-government; their interests could best be looked after by an uncorruptible aristocracy truly devoted to the welfare of the nation. Their historical writings, then, represented a Federalist-Whig-Republican point of view. Consequently they were in most respects highly critical of and hostile toward Jackson.

By the beginning of the twentieth century the study of history in the United States had begun to undergo a profound transformation. No longer did eastern patricians dominate historical writing. Instead, their places were taken by younger scholars, many of whom came from different parts of the country and did not hold aristocratic elitist views. These younger historians saw in their discipline both a means of illuminating contemporary problems and providing guidelines for future action. Staunch believers in democracy and progress they tended to favor those leaders and movements that had contributed the most to the growing democratization of the American people and their institutions. Unlike the patricians they did not write about American history in terms of decline from some supposed earlier golden age. On the contrary, they wrote American history in terms of protracted conflict between the people and the special interests, between the forces of democracy as against aristocracy, so that each epoch brought their country closer and closer to what they felt was its true democratic destiny. These historians, most of whom were part of the Progressive

---

[4]Hermann E. von Holst, *The Constitutional and Political History of the United States*, 8 vols. (Chicago, 1876–1892), 2:77.

[5]Parton, *Life of Andrew Jackson*, 3:700.

school of American historiography, began to break with the views of the older patrician school. In doing so they set the stage for a radical reevaluation of Jackson and his role in American history.

The changing attitude toward Andrew Jackson first became evident in the writings of Frederick Jackson Turner, one of the earliest of the great Progressive historians. Just as Parton and other patrician historians leaned toward aristocracy, so Turner leaned toward democracy. Indeed, his famous paper on the significance of the frontier in American history in 1893 was an effort to differentiate Americans from Europeans by emphasizing the democratizing influence of a frontier environment. According to Turner, Andrew Jackson was in some ways the logical culmination of the triumph of democratic values in the United States. "On the whole," Turner wrote, "it must be said that Jackson's Presidency was more representative of the America of his time than would have been that of any of his rivals. The instincts of the American people in supporting him conformed to the general drift of the tendencies of this New World democracy—a democracy which preferred persons to property, an active share by the people in government to the greater system and efficiency of a scientific administration by experts or by an established elite who dealt with the people from above."[6]

From the turn of the century until the end of World War II the Progressive school interpretation of Jacksonian Democracy remained dominant among American historians. In numerous books and articles scholars contributed to the growing identification between the triumph of political democracy and the accession of Jackson to the presidency. Even the supposed introduction of the spoils system—a development that patrician historians had regarded as an unmitigated disaster—began to be studied in a new light. The spoils system, Progressive historians emphasized, was both a reflection and a result of a democracy. Prior to Jackson public office had been monopolized by a small social and economic elite who had regarded government as their own private preserve. But the introduction of universal manhood suffrage and the emergence of a broad-based two-party system destroyed the monopoly of this elite and threw open governmental office to all persons regardless of their class or background. The spoils system, then, was the democratic alternative to an elitist monopoly. Far from abhorring the spoils system Progressive historians saw it as the logical consequence of democracy even though they recognized that it was, under certain conditions, susceptible to abuses.

The culmination of the Progressive interpretation of Jacksonian Democracy came in 1945 when Arthur M. Schlesinger, Jr., published

---

[6]Frederick Jackson Turner, *The United States 1830–1850: The Nation and Its Sections* (New York, 1935), p. 28.

his Pulitzer Prize–winning study *The Age of Jackson*. This book immediately became the starting point for historiographical controversy and
scholars, generally speaking, fell into either the pro- or anti-Schlesinger
camp. Indeed, so great was the impact of this book that much of the
current debate over Jacksonian Democracy may be dated from the publication of *The Age of Jackson*.

What Schlesinger succeeded in doing was to sharpen and elucidate
in a brilliant and provocative manner the Progressive school interpretation of the Jacksonian era. While his Progressive predecessors had
regarded Jackson and democracy as related subjects, they had never
clearly spelled out the nature of the relationship in other than general
and vague terms. Earlier Progressive historians, for example, had assumed that throughout most of American history economic opportunity had prevented a potential plutocracy from consolidating its rule.
Although concerned over the growing disparities between rich and
poor in twentieth-century America, they believed that periodic re-
newals of the democratic faith would modify or ameliorate the overt
class struggles that wracked European society. Like most middle-class
Americans they disliked open class conflict; in their historical writings, therefore, they played down open class strife and stressed instead
a sectional conflict between the democratic West, the capitalist Northeast, and the aristocratic slave-owning South.

Schlesinger, on the other hand, minimized sectional conflict as the
key to an understanding of American politics during the 1830s. "It
seems clear now," he argued, "that more can be understood about Jacksonian democracy if it is regarded as a problem not of sections but of
classes."[7] In his eyes the impetus behind Jackson came from noncapi-
talists, farmers, and workingmen, who were reacting to the economic
hardships of the period as well as to the domination of business interests seeking to extend their control over the economy. Where Turner
and other sectional historians had emphasized the support that Jackson drew from the West, Schlesinger argued that it was the eastern
urban working class that had played the more important role.

Schlesinger's interpretation of Jacksonian Democracy in terms of
class conflict was set within a broader framework of his understanding
of American history as a whole. The Jacksonian era, Schlesinger maintained, was simply one phase in the continual conflict between liberalism and conservatism in America. American democracy, he wrote, had
always accepted the idea of an enduring struggle among competing
groups for control of the state. Such a struggle was one of the guarantees of liberty, for it prevented the domination of the government by
any single group. "The business community," Schlesinger forcefully
remarked, "has been ordinarily the most powerful of these groups, and

---

[7]Arthur M. Schlesinger, Jr., *The Age of Jackson* (Boston, 1945), p. 263.

liberalism in America has been ordinarily the movement on the part of the other sections of society to restrain the power of the business community. This was the tradition of Jefferson and Jackson, and it has been the basic meaning of American liberalism."[8]

Within this framework Schlesinger's approach to Jackson and his followers was highly favorable. Jackson's attack on the Second Bank of the United States was justified, for the bank, although performing public functions, was completely independent of popular control. Indeed the bank symbolized the alliance between the federal government and the business community. Although Schlesinger clearly pointed out that antipathy toward Nicholas Biddle and the bank came from diverse, even opposing forces, his point was that the bank war represented a phase in the struggle to restrain and curtail the power of the business community. In this sense Jackson and Jacksonian Democracy could only be understood and interpreted within the liberal reformist tradition. The first selection in this chapter is taken from a recent retrospective analysis by Schlesinger of his book.

Schlesinger's interpretation of Jacksonian Democracy, however, did not long go unchallenged. Indeed within two years after the publication of *The Age of Jackson* a number of scholars expressed their dissent in no uncertain terms. While few of these critics could agree on an alternative hypothesis, they concurred that Schlesinger's democratic and class conflict hypothesis was not substantiated by the facts. The result was an extended debate among American historians over the problem of explaining the nature and significance of Jacksonian Democracy.

Generally speaking, Schlesinger's critics fell into two general schools. The first, known as the entrepreneurial school, maintained that Jackson did not represent the great masses of people who were attempting to curb the power and authority of the business community. On the contrary, the Jacksonians themselves were middle-class entrepreneurs and businessmen seeking to free themselves from the restraining hand of government and who sought to embark on ventures that would bring them immediate wealth regardless of the human and social costs involved. The second tradition in American historiography that emerged after 1945 went even further and denied the existence of a movement known as Jacksonian Democracy. The political struggles of the 1830s, argued some of these historians, revolved around local issues and a desire for public office; no ideological divisions whatsoever were involved.

The first criticisms from the entrepreneurial school came shortly after Schlesinger had published *The Age of Jackson*. In a series of articles and then in a Pulitzer Prize–winning book, Bray Hammond, a

[8]*Ibid.*, p. 505.

scholarly official of the Federal Reserve Board, took to task Schlesinger's interpretation of the Second Bank of the United States. Hammond denied Schlesinger's contention that the bank was "the keystone in the alliance between the government and the business community."[9] He argued instead that this institution performed the role of a central bank—that is, it was a responsible regulatory agency that had as its function the prevention of disastrous, periodic economic crises by pursuing sound monetary and fiscal policies. However, within the Democratic party, Hammond wrote, there existed a rising group of entrepreneurs who resented the obstacles that prevented them from embarking on speculative ventures that would bring them quick wealth. They resented particularly the Second Bank of the United States, in part because its sound monetary policy hampered speculative enterprises, and in part because the bank was controlled by Philadelphia interests. These entrepreneurs—centered in New York State and particularly New York City (and Wall Street)—wanted to destroy the national power of the bank in order to further their own economic interests.

In Andrew Jackson, according to Hammond, these rising entrepreneurs found their champion. For Jackson seemed to epitomize the rising tide of democracy in the United States. The appeal of the Jacksonians was extraordinarily broad, for it was phrased in traditional agrarian, democratic, and individualistic terms. Jackson, who never clearly comprehended the issues involved, was persuaded that the bank, by virtue of its privileged position, was destroying economic opportunity. Hence he destroyed the bank. But the result was more than the end of a single financial institution; the power of the federal government to regulate the economy through fiscal and economic policy was thereby greatly diminished. Consequently American society throughout the nineteenth century was subjected to the extreme ups and downs of the business cycle, with all of the human suffering and other undesirable effects that attended periodic depressions. Indeed, by the beginning of the twentieth century the federal government was forced, once again, to reassert the type of financial control required in any modern complex industrial nation. The price of industrialization during the nineteenth century, Hammond concluded, was much greater than it might have been had the bank been able to continue its regulatory activities.[10]

Hammond's thesis, of course, was in some respects diametrically opposed to that of Schlesinger, who had seen Jackson as the champion

----

[9]*Ibid.,* p. 76.

[10]Hammond's most extended discussion of Jacksonian Democracy appeared in his *Banks and Politics in America: From the Revolution to the Civil War* (Princeton, 1957), pp. 286 ff.

of the masses. Hammond, on the other hand, saw Jackson and his followers as middle-class entrepreneurs committed to a laissez-faire policy solely to benefit their own narrow ends. In this sense Jacksonian Democracy was not strictly a democratic movement; it was a movement by expectant capitalists seeking only to free themselves from government restraint.

Oddly enough the entrepreneurial school's interpretation of Jackson and that of Schlesinger had a great deal in common. Both Schlesinger and his entrepreneurial critics viewed Jacksonian Democracy in terms of classes; both rejected an exclusively agrarian approach to the Jacksonians; and both emphasized the urban sources of the movement. Despite these seeming similarities the two came to sharply differing conclusions. By emphasizing the middle-class sources of Jacksonian Democracy the entrepreneurial historians were, in effect, denying that the movement was in the American liberal tradition as Schlesinger had claimed. Instead of championing the cause of the people Jackson was upholding the cause of liberal capitalism. Thus the political struggles of the 1830s, these scholars emphasized, could not be viewed within a class framework that pitted the people against business and other special interests; some other hypothesis would have to be found in order to make some sense out of the politics and personalities of that era.

Hammond's entrepreneurial approach was echoed in one form or another by other historians, notably Richard Hofstadter and Joseph Dorfman, both of whom saw in Jackson a president who was fundamentally probusiness in his outlook. In *The American Political Tradition and the Men Who Made It*, Hofstadter entitled one of his chapters "Andrew Jackson and the Rise of Liberal Capitalism." The Jacksonian movement, he emphasized, was "a phase in the expansion of liberated capitalism" and "was closely linked to the ambitions of the small capitalist." To Hofstadter the popular hatred of privilege and the dominant laissez-faire ideology—both of which came together in Jacksonian Democracy—made an unhappy combination. Their convergence in a single political movement created a mythology that defined democracy in terms of a weak central government, thereby permitting powerful economic interests a disproportionate share of influence in questions involving national policy.[11]

The reaction against the Progressive school interpretation of Jacksonian Democracy by entrepreneurial historians was also reinforced after 1945 by neoconservative historians, who rejected a class analysis of history and emphasized instead a basic consensus that supposedly united all Americans. In the United States, these historians argued,

---

[11]Richard Hofstadter, *The American Political Tradition and the Men Who Made It* (New York, 1948), pp. 55–63.

politics never revolved around ideological and class conflicts precisely because Americans shared a common outlook founded on Lockean middle-class liberalism. Reacting to the external threat posed to American institutions by the Soviet Union in particular and Marxism in general, the work of these historians reflected the emphasis on national unity so characteristic of the postwar era. The rejection of a clear class interpretation of Jacksonian politics was further reinforced by the work of historians who were influenced by the quantitative studies undertaken in other social science disciplines, especially political science, and who attempted to analyze party struggles by gathering and analyzing aggregate voting behavior of large numbers of individuals. Their statistical findings raised some serious questions about the validity of an interpretation that relied on a simple class division and the platforms and statements of parties and leaders.

Although neoconservative and quantitative-minded historians rejected a class conflict analysis of Jacksonian Democracy, they were set apart from the entrepreneurial school, which viewed the period in terms of a struggle between competing economic groups. The entrepreneurial school, it will be recalled, viewed Jackson as a symbol of the rising middle class in American civilization. The basic struggle in the 1830s, they suggested, was not between the haves and the havenots, but between two sets of capitalists—between newer entrepreneurs seeking to free themselves of the shackles imposed by the government regulation that was exercised through the Second Bank of the United States, and the older and more conservative entrepreneurs seeking to guide economic development through a neomercantilist policy that gave the central government an important role in economic affairs.

These newer historians, however went far beyond the approach of the entrepreneurial school in rejecting a class-conflict approach altogether. Although they conceded that the entrepreneurial historians had made a significant contribution in emphasizing the middle-class rather then the lower-class nature of the Jacksonian movement, these scholars believed that the movement had to be interpreted within a different framework. Consequently they began to advance their own explanations of the nature of Jacksonian Democracy, its sources, its development, and its significance in American history.

Some historians, to cite one example, began to deal with the Jacksonian era within a psychological framework. Influenced by work done in the social and behavioral sciences, they sought to apply certain concepts from these disciplines in such a way as to arrive at new insights in the study of history. The idea of reform was particularly susceptible to a psychological analysis, for historians had long been interested in understanding the motivation and behavior of various types of reformers.

In the hands of this psychologically oriented school of historians, the Jacksonians could only be understood in terms of status insecurity. The participation of the Jacksonians in various reform efforts, including their attack on the Second Bank of the United States, resulted not from their ideology but rather from their feelings of anxiety regarding their status in society. Reform served as a compensation for this insecurity and gave them an alternative outlet for self-expression. What these scholars were implying was that the Jacksonians resorted to reform activities because of their inability to adjust to the changing ways of American society. Reform, in effect, served largely as a therapeutic function to calm their fears regarding their own status insecurity. Within such a framework the psychological school reduced all issues to psychological terms.

The most sophisticated example of the psychological interpretation of Jacksonian Democracy was Marvin Meyers' prize-winning book *The Jacksonian Persuasion*. Meyers argued that the Jacksonians wanted to preserve the virtues of a simple agrarian republic without having to sacrifice the rewards and conveniences of modern capitalism. By the 1830s, Meyers suggested, the United States was already on the road toward industrialization. The Jacksonians, together with many of their supporters, were unprepared for all of the changes taking place in their society—changes that were undermining traditional values and giving rise to unfamiliar and unwelcome institutions. Their response was a crusade to try and restore the virtues of the simple agrarian republic that had supposedly existed about the time of the American Revolution. The enemy, according to Jackson and his followers, was best personified in the Second Bank of the United States, for this institution did not create true wealth, but merely represented a *"paper* money power, the *corporate* money power—i.e., concentrations of wealth arising suddenly from financial manipulation and special privilege, ill-gotten gains." Because the bank was corrupting the plain republican order that they held so dear, the Jacksonians decided to cut out this source of corruption in the body politic. Herein, Meyers concluded, lay a paradox. The Jacksonians believed that in attacking the bank they were destroying an institution that menaced their idealized agrarian republic; in reality, they were destroying a regulatory institution, thereby paving the way for the triumph of laissez-faire capitalism.[12]

Historians of the psychological school, of course, were considerably indebted to their predecessors. Meyers, for example, had accepted Schlesinger's description of Jacksonian political rhetoric as well as Hammond's argument that Jacksonian Democracy implied laissez-faire capitalism. Nevertheless, his synthesis simply reduced the Jacksonian movement to a set of psychological adjustments; one could not understand Jackson and his followers as part of a long and viable re-

---

[12]Marvin Meyers, *The Jacksonian Persuasion: Politics and Belief* (Stanford, 1957).

form tradition. Nor were class conflicts determining factors in the movement. The ferment during the Jacksonian era was the result of competition for status and position by certain groups within society rather than competition between classes.

The psychological interpretation of Jacksonian Democracy was only one approach taken by post-1945 historians. Within the next two decades another group of scholars went farther; they denied that Jacksonian Democracy, as an organized movement or even a concept, ever existed. They argued instead that American historians who had utilized the concept had been influenced by their commitment to a democratic ideology. Such a commitment had led these historians to read their own values back into the past, thereby making Andrew Jackson a symbolic champion of the people in what they saw as a perennial struggle against the business class and other special interests. An examination of the sources, these historians emphasized, would completely discredit the Progressive school interpretation of Jacksonian Democracy.

But if Andrew Jackson was neither the champion of the people nor even the representative of the emerging laissez-faire capitalism, then how could the politics of the 1830s be interpreted? In answering this question, these historians tended to borrow heavily from the behavioral sciences and to use quantitative techniques in order to demonstrate that the American people were not divided along class and ideological lines. In this respect their work paralleled the suffrage studies of Robert E. Brown and other colonial historians who had argued that seventeenth- and eighteenth-century America was already a middle-class democratic society. If American society was obviously democratic by the 1820s, Jackson could hardly be considered within a democratic reformist tradition.

Thus Richard P. McCormick, in several studies of voting behavior during the Jacksonian era, challenged the thesis that an unprecedented upsurge in voting had been responsible for Jackson's victories in 1828 and 1832. Indeed, McCormick argued, the real upsurge in voter participation came after Jackson was out of office in 1840. The growth of what he called the second American party system (to distinguish it from the Federalist and Jeffersonian party system) was not precipitated by ideological or class issues. It originated rather in the successive presidential contests between 1824 and 1840. "It did not emerge," McCormick wrote, "from cleavages within Congress, nor from any polarization of attitudes on specific public issues, nor did it represent merely the revival in new form of pre-existing party alignments. The second party system did not spring into existence at any one time. Rather, new party alignments appeared at different times from region to region. The most influential factor determining when alignments appeared within a particular region was the regional identifications of the presidential candidates. As changes occurred in the personnel involved in the contest for the presidency, corresponding changes took place in regional party alignments. New England, for example, was politically monolithic in support of John Quincy Adams, but when Clay was substituted for Adams, a two-party situation resulted. The South was monolithic behind Jackson, but when he was replaced by Van Buren, the South divided into two parties."[13]

More recently McCormick defined what he calls the "Presidential Game"—a contest conducted according to definable (but changing) rules. In brief, he argues that for a variety of reasons the method of selecting a president under the federal Constitution has changed sharply in practice if not in law. The framers of the Constitution hoped to make the presidency into an office that would transcend the factionalism and corruption inherent in politics. But the first four presidential elections demonstrated that the rules of the game were uncertain and hazardous. A second version of the game developed with the election of Thomas Jefferson; Virginians dominated the presidency for the next twenty-four years. In turn the "Virginia game" was succeeded by the "game of faction," which held sway briefly from 1824 to 1832. The final version—the "party game"—came into existence in 1832 and lasted until after World War II. The implications of McCormick's structural argument are obvious: Jacksonian Democracy, in terms of a distinct ideological party apparatus, never existed.[14]

McCormick, nevertheless, was cognizant of the economic and social forces that were transforming America during these decades. Such changes, he observed in an article reprinted as the second selection in this chapter, actually intensified regional differences and threatened the very existence of the union. Jackson, cognizant of the dangers posed by such issues as slavery and the tariff, worked assiduously to keep interregional conflicts out of national politics. Individuals, he insisted, should rely on the natural order rather than the contrivances of government. At the very time that government activity declined popular participation in the electoral system increased. Hence the price of union was "immobilism"—a characteristic that was to have profound consequences when the slavery issue could no longer be evaded.

Others also insisted that the age of Jackson was simply too heterogeneous and defied simple labeling. In a study of the distribution of wealth during this era Edward Pessen emphasized the theme of in-

---

[13]Richard P. McCormick, *The Second American Party System: Party Formation in the Jacksonian Era* (Chapel Hill, 1966), p. 13. See also McCormick's two articles, "New Perspectives on Jacksonian Politics," *American Historical Review* 65 (January 1960): 288–301, and "Suffrage Classes and Party Alignments: A Study in Voter Behavior," *Mississippi Valley Historical Review* 46 (December 1959):397–410.

[14]Richard P. McCormick, *The Presidential Game: The Origins of American Presidential Politics* (New York, 1982).

equality rather than equality. Wealth, rather then being widely distributed, was becoming ever more concentrated, and the nation's social structure more rigid and less fluid. Those who succeeded were generally born into affluent families. If society was becoming more unequal, Pessen asked, how can historians continue to equate the age of Jackson with egalitarianism? Indeed, in an earlier work he noted that there was something to be said for calling the Jacksonian period "an age of materialism and opportunism, reckless speculation and erratic growth, unabashed vulgarity, and a politic, *seeming* deference to the common man by the uncommon men who actually ran things."[15]

In an equally significant work Lee Benson sifted the focus from political parties to the electorate. Rejecting a socioeconomic approach, Benson was among the earliest historians to emphasize the role of national origins and religion as among the most important determinants of voting behavior. Influenced by both behavioral theory developed in the social science disciplines and quantification, he attempted to demonstrate that voting behavior was due in large measure to basic differences in religious values and world views. Ethnic and cultural differences, he insisted, helped to shape the voters' perceptions of issues and thus to determine party affiliation. Drawing upon the work of the sociologist Robert K. Merton, Benson also argued that homogeneous groups often affiliated with one party because the other party already claimed the allegiance of groups with differing ethnic and religious characteristics and holding dissimilar views on moral and cultural issues. Jacksonian Democracy, he concluded, was a fiction created by American historians, and in *The Concept of Jacksonian Democracy: New York as a Test Case* he attempted to prove the validity of the proposition that since the 1820s "ethnic and religious differences have tended to be *relatively* the most important sources of political differences." In succeeding years others followed Benson's lead in developing an ethnocultural interpretation of American politics, thus vitiating the very reality of Jacksonian Democracy as a conceptual construct.[16]

---

[15]Edward Pessen, "The Egalitarian Myth and the American Social Reality: Wealth, Mobility, and Equality in the 'Era of the Common Man,'" *American Historical Review* 76 (October 1971):989–1034, and *Jacksonian America: Society, Personality and Politics* (Homewood, Ill., 1969), pp. 350–351. Surprisingly enough, New Left scholars have all but ignored the Jacksonian era. One exception is Michael A. Lebowitz, "The Jacksonians: Paradox Lost?," in *Towards a New Past: Dissenting Essays in American History*, Barton J. Bernstein, ed. (New York, 1968), pp. 65–89.

[16]Lee Benson, *The Concept of Jacksonian Democracy: New York as a Test Case* (Princeton, 1961). For a more recent discussion by Benson of the Jacksonian period see his essay "Middle Period Historiography: What Is to Be Done," in *American History: Retrospect and Prospect*, George A. Billias and Gerald N. Grob, eds. (New York, 1971), pp. 154–190. For a perceptive discussion of the ethnocultural approach to nineteenth-century American political history see Richard L. McCormick, "Ethno-Cultural Interpretations of Nineteenth-Century American Voting Behavior," *Political Science Quarterly* 89 (June 1974):351–377.

Benson, moreover, categorically denied the very existence of an organized and cohesive reform movement centered around Andrew Jackson and his followers. Indeed he insisted that the program of the Jacksonian party—which included states' rights, a strong executive leadership, freedom of conscience, and the idea of representative government—could hardly be equated with democracy. Such a program, he even suggested, was the negation of the democratic, egalitarian, and humanitarian movements that emerged during the nineteenth century. As an alternative hypothesis, Benson suggested that the era be named the "Age of Egalitarianism." Ideological changes, a phenomenal growth of the nation, and a high rate of physical mobility all combined to increase sharply the opportunities available to Americans and hence produced a more egalitarian society by 1860.

In recent years historians have increasingly rejected simple dualisms and explanations. As Ronald P. Formisano noted in a recent review of the literature, Whigs and Democrats *did* diverge in their conception of the individual, society, and relationship between government and the economy, but the patterns of divergence were complex rather than simple. "It is unlikely, however," he noted, "that parties in this period will be fitted to a liberal-conservative schema or that Jackson and his opponents will be divided again into radical democrats and aristocrats. No single ideological scheme will do to order the political, social, and cultural conflicts of that world, and certainly none exists which would allow scholars to vote comfortably for either of those parties."[17]

In a similar vein, some scholars have insisted that the consequences of actions by such political leaders as Andrew Jackson have been exaggerated. In an important and seminal study of the Jacksonian economy and the cycle of inflation, crisis, and deflation, Peter Temin maintained that the role of Jackson was far less than contemporaries believed; historians also erred in making Jackson a prime mover on the economic scene. "His policies," Temin concluded, "did not help the economy to adjust to the harsh requirements of external forces, but they were of little importance besides these far stronger influences."[18]

Despite the criticisms of the very concept of Jacksonian Democracy, the conviction that there were significant ideological and programmatic differences between parties have persisted. The Whigs, according to Lawrence F. Kohl, represented the emerging commercial society; the Democrats were unalterably opposed. Others emphasized

---

[17]Ronald P. Formisano, "Toward a Reorientation of Jacksonian Politics: A Review of the Literature, 1959–1975," *Journal of American History* 63 (June 1975):64. See also Formisano's *The Transformation of Popular Culture: Massachusetts Parties, 1790s–1840s* (New York, 1983).

[18]Peter Temin, *The Jacksonian Economy* (New York, 1969), p. 176.

the Whig commitment to entrepreneurial values, as compared with their opponent's faith in equality.[19]

Nor have more traditional explanations of Jackson's presidency disappeared from view. Richard B. Latner, for example, emphasized that the election of 1828 represented the rise of the West as an integral partner of the second American party system. Conceding his debt to Frederick Jackson Turner, Latner nevertheless rejected any simple generalizations about the role of sections or the importance of frontier democracy. Instead he found in Andrew Jackson the prototype of the modern president; the "Kitchen Cabinet" was the counterpart of the modern presidential bureaucracy that emerged during the twentieth century. Jackson's agenda, moreover, was directed toward the restoration of Jeffersonian principles to government. In effect, Latner synthesized Turner's emphasis on the importance of the West with Schlesinger's interpretation of Jackson as a part of America's liberal tradition.[20]

Similarly, Robert V. Remini returned to several older themes in a masterful multivolume biography of Andrew Jackson. Remini insisted that Jackson did indeed symbolize the age that bore his name. Early and mid-nineteenth-century American history reflected three major themes: empire, democracy, and freedom. By strengthening the office of the presidency, Jackson furthered the march of democracy. In this sense Remini returned at least in part to the themes associated with Turner.[21]

The absence of broad synthetic works centered around the concept of Jacksonian Democracy, however, is not to suggest that interest in this subject has disappeared. On the contrary, studies of individual states and communities have shed considerable light on economic, political, and social developments.[22] In *Chants Democratic*, for example, Sean Wilentz attempted to demonstrate that working-class political movements in New York City during the 1830s were class-based and directed against an emerging capitalism. Influenced by the "new social

---

[19]Lawrence F. Kohl, *The Politics of Individualism: Parties and the American Character in the Jacksonian Era* (New York, 1989); Daniel W. Howe, *The Political Culture of the American Whigs* (Chicago, 1979); John Ashworth, *'Agrarians' and 'Aristocrats': Party Political Ideology in the United States* (London, 1983).

[20]Richard B. Latner, *The Presidency of Andrew Jackson: White House Politics, 1829–1837* (Athens, Ga., 1979).

[21]Robert V. Remini, *Andrew Jackson and the Course of American Empire, 1767–1821* (New York, 1977); *Andrew Jackson and the Course of American Freedom, 1822–1832* (New York, 1981); and *Andrew Jackson and the Course of American Democracy 1833–1845* (New York, 1984).

[22]Recent works on the Jacksonian period include M. J. Heale, *The Presidential Quest: Candidates and Images in American Political Culture* (London, 1982); Daniel Feller, *The Public Lands in Jacksonian Politics* (Madison, 1984); Amy Bridges, *A City in the Republic: Antebellum New York and the Origins of Machine Politics* (New York, 1984); and Richard E. Ellis, *The Union at Risk: Jacksonian Democracy, States' Rights and the Nullification Crisis* (New York, 1987).

history," Wilentz was also aware of the elements that impeded the unity of workers, including nativism, sex, and race. In effect, his book represented an effort to synthesize several older historiographical traditions that emphasized class and conflict with some of the insights of the "new social history."[23]

In a recent review of the literature, Daniel Feller has suggested that a new synthesis is in the making. Its outlines, though yet vague, nevertheless point in a particular direction. The Jacksonian party system "arose in response to the transformation of the market and class relationships accompanying the transportation revolution." The differences between Whigs and Democrats were real and not imagined. In its extreme forms, Whiggery was identified with aristocrats, innovators, social disciplinarians, entrepreneurs, and towns, where Democracy was more closely affiliated with agrarians, traditionalists, libertarians, laborers, and the countryside. Oftentimes party differences were complicated by ethnic and religious differences, and those who fought for fundamental social changes (e.g., abolitionists or working-class radicals) had to operate independently of the party system. The second party system, Feller concluded, was the vehicle that forged a consensus on the outlines of a democratic capitalist society, thereby resolving conflict within a political system.[24] If it becomes a reality, such a synthesis would incorporate the works of such different scholars as Turner, Schlesinger, and Benson.

Considering the ways in which historians have approached the Jacksonian era, is it possible to offer any judgment about their relative worth? Was the Progressive school correct in arguing that Jackson and his followers represented the people in their struggle against privilege and vested interests, and that the movement was one phase in the continuing conflict for political, social, and economic democracy? Or were entrepreneurial historians right to stress the identification of the Jacksonians with laissez-faire capitalism? Were both partially right and wrong, as some recent historians have insisted? Was national politics simply a struggle between competing electoral machines? Did voter preferences reflect ethnic and cultural rather than class differences? Or was class the most significant element even though modified by ethnic and religious elements? Above all, is Jacksonian Democracy an appropriate designation for this important era of American history?[25]

---

[23]Sean Wilentz, *Chants Democratic: New York City and the Rise of the American Working Class, 1788-1850* (New York, 1984). See also Wilentz's article, "On Class and Politics in Jacksonian America," *Reviews in American History* 10 (December 1982):45–63.

[24]Daniel Feller, "Politics and Society: Toward a Jacksonian Synthesis," *Journal of the Early Republic* 10 (Summer 1990):135–161.

[25]For a periodization of nineteenth-century political history that all but ignores the Jacksonian era as a distinct entity, see Richard L. McCormick, "The Party Period and Public Policy: An Exploratory Hypothesis," *Journal of American History* 66 (September 1979):279–298.

Arthur M. Schlesinger, Jr.

ARTHUR M. SCHLESINGER, JR. (1917–   ) *is Albert Schweitzer Professor of the Humanities at the City University of New York. He was also a special assistant to President John F. Kennedy. Among his many published books are* The Age of Jackson *(1945),* The Age of Roosevelt, 3 vols. *(1957–1960),* A Thousand Days: John F. Kennedy in the White House *(1965), and* Robert Kennedy and His Times *(1978).*

My involvement with the age of Jackson began more than half a century ago. Seeking a subject for an honors essay as an undergraduate at Harvard College in the autumn of 1937, I chose the formidable nineteenth-century American intellectual Orestes A. Brownson. Brownson was a man of many careers—preacher, editor, Transcendentalist fellow traveler, Jacksonian reformer, Catholic convert—and an episode in his Jacksonian phase struck me as of curious interest.

In 1838 Brownson's services in the Jacksonian cause had been rewarded by his appointment as inspector of a government hospital. The arrangement permitted him to continue editing a magazine; and when Jackson's friend and successor President Martin Van Buren ran for re-election in the picturesque "Tippecanoe and Tyler too" contest of 1840, Brownson created considerable embarrassment for his fellow Democrats by writing an inflammatory essay entitled "The Laboring Classes." After describing the exploitation of the workers, Brownson raised the specter of "that most dreaded of all wars, the war of the poor against the rich, a war which, however long it may be delayed, will come, and come with all its horrors." To avert that war, he said, the age must recognize its historic responsibility. "Our business is to emancipate the proletaries, as the past has emancipated the slaves."

Reading "The Laboring Classes" a century later, I was struck by Brownson's drastic class analysis. How had it come about that, eight years before Marx and Engels produced *The Communist Manifesto*, a Jacksonian Democrat in far-off America expressed such "Marxist" views in such "Marxist" language? Brownson moreover, had received his government job from the historian George Bancroft, who, as collector of the port of Boston, was Van Buren's man in Massachusetts, and

---

Arthur M. Schlesinger, Jr., "The Ages of Jackson," *New York Review of Books*, December 7, 1989, 48–51. Reprinted with permission from *The New York Review of Books*. Copyright © 1989 Nyrev, Inc. Adapted from the introduction to the American Past edition of "The Age of Jackson" published by the Book-of-the-Month Club © 1989.

Bancroft evidently thought along similar lines. "The feud between the capitalist and laborer, the house of Have and the house of Want," Bancroft had written, "is as old as social union. . . . It is now for the yeomanry and the mechanics to march at the head of civilization. The merchants and the lawyers, that is, the moneyed interest broke up feudalism. The day for the multitude has now dawned."

Jackson had conventionally been seen as a champion of the frontier; his presidency as the eruption of the backwoods west into national power. Yet it appeared that eastern intellectuals like Brownson and Bancroft had their own stake in the Jacksonian uprising. Moreover, was not someone like Henry Clay of Kentucky quite as representative of the frontier as Andrew Jackson of Tennessee? And Clay, as the champion of the American System of national development, based on the protective tariff, the United States Bank, and federal aid for internal improvement, was Jackson's mortal political antagonist.

If Jacksonianism meant no more than the surge of uncouth backwoodsmen onto the national scene, why were so many leading writers and artists of the day—not only Bancroft and Brownson but James Fenimore Cooper, Nathaniel Hawthorne, William Cullen Bryant, Washington Irving, Walt Whitman, James Kirke Paulding, the actor Edwin Forrest, the sculptors Horatio Greenough and Hiram Powers—ardent Jacksonians? And if the frontier was the force driving the Jacksonian upheaval, how to account for the preoccupation in the pamphlet literature by Jackson's supporters with problems of a commercial society— with monopoly, with banking, with the business cycle, with the unequal distribution of the fruits of labor, with workingmen, with trade unions, with class conflict? How to account for the hatred the business community showed for Jackson and his works?

The Age of Jackson sought to combine narrative and analysis in a fresh look at the Jacksonian revolution. Historians had nearly all agreed that Jacksonian democracy was a frontier phenomenon, but they had vigorously disagreed on whether this was a good or bad thing. Judgment on the merits had varied according to the political climate. When Jackson was in the White House, respectable opinion had seen him as a rude and violent westerner who introduced the spoils system, wrecked the banking system, invited the unwashed mob to Washington, and hastened the degradation of the democratic dogma. This was the view expounded more genially by James Parton a quarter century later in his delightful and still valuable three-volume biography of Jackson (1860–1861). It was reaffirmed in the long conservative interlude after the Civil War by the sociologist William Graham Sumner in the incisive biography he wrote for the American Statesmen series in 1882.

The Populist revolt in the 1890s followed by the Progressive movement in the early twentieth century generated new perspectives.

Frederick Jackson Turner argued the decisive significance of the western frontier in the rise of American democracy. Charles A. Beard offered an economic interpretation of the Constitution and analyzed the economic origins of Jeffersonian democracy. A new school of Progressive historians, seeking precedents for Theodore Roosevelt and Woodrow Wilson, ironically found more to praise in Jackson than TR and Wilson had done in their own days as historians. John Spencer Bassett in his excellent scholarly biography (1911), while expressing reservations about some of Jackson's actions and policies, was typical in saluting "his brave, frank, masterly leadership of the democratic movement which then established itself in our life." Writing a quarter century later under the shadow of the second Roosevelt, Marquis James in his vivid and detailed biography (1933, 1937) was almost unreserved in commendation.

Still, the Progressive historians mostly agreed with their conservative predecessors in seeing Jacksonian politics as essentially a conflict of sections rather than of classes and the Jacksonian victory as a triumph of western ideals. Beard in his *Rise of American Civilization* described the Jacksonian movement as "a triumphant farmer-labor party," but even Beard held to the Turner thesis of the frontier origins of Jacksonian democracy.

The Age of Jackson took a different tack. It argued that more could be understood about Jacksonian democracy if it were regarded as a problem not of sections but of classes. As Jacksonian policies evolved, I contended, they were increasingly shaped not by the needs and demands of the frontier but by the needs and demands of workingmen, small farmers, and intellectuals in the East. Class conflict, for example, was hardly a feature of the far frontier, yet it was a favorite Jacksonian theme. Frontiers breed equality and individualism. Class resentments arise in a developed and stratified economic order. It was the East, not the frontier, that had the bitter experience of shrinking opportunity, growing inequality, and hardening class lines. *The Age of Jackson* further contended that Jacksonian democracy constituted the second phase, Jeffersonianism having been the first, of the perennial struggle between the business community and the rest of society for control of the state, a struggle I saw as the basic meaning of American liberalism and as the guarantee of freedom in a capitalist democracy.

Like historians before me, I too was reflecting the politics of my time. Growing up in the 1930s, I was conditioned politically by the passions of the New Deal era. J. Franklin Jameson said of George Bancroft that his history voted for Jackson. Some have said of me that my history votes for FDR, and I guess there is something to that.

Conservatives in the angry 1930s used to fulminate against the New Deal as "un-American." I wanted to show that, far from importing foreign ideas, FDR was acting in a robustly American spirit and tradition. Jackson's war against Nicholas Biddle and the Second Bank of the United States as the instrumentality of the concentrated money power seemed an earlier and simpler version of the battles waged by Roosevelt against the "economic royalists" of my own day for control of national policy. The two presidents, it appeared, had much the same array of supporters and much the same array of enemies. (Years later I came upon a letter FDR had written to Colonel Edward M. House, Woodrow Wilson's *homme de confiance,* in November 1933. "The real truth of the matter," Roosevelt told House, "is, as you and I know, that a financial element in the larger centers has owned the Government ever since the days of Andrew Jackson—and I am not wholly excepting the Administration of W.W. The country is going through a repetition of Jackson's fight with the Bank of the United States—only on a far bigger and broader basis.")

The Age of Jackson was published in September 1945 while I was still in the army in Europe. The first reviews appeared two weeks after the surrender of Japan. Victory had vindicated the cause of liberal democracy. Now the question of democracy's capacity to manage an uncertain future was much in people's minds.

It was a propitious moment for a book about the American democratic tradition. Some families sent it to sons or husbands overseas who, like the author, were awaiting redeployment to the United States and demobilization. Over the years people have told me how they read *The Age of Jackson* in the South Pacific or the Aleutians or on transports on the way home.

Among historians *The Age of Jackson* has had its ups and downs. Its great value was that it helped reawaken professional interest in a complex and abundant period of American history. It stirred controversy, and controversy is always fruitful for historians. The initial reception was friendly. But soon objections were filed against one or another aspect of the book's argument. By the early 1950s, the New Deal impulse was running its course. The nation was tired of wrangling and eager for healing. The onset of the cold war increased the felt need to affirm national cohesion and unity. President Eisenhower embodied the new mood. Progressive history, with its emphasis on conflict, began to give way to the delineation and, for some historians, celebration of the American consensus.

Consensus historians contended that the beliefs that united Americans—private property, free enterprise, individual opportunity, limited government—were far more significant that the arguments that occasionally divided them. Those notorious confrontations beloved of progressive historians—between Jefferson and Hamilton, or Jackson and Nicholas Biddle, or FDR and Herbert Hoover—were dismissed as no more than family quarrels. Unlike the great revolutions of Europe, American political conflicts, the Civil War always excepted, were over nuances, not over basic shifts in ideas and power.

Scrutinized through the lenses of consensus history, the fierce political and ideological battles of the age of Jackson evaporated into inconsequence. Jacksonian Democrats and their Whig opponents, Richard Hofstadter and Bray Hammond explained, were all entrepreneurs together, all expectant capitalists, all plunged in the acquisitive scramble, all men on the make fighting sham battles to advance individual fortunes. Or, in Lee Benson's version, ethnicity and religion were far more powerful determinants of voting than economic interests or political ideas. As for the drastic ideologies and the fusillades of apocalyptic denunciation, this alarmist rhetoric, as Benson put it in a major tract of the ethnocultural school, was no more than "campaign claptrap." The consensus interpretation was eventually pressed to the point where it almost obliterated the differences between the Jacksonians and the Whigs and left the bitter political tone of the age of Jackson a mystery.

Now, as *The Age of Jackson* makes clear, there were indeed entrepreneurial hustlers in the Jacksonian coalition of the 1830s. There were state banking interests, southern planters, western inflationists, eastern businessmen on the way up. As a movement, Jacksonian democracy included opportunists out for a fast buck as well as radical democrats committed to pure doctrine. The same thing, *mutatis mutandis*, could be said of the Roosevelt coalition of the 1930s. Yet it seems to me hard to argue that Jacksonianism, or the New Deal for that matter, was essentially the philosophy of acquisitive enterprise. To identify Jackson with Biddle (or Herbert Hoover with FDR) would be to drain meaning from American political conflict. Analysis depends on the capacity to draw distinctions.

If the Jacksonians were a rabble of grasping entrepreneurs, who were the Whigs? If Jacksonian democracy served the interests of liberated capitalism, why were so many capitalists so ferociously against it? If many of the self-styled "workingmen" of Jackson's day were not, in fact, workers at all but small proprietors on their way up, why should they define themselves as members of the working class and carry on so about the rich? If Americans of the 1830s were all dedicated to the same capitalist ends, what in the world were the rhetoric of Orestes Brownson and George Bancroft and the savage political conflict of the Jackson era all about?

These were questions the entrepreneurial thesis failed to answer. I have no doubt that historians writing, as I did, in the 1930s and early 1940s, with New Deal struggles reverberating in our minds, tended to exaggerate conflict in the American past. But I have no doubt either that historians writing in the 1950s tended to exaggerate consensus in the American past. However much they may have had in common, Jackson and Nicholas Biddle and their respective followers disagreed vehemently on *something*.

The consensus interpretation foundered eventually on its "campaign claptrap" assumption, that is that the Jacksonians and Whigs of the 1830s did not know, or mean, what they were talking about when they claimed that great differences divided them—that their words misrepresented their real thoughts and motives and that what they said about why they were doing what they were doing was either self-deceived or cynical; in any case, historically worthless.

Now our vanity as historians is to suppose that we understand better than the people who were there what the shouting was about. It is true enough that scholars looking back can know some things better than contemporary participants did. But 20-20 hindsight can be carried too far. Too often we suggest that those poor chaps in the past may have thought they were acting for one set of reasons; but we, so much wiser, *know* they were acting for quite other reasons. This reductionism denies historical figures the validity of their own judgments and thereby denies their human dignity—and of course invites future historians to practice the same reductionism on us. When participants explain in urgent words why they lived, fought, and bled, is it not intellectual arrogance for historians to reject their testimony?

What then was the source of the intense sense of conflict? My surmise is that it had to do with the basic question of a democratic polity: Who is to control the state? The clarity of this point is obscured, however, by confusion with a separate question: What is the proper role of the state?

On the second question, Jackson regarded himself as a Jeffersonian who believed—or believed he believed—that that government was best which governed least. His purpose, he said, was

> to persuade my countrymen, so far as I may, that it is not in a splen-
> did government supported by powerful monopolies and aristocratical
> establishments that they will find happiness, but in a plain system,
> void of pomp, protecting all and granting favors to none, dispensing
> its blessings, like the dews of Heaven, unseen and unfelt save in the
> freshness and bounty they contribute to produce.

This was what I call "the Jeffersonian myth" in the last chapter of *The Age of Jackson*. As Marvin Meyers showed in his book *The Jacksonian Persuasion* (1957), the Jeffersonian myth was an essential part of the Jacksonian appeal—a potent appeal, in a time of wrenching economic change, to the frugal virtues of the old republic against the rising luxury, corruption, and concentrated money power.

In doctrine the Jacksonians were indisputably antistatist. On this level, my critics have a point when they claim the Whigs, and not the

Jacksonians, as the real forerunners of the New Deal. The tradition of affirmative government was the tradition of Hamilton, not of Jefferson. Hamilton's faith in the dynamics of individual acquisition was always tempered by an expectation of government control. Americans, he wrote, had "a certain fermentation of mind, a certain activity of speculation and enterprise which, if properly directed, may be made subservient to useful purposes but which, if left entirely to itself, may be attended with pernicious effect." Subsequent statesmen in this tradition, especially John Quincy Adams and Henry Clay, elaborated the Hamiltonian vision into what Clay called the American System—a great dream of economic development under the leadership of the national state.

When I wrote *The Age of Jackson*, "economic development" was not the issue that it became in the postwar years. The end of colonialism after the war and the emergence of independent states in the third world created new scholarly interest in the way a nation establishes its identity, evolves its political institutions, and achieves its economic growth. Analysis of this process gave historians new perspectives and insights.

Looking back, I think I did Hamilton, Adams, and Clay a good deal less than justice in *The Age of Jackson*. It is true that the American System, with its program of internal improvements, a protective tariff, and Biddle's Bank of the United States, was designed to benefit the business classes; but this was not the whole truth. The Whig program was also designed to benefit the nation and to accelerate the pace of economic growth. In retrospect the Hamiltonians had a sounder conception of the role of government and a more constructive policy of economic development than the antistatist Jacksonians.

While I am confessing error, I must say a word too for Jackson's allies in the war against the Bank, the wildcat bankers and their poorly secured paper notes. As Bray Hammond acidly pointed out in his able if misleading book *Banks and Politics in America from the Revolution to the Civil War* (1957), I knew very little about money when I wrote *The Age of Jackson*. My bias was rather in favor of the hard-money policy—that is, the maintenance of a stable ratio between paper and specie—and certainly against the unrestrained issue of paper notes by banks. As I now reflect on the Jacksonian period, having been enlightened in the years between by kindly instruction from John Kenneth Galbraith and the late Seymour Harris, I am less distressed by wildcat banking. The hard-money policy, systematically pursued, would have held back development. Wildcat banking enlarged the means of payment and stimulated growth. And as Peter Temin demonstrated in his admirable *The Jacksonian Economy* (1969), the inflation and subsequent depression of the 1830s were caused not by Jackson's termination of the Bank of the United States and consequent uncontrolled overissue of notes by wildcat bankers, but by international monetary factors beyond Jackson's control.

Saying that the Jacksonian doctrine was antistatist does not dispose, however, of the question: Who is to control the state? It does not even dispose of the other question: What is the proper role of the state?

The Jacksonians objected to the state because, as the radical editor William Leggett wrote at the time, the power of the state was "always" exercised "for the exclusive benefit of wealth. It was never wielded on behalf of the community." Governmental power in support of special privilege had to be stopped: hence Jackson's war against the Bank and the Maysville veto, his veto of a bill providing for federal purchase of stock in a Kentucky turnpike corporation. But government power wielded on behalf of the community would be another matter. Here the second question merges with the first: Who is to control the state? The Jacksonians were hostile to government intervention in the interests of the rich, not to government intervention per se. Where the Jeffersonians had supposed that governments would infallibly abuse power, Jackson in his Farewell address on March 4, 1837, relegated such abuse to the category of "extreme cases, which we have no reason to apprehend in a Government where the power is in the hands of a patriotic people."

Coming to the White House as a proclaimed foe of strong national government, Jackson, for all his Jeffersonian professions, left the national government stronger than ever before when he departed eight years later. In effect, he reinvented the presidency, changing the office from a rather passive and distant magistracy to an active agency of energy, initiative, and leadership. Executive deference to Congress was over, at least for a while. "The President," Jackson said, "is the direct representative of the American people"—more so, by implication, than the Congress. In this conviction, he appealed over the heads of Congress to the people, as in his veto message refusing to recharter the Bank of the US—"a manifesto of anarchy," Biddle called it, "such as Marat or Robespierre might have issued to the mob of the Faubourg St. Antoine." Indeed, he vetoed more bills than all his predecessors put together and did so on grounds of policy and not solely, as they had done, on presumptions of unconstitutionality. Though scholarship has shown that his exploits as a spoilsman were considerable exaggerated, he established the principle that the executive branch should be responsive to the purposes of the president. And he effectively took away control of national politics from Congress and delivered it to the mass political party. Presidential candidates hereafter were chosen not by congressional caucuses but by national conventions.

Even more important, Jackson took two decisive steps to affirm the supremacy of the national government—one against a rebellious state, South Carolina, the other against the most powerful private cor-

poration in the country. I mean, of course, Jackson's proclamation condemning South Carolina's attempt to nullify the Tariff Act of 1832 and
the Bank veto. Had South Carolina got away with nullification, had
Biddle shown that the bank of the United States was more powerful
than the government of the United States, the implications for the future of the republic would have been considerable. "The Bank of the
United States," Jackson told his cabinet in words that might also have
applied to the state of South Carolina, "is in itself a Government
which has gradually increased its strength from the day of its establishment. The question between it and the people has become one of
power." Jackson, in mastering these two profound challenges to federal
authority, established that authority more firmly than ever.

That is why Henry Clay, in calling on the Senate to censure Jackson for the removal of federal funds from the US Bank, made his pas-
sionate cry in 1833, "We are in the midst of a revolution, hitherto
bloodless, but rapidly tending toward a total change of the pure republican character of the government, and to the concentration of all
power in the hands of one man." Even a Jacksonian like Brownson
exclaimed with alarm at Jackson's "tendency to Centralization and his
evident learning to *Bureaucraticy*"; Jackson had made more rapid
strides toward "Centralization and to the Bureaucratic system than
even the most sensitive nullifier has yet suspected." Another young
Jacksonian, that intelligent rogue Ben Butler of Massachusetts, wrote
in his memoirs that, while had had been "dazzled with the brilliancy
of Jackson's administration . . . I early had sense enough to see that it
conflicted, in a very considerable degree, with the teachings of Jefferson."

In the years since *The Age of Jackson* such scholars as J. G. A.
Pocock and Gordon Wood have given new clarity to the competing
visions of "republicanism" and "liberalism" in the first generation of
independence. Republicanism called on citizens to subordinate their
individual interests to public virtue and the common good. Liberalism
argued that citizens in pursuing their individual interests promoted
the common good. Historians disagree about the proportions in which
republicanism and liberalism were mingled in the revolutionary mind
and about the time when liberalism drove republicanism out. In any
event, as Jackson once told James K. Polk, "My political creed . . . was
formed in the old republican school."

The old republican creed, as Robert V. Remini persuasively shows
in his fine recent biography of Jackson, nourished Jackson's commitment to public virtue and sanctioned government action to secure the
common good. Roger B. Taney, who served Jackson as attorney general
and as secretary of the treasury and whom Jackson thereafter made
chief justice, summed up the point when the Supreme Court vindicated the right of the state of Massachusetts to construct a free bridge

over the Charles River at the expense of a privately owned toll bridge. "The object and end of all government," Taney wrote for the Court, "is to promote the happiness and prosperity of the community . . . and it can never be assumed, that the government intended to diminish its power of accomplishing the end for which it was created."

Under the banner of antistatism, the Jacksonians carried on an aggressive program of government intervention and regulation. Intervention was required to dismantle existing structures of privilege, starting of course with the Bank of the United States. "A good deal of positive government," wrote John L. O'Sullivan, the editor of the *Democratic Review*, "may be yet wanted to undo the manifold mischiefs of past misgovernment." Regulation was required to prevent banks and corporations from erecting a new structure of privilege. "It is the duty of every government," Jackson said, "so to regulate its currency as to protect this numerous [laboring] class as far as practicable from the impositions of avarice and fraud" and to prevent the use of "the paper money system . . . as an engine to undermine your free institutions."

In practice, the answer to the question of the proper role of the state depended for the Jacksonians on the answer to the question who controlled the state; and this is what the fight in the age of Jackson was all about.

If one supposed that the Jacksonians and Whigs meant what they said about each other at the time, it was hard to accept the consensus thesis in either its entrepreneurial or ethnocultural variants. Changes in the political weather once more encouraged changes in historical interpretation. The tumult and violence of the 1960s, intensified doubts about the famous American consensus. If there were real disagreements in the 1960s, might not there also have been real disagreements in the 1830s?

James Roger Sharp in *The Jacksonians versus the Bank* (1970), John M. McFaul in *The Politics of Jacksonian Finance* (1972), and William G. Shade in *Banks or No Banks: The Money Question in Western Politics* (1972) soon demonstrated that the Jacksonians were determined to regulate and reform the banking system. The denial of recharter to the Bank of the United States did not mean, as the entrepreneurial school had contended, a license for unrestrained state banking. Federal funds were now deposited in state banks; but, as Professor McFaul showed, Secretary of the Treasury Taney moved quickly to issue new regulations, to assume central banking functions, and to reward "financial stability rather than political fidelity" in the allocation of government deposits. Deposit banking itself, Professor Remini had noted, "represented an enormous extension of executive power."

"It behooves you," Jackson said in his Farewell Address, ". . . to be watchful in your States as well as in the Federal Government." When

Jackson's program of national control of the deposit bank system failed, the battle to regulate banking shifted to the states, where Jacksonians called for governmental inspection and audit of bank records, amendment of bank charters, elimination of small notes and of limited liability, requirements of a specie reserve for circulation and discount. Van Buren's proposal that government funds be placed in federal subtreasuries, finally enacted in 1840, sought to give regulatory provisions, especially control over state bank notes, federal status. These reforms, Professor Sharp wrote,

> *were aimed at one objective—the restriction or elimination of the virtually unlimited power that antebellum bankers had over prices, the money supply, and the economic cycle. By insisting upon a currency with a larger specie base . . . the Democrats hoped to establish specie as a kind of internal regulating device in the American banking system. The relatively stable and more responsible conduct of the country's banks from the early 1840s to the Civil War was due in large part to Democratic sponsored bank reforms and the vigorous hard-money critique.*

Most scholars today, I believe, would agree with the Jacksonians and Whigs of the 1830s that the two parties represented very different attitudes toward business and, to a degree, different classes. "The entrepreneurial thesis, as it applies to Jacksonian democracy," Professor McFaul concluded, "requires severe modification if not abandonment." "The Democratic party," Professor Sharp wrote, "did not engage in the battle over banks and currency as the party of the entrepreneur. . . . The Whigs were the champions of the banks against the 'radicalism' of the Jacksonians. Despite internal feuding, the main body of the Democratic party supported radical reform of the banks." "In the ideological universe of Jacksonian America," Dr. John Ashworth wrote in *"Agrarians" and "Aristocrats": Party Political Ideology in the United States, 1837–1846,*

> *democracy and capitalism were in conflict. Unless this fundamental truth is recognized the politics of the age will remain ultimately incomprehensible. . . . More obviously anti-entrepreneurial than entrepreneurial, more nearly anti-capitalist than pro-capitalist, and more overtly radical than conservative, Jacksonian Democracy was an avowedly egalitarian movement which sought to utilize the power that democracy gave to the individual in order to resist those social and political forces which took it away.*

"The evidence of the radical period," Professor Cole said of New Hampshire, ". . . suggests that Arthur Schlesinger's interpretation of Jacksonian democracy is more accurate than that of the entrepreneurial historians." It seems, after all, that there was a struggle between the business community and the rest of society over who should control the state.

Every generation produces its own portrait of Jackson: Parton in the 1860s, Sumner in 1882, Bassett in 1911, James in the 1930s. This generation has been splendidly served by Robert V. Remini's three volumes published between 1977 and 1984 and followed in 1988 by the author's one-volume abridgment. Professor Remini used the concept of "republicanism" most effectively to illuminate Jackson's character and policies and saw Jackson's presidency as a vindication of the right of the majority to govern the nation. While critical of Jackson in many respects, he concluded that the entrepreneurial school was "wrong about the Jacksonian movement and wrong about Jackson's place in American history." Bray Hammond was "totally wrong respecting Jackson's role and involvement in the Bank War." When Jackson talked about workers, he did not mean entrepreneurs or rising capitalists; he "referred to urban workers to a very large extent," Jackson's public statements were not "claptrap." Professor Remini affirmed "Jackson's right to many of the claims advanced for him by the Progressive and New Deal historians."

I do not suggest that the reaction against the consensus interpretation of Jacksonian democracy represents a total vindication of *The Age of Jackson*. I well know the infirmities of the work. History reflects the age. As new preoccupations seize historians in the present, we discern new possibilities in the past. In this sense, the present persistently re-creates the past. When I wrote *The Age of Jackson*, the predicament of women, of blacks, of Indians was shamefully out of mind. The perspective of 1990 is bound to be different from that of 1940. So, one may be sure, will be the perspective of 2040.

The Jacksonian era, moreover, is filled with ambiguities that invite perpetual debate. The ideological situation was deeply confused. As the business community was dimly retreating from the Hamiltonian faith in affirmative government, so those who sought to limit business power were dimly retreating from the Jeffersonian faith in negative government. Neither side was prepared to redefine its principles and policies. It is this very complexity and obscurity, along with the fierceness of the polemics and the brilliance of the protagonists, that make the age of Jackson so endlessly fascinating for the historian—and insure that each generation will continue to reach back into this rich and exciting time to fashion its own image of Jacksonian democracy.

Richard P. McCormick

RICHARD P. McCORMICK (1916–   ) *is emeritus university professor of history at Rutgers University. He has written widely on the American political system; his books include* Experiment in Independence *(1950),* The Second American Party System (1966), and The Presidential Game *(1982).*

Many narratives have been constructed by historians about the political course of the United States in the antebellum decades. Whether they center on the tumults of the Age of Jackson or on the grander drama of the coming of the Civil War, these accounts are more distinguished by their variety than by their congruence. In our frail efforts to reconstruct the past, we seem to be fated to speak in a multiplicity of voices, if we are to speak at all. It is with the humility—and yet the boldness—engendered by these observations that I venture to retell a familiar story. My discourse deals with that vague entity once termed "the Union" and the dominant strategy that was devised to preserve it.

We pick up the story in 1832, the centennial of George Washington's birth. Congress was inspired by the occasion to revive the plan that had been proposed soon after the death of the Father of His Country to remove the venerable remains from Mt. Vernon and reinter them in the Capitol. But southern congressmen, led by patriotic Virginians, raised objections. Contemplating the possible dissolution of the Union, they were revolted by the prospect of Washington being entombed on foreign soil. Their fears, voiced midway between the hero's death and the firing on Fort Sumter, were symptomatic of the fragility of the Union. "I now disbelieve its duration for twenty years," former President John Quincy Adams confided to his diary, "and doubt its continuance for five."

Washington himself had recognized that sentiment for national unity was weak. In his Farewell Address he had invoked all of his prestige and marshaled every argument to urge his distracted countrymen to give their allegiance to the Union. But even he could not speak with full confidence. "Is there doubt, whether a common government can embrace so large a sphere?" he queried. "Let Experience solve it. . . . 'Tis well worth a fair and full experiment."

Richard P. McCormick, "The Jacksonian Strategy," *Journal of the Early Republic* 10 (Spring 1990):1–17. Reprinted by permission of the *Journal of the Early Republic.*

Concern about the durability of the Union long weighed oppressively on the minds of national statesmen. They were aware, as Daniel Boorstin put it, that the Union "had not been born in any ecstasy of nationalist passion." Rather it had been an incidental byproduct of the movement of protest against British policies in 1774. The Founders, and those of their successors who were committed to maintaining the Union, were conscious of threats to its persistence. Chief among these were the attachments citizens had to their respective states and the rivalry among distinctive regional subcultures. Strains on the Union were evident from its inception, but I shall look especially at their manifestations after 1820. I shall consider how anxiety about the preservation of the Union influenced policies, politics, and parties during what, for want of a better term, we still label the Age of Jackson. One product of this anxiety was what I shall call the Jacksonian strategy.

The term "Union" acquired currency during the American Revolution. It referred to the political arrangement among the states, at first in the Continental Congress and then, more formally, under the Articles of Confederation. In the postwar years a small but influential political elite viewed the course of public affairs with growing apprehension. These men, who had acquired a nationalist perspective while serving the revolutionary cause, promoted the calling of the Constitutional Convention and dominated its deliberations. Although the Framers were inspired in varying degrees by a commitment to a national political community, they took a realistic view of existing conditions that obliged them to devise a Union which was hedged about by qualifications and clouded by ambiguities.

Because of the strong claims of the states on the loyalties of their citizens, it had to be a *federal* Union, a Union based on dual allegiance. Because there were also regional subcultures with divergent interests, compromises were adopted that were intended to prevent any one region from acquiring dominance within the political system. Elaborately contrived checks and balances operated to place obstacles in the way of rule by simple majorities. To assure that the states remained viable entities, the powers of the federal government were limited with as much precision as possible. The result was a blueprint for a novel, untested kind of polity. It was to be "a more perfect Union" (if one can conceive of degrees of perfection), but what arguments could be advanced to make it acceptable? What appeals would be most effective in engendering support for the Union?

For answers, we turn as usual to the persuasive voice of "Publius" in *The Federalist*. The first thirteen essays were all devoted to urging the *utility* of the Union, as well as "the certain evils, and the probable dangers, to which every State will be exposed from its dissolution." Union would be useful in providing for defense against a hostile world, in preventing "frequent and violent contests among the states," in guarding against domestic insurrection, and, in the words of Madison, as a "republican remedy for the diseases most incident to republican government." Other numbers went on to explain how useful the Union would be in promoting commerce, maintaining a navy, raising revenue, and fostering economy in government.

This theme of the utility of the Union, a distinctly pragmatic appeal, is striking. It was to be repeated again and again by American statesmen down to the Civil War. Union was expedient. It was a means through which certain benefits could be achieved and dreadful evils averted by every state and every interest. But implicit in this rhetoric was the element of calculation. Members of the Union, most particularly the states, could weigh the benefits and the costs of remaining in the Union. Thus their commitment to the Union was conditional. If they concluded that their vital interests were being endangered, they might seek to alter the character of the Union or, as a final resort, withdraw from it.

A Virginia congressman put the matter succinctly during the Missouri debate in 1820:

> *Sir, I am attached to the Union; but it is a rational attachment. . . .*
> *I am attached to the Union because I believe it calculated to serve*
> *the political rights, tranquillity, and happiness of this country. The*
> *moment the Union shall fail to secure and promote these objects, I*
> *shall detest it, as I would any other species of despotism.*

The word "Union" was of critical importance in the American political vocabulary before the Civil War, although it is archaic today. It had great symbolic meaning and was employed in preference to such terms as "republic" or "nation" to evoke a sense of community. More than the flag, to which we now pledge allegiance, or the anthem, which we attempt to sing on all public occasions, it was the supreme object of general loyalty. Like most important symbols, however, its meaning was ambiguous. Yet its very vagueness lent it strength, for it could evoke positive sentiments from men of such diverse political orientations as Andrew Jackson, Henry Clay, and John C. Calhoun.

The bounds of Union were tested, if not strained, in the early decades of the new republic. We need only recall the doctrines expounded in the Kentucky and Virginia Resolutions, Washington's dire warnings about the consequences of sectional parties, and the bitterness of the election of 1800. Even more ominous was the growing sense of alienation in New England, which found its ultimate expression in the Hartford Convention. Frustrated and angered by southern domination of the federal government, those in attendance calculated the utility of the Union to their regional subculture and found it wanting. The remedy they demanded was a remodeled Union, and to that end they proposed several constitutional amendments. With Jackson's victory at New Orleans and the termination of the War of 1812, the crisis quickly passed, but it was indicative of what could happen when inter-regional antagonisms reached a critical stage.

For a brief period after the war, partisanship moderated, national sentiments rose, and the Union seemed to acquire new strength. Presidents Madison and Monroe even encouraged positive governmental actions such as a protective tariff, a national bank, a respectable military establishment, a vigorous commercial policy, and internal improvements. Perhaps through such an "American System" confidence in the utility of the Union could be enhanced.

This strategy was carried forward by President John Quincy Adams, who recommended to Congress a vast program for "promoting the improvement of agriculture, commerce, and manufactures, the cultivation and encouragement of the mechanic and of the elegant arts, the advancement of literature, and the progress of the sciences, ornamental and profound. . . ." But as his term drew to a close, his grandiose vision of national enterprise was replaced by the nightmare of disunion. Shocked by southern reaction to the Tariff of 1828 and the doctrine set forth anonymously in the "Exposition and Protest," Adams was forced to confront the horror of nullification. He did not agree that a state could pronounce an act of Congress unconstitutional, but if a state should persist in its defiance, he sadly observed, "patriotism and philanthropy turn their eyes from the condition in which the parties would be placed. . . ." President Buchanan was to reach much the same conclusion as he confronted the disintegration of the Union in 1861.

It is doubtful that Adams understood the profound changes that were under way in the United States. Elements of continuity that had extended from 1787 into the 1820s were fading. The persistence of the revolutionary generation, with its dedication to the organic concept of a national community; the relative insulation of federal authorities from popular control; the reluctance to accord legitimacy to political parties; and the strong disposition of political leaders to arrange and honor sectional compromises were all characteristic of an era that was passing.

Meanwhile, the nation was being transformed under the impact of the transportation revolution, the rise of the factory system, mounting immigration, a surge of settlers into the farthest expanses of the West, and a comparable movement into burgeoning cities. Distinctive influences shaped the South, as it became the Cotton Kingdom and extended its plantation economy and peculiar institution of slavery into the Gulf states.

Everything seemed to be in flux. What John Higham described as a "spirit of boundlessness" marked a new American outlook. In order to identify the attitude that seemed most to define the popular psyche, the discerning foreign observer, Alexis de Tocqueville, introduced the term "individualism." Within the context of American democracy, individualism rejected the concept of the organic community, gave new dimensions to the idea of equality, and exalted the freedom of the individual above all other values.

This altered environment did not lessen differences between regional subcultures; rather it enhanced them. The South became increasingly differentiated from the rest of the nation. It clung to values and institutions that were to seem ever more anomalous to the northern majority. It became more self-conscious, apprehensive, and—on occasions—more militant. The region had been deeply affected by the unprecedented assaults on slavery during the protracted debates over the Missouri question. Its darkest fears had been aroused in 1831 by the slave insurrection led by Nat Turner. In the same year the abolitionist movement, signalized by the appearance of William Lloyd Garrison's *Liberator,* raised the potential for discord.

Since the inception of the Union, national statesmen had taken account of dangers inherent in regional antagonisms. They sought to moderate or control them by devising such institutional arrangements as were incorporated in the Constitution and by sanctioning accommodative norms of political behavior. Thus the practice developed of having a presidential candidate from one region coupled with a vice-presidential candidate from another, making cabinet appointments with a similar consideration in mind, and holding the number of free and slave states equal. It was in this spirit, too, that Washington issued his solemn warning against the dangers of sectional parties. Later, other leaders declaimed against the introduction of the slavery issue into the national political arena. Over and over there were appeals to the utility of the Union and related pleas for mutual forbearance and compromise to preserve the Union.

Different and conflicting meanings, however, were to be given to that key symbolic word: union. Was it a union of sovereign states, or of the people of the states, or of the people of the United States? Had union preceded, or followed, the formation of the states? Was union an expedient means to an end, or was it an end in itself? Was union essential to democracy—as Lincoln would insist—or was it antithetical to democracy? Was union an experiment, or did it represent an irrevocable commitment? Each of these questions was the subject of unending debate. The meaning of union could not be resolved. The term itself reflected the contradictions within the political system that contributed to its frailty.

As Andrew Jackson approached the end of his turbulent administration, he decided to follow the example of Washington and issue a "farewell address." Soliciting the assistance of his confidant, Chief Justice Roger B. Taney, Jackson explained what he had in mind, and revealed the overriding concern that had shaped his policies and actions as president:

> *The events of my administration necessarily bring into review, that object of all absorbing interest, our* glorious Union—*the multiplied schemes which ambitious and factious spirits have devised to dissolve it and throw our country into anarchy, is a point which . . . has . . . commanded the deepest solicitude during my term of service, [and] ought to be treated as preeminently important. How to impress the public with an adequate aversion to the sectional jealousies, the sectional parties, and sectional preferences which centuring on mischievous and intrigueing individuals gave them power to disturb and shake our happy confederacy, is a matter which has occupied my own thoughts greatly. . . .*

Jackson was not hallucinating when he perceived dangers to the Union. The "happy confederacy" had been shaken by his break with Calhoun, by the impassioned oratory of the Webster-Hayne debate, and by the furor that led up to the Compromise Tariff of 1833 and the Force Bill. Then came the bitter controversy over antislavery petitions, which was only partially stilled by the gag rule, and the flare-up over the matter of preventing the use of the mails to distribute abolitionist literature in the South. And in 1836 Jackson's anointed successor had to confront a sectional candidate—Hugh Lawson White—in the South. There was abundant evidence that "sectional jealousies, the sectional parties, and sectional preferences" were threatening the Union.

Jackson's devotion to the Union, whatever its source, was fervent, though tinged with a pro-southern bias. It deeply influenced his conduct as president. If we reexamine the policies of his administration in this context, we can discern the outlines of a generalized strategy that he followed in attempting to reduce stress on the bonds of Union. The strategy that he and his associates defined and elaborated became embedded in the creed of the Democratic party down to its fateful disruption in 1860.

The salient features of the Jacksonian strategy as it evolved over eight tempestuous years can be compressed into a few principles. Issues that aroused inter-regional conflicts—"jarring issues," Jackson called them—must be kept out of the political system. To that end, he insisted on limiting federal activity to bounds even narrower than those defined by his predecessors. He constantly reiterated the same theme: "The successful operation of the federal system can only be preserved by confining it to the few and simple, but yet important, objects for which it was designed." The government's true strength, he later declared, "consists in leaving individuals and States as much as possible to themselves—in making itself felt, not in its power, but in its beneficence; not in its control, but in its protection; not in binding the States more closely to the center, but leaving each unobstructed in its proper orbit." Or again: "To suppose that because our Government has been instituted for the benefit of the people it must therefore have the power to do whatever may seem to conduce to the public good is an error into which even honest minds are the apt to fall."

Jackson devoted much of his energy as president to playing the role of gatekeeper and censor in his endeavor to reduce strains on the government. He enhanced his authority in these roles by insistently claiming that he, and he alone, represented the whole American people. Thus he could inform his cabinet after the election of 1832: "Whatever may be the opinion of others, the President considers his reelection as a decision of the people against the bank." No previous president had approached Jackson's assertiveness in depicting himself as the tribune of the people. None employed the veto more aggressively.

The third and crucial element in the Jacksonian strategy was the formulation of a dogma to persuade the people that they must not make demands on government. The rhetoric was two-pronged. Jackson propagated the idea that every positive act of government favored some special interest or, even more specifically, favored the wealthy at the expense of the poor. He charged in his Bank Veto message that

> *Many of our rich men have not been content with equal protection and equal benefits, but have besought us to make them richer by act of Congress. By attempting to gratify their desires, we have ... arrayed section against section, interest against interest, and man against man, in fearful commotion which threatens to shake the foundations of our Union.*

In a complementary vein, he extolled the virtues of unhampered free enterprise, of individualism, and of reliance on the natural order, rather than on the artificial contrivances of government. By these appeals, he sought to strengthen existing cultural inhibitions against reliance on the political system as a source of private benefits.

Finally, Jackson was more vociferous than any of his predecessors in constantly warning against the dangers of disunion. "Our Federal Union, it must be preserved" was not only his celebrated challenge to Calhoun but also his oft-proclaimed creed. "If we should fail," he wrote at the height of the nullification crisis in 1833, "and our blessed union be dissolved, ... civil wars, blood, and destruction must be our unfortunate lot, and despotism will again triumph over the world. But my friend, the union shall be preserved, or I perish with it ...." In his Farewell Address, he deplored efforts "to excite the *south* against the *north,* and the *north* against the *south,* and to force into the controversy the most delicate and exciting topics ...." Jackson concluded that it was "impossible to look on the consequences that would inevitably follow the destruction of this government and not feel indignant when we hear cold calculations about the value of the union, and have so constantly before us a line of conduct so well calculated to weaken its ties."

In short, Jackson sought to persuade his fellow citizens that the ineffectuality of the government was a virtue. Tocqueville, for one, viewed the operation of this strategy with dismay. "I am strangely mistaken," he wrote, "if the Federal government of the United States is not constantly losing strength, retiring gradually from public affairs, and narrowing the circle of action." In his eyes the Union presented "no definite object to patriotic feeling"; it was an accident which would last only so long as circumstances favored it. Although he astutely observed the consequences of the Jacksonian strategy, he was less aware of its rationale. The Jacksonians believed that only be reducing stressful demands on the political system could the Union be preserved.

At this point we confront a paradox. Popular participation in the political system soared while the level of governmental activity declined. Presidential elections, in particular, aroused tremendous excitement. How can these manifestations of popular interest and involvement be reconciled with reduced outputs? How can we account for the enigma of a non-demanding democracy?

We cannot explore the manifold dimensions of this intriguing problem here, but one aspect of it merits comment. This has to do with the nature of the second American party system. Although it was shaped in its formative years by sectional influences, there were by 1840 two parties that competed with each other in every state and rallied national followings in the quadrennial contests for the presidency. The parties developed elaborate, state-based organizations that required for their staffing huge numbers of volunteer workers. Through a variety of appeals, voters were induced to adopt partisan identities. Campaigns took on a flamboyant, spectacular style, involving the use of symbols, rituals, and mass participation. In a manner that would have been unthinkable a generation earlier, candidates were popularized by nicknames, such as "Old Hickory," "Old Tip," "Harry of the West," and "Old Rough and Ready." Elections became psychodramas, with voters exhibiting the manic behavioral characteristics of modern-day sports fans.

What motivated party activists and enthusiastic partisans to devote so much emotional energy to election campaigns remains a debatable question. Surely the voters' perceptions of what was at stake in the contests and the closeness of inter-party competition stimulated their involvement. But there is the possibility that voters were attracted to the electoral arena by the prospect of the immediate satisfactions to be gained by engaging in mass activism as well as by the benefits they expected to receive by influencing public policy. Party symbols and rituals filled a need met in other cultures by such institutions as the church and the military, or even by the trappings of royalty. Elections offered a cathartic experience. Positions in the party hierarchy conferred status, or furnished absorbing roles, to tens of thousands of relatively humble men. Exertions in behalf of one's party could bring tangible rewards in the form of jobs and contracts. Herein may lie an explanation for the paradox of low governmental activity associated with high participation.

So long as the parties remained national in scope, they served to moderate inter-regional strains on the Union. Especially during presidential campaigns, they had to close ranks by adroitly managing—or masking—their internal differences, which so commonly involved sectional issues. A similar imperative operated in Congress, where inter-regional accommodation was required in the interest of party unity. On such matters as land policy, internal improvements, and the tariff, both parties succeeded over time in elaborating positions that were sufficiently flexible—and included enough options—to minimize intra-party discord.

Whigs and Democrats also engaged in inter-party collaboration when confronted with potentially disruptive questions. In this spirit they could agree on a compromise tariff in 1833 as part of an arrangement to deal with southern discontent. They joined in sanctioning the gag rule to keep antislavery petitions out of Congress. They indulged for nearly a decade in mutual avoidance of Texan annexation. Both solemnly pledged to accept the finality of the Compromise of 1850.

In particular, responsible leaders of both parties sought to enforce the norm that banned the slavery issue from national politics. Violations of that norm would not only threaten their parties; they would endanger the Union. "Experience has abundantly taught us," warned President William Henry Harrison, "that the agitation by citizens of one part of the Union of a subject not confined to the General Government . . . is productive of no other consequences than bitterness, alienation, discord, and injury to the very cause which is intended to be advanced." President Polk was even more explicit in denouncing those who sought to destroy slavery: "All must see that if it were possible for them to be successful in attaining their object the dissolution of the Union and the consequent destruction of our happy form of government must speedily follow." The compromises of the Constitution must be adhered to faithfully, sectional jealousies must be avoided, and the activities of the federal government must be held to the barest minimum.

Although responsible leaders of both parties upheld the norms that were deemed to be essential to inter-regional harmony, some whose party attachments were less binding defied them. Thus John Quincy Adams insistently pressed his attack on the gag rule, John Tyler forced the issue of Texan annexation on a reluctant Congress, David Wilmot brought forth his explosive proviso, and John C. Calhoun concocted his doctrine of "positive protection." Outside the political mainstream, the Liberty party in 1844, the Free Soil party in 1848, and the Free Democratic party in 1852 all gave voice to the attack on slavery. Ahead lay William H. Seward's "higher law" manifesto. How long could sectional jealousies be suppressed or compromised by a political elite committed to preserving the second party system—and the Union?

In time, the Jacksonian strategy produced a dilemma. Based as it was on the belief that "jarring issues" must be kept out of the political system, it gave rise to the danger that dissolution could result from its inability to address the insistent demands of particular regions or interest groups. By 1852 the Whig party, ridden with regional discord, adopted a platform that was scarcely distinguishable from that of the Democrats. It represented not only a bipartisan agreement to depoliticize the slavery issue but also the acceptance of the substance of the Jacksonian strategy.

For both parties, then, the price of union was to be immobilism, or the inability to deal with demands put forth by conflicting interests in the nation. The deadlock was to be broken, of course, by the formation of the Republican party and the attendant disruption of the Democracy. The agreement of political elites to suppress or evade regionally divisive issues in the interest of preserving the Union could no longer be maintained.

My brief narrative has focused on the strategy that was devised by the Jacksonians to sustain a fragile Union. Union, rather than nation, was the term used to define a sense of communal allegiance; the contested meanings that were associated with it were symptomatic of its ambiguity. As a symbolic word, union reflected the discord and anxiety that marred the American's sense of nationhood. The main appeal in its behalf centered on its utility, thereby introducing the element of calculation. Because rival regional subcultures differed in their assessments of the value of the Union, its persistence was threatened. Such a Union could be maintained only if political elites agreed to respect certain norms that would serve to moderate, suppress, or compromise critical differences.

The perception that the Union was fragile conditioned the behavior of political leaders at the national level. Their concern for the maintenance of the Union influenced the formulation of public policy, the operation of the second party system, and the conduct of politics. The Jacksonian strategy represented an effort to reduce stress on the Union. The consequence was that by the 1850s the federal government was becoming immobilized; it was incapable of addressing or resolving the competing demands of the divergent subcultures. The Union was still intact. Statesmen were still extolling its utility and pleading for its support. But time-honored norms were being challenged, the will to effect compromises was fading, and a new majority was soon to form on the ruins of the second party system. Ahead lay the demise of the ill-fated Union and its replacement by a reconstituted political nation.

☆ 8 ☆

Mid-Nineteenth-Century Reform

CREATIVE OR FUTILE?

"In the history of the world the doctrine of Reform had never such scope as at the present hour," confided Ralph Waldo Emerson in his journal in 1840. In the past, he noted, many institutions had been accorded respect. "But now all these & all else hear the trumpet & are rushing to judgment. Christianity must quickly take a niche that waits for it in the Pantheon of the past, and figure as Mythology henceforward and not a kingdom, town, statute, rite, calling, man, woman, or child, but is threatened by the new spirit."[1] Such was the bewildering array of reform movements that nothing and no one escaped their influence.

The reform movements that swept across America during the first half of the nineteenth century took a variety of forms. The most famous was the antislavery crusade. Less known ones, but equally important, were the movements to improve the condition of such groups as the blind, the inebriate, the deaf, the insane, the convict, and other unfortunate members of society. Some of these reform movements were intended to help individuals and groups powerless to change their condition; others had broader social and humanitarian goals, including the abolition of war, the remaking of society by establishing model utopian communities, the establishment of greater equality between the sexes, and the founding of a free system of universal education. Thus reform was characterized by heterogeneity in form as well as in function.

It is equally difficult to categorize the ideologies of those involved in reform movements. Some saw social evils arising out of improvi-

---

[1] *The Journals and Miscellaneous Notebooks of Ralph Waldo Emerson*, 16 vols. to date (Cambridge, Mass., 1960–1982), 7:403. This quote was later incorporated into Emerson's essay entitled "Man the Reformer."

dent and immoral behavior on the part of the individual. Others believed that an imperfect environment was at fault and that a meaningful solution to the problem at hand involved structural changes in American society. A few viewed reform as being conservative in nature in that it would diminish class rivalries and antagonisms, thereby preserving a fundamentally good and moral social order; others saw reform in more radical terms and urged fundamental changes in the fabric and structure of society. Similarly there was little agreement about the use of the state to effect reform, for some regarded state intervention as an absolute necessity while others felt that reform efforts should be confined to private endeavors.

Although reform movements were heterogeneous in nature, there were a few themes common to them all. In the first place, all reformers by definition were optimists. In their eyes no problem was so difficult that it could not be solved; no evil was so extreme as to be ineradicable; no person was so sinful as to be unredeemable; no situation was so far gone as to be beyond control; and no illness was so severe as to be incurable. Second, an extraordinarily large number of them held strong religious convictions. Although disinterested in and even hostile to the fine points of doctrinal dispute, most were motivated by a firm sense of obligation and stewardship. All individuals, they argued, were under a moral law that gave them a responsibility for the welfare of their fellow man. No individual could ignore this obligation. Third, most reformers believed that science and reason complemented rather than contradicted religious faith. Indeed, reason and science provided the means of fulfilling the moral and religious obligations that bound all individuals. Finally, most reformers recognized the complexity and interdependency of society. Consequently they were catholic in their concerns and shared one other characteristic: they were frequently involved in more than one type of reform. Horace Mann, for example, first came to national attention as a crusader on behalf of the mentally ill. But he turned later to educational reform partly out of his conviction that the evils and diseases that manifested themselves in later life could be minimized or prevented by proper education and training during youth when the individual's character was unformed and pliable rather than fixed. Mann's broad interests were fairly typical, for he—like most activists—recognized that a multifaceted attack on existing evils was indispensable for social betterment.

Many of the intended beneficiaries of reform, it should be noted, were either from the lower classes or else included a disproportionately high percentage of poor. Responsibility for the welfare of such lower-class groups was generally entrusted to those individuals in more fortunate straits—if only because of the inability of these dependent groups to change significantly the conditions under which they lived. Slaves, for example, were in no position to help bring about their own liberation. Nor could mentally-ill persons, orphans, drunkards, or convicts agitate for the establishment or improvement of institutions that would benefit them. Moreover, reformers had to have both leisure time and a sufficient income to permit them to pursue their careers as social activists. Reform movements, therefore, drew much of their inspiration and personnel from the ranks of the middle class and the well-to-do.

Though few middle-class reformers embarked on their activistic careers with a clear and cohesive ideology, their experiences with evils often led to sophisticated social analyses. An analytical approach, however, often had a self-extending mechanism, in that it was difficult to deal with an individual problem without bringing under scrutiny broader institutional arrangements and structures. The result was a searching analysis that frequently involved judgments about the basic morality or immorality of American society, a judgment that was certain to engender conflict and controversy. Those active in the woman's rights movement, to offer one illustration, found it difficult to discuss that issue without becoming involved in an examination of the larger society in which they lived. Aside from goals, reformers also had to face the question of means. What tactics were appropriate to the problem? What should be done if slaveowners refused to countenance the idea of abolishing slavery, or inebriates to discontinue the use of liquor?

It is clear that most mid-nineteenth-century reformers found it difficult, if not impossible, to avoid making judgments about their country. And such judgments inevitably either confirmed or repudiated time-honored values concerning the legitimacy or illegitimacy of institutional relationships within American society. Whatever the case, it is clear that the searching analysis of the fabric of society that was under way during the first half of the nineteenth century did not occur solely within a framework of reason and rationality. Few individuals and groups, after all, possessed the confidence and self-restraint that enabled them to discuss the issues with which they were concerned without becoming emotionally involved. Reformers often experienced an intense internal conflict if only because their vision concerning what American society was and what it should be were often so wide apart. Abolitionists, for example, saw slavery not only in terms of immorality per se, but as an institution that ultimately corrupted most of Southern society and tainted even those who remained neutral. Southerners, on the other hand, saw abolitionists as a collection of fanatics who did not understand either the slave or the South and who were intent on forcing all others to conform to their own unique definitions of morality and justice.

Just as Americans between 1800 and 1860 argued and fought over various visions of what constituted a just and moral society, so historians have argued over the nature, sources, and intentions of reformers. Indeed, those historians undertaking a study of individuals and groups seeking changes in American society sooner or later became involved in judgments about these reformers, including their means, goals, and even reasons for becoming social activists. The result has been a bewildering multiplicity of interpretations of the many reform movements that developed during the first half of the nineteenth century, interpretations that more often than not reflected the personal values of the historians writing about the problem.

The writing of American history in the twentieth century was dominated by scholars who held a liberal ideology and who tended to interpret the past in terms of a struggle between the mass of people on the one hand and narrow, selfish, and grasping special interests on the other. It was not surprising, therefore, that reformers and reform movements were generally held in high esteem. "In that time, if ever in American history," wrote Alice F. Tyler in her comprehensive study of antebellum reform, "the spirit of man seemed free and the individual could assert his independence of choice in matters of faith and theory. The militant democracy of the period was a declaration of faith in man and in the perfectibility of his institutions. The idea of progress so inherent in the American way of life and so much a part of the philosophy of the age was at the same time a challenge to traditional beliefs and institutions and an impetus to experimentation with new theories and humanitarian reforms."[2] The origins of reform, she argued, were to be found in the interaction of Enlightenment rationalism, religious revivalism, transcendentalism, and the democratization of society that resulted from the impress of the frontier.

Scholars within the Progressive school tradition held diverse views about the nature and origin of early-nineteenth-century reform. Arthur E. Bestor, Jr., for example, insisted that the communitarian movement of this era reflected a unique social context. Unlike Tyler he did not trace the origins of the communitarian experiments to a frontier experience, nor did he perceive of a shared tradition that bound together reformers in different eras of American history. A majority of these novel communities did not arise on the frontier, nor was communitarian thinking a product of the westward movement. Communitarianism rather reflected a faith that the establishment and success of small modern communities would ultimately lead to a vast social reorganization that would transform American society. Most Americans believed in the plasticity of institutions, and the West seemed to provide living proof that social forms were neither rigid nor fixed. Thus the formation of model communities would act as a demonstration

---

[2]Alice Felt Tyler, *Freedom's Ferment: Phases of American Social History from the Colonial Period to the Outbreak of the Civil War* (Minneapolis, 1944), p. 1.

project in a society that was not yet fixed and rigid. In this sense, concluded Bestor, early-nineteenth-century reformers faced fundamentally different problems than did their late-nineteenth-century successors who had to confront the task of altering institutions already firmly established.[3]

Although most accounts seemed generally favorable toward antebellum reform, more often than not they were critical of specific movements. Not all reform movements, argued some historians, were necessarily for the good. The temperance crusade, after all, was led by narrow-minded and bigoted individuals seeking to impose their own moral code upon the rest of the people. Indeed, Tyler, in her generally sympathetic survey of reform, noted that in back of the temperance crusade "lay the danger, ever present in a democracy, of the infringement by a majority of the rights of a minority and the further dangers inherent in the use of force to settle a moral issue." Equally distasteful to historians was the strong current of nativism—a movement that took a marked anti-Catholic turn during and after the 1830s and which entered politics in the form of the Know-Nothing or Native American party during the 1850s. Most scholars found it difficult to deal with this movement and its accompanying intolerance, which seemed to set it apart from the general current of reform.[4] Much the same pattern was true of abolitionism. Virtually no scholar defended slavery yet a large number were extraordinarily critical of the abolitionist movement because of its fanaticism and intolerance.

Indeed, abolitionism offers a dramatic illustration of the way in which historians have interpreted the past in terms of their own values and the concerns of the present. To Northerners writing in the 1870s and 1880s the abolitionists were courageous men and women who were so convinced that slavery was immoral that they were willing to dedicate their lives to its elimination in spite of being ostracized and even endangered by the hostility of their outraged countrymen. Many of these early writers, of course, had themselves been participants in the Civil War; their works in part represented both an explanation and a justification for their actions. Southerners, on the other hand, flatly laid the blame for the Civil War at the doorstep of the abolitionists. Some even charged that the intolerance and fanaticism of the abolitionists had aborted a moderate and sensible emancipation movement that had been under way in the South. Such was the position of Robert

---

[3]Arthur E. Bestor, Jr., "Patent-Office Models of the Good Society: Some Relationships Between Social Reform and Westward Expansion," *American Historical Review* 58 (April 1953):505–526. See also Bestor's *Backwoods Utopias: The Sectarian and Owenite Phases of Communitarian Socialism in America, 1663–1829* (Philadelphia, 1950).

[4]Tyler, *Freedom's Ferment*, p. 359. See especially Ray Allen Billington, *The Protestant Crusade 1800–1860: A Study of the Origins of American Nativism* (New York, 1938).

E. Lee, who told a reporter in 1866 that he had always favored emancipation, and that in Virginia "the feeling had been strongly inclined in the same direction, till the ill-judged enthusiasms (amounting to rancour) of the abolitionists in the North had turned the Southern tide of feeling in the other direction."[5]

The Southern view of abolitionism by the early part of the twentieth century had become the dominant tradition in American historiography. One reason for this in part was that a significant number of scholars came from the South and shared the outlook and loyalties of that section. Since they placed the blame for the coming of the Civil War on the North, they tended to treat the abolitionists as an irresponsible group who had stirred up sectional animosities to the point where an armed confrontation was all but inevitable. Thus in his discussion of the causes of the Civil War, Frank L. Owsley (in his presidential address before the Southern Historical Association in 1940) condemned the abolitionists in harsh and unequivocal terms. "One has to seek in the unrestrained and furious invective of the present totalitarians," he stated, "to find a near parallel to the language that the abolitionists and their political fellow travelers used in denouncing the South and its way of life. Indeed, as far as I have been able to ascertain, neither Dr. Goebbels nor Virginio Gayda nor Stalin's propaganda agents have as yet been able to plumb the depths of vulgarity and obscenity reached and maintained by George Bourne, Stephen Foster, Wendell Phillips, Charles Sumner, and other abolitionists of note. . . . Neither time nor good taste permits any real analysis of this torrent of coarse abuse; but let it be said again that nothing equal to it has been encountered in the language of insult used between the nations today—even those at war with one another."[6]

But not all the hostility of historians toward the abolitionists can be attributed to sectional partisanship alone, since many of these scholars came from other regions of the country. The dislike of these individuals arose not out of sympathy with the institution of slavery, but rather out of a distaste of the fanaticism of the abolitionists and their incessant quarrels over tactics and programs. Moreover, historians reflected some of the general apathy—even hostility—toward the plight of black Americans that was characteristic of the first three or so decades of the twentieth century, a fact that made it all the more difficult to attribute wisdom or sincerity to the abolitionist movement. A few scholars also noted that not all abolitionists were

---

[5]Robert E. Lee, *Recollections and Letters of General Robert E. Lee* (New York, 1924), p. 231, cited in Fawn M. Brodie, "Who Defends the Abolitionists?" in *The Antislavery Vanguard: New Essays on the Abolitionists,* Martin Duberman, ed. (Princeton, 1965), p. 58

[6]Frank L. Owsley, "The Fundamental Cause of the Civil War: Egocentric Sectionalism," *Journal of Southern History* 7 (February 1941):16–17.

committed to the proposition that blacks and whites were equal. Consequently the allegation that abolitionists were "insincere" and "hypocritical" seemed to have some substance. The result was a constant and subtle denigration of the abolitionist movement in historical literature.

In one highly influential study published in 1933, for example, Gilbert H. Barnes argued that abolitionism was an outgrowth of the evangelical religious revivals of the 1820s and 1830s that could be linked to such preachers as the Reverend Charles Grandison Finney. Associated with these revivals was a spirit of reform that led some individuals to regard their own moral regeneration as evidence of the need to redeem sinners elsewhere. The concern of the abolitionists, noted Barnes, "was not the abolition of slavery, it was 'the duty of rebuke which every inhabitant of the Free States owes to every slaveholder.' Denunciation of the evil came first; reform of the evil was incidental to that primary obligation."[7] The portrait that Barnes drew of some of the abolitionists was scarcely flattering.

Another reason for the denigration of the abolitionists was the use by scholars of insights and concepts borrowed from the social and behavioral sciences to inquire into the motives of reformers. It was not difficult to interpret fanaticism in psychiatric terms and thus reduce abolitionism to a form of social or psychological pathology. Hazel Wolf, for example, described the behavior of individual abolitionists as obsessive and paranoic in nature. All of them, she wrote, were "eagerly bidding for a martyr's crown."[8] David Donald, in an essay that has become a classic since its publication in 1956, resorted to social psychology to explain the behavior of the abolitionists as a reform group:

> *Descended from old and socially dominant Northeastern families, reared in a faith of aggressive piety and moral endeavor, educated for conservative leadership, these young men and women who reached maturity in the 1830s faced a strange and hostile world. Social and economic leadership was being transferred from the country to the city, from the farmer to the manufacturer, from the preacher to the corporation attorney. Too distinguished a family, too gentle an education, too nice a morality were handicaps in a bustling world of business. Expecting to lead, these young people found no followers. They were an elite without function, a displaced class in American society.*
>
> > *Some—like Daniel Webster—made their terms with the new order and lent their talents and their family names to the greater glorification of the god of trade. But many of the young men were unable*

---

[7]Gilbert H. Barnes, *The Antislavery Impulse 1830–1844* (New York, 1933), p. 25.

[8]Hazel C. Wolf, *On Freedom's Altar: The Martyr Complex in the Abolition Movement* (Madison, Wis., 1952), p. 4.

to overcome their traditional disdain for the new money-grubbing
class that was beginning to rule. In these plebeian days they could
not be successful in politics; family tradition and education pro-
hibited idleness; and agitation allowed the only chance for personal
and social self-fulfillment. . . .

They did not support radical economic reforms because funda-
mentally these young men and women had no serious quarrel with
the capitalistic system of private ownership and control of property.
What they did question, and what they did rue, was the transfer of
leadership to the wrong groups in society, and their appeal for reform
was a strident call for their own class to re-exert its former social
dominance. Some fought for prison reform; some for women's rights;
some for world peace; but ultimately most came to make
that natural identification between moneyed aristocracy, textile-
manufacturing, and Southern slave-grown cotton. An attack on slav-
ery was their best, if quite unconscious, attack upon the new indus-
trial system.[9]

While the majority of historians were unfriendly in their treatment
of the abolitionists, the older and more favorable views held by Northern writers in the 1860s and 1870s did not completely disappear. Indeed, by the late 1930s—especially when it began to be increasingly
apparent that the problem of black-white relationships was becoming
more and more tense as a result of a growing militancy within the
black community and the general discrediting of racist theory—the beginnings of a change in the existing unfavorable portrait of abolitionism began to be evident. Dwight L. Dumond, for example, showed considerable sympathy for the abolitionists in his study of the origins of
the Civil War in 1939.[10] The broadening of the civil rights movement
and the struggle for equality in the 1950s and 1960s further shifted
the framework of the debate, for it was difficult, if not impossible, for
historians to avoid dealing with the tragedy of black-white relationships in America. Indeed, by the 1960s a significant number of historians clearly sympathized with the abolitionists, and their approach
now seemed to be dominant. In a major study on antislavery in 1961
Dumond began by stating his own viewpoint in clear and straightforward language:

The course of the men and women who dedicated their lives to ar-
resting the spread of slavery was marvelously direct and straight-
forward. They denounced it as a sin which could only be remedied

---

[9]David Donald, *Lincoln Reconsidered: Essays on the Civil War Era* (New York, 1956), pp. 33–34. For a critique of Donald's thesis see Robert A. Skotheim, "A Note on Historical Method: David Donald's 'Toward a Reconsideration of Abolitionists,'" *Journal of Southern History* 25 (August 1959):356–365.

[10]Dwight L. Dumond, *Antislavery Origins of the Civil War in the United States* (Ann Arbor, 1939).

*by unconditional repentance and retributive justice. They de-
nounced it as antithetical to the foundation principles of the nation,
contrary to both natural law and moral law. . . .*

    *These people were neither fanatics nor incendiaries. They ap-
pealed to the minds and consciences of men. They precipitated an
intellectual and moral crusade for social reform, for the rescue of a
noble people, for the redemption of democracy.*[11]

Dumond was not alone in rehabilitating the abolitionists. Aside
from the publication of numerous favorable biographies, there was a
clear tendency to write about the movement in friendly, even glowing,
terms. One book of essays by various authorities in 1965 explicitly
rejected earlier views of abolitionism as a movement of maladjusted
and evil fanatics. Indeed, in the concluding essay Howard Zinn argued
that abolitionist radicalism was highly constructive when compared
with the extreme inhumanity of slavery.[12] Similarly, Donald G. Mathews, who analyzed the arguments and rhetoric of the abolitionists,
concluded that they were neither irrational nor fanatic. The abolitionists as agitators were not attempting to change the values of Americans—rather they were trying to extend them to human beings who
were generally considered to be outside of society. Nor were the men
and women who spent much of their lives fighting against slavery
guilty of oversimplification, according to Mathews. They freely admitted that many slaveholders were good people, that not all were sinners,
and that slavery was a complex institution. Nevertheless slavery involved the exercise of arbitrary and absolute power. Such power enabled good Southerners to live with an immoral and evil institution.
The absolute power of whites over blacks, moreover, corrupted not
only individuals, but the South as a section as well as the entire nation.
The abolitionists ultimately rejected the idea that proper social agitation was ameliorative. They opted instead for an ideology that sought
to change society so that there would be no oppression of one human
being by another. Mathews's interpretation reflected the more sympathetic views of abolitionism characteristic of historical literature during the last few decades.[13]

    Historians, however, have not treated all reform movements in the
same manner as they have abolitionists. Indeed, during the 1950s and
1960s, when fissures and flaws in American society began to appear
more pronounced, scholars began to view the reform movements of

---

[11]Dwight L. Dumond, *Antislavery: The Crusade for Freedom in America* (Ann
Arbor, 1961), p.v.

[12]Martin Duberman, ed., *The Antislavery Vanguard: New Essays on the Abolitionists* (Princeton, 1965), pp. 417–451.

[13]Donald G. Mathews, "The Abolitionist on Slavery: The Critique Behind the Social
Movement," *Journal of Southern History* 23 (May 1967):163–182.

the mid-nineteenth century as harbingers of many of the unsolved dilemmas and problems of the present day. The theme of social control, to cite one example, tended to loom larger even in the writings of scholars who were in no way identified with the hostile critique of American history associated with the New Left school of historiography. Historians began to suggest that the motivation behind the actions of many reformers, either consciously or unconsciously, was to impose some form of social control over those whom they were ostensibly trying to help.

Religious benevolence—clearly a major theme in mid-nineteenth-century America—underwent a sharp reevaluation. For example, Clifford S. Griffin, noting the phenomenal increase in the number of national societies established for such benevolent purposes as education, conversion, temperance, peace, antislavery, moral reform, and the dissemination of the Bible, saw in them more than merely the disinterested exercise of charitable impulses. As more and more people confronted political and social upheavals, and the homogeneity of American society splintered before their very eyes, many turned to religion—especially Protestantism—as the only social force capable of restoring "stability and order, sobriety and safety." A theocratic state where moral legislation buttressed and embodied a religious code was clearly impossible to institute within the United States. Both clergymen and laymen, therefore, turned to new national societies they founded for theocratic purposes. Such societies, organized to promote religious benevolence and charity, embodied also a belief on the part of their trustees that God wished all men to obey His laws, and that these societies were the proper and legitimate interpreters of God's laws. Most of the leaders of these societies were relatively well-to-do, and viewed religious benevolence as a means of social control. "Religion and morality, as dispensed by the benevolent societies throughout the seemingly chaotic nation," argued Griffin, "became a means of establishing secular order." That this version of morality strengthened the status quo and ensured the retention of power in the hands of affluent groups was hardly surprising.[14]

In a similar vein Michael Katz was critical of those historians who had interpreted the educational reform movement as merely an outgrowth of mid-nineteenth-century humanitarian zeal and the extension of political democracy. "Very simply," he wrote, "the extension and reform of education in the mid-nineteenth century were not a

---

[14]Clifford S. Griffin, *Their Brothers' Keepers: Moral Stewardship in the United States, 1800–1855* (New Brunswick, N.J., 1960), pp. x-xiii. In recent years some historians have sharply modified the social control interpretation of recent benevolence by emphasizing that the effort to establish a general standard of right conduct is characteristic of many groups. See Paul Boyer, *Urban Masses and Moral Order in America 1820–1920* (Cambridge, Mass., 1978).

potpourri of democracy, rationalism, and humanitarianism. They were the attempt of a coalition of the social leaders, status-anxious parents, and status-hungry educators to impose educational innovation, each for their own reasons, upon a reluctant community."[15] Those community leaders promoting education sought a school system that would simultaneously harmonize America's economic growth with a business-oriented value system that would prevent the violent consequences that had accompanied the rise of industrialism in countries such as England. Educational reform, moreover, was not a consequence of a broad and diverse coalition of various social and economic groups; rather it was imposed on a society by leaders who identified education with their own interests and values. Consequently education did not gain the allegiance of working- and lower-class groups, who reacted adversely precisely because the schools obviously did not serve their particular needs. After analyzing a number of local case studies in Massachusetts, Katz concluded that urban school reformers failed to achieve their goals.

> The schools failed to reach their ends, first, because those ends were impossible to fulfill. They failed, second, because of the style of educational development. Educational reform and innovation represented the imposition by social leaders of schooling upon a reluctant, uncomprehending, skeptical, and sometimes . . . hostile citizenry. Social and cultural antagonisms that delayed and made difficult the achievement of innovation could not be simply erased after new schools had been built. From on high the school committees, representing the social and financial leadership of towns and cities, excoriated the working-class parents. They founded schools with a sense of superiority, not compassion. They forced education, and they forced it fast and hard; no time was allowed for the community to accustom itself to novel institutions or ideas about the length of school life. School committees hoped to serve their own ends and the ends of the status-seeking parents that supported them; one of those ends involved the unification of urban society. Ironically, their ideology and style could not have been better designed to alienate the very people whom they strove to accommodate in a more closely knit social order. In making the urban school, educational promoters of the mid-nineteenth century fostered an estrangement between the school and the working-class community that has persisted to become one of the greatest challenges to reformers of our own times.[16]

The themes of social control and imposition of reform have by no means been confined to religious benevolence or education. Joseph R. Gusfield, a sociologist by profession, analyzed the temperance move-

---

[15]Michael B. Katz, *The Irony of Early School Reform: Educational Innovation in Mid-Nineteenth-Century Massachusetts* (Cambridge, Mass., 1968), p. 218.

[16]*Ibid.*, p. 112.

ment in much the same manner as Donald, Griffin, and Katz viewed their reform movements. To Gusfield temperance was a "symbolic crusade" in that it had unconscious roots far removed from the outward form that it took. Issues of moral reform, in his eyes, represented the manner in which a cultural group acts to preserve, defend, and enhance the dominance and prestige of its own style of living within a total society. During the federal era temperance attracted a declining social elite bent on retaining its power and leadership. This elite "sought to make Americans into a clean, sober, godly, and decorous people"—a people that reflected the values of New England Federalists themselves. By the 1840s temperance had become a reflection of the tensions between native Americans and immigrants or between Protestants and Catholics. Those who favored temperance, in short, saw the curtailment of the use of liquor as a means "of solving the problems presented by an immigrant, urban poor whose culture clashed with American Protestantism." Similarly, David J. Rothman insisted that fear of social disorder in the early nineteenth century led elite groups to espouse institutional solutions in the hope of controlling deviant behavior by predominantly lower-class groups. Prisons, mental hospitals, and almshouses, he observed, were not the fruits of benevolent reform; they reflected rather a desire to control and to change behavior through the application of institutional solutions. Precisely because of their emphasis on discipline, order, and obedience, these institutions quickly became custodial in nature; they were the places to which society relegated a large number of socially undesirable persons and groups.[17]

In the first selection in this chapter Michael B. Katz attempts to explain the early-nineteenth-century origins of the "Institutional State." In relating social context, social position, ideology, and policy, he employs the concept of *deviance* in a retrospective manner. Deviancy, Katz argues, is at least a political or social category. In the early nineteenth century its meaning was altered at precisely the same time that the mercantile-peasant economy was being superseded by a commercial capitalist economy. As capitalism (which is distinct from industrialism) spread, social relations changed and a new dependent population was created. Traditional means of caring for dependent groups declined and were replaced by institutions devoted to the care of the casualties of the new social order. Reflecting their social origins these

---

[17]Joseph R. Gusfield, *Symbolic Crusade: Status Politics and the American Temperance Movement* (Urbana, Ill., 1963), pp. 5–6, and David J. Rothman, *The Discovery of the Asylum: Social Order and Disorder in the New Republic* (Boston, 1971). For a somewhat different interpretation from Rothman's, see Gerald N. Grob, *Mental Institutions in America: Social Policy to 1875* (New York, 1973), and Nancy Tomes, *A Generous Confidence: Thomas Story Kirkbride and the Art of Asylum-Keeping, 1840–1883* (New York, 1984).

institutions sought to reshape character along certain lines. The ideal components of character in a capitalist society, Katz notes, were sensual restraint, dependability, a willingness to work, and acceptance of the social order and one's position within it. Those who could not function within capitalism were swept into custodial institutions; by the single standard of capitalism they were unworthy and unproductive. The dismal legacy of the institutional activists of the early nineteenth century, Katz concludes, is still with us.[18]

Much of the literature pertaining to reform, therefore, has been as much a commentary on the values held by the individual historian as it has been the creation of a supposedly objective past. Those historians who shared the ideals, values, vision, and tactics of a particular reform movement have generally written about it in a favorable and approving manner. Those who disagreed tended to find unconscious or semiconscious forces at work that made reform an instrument of social control, often by well-to-do groups seeking to retain or extend their power and authority. Within this framework the historian, in effect, had taken on the role of social critic.

Nevertheless some historians found such an approach too limiting or circumscribed to serve as a satisfactory means of explaining reform movements. To classify some reforms as good (i.e., abolitionism) and others as less than good (i.e., temperance, religious benevolence, and education) posed some difficulties. One such difficulty arose out of the fact that reformers tended to be eclectic rather than narrow in their concerns. More often than not, an individual active in one reform movement was likely to be active in several others, though perhaps not with the same degree of intensity or involvement. Horace Mann and Samuel Gridley Howe, to cite only two cases, were active in educational reform, in movements to establish facilities for the mentally ill and deaf, dumb, and blind, as well as abolitionism. To characterize one of these movements as "bad" and another as "good" raised serious intellectual problems.

A "good-bad" dichotomy also tended to obscure for some historians a more general issue; namely, what was responsible for the pervasiveness of reform during the first half of the nineteenth century? Had there been only a few reform movements each could have been explained in terms of a particular and specific situation. Abolitionism, for example, could be viewed simply as a response to the existence of slavery. But the fact of the matter was that considerably more than a dozen reform movements were operating during the first five decades

---

[18]For an effort to synthesize all of the nineteenth century within a quasi-Marxian model that emphasizes a two-class system, see Michael B. Katz, Michael J. Doucet, and Mark J. Stern, *The Social Organization of Early Industrial Capitalism* (Cambridge, Mass., 1982).

of the nineteenth century. Was it not plausible to argue that something within American society that transcended a particular evil or void was responsible for this state of affairs?

To Merle Curti, a scholar writing within the Progressive tradition of American history in the early 1940s, the roots of reform were to be found in a complex combination of Enlightenment beliefs—faith in reason, natural law, and the idea of progress—and a liberal humanitarian religion that assumed the goodness of humans and the perfectibility of the individual. Two other intellectual trends also played a role in stimulating reform: romanticism, with its enthusiasm for each one as a human being without reference to a person's status in terms of inheritance and education; and utilitarianism, which insisted that all institutions be judged by standards of social utility rather than tradition or custom. Social and economic tensions—especially those brought on by the recurring swings in the business cycle, likewise stimulated individual reform movements. Labor leaders, to cite but one example, fought against exploitation by employers (including slave-owners), and added their voices to the movement for free public education because education clearly served the needs of their constituents. All these considerations gave rise to a current of reform that drew strength and sustenance from all strata of American society.[19]

Many scholars, however, were less confident about Curti's conclusions regarding reformers and reform. Not all reform movements, they noted, necessarily resulted in a good outcome. It was true that certain institutions—notably slavery—were abolished. Yet those who had fought to do away with slavery failed to eradicate the roots of racial prejudice that gave rise to a crisis of massive proportions in the United States in the mid-twentieth century. In his seminal work on slavery, published in 1959, Stanley M. Elkins provided a major reinterpretation of the abolitionists in particular and reformers in general. To Elkins the most distinctive feature of American society in the early nineteenth century was the general breakdown of a number of key social institutions. The older establishments that had stood for order and stability—the church, the bar, the Federalist party, the Eastern merchant aristocracy—had been stripped of their power by the 1830s and replaced by an almost mystical faith in the individual. With formal institutions losing their influence, a new kind of reformer emerged who did not rely upon such agencies to bring about social change. The pressures on such an individual were not the concrete demands of an institution or organization; there was no necessity to consider the needs of a clientele and there was no urge to spell out a program that was sound both tactically and strategically. On the contrary, reformers tended to

---

[19]Merle Curti, *The Growth of American Thought* (3rd ed., New York, 1964), esp. Chap. 15. The first edition of this book appeared in 1943.

be so free that their thinking was "erratic, emotional, compulsive, and abstract." Above all, they became preoccupied with a sense of self-guilt regarding society's problems. The result was an emotional demand for a total solution. When abolitionists sought to abolish slavery, for example, they did not feel impelled to discuss institutional arrangements in their proposed solutions to the problem. They treated slavery not as a concrete social issue but as a moral abstraction. Protest, therefore, occurred in an institutional vacuum, and reformers were never called upon to test their ideas in concrete situations or offer programmatic solutions. Out of Elkins's interpretation emerged a more generalized description of the abstract and moral nature of American reform and its failure to come to grips with concrete and specific problems.[20]

In an influential article, published in 1965, John L. Thomas attempted to synthesize many of the diverse and even conflicting interpretations of antebellum reform. Beginning originally as a romantic faith in perfectibility and confined to religious institutions, wrote Thomas, reform quickly overflowed its barriers and spread across society and politics. Defining social sin as the sum total of individual sin, reformers worked to regenerate and to educate individuals. Moral regeneration of the individual, then, would lead ultimately to the disappearance of social problems. Reform, therefore, involved a broad moral crusade but with a strong anti-institutional bias since it was based on the concept of the free and regenerate individual. In an important sense Thomas agreed with Elkins about the nature of mid-nineteenth-century reform. Even the communitarian experiments, Thomas noted, were anti-institutional solutions, for they involved an abandonment of political and religious institutions in favor of an ideal society giving full rein to the free individual. More recently Robert H. Walker went even further in an effort to develop a three-stage typology of American reform. Mode I included movements designed to promote a greater measure of "politico-economic democracy"; Mode II was directed toward the integration of large groups excluded from the mainstream of American life; and Mode III involved utopian alternatives to the existing social system.[21]

---

[20]Stanley M. Elkins, *Slavery: A Problem in American Insitutional and Intellectual Life* (Chicago, 1959), pp. 140–222. Several historians, on the other hand, have argued that reformers and abolitionists were more realistic than most of their countrymen. See in particular Aileen S. Kraditor, *Means and Ends in American Abolitionism: Garrison and His Critics on Strategy and Tactics, 1834–1850* (New York, 1969), and James M. McPherson, *The Struggle for Equality: Abolitionists and the Negro in the Civil War and Reconstruction* (Princeton, 1964).

[21]John L. Thomas, "Romantic Reform in America, 1815–1865," *American Quarterly* 17 (Winter 1965):656–681; Robert H. Walker, *Reform in America: The Continuing Frontier* (Lexington, 1985). In *American Reformers 1815–1860* (New York, 1978), Ronald G. Walters explored social and cultural conditions that permitted reformers to perceive reality as they did.

Recent students of abolitionism also emphasized the social and cultural context of the movement and the concern of individual abolitionists with the realization of self. In 1976, for example, Ronald G. Walters published a study of antislavery after 1830 that emphasized the interplay between individuals and culture. Three years later Lewis Perry and Michael Fellman brought out a collection of essays by different historians representative of this trend. This work, together with several others, dealt with the desire of abolitionists to create an atomistic universe of free and autonomous individuals, each able to realize his own destiny and free from social constraints. And in 1982 Lawrence J. Friedman attempted to depict the inner experiences of abolitionists from their youthful beginnings to their later careers by employing a novel typology. In place of radical, conservative, and other more familiar categories Friedman substituted categories that began with inner elements and moved outward to immersion in social and political conflicts. In pointing to the relationship between abolitionism and mid-nineteenth century religious, civic, and moral culture, recent scholars have also drawn a parallel between antislavery and the developing capitalist order; autonomous individuals seeking self-ealization prepared the way for the primacy of the marketplace as the guiding element in American society.[22]

Fascination with reformers and reform movements remained as strong as ever in the 1960s and 1970s, if only because of the seeming relevance to present-day concerns. It was by no means unexpected, therefore, that social and ideological currents of these decades subtly began to alter perceptions of America's reform tradition. Just as the civil rights movement helped to develop a more sympathetic portrait of the abolitionists, so the women's movement helped to transform the ways in which historians interpreted earlier efforts to further social change.

No longer concerned—as were their predecessors in the nineteenth and early twentieth century—with the legal right to vote, many women in the 1960s and 1970s began to demand equality in the full meaning of that term. In so doing they questioned traditional institutional arrangements that made the home and the family the primary responsibility of females. The general concern with patterns of dis-

---

[22]Ronald G. Walters, *The Antislavery Appeal: American Abolitionism After 1830* (Baltimore, 1976); Lewis Perry and Michael Fellman, eds., *Antislavery Reconsidered: New Perspectives on the Abolitionists* (Baton Rouge, 1979); Peter F. Walker, *Moral Choices: Memory, Desire, and Imagination in Nineteenth-Century American Abolition* (Baton Rouge, 1978); Lewis Perry, *Childhood, Marriage, and Reform: Henry Clarke Wright 1797–1870* (Chicago, 1980); Lawrence J. Friedman, *Gregarious Saints: Self and Community in American Abolitionism 1830–1870* (New York, 1982). See also John R. McKivigan, *The War Against Proslavery Religion: Abolitionism and the Northern Churches, 1830–1865* (Ithaca, 1984), and James H. Moorhead, *American Apocalypse: Yankee Protestants and the Civil War, 1860–1869* (New Haven, 1978).

crimination and unanswered questions about the status of women, past and present, left an especially strong mark on many of the nation's colleges and universities as well as on a number of academic disciplines. Out of this concern came a new field of research, namely, women's history. The growing importance of social history merely reinforced interest in the history of a group that in the past had been neglected by scholars concerned with political and diplomatic themes.

Although the new emphasis on women focused attention on the history of sex roles and the family in particular, it also created some novel ways of interpreting familiar data. It had long been known, for example, that women played important roles in philanthropic and charitable organizations. Few historians, however, paid attention to the women who took active parts in these organizations. Given the heightened interest in women, it was not surprising that some historians would begin to follow new paths and raise novel questions that ultimately reshaped the ways in which antebellum reform was perceived.

Indicative of the newer trends was Carroll Smith-Rosenberg's study of the early history of the anti-prostitution New York Female Moral Reform Society, which was founded in 1834. As she attempted to demonstrate, the women who joined this organization were not simply protesting against prostitution; they simultaneously developed an ideology based upon female autonomy that rejected male dominance and insisted upon the right of women to change male behavior. When men behaved in immoral and illegal ways, women had the right and the duty to leave the confines of their homes and to work to purify the male-dominated society. In a like vein, other historians suggested that temperance reform embodied an implicit attack on a male-dominated culture marked by violence and this represented in part an effort to empower women.[23]

The second selection in this chapter by Lori D. Ginzberg is indicative of the changing interpretations of antebellum reform. Women, she observed, played a central role in both the development and in the means proposed to effect basic social changes. In the 1830s women emphasized moral suasion. The failure to eradicate social evils led them to focus on politics and institutional change by the 1850s. Ironically, this shift tended to narrow the goals of social activism.

---

[23]Carroll Smith-Rosenberg, "Beauty, the Beast and the Militant Woman: A Case Study in Sex Roles and Social Stress in Jacksonian America," *American Quarterly* 23 (October 1971): 562–584; Jed Dannenbaum, *Drink and Disorder: Temperance Reform in Cincinnati from the Washingtonian Revival to the WCTU* (Urbana, 1984). See also Kathryn K. Sklar, *Catharine Beecher: A Study in American Domesticity* (New Haven, 1973); Nancy Cott, *The Bonds of Womanhood: "Woman's Sphere" in New England, 1730–1835* (New Haven, 1977); and Suzanne Lebsock, *The Free Women of Petersburg: Status and Culture in a Southern Town, 1784–1860* (New York, 1984).

In surveying this large body of scholarship dealing with antebellum reform, one is struck by its ambivalent nature. On the one hand, the idea of reform has always appealed to historians, most of whom have been sympathetic to a liberal, reformist, secular ideology. On the other hand, these same historians could not help but note that mid-nineteenth-century reform movements had failed in the sense that later generations of Americans (including their own) were confronting many of the same problems. The approach to reform inevitably implied an implicit judgment of failure.

The theme that reform had failed tended to vary in intensity; the greater the perception of unresolved problems in their own society the more likely were historians prone to see earlier reform movements in terms of their shortcomings. Consequently—with some exceptions—scholars since the 1950s have tended to emphasize the failures of reform rather than its achievements. Yet these same scholars have often been vague about the standards which they were employing in judging the past. The result has been to complicate further the task of evaluating antebellum reform; hard and fast criteria seemed lacking, and most scholars appeared to be employing a personal and often implicit subjective standard in their evaluations.

As long as Americans continue to disagree over what constitutes the proper framework and structure of their society, the nature of antebellum reform will continue to be a controversial subject among historians. In examining activists who sought to change society in the past, historians will probably ask the same questions as their predecessors and contemporaries. What was the nature of mid-nineteenth-century reform? Were the goals of reformers conservative or radical? Were reformers responding to objective social evils? Or did their activities embody psychological and group frustration? Did these reformers really achieve their objectives? If not, who or what was responsible for their failures? Were the tactics of reformers appropriate to the goals and objectives they were seeking? Were the American people prepared to organize their society in such a way that justice would be granted in an equitable manner? These are only a few of the issues that scholars have faced and probably would continue to face when dealing with the problem of antebellum reform.

Michael B. Katz

MICHAEL B. KATZ (1939–   ) *is professor of education and history at the University of Pennsylvania. His books include* The Irony of Early School Reform *(1968),* Class, Bureaucracy and Schools *(1971),* The People of Hamilton, Canada West *(1975),* The Social Organization of Early Industrial Capitalism *(1982), and* Poverty and Policy in American History *(1983).*

We live in an institutional state. Our lives spin outwards from the hospitals where we are born, to the school systems that dominate our youth, through the bureaucracies for which we work, and back again to the hospitals in which we die. If we stray, falter, or lose our grip, we are led or coerced towards the institutions of mental health, justice, or public welfare. Specialists in obstetrics, pediatrics, education, crime, mental illness, unemployment, recreation, to name only some of the most obvious, wait in the yellow pages to offer their expertise in the service of our well-being. Characteristically, we respond to a widespread problem through the creation of an institution, the training of specialists, and the certification of their monopoly over a part of our lives.

We accept institutions and experts as inevitable, almost eternal. That, after all, is the way the world works. It is hard—almost impossible—for us to recall that they are a modern invention.

In North America prior to the nineteenth century few experts or specialized institutions existed. The sick, the insane, and the poor mixed indiscriminately within relatively undifferentiated almshouses. Criminals of all ages and varieties remained in prison for fairly short periods awaiting trial. If guilty they were punished, not by long incarceration but by fine, whipping, or execution. Dependent or troublesome strangers did not receive much charity; they were simply warned out of town. Children learned to read in a variety of ways and attended schools irregularly. In short, families and communities coped with social and personal problems traditionally and informally.

Everything changed within fifty to seventy-five years. By the last quarter of the nineteenth century, specialized institutions were dealing with crime, poverty, disease, mental illness, juvenile delinquency, the blind, the deaf and dumb, and the ignorant. Institutions prolifer-

---

Michael B. Katz, "Origins of the Institutional State," *Marxist Perspectives* 1 (Winter 1978):6–22. Reprinted by permission of *Marxist Perspectives* and Michael B. Katz.

ated so rapidly that by the 1860s some states began to create Boards of State Charities to coordinate and rationalize public welfare.

The treatment of crime, poverty, ignorance, and disease repeated the same story with different details. Institutions suddenly came to dominate public life in a radical departure in social policy. Aside from their sudden creation, most new public institutions experienced a similar cycle of development during their early histories: a shift from reform to custody. Mental hospitals, school systems, reformatories, and penitentiaries began optimistically with assumptions about the tractability of problems and the malleability of human nature. Early promoters expected them to transform society through their effect upon individual personalities. In some instances, as in the case of early mental hospitals or the first reformatory for young women, the optimism appeared justified for a few years. However, institutions, as even their supporters soon came to admit, could not work miracles. Rates of recovery remained low, recidivism high; school systems did not eliminate poverty and vice; ungrateful inmates even, on occasion, set their institutions on fire.

The public had invested heavily in new institutions that a reasonable person might conclude were failures. Nonetheless, the newly created institutional managers did not intend either to admit failure or to abandon the intricate hierarchical professional worlds they had created. Instead, they altered their justification: Mental illness and crime frequently arose from heredity and were incurable; lower-class children were incorrigible; paupers genetically unable and unwilling to work. Institutions existed to keep deviants off the streets; to prevent a glut on the labor market; to contain, not cure, the ills of society. This shift from reform to custody characterized the history of reformatories, mental hospitals, prisons, and school systems within the first two or three decades of their existence.

Social historians disagree about the impulse underlying institutional development. Why did the institutional State emerge at the time and in the manner it did? The question is straightforward, the answer complex and elusive. Actually, two sets of events must be explained: the origins and founding of institutions and the shift from reform to custody. Here, I shall consider only the former and attempt to show a connection between the origins of institutions and the early history of capitalism in North America.

First, consider the pattern and timing of institutional development. The new institutions of the early nineteenth century divide into various groups. Those on which historians have focused most sharply treated deviance: mental hospitals, poorhouses, reformatories, penitentiaries. The first mental hospital, the private McLean's, opened in 1818, followed by the first state hospital in Worcester, Massachusetts, in 1835. The first reformatory, also a private corporation, the New

York House of Refuge, opened in 1825; the first state reform school incarcerated its first boys in 1848. Both Massachusetts and New York established a network of poorhouses in the 1820s as a result of the famous Quincy and Yates reports which urged the virtual abolition of outdoor relief. In Ontario the provincial penitentiary opened in 1835 and the lunatic asylum in 1850.

New institutions were not solely residential nor did they serve only those whom we today label deviant. The most notable of the non-residential institutions designed to service a clearly defined sector of more ordinary people was the public school. Nineteenth-century educational promoters equated ignorance with deviance and both with poverty, but they intended public schools to serve a broader portion of the population than the children of the slums. And public schooling became especially popular among the middle classes. Tax-supported schools of sorts certainly had existed for centuries. The novelty during the nineteenth century rested in the creation of systems of public education—age-graded, finely articulated, nominally universal institutions presided over by specially trained experts and administrators. In New York City the system of public schools began with the organization of the Free School Society in 1805. The first state board of education was established in Massachusetts in 1837 and the Superintendency of Public Instruction in the Provinces of Canada in 1841. By 1880 elaborate, hierarchical educational systems existed in most urban centers.

New or novel institutions served other groups as well. Private boarding schools for the children of the rich developed in the antebellum period in the United States. The most influential of them, according to their historian, was St. Paul's, started in Concord, New Hampshire, in 1855. Indeed, it is fascinating to observe the parallels between private academies and other institutions. In their educational philosophy, organizational ideal, and theory of human nature, early reform schools resembled nothing so much as academies for the poor.

Within New York City, as Alan Horlick has shown, merchants developed a series of institutions to control and socialize the incoming hordes of young, aggressive, and undeferential clerks. This effort gave rise during the early nineteenth century to the YMCA, the Mercantile Library Association, and similar organizations.

The first general hospitals opened in 1752 in Philadelphia, in 1792 in New York City, and in 1821 in Boston. Construed primarily as charities, early hospitals were supposed to cure both the physical and moral afflictions of the poor who composed their patient populations. As with schools, prisons, or reformatories, the purposes of early hospitals included the reformation of character, and, like the sponsors of other institutions, hospital supporters compounded poverty, crime, ignorance, and disease into a single amalgam. Hospitals proved no more able than schools, prisons, or reformatories to uplift social character, and by the 1870s their purpose narrowed to the treatment of specific diseases. At the same time the internal development of hospitals traced a path similar to that followed in other institutions: a growth in size and complexity accompanied by an emphasis upon professional management increasingly divorced from lay influence.

At the most intimate level even the family reflected the thrust of institutional development in more public spheres. Decreasingly the place of both work and residence, with boundaries more tightly drawn between itself and the community, and decreasingly the custodian of the deviant and deficient, the family—the working-class as well as the middle-class family—became a sharply delimited haven, a specialized agency for the nurture of the young. Within families sex roles became more clearly defined, and by the mid-nineteenth century Catharine Beecher, among others, was attempting to certify the institutionalization of the home through the conversion of domesticity into a science.

In sum, the institutional explosion did not issue directly or solely from state sponsorship, nor were institutions directed only towards deviance or solely asylums. More accurately, institutional development during the early and middle nineteenth century should be described as the creation of formal organizations with specialized clienteles and a reformist, or characterbuilding, purpose.

Institutions were not in themselves novel. Poorhouses had existed in colonial New England. Indeed, Foucault labels the seventeenth century the age of the great confinement. Nonetheless, the use of institutions as deliberate agencies of social policy, their specialization, and their emphasis upon the formation or reformation of character represented a new departure in modern history.

Most major social institutions originated in a two-stage process. They commenced as private corporations to serve public purposes but within a few decades were imitated, superseded, augmented, or expanded by the State. The transition from voluntarism to the State did not represent a simple evolution. Certainly, the magnitude of the problems undertaken by early voluntary corporations—the alleviation of poverty, mental illness, delinquency, ignorance—strained private resources. Financially, voluntary corporations, however, did not rely solely, or, in many cases, at all, upon private contributions. Rather, they commonly received public funds. The assumption of primary responsibility for the operation as well as the funding of institutions, consequently, represented a shift in generally acceptable models for public organization. Elsewhere, I have called this shift the transition from paternalistic and corporate voluntarism to incipient bureaucracy. Voluntarism upheld an ideal of organizations controlled by self-perpetuating corporations of wealthy, enlightened, public-spirited citizens, essentially limited in size, staffed by talented generalists. The shift to the State reflected a belief that public funding required public control, a commitment to expansion of scale, and an emphasis upon the importance of specialized, expert administration.

The shift from voluntarism to the State appears in the New York House of Refuge, the McLean Hospital, the New York Free School Society, and another interesting variant, the Boston Primary School Committee. When these voluntary corporations went public they often altered their purpose as well as their form. In the case of mental hospitals, the entrance of the State meant the extension of service from the well-to-do served by McLean's to the poor treated at Worcester; in the case of public schools the opposite occurred, as school promoters sought to incorporate the children of the affluent into the free schools, which in their early years had suffered from their association with pauperism and charity. Both the mental hospitals and the public schools illustrate an attempt to broaden the social composition of public institutions.

The early history of hospitals formed an instructive, if partial, exception to the shift away from corporate voluntarism. The great early hospitals in Philadelphia, New York, and Boston, to name three, remained under the control of private, nonprofit corporations. When public representatives wanted hospitals to expand their size, role, or scope, they could not bring them under State control. Rather, they sometimes had to establish parallel institutions. In Boston in the 1860s the board and staff of the Massachusetts General Hospital fought against the creation of Boston City Hospital, which they explicitly viewed as an institution more "democratic" and more accessible to public influence in such important ways as admission procedures and internal routines like visiting hours. The social group that wanted Boston City was not the very poor served by Massachusetts General but the skilled workers, petty proprietors, and clerks who were less welcome at the older hospital yet unable to afford easily the cost of medical care at home. The reason that hospitals remained under private control probably rests in their relation to the medical profession. Often, physicians instigated the founding of hospitals and played the principal roles not only in a strictly professional capacity but also in institutional design and administration. Hospitals differed from other major social institutions in that a prestigious, prosperous, and generally cohesive corps of professionals preceded their establishment. By contrast, mental hospitals and schools, to take two examples, created two new professions. The founding of mental hospitals and school systems, therefore, much more than of general hospitals, depended upon lay support, and they consequently remained much more susceptible to public influence during their early years.

Although private hospitals did not go public, they still reflected one process that characterized other institutions: the shift in the social origins of their clientele. For years hospital supporters had tried to broaden the social composition of the patient population, but, as in the case of early public education, the aura of charity clung to hospitals. In sharp contrast to public schools, however, hospitals were unable to shed that aura until a series of demographic changes and medical advances coalesced during the late nineteenth and early twentieth centuries. The transition from home to hospital care by the affluent was symbolized dramatically by the construction of the expensive and luxurious Phillips House as a branch of the Massachusetts General in 1817.

The supersession of corporate voluntarism reflected the increasingly sharp distinction between public and private, which formed part of a larger theme in social development: the drawing of sharp boundaries between the elements of social organization; the separation of family and community; the division of community into discrete and specialized functions.

The connection that exists between the emergence of modern society and the expansive specialization of both public and private institutions remains open to interpretation. How are we to account, in this case, for the origins of public institutions? What, precisely, did they signify?

Historians currently offer two principal, competing interpretations, which, put crudely, can be called the fear of social disorder versus the humanitarian impulse. The most notable exponent of the former is David Rothman, of the latter, Gerald Grob. Here I must risk some violence to their complex and subtle work in order to highlight the central point in contention and the problems left unresolved. Although Grob has attacked Rothman, the two share much common ground, as Rothman points out in a review of Grob's most recent book. Both tell a similar story and even stress many of the same factors, but they differ in the interpretation they give to events and, ultimately, in the meaning they assign to American history in the formative years between the Revolution and the Civil War.

Rothman argues that the fear of disorder arising from the breakdown of traditional communal controls spurred the discovery of the asylum. He writes, "The response in the Jacksonian period to the deviant and the dependent was first and foremost a vigorous attempt to promote the stability of the society at a moment when traditional ideas and practices appeared outmoded, constricted, and ineffective . . . all represented an effort to insure the cohesion of the community in new and changing circumstances." Elsewhere he asserts, "under the influence of demographic, economic and intellectual developments, they [Americans] perceived that the traditional mechanisms of social control were obsolete."

Grob emphasizes the individualist philosophy and humanitarian impulses that arose from the Second Awakening. Although he cannot deny the pervasive fear of social disorder or the manifest influence of class in the social origins of reformers, he argues:

Since the absence of broad theoretical models relating to public policy made it difficult to gather or to use empirical data in a meaningful way, policy often reflected external factors such as unconscious class interests or similar social assumptions that were never questioned. This is not to imply that mid-nineteenth century legislators and administrators were deficient in intelligence or malevolent in character. It is only to say that lack of theory and methodology often led to the adoption of policies that in the long run had results which were quite at variance with the intentions of those involved in their formulation.

Grob's arresting and partly true statement rests on the assumption that knowledge—hard data—scientific in character and free from bias does in fact exist and awaits discovery by students of deviance and dependence. It assumes further that the acquisition of scientific knowledge automatically leads to rational, humanitarian solutions framed in the best interests of the people to which they were directed. The history of social and behavioral science should make us skeptical.

Five problems, which appear in varying degrees in different accounts, underlie most formulations of both the social disorder and humanitarian interpretations, the very problems that appear in most attempts to explain early-nineteenth-century social reforms and institutional creation.

First, most interpretations do not provide a link between institutions created for deviants and the other institutional developments of the time. An adequate interpretation must encompass not only the asylum, not only prisons, mental hospitals, and poorhouses, but also public schools, academies, the YMCA, and, ultimately, the family. Striking parallels exist between the timing, theory, and shape of those developments which affect deviants, dependents, children, adolescents, and families. An understanding of any of them depends upon an exploration of their interconnection.

Second, definitions of disorder usually remain loose. Scholars invoke industrialization and urbanization, but these broad concepts mask as much as they reveal. What was it, exactly, about the development of cities that created social disorder? What type of mechanisms broke down, when, and why? The arrival of hundreds of thousands of impoverished immigrants might explain a heightened concern with poverty or account for some of the nervousness on the part of genteel natives, but it assists little in an attempt to comprehend the origins of academies or even the special attention paid to the mentally ill.

Third, the way in which historical context intersects with the perception of people differentially situated in the social order usually remains unclear. The exact relation between the periodization of socio-economic and institutional development rarely is made explicit, and the identity of institutional sponsors and opponents—and opposition did exist—remains unclear in most accounts. We are left with David Rothman's "Americans," surely a category within which significant differences of opinion existed. But which Americans wanted the asylum? How did their perceptions influence public policy?

There are, however, few, if any, historical subjects more treacherous than human motivation—thus, the fourth problem with existing interpretations. They simplistically use models of individual behavior. They confuse, that is, the analysis of individual motivation with the analysis of class. Class analysis does not deny that individuals believe they do good works. It regards individual sincerity as irrelevant. Class analysis concerns the actions of groups and the relation between activity and class position. It does not deny the role of religion or tradition in the formulation and expression of class action. The theory of class is neither crudely reductionist nor contradicted by the existence of deeply felt humanitarian conviction. To argue that institutional promoters believed they were acting in the best interests of the poor, the criminal, the mentally ill, or the ignorant, and to leave the argument there, is not to refute a class analysis but merely to finesse it.

The reluctance to probe the interconnections between social context, social position, ideology, and policy underlies the fifth problem. Most accounts of institutional development and social reform uncritically accept the interpretation of problems offered by institutional promoters and social reformers. They fail to question the description of crime, poverty, mental illness, or illiteracy offered in official sources. Thus, Grob simply accepts the proposition that immigrants were more prone than others to insanity and does not probe the social characteristics shaping definitions of mental illness. Other historians similarly accept the proposition that crime increased disproportionately in early-nineteenth-century cities, that industrialization eroded the stability of the lower-class family, or that, as Oscar Handlin has written, the Irish were degraded.

The acceptance of official descriptions of reality ignores important considerations. First, deviance is at least partly a social or political category and cannot be defined as a universal. It is the product of prevailing laws, customs, and views. Second, institutional promoters sometimes gauged popular sentiments inaccurately. The poor occasionally used new institutions in ways that violated the purposes and perceptions of their sponsors. For example, parents themselves provided the largest source of commitments to reform schools. The working-class family, however, was not breaking down. Rather, poor parents turned to reform schools, which had not yet acquired their present stigma, precisely as other and more affluent parents turned to academies as places that would remove their refractory children from trouble and educate them at the same time. Other poor parents used reform schools in difficult periods as places in which children could stay safely during episodes of family crisis. The people at whom institutions were directed were not inert or passive. The image of degradation and helplessness that emerges from institutional promoters must be treated, always, with skepticism. Indeed, wherever historians have looked with care—and the recent historiography of slavery has been especially rich in this regard—severe disjunctions emerge between official perception of client populations and their actual behavior.

Thus, a new interpretation of the origin of the institutional State should be set within a revised framework of North American social development between the late eighteenth and the middle nineteenth century. In particular, it should rest on a substitution of a three-stage for the more familiar two-stage paradigm that underlies much of North American history. The focus of the revised framework should be the spread of wage labor and the values associated with capitalism rather than urbanization and industrialization.

Most North American history rests on a simple two-stage paradigm—a shift from a preindustrial to an industrial society or from rural to urban life—which obscures the relationship between institutions and social change. For, though the transformation of economic structures and the creation of institutions did take place at roughly the same period, attempts to construct causal models or to develop tight and coherent explanations usually appear mechanistic or vague.

When a three-stage paradigm replaces the two-stage one, the connection between social change and institutional creation becomes tighter. In the three-stage paradigm North America shifted from a peculiar variety of a mercantile-peasant economy to an economy dominated by commercial capital to industrial capitalism. Though the pace of change varied from region to region and stages overlapped each other, the most important aspect of the late eighteenth and early nineteenth centuries was not industrialization or urbanization but, rather, the spread of capitalism defined, in Maurice Dobb's words, as "not simply a system of production for the market . . . but a system under which labour-power had itself become a commodity and was bought and sold on the market like any other object of exchange." Capitalism was the necessary, though conceptually distinct, antecedent of industrialization.

Consider the following as reflections of the spread of capitalist relations prior to industrialization. Between 1796 and 1855, prior to industrialization, the most striking change in New York City's occupational structure, according to Carl Kaestle's figures, was the increase in the proportion of men who listed themselves simply as laborers—an increase from 5.5 percent to 27.4 percent. Moreover, apprenticeship, whose emphasis on bound labor is incompatible with capitalism, had ceased to function with anything like its traditional character well before industrialization. In both Buffalo, New York, and Hamilton, Ontario, prior to their industrialization, there were about eleven skilled wage workers and several semiskilled and unskilled ones for every independent master or manufacturer. From a different point of view one historian recently has pointed to an unmistakable increase in the wandering of the poor from place to place in late-eighteenth-century Massachusetts. The expansion of commerce in this period has been documented extensively, and it was in this era that state governments exchanged their essentially mercantilist policies for reliance upon competition and private initiative to regulate the economy.

The problem, thus, becomes one of formulating the connection between the development of capitalism and the spread of institutions. The drive towards institutional development preceded the industrial takeoff in the Northeast. Any interpretation based upon industrialization must fall simply upon considerations of time. A much better temporal connection exists between institutional origins and the spread of capitalist relations of production.

The most profound statement of the relation between capitalism and the institutional State occurs in the remarkable book by the late Harry Braverman, *Labor and Monopoly Capital*. It is worth considering in detail:

> *The ebbing of family facilities, and of family, community, and neighborly feelings upon which the performance of many social functions formerly depended, leaves a void. As the family members, more of them now at work away from home, become less and less able to care for each other in time of need, and as the ties of neighborhood, community and friendship are reinterpreted on a narrower scale to exclude onerous responsibilities, the care of humans for each other becomes increasingly institutionalized. At the same time, the human detritus of the urban civilization increases, not just because of the aged population, its life prolonged by the progress of medicine grows ever larger; those who need care include children—not only those who cannot "function" smoothly but even the "normal" ones whose only defect is their tender age. Whole new strata of the helpless and dependent are created, or familiar old ones enlarged enormously: the proportion of "mentally ill" or "deficient," the "criminals," the pauperized layers at the bottom of society, all representing varieties of crumbling under the pressures of capitalist urbanism and the conditions of capitalist employment or unemployment. In addition, the pressures of urban life grow more intense and it becomes harder to care for any who need care in the conditions of the jungle of the cities. Since no care is forthcoming from an atomized community, and since the family cannot bear all such encumbrances if it is to strip for action in order to survive and "succeed" in the market soci-*

ety, the care of all these layers becomes institutionalized, often in the most barbarous and oppressive forms. Thus understood, the massive growth of institutions stretching all the way from schools and hospitals on the one side to prisons and madhouses on the other represents not just the progress of medicine, education, or crime prevention, but the clearing of the marketplace of all but the "economically active" and "functioning" members of society. . . .

Note that Braverman isolates three processes that link capitalism and institutions: (1) the absolute growth of a dependent population through underemployment, accidents, and other means; (2) the end of traditional ways of caring for dependents; (3) the creation of new types of dependents—not just the sick, poor, or criminal, but all who are economically unproductive and, as a consequence, put out of the way and out of sight. In fact, all three processes can be shown clearly at work in late-eighteenth- and early-nineteenth-century North America. Take some examples:

First, the rise in transiency. By the early nineteenth century a highly mobile class of wage laborers, cut off from close ties with any communities, drifted about and between cities. Living for the most part in nuclear families, with no personal or communal resources for the periods of recurrent poverty or frequent disaster that disfigured their lives, they swelled the dependent class.

The recognition that transiency had become a widespread way of life impelled the reform of the poor laws called for by the Quincy and Yates reports in Massachusetts and New York during the second decade of the nineteenth century. Previously, counties had retained legal responsibility for their own poor almost wherever they wandered. Poor strangers were warned out of town or shipped back to the communities from which they came. But after a point who could claim that any particular community could be considered home for the poor who wandered through it? The upsurge in population movement made obsolete the concept of a community of origin, and the very size of the problem meant that the customary practice would produce an endless stream of poor people shipped back and forth between counties. The sensible solution appeared to be to end the traditional practice and to require each county to support the poor within its boundaries, whatever their place of origin, in a new network of poorhouses strung out across the state.

The problem of the poor illustrates both the growth of dependency and breakdown of traditional ways of coping with poverty. Other developments underscore another process—the creation of new categories of dependency. One of these categories was youth. In earlier times the life cycle of young people had followed a clear and well-defined sequence. At no point in their lives were they uncertain how they should spend their time or in what setting they should live. But the erosion of apprenticeship and, contrary to popular belief, the lack of wage work for young men in the early phase of capitalist development, occurred before the creation of any set of institutions to contain or instruct them. In consequence, young people in the nineteenth-century city faced a crisis that cut across class lines. In the 1820s, for instance, a group of Boston merchants gathered at the home of William Ellery Channing to discuss their anxieties about their sons, no longer needed in the countinghouse or on shipboard at the age of fourteen. The result of that meeting was Boston English High School. In Hamilton, Ontario, the rapid creation of a public school system with special provisions for adolescent students followed the period in which the crisis of idle youth became most acute. Similarly, the disruption of traditional career patterns and living arrangements for young men in New York City provoked worried merchants to create new institutions to guide their behavior and refine their manners.

The nineteenth century's institutionalized population represented the casualties of a new social order: landless workers exposed without buffers to poverty and job-related accidents; men broken by the strain of achievement in a competitive, insecure world; women driven to desperation by the enforced repression inherent in contemporary ideals of domesticity; or even children—casualties on account of their age. But how did institutions assume the shape they did? Why did the response to problems take the form not simply of institutions but of ones specialized in organization and reformist in intent?

Peter Dobkin Hall offers an answer applicable to the early, voluntarist stage of institutional development. After the Revolution, he argues, merchants sought to expand the scope of their activities. To do so, they had to increase specialization, pool risks, create joint-stock corporations, and accumulate capital outside of family firms:

> The disengagement of capital from family firms was achieved through two fundamental innovations in the means of wealth transmission: the testamentary trust and the charitable endowment. Under testamentary trusts it became possible for testators to entirely avoid the partible division of their estates. . . . The charitable endowment was also a kind of trust. Through it moneys could be left in perpetuity to trustees or to a corporate body for the accomplishment of a variety of social welfare purposes—most of which had, in Massachusetts, been traditionally carried out through families. Once the merchants began to search for means of disengaging capital from familial concerns, they quickly recognized the usefulness of charitable endowments both for the accumulation of capital and for relieving their families from the burdens of welfare activity.

The specialization in mercantile life between institutions for credit, insurance, wholesaling, retailing, warehousing, and other activities reflected the division of labor that characterizes capitalist development. That division, as Marx observed, takes opposite forms in social life and in industry. Within manufacturing the division of labor results from the combination of previously distinct operations into one process. By contrast, the social division of labor requires the decomposition of tasks—all originally performed by the family—into separate organizations. "In one case," wrote Marx, "it is the making dependent what was before independent; in the other case the making independent what was before dependent." Equally, with cotton mills, foundries, or shoe factories, new social institutions—schools, penitentiaries, mental hospitals, reformatories—exemplified in their own way the division of labor as the dynamic organizational principle of their age.

The spread of what Christopher Lasch called the "single standard of honor" accompanied the early history of capitalism in North America. By that standard the unproductive became more than a nuisance; they became unworthy. In an attempt to raise their usefulness, the unproductive were swept into massive brick structures that looked distressingly like factories and there taught those lessons in social and economic behavior which, it was hoped, would facilitate their reentry into real workplaces. The depressing sameness about the look of schools, prisons, mental hospitals, and factories belied the sentimentality of the age. The romantic proclamation of the child's innocence, purity, and potential masked the disdain and exasperation that designed urban schools or reformatories. As in the case of children, a transmutation of disdain into purity justified the confinement of women in the institution called home. Indeed, the unwillingness to acknowledge confinement as nasty proved a remarkable feature of early nineteenth-century institutional promotion. But promoters protested too much: Their love for, or at least neutrality towards, those they would incarcerate sounds hollow when echoing through the halls of a nineteenth-century mental hospital, prison, or school. We do no better today, though our particular specialty is perhaps the aged. We construct ghettos for the aged, ostensibly because they want them. In fact, we want to have them out of the way. The single standard of honor remains our legacy and our trademark.

Early capitalist development was experienced by the immediate heirs of the Enlightenment and the Revolution—by people swept simultaneously by optimistic theories of human nature and evangelical religion. Their intellectual and religious heritage composed complex lenses through which people filtered their perceptions of social and economic change. The refraction undoubtedly contributed to their interpretation of crime, poverty, mental illness, ignorance, and youth as conditions of character. Imbued with a belief in progress and committed to either a secular or spiritual millennium, institutional promoters approached their work optimistically, defining their task as the shaping of souls. Nonetheless, characters were to be shaped to a standard with clear components: sensual restraint, dependability, willingness to work, acquiescence in the legitimacy of the social order, and acceptance of one's place within it—all serviceable traits in early capitalist America.

One example, sums up the problem of character, its relation to social institutions, to cultural definitions of deviance, and to the personal strain exacted by early capitalism: the trouble with the first patient admitted to the New York State Lunatic Asylum when it opened on January 14, 1843. He thought he was Tom Paine.

Lori D. Ginzberg

LORI D. GINZBERG (1957–   ) *is assistant professor of history and women's studies at Pennsylvania State University. She is the author of* Women and the Work of Benevolence: Morality, Politics, and Class in the Nineteenth Century United States *(1990).*

As a result of the Second Great Awakening of the 1820s and early 1830s, a millennial spirit pervaded efforts at transforming United States society. Abolitionists, vegetarians, temperance activists, and crusaders against "male lust"—"ultraists" in nineteenth-century terms—sought not merely social change but spiritual transformation, the moral regeneration of the world. That evangelical impulse, as numerous historians have argued, provided the framework in which radical social change was articulated in the antebellum period. American middle-class radicalism in the 1830s and 1840s evolved in a religious context, one in which the regeneration of individuals would precede—and assure—the salvation of society.

Women played a central role both in the ideology and in the means of the proposed national transformation. Viewed as inherently moral, women were to instruct by example and to participate in movements for social, or moral, change. Moral suasion, the chosen means for those who sought nothing less than the transformation of the public soul, conformed both to women's supposed qualities and to the nature of their access to those in power.

Lori D. Ginzberg, "'Moral Suasion is Moral Balderdash': Women, Politics, and Social Activism in the 1850s," *Journal of American History* 73 (December 1986). Reprinted with the permission of the *Journal of American History.*

For a brief period in the 1830s, ultraist women called on men to adhere to a single—"female"—standard of behavior in the interest of social change. Being voteless and, in theory, nonpartisan was part of the radical vision, and votelessness was a choice made with pride. "Far be it from me to encourage women to vote," declared Lucretia Mott in an early speech asserting women's right to do so, "or to take an active part in politics in the present state of our government. . . . Would that man, too, would have no participation in a government recognizing the life-taking principle." "As to [women's] ever becoming partisans, i.e., sacrificing principles to power or interest," wrote Angelina Grimké, "I reprobate this under all circumstances, and in *both* sexes." Access to the political process itself—long assumed by relatively elite and conservative women who petitioned legislators for legal changes, state funds, and corporate status for their organizations—represented to more radical activists the privileges of class, the advocacy of a traditional cause, and narrowness of vision. For ultraists, the adoption of "practical" means for change represented a retreat from principle, from the ideal of an aggressively Christian and implicitly "female" identity that would be shared by all. To those who believed that governments were ineffective at implementing fundamental change, "moral" power was the only kind worth exerting.

By the late 1840s, however, all but a few of the most "ultra" of reformers agreed that moral suasion had failed to transform society. Increasingly, reformers turned to electoral means and to institutional settings through which to consolidate the work of the previous decades. For women, who had been at the heart of the earlier movements, the shifting context of reform was especially momentous.

Two trends in the 1850s helped redefine both the rhetorical and the actual association of women with benevolent change. First, women reformers faced a narrowing definition of political action that emphasized electoral activity rather than the traditional forms of lobbying in which women had participated. As moral suasion became a less convincing call to action, ultraist women's influence in benevolent movements declined. Women became less prominent in a number of activities, such as petitioning, in which they had participated fully in the earlier decades. Voteless, women discovered that benevolent work's growing dependence on electoral means had by the 1850s rendered "female" means for change less effective and thus less popular.

At the same time, more conservative benevolent activists increasingly sought to alleviate social and moral conditions by founding benevolent institutions, often in close alliance with men. Earlier, women had refused male offers of organizational "assistance": When an 1803 legislative committee suggested that the "ladies" of the Boston Female Asylum permit male trustees to control their funds, the female managers "firmly opposed" the attempt to limit their autonomy, and the suggestion was withdrawn, apparently with little dispute. But in 1849, for example, the American Female Guardian Society engaged an advisory board composed of men. Conservative women's new reliance on male advisers suggests that they too were finding traditional female avenues to political and economic favors inadequate.

Both trends affected reformers' commitment to broad social change, for the narrower focus on elections and on institutions corresponded to a declining faith in the moral transformation of American society. To many women in the "utilitarian" 1850s, who came to accept both the brick and stone of institutionalized benevolence and the new emphasis on electoral results, movements that called on slave-owners to free the slaves, drunkards to reject liquor, and seducers to protect the innocent had, quite simply, failed. Substantial changes in the work of activists across the benevolent spectrum signified a more limited, if perhaps more realistic, vision of the possibilities for social change, as benevolent activists sought to restrain the sins they had been unable to eradicate.

The changing nature of politics itself made the commitment to a nonvoting position increasingly anachronistic. Political parties organized unprecedented numbers of voters in the antebellum decades, and voters behaved as if voting mattered. Interest in presidential politics in particular increased greatly. The growing prestige of the vote is seen in the rising percentage of eligible voters who actually bothered to cast ballots. Fewer than 30 percent of adult white males, an unusually small percentage, voted in the presidential election of 1824; in 1828 more than 57 percent did. Voter turnout continued to rise dramatically. In 1840 more than 80 percent of eligible voters, which by then included virtually all white men, went to the polls. Only once more in the antebellum period did the percentage of voters casting ballots in a presidential election top 80 percent (81.2 percent in 1860), but only once did it fall below 70 percent (69.6 percent in 1852). Increased voter participation was even more pronounced in some northeastern states.

The editors of the *History of Woman Suffrage* recognized that a significant change in the popular perception of elections occurred in 1840, when women began to attend "political meetings, as with the introduction of moral questions into legislation, they had manifested an increasing interest in government." In keeping with the growing concern for electoral politics, activist movements increasingly framed their conception of social change in terms of electoral means and goals. The 1850s witnessed a burst of legislative activity on the part of women; hundreds and thousands demanded their civil and political rights and joined men in appealing for laws against alcohol, for removal of politicians and judges, and for corporate charters and funds for their organizations. Women's interest in legislation introduced them to a wider range of political issues. As one writer for the *Lily* commented sarcastically, "The women of Seneca Falls have so far dared to outstep their sphere as to go by scores and hundreds to the political meetings recently held to discuss the constitutionality of the Canal Bill, and to pass upon the conduct of the resigning Senators! And what is more strange still, the men consented to it. . . . Yes, our ladies have mingled at political meetings with the 'low rabble' who go to the polls." The *Una* published regular and varied reports from a correspondent in the visitors' gallery of the United States Senate. In 1854, for the benefit of its largely female readership, the paper added a column entitled "Acts of Legislatures."

Gradually ultraists among both sexes, including the most unyielding of "nonvoters," shifted their enthusiasm to elections in the decade or so before the Civil War. "I am rejoiced to say that Henry is heart and soul in the Republican movement," wrote Elizabeth Cady Stanton to Susan B. Anthony, adding that she herself had "attended all the Republican meetings." Such intense interest in electoral politics characterized the decade that Martha Coffin Wright feared for the attendance at the 1856 Woman's Rights Convention: "[The] engrossing subject of the coming elections," she wrote worriedly to Anthony, "will distract somewhat from the interest of anything not strictly political." Reformers' growing dependence on and interest in electoral politics underscored the powerlessness of a nonvoting position.

The temperance movement provides perhaps the best example of the decidedly "partisan political turn" taken by reformers in the late 1840s and the 1850s. Ironically, the shift toward electoral politics coincided with the entrance of significant numbers of women into temperance work and with the beginning of a long history of viewing temperance as a woman's issue. Its timing suggests that temperance women might have early become convinced of their own growing need for the ballot. Those women most identified with antebellum temperance— Mary C. Vaughan, Amelia Bloomer, and Susan B. Anthony—turned quickly to the emerging woman's movement's demand for suffrage for a new source of authority.

The *Lily*, Amelia Bloomer's paper, most self-consciously reflected the connection between the temperance movement of the 1850s and women's emerging recognition of the value of suffrage. "We have not much faith in moral suasion for the rumseller," the paper admitted in its third issue, as it advocated legislative solutions to problems associated with drunkenness. Over time, contributors—including the vociferous, although not typical, Elizabeth Cady Stanton—demanded that women have a share in the making of laws to restrict the sale of liquor and to permit wives to divorce intemperate men. The paper's tone broke sharply from that of the previous decade, when reformers had encouraged petitioning as a "moral" tool. "Why shall [women] be left only the poor resource of petition?" wondered one article. "For even petitions, when they are from women, without the elective franchise to give them backbone, are of but little consequence."

Because of the temperance movement's outspokenness about the importance of electoral politics, temperance women were indeed relatively willing to express what Amelia Bloomer called "a strong woman's-rights sentiment." In Buffalo, New York, she wrote, "all feel that the only way in which women can do anything effectually in this cause is through the ballot-box, and they feel themselves fettered by being denied the right to thus speak their sentiments in a manner that could not be misunderstood." As early as 1846 "fourteen hundred women from Monroe County [New York] 'bemoaned their lack of the ballot,' and 'petitioned voters to safeguard their welfare at the polls' by voting for candidates opposed to the liquor traffic." Indeed, it was through frustration with temperance men and the "senseless, hopeless work that man points out for woman to do" that Susan B. Anthony became a supporter of woman suffrage.

Many benevolent women, still convinced that the broadest possible social change would be achieved by "female" means, were dismayed by the trend toward electoral means and eschewed the demand for woman suffrage. Only a few women, such as Elizabeth Cady Stanton, had always been aware of the dual nature of moral suasion, its power and its weakness, and had labeled "nonpolitical" means a screen set up by conservative men who smugly advised more radical women to "'pray over it.'" More had doubted whether the vote was a tool that could advance a moral cause: "It is with reluctance that I make the demand for the political rights of women," admitted Lucretia Mott. Even as they moved into suffrage activity, some women continued to insist that only in moral suasion lay the possibilities for a major social transformation and for an enlarged female influence. By the 1850s, however, the radical possibilities of that analysis, like the evangelical fervor that had nurtured it, had been exhausted, and some advocates of social change looked more to the ballot for assistance.

Those who turned to electoral means and goals continued to express ambivalence about partisanship, that buzzword of moral compromise. Within the antislavery movement, for example, even abolitionists who embraced the idea of a third party worried over what partisanship would do to their souls. Women, who did not benefit directly from political victory, sought to take the moral high ground in the electoral contest. Antoinette Brown, who "like her father, was a 'voting abolitionist'" and who had campaigned actively for Gerrit Smith's election to Congress, told Lucy Stone that she "should hate to sink so low as to become a common vulgar politician. Let me first be a [nonvoting] Garrisonian ten times over. I say, Lucy, I pray you won't get converted to such politics as the world at large advocates." Brown had reason to worry; conversions to "such politics as the world at large advocates" were becoming more frequent every day. . . .

That transition was reflected in the work of individual women who consolidated decades-old benevolent organizations in new settings that signified both stability and more limited goals. For example, Abby Hopper Gibbons, abolitionist, prison reformer, and frequent and effective lobbyist, increasingly turned to institutional contexts in which to achieve her benevolent ends. In 1854, following a dispute with male colleagues over conflicting prerogatives, the Female Department of the Prison Association of New York, with Gibbons as president, formed an independent Women's Prison Association and Home. At the same time, Gibbons became president of the Industrial School for German girls, under the auspices of the Children's Aid Society of New York. Virtually all of her work in the 1850s was geared toward building and promoting those institutions. Gibbons was unusual in that she maintained contact with abolitionist and woman's rights circles. Her almost exclusive focus on institutional and legislative means, however, was characteristic of the time.

Even activists who united for the purpose of lobbying for legislation occasionally ended up building institutions. In January 1847 a group of women, leading ultraists such as Lucretia Mott, Abby Kimber Burleigh, Mary Grew, and Sarah Pugh among them, organized in Philadelphia to petition the state legislature for the abolition of capital punishment. After sending off almost twelve thousand signatures a mere six weeks later, the women eagerly applauded the suggestion made by one of their number that they "open a house for the reformation, employment, and instruction of females, who had led immoral lives." By October they had formulated a plan for the new undertaking, purchased a building, recruited 346 women as members, and opened a house of industry. By the following April they had acquired an act of incorporation and a $1,300 mortgage and were on their way to becoming a respected, established institution in the city. In 1854, as evidence of that status, the Pennsylvania legislature granted the Rosine Association an annual appropriation of $3,000.

More conservative and elite women avoided the questionable connotations of aiming their efforts at prostitutes and pursued the tradition of aiding the "worthy poor." Still they, like members of the Rosine Association, focused on establishing institutions. By mid-decade, industrial schools and houses of industry had sprouted throughout urban areas. The American Female Guardian Society (AFGS) alone sponsored a number of industrial schools in New York City and elsewhere in addition to its Home for the Friendless and House of Industry. Numerous older institutions celebrated their growth and stability by moving into larger buildings in the 1850s. The New Haven Orphan Asylum did so in 1853. The AFGS dedicated its first building in 1848 and opened a larger one in 1857. Sketches of those imposing structures constitute the frontispiece of many an annual report, capturing in a picture a changing intellectual and physical environment that the women saw little need to explain. . . .

Both the trend toward electoral means and that toward institutional structures tended to weaken women's overall position in benevolent movements and to narrow the goals of social activism. The rhetorical evidence of women's displacement is clear: Rarely does a student of the 1850s come across calls to men to adopt the standard set by "female" virtues and female votelessness. Even for women working in all or predominantly female institutions, the change in rhetoric signaled an altered context—a waning of authority based on the special morality of "female" values. Indeed, "female" virtue was coming to be seen as just that: an exclusively female quality to be applied within those settings that continued to be dominated by women rather than to be inculcated in the world at large. The prestige of female influence, so celebrated in the form of moral suasion a decade earlier, was seriously threatened at the same time that the focus on elections and on institutions narrowed the goals of benevolence itself. Increasingly those who had once called for the regeneration of the world through "female" virtues relied on asylums and on laws as pragmatic steps to a more limited transformation.

As the goals that activist women sought became more frequently confined to legislation and the issues that absorbed the nation increasingly focused on elections and on the federal government, some women came to feel acutely the limitations of their disfranchisement. The fact that activists recognized voting as an essential tool suggests a new interpretation of the call for woman suffrage made by a small group of women in 1848. The changing political context of the era, rather than simply a sudden awareness of the injustices of women's status, was central to women's demand for the ballot.

The most forward-looking movement of the day, the emerging woman's rights movements, constituted a wholly new route for women, one that advanced explicitly electoral rather than "moral" means for effecting social change. Women active in the movement understood the limitations placed on their work by the ideology of benevolent womanhood and by the strategy of moral suasion. At the same time, woman's rights activists engaged in a rhetorical displacement of "female" virtues: They demanded, in essence, that women's status be raised to a level of equality with men rather than that men should aspire to the standard supposedly set by women. Determined to use the essential tools of electoral change, they adopted a political rather than a moral definition of status. For them, the growing centrality of electoral politics underscored the irony of extolling the virtues of a nonvoting stance. Female influence seemed to have lost its power of persuasion. . . .

The Civil War and the immediate postwar decades would make even clearer how benevolence itself had changed. As their work in the 1850s anticipated, reformers became political activists in a secular society. The women who reached adulthood in the 1850s, launched their careers during the Civil War, and worked on postwar charity boards and committees composed of elite women and men virtually never used the imagery of gender in their public work. Indeed, the founders of postwar charity undermined those traditional images in their very dependence on the wartime principles of efficiency, order, and unsentimental discipline. The State Charities Aid Association of New York, for example, founded by Louisa Lee Schuyler, stressed its freedom from "weak or sickly sentimentality" so closely associated with "a gathering of sympathetic women." Benevolent workers had become liberals who, according to David Montgomery, "sought to bring under the sway of science the management of the social order itself." In close alliance with state governments, they set about creating institutional settings for the "social welfare" programs that would be the focus of a later generation.

By the postwar period the genteel Protestant reformers of antislavery heritage were no longer on the radical cutting edge of United States society. Organizations such as Josephine Shaw Lowell's Charity Organization Society, with its emphasis on science and business principles, helped recast benevolent discourse from a radical call for the moral transformation of society into a conservative defense of the class privilege of benevolent leaders. "Outraged respectability" found an outlet in the new journal the *Nation*, which, although founded by abolitionists James Miller McKim and William Lloyd Garrison, Jr., "opposed nearly all the political economic movements of that period." One of the *Nation*'s primary goals was to find "means of checking the popular passions, which it felt were largely manifestations of ignorance and sin" and which were increasingly defined in class terms.

Workers' and farmers' organizations came to represent the radical voice of United States society after the Civil War. Laying claim to the utopianism that the middle class had rejected, they often adopted the ideals of earlier reformers. "[T]he Christian perfectionism of pre-Civil War evangelical and reform movements," asserts Herbert G. Gutman, "lingered on among many discontented postbellum workers." Middle-class liberals, in contrast, found themselves defending a distasteful "procorporation credo." Depressions, strikes, corruption, and noticeably greater extremes of wealth—all played a role in transforming the context in which middle-class Protestants had once sought a grand moral change in society. Slavery no longer provided an issue around which ultraists could rally their moral forces. Battles between classes and regions cornered the middle class in a defense of privilege based on a growing conviction of human nature's imperfectability. Even the demand for woman suffrage was losing its radical associations as more conservative women became convinced of the value of the vote in their own work. The 1870s and 1880s were a conservative time, as the middle class engaged in a backlash against both prewar utopianism and the radical possibilities of abolition. "Many persons who have been Radicals all their lives," wrote the *Nation*'s editor E. L. Godkin in 1871, "are in doubt whether to be Radical any longer." . . .

The ideology of women's unique moral calling thus seemed to have lost its radical potential as a means of social change. Virtue itself came to be treated as solely, even biologically, women's responsibility, rather than as a model to which men should aspire. The belief that human perfectability was possible through female benevolence was as anachronistic in the postwar decades as the utopian impulse that had inspired it. Not until the Progressive decades would elite Protestant women such as Grace Hoadley Dodge and Jane Addams again infuse social reform with the rhetoric of female virtue and moral righteousness.

The reemergence of a radical voice among middle-class Protestants in the late 1880s suggests the cyclical nature of the history of social reform in the United States. Commonly, reform activity has moved from an agitational focus on the transformation of individuals to an emphasis on electoral and institutional solutions. For example, ultraist reform in the 1830s emerged in part as a reaction against the conservative political tactics of the Benevolent Empire, only to return to political strategies in the 1850s with the decline of moral suasion. Certainly the woman suffrage movement abandoned its concern for broad social change to campaign for suffrage alone. Mainstream suffragists defended their increasingly racist rhetoric and rigid class and ethnic bias on the basis of the difficulty of achieving their exclusively legislative goal.

Similarly, the Progressive movement of the turn of this century, the civil rights movement of the 1950s and 1960s, and the women's movement of the 1960s and 1970s experienced a shift in focus as each moved from an effort to achieve what might loosely be called a moral transformation to a narrower concentration on electoral politics. To the extent that those movements have been absorbed into the electoral process at the expense of other forms of action, they may have both limited their vision of social change and isolated less powerful groups within them.

That is not to say that a vision of social change that proscribes electoral politics—such as that advanced by many ultraists in the 1830s—can necessarily be productive of change in other political contexts. The belief that only in moral change lay the broadest female power, for example, is far less convincing in our own time than it was in the 1830s, when the power of government and other institutions was far less pervasive and the rigidity of class boundaries less daunting. Reformers' adoption of electoral means and goals, however, though it has seemed to democratize the holding of political power, has involved tradeoffs: As the history of benevolent reform during the 1850s illustrates, electoral politics has tended to isolate groups with limited access to those in authority, to redefine the nature of social reform, and to limit the vision of reformers themselves.

☆ 9 ☆

American Slavery

BENIGN OR MALIGNANT?

Although Americans of the mid-nineteenth century were prone to glorify their nation and its institutions, they were also aware that millions of blacks remained enslaved and possessed none of the legal rights and privileges promised to citizens by the Declaration of Independence. Paradoxically, a people who prided themselves on having created one of the freest societies in the world also sanctioned slavery—an institution that many other nations less free had long since abolished.

The existence of the "peculiar institution," of course, played a crucial role in American history. In the Constitutional Convention of 1787 the founding fathers were forced to deal with its presence. Despite subsequent efforts at suppression the slavery controversy would not remain quiescent. The presumed compromise settlements of 1820 and 1850 proved transitory. Ultimately it took a long and bloody civil war to end the legal existence of the "peculiar institution." Even after that war the problems posed by the presence of a black minority in a predominantly white society continued to plague generations of Americans from the Civil War to the present.

Just as Northerners and Southerners debated the morality and legitimacy of slavery in antebellum decades, so too have later historians disagreed over the nature of the "peculiar institution." Controversy rather than consensus characterizes the debates among historians. Scholars cannot agree on the origins of slavery; they debate why it was that only blacks were enslaved, and Indians and indentured servants were not. They disagree as to whether racism preceded slavery, or if racial prejudice developed as a rationalization of an already established institution.[1] Similarly, historians continue to debate the nature of slavery and its immediate and enduring impact upon black Americans.

---

[1]cf. Oscar and Mary F. Handlin, "Origins of the Southern Labor System," *William and Mary Quarterly*, 3d ser. 7 (1950):199–222; Winthrop D. Jordan, *White Over Black:*

The framework for the historical debate over slavery was first established by the participants in the controversy in the decades preceding the Civil War. Northerners bent on making a strong case against slavery were prone to seek out those facts that buttressed their positions. Southerners, on the other hand, were equally determined to show the beneficence of their "peculiar institution." Similarly, the large number of eyewitness accounts of travelers in the South tended to reflect personal views regarding the morality or immorality of slavery. From the very beginning, therefore, questions about the nature of slavery tended to be discussed within a predominantly moral framework.

The first serious scholarly effort to delineate the nature of slavery came from a group of historians who came to the fore in the 1880s and 1890s. Being a generation removed from the Civil War they were less involved emotionally in the issue. These scholars tended to view the end of slavery as a blessing to both North and South. The Civil War, once and for all, had sealed the bonds of unity in blood, and had created a single nation rather than a collection of sovereign states. Nationalistic in their orientation, these historians developed an interpretation of slavery similar in many respects to the one held by some prewar antislavery partisans.

James Ford Rhodes, a businessman turned historian who published a major multivolume history of the United States covering the period from 1850 to 1877, was perhaps typical of this nationalist school of scholars. His first volume began with an unequivocal statement of his position: slavery was an immoral institution. Rhodes's treatment of slavery was little more than a restatement of Henry Clay's famous dictum that "slavery is a curse to the master and a wrong to the slave." He cited evidence that blacks were often overworked and underfed. The institution was brutalizing; the slave and slave family lacked any legal rights to afford a measure of protection against the arbitrary and often cruel behavior by white masters. Pointing to the sexual exploitation of black women, Rhodes insisted that slavery had debased the entire nation.[2] His study established the pattern for much of the subsequent treatment of American slavery by historians.

Surprisingly enough Rhodes's work gained general acceptance not only among Northern historians but among Southern scholars as well. Southerners were willing to condemn slavery as a reactionary institution that inhibited the economic development of their section. They

---

American Attitudes Toward the Negro, 1550–1812 (Chapel Hill, 1968); and Edmund S. Morgan, American Slavery, American Freedom: The Ordeal of Colonial Viriginia (New York, 1975).

[2] James Ford Rhodes, History of the United States from the Compromise of 1850 to the Final Restoration of Home Rule in the South in 1877, 7 vols. (New York, 1893–1906), 1.

now welcomed its abolition, and looked forward to a new era of prosperity in which the South would share in the nation's industrial progress. Rhodes's hostility toward the Radical Reconstruction program after 1865 and his willingness to acquiecse in the right of Southern whites to deal with the race question as they saw fit made his views acceptable in that part of the country.

For nearly a quarter of a century, the historical view of slavery followed the pattern set forth by Rhodes and other nationalist scholars. In 1918, however, Ulrich Bonnell Phillips—undoubtedly the most important historian of the antebellum South—published his *American Negro Slavery*. From that moment the debate over slavery assumed a somewhat different form. Subsequent historians, whatever their views, had to take Phillip's work into account. Indeed, it may not be too much to claim that the vitality of the historiographical debate over slavery was due in large measure to Phillips's pioneering contributions.

Born in Georgia in 1877, Phillips attended the state university and then went on to receive his doctorate at Columbia University. Rather than return to the South he accepted an offer from the University of Wisconsin, then a center of American Progressivism. Phillips adopted many of the tenets of Progressivism; as a scholar he attempted to break with the emphasis on political and legal events and to study the underlying social and economic factors responsible for shaping the nation's history. Aside from his commitment to much of the ideology of Progressivism, Phillips was an indefatigable researcher; his work was marked by deep and intensive study of original sources drawn from plantation records.

Phillips's view of slavery grew out of his general interpretation of antebellum Southern society. Focusing on the plantation system he sought to demonstrate that it was much more than a system on landholding or of racial exploitation. The plantation was rather a complete social system in which paternalism and capitalism went hand in hand. Indeed, his commentaries on the new postwar South tended to be highly critical because he believed that industrial capitalism without any redeeming humane and paternalistic features was cruel and harsh. His sympathetic portrayal of the Old South, as Eugene Genovese remarked, was "an appeal for the incorporation of the more humane and rational values of pre-bourgeois culture into modern industrial life."

Slavery, according to Phillips, was above all a system of education. Sharing the racial views held by many Southerners and Northerners (particularly those who believed in the Progressive ideology), Phillips viewed blacks as a docile, childlike people who required the care and guidance of paternalistic whites. In this sense he rejected another stereotype held by many of his contemporaries who feared and hated blacks. Bringing together massive evidence from original sources Phillips painted a subtle and complex portrait of slavery that repudiated the older allegations that the system was inhumane and cruel. Indeed, he emphasized over and over again the profound human relationship that existed between paternal white masters and faithful and childlike black slaves. Yet Phillips, despite the sharp differences in interpretation, owed a significant debt to earlier scholars like Rhodes, for his categories in studying slavery—labor, food, clothing, shelter, care, and the profitability of the system—were precisely the same as those of his predecessor. *American Negro Slavery,* then, was both a sympathetic portrait of the past and commentary on a harsh and impersonal present.[3] For nearly a generation Phillips's view of slavery remained the dominant one. Scholars who followed in his footsteps made a few revisions, but none altered the general picture he had so skillfully sketched. One of the few exceptions was Herbert Aptheker's study of slave revolts in 1943. Aptheker challenged Phillips's portrait of docile slaves and insisted that "discontent and rebelliousness" was more characteristic.[4]

At the same time that Phillips's interpretation of slavery was becoming dominant, a reaction began setting in against the prevailing theories of race. The work of figures like Franz Boas and others had begun to undermine racial interpretations of culture; an emphasis on environment slowly began to replace the earlier belief in the primacy of race. The experiences of the 1930s and 1940s further discredited racist theories, particularly after the ramifications of this doctrine were revealed by events in Nazi Germany. The political ideologies of these decades, moreover, involved a rejection of race theory on both scientific and philosophical grounds. In view of these developments, it was not surprising that the interpretation espoused by Phillips began to be challenged by critics who did not share his historical, racial, or political ideas.

The attack on Phillips and the efforts to discredit *American Negro Slavery,* oddly enough, did not alter the framework within which the debate over slavery took place. Indeed, critics accepted the same categories of analysis employed by Phillips and his predecessors. Their differences with him were largely moral in character. Where Phillips painted a portrait of a harmonious, interdependent, and humane system, his detractors emphasized the cruel and arbitrary nature of slavery, its economic and sexual exploitation, and the degree to which blacks resisted the abominations practiced by their masters. Moreover,

---

[3]For sympathetic evaluations of Phillips's achievements see Eugene D. Genovese, "Race and Class in Southern History: An Appraisal of the Work of Ulrich Bonnell Phillips," *Agricultural History* 41 (October 1967):345–358, and Daniel J. Singal, "Ulrich Bonnell Phillips: The Old South as the New," *Journal of American History* 63 (March 1977):871–891.

[4]Herbert Aptheker, *American Negro Slave Revolts* (New York, 1943).

Phillips's research methodology came under careful scrutiny. Richard Hofstadter, in an article published in 1944, argued that *American Negro Slavery* was flawed because its thesis rested on a faulty sampling of plantation records. Most slaves lived on smaller plantations or farms, Hofstadter noted, whereas Phillips used records of large plantations.[5]

The attack on Phillips culminated in 1956 when Kenneth M. Stampp published *The Peculiar Institution*. Stampp, some years earlier, had become convinced that the time was ripe for a complete reappraisal of the subject. Besides the problems of a biased sample of plantation records and a reluctance to use unfavorable contemporary travel accounts, Stampp charged, Phillips had accepted without question assumptions about the supposed inferiority of blacks.[6] *The Peculiar Institution*, then, was written specifically to revise *American Negro Slavery*. In place of a harmonious antebellum South, Stampp pictured a system of labor that rested upon the simple element of force. In a chapter entitled "To Make Them Stand in Fear," he argued that, without the power to punish, the system of bondage could not have been sustained.

Yet Stampp was unable to break out of the mold within which the debate over slavery had taken place; his analytical categories were virtually identical to those of Rhodes and Phillips. The difference—which was by no means insignificant—was that Stampp's view of slavery was quite similar to that held by Northern abolitionists.

The Peculiar Institution summed up nearly a century of historical controversy. Its author, as a matter of fact, was forced by his own evidence to qualify any sweeping generalization about slavery. He conceded that the "only generalization that can be made with relative confidence is that some masters were harsh and frugal, others were mild and generous, and the rest ran the whole gamut in between." Moreover, Stampp's egalitarian commitment led him to see slavery not through the eyes of slaves (an admittedly difficult task) but through the eyes of whites. "Negroes," he wrote in his introduction, "*are*, after all, only white men with black skins, nothing more, nothing less."[7]

Shortly after Stampp published his book the debate over slavery took a new shape. There were a number of reasons for this transformation. No doubt the diminishing returns within the traditional conceptual framework played a role. More important, historians and social scientists were beginning to raise certain kinds of issues about the na-

---

[5]Richard Hofstadter, "U. B. Phillips and the Plantation Legend," *Journal of Negro History* 29 (April 1944):109–124. The criticisms of Phillips can be followed in the pages of the *Journal of Negro History*.

[6]Kenneth M. Stampp, "The Historian and Southern Negro Slavery," *American Historical Review* 57 (April 1952):613–624.

[7]Kenneth M. Stampp, *The Peculiar Institution: Slavery in the Ante-Bellum South* (New York, 1956), pp. vii, 616.

ture of the black experience in America that resulted in some radical rethinking about slavery. Computer technology also made it possible for the first time to use data in ways that were previously impracticable. But perhaps the most significant factor was the changes in the intellectual milieu of the late 1950s and the period thereafter. During the civil rights movement, blacks and whites alike challenged the prevailing patterns of social and economic relations between the races. The ensuing reorientation of social and political thought quickly influenced the writing of American history. Slavery became one of the most vital and controversial subjects in American history, and the evidence is strong that the subject will continue to be of great interest to future scholars.

The first major challenge to traditional historiography came in 1959 when Stanley Elkins published a brief study entitled *Slavery: A Problem in American Institutional and Intellectual Life.* Elkins's book was not based on new data. Indeed, when compared with Stampp's *The Peculiar Institution,* it was evident that *Slavery* was written without significant research in existing primary sources. What Elkins did—and herein lay the significance of his work—was to pose a series of questions that moved the debate over the nature of slavery to a totally new plane.

Elkins began his study by noting that the abolition of slavery in Latin America had not left the severe race problem faced by the United States. Intrigued by this observation, Elkins concluded that it was the absence of countervailing institutions in the United States such as a strong national church that permitted slavery to develop without any obstructions that might mitigate its power. Second, Elkins stressed the harshness of American slavery and argued that it had a devastating impact on the black personality. He insisted that the Black Sambo stereotype—the shuffling, happy-go-lucky, not very intelligent black— had a basis in fact. Elkins used the analogy of the Nazi concentration camps to demonstrate that total, or totalitarian, institutions could reduce their inmates to perpetual childlike dependency. Hence the all-encompassing institution of slavery had given rise to the Sambo personality type. Inplicit in Elkins's work was the belief that slavery victimized blacks by stripping them of their African heritage, making them dependent on whites, and preventing them from forming any cohesive family structure. The first selection in this chapter is a section from Elkins's book.

Elkins's thesis seemed acceptable to historians and other Americans, at first, partly because it undermined still further a racial ideology that had assumed the innate inferiority of blacks. By stressing that blacks were victims of slavery, Elkins repudiated the more benign view of that institution and even made Stampp's unflattering description far less potent. Morever, Elkins appeared to provide intellectual support for compensatory social and economic programs in the 1960s designed to help blacks overcome residual effects of slavery. Elkins implicitly placed the responsibility for the nation's racial dilemmas squarely upon whites by picturing blacks as unwilling victims of white transgressions.

Elkins's book had (and still has) a profound influence. First, it raised questions heretofore neglected, such as the relationship between slavery and subsequent racial conflict. Second, it inspired a group of scholars to undertake studies of comparative slave systems in order to answer some questions posed by Elkins. Third, it placed the slavery debate within a new conceptual framework, for Elkins had focused less on slavery as an institution and more upon blacks themselves. Finally, Elkins—more than his colleagues—had linked history with other social science disciplines.[8]

Yet within a few years after the appearance of his book, Elkins found himself under attack from both within and outside his discipline. Some historians were concerned about the book's facile use of hypotheses taken from the other social sciences and its relative neglect of data from primary sources. Others felt that Elkins had made too much of the Sambo stereotype; evidence of slave resistance seemed to disprove the thesis that blacks had been reduced to childlike dependency. Still others, though not explicitly contradicting Elkins, produced studies that demonstrated that slavery was a far more complex institution than Elkins implied. Richard C. Wade's study of urban slavery, for example, showed that there were behavioral differences between urban black slaves and those who labored on plantations and farms. Conceding that urban slavery was in a state of decline before the Civil War because of the difficulties in maintaining social control, Wade's portrait of urban slaves was not always in agreement with Elkins's Sambo stereotype.[9]

The major assault on Elkins, however, came from outside the ranks of historians. By the mid-1960s a number of ideologies had emerged within the black community. Although integration was still the dominant goal for most blacks, a significant number of them turned inward and articulated black nationalist or other separatist points of view. Bitter at continued white resistance to black demands

---

[8]See Ann J. Lane, ed., *The Debate Over Slavery: Stanley Elkins and His Critics* (Urbana, Ill. 1971), and Kenneth M. Stampp, "Rebels and Sambos: The Search for the Negro's Personality in Slavery," *Journal of Southern History* 27 (August 1971):367–392. For examples of the recent concern with comparative slave systems see Herbert S. Klein, *Slavery in the Americas: A Comparative Study of Cuba and Virginia* (Chicago, 1967); Carl N. Degler, *Neither Black nor White: Slavery and Race Relations in Brazil and the United States* (New York, 1971); and David Brion Davis, *The Problem of Slavery in Western Culture* (Ithaca, 1966), and *The Problem of Slavery in the Age of Revolution* (Ithaca, 1975).

[9]Richard C. Wade, *Slavery in the Cities: The South 1820–1860* (New York, 1964).

for full equality, they rejected the goal of integration and assimilation as inappropriate and unattainable. To such spokesmen Elkins's Sambo stereotype undermined the search for a usable past that emphasized instead black achievement and black pride in the face of unremitting white oppression. Moreover, some blacks (and whites) did not care for a thesis that emphasized deprivation. They felt it was simply a sophisticated restatement of racism because it placed part of the responsibility or blame upon the deprived group. Finally, some radicals were hostile to the Sambo image. They posited the idea of perpetual conflict between the oppressors and oppressed, and acceptance of the concept of a docile and nonresisting slave would contradict their own ideological position.

Disagreement with Elkins's view of slave personality and his emphasis on the absence of resistance to white pressure soon led some scholars to study anew the actual life of slaves on plantations. Previous scholarship dealing with slavery, of course, was largely dependent on predominantly *white* sources, including plantation records, newspapers, manuscripts, court records, and travel accounts. The newer scholarship, however, was based on hitherto neglected sources, including a significant number of slave narratives published both before and after the Civil War. During the depression of the 1930s, moreover, the Federal Writers' Project of the Works Projects Administration had subsidized an oral history project in which more than two thousand ex-slaves who were still alive were interviewed. Using these and other sources, historians began to raise some new questions. If, for example, the control of whites was so complete, why did some slaves run away and others engage in all kinds of covert resistance? What kind of institutional structures developed within the slave community? To what degree were these black institutions partly or fully autonomous? Influenced by the "new social history," scholars began to study slave society not as one created by whites but as one that represented to some degree the hopes, aspirations, and thoughts of blacks.

Indicative of the newer approach was the publication in 1972 of two works. The first, *From Sundown to Sunup: The Making of the Black Community*, was based upon the interviews with ex-slaves during the 1930s. Its author, George P. Rawick, also edited eighteen additional volumes printing the text of the interviews. Rawick emphasized that slaves were not passive; he insisted that plantation life showed considerable interaction between whites and blacks. Forcibly removed from Africa, blacks created a way of life that fused their African heritage with the "social forms and behavior patterns" of Southern society. The slave personality, Rawick emphasized, was ambivalent. On the one hand slaves were submissive and accepted the belief that one deserved to be a slave. On the other hand they demonstrated the kind of anger that served as a protection against infantilization and dependency. Blacks, concluded Rawick, "developed an independent community and culture which molded the slave personality" and permitted a measure of autonomy.[10]

In a similar vein, John Blassingame's *The Slave Community: Plantation Life in the Ante-Bellum South* described a social setting in which slaves employed a variety of means to circumscribe and inhibit white authority. Family ties among slaves persisted, thus creating a partial protective shield. Blacks also developed and retained religious and mythological beliefs that enabled them to maintain a high degree of autonomy. Slowly but surely the focus of the debate over slavery began a shift of emphasis away from white slaveowners and toward the slaves themselves.[11]

The works of Rawick and Blassingame were received without fanfare or extended debate. Although some criticisms were raised, their contributions were relatively noncontroversial. The same was not true of a book by Robert Fogel and Stanley L. Engerman, *Time on the Cross: The Economics of American Negro Slavery,* which appeared in 1974. Based on quantified data, computer-based analysis, and modern economic theory, Fogel and Engerman presented an interpretation of slavery that set off a fierce and heated debate. Purportedly rejecting virtually every previous work on slavery, the two "new economic historians" presented what seemed to be a series of novel findings about the institution.

Slavery, the two authors emphasized, was not an economically backward system kept in existence by plantation owners unaware of their true interest. On the contrary, Southern slave agriculture was highly efficient on the eve of the Civil War. "Economies of large-scale operation, effective management, and intensive utilization of labor and capital made southern slave agriculture 35 percent more efficient than the northern system of family farming." Nor were slaves Sambo-like caricatures; they were hardworking individuals who within the limitations of bondage were able to pursue their own self-interest precisely because they internalized the capitalist values of their masters. Slaveowners encouraged stable black families, rejected the idea of indiscriminate force, did not sexually abuse black women, and provided—by the standards of that era—adequate food, clothing, and shelter. Slavery, therefore, was a model of capitalist efficiency. Within its framework blacks learned and accepted the tenets of the "Protestant ethic" of work. They received, in return, incentives in the form of ma-

---

[10]George P. Rawick, *From Sundown to Sunup: The Making of the Black Community* (Westport, 1972), and *The American Slave: A Composite Autobiography,* 18 vols. (Westport, Conn., 1972).

[11]John W. Blassingame, *The Slave Community: Plantation Life in the Ante-Bellum South* (New York, 1972).

terial rewards, opportunities for upward mobility within the plantation hierarchy, and a chance to create their own stable families. Although Fogel and Engerman in no way diminished the moral evil of slavery, they claimed their goal was "to strike down the view that black Americans were without culture, without achievement, and without development for their first two hundred and fifty years on American soil." A major corollary to their view of slavery was their conclusion that in the century following its abolition white Americans systematically attacked and degraded black citizens. Whites drove freed blacks out of skilled occupations, paid them minimal wages, limited their access to education, and imposed a rigid system of segregation that deprived them of many of the opportunities available to whites. In a recent work, Fogel extended these earlier findings, albeit in modified form. Nevertheless, he continued to insist that slavery was destroyed by political and moral forces rather than economic weaknesses.[12]

Time on the Cross immediately became the object of an acrimonious debate. Some condemned the hypothesis that slaves willingly accepted white-imposed values. Others attacked the way in which the two authors used historical data to reach flawed conclusions. Still others were unwilling to accept many of the underlying assumptions of the two authors. Indeed, within a short period of time the literature criticizing *Time on the Cross* was enormous.[13]

At precisely the same time that *Time on the Cross* appeared Eugene D. Genovese published *Roll, Jordan, Roll: The World the Slaves Made.* Genovese, who had already written some distinguished works on the antebellum South, denied in his book that slavery was to be understood within the context of modern capitalism. The key to an understanding of the peculiar institution, he insisted, was to be found in the crucial concept of *paternalism.* The destinies of masters and slaves were linked by a set of mutual duties and responsibilities comparable in many ways to the arrangements between lords and serfs under the feudal system. Whites exploited and controlled the labor of socially inferior blacks and, in return, provided them with the basic necessities of life. To blacks slavery meant a recognition of their basic humanity, and this gave them a claim upon their masters. This claim could be manipulated by slaves who accepted the concessions offered to them by their masters and molded them to suit themselves. Within the limitations of the legal system of bondage, therefore, blacks were

---

[12]Robert W. Fogel and Stanley L. Engerman, *Time on the Cross: The Economics of American Slavery,* 2 vols. (Boston, 1974); Fogel, *Without Consent or Contract: The Rise and Fall of American Slavery* (New York, 1989).

[13]See Herbert G. Gutman, *Slavery and the Numbers Game: A Critique of Time on the Cross* (Urbana, Ill., 1975), and Paul A. David et al., *Reckoning With Slavery: A Critical Study in the Quantitative History of American Negro Slavery* (New York, 1976).

able to create their own culture. Genovese particularly emphasized slave religion because its affirmation of life served as a weapon for "personal and community survival." The price the blacks paid for this partial autonomy was the development of a nonrevolutionary and pre-political consciousness.[14]

In keeping with the newer focus upon the autonomy of slave society as contrasted with the earlier emphasis on dependency, Herbert G. Gutman in 1976 published his study of the black family. Gutman had been one of the most severe critics of *Time on the Cross,* and he wrote a book-length critique which attacked Fogel and Engerman precisely because of their claims of "black achievement under adversity." In *The Black Family in Slavery and Freedom, 1750–1925,* Gutman offered his own views, which, surprisingly enough, were not at all at variance with Fogel and Engerman or, for that matter, with Rawick, Blassingame, or Genovese.

Like many recent "new social historians" Gutman stressed the ability of blacks to adapt themselves to oppression in their own unique ways. In this respect he rejected the claims of Elkins and others about the debilitating impact of slavery upon its unwilling victims. Yet Gutman at the same time denied that plantation capitalism (Fogel and Engerman) and paternalism (Genovese) were necessary components in the process of adaptation. Slaves were able to create their own society not by reacting to white offers of rewards or by molding the concessions granted them by their masters, but rather by developing a sophisticated family and kinship network that transmitted the Afro-American heritage from generation to generation. The black family, in effect, served to cushion the shock of being uprooted from Africa. If parents were separated from their children by being sold, other relatives became surrogate parents to the remaining children. The stability of the black family rested upon a closely knit nuclear arrangement. Adultery after wedlock, for example, was infrequent. These family values were not imposed by white masters, according to Gutman, for they were rooted in the African cultural inheritance. Blacks were more loyal to each other than were whites, moreover, because the community was the basic means of survival.[15]

The debate over the nature of slavery took a somewhat different turn with the publication in 1977 of Lawrence Levine's *Black Culture and Black Consciousness: Afro-American Folk Thought from Slavery to Freedom.* Rather than utilizing standard plantation and demo-

---

[14]Genovese's major works include *The Political Economy of Slavery: Studies in the Economy & Society of the Slave South* (New York, 1965), *The World the Slaveholders Made: Two Essays in Interpretation* (New York, 1969), and *Roll, Jordan, Roll: The World the Slaves Made* (New York, 1974).

[15]Herbert G. Gutman, *The Black Family in Slavery and Freedom, 1750–1925* (New York, 1976).

graphic records, Levine uncovered and studied thousands of black songs, folktales, jokes, and games in an effort to penetrate into the minds and personalities of individuals who left few written records. Levine emphatically rejected Elkins's claim that slavery destroyed black culture and thus helped to create a dependent childlike individual. On the contrary, Levine insisted the evidence suggested that blacks preserved communal values amidst the harsh restrictions of a slave environment. A decade later Sterling Stuckey went even further and argued that an African heritage and nationalism "bound slaves together and sustained them under the brutal conditions of oppression." Indeed, ethnic differences were all but submerged by a common African heritage that defined black culture and shaped the black experience in America.[16]

The newer emphasis on slave society and culture has had several curious results. One has been the subtle transformation of slavery from an ugly and malignant system to an institution that is somewhat more benign in its character. This is not to imply that scholars like Fogel, Engerman, Genovese, and Gutman are in any way sympathetic to slavery, for all of them concede without reservation its immorality. But by focusing on the ability of black slaves to create a partially autonomous culture and society they implicitly diminish the authority of dominant white masters whose control was less than complete. Ironically, the emphasis on an indigenous black culture moved contemporary scholarship closer to Ulrich Bonnell Phillips, who had emphasized the contentment of blacks under slavery. Recent scholars, of course, take a quite different approach, but there is a distinct implication in their work that whites did not control many major elements in the lives of their slaves, who exercised considerable authority in determining their personal and familial relations. Compared with the Stampp and Elkins interpretation of slavery, these more recent works diminish, in part, the tragic view of slavery as an institution.

There is little doubt also that the parameters of the lively debate over the nature of slavery has been defined by a strong intellectual current that emphasizes the autonomy rather than the dependence of the American black experience. White scholars have been extremely sensitive to charges (particularly by blacks) that they have made the history of blacks a mere appendage of white actions and behavior. Consequently the emphasis on a unique and separate black identity and culture has had the effect of diminishing the importance of the white man's oppression as a major determinant in black history. By way of

---

[16]Lawrence W. Levine, *Black Culture and Black Consciousness: Afro-American Folk Thought from Slavery to Freedom* (New York, 1977); Sterling Stuckey, *Slave Culture: Nationalist Theory and the Foundations of Black America* (New York, 1987).

contrast, the Stampp-Elkins approach emphasized white responsibility for black problems.[17]

Many of the interpretations of slavery since the 1950s tended to treat the "peculiar institution" as a single unit; with only an occasional exception historians did not distinguish between time and place. In 1980, however, Ira Berlin threw down an explicit challenge to his colleagues. In a significant article in the *American Historical Review* he noted that "time and space"—the "traditional boundaries of historical inquiry"—had been largely ignored by American historians, most of whom had produced a "static vision of slave culture." In a detailed examination of seventeenth- and eighteenth-century slavery Berlin went on to identify three distinct slave systems: a Northern nonplantation system; and two Southern plantation systems, one in the Chesapeake Bay region and the other in the Carolina and Georgia low country. In each of these areas slavery developed in a unique manner; the differences had important consequences for black culture and society.

In the North, according to Berlin, acculturation incorporated blacks into American society while at the same time making them acutely conscious of their African past. Whites, who outnumbered blacks by a wide margin, allowed their slaves considerable autonomy. In the Southern low country, on the other hand, blacks were deeply divided; urban blacks pressed for incorporation into white society while plantation blacks remained physically separated and estranged from the Anglo-American world and closer to their African roots. In the Chesapeake region a single unified Afro-American culture emerged. Because of the impress of white paternalism, Afro-American culture paralleled Anglo-American culture; the African heritage was submerged. Berlin's analysis constituted an explicit and clear challenge to the parameters of the debate over slavery from the 1950s through the 1970s. "If slave society during the colonial era can be comprehended only through a careful delineation of temporal and spatial differences among Northern, Chesapeake, and low-country colonies," Berlin observed, "a similar division will be necessary for a full understanding of black life in nineteenth-century America. The actions of black people during the American Revolution, the Civil War, and the long years of bondage between these two cataclysmic events cannot be understood merely as a function of the dynamics of slavery or the possibilities of liberty, but must be viewed within the specific social circumstances and cultural traditions of black people. These varied

---

[17]For some recent discussions of this point see Stanley M. Elkins, *Slavery: A Problem in American Institutional and Intellectual Life* (3rd ed., Chicago, 1976), pp. 223–302, and George M. Fredrickson, "The Gutman Report," *New York Review of Books* 23 (September 30, 1976):18–23.

from time to time and from place to place. Thus no matter how complete recent studies of black life appear, they are limited to the extent that they provide a static and singular vision of a dynamic and complex society."[18]

Berlin was by no means alone in seeking to break with the traditional paradigm. Albert J. Raboteau and Margaret W. Creel, for example, focused on religion in an effort to understand the ethos of slaves. Creel in particular argued that slaves retained crucial elements of their African religious heritage, which they fused with a peculiar interpretation of Christianity. These religious beliefs served in turn as a means of opposing repression. The rise of women's history also led to a new concern with the experiences of female slaves. Deborah White demonstrated that the lives of male and female slaves were by no means identical. Females were less likely to run away because of maternal responsibilities; they were not dependent on black males; and they forged close bonds with other female slaves. In another important work Elizabeth Fox-Genovese emphasized that patriarchal households defined the entire slaveholding South, thus affecting the lives of both white and black slaves.[19]

A concern with the inner lives of blacks also stimulated research in old and new sources in an effort to develop a more sophisticated understanding of an elusive but important subject, namely, the impact of slavery on the personality and behavior of blacks. Employing an honor-shame dichotomy, Bertram Wyatt-Brown described a society in which male slaves varied their roles, depending on situational pressures. In his eyes the psychological costs of slavery were far higher than is generally realized, for repression led to communal mistrust and heightened the social and psychological stresses and tensions of slavery.[20] The second selection in this chapter is from an essay by Wyatt-Brown.

In evaluating the competing interpretations of American slavery it is important to understand that more than historical considerations are involved. Any judgment upon the nature of slavery implicitly offers a judgment of the present and a prescription for the future. To emphasize the harshness of slavery and the dependence of its victims

---

[18]Ira Berlin, "Time, Space, and the Evolution of Afro-American Society on British Mainland North America," *American Historical Review* 85 (February 1980):44–78.

[19]Albert J. Raboteau, *Slave Religion: The "Invisible Institution" in the Antebellum South* (New York, 1978); Margaret W. Creel, *"A Peculiar People": Slave Religion and Community-Culture Among the Gullahs* (New York, 1988); Deborah G. White, *Ar'n't I a Woman? Female Slaves in the Plantation South* (New York, 1985); Elizabeth Fox-Genovese, *Within the Plantation Household: Black and White Women of the Old South* (Chapel Hill, 1988).

[20]See also Bertram Wyatt-Brown's *Southern Honor: Ethics and Behavior in the Old South* (New York, 1982).

is to maximize the white man's responsibility. On the other hand to down-play the effectiveness of white authority is to move toward a position that concedes black autonomy and hence accepts the view that responsibility for post-Civil War developments rests in part with blacks.

Which of the various viewpoints of slavery are correct? Were slaves contented or discontented under slavery? In what ways were they successful in resisting the efforts of their masters to make them totally dependent human beings? To what degree did an autonomous black culture and social order develop during slavery? Was slavery a prebourgeois feudal system or a modern version of rational capitalism? What was the nature of the master-slave relationship? Is it possible to generalize about the lives of several millions of individuals under slavery? Must historians begin to distinguish between the common and the unique elements of the institution of slavery in terms of time and space? The answers to these questions undoubtedly will rest upon the continued analysis of surviving sources. But to a considerable degree they will rest also upon the attitudes and values of historians, whose own personal commitments play a role in shaping their perceptions of the past and their view of the present and future.

Stanley Elkins

STANLEY ELKINS (1925–   ) *is professor of history at Smith College. In addition to his influential book on slavery, he has published a number of articles and edited with Eric McKitrick* The Hofstadter Aegis: A Memorial *(1974).*

It will be assumed that there were elements in the very structure of the plantation system—its "closed" character—that could sustain infantilism as a normal feature of behavior. These elements, having less to do with "cruelty" per se than simply with the sanctions of authority, were effective and pervasive enough to require that such infantilism be characterized as something much more basic than mere "accommodation." It will be assumed that the sanctions of the system were in themselves sufficient to produce a recognizable personality type.

It should be understood that to identify a social type in this sense is still to generalize on a fairly crude level—and to insist for a limited purpose on the legitimacy of such generalizing is by no means to deny that, on more refined levels, a great profusion of individual types might have been observed in slave society. Nor need it be claimed that the "Sambo" type, even in the relatively crude sense employed here, was a universal type. It was, however, a plantation type, and a plantation existence embraced well over half the slave population. Two kinds of material will be used in the effort to picture the mechanisms whereby this adjustment to absolute power—an adjustment whose end product included infantile features of behavior—may have been effected. One is drawn from the theoretical knowledge presently available in social psychology, and the other, in the form of an analogy, is derived from some of the data that have come out of the German concentration camps. It is recognized in most theory that social behavior is regulated in some general way by adjustment to symbols of authority—however diversely "authority" may be defined either in theory or in culture itself—and that such adjustment is closely related to the very formation of personality. A corollary would be, of course, that the more diverse those symbols of authority may be, the greater is the permissible variety of adjustment to them—and the wider the margin of individuality,

---

Stanley Elkins, *Slavery: A Problem in American Institutional and Intellectual Life* (Chicago, 1959), pp. 86–89 and 115–39. Reprinted by permission of the author and The University of Chicago Press. Copyright 1959 by The University of Chicago Press.

consequently, in the development of the self. The question here has to do with the wideness or narrowness of that margin on the antebellum plantation.

The other body of material, involving an experience undergone by several million men and women in the concentration camps of our own time, contains certain items of relevance to the problem here being considered. The experience was analogous to that of slavery and was one in which wide-scale instances of infantilization were observed. The material is sufficiently detailed, and sufficiently documented by men who not only took part in the experience itself but who were versed in the use of psychological theory for analyzing it, that the advantages of drawing upon such data for purposes of analogy seem to outweigh the possible risks.

The introduction of this second body of material must to a certain extent govern the theoretical strategy itself. It has been recognized both implicitly and explicitly that the psychic impact and effects of the concentration-camp experience were not anticipated in existing theory and that consequently such theory would require some major supplementation. It might be added, parenthetically, that almost any published discussion of this modern Inferno, no matter how learned, demonstrates how "theory," operating at such a level of shared human experience, tends to shed much of its technical trappings and to take on an almost literary quality. The experience showed, in any event, that infantile personality features could be induced in a relatively short time among large numbers of adult human beings coming from very diverse backgrounds. The particular strain which was thus placed upon prior theory consisted in the need to make room not only for the cultural and environmental sanctions that sustain personality (which in a sense Freudian theory already had) but also for a virtually unanticipated problem: actual change in the personality of masses of adults. It forced a reappraisal and new appreciation of how completely and effectively prior cultural sanctions for behavior and personality could be detached to make way for new and different sanctions, and of how adjustments could be made by individuals to a species of authority vastly different from any previously known. The revelation for theory was the process of detachment.

These cues, accordingly, will guide the argument on Negro slavery. Several million people were detached with a peculiar effectiveness from a great variety of cultural backgrounds in Africa—a detachment operating with infinitely more effectiveness upon those brought to North America than upon those who came to Latin America. It was achieved partly by the shock experience inherent in the very mode of procurement but more specifically by the type of authority system to which they were introduced and to which they had to adjust for physical and psychic survival. The new adjustment, to absolute power in a closed system, involved infantilization, and the detachment was so complete that little trace of prior (and thus alternative) cultural sanctions for behavior and personality remained for the descendants of the first generation. For them, adjustment to clear and omnipresent authority could be more or less automatic—as much so, or as little, as it is for anyone whose adjustment to a social system begins at birth and to whom that system represents normality. We do not know how generally a full adjustment was made by the first generation of fresh slaves from Africa. But we do know—from a modern experience—that such an adjustment is possible, not only within the same generation but within two or three years. This proved possible for people in a full state of complex civilization, for men and women who were not black and not savages. . . . The immense revelation for psychology in the concentration-camp literature has been the discovery of how elements of dramatic personality change could be brought about in masses of individuals. And yet it is not proper that the crude fact of "change" alone should dominate the conceptual image with which one emerges from this problem. "Change" per se, change that does not go beyond itself, is productive of nothing; it leaves only destruction, shock, and howling bedlam behind it unless some future basis of stability and order lies waiting to guarantee it and give it reality. So it is with the human psyche, which is apparently capable of making terms with a state other than liberty as we know it. The very dramatic features of the process just described may upset the nicety of this point. There is the related danger, moreover, of unduly stressing the individual psychology of the problem at the expense of its social psychology.

These hazards might be minimized by maintaining a conceptual distinction between two phases of the group experience. The process of detachment from prior standards of behavior and value is one of them, and is doubtless the more striking, but there must be another one. That such detachment can, by extension, involve the whole scope of an individual's culture is an implication for which the vocabulary of individual psychology was caught somewhat unawares. Fluctuations in the state of the individual psyche could formerly be dealt with, or so it seemed, while taking for granted the more or less static nature of social organization, and with a minimum of reference to its features. That such organization might itself become an important variable was therefore a possibility not highly developed in theory, focused as theory was upon individual case histories to the invariable minimization of social and cultural setting. The other phase of the experience should be considered as the "stability" side of the problem, that phase which stabilized what the "shock" phase only opened the way for. This was essentially a process of adjustment to a standard of social normality, though in this case a drastic *re*adjustment and compressed within a very short time—a process which under typical conditions of individual and group existence is supposed to begin at birth and last a lifetime and be transmitted in many and diffuse ways from generation to generation. The adjustment is assumed to be slow and organic, and it normally is. Its numerous aspects extend much beyond psychology; those aspects have in the past been treated at great leisure within the rich provinces not only of psychology but of history, sociology, and literature as well. What rearrangement and compression of those provinces may be needed to accommodate a mass experience that not only involved profound individual shock but also required rapid assimilation to a drastically different form of social organization, can hardly be known. But perhaps the most conservative beginning may be made with existing psychological theory.

The theoretical system whose terminology was orthodox for most of the Europeans who have written about the camps was that of Freud. It was necessary for them to do a certain amount of improvising, since the scheme's existing framework provided only the narrowest leeway for dealing with such radical concepts as out-and-out change in personality. This was due to two kinds of limitations which the Freudian vocabulary places upon the notion of the "self." One is that the superego—that part of the self involved in social relationships, social values, expectations of others, and so on—is conceived as only a small and highly refined part of the "total" self. The other is the assumption that the content and character of the superego is laid down in childhood and undergoes relatively little basic alteration thereafter. Yet a Freudian diagnosis of the concentration-camp inmate—whose social self, or superego, did appear to change and who seemed basically changed thereby, is, given these limitations, still possible. Elie Cohen, whose analysis is the most thorough of these, specifically states that "the superego acquired new values in a concentration camp." The old values, according to Dr. Cohen, were first silenced by the shocks which produced "acute depersonalization" (the subject-object split: "It is not the real 'me' who is undergoing this"), and by the powerful drives of hunger and survival. Old values, thus set aside, could be replaced by new ones. It was a process made possible by "infantile regression"—regression to a previous condition of childlike dependency in which parental prohibitions once more became all-powerful and in which parental judgments might once more be internalized. In this way a new "father-image," personified in the SS guard, came into being. That the prisoner's identification with the SS could be so positive is explained by still another mechanism: the principle of "identification with the aggressor." "A child," as Anna Freud writes, "interjects some characteristic of an anxiety-object and so assimilates an anxiety-experience which he has just undergone. . . . By impersonating the aggressor, assuming his attributes or imitating his aggression, the child transforms himself from the person threatened into the person who makes the threat." In short, the child's only "defense" in the presence of a cruel, all-powerful father is the psychic defense of identification.

Now one could, still retaining the Freudian language, represent all this in somewhat less cumbersome terms by a slight modification of the metaphor. It could simply be said that under great stress the super-ego, like a bucket, is violently emptied of content and acquires, in a radically changed setting, new content. It would thus not be necessary to postulate a literal "regression" to childhood in order for this to occur. Something of the sort is suggested by Leo Alexander. "The psychiatrist stands in amazement," he writes, "before the thoroughness and completeness with which this perversion of essential superego values was accomplished in adults . . . [and] it may be that the decisive importance of childhood and youth in the formation of [these] values may have been overrated by psychiatrists in a society in which allegiance to these values in normal adult life was taken too much for granted because of the stability, religiousness, legality, and security of the 19th Century and early 20th Century society."

A second theoretical scheme is better prepared for crisis and more closely geared to social environment than the Freudian adaptation indicated above, and it may consequently be more suitable for accommodating not only the concentration-camp experience but also the more general problem of plantation slave personality. This is the "interpersonal theory" developed by the late Harry Stack Sullivan. One may view this body of work as the response to a peculiarly American set of needs. The system of Freud, so aptly designed for a European society the stability of whose institutional and status relationships could always to a large extent be taken for granted, turns out to be less clearly adapted to the culture of the United States. The American psychiatrist has had to deal with individuals in a culture where the diffuse, shifting, and often uncertain quality of such relationships has always been more pronounced than in Europe. He has come to appreciate the extent to which these relationships actually support the individual's psychic balance—the full extent, that is, to which the self is "social" in its nature. Thus a psychology whose terms are flexible enough to permit altering social relationships to make actual differences in character structure would be a psychology especially promising for dealing with the present problem.

Sullivan's great contribution was to offer a concept whereby the really critical determinants of personality might be isolated for purposes of observation. Out of the hopelessly immense totality of "influences" which in one way or another go to make up the personality, or "self," Sullivan designated one—the estimations and expectations of others—as the one promising to unlock the most secrets. He then made a second elimination: the *majority* of "others" in one's existence may for theoretical purposes be neglected; what counts is who the *sig-*

nificant others are. Here, "significant others" may be understood very crudely to mean those individuals who hold, or seem to hold, the keys to security in one's own personal situation, whatever its nature. Now as to the psychic processes whereby these "significant others" become an actual part of the personality, it may be said that the very sense of "self" first emerges in connection with anxiety about the attitudes of the most important persons in one's life (initially, the mother, father, and their surrogates—persons of more or less absolute authority), and automatic attempts are set in motion to adjust to these attitudes. In this way their approval, their disapproval, their estimates and appraisals, and indeed a whole range of their expectations become as it were internalized, and are reflected in one's very character. Of course as one "grows up," one acquires more and more significant others whose attitudes are diffuse and may indeed compete, and thus "significance," in Sullivan's sense, becomes subtler and less easy to define. The personality exfoliates; it takes on traits of distinction and, as we say, "individuality." The impact of particular significant others is less dramatic than in early life. But the pattern is a continuing one; new significant others do still appear, and theoretically it is conceivable that even in mature life the personality might be visibly affected by the arrival of such a one—supposing that this new significant other were vested with sufficient authority and power. In any event there are possibilities for fluidity and actual change inherent in this concept which earlier schemes have lacked.

The purest form of the process is to be observed in the development of children, not so much because of their "immaturity" as such (though their plasticity is great and the imprint of early experience goes deep), but rather because for them there are fewer significant others. For this reason—because the pattern is simpler and more easily controlled—much of Sullivan's attention was devoted to what happens in childhood. In any case let us say that unlike the adult, the child, being drastically limited in the selection of significant others, must operate in a "closed system."

Such are the elements which make for order and balance in the normal self: "significant others" plus "anxiety" in a special sense— conceived with not simply disruptive but also guiding, warning functions. The structure of "interpersonal" theory thus has considerable room in it for conceptions of guided change—change for either beneficent or malevolent ends. One technique for managing such change would of course be the orthodox one of psychoanalysis; another, the actual changing of significant others. Patrick Mullahy, a leading exponent of Sullivan, believes that in group therapy much is possible along these lines. A demonic test of the whole hypothesis is available in the concentration camp.

Consider the camp prisoner—not the one who fell by the wayside but the one who was eventually to survive; consider the ways in which he was forced to adjust to the one significant other which he now had—the SS guard, who held absolute dominion over every aspect of his life. The very shock of his introduction was perfectly designed to dramatize this fact; he was brutally maltreated ("as by a cruel father"); the shadow of resistance would bring instant death. Daily life in the camp, with its fear and tensions, taught over and over the lesson of absolute power. It prepared the personality for a drastic shift in standards. It crushed whatever anxieties might have been drawn from prior standards; such standards had become meaningless. It focused the prisoner's attention constantly on the moods, attitudes, and standards of the only man who mattered. A truly childlike situation was thus created: utter and abject dependency on one, or on a rigidly limited few, significant others. All the conditions which in normal life would give the individual leeway—which allowed him to defend himself against a new and hostile significant other, no matter how powerful— were absent in the camp. No competition of significant others was possible; the prisoner's comrades for practical purposes were helpless to assist him. He had no degree of independence, no lines to the outside, in any matter. Everything, every vital concern, focused on the SS: food, warmth, security, freedom from pain, all depended on the omnipotent significant other, all had to be worked out within the closed system. Nowhere was there a shred of privacy; everything one did was subject to SS supervision. The pressure was never absent. It is thus no wonder that the prisoners should become "as children." It is no wonder that their obedience became unquestioning, that they did not revolt, that they could not "hate" their masters. Their masters' attitudes had become *internalized* as a part of their very selves; those attitudes and standards now dominated all others that they had. They had, indeed, been "changed."

There still exists a third conceptual framework within which these phenomena may be considered. It is to be found in the growing field of "role psychology." This psychology is not at all incompatible with interpersonal theory; the two might easily be fitted into the same system. But it might be strategically desirable, for several reasons, to segregate them for purposes of discussion. One such reason is the extraordinary degree to which role psychology shifts the focus of attention upon the individual's cultural and institutional environment rather than upon his "self." At the same time it gives us a manageable concept—that of "role"—for mediating between the two. As a mechanism, the role enables us to isolate the unique contribution of culture and institutions toward maintaining the psychic balance of the individual. In it, we see formalized for the individual a range of choices in models of behavior and expression, each with its particular style, quality, and attributes. The relationship between the "role" and the "self," though not yet clear, is intimate; it is at least possible at certain levels of inquiry to look upon the individual as the variable and upon the roles extended him as the stable factor. We thus have a potentially durable link between individual psychology and the study of culture. It might even be said, inasmuch as its key term is directly borrowed from the theater, the role psychology offers in workable form is the long-awaited connection—apparently missed by Ernest Jones in his *Hamlet* study—between the insights of the classical dramatists and those of the contemporary social theorist. But be that as it may, for our present problem, the concentration camp, it suggests the most flexible account of how the ex-prisoners may have succeeded in resuming their places in normal life.

Let us note certain of the leading terms. A "social role" is definable in its simplest sense as the behavior expected of persons specifically located in specific social groups. A distinction is kept between "expectations" and "behavior"; the expectations of a role (embodied in the "script") theoretically exist in advance and are defined by the organization, the institution, or by society at large. Behavior (the "performance") refers to the manner in which the role is played. Another distinction involves the roles which are "pervasive" and those which are "limited." A pervasive role is extensive in scope ("female citizen") and not only influences but also sets bounds upon the other sorts of roles available to the individual ("mother," "nurse," but not "husband," "soldier"); a limited role ("purchaser," "patient") is transitory and intermittent. A further concept is that of "role clarity." Some roles are more specifically defined than others; their impact upon performance (and, indeed, upon the personality of the performer) depends on the clarity of their definition. Finally, it is asserted that those roles which carry with them the clearest and most automatic rewards and punishments are those which will be (as it were) most "artistically" played.

What sorts of things might this explain? It might illuminate the process whereby the child develops his personality in terms not only of the roles which his parents offer him but of those which he "picks up" elsewhere and tries on. It could show how society, in its coercive character, lays down patterns of behavior with which it expects the individual to comply. It suggests the way in which society, now turning its benevolent face to the individual, tenders him alternatives and defines for him the style appropriate to their fulfillment. It provides us with a further term for the definition of personality itself: there appears an extent to which we can say that personality is actually made up of the roles which the individual plays. And here, once more assuming "change" to be possible, we have in certain ways the least cumbersome terms for plotting its course.

The application of the model to the concentration camp should be simple and obvious. What was expected of the man entering the role of camp prisoner was laid down for him upon arrival:

> *Here you are not in a penitentiary or prison but in a place of instruction.*
> *Order and discipline are here the highest law. If you ever want to see*
> *freedom again, you must submit to a severe training. . . . But woe to*
> *those who do not obey our iron discipline. Our methods are thorough!*
> *Here there is no compromise and no mercy. The slightest resistance*
> *will be ruthlessly suppressed. Here we sweep with an iron broom!*

Expectation and performance must coincide exactly; the lines were to be read literally; the missing of a single cue meant extinction. The role was pervasive; it vetoed any other role and smashed all prior ones. "Role clarity"—the clarity here was blinding; its definition was burned into the prisoner by every detail of his existence.

> *In normal life the adult enjoys a certain measure of independence;*
> *within the limits set by society he had a considerable measure of lib-*
> *erty. Nobody orders him when and what to eat, where to take up his*
> *residence or what to wear, neither to take his rest on Sunday nor when*
> *to have his bath, nor when to go to bed. He is not beaten during his*
> *work, he need not ask permission to go to the W.C., he is not continu-*
> *ally kept on the run, he does not feel that the work he is doing is silly*
> *or childish, he is not confined behind barbed wire, he is not counted*
> *twice a day or more, he is not left unprotected against the actions of*
> *his fellow citizens, he looks after his family and the education of his*
> *children.*
>
> *How altogether different was the life of the concentration-camp*
> *prisoner! What to do during each part of the day was arranged for him,*
> *the decisions were made about him from which there was no appeal.*
> *He was impotent and suffered from bedwetting, and because of his*
> *chronic diarrhea he soiled his underwear. . . . The dependence of the*
> *prisoner on the SS . . . may be compared to the dependence of children*
> *on their parents. . . .*

The impact of this role, coinciding as it does in a hundred ways with that of the child, has already been observed. Its rewards were brutally simple—life rather than death; its punishments were automatic. By the survivors it was—it had to be—a role *well played.*

Nor was it simple, upon liberation, to shed the role. Many of the inmates, to be sure, did have prior roles which they could resume, former significant others to whom they might reorient themselves, a repressed superego which might once more be resurrected. To this extent they were not "lost souls." But to the extent that their entire personalities, their total selves, had been involved in this experience, to the extent that old arrangements had been disrupted, that society itself had been overturned while they had been away, a "return" was fraught with innumerable obstacles.

It is hoped that the very hideousness of a special example of slavery has not disqualified it as a test for certain features of a far milder and more benevolent form of slavery. But it should still be possible to say, with regard to the individuals who lived as slaves within the respective systems, that just as on one level there is every difference between a wretched childhood and a carefree one, there are, for other purposes, limited features which the one may be said to have shared with the other.

Both were closed systems from which all standards based on prior connections had been effectively detached. A working adjustment to either system required a childlike conformity, a limited choice of "significant others." Cruelty per se cannot be considered the primary key of this; of far greater importance was the simple "closedness" of the system, in which all lines of authority descended from the master and in which alternative social bases that might have supported alternative standards were systematically suppressed. The individual, consequently, for his very psychic security, had to picture his master in some way as the "good father," even when, as in the concentration camp, it made no sense at all. But why should it not have made sense for many a simple plantation Negro whose master did exhibit, in all the ways that could be expected, the features of the good father who was really "good"? If the concentration camp could produce in two or three years the results that it did, one wonders how much more pervasive must have been those attitudes, expectations, and values which had, certainly, their benevolent side and which were accepted and transmitted over generations.

For the Negro child, in particular, the plantation offered no really satisfactory father-image other than the master. The "real" father was virtually without authority over his child, since discipline, parental responsibility, and control of rewards and punishments all rested in other hands; the slave father could not even protect the mother of his children except by appealing directly to the master. Indeed, the mother's own role loomed far larger for the slave child than did that of the father. She controlled those few activities—household care, preparation of food, and rearing of children—that were left to the slave family. For that matter, the very etiquette of plantation life removed even the honorific attributes of fatherhood from the Negro male, who was addressed as "boy"— until, when the vigorous years of his prime were past, he was allowed to assume the title of "uncle."

From the master's viewpoint, slaves had been defined in law as property, and the master's power over his property must be absolute. But then this property was still human property. These slaves might never be quite as human as *he* was, but still there were certain standards that could be laid down for their behavior: obedience, fidelity, humility, docility, cheerfulness, and so on. Industry and diligence would of course be demanded, but a final element in the master's situation would undoubtedly qualify that expectation. Absolute power for him meant absolute dependency for the slave—the dependency not of the developing child but of the perpetual child. For the master, the role most aptly fitting such a relationship would naturally be that of the father. As a father he could be either harsh or kind, as he chose, but as a *wise* father he would have, we may suspect, a sense of the limits of his situation. He must be ready to cope with *all* the qualities of the child, exasperating as well as ingratiating. He might conceivably have to expect in this child—besides his loyalty, docility, humility, cheerfulness, and (under supervision) his diligence—such additional qualities as irresponsibility, playfulness, silliness, laziness, and (quite possibly) tendencies to lying and stealing. Should the entire prediction prove accurate, the result would be something resembling "Sambo."

The social and psychological sanctions of role-playing may in the last analysis prove to be the most satisfactory of the several approaches to Sambo, for, without doubt, of all the roles in American life that of Sambo was by far the most pervasive. The outlines of the role might be sketched in by crude necessity, but what of the finer shades? The sanctions against overstepping it were bleak enough, but the rewards—the sweet applause, as it were, for performing it with sincerity and feeling— were something to be appreciated on quite another level. The law, untuned to the deeper harmonies, could command the player to be present for the occasion, and the whip might even warn against his missing the grosser cues, but could those things really insure the performance that melted all hearts? Yet there was many and many a performance, and the audiences (whose standards were high) appear to have been for the most part well pleased. They were actually viewing their own masterpiece. Much labor had been lavished upon this chef d'oeuvre, the most genial resources of Southern society had been available for the work; touch after touch had been applied throughout the years, and the result—embodied not in the unfeeling law but in the richest layers of Southern lore—had been the product of an exquisitely rounded collective creativity. And indeed, in a sense that somehow transcended the merely ironic, it was a labor of love. "I love the simple and unadulterated slave, with his geniality, his mirth, his swagger, and his nonsense," wrote Edward Pollard. "I love to look upon his countenance shining with content and grease; I love to study his affectionate heart; I love to mark that peculiarity in him, which beneath all his buffoonery exhibits him as a creature of the tenderest sensibilities, mingling his joys and his sorrows with those of his master's home." Love, even on those terms, was surely no inconsequential reward.

But what were the terms? The Negro was to be a child forever. "The Negro . . . in his true nature, is always a boy, let him be ever so old. . . ." "He is . . . a dependent upon the white race; dependent for guidance and direction even to the procurement of his most indispensable necessaries. Apart from this protection he has the helplessness of a child—without foresight, without faculty of contrivance, without thrift of any kind." Not only was he a child; he was a happy child. Few Southern writers

failed to describe with obvious fondness the bubbling gaiety of a plantation holiday or the perpetual good humor that seemed to mark the Negro
character, the good humor of an everlasting childhood.

The role, of course, must have been rather harder for the earliest generations of slaves to learn. "Accommodation," according to John Dol-
lard, "involves the renunciation of protest or aggression against undesirable conditions of life and the organization of the character so that
protest does not appear, but acceptance does. It may come to pass in the
end that the unwelcome force is idealized, that one identifies with it and
takes it into the personality; it sometimes even happens that what is at
first resented and feared is finally loved."

Might the process, on the other hand, be reversed? It is hard to imagine its being reversed overnight. The same role might still be played in
the years after slavery—we are told that it was—and yet it was played
to more vulgar audiences with cruder standards, who paid much less for
what they saw. The lines might be repeated more and more mechani-
cally, with less and less conviction; the incentives to perfection could
become hazy and blurred, and the excellent old piece could degenerate
over time into low farce. There could come a point, conceivably, with
the old zest gone, that it was not longer worth the candle. The day might
come at last when it dawned on a man's full waking consciousness that
he had really grown up, that he was, after all, only playing a part.

One might say a great deal more than has been said here about mass
behavior and mass manifestations of personality, and the picture would
still amount to little more than a grotesque cartoon of humanity were
not some recognition given to the ineffable difference made in any social
system by men and women possessing what is recognized, anywhere and
at any time, simply as character. With that, one arrives at something too
qualitatively fine to come very much within the crude categories of the
present discussion; but although it is impossible to generalize with any
proper justice about the incidence of "character" in its moral irreducible, individual sense, it may still be possible to conclude with a note or
two on the social conditions, the breadth or narrowness of their compass, within which character can find expression.

Why should it be, turning once more to Latin America, that there
one finds no Sambo, no social tradition, that is, in which slaves were defined by virtually complete consensus as children incapable of being
trusted with the full privileges of freedom and adulthood? There, the system surely had its brutalities. The slaves arriving there from Africa had
also undergone the capture, the sale, the Middle Passage. They too had
been uprooted from a prior culture, from a life very different from the one
in which they now found themselves. There, however, the system was
not closed.

Here again the concentration camp, paradoxically enough, can be instructive. There were in the camps a very small minority of the survivors

who had undergone an experience different in crucial ways from that of the others, an experience which protected them from the full impact of the closed system. These people, mainly by virtue of wretched little jobs in the camp administration which offered them a minute measure of privilege, were able to carry on "underground" activities. In a practical sense the actual operations of such "undergrounds" as were possible may seem to us unheroic and limited: stealing blankets; "organizing" a few bandages, a little medicine from the camp hospital; black market arrangements with a guard for a bit of extra food and protection for oneself and one's comrades; the circulation of news; and other such apparently trifling activities. But for the psychological balance of those involved, such activities were vital; they made possible a fundamentally different adjustment to the camp. To a prisoner so engaged, there were others who mattered, who gave real point to his existence—the SS was no longer the "only" one. Conversely, the role of the child was not the only one he played. He could take initiative; he could give as well as receive protection; he did things which had meaning in adult terms. He had, in short, alternative roles; this was a fact which made such a prisoner's transition from his old life to that of the camp less agonizing and destructive; those very prisoners, moreover, appear to have been the ones who could, upon liberation, resume normal lives most easily. It is, in fact, these people—not those of the ranks—who have described the camps to us.

It was just such a difference—indeed, a much greater one—that separated the typical slave in Latin America from the typical slave in the United States. Though he too had experienced the Middle Passage, he was entering a society where alternatives were significantly more diverse than those awaiting his kinsman in North America. Concerned in some sense with his status were distinct and at certain points competing institutions. This involved multiple and often competing "significant others." His master was, of course, clearly the chief one—but not the only one. There could, in fact, be a considerable number: the friar who boarded his ship to examine his conscience, the confessor; the priest who made the rounds and who might report irregularities in the treatment to the *procurador*; the zealous Jesuit quick to resent a master's intrusion upon such sacred matters as marriage and worship (a resentment of no small consequence to the master); the local magistrate, with his eye on the king's official protector of slaves, who would find himself in trouble were the laws too widely evaded; the king's informer who received one-third of the fines. For the slave the result was a certain latitude; the lines did not all converge on one man; the slave's personality, accordingly, did not have to focus on a single role. He was, true enough, primarily a slave. Yet he might in fact perform multiple roles. He could be a husband and a father (for the American slave these roles had virtually no meaning); open to him also were such activities as artisan, peddler, petty merchant, truck gardener (the law reserved to him the necessary time and a share of the proceeds, but such arrangements were against the law for Sambo); he could be a communicant in the church, a member of a religious fraternity (roles guaranteed by the most powerful institution in Latin America—comparable privileges in the American South depended on a master's pleasure). These roles were all legitimized and protected *outside* the plantation; they offered a diversity of channels for the development of personality. Not only did the individual have multiple roles open to him as a slave, but the very nature of these roles made possible a certain range of aspirations should he some day become free. He could have a fantasy life not limited to catfish and watermelons; it was within his conception to become a priest, an independent farmer, a successful merchant, a military officer. The slave could actually—to an extent quite unthinkable in the United States—conceive himself *as a rebel*. Bloody slave revolts, actual wars, took place in Latin America; nothing on this order occurred in the United States. But even without a rebellion, society here had a network of customary arrangements, rooted in antiquity, which made possible at many points a smooth transition of status from slave to free and which provided much social space for the exfoliation of individual character.

To the typical slave on the antebellum plantation in the United States, society of course offered no such alternatives. But that is hardly to say that something of an "underground"—something rather more, indeed, than an underground—could not exist in Southern slave society. And there were those in it who hardly fitted the picture of "Sambo."

The American slave system, compared with that of Latin America, was closed and circumscribed, but, like all social systems, its arrangements were less perfect in practice than they appeared to be in theory. It was possible for significant numbers of slaves, in varying degrees, to escape the full impact of the system and its coercions upon personality. The house servant, the urban mechanic, the slave who arranged his own employment and paid his master a stipulated sum each week, were all figuratively members of the "underground." Even among those working on large plantations, the skilled craftsman or the responsible slave foreman had a measure of independence not shared by his simpler brethren. Even the single slave family owned by a small farmer had a status much closer to that of house servants than to that of a plantation labor gang. For all such people there was a margin of space denied to the majority; the system's authority-structure claimed their bodies but not quite their souls.

Out of such groups an individual as complex and highly developed as William Johnson, the Natchez barber, might emerge. Johnson's diary reveals a personality that one recognizes instantly as a type—but a type whose values came from a sector of society very different from that which formed Sambo. Johnson is the young man on the make, the ambitious free-enterpriser of American legend. He began life as a slave, was manumitted at the age of eleven, and rose from a poor apprentice barber to become one of the wealthiest and most influential Negroes in antebellum Mississippi. He was respected by white and black alike, and counted among his friends some of the leading public men of the state.

It is of great interest to note that although the danger of slave revolts (like Communist conspiracies in our own day) was much overrated by touchy Southerners; the revolts that actually did occur were in no instance planned by plantation laborers but rather by Negroes whose qualities of leadership were developed well outside the full coercions of the plantation authority-system. Gabriel, who led the revolt of 1800, was a blacksmith who lived a few miles outside Richmond; Denmark Vesey, leading spirit of the 1822 plot at Charleston, was a freed Negro artisan who had been born in Africa and served several years aboard a slave-trading vessel; and Nat Turner, the Virginia slave who fomented the massacre of 1831, was a literate preacher of recognized intelligence. Of the plots that have been convincingly substantiated (whether they came to anything or not), the majority originated in urban centers.

For a time during Reconstruction, a Negro elite of sorts did emerge in the South. Many of its members were Northern Negroes, but the Southern ex-slaves who also comprised it seem in general to have emerged from the categories just indicated. Vernon Wharton, writing of Mississippi, says:

> A large portion of the minor Negro leaders were preachers, lawyers, or teachers from the free states or from Canada. Their education and their independent attitude gained for them immediate favor and leadership. Of the natives who became their rivals, the majority had been urban slaves, blacksmiths, carpenters, clerks, or waiters in hotels and boarding houses; a few of them had been favored body-servants of affluent whites.

The William Johnsons and Denmark Veseys have been accorded, though belatedly, their due honor. They are, indeed, all too easily identified, thanks to the system that enabled them as individuals to be so conspicuous and so exceptional and, as members of a group, so few.

Bertram Wyatt-Brown

BERTRAM WYATT-BROWN (1932–   ) *is professor of history at the University of Florida. He is the author of a number of books and articles on antebellum America, including* Lewis Tappan and the Evangelical War Against Slavery *(1969) and* Southern Honor: Ethics and Behavior in the Old South *(1982).*

In August 1788, Thomas Foster, a dirt farmer of Spanish Natchez, purchased for $930 two slaves—"dos negros brutos," the deed said, meaning that they were recent imports from Africa. One of the slaves was named Samba, "second son" in the Fullah language of his native locale in the Futa Jallon country of modern Guinea. The other captive had a much more unusual name and finer pedigree: Abd-al-Rahman Ibrahima. He was the son of Sori, the *alimami*, or theocratic ruler, of the Fulani tribal group, whose capital was Timbo, an inland center that traded with distant Timbuktu, where Ibrahima had received Islamic training. Some months earlier, at the head of a cavalry detachment in his father's army, Ibrahima had been assigned to punish coastal tribesmen interfering with Fulani trade. He had been ambushed, captured, and sold to *slattees,* or native African slave traders.

Through some means, Ibrahima conveyed to Foster the possibilities of ransom for himself in cattle and other valuables, perhaps including slaves, of which there was a great supply in Futa Jallon. But Foster had more immediate prospects in mind. The master dubbed his new prize "Prince" and at once had Ibrahima's long plaits of hair cut, although it took several men to restrain him. Intentionally or not, Foster had deeply shamed his black antagonist. In Ibrahima's eyes, he, a Fulani warrior, had sunk to the level of a tribal youngster.

Other and worse humiliations followed when Ibrahima refused to work. The Fulani were pastoral folk among whom even the lowliest herdsman looked on manual labor with disdain. Agricultural work was the task of the Jalunke, many of whom the Fulani had conquered and enslaved. After one of several whippings, Ibrahima ran off to the woods. Like most runaways, African or Creole, he probably did not stray too far from the Fosters' five-acre clearing. Weeks passed, and Ibrahima realized the hopelessness of his situation. Since suicide was a serious violation

---

Bertram Wyatt-Brown, "The Mask of Obedience: Male Slave Psychology in the Old South," *American Historical Review* 93 (December 1988):1228–1252. Reprinted with the permission of Bertram Wyatt-Brown.

of the Koran, he was left to assume that Allah had intended his predicament. According to a story long remembered in Natchez, he appeared in the doorway when Thomas Foster's wife Sarah was alone. Looking up, she saw the tall and ragged frame of the missing slave, eyes fierce and staring. But rather than recoil in terror, she smiled, according to the story, and offered her hand in greeting. Ibrahima took it, then knelt on the floor and placed her foot on his neck.

Ibrahima's experience with bondage offers us clues about male slave psychology. The discussion is best limited, it should be added, to male slaves because they were considered the most troublesome, and therefore on them fell the greater demands for signals of full compliance. For newly acquired Africans, the requirement of docility and abject obedience, masters believed, had to replace traits associated with manly independence and self-direction. For those males born in slavery, dangerous signs of resentment or resistance were bound to meet prompt reprisal. In the struggle for control, masters ordinarily had less reason to fear open rebellion from their female property: the women could be coerced with threats against their men or their young. Slaveholders expected that the women would fall into line if the men were subdued and that mothers would raise their children with an understanding of the system and their circumscribed roles in it.

Few anecdotes—or even legends—explain how newly arrived Africans reacted to this regimen, which commanded not only their labor but also their change of behavior, even personality. We are accustomed to think in terms of stereotypical and anonymous figures like Samba, the other slave that the New Orleans trader had sold to Foster. Yet there was a connection between the Timbo prince's bad luck and what has come to be called "samboism," the expression of complete servility. In fact, Ibrahima's gesture of submission can symbolize for us that process of learning the demands of servitude as well as what servitude meant for the millions once in bondage. Although they learned subservience, Ibrahima and countless other blacks retained independent judgment. As Erik Erikson has pointed out, "it takes a well established identity to tolerate radical change." The Fulani warrior had that kind of resiliency, pride, and dignity. His religion and former place in African society prepared him to make the best of things without losing his sense of who he was.

More important to our purposes, community life in American slave culture, as in all societies, can be rendered unstable with differing effects on individual members, as circumstance, temperament, and the general situation shape their responses. Under oppressive conditions, which traits are most affected may be subject to debate, but the issue of damage itself must be faced. We simply cannot continue expatiating on the riches of black culture without also examining the social and psychological tensions that slavery entailed. . . .

Africans transported to the Western world were already acquainted with the dictates of absolute rule and absolute servility, the latter a condition that encouraged a resignation severely inhibiting thoughts of rebellion. Slave rebellions were as rare in Africa as they were in North America, perhaps because Americans combined a familial bondage—the African mode—with commercial cropping on relatively small estates. The purely commercial, impersonal, and large-scale plantations in the West Indies, by contrast, resulted in much greater degrees of unrest.

The African past and the servile present that Ibrahima symbolizes had in common a cultural pattern both parties understood: the ethic of honor and shame. Indeed, the culture from which Ibrahima—and so many of the blacks enslaved in early America—came resembled much more the honor-shame paradigm I have proposed for the white South than the conscience-guilt model of the northern section. But the power exercised over the slaves complicated the situation. Slaves were forced by circumstance to adopt the amoral posture of shamelessness, a pose intended to avoid the excesses of their victimization but that resulted in personal and social instability for them. Three major types of servility can be distinguished. The first is exemplified by Ibrahima—ritualized compliance in which self-regard is retained. The second is the socialization of subordination, a natural acceptance of circumstance that involves the incorporation of shame. The third type of subordination is the adoption of "samboism," as it may be called, or shamelessness. None of the forms of subservience is exclusive, for each merges into another with as much variation and contradictoriness as might be found in any individual. Samboism was a disengagement from, a denial of, the conventional ethic, though a part of the social order that both whites and blacks recognized. As a strategy for dealing with whites, samboism did not in itself signify mental aberration or perversion. It did, however, involve character disorder, an insensitivity to others, and a dangerous selfishness. The untroubled sambos served masters and themselves, sowing suspicion in the quarters and thus adding to the troubles of all. In other words, the slave who played sambo did not suffer much psychic injury, because, lacking a sense of morality at the time of taking the role, he lacked conflict. It was instead slaves of some sensitivity who had the real dilemma: how to maintain dignity in the face of shamelessness by masters and even by fellow slaves. In fact, both shame, as accepted by the slave, and shamelessness, as sometimes adopted, were involved in community but not necessarily personal instability. In poorly run or cruelly mismanaged plantation households, however, emotional confusion, misdirected violence or scapegoating out of repressed anger, severe or mild depression, self-contempt, and collective paranoia and mistrust could easily arise.

First, let us review the chief aspects of the honor-shame culture. It differs from the conscience-guilt style of conduct—the introspective, democratic, and individualized patterns that we like to think guide our own lives. "Whereas," wrote Gerhard Piers, "guilt is generated whenever a boundary . . . is touched or transgressed, shame occurs when a goal . . . is not being reached. It thus indicates a real 'short-coming.' Guilt anxiety accompanies transgression." On the other hand, shame involves a total failure of the individual: the incapacity to do, think, and feel the "right" way after recognizing the low opinion and disrespect in which one is held by others, who have respect and power. The excitation of shame involves a sense of defenselessness against the opinion and possibly the physical threats of others who claim superiority. Still more serious, a person shamed also suffers, as Norbert Elias, the German sociologist, pointed out, an internal conflict "with the part of himself that represents this social opinion. It is a conflict within his own personality; he recognizes himself as inferior." In the case of the male slave, shame operates to affect his relations with other slaves whose good opinion he wishes to have in order to enhance his own self-esteem. To some extent, shame also conditions him to seek the good will of his master, so that the master is less likely to shame him in front of his fellow slaves and the white world as well.

Just as shame and guilt are distinct, so too are honor and conscience. Here, honor refers to the expression of power through the prism of reputation and rank based on such factors as gender, skin color, age, wealth, and lineage, rather than on meritocratic criteria. Those who deviate from the accepted moral standards appropriate to their rank or who, by their race, color, or lowly occupation, are rejected by the group are subject to the sanctions of shame. Honor distinguishes between kin and alien, friend and enemy, in very obvious terms. Group and personal esteem is tied to family and to friendship as well as to vengeance against betrayers of one or both. It follows that kinlessness and friendlessness are the marks of shame and disgrace in all honor cultures. For Africans like Ibrahima, the great fear was "unhappy solitude," the dread of being alone. The same was also characteristic of white southern life.

Deference to illegitimate authority could not be countenanced by a man of honor. That was a principle that Ibrahima had come to live by. But, if enslavement was one's fate, the Fulani tribesman believed resignation to be the only response possible because divine forces had ordained it. The gesture that Ibrahima employed was the traditional emblem of unconditional surrender in West Africa. Orlando Patterson has called enslavement "social death," a literal reprieve from actual death. By formalizing his subjection in this way, however, Ibrahima was not merely prolonging his life. He was helping to smooth out the hills and valleys of his emotions into a level plain. Rituals serve to inhibit and control wild feelings of total despair. Similar if less dramatic rituals of slave deference served that function for other slaves. Since honor was something that all whites shared in contrast to the shame of all blacks, acts of homage lent—or were intended to lend—predictability to a situation that offered no permanent security.

For Ibrahima, the act of subjection was the beginning of unlearning his old self and teaching himself to present a new face of conformity. But he determined not to confess to dishonor, not to lose self-control. The Fulani people from which he came were well versed in the connection between male honor and the ideal of emotional restraint. To lose control was to forfeit honor and authority, to acknowledge unmanliness. No doubt, his success in maintaining dignity prompted his master to recognize his leadership qualities. Ibrahima became Thomas Foster's chief driver, to whom other slaves, some of them also from Futa Jallon, had to defer.

The second category of subservience, the inculcation of shame, can also be illustrated by reference to the Fulani experience in Africa. In the Fulani areas, the condition of slavery was one that anthropologist Paul Riesman argued "most clearly expressed everything that is the opposite of Fulani." Slaves and captives belonging to that people were labeled "black, fat, coarse, naive, irresponsible, uncultivated, shameless, dominated by their needs and their emotions." Slavery was a status given to strangers who were captured or bought; they became and remained kinless and subordinate, a traumatic experience in a society based on lineage and kinship networks.

More to our purposes are the slaves born into that condition in another Fulani corner of West Africa today. Anthropologist Bernd Baldus has recently studied the slave systems of Fulani herdsmen in the Borgu region of northern Benin. The Batomba are agriculturalists and have lived side by side with the Fulani since Fulani migrations began in the eighteenth century. Like other West Africans, the Batomba have long believed that, if a child's teeth appeared first in the upper jaw, fearful disaster would afflict the kinspeople and tribe. Parents underwent rites of purification, but the affected babies were killed. After the Fulani had settled, the Batomba gave or sold the infants as slaves to their new pastoral neighbors, whose Islamic beliefs did not include the dental taboo.

Called *machube* (singular: *machudo*), the stigmatized slaves and their descendants thereafter stood lower than those subject to three other forms of servitude in the area. As a result, when slaves of Borgu were freed under French colonial rule eighty-odd years ago, the *machube* continued in bondage more or less by force of custom alone. (Except briefly and ineffectively at the time of official abolition, they have not risen up against their masters.) Today, the Fulani use neither physical nor legal means of coercion to enforce their will. When Baldus recently interviewed the slaves, he found that they had internalized their lowly status, ranking themselves below the Fulani and Batomba. Baldus discovered that the *machube* blamed themselves, not their superiors, for their plight. Their sense of humiliation was so powerful that, much abashed, they hesitated to account for their bondage until the anthropologist explained that he already knew. Somehow, the *machube* were convinced that the Fulani provided them with special status. Whereas a Fulani master assumes authority as a right, a *machudo* accepts slavery out of a mixture of awe for Fulani magic and a sense of gratitude. Said one: "I work for the Pullo [another term for Fulani] because he has taken me as a child from the Batomba. He has raised me, washed me, he has given me milk . . . For this reason, as a sign of recognition, one carries out all his commands. . . .

Internalization of the master's values was often so complete that slaves ignored opportunities to escape. Josiah Henson, a slave who eventually escaped to freedom, lamented that in his youth he, like other country blacks, had long assumed the legitimacy of his own bondage. Moving his property prior to a sheriff's sale, his master had assigned Henson to guide some eighteen slaves from Virginia to Kentucky. "My pride was aroused in view of the importance of my responsibility, and heart and soul I became identified with my master's project of running off his negroes." Even though they floated past the wharves of Cincinnati, where crowds of free blacks urged them to flee, Henson suppressed excited talk of freedom. As he sadly recalled, he "had a sentiment of honor on the subject." Accustomed to obedience and "too degraded and ignorant of the advantages of liberty to know what they were forfeiting," the crew heeded his orders, and the barge journeyed southward. The incident was tragic, as Henson later realized in anguish, but most understandable. Plantation blacks who had little experience with autonomy were seldom quick to repudiate a humble conservatism that had long served as a means of survival. . . .

The third ingredient in the framework of male subservience is the traditional sambo himself—one not so habitually deferential as the *machudo* example nor so reserved and dignified as Ibrahima. Elkins erred in defining this character as a whole personality. Sambo was in fact a guise, adopted and cast aside as needed. When a slave took the role—some resorting to it more often than others—he made use of the third proposition in the system of honor and shame, namely, shamelessness. As Elkins correctly argued, naked power, unchecked by any custom or institutional restraint, morally but not necessarily emotionally deforms both victimizer and victim. In other words, repudiation of ordinary and mediated ethics on the master's part could have induced an excessive servility and sense of unworthiness on the part of the slave. As Anthony F. C. Wallace has noted, "shame—awareness of incompetence in any sphere, whether growing from self-observation or information from others—may arouse so much anxiety as to inhibit further the person's competence." Such individuals were probably rare in the slave quarters, because most could find some skill or expertise to counteract the contempt of the whites.

Even though Elkins failed to recognize the different responses that slavery could elicit, he was essentially right that Sambo behavior was authentic—but as ritual behavior, similar to but not identical with Ibrahima's alleged gesture. A reminder of how well this model of servility could be acted out appears in the diary of that remarkable South Carolinian, Mary Chesnut, at the close of the war:

> *We had a wonderful scene here last Sunday—an old African—who heard he was free & did not at his helpless old age relish the idea. So he wept & prayed, kissed hands, rolled over on the floor until the boards of the piazza were drenched with his tears. He seemed to worship his master & evidently regarded the white race as some superior order of beings, he prostrated himself so humbly.*

The whites rewarded his gratifying performance with a blanket and other throwaways. The observers knew how insincere the beggar was, and all parties involved appreciated his immunity from moral responsibility in adopting the role.

The samboism of the roguish, coarse, and deceitful slave describes only one role slaves might play, but in all honor-shame societies in which slavery is a key institution, one finds the same ritualized and highly expressive practice: in Muscovite Russia, Greece, and Rome, in Brazil, the West Indies, in fact, nearly everywhere save parts of Asia. In all such societies, the slave was perceived as childlike and womanlike in character, only more so—violent (when spoiled) but usually passive, even affectionate.

The necessity for adopting the trickster role lay in the unpredictability of the master's behavior, a point that Elkins convincingly made. The slaveholder could be shameless in rule and the slave shameless in protestations of dependency, driven by the emotions of the moment in a childish way. The survivor was the conscienceless "chameleon" who adopted the coloration that the totalitarian slave regime—or the master's whim—imposed. An example from contemporary society appears in Nien Cheng's *Life and Death in Shanghai*. In Communist China, "chameleon" is the term used for those able to adjust quickly to authoritarian changes of policy. Both southern slaveowner and servant could act with a lack of decorous inhibition and yet not be mentally "damaged" or neurotic. . . .

Thus a range of different degrees of deference and inner acceptance existed, with each slave adopting or, at times, rejecting servility as the plantation environment, personal temperament, mood, and even unconscious motive allowed. A small number may well have fit Elkins' unhappy description and lived lives of self-deprecation and deception. At the other, more inspired, extreme of samboism, some slaves took positive delight in the jesting, roguish performance. Almost all varieties of servility involved some degree of shamelessness, for that signaled an inner contempt for the values of honor on which the master rested his authority. But, in dealing with each other as opposed to the requirements of slavery, slaves avoided extremes for the most part. Some gave out contradictory or ambivalent signals. Such, for instance, was "Runaway Dennis," a slave belonging to Katherine Du Pre Lumpkin's grandfather in middle Georgia. Dennis so constantly quarreled with fellow slaves that they "'fought shy' of him" but protected him as well, she recalled from family retellings. When called to account by the black driver, the overseer, or the owner, Dennis would vanish. None of the slaves ever betrayed his whereabouts. He "shamefacedly" reappeared only when word reached him through the quarters that he had been promised amnesty, usually through the intercession of Lumpkin's grandmother, whom he revered. For a short time, Dennis was once more a model of conscientiousness and servile compliance. After freedom, the unreconstructed former slave remained as "friendless" in the black community as he had been during slavery but showed his loyalty to Lumpkin by voting Democratic. . . .

To escape the dictates of shame and humiliation, then, male slaves had to repress emotions and maintain confident behavior under pressure. But, even so, the unpredictability of masters, the difficulty of avoiding white surveillance, the powerlessness of any slave in jeopardy could result in self-devaluation and especially doubt, what Erikson called "the brother of shame." Ball explained these feelings in the case of his own family under slavery. Helpless to prevent the sale of his wife, Ball's father, once a man "of a gay social temper," turned "gloomy and morose . . . and spent nearly all his leisure time with my grandfather, who claimed kindred with some royal family in Africa." To avoid sale himself, Ball's father had to run away, and only the grandfather remained to raise the boy, doing his best to endow Ball with a sense of selfhood based, like Ibrahima's, on the family lineage.

The male slave's abuse of women—sexual violence, desertion, insult—recapitulated white men's assaults on the black male ego, even as it arose from feelings of personal dissatisfaction. These emotions of rage, depression, and stony resentment—often inwardly directed and involving alcoholism—are constantly emphasized in modern black autobiography and fiction, sources that put in artistic form some realities of black alienation. The situation was the classic issue of neurotic conflict as Karen Horney portrayed it in *Neurosis and Human Growth*. Although condemned for his unrealistic portrait of the historical Nat Turner, William Styron presented a picture of anarchic cruelty as the basis for such reactions, cruelty that blacks adopted in whole or in part to protect selfhood. The very pecking order of the plantation—mirror image in the slave quarters of the patriarchal, male-dominated, honor-obsessed rankings of the white society—encouraged shamelessness, disesteem of others, and self-abnegation. Household servants were contemptuous of field hands, drivers of their underlings, lowly male slaves of their women, and women of the inferior members of their own sex. Accepting white standards of physical beauty, slaves often expressed a preference for light skin.

Deep mistrust and rivalry rent the harmony of the slave quarters. Such problems had potentially tragic consequences. The darker side of "shamelessness," for instance, was that busy sambos made untrustworthy companions. They might have been and probably were emotionally undamaged. The male slave who acted the part but felt it contrary to his nature was a likely victim of his own rage and conflict. But an imperviousness to moral controls made the effective trickster dangerous to the stability of the slave community. In a novel, W. E. B. Du Bois created one such figure named Johnson, whom a Colonel Cresswell called "'a faithful nigger.' He was one of those constitutionally timid creatures," the narrator said, "into whom the servility of his fathers had sunk so deep that it had become second nature," but to the other Negroes, "he was a 'white folks' nigger,' to be despised and feared." According to a recent study, Du Bois believed that the psychic damage of slavery was "an intense self-hatred" that made "racial solidarity an alien concept." Distrust and insecurity among blacks themselves multiplied as a result. Of course, it is possible that sambo-like behavior—playing dumb or unconcerned—could well mask other designs or fool the white onlooker—to the satisfaction of the performer and his colleagues. Nonetheless, one wonders how much effort, time, and emotional stress had to be directed toward self-protection alone, leaving less energy for more creative pursuits and self-development. What saved the situation from complete demoralization was the strength of family ties in a wide, extended-family kinship network characteristic of both North American black and African culture. Although circumstances differed on both continents, sources of security outside the family were not available. In the American South, it did not pay to trust others in the quarters under such circumstances. Du Bois observed that blacks responded to the disruptive, unreliable world around them with a "double-consciousness," that is, a "sense of always looking at one's self through the eyes of others, of measuring one's soul by the tape of a world that looks on in amused contempt and pity." How different from the studied and voluntary doubleness of the stage actor.

Equally damaging was the sheer physical punishment that masters could inflict. The point is so obvious that I hesitate to belabor it, but even the most knowledgeable historians of slavery have underestimated its frequency and psychological effects. The prospect of 150 lashes would make almost anyone a cringing coward. In fact, slaves exercised remarkable control. Their fortitude certainly had African roots. In some tribes, thrashing ceremonies, called in northern Nigeria the *sheriya*, tested stoic manhood. In any event, the physical effects could be very severe even under law rather than simply under the arbitrary passion of an irate master. Corydon Fuller, a pious young bookseller traveling through Louisiana, recorded that, in Claiborne Parish, Louisiana, 1858, a slave who had inadvertently struck his mistress in the face with a bridle was sentenced to *"one thousand* lashes to be inflicted 100 each day for ten days. Many think he will die." Such punishments were scarcely everyday occurrences, but neither were they rare.

From the psychological point of view, whippings had three major effects. They degraded the victim, shut down more normal communications, but, most important of all, compelled the victim to repress the inevitable anger felt toward those responsible for the pain and disgrace. As a result, even the merest hint of violence obliged the victim to retreat into as complaint a pose as could be managed. Edward Wilmot Blyden, an early nationalist and advocate for Liberian settlement, declared, "We have been taught a cringing servility. We have been drilled into contentment with the most undignified circumstances." White oppression stirred both compliance and fierce resentment, as Genovese explained in *Roll, Jordan, Roll.*

In addition, less physically injurious cruelties abounded. We need not mention the threat of sale and separation from family and community, a sudden and often unpredictable event with sorrows hard to imagine. Also, masters sometimes used shaming rites, ones that could enlist the other slaves into enjoying the spectacle, thereby doubling the misery while keeping the slaves disunited. Bennet Barrow, a slaveholder of Louisiana, once threatened to put an offending slave on a scaffold in the yard, wearing a red flannel cap. In another example, a slave with an insatiable craving had stolen an enormous seed pumpkin from his master's patch. The other slaves told on him, and the master easily recovered the unconcealable object. He made the slave eat a "big bowl of pumpkin sauce." The old slave who recalled the incident declared, "it am funny to see that colored gentleman with pumpkin smear on he face and tears running down he face. After that us children call him Master Pumpkin, and Master have no more trouble with stealing he seed pumpkins."

With all the psychological, social, political, military, economic, and educational advantages that whites wielded, slaves could scarcely avoid feelings of oppression—and therefore of repression in a part of their social personality. To be sure, an essential self remained inviolable. Behind the mask of docility, the male slave was still himself and gave the lie to southern claims of "knowing" their blacks. As W. J. Cash pointed out, "even the most unreflecting must sometimes feel suddenly, in dealing with him, that they were looking at a blank wall, that behind that grinning face a veil was drawn which no white man might certainly know he had penetrated." And yet the cost of building that impenetrable wall was high: repressing the hatred of the oppressors, bearing the slave's own powerlessness and the slavishness of other blacks. Male honor was richly prized in the slave quarters, and a defense of it established rank among fellow slaves. But slave honor was confined to the slave quarters, a restriction that may have made them all the more brutal out of frustration. Judge Nash of the North Carolina Supreme Court once declared that the slaves "sometimes kill each other in heat of blood, being sensible to the dishonor in their own caste of crouching in submission to one of themselves." Such behavior betokened a self-despising that sought a scapegoat in another person. For instance, Dan Josiah Lockhart, a fugitive in Canada, but once a plantation driver, admitted, "I was harder on the servants than [my master] wanted I should be." From his account, he was clearly taking out his resentment against his owner for selling his wife to a farmer an unreachable eight miles away.

Another sign of self-hatred can be located in the examples of sabotage or apparent plantation "accidents" that historians have largely attributed to motives of subversion rather than to racist ideas of black "laziness" and irresponsibility. For instance, James Redpath, a journalist with strong antislavery convictions, reported that, on a trip through the South, he had witnessed a slave drayman lashing the horses legs unmercifully as they hauled uphill a two-ton load of plaster. "This is a fair specimen of the style in which Negroes treat stock," he remarked. Frederick Law Olmsted offered similar testimony. Planters, he said, used mules more often than horses because "horses cannot bear the treatment they always must get from negroes" whereas "mules will bear the cudgeling." To take out disappointments on a hoe or horse would, then, be less politically calculated than an impulsive expression of anger against personal miseries in the quarters as well as in the slave system itself. We are unlikely ever to know.

Likewise, historians understand little about how mothers reared their slave children. One suspects that at some point early affection had to give way to stern and perhaps arbitrary discipline—a cuffing without explanation—to turn the child toward automatic obedience and toward staying out of trouble with the white man. Male children more than female would have to be so trained. Wright implied in *Black Boy*, his autobiographical novel, that the reason why his mother, grandmother, and other family elders cuffed, slapped, and beat him was not only a venting of their own miseries against a smaller creature but also an expression of a desperate love for him: without such treatment to curb his uncalculating independence, he would surely one day become, they thought, a white mob's victim. "How many mothers and fathers had to punish severely children they loved so as to instill in them the do's and don'ts of a hideous power system in which a mistake could cost lives?" asked Genovese.

Evidence of similar patterns in the experience of the Fulani slaves provides further insight. Bernd Baldus noted that the Fulani and Batomba superiors consider the *machudo* slave "uncivilized" or "wild."

The *machube* are demoralized to the point of extreme aggressiveness toward each other. They never assault the mocking rulers but instead fall on one another in often fierce violence. "Mistrust" and lack of internalized controls are "pervasive, covering even close social ties among neighbors, friends, or family members." The experience of the *machube* was different from that of American slaves, who had the benefit of a Christian humanitarianism and more sophisticated attitudes with which to forge the bonds of a community. But such unhappy conditions could well have existed on those plantations where masters sought to destroy any sense of black collectivity.

In the last few years, the darker side of slave life has regained scholars' notice, but generally historians place the emphasis on the remarkable endurance and even joyousness that slaves extracted from harsh conditions. Significant and valid though the brighter view is, the costs of honor, shame, and shamelessness should not be ignored. If repression and its manifestations in inappropriate ways was one of the chief emotional problems of bondage, another was the related problem of communal mistrust and its effect on the social personality of the slave. . . .

☆ 10 ☆

The Civil War

REPRESSIBLE OR IRREPRESSIBLE?

Few events in American history have been studied more than the Civil War. Scarcely a year passes that does not see the publication of a wave of books and articles dealing with the war as well as the events leading up to it. So widespread has been interest in the origins and consequences of the conflict that many organizations as well as journals have been founded expressly for the purpose of furthering additional research and stimulating popular and professional interest in this subject. Indeed, to refer to the "cult" of the Civil War enthusiasts is not to exaggerate the intense interest that this topic has generated.

One of the reasons for the enduring interest in the Civil War era undoubtedly lies in the fact that this conflict pitted Americans against Americans. Under such circumstances responsibility for the coming of the war could not easily be placed on an external foe or upon factors beyond the control of Americans. The symbolic influence of the conflict as a major dividing line in American history also helps to explain the continued fascination with this problem. To American historians the Civil War bears the same relationship to American people as the French Revolution to Frenchmen, the English civil war to Englishmen, and the Russian Revolution to Russians. Questions involving vital national issues seemed to be at stake: the problem of nationalism versus states' rights and sectionalism; the role the war played in promoting industrialization and urbanization; and the status blacks were to have in American society.

Despite the vast body of published material dealing with the Civil War, however, historians have been unable to come to any agreement as to why the war occurred in the first place. "Historians, whatever their predispositions," noted a famous scholar nearly fifty years ago," assign to the Civil War causes ranging from one simple force or phenomenon to patterns so complex and manifold that they include, intricately interwoven, all the important movements, thoughts, and actions of the decades before 1861."[1] This comment is as true today as it was when it was first written. Disagreements among historians over the problem of Civil War causation seem to be as sharp today as they were when the conflict began over a century ago.

The disagreement over the coming of the conflict was hardly surprising; Americans have traditionally engaged in a debate over all of the wars in which they participated. Historians still argue over the desirability or wisdom of America's participation in World Wars I and II; they discuss the War of 1812, the Mexican War, and the Spanish-American War in terms of American aggression—thereby questioning the desirability and morality of these conflicts; and they debate the question of whether or not the Korean War and Vietnam War were due to the ineptitude of America's foreign policies. The Civil War, however, has undoubtedly been the most controversial of all of these conflicts insofar as scholars were concerned. Unlike the American Revolution—whose good and beneficent results few ever questioned—American historians have, by and large, never been fully convinced that the war was necessary or that its results were worthwhile. Consequently they have continued to seek to fix responsibility for its causes upon specific groups or institutions.

In the three decades following the end of fighting in 1865, many authors published their own evaluations of the causes of the war. Most of these early writers themselves had participated in one way or another in the war; their books represented an attempt to justify their own actions or those of their respective sections. When they looked at the war, therefore, they viewed it in terms of a conspiracy. Northern writers portrayed Southern secessionists as men dedicated to the advance of the cause of slavery, regardless of the harm to the rest of the nation. The slave power, wrote Henry Wilson in a famous book published in the 1870s, "after aggressive warfare of more than two generations upon the vital and animating spirit of republican institutions, upon the cherished and hallowed sentiments of a Christian people, upon the enduring interests and lasting renown of the Republic organized treasonable conspiracies, raised the standard of revolution, and plunged the nation into a bloody contest for the preservation of its threatened life."[2] To most Northern writers the war resulted from a conspiracy of slaveowners committed to an immoral institution; the North was defending the Union and the Constitution against the unprovoked and immoral aggression of the South.

---

[1] Howard K. Beale, "What Historians Have Said About the Causes of the Civil War," in *Theory and Practice in Historical Study: A Report of the Committee on Historiography,* Social Science Research Council, Bulletin 54 (1946):55

[2] Henry Wilson, *History of the Rise and Fall of the Slave Power in America,* 3 vols. (Boston, 1872–1877), 1:vi–vii.

Southern writers, on the other hand, depicted an aggressive North determined to destroy the South and its institutions. The war, they insisted, was not a moral conflict over the issue of slavery; slavery was the occasion of the conflict, not its cause. The basic cause of the war was the unconstitutional and aggressive acts of the North, which used its power for political and economic gain. Although Southerners denied that the war had stemmed from differences over slavery, they did argue that both sections had differing and incompatible ways of life. One of the basic factors leading to hostilities, therefore, was the North's domineering attitude toward the South. Thus Abraham Lincoln and the Republican party deliberately provoked the conflict by their aggressive and unwarranted actions in 1860 and 1861, thereby forcing the South to defend the Constitution as well as its rights. For this reason Southerners refused to accept the term "Civil War" or the "War of the Great Rebellion"; both implied that the South was wrong. Instead they used the designation "War Between the States," which seemed to justify the Southern emphasis on states' rights and local autonomy.

While Northern and Southern partisans were attacking each other a third school of writers was developing the concept of a "needless" or "avoidable" conflict. The origins of this approach to the problem of Civil War interpretation arose first among those individuals who had been critical of the activities of both Northern and Southern statesmen between 1860 and 1865. President James Buchanan, for example, argued in 1865 that the cause of the Civil War was to be found in "the long, active, and persistent hostility of the Northern Abolitionists, both in and out of Congress, against Southern slavery, until the final triumph of President Lincoln; and on the other hand, the corresponding antagonism and violence with which the advocates of slavery resisted these efforts, and vindicated its preservation and extension up till the period of secession."[3] Implied in Buchanan's statement was the assumption that the war need not have taken place had it not been for Northern fanatics and, to a lesser extent, Southern extremists. To put it another way, there was no substantive issue important enough in 1861 to necessitate a resort to arms; the war had been brought on by extremists on both sides.

These three contemporary views of the causes of the Civil War set the stage for the historical debate that began at the end of the nineteenth century and continues right down to the present. Despite massive research into the sources, both published and unpublished, historians continued to divide into competing and antagonistic schools. It was not that scholars disagreed over what constituted the "facts" in

---

[3]James Buchanan, *The Administration on the Eve of the Rebellion: A History of Four Years Before the War* (London, 1865), p. iv.

each case; indeed, their data, whatever school they belonged to, were remarkably similar. What divided them was the different way in which they read and interpreted the data.

The first serious attempts to explain the coming of the Civil War in a way that was free from the bitterness of contemporary accounts came from the writings of the postwar generation of historians who came to maturity in the 1890s. To them the Civil War was "history" rather than a part of current events. Most of them had been very young when the war began; their memories of the war years were not as personally and emotionally involved as were their parents'. The writings of this later generation reflected a decline in the heated partisanship characteristic of earlier accounts.

These scholars were influenced also by the rising tide of American nationalism during the 1890s and early part of the twentieth century. By that time both North and South had come to the conclusion that the outcome of the Civil War had been a blessing in disguise. Not only had the slavery issue disappeared, but the intense sectional strife that had inhibited the growth of the nation at large had been laid to rest. After the war the stage was set for the phenomenal industrial growth of the United States, a development that made the nation a world power by the turn of the century. Even more significant, the war had tested the mettle and fiber of all Americans; they had not been found wanting. While the nationalist school did not gloss over the war, they began to present a more balanced and less partisan picture of an event that had cemented for all time the bonds of American nationality.

One of the first—and in some respects the most influential—works in the nationalist tradition was written by James Ford Rhodes whose multivolume history of the United States from 1850 to 1877 became a classic. Like many of his Northern predecessors Rhodes accepted the idea that slavery was the basic cause of the war. He rejected the claim by Southerners that they had been persecuted; instead he argued that the South had fought the war to extend slavery. In his eyes, however, slavery was an immoral institution. The Civil War, Rhodes concluded, involved an "irrepressible conflict" between North and South, and the South had been clearly in the wrong.

Despite his obvious Northern sympathies Rhodes modified considerably his own partisan approach in his discussion of the South and its peculiar institution. Slavery had prospered, he wrote, because of technological progress; the cotton gin had prevented the peaceful abolition of slavery. Moreover, both England and New England had played an important role in the preservation of slavery; their citizens had purchased slave-grown cotton without any moral compunctions. Rhodes also distinguished between the institution of slavery and individual slaveowners; he absolved the latter of any crime and insisted that they were deserving of sympathy rather than of censure. Indeed, Rhodes's discussion of the South was by no means hostile; he found much to praise in his descriptions of Southern life. To Rhodes the Civil War came about through the collision of impersonal forces, not individuals; out of the conflict, he concluded, had emerged a modern united America.

Rhodes's general approach was followed by other nationalist historians, many of whom were native Southerners. To the nationalist school the causes of war were less important than its results. Southern scholars, for example, emphasized nationalism, sectional reconciliation, and the integration of the South into national life so that their section was able to share in the blessings of industrialization and prosperity. There writers were not critical of the South—they unabashedly loved their region—but they were critical of slavery and secession. Their condemnation of slavery, however, did not rest on a moral foundation that accepted blacks as the equals of whites. Instead they condemned the peculiar institution because it had prevented the South from making progress in industrial, economic, social, and cultural matters. Woodrow Wilson, for example (who prior to entering public life had achieved a national reputation as a historian), emphasized the development of American nationalism in many of his works. Unfortunately, he concluded, the South remained outside the rising spirit of nationalism precisely because of slavery; consequently it developed differently from the rest of the country. The result, according to Wilson, was the Civil War—a conflict that came about because differences between North and South "were removable in no other way."

Generally speaking, nationalist historians often wrote about the Civil War in terms of an "irrepressible conflict." The sectional approach to history that developed in the early part of the twentieth century tended to reinforce this concept. The conflict between North and South, some historians argued, was basically one that grew out of sectional differences on issues of national policy—of which slavery was but one issue. "By the middle of the [nineteenth] century," wrote Edward Channing, one of America's most distinguished historians, "two distinct social organizations had developed within the United States, the one in the South and the other in the North. Southern society was based on the production of staple agricultural crops by slave labor. Northern society was bottomed on varied employments—agricultural, mechanical, and commercial—all carried on under the wage system. Two such divergent forms of society could not continue indefinitely to live side by side within the walls of one government. . . . One or the other of these societies must perish, or both must secure complete equality . . . or the two societies must separate absolutely and live each by itself under its own government."[4]

---

[4]Edward Channing, *A History of the United States*, 6 vols. (New York, 1905-1925), 6:3–4, and James Ford Rhodes, *History of the United States from the Compromise of*

Those historians who wrote within the nationalist tradition obviously approved of the outcome of the Civil War. Most of them felt that the growth of industry—a development that dated from the Civil War—was good. Few of these scholars were interested in social reform nor were they antibusiness in their ideological views. Rhodes had been a businessman before taking up the study of history, and he shared the conservative outlook of many late nineteenth-century businessmen. Wilson in the 1890s was a conservative Democrat of the Cleveland stripe; his conversion to Progressivism did not occur until later. Even Channing was not noted for being antibusiness. All of these nationalist historians, therefore, were pleased with developments after 1865. The climate of opinion around the turn of the century was such that few took occasion to protest the fact that blacks had not yet achieved a measure of equality with whites. Like most white Americans, many of these scholars—though by no means all—believed blacks to be inferior beings. Such a belief seemed to them to be buttressed by contemporary scientific findings. They therefore accepted the subordinate role of blacks in American society as a natural development.

By the early twentieth century the dominance of the nationalist school of Civil War historiography began to face a formidable challenge from the rising Progressive school. As we have already seen the Progressive school had developed during the period of domestic reform around the turn of the century. Concerned with contemporary social problems, particularly those involving injustices in society arising out of a maldistribution of wealth and power, Progressive historians attempted to provide answers to these problems by showing how they had developed in the past. Thus they began to restudy American history in terms of a conflict between democracy and aristocracy, between the have-nots and the haves in American society. Led by men like Charles A. Beard and others, these scholars emphasized not the development of a beneficent nationalism, but the emergence of democracy, particularly economic democracy. Consequently they divided America's past into alternating periods of reform and reaction—a cycle that was generated by class and social conflict in each instance.

In the writings of these historians the Civil War began to be studied within a new framework. Perhaps the most lucid and influential Progressive interpretation of the Civil War came from the pen of Charles and Mary Beard, who published in 1927 their famous Progressive synthesis of American history, *The Rise of American Civilization*. To the Beards the resort to arms in 1861 precipitated by secession was merely a facade for a much more deeply rooted conflict. Stripped of all nonessentials, they emphasized, the Civil War "was a social war, end-

---

1850 to the Final Restoration of Home Rule in the South in 1877, 7 vols. (New York, 1893-1906).

ing in the unquestioned establishment of a new power in the government, making vast changes in the arrangement of classes, in the accumulation and distribution of wealth, in the course of industrial development, and in the Constitution inherited from the Fathers. . . . In any event neither accident nor rhetoric should be allowed to obscure the intrinsic character of that struggle. If the operations by which the middle classes of England broke the power of the king and the aristocracy are to be known collectively as the Puritan Revolution, if the series of acts by which the bourgeois and peasants of France overthrew the king, nobility and clergy is to be called the French Revolution, then accuracy compels us to characterize by the same term the social cataclysm in which the capitalists, laborers, and farmers of the North and West drove from power in the national government the planting aristocracy of the South."[5]

Unlike the nationalist interpretation, a Progressive synthesis such as that of the Beards condemned the results of the Civil War in no uncertain terms. Between 1865 and 1900 the American economy came to be dominated by ruthless and immoral capitalists who thought of nothing but their own aggrandizement. To Matthew Josephson, a writer in the Progressive tradition, the postwar era saw the rise to power of the great "Robber Barons." "Under their hands the renovation of our economic life proceeded relentlessly; large-scale production replaced the scattered, decentralized mode of production; industrial enterprises became more concentrated, more 'efficient' technically, and essentially 'cooperative,' where they had been purely individualistic and lamentably wasteful. But all this revolutionizing effort is branded with the motive of private gain on the part of the new captains of industry. To organize and exploit the resources of a nation upon a gigantic scale, to regiment its farmers and workers into harmonious corps of producers, and to do this only in the name of an uncontrolled appetite for private profit—here surely is the great inherent contradiction whence so much disaster, outrage and misery has flowed."[6] Such an approach to the Civil War and the postwar era seemed to be written to provide the rationale for some democratic reforms lest America become the private preserve of a small group of capitalists.

While the Beardian economic interpretation of the Civil War was growing in importance during the depression decade of the 1930s, a small group of Marxian historians were going far beyond the Beards in stressing the importance of economic factors. These scholars were convinced that the end of the capitalistic system was fast approaching.

---

[5]Charles A. and Mary R. Beard, *The Rise of American Civilization*, 2 vols. (New York, 1927), 2:53–54.

[6]Matthew Josephson, *The Robber Barons: The Great American Capitalists 1861–1901* (New York, 1934), p.viii.

They therefore periodized American history within a Marxian framework; each successive stage brought the nation closer and closer to the inevitable and final proletarian revolution. The place of the Civil War within this framework was clear; the Civil War was indeed—as the Beards claimed—a "Second American Revolution." Unlike the Beards, however, Marxist historians were not critical of the results of war. The war, they emphasized, had destroyed the slave power and prepared the ground for the triumph of capitalism—a necessary concomitant to the inevitable triumph of the proletariat. "The sectional nature of the conflict and the geographical division of the contending classes," one Marxian scholar wrote, "have obscured the essential revolutionary nature of the Civil War. But this conflict was basically a revolution of a bourgeois democratic character, in which the bourgeoisie was fighting for power against the landed aristocracy. . . . The destruction of the slave power was the basis for real national unity and the further development of capitalism, which would produce conditions most favorable for the growth of the labor movement. . . . The stage was being cleared of outworn and hackneyed properties to make way for a new and contemporary drama in which the chief protagonists would be the bourgeoisie and the proletariat."[7]

While the economic interpretation was flowering during the depression of the 1930s, two other schools of historical scholarship arose to make their own evaluations of the Civil War. The first of these schools came out of the resurgence of interest of native Southerners in their own section. The reawakened interest in the South, which took the form of a loosely defined and generally romantic movement, had a variety of sources. Taken as a whole, however, the movement attempted to portray the Southern way of life as being far better than the urbanized and industrialized way of life that seemed characteristic of twentieth-century America. Symbolic of the resurgence of Southern nationalism was the publication in 1930 of I'll Take My Stand—a symposium written by twelve Southern intellectuals seeking to show the superiority of the agrarian South over the industrial North. Southerners, in addition, were increasingly sensitive to the vast body of literature critical of their section which had originated in other regions of the nation. Consequently some Southerners began to undertake a reappraisal of the relations between the South and the rest of the country in order to vindicate their section.

The rise of Southern nationalism in the 1930s was sharply mirrored in the historical treatment of the South by its native historians. Such scholars as Ulrich B. Phillips, Charles W. Ramsdell, and Frank L. Owsley set out to portray the South in a far more sympathetic light

---

[7]James S. Allen, Reconstruction: The Battle for Democracy 1865–1876 (New York, 1937), pp. 18 and 26–28. The quotations are taken from the 1955 edition of this work.

than any of their predecessors. When they wrote about the Civil War, therefore, they exonerated the South and blamed the North. In some ways their writings resembled the contemporary Confederate accounts written in the 1860s and 1870s; these twentieth-century scholars tended to idealize the South and its institutions while at the same time portraying the North in hostile, even savage, terms.

In an article published in 1941, for example, Owsley argued that the basic cause of the Civil War was the "egocentric sectionalism" of the North. The North, he charged, considered itself the nation; it destroyed the sectional balance of power by insisting on its own dominance; and it failed to recognize "the dignity and self-respect of the people in other sections." Owsley was particularly critical of the abolitionists, whom he accused of arousing the entire population of the North by their savage lies. He denied that slavery was the cause of the war.[8] Actually his position combined the Beardian interpretation of the Civil War as a conflict between an agrarian South and an industrial North with the older claims of Southerners in the 1860s that the North was seeking the destruction of the South and its beneficent institutions and superior way of life.

The second school of Civil War historiography that flourished in the 1930s and 1940s was the revisionist school. Unlike the followers of Beard or those historians seeking to vindicate the South, revisionist scholars approached the problem within a quite different framework. Their basic assumption was that wars in general and the Civil War in particular were evil. Even more significant was their underlying belief that the war had been avoidable and that there had been genuine alternatives facing the political leaders in both sections.

It is not difficult to understand why some scholars held such views during these years. The United States, after all, had gone to war in 1917 supposedly to make the world safe for democracy and to achieve other laudatory and moral objectives. Instead of finding a brave new world, however, the postwar generation saw their idealistic hopes dashed by a supposedly unjust and unfair Versailles peace treaty that caused the rise of totalitarian and dictatorial regimes throughout the world. Americans during 1930s were deeply disillusioned with the results of World War I; they were even more concerned about staying out of future conflicts that seemed to be in the offing. Hence revisionist historians examined the causes of the Civil War at a time when war as a means of solving problems was not considered to be a sound solution.

---

[8]Frank L. Owsley, "The Fundamental Cause of the Civil War: Egocentric Sectionalism," *Journal of Southern History* 7 (February 1941):3–18. Owsley had also argued in 1930 that slavery was primarily a racial rather than an ethical issue. The blacks of the South, he had written, were "cannibals and barbarians"; slavery was simply a system of racial discipline. See Owsley, "The Irrepressible Conflict," in Twelve Southerners, *I'll Take My Stand* (New York, 1930), pp. 77–78.

Some revisionists came to the conclusion that the Civil War had been an "avoidable" or "repressible" conflict. The belief that the conflict could have been averted was already evident in some scholarly works published during the 1920s which had begun the task of rehabilitating the reputations of those moderates in 1860 and 1861 who had struggled so valiantly to find a peaceable way out of the impasse. The biographers of James Buchanan and Stephen A. Douglas, for example, had argued that a peaceable solution could have been found had Americans heeded the advice and example of these two leading statesmen. Conversely, the extremists on both sides—particularly Northern abolitionists—were condemned for their role in bringing on the war and all that followed.[9]

The most mature formulation of the revisionist hypothesis, however, came from the pens of Avery Craven and James G. Randall in the years just before Pearl Harbor. Both of these distinguished scholars hated war in general; both were convinced that the results of war never approximated the supposedly noble objectives for which such conflicts were fought; both regarded war as abnormal and peace as normal; and both equated war with pathological emotionalism and irrationalism. Given these assumptions it was understandable that these two historians should have rejected many other interpretations that had been offered about the causes of the Civil War. For both Craven and Randall were convinced that the Civil War was a "repressible conflict"; they therefore explained the coming of the war in terms of a failure on the part of the generation of the 1850s and 1860s.

Craven, for example, argued that sectional differences—economic, social, political—could not explain the causes of the war; many countries had pronounced sectional dissimilarities without having had civil strife. Nor was slavery the cause of the war. "If it had not become a symbol first of sectional differences and then of southern depravity, or superiority, according to the point of view—it might have been faced as a national question and dealt with as successfully as the South American countries dealt with the same problem."[10] The war, Craven maintained, occurred because normal sectional differences—which were not serious and could have been resolved through political means—were magnified and emotionalized until they could no longer be dealt with in rational terms. "Stripped of false assumptions, the tragedy of the nation in bloody strife from 1861 to 1865 must, in large part, be charged to a generation of well-meaning Americans, who, busy

---

[9]For typical examples see the following works: Philip G. Auchampaugh, *James Buchanan and His Cabinet on the Eve of Secession* (Lancaster, Pa., 1926); George Fort Milton, *The Eve of Conflict: Stephen A. Douglas and the Needless War* (New York, 1934); and Gilbert H. Barnes, *The Antislavery Impulse, 1830–1844* (New York, 1933).

[10]Avery Craven, *The Repressible Conflict 1830-1861* (Baton Rouge, 1939), p. 64.

with the task of getting ahead, permitted their shortsighted politicians, their overzealous editors, and their pious reformers to emotionalize real and potential differences and to conjure up distorted impressions of those who dwelt in other parts of the nation. For more than two decades these molders of public opinion steadily created the fiction of two distinct peoples contending for the right to preserve and expand their sacred cultures. . . . They awakened new fears and led men to hate. In time a people came to believe that social security, constitutional government and the freedom of all men were at stake in their sectional differences; that the issues were between right and wrong; good and evil. Opponents became devils in human form. Good men had no choice but to kill and to be killed."[11]

Like Craven, Randall also rejected an approach that romanticized war. Realists, he suggested, would not use the term "war," but rather *organized murder* or *human slaughterhouse*. The war was indeed a "needless one," for the Union could have been continued and slavery abolished without the conflict. Its causes, according to Randall, could only be understood within a pathological framework; it was a proper subject for social psychiatry. Without abnormality, bogus leadership, or inordinate ambition, war would not have occurred; no issues were so vital as to require a violent resolution. Responsibility for the Civil War, concluded Randall, must be placed at the feet of a "blundering generation."[12]

Although the revisionist "needless war" approach remained popular throughout the 1940s and even afterward,[13] some historians began to attack its basic premises in sharp terms. While wars could never be good in themselves, these scholars argued, not to go to war in certain cases was even a far greater evil. Pointing to World War II, Samuel Eliot Morison—one of America's most distinguished historians—argued in his presidential address before the American Historical Association that "war does accomplish something, that war is better than servitude, that war has been an inescapable aspect of the human story."[14] Influenced by the rise of totalitarian regimes, Morison and other scholars insisted that war could indeed involve fundamental moral and ethical issues that could not be compromised. Moreover, some of these historians were influenced by the writings of Reinhold Niebuhr and

---

[11]Avery Craven, *The Coming of the Civil War* (New York, 1942), p. 2.

[12]J. G. Randall, "The Blundering Generation," *Mississippi Valley Historical Review* 27 (June 1940):4–16.

[13]Two outstanding revisionist works published after the end of World War II include Roy F. Nichols, *The Disruption of American Democracy* (New York, 1948), and Kenneth M. Stampp, *And the War Came: The North and the Secession Crisis 1860–1861* (Baton Rouge, 1950).

[14]Samuel Eliot Morison, "Faith of a Historian," *American Historical Review* 56 (January 1951):267.

other theologians and philosophers who had insisted that evil was a reality within the framework of human experience and had to be taken into account in any adequate explanation of past events. Armed confrontations were occasionally necessary precisely because of man's egotistical and sinful nature. Finally, the growing demands since the 1940s that blacks be given the same rights as white Americans also contributed to the reevaluation of the problem of the coming of the Civil War.

The criticisms of antiwar historians were most cogently put in an influential article by Arthur M. Schlesinger, Jr. Schlesinger was particularly hostile to the revisionist thesis, especially as presented by Craven and Randall. To rebut their hypothesis he asked one specific question: If the war could have been avoided, what course should American leaders have followed? Noting that none of the revisionists had ever spelled out the proper policies that contemporary figures should have adopted, Schlesinger listed three possible alternatives: that the South might have abolished slavery by itself if left alone; that slavery would have died because it was economically unsound; or that the North might have offered some form of emancipated compensation. Finding that all three of these possibilities were either inadequate or unattainable, Schlesinger charged that revisionism "is connected with the modern tendency to seek in optimistic sentimentalism an escape from the severe demands of moral decision; that it is the offspring of our modern sentimentality which at once evades the essential moral problems in the name of a superficial objectivity and asserts their unimportance in the name of an invincible progress." The South was indeed becoming a closed society by the time of the Civil War; its citizens, in defending their evil institution, had posed moral differences too profound to be solved by political compromise. In effect, Schlesinger insisted that the revisionists glossed over slavery because of their own belief that war could never involve real issues. Human conflict, he concluded, is a perennial concomitant of human behavior; to write as though it never existed is to rule out one of the moral dimensions of humanity.[15]

At about the same time that Schlesinger was attacking the revisionists, Allan Nevins's magisterial history of the United States from the 1840s through the 1860s was beginning to appear. In the *Ordeal of the Union* Nevins combined elements from both the nationalist and revisionist traditions (although the former was clearly more dominant). Conceding that economic factors were involved in the coming of war, he nevertheless rejected an economic interpretation. The Civil War, wrote Nevins, "should have been avoidable," but "the problem

---

[15]Arthur M. Schlesinger, Jr., "The Causes of the Civil War: A Note on Historical Sentimentalism," *Partisan Review* 16 (October 1949):969–981.

of slavery *with its complementary problem of race-adjustment"* involved basic differences between North and South. Given the refusal of the South to take some step in the direction of ending slavery, the Civil War then followed. The first selection in this chapter is from Nevins's second volume.

Although the debate over the causes of the Civil War remained embedded within a somewhat static conceptual framework,[16] developments within the historical profession during and after the 1960s slowly began to undermine traditional approaches and questions. The rise of the "new political history" (an approach that emphasized the social basis of politics and employed quantitative techniques) led some to de-emphasize the issue of slavery in terms of its relationship to the totality of American society. These scholars insisted that the behavior of Americans and their political parties in the two decades preceding the Civil War involved more than merely a reaction to the challenges posed by the existence of slavery. Some emphasized the role of religion and culture in shaping political ideology and voting behavior; others examined the war within the framework of a modernizing society. Slowly but surely the Civil War was brought back and integrated with other significant elements in American history. The problem of slavery in the territories, though by no means ignored, lost its central position as historians began to study social, cultural, ethnic, and religious cleavages, voting behavior, voter participation, and political ideology.[17]

Historians, Joel H. Silbey charged in 1964, erred in subordinating the two antebellum decades to the coming of war in 1861. In a series of subsequent essays, he insisted that competing ethnic, religious, and cultural traditions and groups were central to political development in the 1840s and 1850s; sectional disputes over slavery occupied a distinctly subordinate position. Antebellum politics revolved around conflicts between natives and immigrants as well as between Protestants and Catholics; struggles over the consumption of liquor were more significant than differences over slavery. Like Lee Benson, Silbey believed that ethnocultural concerns transcended differences between classes and sections.[18]

In a similar vein Michael F. Holt, who combined a behavioral with an ideological analysis, conceded that the sectional conflict over slavery was crucial. Nevertheless, he de-emphasized the conflict over the

---

[16]Indeed, David Donald wrote in 1960 that historians were no longer concerned with the causes of the Civil War. See his article "American Historians and the Causes of the Civil War," *South Atlantic Quarterly* 59 (Summer 1960):351–355.

[17]See Eric Foner, "The Causes of the American Civil War: Recent Interpretations and New Directions," *Civil War History* 20 (September 1974):194–214.

[18]Joel H. Silbey's essays have been collected in *The Partisan Imperative: The Dynamics of American Politics Before the Civil War* (New York, 1985). See also his *The Shrine of Party: Congressional Voting Behavior, 1841–1852* (Pittsburgh, 1967).

institution of slavery. Most Americans, Holt insisted, were preoccupied with their republican ideology and alleged threats to its survival. Fearful that republican society might be undermined by corruption, white Americans were determined to pursue self-government, liberty, and equality. During the 1950s, however, the second party system collapsed, and

> *a sense of crisis developed that government was beyond control of the people, that it had become a threatening power dominated by some gigantic conspiracy, and hence that republican institutions were under attack. Politicians in the North and South responded to this sense of crisis by making an enemy in the other section the chief menace to republicanism who would enslave the residents of their own section. As a result, sectional antagonism became much more inflamed in the 1850s than it had ever been. Along with Know Nothingism, this strategy restored a sense of political efficacy in most of the nation, because antirepublicanism devils were associated with rival parties that could be stopped simply by voting against them. In the Deep South, however, no internal enemy was identified who could be defeated through the normal political process. Men there thought that more drastic action was necessary to escape slavery. The consequence was secession and a tragic Civil War.[19]*

Yet the traditional view that slavery was somehow central to the coming of war has persisted in various forms. In a study of the ideology of the Republican party, Eric Foner insisted that the concept of "free labor" was central. Republicans believed in the concept of an open and mobile society that rewarded work. They might disagree on specific issues, but were united in their conviction that slavery was incompatible with free labor and would sooner or later have to disappear. Unlike Silby and Holt, Foner suggested that nativism was only of marginal significance.[20]

The second selection in this chapter, by Eric Foner, illustrates at least some of the newer trends in Civil War historiography. In the half century following the adoption of the federal Constitution, argues Foner, the political system functioned "as a mechanism for relieving social tensions, ordering group conflict, and integrating the society." By the 1830s and 1840s a new element had entered the national scene, namely, the creation of distinct party structures that channeled voter participation in politics. Although Jacksonian politics were for the most part nonideological, they did help to create a link between the people and their government. But this very link had serious implications for underlying sectional antagonisms, for it made possible the

---

[19]Michael F. Holt, *The Political Crisis of the 1850s* (New York, 1978), pp. 258–259.

[20]Eric Foner, *Free Soil, Free Labor, Free Men: The Ideology of the Republican Party Before the Civil War* (New York, 1970).

emergence of sectional agitators in both the North and the South who hoped to force public opinion—and hence government—to confront the issue of slavery. The result was a polarization of American politics along ideological lines and an inability on the part of the political system to resolve basic differences between the sections. In both the North and the South an ideological coalition emerged that was completely antithetical to the idea of national unity and national integration on other than its own terms. The Civil War, concludes Foner, accomplished the goal originally envisaged by the founding fathers when they wrote the Constitution and established a unique political system—the creation of a single nation. Although aware of the paramount importance of the slavery issue, Foner's interpretation rests upon his conviction that the causes of the Civil War cannot be isolated from the nature of the American political system and the social and economic values that became the foundation of competing ideologies.

Although broad overarching interpretations of Civil War causation seem to have fallen out of favor, historians continue to be fascinated with antebellum politics. A number of recent studies have demonstrated that sectional antagonisms were exacerbated by seemingly extraneous events. In a volume dealing with the panic of 1857 James L. Huston attempted to demonstrate how economic difficulties reinforced and intensified sectional conflicts. In a like manner Mark W. Summers depicted the manner in which pervasive corruption undermined the legitimacy of political institutions. The Republican party was the beneficiary; it exploited the fears that a "slave power conspiracy" was bent on destroying representative democratic institutions, thus strengthening its appeal among the northern electorate. And in a sophisticated narrative study of the year 1857, Kenneth M. Stampp emphasized the rigidity and ineptitude of President James Buchanan. This president supported a proslavery minority in the struggle to determine whether Kansas would be admitted as a slave or free state. In so doing he split his party and prepared the ground for the triumph of the Republican party in the ensuing presidential election.[21]

By the 1990s the problem of Civil War causation seemed as complex as ever. Given all of the conflicting schools of thought, how can the student select and choose in order to arrive at a more "objective" view of the war? The answer to this question is difficult indeed; sooner or later students will have to cope with the same problems that confronted historians for nearly a century. Was the North, for example, fighting the war solely on moral grounds? Were Southern leaders deter-

---

[21]James L. Huston, *The Panic of 1857 and the Coming of the Civil War* (Baton Rouge, 1987); Mark W. Summers, *The Plundering Generation: Corruption and the Crisis of the Union, 1849–1861* (New York, 1987); Kenneth M. Stampp, *America in 1857: A Nation on the Brink* (New York, 1990). See also William E. Gienapp, *The Origins of the Republican Party, 1852–1856* (New York, 1987).

mined to have their own way in 1861, even if it meant the destruction of the Union? What role did social and economic differences play in the coming of the war? Is it appropriate even to ask the question as to whether the war was a repressible or irrepressible conflict? Did American leaders fail because of their inability to deal with the issues in a statesmanlike and rational framework? How did such variables as religion, ethnicity, and culture influence ideology and national political structures and elections?

Nearly four decades ago one historian surveying the many ways that his colleagues had approached the problem of the Civil War noted with concern that "the further the Civil War receded into the past, the greater the strength of the emotions with which these divergent viewpoints were held." The reason for this anomalous situation, he suggested, was that American historians still found the issues of the 1850s and 1860s of contemporary concern; as long as historians wrote about the role of blacks in American society, debated the wisdom of fighting wars, and studied majority rule and minority rights, the causes of the Civil War would remain a matter of dispute.[22] In a certain sense his comments remain applicable to the present. Yet recent contributions to Civil War historiography suggest that contemporary scholars are in the process of creating a new synthesis that relates the moral controversy over slavery to a variety of other social, political, and economic structures that were slowly giving the nation its basic configuration. In so doing they have transferred the issue of Civil War causation from a largely moral domain that seeks understanding and explanations rather than condemnation. Only the future will tell whether this newer approach will bring us closer to a more satisfying answer to this vexing historical problem.

---

[22]Thomas J. Pressly, *Americans Interpret Their Civil War* (Princeton, 1954), pp. 321–323.

Allan Nevins

ALLAN NEVINS (1890–1971) *was professor of history at Colum-bia University. He was one of the most prolific American historians of the twentieth century. In addition to his multivolume study of the Civil War era, he also wrote biographies of John D. Rockefeller and Henry Ford, among many other books.*

Great and complex events have great and complex causes. Burke, in his *Reflections on the Revolution in France,* wrote that "a state without the means of some change is without the means of its conservation," and that a constant reconciliation of "the two principles of conservation and correction" is indispensable to healthy national growth. It is safe to say that every such revolutionary era as that on which the United States entered in 1860 finds its genesis in an inadequate adjustment of these two forces. It is also safe to say that when a tragic national failure occurs, it is largely a failure of leadership. "Brains are of three orders," wrote Machiavelli, "those that understand of themselves, those that understand when another shows them, and those that understand neither by themselves nor by the showing of others." Ferment and change must steadily be controlled; the real must, as Bryce said, be kept resting on the ideal; and if disaster is to be avoided, wise leaders must help thoughtless men to understand, and direct the action of invincibly ignorant men. Necessary reforms may be obstructed in various ways; by sheer inertia, by tyranny and class selfishness, or by the application of compromise to basic principles— this last being in Lowell's view the main cause of the Civil War. Ordinarily the obstruction arises from a combination of all these elements. To explain the failure of American leadership in 1846–1861, and the revolution that ensued, is a baffling complicated problem.

Looking backward from the verge of war in March, 1861, Americans could survey a series of ill-fated decisions by their chosen agents. One unfortunate decision was embodied in Douglas's Kansas-Nebraska Act of 1854. Had an overwhelming majority of Americans been ready to accept the squatter sovereignty principle, this law might have proved a statesmanlike stroke; but it was so certain that powerful elements North and South would resist it to the last that it accentu-

---

ated the strife and confusion. Another disastrous decision was made by Taney and his associates in the Dred Scott pronouncement of 1857. Still another was made by Buchanan when he weakly accepted the Lecompton Constitution and tried to force that fraudulent document through Congress. The Northern legislatures which passed Personal Liberty Acts made an unhappy decision. Most irresponsible, wanton, and disastrous of all was the decision of those Southern leaders who in 1858–1860 turned to the provocative demand for Congressional protection of slavery in all the Territories of the republic. Still other errors might be named. Obviously, however, it is the forces behind these decisions which demand our study; the waters pouring down the gorge, not the rocks which threw their spray into the air.

At this point we meet a confused clamor of voices as various students attempt an explanation of the tragic denouement of 1861. Some writers are as content with a simple explanation as Lord Clarendon was when he attributed the English Civil War to the desire of Parliament for an egregious domination of the government. The bloody conflict, declared James Ford Rhodes, had "a single cause, slavery." He was but echoing what Henry Wilson and other early historians had written, that the aggressions of the Slave Power offered the central explanation. That opinion had been challenged as early as 1861 by the London *Saturday Review*, which remarked that "slavery is but a surface question in American politics," and by such Southern propagandists as Yancey, who tried to popularize a commercial theory of the war, emphasizing a supposed Southern revolt against the tariff and other Yankee exactions. A later school of writers was to find the key to the tragedy in an inexorable conflict between the business-minded North and the agrarian-minded South, a thrusting industrialism colliding with a rather static agricultural society. Still another group of writers has accepted the theory that the war resulted from psychological causes. They declare that agitators, propagandists, and alarmists on both sides, exaggerating the real differences of interest, created a state of mind, a hysterical excitement, which made armed conflict inevitable.

At the very outset of the war Senator Mason of Virginia, writing to his daughter, asserted that two systems of society were in conflict; systems, he implied, as different as those of Carthage and Rome, Protestant Holland and Catholic Spain. That view, too, was later to be elaborated by a considerable school of writers. Two separate nations they declared, had arisen within the United States in 1861, much as two separate nations had emerged within the first British Empire by 1776. Contrasting ways of life, rival group consciousness, divergent hopes and fears made a movement for separation logical; and the minority people, believing its peculiar civilization in danger of suppression, began a war for independence. We are told, indeed, that two types of nationalism came into conflict: a Northern nationalism which wished to preserve the unity of the whole republic, and a Southern nationalism intent on creating an entirely new republic.

It is evident that some of these explanations deal with merely superficial phenomena, and that others, when taken separately, represent but subsidiary elements in the play of forces. Slavery was a great fact; the demands of Northern industrialism constituted a great fact; sectional hysteria was a great fact. But do they not perhaps relate themselves to some profounder underlying cause? This question has inspired one student to suggest that "the confusion of a growing state" may offer the fundamental explanation of the drift to war; an unsatisfactory hypothesis, for westward growth, railroad growth, business growth, and cultural growth, however much attended with "confusion," were unifying factors, and it was not the new-made West but old-settled South Carolina which led in the schism.

One fact needs emphatic statement: of all the monistic explanations for the drift to war, that posited upon supposed economic causes is the flimsiest. This theory was sharply rejected at the time by so astute an observer as Alexander H. Stephens. South Carolina, he wrote his brother on New Year's Day, 1861, was seceding from a tariff "which is just what her own Senators and members in Congress made it." As for the charges of consolidation and despotism made by some Carolinians, he thought they arose from peevishness rather than a calm analysis of facts. "The truth is, the South, almost in mass, has voted, I think, for every measure of general legislation that has passed both houses and become law for the last ten years." The South, far from groaning under tyranny, had controlled the government almost from its beginning, and Stephens believed that its only real grievance lay in the Northern refusal to return fugitive slaves and to stop the antislavery agitation. "All other complaints are founded on threatened dangers which may never come, and which I feel very sure would be averted if the South would pursue a judicious and wise course." Stephens was right. It was true that the whole tendency of federal legislation 1842–1860 was toward free trade; true that the tariff in force when secession began was largely Southern-made; true that it was the lowest tariff the country had known since 1816; true that it cost a nation of 30 million people but $60 million in indirect revenue; true that without secession no new tariff law, obnoxious to the Democratic party, could have passed before 1863—if then.

In the official explanations which one Southern state after another published for its secession, economic grievances are either omitted entirely or given minor position. There were few such supposed grievances which the agricultural states of Illinois, Iowa, Indiana, Wisconsin, and Minnesota did not share with the South—and they never threatened to secede. Charles A. Beard finds the taproot of the war in the resistance of the planter interest to Northern demands enlarging the old Hamilton-Webster policy. The South was adamant in standing for "no high protective tariffs, no ship subsidies, no national banking and currency system; in short, none of the measures which business enterprise deemed essential to its progress." But the Republican platform in 1856 was silent on the tariff; in 1860 it carried a milk-and-water statement on the subject which western Republicans took, mild as it was, with a wry face; the incoming president was little interested in the tariff; and any harsh legislation was impossible. Ship subsidies were not an issue in the campaign of 1860. Neither were a national banking system and a national currency system. They were not mentioned in the Republican platform nor discussed by party debaters. The Pacific Railroad was advocated both by the Douglas Democrats and the Republicans; and it is noteworthy that Seward and Douglas were for building both a Northern and a Southern line. In short, the divisive economic issues are easily exaggerated. At the same time, the unifying economic factors were both numerous and powerful. North and South had economies which were largely complementary. It was no misfortune to the South that Massachusetts cotton mills wanted its staple, and that New York ironmasters like Hewitt were eager to sell rails dirtcheap to Southern railway builders; and sober businessmen on both sides, merchants, bankers, and manufacturers, were the men most anxious to keep the peace and hold the Union together.

We must seek further for an explanation; and in so doing, we must give special weight to the observations of penetrating leaders of the time, who knew at firsthand the spirit of the people. Henry J. Raymond, moderate editor of the *New York Times*, a sagacious man who disliked Northern abolitionists and Southern radicals, wrote in January 1860 an analysis of the impending conflict which attributed it to a competition for power.

> In every country there must be a just and equal balance of powers in the government, an equal distribution of the national forces. Each section and each interest must exercise its due share of influence and control. It is always more or less difficult to preserve their just equipoise, and the larger the country, and the more varied its great interests, the more difficult does the task become, and the greater the shock and disturbance caused by an attempt to adjust it when once disturbed. I believe I state only what is generally conceded to be a fact, when I say that the growth of the Northern States in population, in wealth, in all the elements of political influence and control, has been out of proportion to their political influence in the Federal Councils. While the Southern States have less that a third of the aggregate population of the Union, their interests have influenced the policy of the government far more than the interests of the Northern States. . . . Now the North has made rapid advances within the last five years, and it naturally claims a proportionate share of influence and power in the affairs of the Confederacy.

>   *It is inevitable that this claim should be put forward, and it is also inevitable that it should be conceded. No party can long resist it; it overrides all parties, and makes them the mere instruments of its will. It is quite as strong today in the heart of the Democratic party of the North as in the Republican ranks and any party which ignores it will lose its hold on the public mind.*
>
>   *Why does the South resist this claim? Not because it is unjust in itself, but because it has become involved with the question of slavery, and has drawn so much of its vigor and vitality from that quarter, that it is almost merged in that issue. The North bases its demand for increased power, in a very great degree, on the action of the government in regard to slavery—and the just and rightful ascendency of the North in the Federal councils comes thus to be regarded as an element of danger to the institutions of the Southern States.*

In brief, Raymond, who held that slavery was a moral wrong, that its economic and social tendencies were vicious, and that the time had come to halt its growth with a view to its final eradication, believed that the contest was primarily one for power, and for the application of that power to the slave system. With this opinion Alexander H. Stephens agreed. The Georgian said he believed slavery both morally and politically right. In his letter to Lincoln on December 30, 1860, he declared that the South did not fear that the new Republican Administration would interfere directly and immediately with slavery in the states. What Southerners did fear was the ultimate result of the shift of power which had just occurred—in its application to slavery:

>   *Now this subject, which is confessedly on all sides outside of the constitutional action of the Government, so far as the States are concerned, is made the "central idea" in the platform of principles announced by the triumphant party. The leading object seems to be simply, and wantonly, if you please, to put the institutions of nearly half the States under the ban of public opinion and national condemnation. This, upon general principles, is quite enough of itself to arouse a spirit not only of general indignation, but of revolt on the part of the proscribed. Let me illustrate. It is generally conceded by the Republicans even, that Congress cannot interfere with slavery in the States. It is equally conceded that Congress cannot interfere with slavery in the States. It is equally conceded that Congress cannot establish any form of religious worship. Now suppose that any one of the present Christian churches or sects prevailed in all the Southern States, but had no existence in any one of the Northern States,— under such circumstances suppose the people of the Northern States should organize a political party, not upon a foreign or domestic policy, but with one leading idea of condemnation of the doctrines and tenets of that particular church, and with an avowed object of preventing its extension into the common Territories, even after the highest judicial tribunal of the land had decided they had no such constitutional power. And suppose that a party so organized should*

*carry a Presidential election. Is it not apparent that a general feeling
of resistance to the success, aims, and objects of such a party would
necessarily and rightfully ensue?*

Raymond and Stephens agreed that the two sections were competing for power; that a momentous transfer of power had just occurred;
and that it held fateful consequences because it was involved with the
issue of slavery, taking authority from a section which believed slavery
moral and healthy, and giving it to a section which held slavery immoral and pernicious. To Stephens this transfer was ground for resuming the ultimate sovereignty of the states. Here we find a somewhat
more complex statement of James Ford Rhodes's thesis that the central
cause of the Civil War lay in slavery. Here, too, we revert to the assertions of Yancey and Lincoln that the vital conflict was between those
who thought slavery right and those who thought it wrong. But this
definition we can accept only if we probe a little deeper for a concept
which both modifies and enlarges the basic source of perplexity and
quarrel.

The main root of the conflict (and there were minor roots) was the
problem of slavery *with its complementary problem of race adjustment;* the main source of the tragedy was the refusal of either section
to face these conjoined problems squarely and pay the heavy costs of
a peaceful settlement. Had it not been for the difference in race, the
slavery issue would have presented no great difficulties. But as the racial gulf existed, the South inarticulately but clearly perceived that
elimination of this issue would still leave it the terrible problem of the
Negro. Those historians who write that if slavery had simply been left
alone it would soon have withered overlook this heavy impediment.
The South as a whole in 1846–1861 was not moving toward emancipation, but away from it. It was not relaxing the laws which guarded
the system, but reinforcing them. It was not ameliorating slavery, but
making it harsher and more implacable. The South was further from
a just solution of the slavery problem in 1830 than it had been in 1789.
It was further from a tenable solution in 1860 than it had been in 1830.
Why was it going from bad to worse? Because Southern leaders refused
to nerve their people to pay the heavy price of race adjustment. These
leaders never made up their mind to deal with the problem as the progressive temper of civilization demanded. They would not adopt the
new outlook which the upward march of mankind required because
they saw that the gradual abolition of slavery would bring a measure
of political privilege; that political privilege would usher in a measure
of economic equality; that on the heels of economic equality would
come a rising social status for the Negro. Southern leadership dared
not ask the people to pay this price.

A heavy responsibility for the failure of America in this period rests with this Southern leadership, which lacked imagination, ability, and courage. But the North was by no means without its full share, for the North equally refused to give a constructive examination to the central question of slavery as linked with race adjustment. This was because of two principal reasons. Most abolitionists and many other sentimental-minded Northerners simply denied that the problem existed. Regarding all Negroes as white men with dark skins, whom a few years of schooling would bring abreast of the dominant race, they thought that no difficult adjustment was required. A much more numerous body of Northerners would have granted that a great and terrible task of race adjustment existed—but they were reluctant to help shoulder any part of it. Take a million or two million Negroes into the Northern States? Indiana, Illinois, and even Kansas were unwilling to take a single additional person of color. Pay tens of millions to help educate and elevate the colored population? Take even a first step by offering to pay the Southern slaveholders some recompense for a gradual liberation of their human property? No Northern politician dared ask his constituents to make so unpopular a sacrifice. The North, like the South, found it easier to drift blindly toward disaster.

The hope of solving the slavery problem without a civil war rested upon several interrelated factors, of which one merits special emphasis. We have said that the South as a whole was laboring to bolster and stiffen slavery—which was much to its discredit. But it is nevertheless true that slavery was dying all around the edges of its domain; it was steadily decaying in Delaware, Maryland, western Virginia, parts of Kentucky, and Missouri. Much of the harshness of Southern legislation in the period sprang from a sense that slavery was in danger from *internal* weaknesses. In no great time Delaware, Maryland, and Missouri were likely to enter the column of free states; and if they did, reducing the roster to twelve, the doom of the institution would be clearly written. Allied with this factor was the rapid comparative increase of Northern strength, and the steady knitting of economic, social, and moral ties between the North and West, leaving the South in a position of manifest inferiority. A Southern Confederacy had a fair fighting chance in 1861; by 1880 it would have had very little. If secession could have been postponed by two decades, natural forces might well have placed a solution full in sight. Then, too, the growing pressure of world sentiment must in time have produced its effect. But to point out these considerations is not suggest that in 1861 a policy of procrastination and appeasement would have done anything but harm. All hope of bringing Southern majority sentiment to a better attitude would have been lost if Lincoln and his party had flinched on the basic issue of the restriction of slavery; for by the seventh decade of nineteenth-century history, the time had come when that demand had to be maintained.

While in indicting leadership we obviously indict the public behind the leaders, we must also lay some blame upon a political environment which gave leadership a poor chance. American parties, under
the pressure of sectional feeling, worked badly. The government suffered greatly, moreover, from the lack of any adequate planning agency.
Congress was not a truly deliberative body, and its committees had
not yet learned to do long-range planning. The president might have
formulated plans, but he never did. For one reason, no president between Polk and Lincoln had either the ability or the prestige required;
for another reason, Fillmore, Pierce, and Buchanan all held that their
duty was merely to execute the laws, not to initiate legislation. Had
the country possessed a ministerial form of government, the Cabinet
in leading the legislature would have been compelled to lay down a
program of real scope concerning slavery. As it was, leadership in
Washington was supplied only spasmodically by men like Clay, Douglas, and Crittenden.

And as we have noted, the rigidity of the American system was at
this time a grave handicap. Twice, in the fall of 1854 and of 1858, the
elections gave a stunning rebuke to the Administration. Under a ministerial system, the old government would probably have gone out and
a new one have come in. In 1854, however, Pierce continued to carry
on the old policies, and in 1858 Buchanan remained the drearily inept
helmsman of the republic. Never in our history were bold, quick planning and a flexible administration of policy more needed; never was
the failure to supply them more complete.

Still another element in the tragic chronicle of the time must be
mentioned. Much that happens in human affairs is accidental. When
a country is guided by true statesmen the role of accident is minimized; when it is not, unforeseen occurrences are numerous and dangerous. In the summer and fall of 1858, as we have seen, the revival of
a conservative opposition party in the upper South, devoted to the
Union, furnished a real gleam of hope. If this opposition had been given
unity and determined leadership, if moderate Southerners had stood
firm against the plot of Yancey and others to disrupt the Democratic
Party, if Floyd had been vigilant enough to read the warning letter
about John Brown and act on it, the situation might even then have
been saved. Instead, John Brown's mad raid fell on public opinion like
a thunderstroke, exasperating men everywhere and dividing North and
South more tragically than ever. The last chance of persuading the
South to submit to an essential step, the containment of slavery, was
gone.

The war, when it came, was not primarily a conflict over state
rights, although that issue had become involved in it. It was not primarily a war born of economic grievances, although many Southerners
had been led to think that they were suffering, or would soon suffer,

economic wrongs. It was not a war created by politicians and publicists who fomented hysteric excitement; for while hysteria was important, we have always to ask what basic reasons made possible the propaganda which aroused it. It was not primarily a war about slavery alone, although that institution seemed to many the grand cause. It was a war over slavery *and* the future position of the Negro race in North America. Was the Negro to be allowed, as a result of the shift of power signalized by Lincoln's election, to take the first step toward an ultimate position of general economic, political, and social equality with the white man? Or was he to be held immobile in a degraded, servile position, unchanging the next hundred years as it had remained essentially unchanged for the hundred years past? These questions were implicit in Lincoln's demand that slavery be placed in a position where the public mind could rest assured of its ultimate extinction.

Evasion by the South, evasion by the North, were no longer possible. The alternatives faced were an unpopular but curative adjustment of the situation by the opposed parties, or a war that would force an adjustment upon the loser. For Americans in 1861, as for many other peoples throughout history, war was easier than wisdom and courage.

Eric Foner

ERIC FONER *(1943–   ) is professor of history at Columbia University. His published works include* Free Soil, Free Labor, Free Men: The Ideology of the Republican Party Before the Civil War *(1970);* Tom Paine and Revolutionary America *(1976), and* Reconstruction: America's Unfinished Revolution, 1863–1877 *(1988).*

It has long been an axiom of political science that political parties help to hold together diverse, heterogeneous societies like our own. Since most major parties in American history have tried, in Seymour Lipset's phrase, to "appear as plausible representatives of the whole society," they have been broad coalitions cutting across lines of class, race, religion, and section. And although party competition requires that there be differences between the major parties, these differences

Eric Foner, "Politics, Ideology, and the Origins of the American Civil War," in *A Nation Divided: Problems and Issues of the Civil War and Reconstruction,* George M. Fredrickson, ed. (Minneapolis, 1975), pp. 15–34. Reprinted with the permission of Burgess Publishing Company.

usually have not been along sharp ideological lines. In fact, the very diversity of American society has inhibited the formation of ideological parties, for such parties assume the existence of a single line of social division along which a majority of the electorate can be mobilized. In a large, heterogeneous society, such a line rarely exists. There are, therefore, strong reasons why, in a two-party system, a major party—or a party aspiring to become "major"—eschew ideology, for the statement of a coherent ideology will set limits to the groups in the electorate the party can hope to mobilize. Under most circumstances, in other words, the party's role as a carrier of a coherent ideology will conflict with its role as an electoral machine bent on winning the widest possible number of votes.

For much of the seventy years preceding the Civil War, the American political system functioned as a mechanism for relieving social tensions, ordering group conflict, and integrating the society. The existence of national political parties, increasingly focused on the contest for the presidency, necessitated alliances between political elites in various sections of the country. A recent study of early American politics notes that "political nationalization was far ahead of economic, cultural, and social nationalization"—that is, that the national political system was itself a major bond of union in a diverse, growing society. But as North and South increasingly took different paths of economic and social development and as, from the 1830s onwards, antagonistic value systems and ideologies grounded in the question of slavery emerged in these sections, the political system inevitably came under severe disruptive pressures. Because they brought into play basic values and moral judgments, the competing sectional ideologies could not be defused by the normal processes of political compromise, nor could they be contained within the existing intersectional political system. Once parties began to reorient themselves on sectional lines, a fundamental necessity of democratic politics—that each party look upon the other as a legitimate alternative government—was destroyed.

When we consider the causes of the sectional conflict, we must ask ourselves not only why civil war came when it did, but why it did not come sooner. How did a divided nation manage to hold itself together for as long as it did? In part, the answer lies in the unifying effects of intersectional political parties. On the level of politics, the coming of the Civil War is the story of the intrusion of sectional ideology into the political system, despite the efforts of political leaders of both parties to keep it out. Once this happened, political competition worked to exacerbate, rather than solve, social and sectional conflicts. For as Frank Sorauf has explained:

> *The party of extensive ideology develops in and reflects the society*
> *in which little consensus prevails on basic social values and institu-*

tions. It betokens deep social disagreements and conflicts. Indeed, the party of ideology that is also a major, competitive party accompanies a politics of almost total concern. Since its ideology defines political issues as including almost every facet of life, it brings to the political system almost every division, every difference, every conflict of any importance in society.

"Parties in this country," wrote a conservative northern Whig in 1855, "heretofore have helped, not delayed, the slow and difficult growth of a consummated nationality." Rufus Choate was lamenting the passing of a bygone era, a time when "our allies were everywhere . . . there were no Alleghenies nor Mississippi rivers in our politics." Party organization and the nature of political conflict had taken on new and unprecedented forms in the 1850s. It is no accident that the break up of the last major intersectional party preceded by less than a year the break up of the Union or that the final crisis was precipitated not by any "overt act," but by a presidential election.

From the beginning of national government, of course, differences of opinion over slavery constituted an important obstacle to the formation of a national community. "The great danger to our general government," as Madison remarked at the Constitutional Convention, "is the great southern and northern interests of the continent, being opposed to each other." "The institution of slavery and its consequences," according to him, was the main "line of discrimination" in convention disputes. As far as slavery was concerned, the Constitution amply fulfilled Lord Acton's dictum that it was an effort to avoid settling basic questions. Aside from the Atlantic slave trade, Congress was given no power to regulate slavery in any way—the framers' main intention seems to have been to place slavery completely outside the national political arena. The only basis on which a national politics could exist—the avoidance of sectional issues—was thus defined at the outset.

Although the slavery question was never completely excluded from political debate in the 1790s, and there was considerable Federalist grumbling about the three-fifths clause of the Constitution after 1800, the first full demonstration of the political possibilities inherent in a sectional attack on slavery occurred in the Missouri controversy of 1819–1821. These debates established a number of precedents which forecast the future course of the slavery extension issue in Congress. Most important was the fact that the issue was able for a time to completely obliterate party lines. In the first votes on slavery in Missouri, virtually every northerner, regardless of party, voted against expansion. It was not surprising, of course, that northern Federalists would try to make political capital out of the issue. What was unexpected was that northern Republicans, many of whom were aggrieved by Virginia's long dominance of the presidency and by the Monroe administration's tariff and internal improvement policies, would unite with the Federalists. As John Quincy Adams observed, the debate "disclosed a secret: it revealed the basis for a new organization of parties. . . . Here was a new party really formed . . . terrible to the whole Union, but portentously terrible to the South." But the final compromise set another important precedent: enough northern Republicans became convinced that the Federalists were making political gains from the debates and that the Union was seriously endangered to break with the sectional block and support a compromise which a majority of northern Congressmen—Republicans and Federalists—opposed. As for the Monroe administration, its semiofficial spokesman, the *National Intelligencer*, pleaded for a return to the policy of avoiding sectional issues, even to the extent of refusing to publish letters which dealt in any way with the subject of slavery.

The Missouri controversy and the election of 1824, in which four candidates contested the presidency, largely drawing support from their home sections, revealed that in the absence of two-party competition, sectional loyalties would constitute the lines of political division. No one recognized this more clearly than the architect of the second-party system, Martin Van Buren. In his well-known letter to Thomas Ritchie of Virginia, Van Buren explained the need for a revival of national two-party politics on precisely this ground: "Party attachment in former times furnished a complete antedote for sectional prejudices by producing counteracting feelings. It was not until that defense had been broken down that the clamor against Southern Influence and African Slavery could be made effectual in the North." Van Buren and many of his generation of politicians had been genuinely frightened by the threats of disunion which echoed through Congress in 1820; they saw national two-party competition as the alternative to sectional conflict and eventual disunion. Ironically, as Richard McCormick has made clear, the creation of the second party system owed as much to sectionalism as to national loyalties. The South, for example, only developed an organized, competitive Whig party in 1835 and 1836 when it became apparent that Jackson, the southern President, had chosen Van Buren, a northerner, as his successor. Once party divisions had emerged, however, they stuck, and by 1840, for one of the very few times in American history, two truly intersectional parties, each united behind a single candidate, competed for the presidency.

The 1830s witnessed a vast expansion of political loyalties and awareness and the creation of party mechanisms to channel voter participation in politics. But the new mass sense of identification with politics had ominous implications for the sectional antagonisms which the party system sought to suppress. The historian of the Missouri Compromise has observed that "if there had been a civil war in 1819–1821 it would have been between the members of Congress, with the rest of the country looking on in amazement." This is only one example of the intellectual and political isolation of Washington from the general populace which James Young has described in *The Washington Community*. The mass, nonideological politics of the Jackson era created the desperately needed link between governors and governed. But this very link made possible the emergence of two kinds of sectional agitators: the abolitionists, who stood outside of politics and hoped to force public opinion—and through it, politicians—to confront the slavery issue, and political agitators, who used politics as a way of heightening sectional self-consciousness and antagonism in the populace at large.

Because of the rise of mass politics and the emergence of these sectional agitators, the 1830s was the decade in which long-standing, latent sectional divisions were suddenly activated, and previously unrelated patterns of derogatory sectional imagery began to emerge into full-blown sectional ideology. Many of the antislavery arguments which gained wide currency in the 1830s had roots stretching back into the eighteenth century. The idea that slavery degraded white labor and retarded economic development, for example, had been voiced by Benjamin Franklin. After 1800, the Federalists, increasingly localized in New England, had developed a fairly coherent critique, not only of the social and economic effects of slavery, but of what Harrison Gray Otis called the divergence of "manners, habits, customs, principles, and ways of thinking" which separated northerners and southerners. And, during the Missouri debates, almost every economic, political, and moral argument against slavery that would be used in the later sectional debate was voiced. In fact, one recurring argument was not picked up later—the warning of northern Congressmen that the South faced the danger of slave rebellion if steps were not taken toward abolition. (As far as I know, only Thaddeus Stevens of Republican spokesmen in the 1850s would explicitly use this line of argument.)

The similarity between Federalist attacks on the South and later abolitionist and Republican arguments, coupled with the fact that many abolitionists—including Garrison, Phillips, the Tappans, and others—came from Federalist backgrounds, has led James Banner to describe abolitionism as "the Massachusetts Federalist ideology come back to life." Yet there was a long road to be travelled from Harrison Gray Otis to William H. Seward, just as there was from Thomas Jefferson to George Fitzhugh. For one thing, the Federalist distrust of democracy, social competition, the Jeffersonian cry of "equal rights," their commitment to social inequality, hierarchy, tradition, and order prevented them from pushing their antislavery views to their logical conclusion. And New England Federalists were inhibited by the requirements of national party organization and competition from voicing antislavery views. In the 1790s, they maintained close ties with southern Federalists, and after 1800 hope of reviving their strength in the South never completely died. Only a party which embraced social mobility and competitive individualism, rejected the permanent subordination of any "rank" in society, and was unburdened by a southern wing could develop a fully coherent antislavery ideology.

An equally important reason why the Federalists did not develop a consistent sectional ideology was that the South in the early part of the nineteenth century shared many of the Federalists' reservations about slavery. The growth of an antislavery ideology, in other words, depended in large measure on the growth of proslavery thought, and, by the same token, it was the abolitionist assault which brought into being the coherent defense of slavery. The opening years of the 1830s, of course, were ones of crisis for the South. The emergence of militant abolitionism, Nat Turner's rebellion, the Virginia debates on slavery, and the nullification crisis suddenly presented assaults to the institution of slavery from within and outside the South. The reaction was the closing of southern society in defense of slavery, "the most thoroughgoing repression of free thought, free speech, and a free press ever witnessed in an American community." At the same time, southerners increasingly abandoned their previous, highly qualified defenses of slavery and embarked on the formulation of the proslavery argument. By 1837, as is well known, John C. Calhoun could thank the abolitionists on precisely this ground:

> This agitation has produced one happy effect at least; it has compelled us at the South to look into the nature and character of this great institution, and to correct many false impressions that even we had entertained in relation to it. Many in the South once believed that it was a moral and political evil; that folly and delusion are gone; we see it now in its true light, and regard it as the most safe and stable basis for free institutions in the world.

The South, of course, was hardly as united as Calhoun asserted. But the progressive rejection of the Jeffersonian tradition, the suppression of civil liberties, and the increasing stridency of the defense of slavery all pushed the South further and further out of the intersectional mainstream, setting it increasingly apart from the rest of the country. Coupled with the Gag Rule and the mobs which broke up abolitionist presses and meetings, the growth of proslavery thought was vital to a new antislavery formulation which emerged in the late 1830s and which had been absent from both the Federalist attacks on slavery and the Missouri debates—the idea of the slave power. The slave power replaced the three-fifths clause as the symbol of southern power, and it was a far more sophisticated and complex formulation. Abolitionists could argue that slavery was not only morally repugnant, it was incompatible with the basic democratic values and liberties of white Americans. As one abolitionist declared, "We commenced the present struggle to obtain the freedom of the slave; we are compelled to continue it to preserve our own." In other words, a process of ideological expansion had begun, fed in large measure by the sequence of response and counterresponse between the competing sectional outlooks. Once this process had begun, it had an internal dynamic which made it extremely difficult to stop. This was especially true because of the emergence of agitators whose avowed purpose was to sharpen sectional conflict, polarize public opinion, and develop sectional ideologies to their logical extremes.

As the 1840s opened, most political leaders still clung to the traditional basis of politics, but the sectional, ideological political agitators formed growing minorities in each section. In the South, there was a small group of outright secessionists and a larger group, led by Calhoun, who were firmly committed to the Union but who viewed sectional organization and self-defense, not the traditional reliance on intersectional political parties, as the surest means of protecting southern interest within the Union. In the North, a small radical group gathered in Congress around John Quincy Adams and Congressmen like Joshua Giddings, William Slade, and Seth Gates—men who represented areas of the most intense abolitionist agitation and whose presence confirmed Garrison's belief that, once public opinion was aroused on the slavery issue, politicians would have to follow step. These radicals were determined to force slavery into every Congressional debate. They were continually frustrated but never suppressed, and the reelection of Giddings in 1842 after his censure and resignation from the House proved that in some districts party discipline was no longer able to control the slavery issue.

The northern political agitators, both Congressmen and Liberty party leaders, also performed the function of developing and popularizing a political rhetoric, especially focused fear of the slave power, which could be seized upon by traditional politicians and large masses of voters if slavery ever entered the center of political conflict.

In the 1840s, this is precisely what happened. As one politician later recalled, "Slavery upon which by common consent no party issue had been made was then obtruded upon the field of party action." It is significant that John Tyler and John C. Calhoun, the two men most responsible for this intrusion, were political outsiders, men without places in the national party structure. Both of their careers were blocked by the major parties but might be advanced if tied to the slavery question in the form of Texas annexation. Once introduced into politics, slavery was there to stay. The Wilmot Proviso, introduced in 1846, had precisely the same effect as the proposal two decades earlier to restrict slavery in Missouri—it completely fractured the major parties along sectional lines. As in 1820, opposition to the expansion of slavery became the way in which a diverse group of northerners expressed their various resentments against a southern-dominated administration. And, as in 1821, a small group of northern Democrats eventually broke with their section, reaffirmed their primary loyalty to the party, and joined with the South to kill the proviso in 1847. In the same year, enough southerners rejected Calhoun's call for united sectional action to doom his personal and sectional ambitions.

But the slavery extension debates of the 1840s had far greater effects on the political system than the Missouri controversy had had. Within each party, they created a significant group of sectional politicians—men whose careers were linked to the slavery question and who would therefore resist its exclusion from future politics. And in the North, the 1840s witnessed the expansion of sectional political rhetoric—as more and more northerners became familiar with the "aggressions" of the slave power and the need to resist them. At the same time, as antislavery ideas expanded, unpopular and divisive elements were weeded out, especially the old alliance of antislavery with demands for the rights of free blacks. Opposition to slavery was already coming to focus on its lowest common denominators—free soil, opposition to the slave power, and union.

The political system reacted to the intrusion of the slavery question in the traditional ways. At first, it tried to suppress it. This is the meaning of the famous letters opposing the immediate annexation of Texas issued by Clay and Van Buren on the same spring day in 1844, probably after consultation on the subject. It was an agreement that slavery was too explosive a question for either party to try to take partisan advantage of it. The agreement, of course, was torpedoed by the defeat of Van Buren for the Democratic nomination, a defeat caused in part by the willingness of his Democratic opponents to use the Texas and slavery questions to discredit Van Buren—thereby violating the previously established rules of political conduct. In the North from 1844 onwards, both parties, particularly the Whigs, tried to defuse the slavery issue and minimize defection to the Liberty party by adopting antisouthern rhetoric. This tended to prevent defections to third parties, but it had the effect of nurturing and legitimating antisouthern sentiment within the ranks of the major parties themselves. After the 1848 election in which northern Whigs and Democrats vied for title of "free soil" to minimize the impact of the Free Soil party, William H. Seward commented, "Antislavery is at length a respectable element in politics."

Both parties also attempted to devise formulas for compromising the divisive issue. For the Whigs, it was "no territory"—an end to expansion would end the question of the spread of slavery. The Democratic answer, first announced by Vice-President Dallas in 1847 and picked up by Lewis Cass, was popular sovereignty or nonintervention:

giving to the people of each territory the right to decide on slavery. As
has often been pointed out, popular sovereignty was an exceedingly
vague and ambiguous doctrine. It was never precisely clear what the
power of a territorial legislature was to be or at what point the question
of slavery was to be decided. But politically such ambiguity was essential (and intentional) if popular sovereignty were to serve as a means
of settling the slavery issue on the traditional basis—by removing it
from national politics and transferring the battleground from Congress
to the territories. Popular sovereignty formed one basis of the compromise of 1850, the last attempt of the political system to expel the disease of sectional ideology by finally settling all the points at which
slavery and national politics intersected.

That compromise was possible in 1850 was testimony to the resiliency of the political system and the continuing ability of party loyalty
to compete with sectional commitments. But the very method of passage revealed how deeply sectional divisions were embedded in party
politics. Because only a small group of Congressmen—mostly north-
western Democrats and southern Whigs—were committed to compromise on every issue, the "omnibus" compromise measure could not
pass. The compromise had to be enacted serially with the small compromise bloc, led by Stephen A. Douglas of Illinois, aligned with first
one sectional bloc then the other, to pass the individual measures.

His role in the passage of the compromise announced the emergence of Douglas as the last of the great Unionists, compromising politicians, the heir of Clay, Webster, and other spokesmen for the center.
And his career, like Webster's, showed that it was no longer possible
to win the confidence of both sections with a combination of extreme
nationalism and the calculated suppression of the slavery issue in national politics. Like his predecessors, Douglas called for a policy of "entire silence on the slavery question," and throughout the 1850s, as
Robert Johannsen has written, his aim was to restore "order and stability to American politics through the agency of a national, conservative
Democratic party." Ultimately, Douglas failed—a traditional career for
the Union was simply not possible in the 1850s—but it is equally true
that in 1860 he was the only presidential candidate to draw significant
support in all parts of the country.

It is, of course, highly ironic that it was Douglas's attempt to extend the principle of popular sovereignty to territory already guaranteed to free labor by the Missouri Compromise which finally shattered
the second party system. We can date almost exactly the final collapse
of that system—February 15, 1854—the day a caucus of southern Whig
Congressmen and Senators decided to support Douglas's Nebraska bill,
despite the fact that they could have united with northern Whigs in
opposition both to the repeal of the Missouri Compromise and the revival of sectional agitation. But in spite of the sectionalization of poli-

tics which occurred after 1854, Douglas continued his attempt to maintain a national basis of party competition. In fact, from one angle of vision, whether politics was to be national or sectional was the basic issue of the Lincoln-Douglas debates of 1858. The Little Giant presented local autonomy—popular sovereignty for states and territories—as the only "national" solution to the slavery question, while Lincoln attempted to destroy this middle ground and force a single, sectional solution on the entire Union. There is a common critique of Douglas's politics, expressed perhaps most persuasively by Allan Nevins, which argues that, as a man with no moral feelings about slavery, Douglas was incapable of recognizing that this moral issue affected millions of northern voters. This, in my opinion, is a serious misunderstanding of Douglas's politics. What he insisted was not that there was no moral question involved in slavery but that it was not the function of the politician to deal in moral judgments. To Lincoln's prediction that the nation could not exist half slave and half free, Douglas replied that it had so existed for seventy years and could continue to do so if northerners stopped trying to impose their own brand of morality upon the South.

Douglas's insistence on the separation of politics and morality was expressed in his oft-quoted statement that—in his role as a politician—he did not care if the people of a territory voted slavery "up or down." As he explained in his Chicago speech of July 1858, just before the opening of the great debates:

> I deny the right of Congress to force a slave-holding state upon an unwilling people. I deny their right to force a free state upon an unwilling people. I deny their right to force a good thing upon a people who are unwilling to receive it. . . . It is no answer to this argument to say that slavery is an evil and hence should not be tolerated. You must allow the people to decide for themselves whether it is a good or an evil.

When Lincoln, therefore, said the real purpose of popular sovereignty was "to educate and mould public opinion, at least northern public opinion, to not care whether slavery is voted down or up," he was, of course, right. For Douglas recognized that moral categories, being essentially uncompromisable, are unassimilable in politics. The only solution to the slavery issue was local autonomy. Whatever a majority of a state or territory wished to do about slavery was right—or at least should not be tampered with by politicians from other areas. To this, Lincoln's only possible reply was the one formulated in the debates—the will of the majority must be tempered by considerations of morality. Slavery was not, he declared, an "*ordinary* matter of domestic concern in the states and territories." Because of its essential immorality, it tainted the entire nation, and its disposition in the territories, and eventually in the entire nation was a matter of national concern to be decided by a national, not a local, majority. As the debates continued, Lincoln increasingly moved to this moral level of the slavery argument: "Everything that emanates from [Douglas] or his co-adjutors, carefully excludes the thought that there is anything wrong with slavery. All their arguments, if you will consider them, will be seen to exclude the thought. . . . If you do admit that it is wrong, Judge Douglas can't logically say that he don't care whether a wrong is voted up or down."

In order to press home the moral argument, moreover, Lincoln had to insist throughout the debates on the basic humanity of the blacks; while Douglas, by the same token, logically had to define blacks as subhuman, or at least, as the Dred Scott decision has insisted, not part of the American "people" included in the Declaration of Independence and the Constitution. Douglas's view of the black, Lincoln declared, conveyed "no vivid impression that the Negro is a human, and consequently has no idea that there can be any moral question in legislating about him." Of course, the standard of morality which Lincoln felt the nation should adopt regarding slavery and the black was the sectional morality of the Republican party.

By 1860, Douglas's local majoritarianism was no more acceptable to southern political leaders than Lincoln's national and moral majoritarianism. The principle of state rights and minority self-determination had always been the first line of defense of slavery from northern interference, but southerners now coupled it with the demand that Congress intervene to establish and guarantee slavery in the territories. The Lecompton fight had clearly demonstrated that southerners would no longer be satisfied with what Douglas hoped the territories would become—free, Democratic states. And the refusal of the Douglas Democrats to accede to southern demands was the culmination of a long history of resentment on the part of northern Democrats, stretching back into the 1840s, at the impossible political dilemma of being caught between increasingly antisouthern constituency pressure and loyalty to an increasingly prosouthern national party. For their part, southern Democrats viewed their northern allies as too weak at home and too tainted with antisouthernism after the Lecompton battle to be relied on to protect southern interests any longer.

As for the Republicans, by the late 1850s they had succeeded in developing a coherent ideology which, despite internal ambiguities and contradictions, incorporated the fundamental values, hopes, and fears of a majority of northerners. As I have argued elsewhere, it rested on a commitment to the northern social order, founded on the dignity and opportunities of free labor, and to social mobility, enterprise, and "progress." It gloried in the same qualities of northern life—materialism, social fluidity, and the dominance of the self-made man—which twenty years earlier had been the source of widespread anxiety and fear in Jacksonian America. And it defined the South as a backward, stagnant, aristocratic society, totally alien in values and social order to the middle-class capitalism of the North.

Some elements of the Republican ideology had roots stretching back into the eighteenth century. Others, especially the Republican emphasis on the threat of the slave power, were relatively new. Northern politics and thought were permeated by the slave power idea in the 1850s. The effect can perhaps be gauged by a brief look at the career of the leading Republican spokesman of the 1850s, William H. Seward. As a political child of upstate New York's burned-over district and antimasonic crusade, Seward had long believed that the Whig party's main political liability was its image as the spokesman of the wealthy and aristocratic. Firmly committed to egalitarian democracy, Seward had attempted to reorient the New York State Whigs into a reformist, egalitarian party, friendly to immigrants and embracing political and economic democracy, but he was always defeated by the party's downstate conservative wing. In the 1840s, he became convinced that the only way for the party to counteract the Democrats' monopoly of the rhetoric of democracy and equality was for the Whigs to embrace antislavery as a party platform.

The slave power idea gave the Republicans the antiaristocratic appeal with which men like Seward had long wished to be associated politically. By fusing older antislavery arguments with the idea that slavery posed a threat to northern free labor and democratic values, it enabled the Republicans to tap the egalitarian outlook which lay at the heart of northern society. At the same time, it enabled Republicans to present antislavery as an essentially conservative reform, an attempt to reestablish the antislavery principles of the founding fathers and rescue the federal government from southern usurpation. And, of course, the slave power idea had a far greater appeal to northern self-interest than arguments based on the plight of black slaves in the South. As the black abolitionist Frederick Douglass noted, "The cry of Free Men was raised, not for the extension of liberty to the black man, but for the protection of liberty of the white."

By the late 1850s, it had become a standard part of Republican rhetoric to accuse the slave power of a long series of transgressions against northern rights and liberties and to predict that, unless halted by effective political action, the ultimate aim of the conspiracy—the complete subordination of the national government to slavery and the suppression of northern liberties—would be accomplished. Like other conspiracy theories, the slave power idea was a way of ordering and interpreting history, assigning clear causes to otherwise inexplicable events, from the Gag Rule to Bleeding Kansas and the Dred Scott decision. It also provided a convenient symbol through which a host of anxieties about the future could be expressed. At the same time, the notion of a black Republican conspiracy to overthrow slavery and southern society had taken hold in the South. These competing conspiratorial outlooks were reflections, not merely of sectional "paranoia," but of the fact that the nation was every day growing apart and into two societies whose ultimate interests were diametrically opposed. The South's fear of black Republicans, despite its exaggerated rhetoric, was based on the realistic assessment that at the heart of Republican aspirations for the nation's future was the restriction and eventual eradication of slavery. And the slave power expressed northerners' conviction, not only that slavery was incompatible with basic democratic values, but that to protect slavery, southerners were determined to control the federal government and use it to foster the expansion of slavery. In summary, the slave power idea was the ideological glue of the Republican party—it enabled them to elect in 1860 a man conservative enough to sweep to victory in every northern state, yet radical enough to trigger the secession crisis.

Did the election of Lincoln pose any real danger to the institution of slavery? In my view, it is only possible to argue that it did not if one takes a completely static—and therefore ahistorical—view of the slavery issue. The expansion of slavery was not simply an issue, it was a fact. By 1860, over half the slaves lived in areas outside the original slave states. At the same time, however, the South had become a permanent and shrinking minority within the nation. And in the majority section, antislavery sentiment had expanded at a phenomenal rate. Within one generation, it had moved from the commitment of a small minority of northerners to the motive force behind a victorious party. That sentiment now demanded the exclusion of slavery from the territories. Who could tell what its demands would be in ten or twenty years? The incoming President had often declared his commitment to the "ultimate extinction" of slavery. In Alton, Illinois, in the heart of the most proslavery area of the North, he had condemned Douglas because "he looks to no end of the institution of slavery." A Lincoln administration seemed likely to be only the beginning of a prolonged period of Republican hegemony. And the succession of generally weak, one-term presidents between 1836 and 1860 did not obscure the great expansion in the potential power of the presidency which had taken place during the administration of Andrew Jackson. Old Hickory had clearly shown that a strong-willed president, backed by a united political party, had tremendous power to shape the affairs of government and to transform into policy his version of majority will.

What was at stake in 1860, as in the entire sectional conflict, was the character of the nation's future. This was one reason Republicans had placed so much stress on the question of the expansion of slavery. Not only was this the most available issue concerning slavery constitutionally open to them, but it involved the nation's future in the most direct way. In the West, the future was *tabula rasa,* and the future course of western development would gravely affect the direction of the entire nation. Now that the territorial issue was settled by Lincoln's election, it seemed likely that the slavery controversy would be transferred back into the southern states themselves. Secessionists, as William Freehling has argued, feared that slavery was weak and vulnerable in the border states, even in Virginia. They feared Republican efforts to encourage the formation of Republican organizations in these areas and the renewal of the long-suppressed internal debate on slavery in the South itself. And, lurking behind these anxieties, may have been fear of antislavery debate reaching the slave quarters, of an undermining of the masters' authority, and, ultimately, of slave rebellion itself. The slaveholders knew, despite the great economic strength of King Cotton, that the existence of slavery as a local institution in a larger free economy demanded an intersectional community consensus, real or enforced. It was this consensus which Lincoln's election seemed to undermine, which is why the secession convention of South Carolina declared, "Experience has proved that slaveholding states cannot be safe in subjection to non-slaveholding states."

More than seventy years before the secession crisis, James Madison had laid down the principles by which a central government and individual and minority liberties could coexist in a large and heterogeneous Union. The very diversity of interests in the nation, he argued in *The Federalist* papers, was the security for the rights of minorities, for it ensured that no one interest would ever gain control of the government. In the 1830s, John C. Calhoun recognized the danger which abolitionism posed to the South—it threatened to rally the North in the way Madison had said would not happen—in terms of one commitment hostile to the interests of the minority South. Moreover, Calhoun recognized, when a majority interest is organized into an effective political party, it can seize control of all the branches of government, overturning the system of constitutional checks and balances which supposedly protected minority rights. Only the principle of the concurrent majority—a veto which each major interest could exercise over policies directly affecting it—could reestablish this constitutional balance.

At the outset of abolitionist crusade, Calhoun had been convinced that, while emancipation must be "resisted at all costs," the South should avoid hasty action until it was "certain that it is the real object, not by a few, but by a very large portion of the non-slaveholding states." By 1850, Calhoun was convinced that "Every portion of the North entertains views more or less hostile to slavery." And by 1860, the election returns demonstrated that this antislavery sentiment, contrary to Madison's expectations, had united in an interest capable of electing a president, despite the fact that it had not the slightest support from the sectional minority. The character of Lincoln's election, in other words, completely overturned the ground rules which were supposed to govern American politics. The South Carolina secession convention expressed secessionists' reaction when it declared that once the sectional Republican party, founded on hostility to southern values and interests, took over control of the federal government, "the guarantees of the Constitution will then no longer exist."

Thus the South came face to face with a conflict between its loyalty to the nation and loyalty to the South—that is, to slavery, which, more than anything else, made the South distinct. David Potter has pointed out that the principle of majority rule implies the existence of a coherent, closely recognizable body of which more than half may be legitimately considered as a majority of the whole. For the South to accept majority rule in 1860, in other words, would have been an affirmation of a common nationality with the North. Certainly, it is true that in terms of ethnicity, language, religion—many of the usual components of nationality—Americans, North and South, were still quite close. On the other hand, one important element, community of interest, was not present. And perhaps most important, the preceding decades had witnessed an escalation of distrust—an erosion of the reciprocal currents of good will so essential for national harmony. "We are not one people," declared the *New York Tribune* in 1855. "We are two peoples. We are a people for Freedom and a people for Slavery. Between the two, conflict is inevitable." We can paraphrase John Adams's famous comment on the American Revolution and apply it to the coming of the Civil War—the separation was complete, in the minds of the people, before the war began. In a sense, the Constitution and national political system had failed in the difficult task of creating a nation—only the Civil War itself would accomplish it.

☆ 11 ☆

The Reconstruction Era

CONSTRUCTIVE OR DESTRUCTIVE?

To students of American history the Civil War years stand in sharp contrast to those of the Reconstruction era. The war years represented a period of heroism and idealism; out of the travail of conflict there emerged a new American nationality that replaced the older sectional and state loyalties. Although the cost in lives and money was frightful, the divisions that had plagued Americans for over half a century were eliminated in the ordeal of fire. Henceforth America would stand as a united country, destined to take its rightful place as one of the leading nations in the world.

The Reconstruction era, on the other hand, conjures up a quite different picture. Just as the war years were dominated by heroism, the postwar period was characterized as being dominated by evil, power-seeking scoundrels intent upon pursuing their narrow self-interest regardless of the cost to either the South or the nation. The result was a tragedy for all Americans—Northerners, Southerners, whites, and blacks alike. Nothing short of a revolution, it seemed, could displace the forces of evil from power and restore the South and the nation to its rightful rulers.

Between 1890 and 1930 few historians would have disagreed with this contrast of the two periods. If anything, most scholars during these years characterized Reconstruction in even harsher terms. Led by Professor William A. Dunning of Columbia University—who literally founded the school of Reconstruction historiography that still bears his name—the historical profession set out to prove that the years following the Civil War were marked by tragedy and pathos because men of good will were momentarily thrust out of power by the forces of evil. This period, in the words of one historian, "were years of revolutionary turmoil. . . . The prevailing note was one of tragedy. . . . Never have American public men in responsible positions, directing the des-

415

tiny of the Nation, been so brutal, hypocritical, and corrupt. . . . The Southern people literally were put to the torture."[1]

Underlying the interpretation of the Dunning school were two important assumptions. The first was that the South should have been restored to the Union quickly and without being exposed to Northern vengeance. Most Southerners, it was argued, had accepted their military defeat gracefully and were prepared to pledge their good faith and loyalty to the Union. Second, responsibility for the freedmen should have been entrusted to white Southerners. Blacks, these historians believed, could never be integrated into American society on an equal plane with whites because of their former slave status and inferior racial characteristics.

Working within the framework of these two assumptions, historians in the Dunning school tradition proceeded to study Reconstruction in terms of a struggle between elements of good and evil. On one side stood the forces of good—Northern and Southern Democrats and Republicans of the Andrew Johnson variety. These men, recognizing the necessity for compassion and leniency, were willing to forget the agonies of war and to forgive the South. On the opposing side were the forces of evil—scalawags, carpetbaggers, and, above all, a group of radical and vindictive Republicans intent upon punishing the South by depriving the native aristocracy of their power and status, thereby ensuring the dominance of the Republican party in that section. Caught in the middle of this struggle were the helpless, impotent, and ignorant blacks, whose votes were sought for sinister purposes by Radical Republicans who had little or no real concern for the welfare of the freedman once he had left the ballot box.

The result of such a political alignment in the South, according to the Dunning school, was disastrous. The Radical carpetbag state governments that came into power proved to be totally incompetent— in part because they included illiterate blacks who were unprepared for the responsibilities of self-government. Still worse, these governments were extraordinarily expensive because they were corrupt. Most of them, indeed, left nothing but a legacy of huge debts. "Saddled with an irresponsible officialdom," one Dunning school historian concluded, "the South was now plunged into debauchery, corruption, and private plundering unbelievable—suggesting that government had been transformed into an engine of destruction."[2]

The decent whites in the South, the Dunning argument continued, united out of sheer desperation to force the carpetbaggers, scalawags,

---

[1] Claude G. Bowers, *The Tragic Era: The Revolution After Lincoln* (Cambridge, Mass., 1929), pp. v–vi.

[2] E. Merton Coulter, *The South During Reconstruction 1865–1877* (Baton Rouge, 1947), p. 148.

and blacks from power. In one state after another Radical rule was eventually overthrown and good government restored. By the time of the presidential campaign of 1876 only three states remained under Radical control. When the dispute over the contested election was resolved, Hayes withdrew the remaining federal troops from the South, and the three last Radical regimes fell from power. Thus the tragic era of Reconstruction came to an end.

For nearly three decades after the turn of the century the Dunning point of view was dominant among most American historians. Many monographs on the history of individual Southern states were published, but most of them simply filled in pertinent details and left the larger picture virtually unchanged. All of these studies, despite their individual differences, agreed that the Reconstruction period had been an abject and dismal failure. Not only had Reconstruction destroyed the two-party system in the South, it had left behind an enduring legacy of bitterness and hatred between the races.

As late as 1942 Albert B. Moore, in his presidential address at the Southern Historical Association, argued that Reconstruction had the effect of converting the South into a colonial appendage of the North. To put it another way, the Reconstruction period was simply one phase of the process whereby the North attempted to remake the South in its own image; it was an attempt by a victor to punish the vanquished. Rejecting completely the assertion that the North was lenient, Moore emphasized property confiscations, mental torture, and vindictive military rule. The political enfranchisement of blacks, which laid the basis for carpetbag government, was to Moore perhaps the most incredible event of an incredible era. The result was the continued exacerbation of Southern economic, political, and social problems. The South, he concluded, was still paying for the dark legacy of Reconstruction in the twentieth century.[3]

In the late 1920s, however, historians began to look at the events between 1865 and 1877 from a new and different perspective. These revisionists—a term that distinguishes them from followers of the Dunning school—were much less certain that Reconstruction was as bad as had been commonly supposed. Influenced by the Progressive school of American historiography—which emphasized underlying economic factors in historical development—the revisionists began to restudy the entire Reconstruction period. As a result they posed a sharp challenge to the Dunning school by changing the interpretive framework of the Reconstruction era.

Generally speaking the revisionists accepted most, if not all, of the findings of the Dunning school. The disagreement between the two

---

[3]Albert B. Moore, "One Hundred Years of Reconstruction in the South," *Journal of Southern History* 9 (May 1943):153–165.

groups, therefore, arose from their different starting assumptions and the consequent interpretation of data rather than over disputed empirical data as such. Unlike the Dunningites, the revisionists could not view events between 1865 and 1877 in terms of a morality play that depicted Reconstruction as a struggle between good and evil, white and black, and Democrats and Radical Republicans. Nor were the revisionists willing to accept the view that responsibility for the freedmen should have been entrusted to native white Southerners. Given these differences it was understandable that the revisionist interpretation should differ sharply from that of the Dunning school.

In 1939 Francis B. Simkins, a distinguished Southern historian who published with Robert Woody in 1932 one of the first revisionist studies, summed up some of the findings of the revisionist school. Pointing out that the overwhelming majority of Southerners lived quietly and peacefully during these years, he emphasized many of the constructive achievements of this era. Simkins, as a matter of fact, denied that the Radical program was radical within the accepted meaning of the word; indeed, the Radicals failed because they did not provide freedmen with a secure economic base. Past historians, he concluded, had given a distorted picture of Reconstruction because they had assumed that blacks were racially inferior. The result was a provincial approach to Reconstruction that was based on ignorance and priggishness. Only by abandoning their biases could historians contribute to a more accurate understanding of the past, thereby making possible rational discussion of one of the nations's most critical dilemmas.[4]

While the revisionists often disagreed as much among themselves as they did with the Dunning school, there were common areas of agreement that gave their writings a certain unity. Most revisionists viewed the problems of American society during these years in a broader context and concluded that they were national rather than sectional in scope. Corruption, to cite but one example, was not confined to the South. It was a national phenomenon in the postwar era and involved all sections, classes, and political parties alike. To single out the South in this regard was patently unfair and ahistorical.[5]

Revisionist historians attempted also to refute many of the familiar assertions of the Dunning school. In the first place, they denied that the Radical governments in the South were always dishonest, incompetent, and inefficient. On the contrary, they claimed, such governments accomplished much of enduring value. The new constitu-

---

[4]Francis B. Simkins, "New Viewpoints of Southern Reconstruction," *Journal of Southern History* 5 (February 1939):49–61.

[5]For a revisionist synthesis see J. G. Randall and David Donald, *The Civil War and Reconstruction* (2d ed., Boston, 1961). The first edition, written by Randall in 1937, was in the Dunning school tradition.

tions written during Reconstruction represented a vast improvement over the older ones and often survived the overthrow of the men who had written them. Radical governments brought about many long-needed social reforms, including state-supported school systems for both blacks and whites, a revision of the judicial system, and improvements in local administration. Above all, these governments operated—at least in theory—on the premise that all men, white and black alike, were entitled to equal political and civil liberties.

Second, the revisionists drew a sharply different portrait of blacks during Reconstruction. They denied that developments in the postwar South resulted from black participation in government or that the freedmen were illiterate, naive, and inexperienced. In no Southern state, they pointed out, did blacks control both houses of the legislature. Moreover, there were no black governors and only one black state supreme court justice. Only two blacks were elected to the United States Senate and fifteen to the House of Representatives. Such statistics hardly supported the charge that the supposed excesses of Reconstruction were due to political activities of black Americans.

Indeed, the revisionists maintained that blacks, as a group, were quite capable of understanding where their own interests lay without disregarding the legitimate interests of others. The freedmen were able to participate at least as intelligently as other groups in the American political process. As Vernon L. Wharton concluded in his pioneering revisionist study of the Negro in Mississippi after the Civil War, there was "little difference . . . in the administration of . . . counties [having blacks on boards of supervisors] and that of counties under Democratic control. . . . Altogether, as governments go, that supplied by the Negro and white Republicans in Mississippi between 1870 and 1876 was not a bad government. . . . With their white Republican colleagues, they gave to the state a government of greatly expanded functions at a cost that was low in comparison with that of almost any other state."[6]

If black Americans were not the dominant group in most Radical governments, where did these governments get their support? In attempting to answer this question revisionists again endeavored to refute the Dunning school contention that these governments were controlled by evil, power-hungry, profit-seeking carpetbaggers and renegade scalawags who used black votes to maintain themselves in power. The stereotype of the carpetbagger and scalawag, according to revisionists, was highly inaccurate and far too simplistic. Carpetbaggers, to take one group, migrated to the South for a variety of reasons—

---

[6]Vernon L. Wharton, *The Negro in Mississippi 1865–1890* (Chapel Hill, 1947), pp. 172 and 179–180. See also Willie Lee Rose, *Rehearsal for Reconstruction: The Port Royal Experiment* (New York, 1964) and Joel Williamson, *After Slavery: The Negro in South Carolina During Reconstruction 1861–1877* (Chapel Hill, 1965).

including the lure of wider and legitimate economic opportunities as well as a desire to serve the former slaves in some humanitarian capacity. The scalawags were an equally diverse group. Within their ranks one could find former Southern unionists and Whigs, lower-class whites who sought to use the Republican party as the vehicle for confiscating the property of the planter aristocrats, and businessmen attracted by the promise of industrialization. The Radical governments, then, had a wide base of indigenous support in most Southern states.[7]

Finally, the revisionists rejected the charge that the Radical governments were extraordinarily expensive and corrupt, or that they had saddled the South with a large public debt. It was true that state expenditures went up sharply after the war. This situation was due, however, to understandable circumstances and not to inefficiency or theft. As in most postwar periods, the partial destruction of certain cities and areas required an infusion of public funds. Deferring regular appropriations during the war years also meant that a backlog of legitimate projects had accumulated. Most important of all, the South for the first time had to provide certain public facilities and social services for its black citizens. Southern states and communities had to build schools and provide other facilities and services for blacks which did not exist before the 1860s and for which public funds had never been expended prior to this time. It is little wonder, then, that there was a rise in spending in the Reconstruction era.

In examining the financial structure of Southern governments between 1865 and 1877, the revisionists also found that the rise in state debts, in some instances, was more apparent than real. Grants to railroad promoters, which in certain states accounted for a large proportion of the increase in the debt, were secured by a mortgage on the railroad property. Thus the rise in the debt was backed by sound collateral. The amount of the debt chargeable to theft, the revisionists maintained, was negligible. Indeed, the restoration governments, which were dominated by supposedly honest Southerners, proved to be far more corrupt than those governments controlled by the Radicals.

Although revisionists agreed that the Dunning interpretation of Reconstruction was inadequate—if not misleading—they had considerable difficulty themselves in synthesizing their own findings. If there was one idea on which the revisionists were united it was their conviction that economic forces, which were related to the growth of an urban and industrialized nation, somehow played a major role during this period. Beneath the political and racial antagonisms of this era, some revisionists argued, lay opposing economic rivalries. Anxious to

---

[7]See Otto H. Olsen, "Reconsidering the Scalawags," *Civil War History* 12 (December 1966):304–320, and Allen W. Trelease, "Who Were the Scalawags?," *Journal of Southern History* 29(November 1963):445–468.

gain an advantage over their competitors, many business interests used politics as the vehicle to further their economic ambitions—especially since the South, like the North and West, was ardently courting businessmen. The result was that economic rivalries were translated into political struggles.[8]

Revisionists also emphasized the crucial issue of race. During Reconstruction many former Whigs joined the Republican party because of its probusiness economic policies. These well-to-do conservatives, at first, were willing to promise blacks civil and political rights in return for their support at the polls. Within the Democratic party, however, lower-class whites, fearful of possible encroachments by blacks upon their social status and economic position, raised the banner of race. Conservatives found their affiliation with the Republican party increasingly uncomfortable, and they slowly began to drift back into the Democratic party. The fact that both parties were under the control of conservatives made it easier for former Republicans to shift their political allegiance. One result of the political alignment was that it left Southern blacks politically isolated and without allies among the whites. When the move to eliminate them from political life in the South got started, blacks could find little support among Southern whites. This political move came at a time when Northerners were disillusioned by the failure of the Radicals to achieve many of their idealistic aims for the freedmen. Tired of conflict and turmoil, Northerners became reconciled to the idea of letting the South work out its own destiny—even if it meant sacrificing the black people. Northern businessmen likewise became convinced that only Southern conservatives could restore order and stability and thus create a favorable environment for investment.

The result was both a polarization of Southern politics along racial rather than economic lines and the emergence of the Democratic party as the white man's party. For whites of lower-class background, the primary goal was to maintain the South as a white man's country. Upper-class whites were also contented with the existing one-party political structure because they were permitted the dominant role in determining the future economic development of their section.

The end of Reconstruction, according to the revisionists, was closely related to the triumph of business values and industrial capitalism. When the contested presidential election of 1876 resulted in an apparent deadlock between Rutherford B. Hayes, the Republican candidate, and Samuel J. Tilden, his Democratic opponent, some prominent

---

[8]Recent historians have once again begun to study the importance of economic factors and rivalries in Reconstruction. See Mark W. Summers, *Railroads, Reconstruction, and the Gospel of Prosperity: Aid Under the Radical Republicans, 1867–77* (Princeton, 1984), and Terry L. Seip, *The South Returns to Congress: Men, Economic Measures, and International Relationships* (Baton Rouge, 1983).

Republicans saw an opportunity to rebuild their party in the South upon a new basis. Instead of basing their party upon propertyless, former slaves, they hoped to attract well-to-do former Whigs who had been forced into the Democratic party as a result of events during the Reconstruction. To accomplish this goal a group of powerful Republican leaders began to work secretly to bring about a political realignment. If Southern Democratic congressmen would not stand in the way of Hayes's election and also provide enough votes to permit the Republicans to organize the House of Representatives, these leaders were willing to promise the South federal subsidies—primarily for railroads—and also to name a Southerner as postmaster general.

The Compromise of 1877, as this political deal was called, was not fully carried out, but its larger implications survived unscathed. As C. Vann Woodward, the revisionist historian who propounded the thesis of such a political bargain, concluded, the compromise "did not restore the old order in the South, nor did it restore the South to parity with other sections. It did assure the dominant whites political autonomy and nonintervention in matters of race policy and promised them a share in the blessings of the new economic order. In return the South became, in effect, a satellite of the dominant region. So long as the Conservative Redeemers held control they scotched any tendency of the South to combine forces with the internal enemies of the new economy—laborites, Western agrarians, reformers. Under the regime of the Redeemers the South became a bulwark instead of a menace to the new order."[9]

After the early 1950s a new school of Reconstruction historiography called "the neorevisionists" emerged. These historians emphasized the moral rather than the economic basis of Reconstruction. The differences between the revisionists and neorevisionists were often minimal since the latter frequently relied upon the findings of the former to reach their conclusions, and it is difficult, if not impossible, to categorize certain historians as belonging to one group or another. Generally speaking, while the neorevisionists accepted many findings of the revisionists, they rejected the idea of interpreting Reconstruction in strictly economic terms. The Republican party, the neorevisionists maintained, was not united on a probusiness economic program; it included individuals and groups holding quite different social and economic views.[10]

In interpreting Reconstruction the neorevisionists stressed the

---

[9]C. Vann Woodward, *Reunion and Reaction: The Compromise of 1877 and the End of Reconstruction* (Boston, 1951), p. 246.

[10]Robert Sharkey, *Money, Class, and Party: An Economic Study of the Civil War and Reconstruction* (Baltimore, 1959), and Irwin Ungar, *The Greenback Era: A Social and Political History of American Finance, 1865–1879* (Princeton, 1964).

critical factor of race as a moral issue. One of the unresolved dilemmas after the Civil War, they claimed, was the exact role that blacks were to play in American society. Within the Republican party a number of factions each offered their own solution to this question. Andrew Johnson, who had been nominated as Lincoln's running mate in 1864 on a Union party ticket despite his Democratic party affiliations, spoke for one segment of the party. To Johnson blacks were incapable of self-government. Consequently he favored the state governments in the South that came back into the Union shortly after the end of the war under his own plan of reconstruction and went along with the Black Codes that denied black Americans many of their civil rights.

Although Johnson was president as well as titular head of the Republican party there was a great deal of opposition to his policies by a group known as the Radicals. Who were the Radical Republicans and what did they stand for? To the Dunning school the Radicals were a group of vindictive politicians who were utterly amoral in their quest for power; they were merely interested in the black man for his vote. To revisionists the Radicals represented, at least in part, the interests of the industrial Northeast—men who wanted to use black votes to prevent the formation of a coalition of Western and Southern agrarian interests against the industrial capitalism of the Northeast.[11]

To the neorevisionists, on the other hand, the Radicals were a much more complex group. Many of the Radicals, they claimed, joined the Republican party in the 1850s for moral and idealistic reasons— their antislavery zeal—rather than for economic motives. These men, seeking to eradicate all vestiges of slavery, were consistent in their demands before and after the war that blacks be given the same rights as white Americans. Their beliefs, of course, brought them to a face-to-face confrontation with President Johnson in the postwar period. In the ensuing struggle the president, because of his political ineptness, soon found himself isolated. Taking advantage of the situation the Radicals first won the support of conservative Republicans and then set out to remake Southern society by transferring political power from the planter class to the freedmen. The program of the Radicals, therefore, was motivated in large measure by idealism and a sincere humanitarian concern.[12]

In 1965 Kenneth M. Stampp published an important synthesis that emphasized the moral dimension of the Reconstruction years. Stampp rejected the traditional stereotype of the average Radical as a figure

---

[11]This point of view was best expressed by Howard K. Beale, one of the fathers of the revisionist school, in *The Critical Year: A Study of Andrew Johnson and Reconstruction* (New York, 1930).

[12]See James H. McPherson, *The Struggle for Equality: Abolitionists and the Negro in the Civil War and Reconstruction* (Princeton, 1964), and Hans L. Trefousse, *The Radical Republicans: Lincoln's Vanguard for Social Justice* (New York, 1969).

motivated by vindictive considerations. He argued that the issues of the 1860s were not artificial ones as the Dunning school had claimed. The central question of the postwar period was the place of the freedmen in American society. President Johnson and his followers believed in the innate racial inferiority of blacks; therefore they rejected any program based upon egalitarian assumptions. The Radicals, on the other hand, took seriously the ideals of equality, natural rights, and democracy. Indeed, most of these men had been closely associated with the antebellum abolitionist crusade. Stampp did not deny that the Radicals had other motives as well, for he admitted that they saw black Americans as valuable additions to the Republican party. But most politicians, he insisted, identify the welfare of the nation with the welfare of their party. To argue that the Radicals had invidious and selfish motives, Stampp concluded, does them a severe injustice and results in a distorted picture of the Reconstruction era.

The Radicals, according to the neorevisionists, ultimately failed in their objectives. Most Americans, harboring conscious and unconscious racial antipathies, were not willing to accept blacks as equals. By the 1870s the North was prepared to abandon blacks to the white South for three reasons: a wish to return to the amicable prewar relations between the sections; a desire to promote industrial investment in the South; and a growing conviction that the cause of black Americans was no longer worth further strife. The tragedy of Reconstruction, the neorevisionists maintained, was not that it occurred, but that it had ended short of achieving the major goal sought by the Radicals.

The struggle over Reconstruction, nevertheless, had not been in vain. In addition to the many achievements of the Radical governments the Radicals had succeeded in securing the adoption of the Fourteenth and Fifteenth amendments. These amendments, in Stampp's words, "which could have been adopted only under the conditions of radical reconstruction, make the blunders of that era, tragic though they were, dwindle into insignificance. For if it was worth four years of civil war to save the Union, it was worth a few years of radical reconstruction to give the American Negro the ultimate promise of equal civil and political rights."[13]

During and after the 1970s neorevisionist scholarship began to take a more pessimistic turn even while interest in Reconstruction remained strong. The pervasiveness of inequality and racial friction during the second half of the twentieth century seemed to highlight the failure of post–Civil War Americans to ensure that blacks would be integrated into the social and political framework of the Union. Yet neorevisionist scholars continued to debate the same issues and problems as their predecessors. To what degree were Americans committed

---

[13]Kenneth M. Stampp, *The Era of Reconstruction* (New York, 1965), p. 215.

to an equal-rights ideology? Why were black Americans left in such a vulnerable position? What was the nature of such political events as the impeachment of Andrew Johnson? Why did Reconstruction come to an end far short of achieving its goals?[14]

To these and other questions neorevisionist historians gave varied answers that demonstrated that few differences had been conclusively resolved. In his study of the Ku Klux Klan, Allen W. Trelease argued that Radical Reconstruction failed because the seeds of biracial democracy fell on barren soil in the South, and the artificial nurture given it by the federal government was ephemeral and quickly discontinued. George C. Rable emphasized the counterrevolutionary guerilla warfare employed by white Southerners concerned with the destruction of the Republican party in the South. Michael Perman insisted that in the context of the political tensions that prevailed in the immediate postwar era, the very moderation that marked presidential and congressional Reconstruction was doomed to fail; only a coercive policy could have succeeded. In a subsequent work Perman emphasized the ways in which the center in both Republican and Democratic parties proved unable to hold together, thus permitting color to become the political line. And in a broad study of national politics William Gillette observed that Reconstruction was so easily reversed because it had always been "fragmentary and fragile."[15]

Nor has interest in the role of Andrew Johnson flagged. Michael Les Benedict, for example, insisted that Johnson was impeached because he seemed to be violating the principle of the separation of powers and because he failed to carry out some key provisions in legislation pertaining to Reconstruction. Hans Trefousse emphasized the degree to which Johnson thwarted radical policies and strengthened conservative forces, thereby facilitating the latter's eventual triumph in the 1870s. Of three other studies of Johnson, two (by Patrick W. Riddleberger and James E. Sefton) emphasized his commitment to sometimes incompatible principles which rendered him impotent, and one (by Albert Castel) accentuated the degree to which his inordinate ambition and desire for power helped to destroy him.[16]

---

[14]For a descriptive analysis of black Americans after slavery that does not deal with Reconstruction as a political event, see Leon F. Litwack's important *Been in the Storm So Long: The Aftermath of Slavery* (New York, 1979).

[15]Allen W. Trelease. *White Terror: The Ku Klux Klan Conspiracy and Southern Reconstruction* (New York, 1971); George C. Rable, *But There Was No Peace: The Role of Violence in the Politics of Reconstruction* (Athens, Ga., 1984); Michael Perman, *Reunion Without Compromise: The South and Reconstruction, 1865–1868* (Cambridge, 1973), and *The Road to Redemption: Southern Politics, 1869–1879* (Chapel Hill, 1984); William Gillette, *Retreat from Reconstruction 1869–1879* (Baton Rouge, 1979), p. 380.

[16]Michael Les Benedict, *The Impeachment and Trial of Andrew Johnson* (New York, 1973); Hans L. Trefousse, *Impeachment of a President: Andrew Johnson, the Blacks, and Reconstruction* (Knoxville, Tenn., 1975); Patrick W. Riddleberger, *1866: The Critical Year Revisited* (Carbondale, Ill., 1979); James E. Sefton, *Andrew Johnson*

In the first selection in this chapter, Robert J. Kaczorowski mirrors some of the themes that have resonated throughout recent Reconstruction historiography. The Thirteenth Amendment abolished slavery, and the Civil Rights Act of 1866 and Fourteenth Amendment conferred citizenship on and secured the civil rights of all Americans irrespective of race or background. Taken together, they represented a revolutionary change in American federalism, for citizenship was no longer within state jurisdiction. Consequently, Congress had authority to protect all citizens in their enjoyment of rights. The radical congressional Republican theory of constitutionalism, according to Kaczorowski, was altered during the 1870s by a Supreme Court bent on retaining a modified theory of state sovereignty, thus permitting partisans of states' rights in the South to reestablish their domination over former slaves.

At the same time that interest in national politics remained high, monographic studies dealing with individual states continued to appear. Here too the traditional dichotomy was evident; some emphasized the degree to which Reconstruction succeeded while others pointed to its failures.[17] In a somewhat novel study of black political leadership in South Carolina that utilized quantitative techniques, Thomas Holt offered a provocative thesis. Holt emphasized the continued persistence of class and caste but argued that the Afro-American population of South Carolina was not an unvariegated classless mass. Black leaders were divided among themselves; their divisions contributed to the fall of the Republican party in the state. Holt's profile of black leadership demonstrated that most owned property and were literate, and 10 percent were professionally or college trained.[18]

The demolition of the older Dunning school by revisionist and neorevisionist scholars did not lead immediately to any broad new consensus. Bernard Weisberger's vivid portrayal more than thirty years ago of "The Dark and Bloody Ground of Reconstruction Historiogra-

---

and the Uses of Constitutional Power (Boston 1980); Albert Castel, The Presidency of Andrew Johnson (Lawrence, Kansas, 1979). See also the following works: Michael Les Benedict's A Compromise of Principle: Congressional Republicans and Reconstruction, 1863–1869 (New York, 1974) and The Fruits of Victory: Alternatives in Restoring the Union, 1865–1877 (Philadelphia, 1975); Dan T. Carter, When the War Was Over: The Failure of Self-Reconstruction in the South, 1865–1867 (Baton Rouge, 1985); and Richard N. Current, Those Terrible Carpetbaggers: A Reinterpretation (New York, 1988).

[17]Jerrell H. Shofner, Nor Is It over Yet: Florida in the Era of Reconstruction, 1863–1877 (Gainesville, Fla., 1974); Joe Gray Taylor, Louisiana Reconstructed, 1863–1877 (Baton Rouge, 1974); William C. Harris, The Day of the Carpetbagger: Republican Reconstruction in Mississippi (Baton Rouge, 1979); Ted Tunnell, Crucible of Reconstruction: War, Radicalism and Race in Louisiana, 1862–1877 (Baton Rouge, 1984).

[18]Thomas Holt, Black over White: Negro Political Leadership in South Carolina during Reconstruction (Urbana, Ill., 1977).

phy" remained a somewhat accurate characterization.[19] The publication of Eric Foner's massive *Reconstruction: America's Unfinished Revolution, 1863–1877* in 1988 was a milestone; the work represented an effort to restore cohesion to a field long fragmented by disputatious conflict rather than consensus. Ironically, Foner's book was part of the New American Nation Series just as William A. Dunning's synthesis of Reconstruction in 1907 appeared in the original American Nation Series.

Although largely ignoring pre-revisionist historiography, Foner's work in many ways hearkened back to the work of W. E. B. Du Bois in the 1930s as well as claims in the 1980s that economics, not race, shaped black-white relations. A major black scholar and activist who turned to Marxism, Du Bois argued that Reconstruction involved an effort to unite Northern workers with Southern blacks. The attempt failed because Southern conservatives employed racial animosities to fragment working-class unity and thus maintain their own class hegemony.[20] Like Du Bois, Foner centered his analysis on class and specifically blacks. Initially Reconstruction was a radical movement that sought the destruction of the South's antebellum social structure. But by the 1870s fear of class conflict in the North led that section's industrial leaders to evince greater sympathy for the South. The result was a resurgence of white domination below the Mason-Dixon line. Centering his work around blacks, Foner emphasized that the free labor ideology that had brought the Republican party into existence was all but decimated by the 1870s, when fear of social conflict and concern with labor led to a virtual abandonment of the equal rights and free labor ideology. However measured, Foner concluded,

> *Reconstruction can only be judged a failure. . . . Events far beyond the control of Southern Republicans—the nature of the national credit and banking systems, the depression of the 1870s, the stagnation of world demand for cotton—severely limited the prospects for far-reaching economic change. The early rejection of federally sponsored land reform left in place a planter class far weaker and less affluent than before the war, but still able to bring its prestige and experience to bear against Reconstruction. Factionalism and corruption, although hardly confined to Southern Republicans, undermined their claim to legitimacy and made it difficult for them to respond effectively to attacks by resolute opponents. The failure to develop an effective long-term appeal to white voters made it increasingly difficult for Republicans to combat the racial politics of the Redeem-*

---

[19]Bernard A. Weisberger, "The Dark and Bloody Ground of Reconstruction Historiography," *Journal of Southern History* 25 (November 1959):427–447.

[20]W. E. B. Du Bois, *Black Reconstruction in America: An Essay Toward a History of the Part Which Black Folk Played in the Attempt to Reconstruct Democracy in America, 1860–1880* (New York, 1935).

ers. None of these factors, however, would have proved decisive with-
out the campaign of violence that turned the electoral tide in many
parts of the South, and the weakening of Northern resolve, itself a
consequence of social and political changes that undermined the free
labor and egalitarian precepts at the heart of Reconstruction policy.[21]

To a considerable extent the differences between the various schools of Reconstruction historiography grew out of the milieu in which each had grown to maturity. The Dunning point of view, for example, originated in the late nineteenth century and flowered in the early part of the twentieth. During these years the vast majority of white Americans assumed that blacks constituted an inferior race, one that was incapable of being fully assimilated into the mainstream. Most Southerners had come to this conclusion well before the Civil War; many Northerners arrived at the same conclusion after the alleged debacle of Reconstruction seemingly vindicated this belief. Racism in America was buttressed further by the claims of the biological and social sciences in the late nineteenth century. Influenced by evolutionary concepts of Darwinism, some scientists argued that blacks were the products of a unique evolutionary course that resulted in the creation of an inferior race. The racial prejudices and stereotypes of many Americans thus received what was believed to be scientific legitimation.

Given these beliefs it is not difficult to understand why the Dunning school interpretation gained widespread acceptance. The attempts by Republican Radicals to give equal rights to a supposedly inferior race did not appear to be sensible; state governments that included black officials and held power in part through black votes were bound to be inefficient, incompetent, and corrupt. Moreover, the Southern claim that responsibility for black people had to be entrusted to whites seemed entirely justifiable. The findings of the Dunning school that Reconstruction was a tragic blunder doomed to failure from the very beginning came as no surprise to early-twentieth-century Americans, most of whom were prepared to believe the worst about blacks.

The revisionist school, on the other hand, originated in a somewhat different climate of opinion. By the 1920s American historiography had come under the influence of the Progressive, or New History, school. Growing out of the dissatisfaction with the older scientific school of historians that emphasized the collection of impartial empirical data and eschewed "subjective" interpretations, this school borrowed heavily from the new social sciences. The New History sought to explain historical change by isolating underlying economic and so-

---

[21]Eric Foner, *Reconstruction: America's Unfinished Revolution, 1863–1877* (New York, 1988), p. 603.

cial forces that transformed institutions and structures. In place of tradition and stability it emphasized change and conflict. Liberal and
democratic in their orientation, Progressive historians attempted to
explain the present in terms of the dynamic and impersonal forces that
had transformed American society.

The revisionists, then, rejected the moralistic tone of the Dunning
school. They sought instead to identify the historical forces responsible for many of the developments following the Civil War. Economic
and social forces, they maintained, were basic in shaping this era. The
real conflict was not between North and South, white and black; it
was between industrial capitalism and agrarianism, with the former
ultimately emerging victorious. Thus the question of the status of
black people in American society was simply a facade for the more
basic conflicts that lay hidden beneath the surface. Reconstruction,
they concluded, was the first phase in the emergence of the United
States as a leading industrial and capitalist nation.

The neorevisionist school, although owing much to the revisionists, was influenced by the egalitarianism of the period following
World War II. Suggestive of changing attitudes toward blacks was the
publication in 1944 of the monumental study by Gunnar Myrdal and
his associates, *An American Dilemma: The Negro Problem and Modern Democracy*. Myrdal, a distinguished Swedish sociologist, was com-
missioned by the Carnegie Foundation in the late 1930s to undertake
a comprehensive study of black Americans. Although emphasizing
that a variety of complex factors were responsible for the depressed
condition of blacks, Myrdal argued that the problem was basically a
moral one. Americans, he wrote, adhered to a political creed that
stressed the equality of all human beings. This ideal, however, was
constantly confronted with the inescapable reality that in the United
States whites refused to accept blacks as their equals. Thus many
Americans were caught in a dilemma between theory and practice; the
result was inner moral conflict. Myrdal's work anticipated, in part, the
thinking behind the civil rights movement of the 1950s and 1960s.

In evaluating events between 1865 and 1877, neorevisionist historians began to shift the focus of their predecessors. The issue of equal
rights for blacks, neorevisionists maintained, was not a false one, even
though it was complicated by economic and other factors. In a real
sense the fundamental problem of Reconstruction was whether or not
white Americans were prepared to accept the freedmen as equal part-
ners. Even though the Radicals ultimately failed in achieving the egalitarian goals, they left an enduring legacy in the forms of the Fourteenth
and Fifteenth amendments. These amendments gave black people citizenship, promised them equal protection under the law, and gave them
the right to vote. That America did not honor these promises in the
decades after Reconstruction in no way detracted from the idealism of

those responsible for these amendments. Indeed, these amendments took on a new meaning as they gave legal sanction to civil rights after 1945.

The emphasis on the experiences of women and minorities as well as interest in non-Western societies have also led some American historians to express doubts about the uniqueness of Reconstruction. Indeed, the very concept of American uniqueness began to be called into question by a younger generation whose confidence in an unbounded future had been undermined by domestic and international problems that at times defied solutions. The result was a new look at an American past within a comparative framework. Slavery, as scholars conceded, was not unique to the United States; it existed in both the Eastern and Western hemispheres as late as the nineteenth century. Nowhere was its legitimacy universally accepted, and its abolition created residual problems everywhere the institution had existed. Similarly, the difficulties experienced by the United States after 1865 were not unique even if the outcomes were different. In the second selection in this chapter George M. Fredrickson compares Reconstruction with the experiences of Jamaica and South Africa. He concludes that white Southerners—for a number of reasons—were less able than Jamaicans or South Africans to make even a limited adjustment to the concept of equality. The result was the development of a racist order in the United States that was not exceeded until the formal adoption of apartheid in South Africa after 1948. Although comparative history has yet to find a broad following, it clearly has the ability to transform in fundamental ways the manner in which Americans perceive of themselves and their past.

Although it is possible to demonstrate that particular interpretations grew out of and reflected their own milieu, historians must still face the larger and more important problem of evaluating the accuracy or inaccuracy of each interpretation.[22] Was Reconstruction, as the Dunning school argued, a tragedy for all Americans? Were the revisionists correct in stressing the achievements as well as the partial failures of this period, and emphasizing fundamental economic factors? Were the neorevisionists justified in insisting that the major issue during Reconstruction was indeed moral in nature? Did the particular structural form of state and national politics preclude effective governmental action in dealing with the problems growing out of emancipation?

---

[22]For a discussion of schools of Reconstruction historiography see the following: Gerald N. Grob, "Reconstruction: An American Morality Play," *American History: Retrospect and Prospect*, George A. Billias and Gerald N. Grob, eds. (New York, 1971), pp. 191–231; Richard O. Curry, "The Civil War and Reconstruction, 1861–1877: A Critical Overview of Recent Trends and Interpretations," *Civil War History* 20 (September 1974):215–238; and Michael Les Benedict, "Equality and Expediency in the Reconstruction Era: A Review Essay," *ibid.* 23 (December 1977):322–335

Was the American experience dissimilar or similar to other nations who also experienced the transition from a slave to a free society?

To answer these questions historians must also deal with a number of subsidiary issues. Should Northerners have forgotten that it took four years of bloody and expensive conflict to keep America united, and welcomed the South back into the Union in 1865 with open arms? Or was it proper for Northern Republicans to lay down certain conditions to ensure that slavery, legal or implied, would never again exist within the United States? What should have been the proper policy for both the federal and state governments to follow with regard to black Americans, and how were the voices of blacks to be heard during policy formation and implementation? Were Southerners justified in their belief that blacks were incapable of caring for themselves and that their future should be left in the hands of whites? Or were the Radicals correct in insisting that blacks had to be given the same legal and political rights enjoyed by all Americans?

The answers to these and similar questions will, in large measure, shape the broader interpretive framework of the Reconstruction era. Although that period is more than a century from our own, some of the basic conflicts common to both remain unresolved and are as pressing as ever. Time and circumstance may have changed; new leaders may have emerged; yet the fundamental dilemma of what role black people should play in American civilization remains a controversial and crucial one.

Robert J. Kaczorowski

ROBERT J. KACZOROWSKI (1938–   ) *is professor of law at* Fordham University School of Law. He is the author of The Politics of Judicial Interpretation *(1985).*

In 1857, the highest court in the United States held that blacks in America possessed no rights, could never become citizens of the United States, and that Congress was powerless to abolish slavery. In the aftermath of these pronouncements, this country fought one of the bloodiest wars in its history. Fewer than ten years after the *Dred Scott* decision, however, Congress and the Northern states accomplished precisely what the Supreme Court declared could not be done, through constitutional amendments and a civil rights statute. The Thirteenth Amendment abolished slavery everywhere in the United States. The Civil Rights Act of 1866 and the Fourteenth Amendment conferred citizenship on and secured the civil rights of all qualified, natural-born, and naturalized Americans, including former slaves and free blacks. The statute declared illegal infringements of certain civil rights made under the pretext of law or custom and authorized the removal of civil and criminal cases from the state to the federal courts whenever Americans were unable to enforce their rights in the state systems of justice. The Fourteenth Amendment also expressly prohibited the states from infringing the rights that Americans enjoyed as citizens of the United States and their rights to due process and equal protection of the law.
. . .

Congressional Republicans believed that the Thirteenth and Fourteenth Amendments and the Civil Rights Act of 1866 represented a revolutionary change in American constitutionalism. A change in federalism was a prerequisite for Congress to legislate for the protection of civil rights, in light of the nineteenth-century concept of federalism. If the status and fundamental rights of citizenship were the rights that individuals enjoyed as citizens of the states, Congress would not have had the authority to legislate for their protection. These fundamental rights would be within the exclusive jurisdiction of the states. The proposal by Congress of a constitutional amendment and a statute that

Robert J. Kaczorowski, "To Begin the Nation Anew: Congress, Citizenship, and Civil Rights after the Civil War," *American Historical Review*, 92 (February 1987):45–68. Reprinted with the permission of Robert J. Kaczorowski and the American Historical Association.

conferred on all Americans the precious status of citizen, enumerated some of the fundamental rights of citizenship, and extended to citizens federally enforceable guarantees for the protection of their civil rights was itself a revolutionary change in American federalism.

The radical change in American constitutionalism represented by the actions of Congress forced congressional Republicans to formulate a legal theory delegating to Congress the authority to secure the status and civil rights of Americans. Republicans explained that sovereignty resided in the national government and included the primary authority to determine the status and secure the rights of all Americans, white as well as black. They interpreted the Thirteenth Amendment as a constitutional guarantee of the status of Americans as free people and therefore as a delegation of authority to Congress to secure the fundamental rights of American citizens. Congressional Republicans reasoned that the amendment, in abolishing slavery, secured liberty and the rights of free people. They equated the status and rights of free people with the status and natural rights of citizens. Congressional Republicans understood the Thirteenth Amendment as a guarantee of the status and rights of citizenship. Applying a Hamiltonian, nationalistic interpretation of the Constitution, which attributed to Congress the authority to secure rights that are recognized or guaranteed by the Constitution, they concluded that the Thirteenth Amendment delegated to Congress the authority to prohibit slavery and, more important, the authority to secure inherent rights of all U.S. citizens against violation from any source in whatever manner Congress deemed appropriate. Thus, James F. Wilson, the representative from Iowa and the House floor manager of the Civil Rights Bill, introduced it with the explanation "that the possession of these rights by the citizen raises by necessary implication the power in Congress to protect them."

Republicans expressed in law their understanding of the scope of the Thirteenth Amendment when they enacted the Civil Rights Act of 1866 and the Fourteenth Amendment. Section 1 of the Civil Rights Act confers citizenship on all qualified American inhabitants and guarantees to all American citizens at least some of the rights the framers believed to be fundamental. They added a similar citizenship clause to the first section of the Fourteenth Amendment in the event that a subsequent Congress repealed the Civil Rights Act. The addition of this clause was also designed to prevent courts from declaring the statute unconstitutional by interpreting the Thirteenth Amendment as a mere abrogation of slavery. The citizenship clause of the Fourteenth Amendment makes explicit the constitutional recognition of the status and natural rights of citizens that its framers believed was implied in the Thirteenth Amendment. The ratification of the Fourteenth Amendment in 1868 thus completed the constitutional revolution regarding citizenship and civil rights. Congressional Republicans legislated to secure the civil rights of Americans in 1866 with the understanding that, with the Thirteenth and then the Fourteenth Amendment, the Constitution of the United States gave to all Americans the fundamental rights of citizenship and delegated to Congress the authority to protect citizens in their enjoyment of these rights.

A striking feature of the framers' intent in 1866 is their adoption of the most radical abolitionist theory of constitutionalism before the Civil War. By 1866, not only radicals but all moderate and even some conservative Republicans supported the efforts of Congress to secure civil rights. This shift reveals the extent to which the Civil War radicalized American politics. A political and constitutional position regarded as extreme and embraced by a very small minority before the Civil War had become mainstream Republicanism by 1866. The position that contemporaries regarded as radical in 1866 was securing the voting rights of blacks. As a matter of law and as a matter of political objectives, most contemporaries distinguished between civil rights and voting rights. The essential reason that Radical Republicans criticized the Fourteenth Amendment as too moderate was its failure to provide the same protection for voting rights as for civil rights.

The full reach of this revolution in constitutionalism could have changed the nature of American government from a federal republic with divided authority to a unitary state. Democratic opponents in Congress recognized the implications of the Republicans' theory of constitutionalism. Democrats objected to the proposed Fourteenth Amendment and Civil Rights Bill precisely because the constitutional theory that these measures encompassed could be used by Congress to destroy the civil and criminal authority of states over their citizens. If, as proponents of civil rights insisted, the Constitution guaranteed the fundamental rights of citizenship, Congress could exercise exclusive jurisdiction over civil rights. National law could supplant state law and the national government could absorb "all reserved state sovereignty and rights." Senator Garret Davis, Democrat from Kentucky, was one of several opponents who objected that "the principles involved in this bill, if they are legitimate and constitutional, would authorize Congress to pass civil and criminal codes for every State of the Union." These views were echoed by the House of Representatives, the White House, and the press.

These positions were a continuation of a constitutional battle that had raged for many years. Before the Civil War, the states had defined the status and secured the rights of the inhabitants of the United States. They performed these functions through state legal institutions, statutes, and courts. Some antebellum legal theorists argued, however, that the primary authority to perform these functions rested with the national government. The question of whether the national or state governments possessed ultimate authority to determine the status and enforce the rights of American inhabitants produced a national political and constitutional debate that centered on slavery and culminated in the South's secession in 1861. Secession, based on the constitutional theory of state sovereignty, made the legal questions of federalism and the locus of sovereignty central issues of the Civil War. The North responded with Abraham Lincoln's theory of national sovereignty, which denied the existence of any state's right to secede. The Emancipation Proclamation added the other central question, namely, which government possessed the primary constitutional authority to determine the status of American inhabitants.

The antebellum constitutional questions of the nature of American federalism, the locus of sovereignty, and the primary authority over the status of Americans were thus joined as political issues in the Civil War. The causes of Unionism, national sovereignty, and emancipation were victorious on the battlefield. Northern Republicans believed that the Civil War had resolved these political and constitutional questions. They soon discovered they were mistaken. Former Confederates tenaciously adhered to a philosophy of state sovereignty and refused to respect national authority. They defiantly resisted the emancipation guaranteed blacks by the Thirteenth Amendment. Southern white supremacists denied the freedmen's freedom by continuing to treat them as if they were slaves. White supremacists frequently met the attempts of freed blacks to assert their constitutionally guaranteed freedom with violent repression and economic intimidation. Moreover, they treated white Unionists and federal officers with disrespect, and resorted to economic intimidation and violence toward them as well.

Local officials in the South sanctioned and legitimized the defiant behavior of individuals and the racial and political customs of communities dominated by whites. In their constitutions and laws, Southern states refused to recognize that blacks were citizens possessing the natural rights of free people. State officers commonly failed or refused to protect the personal safety and property of blacks. They similarly refused to extend this protection to whites who were political allies or federal agents of blacks. When Southern blacks and politically unpopular whites were the victims of crimes, they could not get sheriffs to arrest, courts to try, or juries to convict the perpetrators. When charged with crimes or sued in the civil courts, blacks seldom received impartial justice. Indeed, white Unionists and freed blacks were prosecuted and sent to prison during peacetime for aiding the U.S. forces during the war. Southern hostility persuaded Northern Republicans and Southern Unionists that secessionist and Confederate sentiments had survived the Civil War. By the end of 1865, the constitutional and political process of restoring the Southern states to the Union had become the problem of preserving the principles for which the war had been fought. . . .

In 1866, the political context of civil rights deprivations compelled Congress to take effective measures to secure the fundamental rights of American citizens. Although Republicans shrank from providing freed blacks with economic independence through land redistribution, they did offer legal recognition of their liberty by securing important rights for their economic autonomy, such as the rights to enter into contracts and to buy and sell property. Congressional Republicans put aside racial prejudice that ordinarily would have precluded the legal enforcement of civil rights. The factors motivating them included the perceived need to preserve the objectives for which so many thousands gave their lives, the obligation to make effective the freedom they had promised to Southern blacks, a sense of elemental fairness and justice, as well as political self-interest. All these objectives were served by providing for the personal safety and security of Southern political allies—civilians of both races and federal officers. The political ideology of the Republican party further diminished the effects of Northern white racism on congressional Republicans. The central ideas of the party were the theory of natural rights, a classic liberalism, and a belief in equal opportunity. The combination served as a concept of American nationalism, distinguishing Republican notions of Unionism and American freedom from the Southern Democratic Conservative ideology of states' rights and slavery.

Northern Republicans decided that the preservation of American nationhood and freedom, as they understood them, required a strong central government to combat the danger posed by Southern recalcitrance. Republican William Lawrence of Ohio invoked political necessity when he warned the House that the congressional protection of civil rights was "essential to preserve national life, and the means of national existence." Withholding this protection would be tantamount to permitting the Southern states to divest citizens of their rights in the aftermath of Appomattox. The editor of the *Philadelphia American* echoed this theme in urging ratification of the Fourteenth Amendment: "If there be one lesson written in bloody letters by the [Civil] War, it is that the national citizenship must be paramount to that of the State. We propose to make it so . . . This citizenship provision is one of the most vital principles developed by the war. Without it we shall inevitably be exposed to new wars of Secession and States rights and nullification." The governor of Wisconsin, Lucius Fairchild, transmitted a copy of the proposed Fourteenth Amendment to the state legislature and urged ratification "because, in view of the terrible events of the past five years, we deem these guarantees necessary to the life of the nation, and we insist that those who saved that life have an undeniable right to demand full guarantees to its future preservation."

The conjunction of political ideology and political necessity resulted in congressional Republicans embracing a revolutionary theory of constitutionalism. To achieve political power in the South, to preserve their wartime objectives of Unionism and freedom for slaves, they insisted that sovereignty resided in the federal government and included primary authority to determine the status and secure the rights of all Americans, white and black. Republican supporters of the Reconstruction amendments and the civil rights statute acknowledged the revolutionary changes they had wrought in American federalism by delegating plenary authority over citizenship and civil rights to the national government. Before the Civil War, the states had exercised almost exclusive jurisdiction over fundamental rights. Under the Thirteenth and Fourteenth Amendments, as Republicans understood them, Congress could conceivably supplant the states in securing civil rights. By virtue of the Constitution's supremacy clause, Congress could exercise exclusive authority over citizenship and civil rights and thereby destroy state authority as a matter of constitutional law. Indeed, Congress exercised this authority when it determined by statute and constitutional amendment which people were citizens and what rights they were to enjoy. The states were deprived of their historical authority to make these decisions. Although congressional Republicans acknowledged the constitutional revolution in which they were engaged, they carefully avoided carrying this revolution to its ultimate conclusion of creating a unitary political structure. Republicans did not wish to supplant the states in providing a foundation for ordinary civil and criminal justice. On the contrary, they consciously preserved federalism by avoiding unnecessary intrusions on state authority over civil rights. Intentionally recognizing concurrent authority, Congress restricted its protection of fundamental rights to situations in which states and localities failed to protect them. . . .

The framers of the Civil Rights Act of 1866 and the Fourteenth Amendment did not intend federal jurisdiction over civil rights to be limited to racially discriminatory state action, as the Supreme Court later held in *Slaughterhouse* and *Cruikshank*. Federal agents who removed cases from local authorities under Section 3 assumed their powers were broad. Judge Adjutant General of the Army, Joseph Holt, for instance, interpreted the statute as authorization for removal in a case in which a former Freedman's Bureau agent claimed that he was being harrassed with a false prosecution in a Louisiana court because of the official assistance he had given to blacks. When the state judge, Edmund Abell, refused to allow the case to be removed to the federal district court, federal officers arrested him and charged him with viola-

ting the Civil Rights Act. In another case, the U.S. Circuit Court held
that white butchers in New Orleans had a claim against a slaughterhouse corporation chartered by the state, which the butchers alleged
had interfered with rights they enjoyed under the Civil Rights Act,
namely, the rights to labor, enter into contracts, and to equal benefit
of the law for protection of person and property. . . .

As the Republican framers understood them, the Thirteenth and
Fourteenth Amendments were constitutionally revolutionary. These
amendments delegated to Congress the authority to render a radical
change in the role of the national government in American life. Congress and the federal courts had not participated to any great extent
before 1860 in guaranteeing the fundamental and personal rights of
citizens. Republicans chose to protect these rights in 1866 by enacting
the Civil Rights Act, which conferred on the federal courts jurisdiction
over and responsibility for enforcing the personal rights of citizens directly when citizens could not do so in the traditional institutions,
namely, the state and local courts.

This new role for national institutions involved radical changes
in constitutional law. Fundamental rights were secured and enforced
through state law before the Civil War, but, afterwards, the civil rights
statutes made fundamental rights a matter of national jurisdiction.
The fundamental rights of citizens were now defined as rights pertaining to U.S. citizenship and, as such, were recognized by the Constitution and laws of the United States. Although the states were expected
to continue in their traditional function of securing civil rights, their
authority was to be shared with Congress and the federal courts. Because federal law was supreme, Congress and the federal courts could
supplant all state authority over personal rights. The framers' legal theory of citizenship and congressional authority over the rights of citizens held the potential of ending federalism and establishing a consolidated, unitary state. That the framers eschewed this extreme
institutional arrangement should not deflect attention from the other
ways in which civil rights amendments and laws of Reconstruction
represented, to the framers and federal legal officers, a revolutionary
constitutionalism and a new American federalism centered in national
authority and national institutions.

In the 1870s, the Supreme Court rejected the revolutionary congressional Republican theory of constitutionalism and read into the
Thirteenth and Fourteenth Amendments the theory of states' rights
promoted by congressional Conservative Democrats. The Court explicitly rejected the broader theory of a congressional civil rights enforcement authority, precisely because it was revolutionary. The Supreme
Court preserved a modified theory of state sovereignty, resurrected a
theory of American federalism based on states' rights, and recognized
primary authority over citizenship and civil rights as residing in the

states. Although American law denied the right of secession, it
adopted other important elements of the antebellum theory of constitutionalism. Congressional framers of the Fourteenth Amendment and
the Civil Rights Act of 1866 may have thought they were reconstructing American government and basing it on a revolutionary constitutional foundation, but the Supreme Court decided against this revolutionary constitutionalism in a reactionary resurgence of states' rights
that resulted in the virtual reenslavement of Southern black Americans.

George M. Fredrickson

GEORGE M. FREDRICKSON (1934–   ) *is professor of history
at Stanford University. He is the author of* The Inner Civil War *(1965),*
The Black Image in the White Mind *(1971), and* White Supremacy: A
Comparative Study in American and South African History *(1981).*

Thirty years have passed since Frank Tannenbaum published the
little book that opened up the study of comparative slavery and race
relations in the Americas. He called it *Slave and Citizen* to show that
his subject was not merely patterns of servitude but also encompassed
what happened after emancipation. The extent to which freedmen
gained citizenship rights or were otherwise incorporated into the societies in which they found themselves was, if anything, more important
to him than how they had fared under slavery. But subsequent historians, who either built on Tannenbaum's work or reacted against it,
have generally been much more concerned with the slave than with
the citizen. Comparative slavery has become a flourishing enterprise,
but the postemancipation responses and adjustments of those who had
formerly been masters and slaves remain relatively undeveloped as
subjects for cross-cultural historical study. This narrowing of concern
may have promoted a clearer perception of slave systems, but it has
also limited our ability to understand the forces involved in the transformation from a racial order based on black slavery to a more ambiguous situation, where formal affirmations of freedom and equality

George M. Fredrickson, "After Emancipation: A Comparative Study of White Responses
to the New Order of Race Relations in the American South, Jamaica & the Cape Colony
of South Africa," in *What Was Freedom's Price?* David G. Sansing, ed. (Jackson, Miss.,
1978), pp. 71–92. Reprinted with permission of the University Press of Mississippi.

clashed with the desire of many whites to institute new forms of racial oppression.

If Tannenbaum's successors have neglected to pursue his interest in the aftermath of slavery, they may have followed him too closely in restricting their comparisons to New World societies. There were in fact colonial slave regimes in the Eastern Hemisphere as well as the Western. Yet there has been no effort by historians to shed light on developments in the United States or other parts of the New World by considering what occurred in places like the Cape Colony of South Africa or the important sugar island of Mauritius in the Indian Ocean. Including new and hitherto unfamiliar cases in our comparative frame of reference might significantly aid our understanding of the processes involved in racial stratification.

One way to further the comparative study of postemancipation race relations, and at the same time enlarge the scope of our geographical awareness, would be to compare local white response to the freeing of slaves and the abolition of legal and political distinctions based on race or color in three areas where this dual process occurred in a relatively sudden, concentrated, and formalized fashion in the middle decades of the nineteenth century—the southern United States, the Cape Colony of South Africa, and Jamaica. In the slave societies of Latin America, the actual emancipation process was actually largely completed through manumission before the formal abolition of slavery; and the legalized racial distinctions of the colonial era, the system of *castas*, had already crumbled by the early nineteenth century under the weight of extensive miscegenation and the demands of prolonged independence struggles. But in the South, the Cape Colony, and Jamaica, whites had to rapidly adjust both to the abolition of slave systems that had shown few signs of eroding away and to the almost simultaneous implementation of a doctrine of legal and political equality that ran counter to local traditions. Hence, they faced a challenge that has no real analogue in the history of Iberian America. By limiting our attention to three multiracial societies of northwest European origin that experienced similar emancipations, we simplify the process of comparative analysis—and perhaps make it more meaningful—by avoiding the kind of gross differences not only in the character of emancipation, but also in cultural and religious traditions, that complicate all comparisons with Latin America. We thus narrow to more manageable size the number of factors that have to be taken into account, and we can devote greater attention to situational or environmental conditions, as opposed to the less tangible realm of inherited cultural values and attitudes.

Since it is an accepted rule of thumb for comparative study that the greater the similarities the more significant the differences, it is important at the outset to chart the common ground. In all three of our instances the new order was imposed from without on an unwilling or at least reluctant white population; the role played by the North in forcing emancipation and Reconstruction on the southern states in the 1860s was played by the British government in both Jamaica and South Africa during the 1830s. As we have seen, the new order involved not merely the abolition of slavery as a legal status but also efforts to place emancipated slaves and other free people of color on a footing of civil and political equality with whites. The South, the Cape, and Jamaica in fact constitute the three principal examples of former slave societies where freedmen and other people of color were, for a time, granted voting rights on the same basis as whites and, to varying degrees, actually exercised those rights within a framework of representative government. But such experiments in civil and political color blindness proved abortive; in all three cases substantive egalitarianism failed to take hold; and white supremacy, in one form or another, was maintained or reestablished.

The common elements in this pattern of development resulted mainly because all three areas were exposed to similar pressures from the metropole or dominant region. Jamaica and the Cape were of course British colonies, and the defeated South of the Reconstruction era was for a time politically subservient to the victorious North. External ideological currents, as well as the willingness of those in power to act on them, shaped the new order and at least temporarily limited local white initiatives to transform or overthrow it.

The most pervasive ideological development affecting these slave societies was the growth in Great Britain and the northern United States of a powerful commitment to free-labor capitalism. This orientation inevitably encouraged a harsh appraisal of local systems of involuntary labor that deviated from the recently sanctified norms of the mother country or dominant section. Once the labor systems of the South, the Cape, or Jamaica were popularly acknowledged in the metropole to be antithetical to capitalistic conceptions of economic progress, the stage was set for the fusion of economic liberalism with another strong intellectual tendency—the philanthropic impulse spawned by the evangelical revivals of the late eighteenth and early nineteenth centuries.

The humanitarian crusade, of which the antislavery movement became a central component, drew its emotional force from the spiritual egalitarianism of the revivals and from a new stress on active "benevolence" in the form of sympathetic action to uplift the downtrodden and convert the unconverted. But, as David Brion Davis suggests in his analysis of the early antislavery movement in England, the humanitarians were also exponents par excellence of emerging bourgeois values, and their ideological lenses tended to filter out the near-at-hand sufferings occasioned by capitalistic development, while clearly reflecting the agonies of slaves or aborigines farther from home. They therefore may have played a major part in giving legitimacy to a rising capitalistic order by contrasting its idealized image with a picture of slave or colonial society as the scene of unmitigated cruelty, barbarism, and immorality.

If Davis's interpretation is correct and if it can be extended both ahead in time and across the Atlantic, it would help explain the momentum that the antislavery movement was able to generate in the American North and the ease with which religious humanitarianism and capitalistic economic attitudes could come together to form an effective antislavery consensus. For northern Republicans of the 1850s, as for British colonial reformers and their evangelical supporters in the 1830s, the slaveholding section may have served as a powerfully evocative "contrast conception," indispensable for validating or legitimating a new order at home.

When the metropolitan free-labor ideology became politically or militarily overpowering, the dominant whites in our three societies were not only forced to abandon slavery but also to eliminate civil and political distinctions based on race or color that had been a by-product of racial servitude. The ultimate failure to achieve the egalitarian promise of the new order was due partly to a decline in the humanitarian component in the capitalistic ideology of the metropole. The waning of humanitarianism, beginning in England in the 1850s and 1860s and in the United States in the 1860s and 1870s, and its eventual replacement by a "tough-minded" racial and social Darwinism, involved a complex process of the popularization of pseudoscientific racism and hereditarianism, a hard-boiled new attitude toward lower-class suffering as the price of progress and the "survival of the fittest," and a widespread disenchantment with the trouble and expense of uplifting "lesser breeds." Whatever the cause of this shift in attitudes, it provided new opportunities to those whites in the South, Jamaica, and the Cape who wished to modify or subvert the new order. The external pressure was either eased or took a new form, and the persisting inequalities in local power and prestige were allowed to solidify, thus thwarting the revolutionary potential of the new order, and white supremacy achieved a new coherence and stability that would prove hardy and long lasting.

The reaction of local whites to the ideological and political pressures exerted by the metropole and its representatives was inspired in each case by the desire to keep as many of their old privileges as possible. Yet, the nature and outcome of the whites' struggle to guarantee their dominance by means other than slavery varied significantly in the three societies. If white supremacy was the common goal, the means used to achieve it and the forms through which white power operated were surprisingly diverse. In fact, a comparative sociologist searching for a typology for differentiating postemancipation white-supremist regimes might find here almost a full range of the possible modes of white domination.

In the American South, to make a long story short, white supremacists vigorously resisted the new order and employed a combination of terror and political mobilization to reestablish rule by a white elite in the 1870s. After about twenty years of maintaining racial subordination by informal pressures and comparatively subtle legal devices, the ruling group resorted in the 1890s and thereafter to legalized segregation and disfranchisement, partly because of new challenges to their hegemony by dissident whites, who were sometimes willing to make political alliances with blacks, and partly because of the unlikelihood of renewed federal intervention in behalf of black equality in the South. The result by 1910 was an elaborately formalized pattern of caste domination, operating under the constitutional cover of "separate but equal" and a qualified franchise, but which in fact assigned flagrantly unequal facilities to blacks and systematically manipulated the voting restrictions to eliminate the black electorate.

In Jamaica, the white colonists tried to adapt to the new order and turn it to their advantage. But their attempts to establish a plantocracy based on free labor and formal equality were seriously hampered by an economic and demographic decline, which had begun under slavery but was greatly exacerbated in the 1840s by the triumph of free trade in England. The fall in the number and prosperity of the white planters and the rise of independent black peasantry that seemed destined to take power help account for the panic of white Jamaica after a local black uprising in 1865. In the wake of the Morant Bay rebellion, the island's Assembly voted itself out of existence and accepted direct rule by the British crown. The period of crown colony administration beginning in 1866 gave to local whites insurance against black domination. The unique solution of the Jamaicans was to place their society under a form of imperial rule designed primarily for colonies composed overwhelmingly of "natives," who allegedly required indefinite guardianship and supervision. In effect they induced the British government—in an era when it was increasingly influenced by the view that Negroes were congenital savages to be ruled with an iron hand—to assume the "white man's burden," thereby relieving themselves of an apparently hopeless task.

The South African response was more complex and in fact involved two disparate solutions to the problem of maintaining white supremacy under the new order. The emancipation of slaves and the liberation of a substantial population of detribalized indigenes from a system of compulsory labor resembling serfdom impelled a portion of the white population to leave the colony and establish independent republics where racial inequality was constitutionally sanctioned and de facto African enslavement, under the guise of "apprenticeship," was widely practiced. A larger segment of the white population remained within the colony and pragmatically adjusted to the new order. In contrast to the Jamaicans, they succeeded in the decades after emancipation in gaining a *greater* measure of self-government; the Cape in fact gained a high degree of local autonomy about the time Jamaica was losing hers and did so without abandoning the principle of legal and political equality associated with emancipation. The franchise established in the Cape when representative government was granted in 1854 was formally color-blind, and no specifically racial distinctions were enacted into law by the new parliament. There were no legal sanctions for segregation or even against miscegenation. Yet a racial hierarchy clearly existed in society if not in law. Although some nonwhites voted, only whites were actually elected to parliament. Whites effectively controlled the economic system and commanded the labor of nonwhites on their own terms. If the South and the Boer republics instituted or reestablished a legalized racial caste system and if white Jamaica accepted imperial guardianship to ossify the status quo, the Cape colonists held the reins of racial power by an astute application of the conventional devices of class rule.

To get a better sense of these differing outcomes, it is useful to imagine a hypothetical traveler visiting the South, Jamaica, and the Cape around the turn of the century. In Dixie he would have seen Jim Crow in full flower with "separate and unequal" dominating all aspects of life. In Jamaica he would have found little overt public discrimination; he would have noticed, however, that almost all power was in the hands of an imperial bureaucracy that showed some paternalistic concern for black welfare but a much greater devotion to the interests of white capital. In Cape Town he would have encountered white politicians appealing to nonwhite voters and an atmosphere of racial fluidity and public mixing, which might have made him wonder if he had taken the wrong ship and ended up in Brazil by mistake. To begin to understand and explain these differing white reactions to the new order and the divergent modes of white supremacy that finally crystallized, we must look more closely first at the contrasting ecological and social settings in which these developments took place and then at differences in the political and ideological circumstances under which the new orders were instituted.

Jamaica was of course a prime example of a tropical exploitation colony. By the time the British took possession from the Spanish in 1655, the indigenous population of Arawak Indians had been exterminated, and slaves were imported from Africa to work on the sugar plantations that soon became the mainspring of the island's economy. Besides the relatively level plantation areas where most of the slaves were concentrated, Jamaica had an extensive and ruggedly mountainous backcountry, which served as a haven for maroons and runaways. By the end of the seventeenth century the local whites were greatly outnumbered by the imported slaves. Throughout the eighteenth century the ratio held firm at about ten to one, and by the time of emancipation in 1834 the gap had widened. Since most white settlers were unattached males, open concubinage with slave women became not only common but socially acceptable. Edward Long, the first historian of Jamaica, noted in the 1770s that "he who should presume to show any displeasure against such a thing as simple fornication would for his pains be accounted a simple blockhead; since not one in twenty can be persuaded that there is either sin or shame in cohabiting with a slave." These liaisons resulted in the growth of a substantial free-colored class, which by the time of emancipation probably outnumbered the whites by about two to one. This important mulatto group served as an intermediate caste during slavery and in general identified more closely with the whites than with the black slaves. During the emancipation era its spokesmen fought with some success for inclusion within the ruling class.

The shrinking population of whites still on the island at the time of abolition did not include the actual owners of most of the plantations. Philip Curtin has estimated that two-thirds or more of the estates under cultivation were owned by absentees residing in England. The influential local whites tended to be agents or managers supervising the plantations of absentees, although most of them owned some land of their own as well. Lower down the social scale were the non-elite whites, the majority of whom were directly dependent on the managerial plantocracy as subordinate supervisory personnel, as "sufficiency men" kept on the plantations mainly as a security measure under laws designed to decrease the likelihood of slave rebellions, and as "jobbers," the small slaveholders whose income was largely derived from hiring out their slaves as supplementary labor for the plantations during busy seasons.

The foremost concern of the local plantocracy was economic survival. Committed to plantation agriculture mainly as a means of gaining enough wealth to return to England as absentee proprietors, they tended to view emancipation in terms of how it affected their dreams of success. Jamaica had been declining economically since the Napoleonic wars, and abolition seemed likely to deliver the *coup de grâce* unless the former slaves could be induced to continue working on the plantations at low wages. Emancipation was therefore viewed primarily as a labor problem, and efforts to solve it were greatly hindered by the existence of an extensive backcountry unsuitable for sugar cultivation but well adapted to semisubsistence farming. Hence, many of the freedmen had the option of deserting the plantations and becoming peasant proprietors, a choice unavailable in most other plantation societies after emancipation.

Unlike Jamaica, the Cape was a colony of permanent settlement with a healthy temperate climate. An outpost of the Dutch East India Company until taken over by the British—temporarily from 1795 to 1803 and permanently in 1806—it was, comparatively speaking, an economic failure and would remain so until the discovery of diamonds and gold in southern Africa in the 1870s and 1880s. Because of the aridity of all but a small fraction of the territory acquired by the company before the 1830s, the agricultural potential was extremely limited. In contrast to Jamaica and the American South, the colony produced no important staples for export during the slave era, and consequently no real plantation system developed. Lack of economic opportunity kept the white population small and widely dispersed; in 1820 there were only forty thousand whites spread out over a vast territory. The whites at this time were outnumbered by the nonwhites in the colony but not by anything like the proportion that existed in Jamaica or that would exist later in South African history. The nonwhites within the borders of the colony comprised thirty thousand imported slaves and about the same number of so-called Hottentots, the largely detribalized descendants of the region's aborigines. Hence, the ratio of nonwhite to white was about one and a half to one, demographically similar to portions of the lower South in the same period. Later in the century the population ratio would change drastically after incorporation into the colony of extensive territories inhabited by Bantu-speaking Africans.

Slavery had been introduced by the Dutch East India Company in the seventeenth century because of a shortage of white labor and the alleged unsuitability of the nomadic Hottentots for sedentary occupations. A substantial proportion of the slaves were East Indians transported from the company's Asian possessions, but a majority seems to have been black Africans imported from Mozambique and Madagascar. Throughout the era of slavery most of them worked as laborers on the wine and grain farms of the limited fertile region of the western Cape or in urban occupations in Cape Town itself. By the middle decades of the eighteenth century, the indigenous Hottentots had been deprived of their cattle and grazing land and were being incorporated into the colonial economy as pastoral serfs, a development reflecting the growth of grazing as a frontier occupation and a basis for rapid white expansion into the semiarid regions to the east and north of the original settlement.

As in Jamaica, the shortage of white females led to extensive race mixture in the seventeenth and eighteenth centuries. But unlike Jamaica, concubinage was not the only acceptable form of interracial union. To a surprising extent Dutch males took women of color as legal spouses and succeeded in having their offspring accepted as part of the white burgher community. But those of mixed origin who were not the products of legal unions or who were simply too dark to be accepted by white society were relegated to a free-colored class, which became the object of increasing racial discrimination by the late eighteenth century. Eventually the free people of color, the emancipated slaves, and the surviving Hottentots would merge to form the Cape Coloreds. But the line between light coloreds and whites would remain vague and permeable. Until recently—some would say up to the present day—"passing for white" was a significant social and even demographic phenomenon in the western Cape.

At the time of emancipation the Bantu-speaking Africans, who now constitute the overwhelming majority of the South African population, were considered an independent people beyond the borders of the colony, although a series of frontier wars reflected a lack of agreement on where the borders actually were. Within the colony, therefore, the various colored groups, which were beginning to coalesce into a conglomerate population of multi-racial origins, did not constitute a relatively privileged intermediate category like the Jamaican mulattoes, but in fact formed the lowest class within the society. The difficulty posed for the settlers by the abolition of slavery and the emancipation of the Hottentots from restrictions on their economic freedom was largely a straightforward labor problem like Jamaica's, involving a similar search for devices short of slavery or serfdom to force the freedmen to return to their former occupations as agricultural laborers. But the freed people in the Cape lacked the Jamaican option of becoming independent peasants, because there was no land in the colony available for small-scale agriculture, and even the semiarid pastoral areas were divided up into large, white-owned holdings. The only alternatives to going back to work for white masters were to emigrate from the colony or take refuge on overcrowded mission stations. Despite the loud complaints of white farmers about "vagrancy," there appears to have been less economic disruption because of emancipation than in Jamaica.

One segment of the white population, however, felt particularly aggrieved by emancipation. The seminomadic frontier graziers or trekboers possessed relatively few slaves, but those they did own represented a major share of their limited wealth. Furthermore, they relied heavily on bonded Hottentots as herdsmen and servants. Accustomed to living in isolated frontier conditions that exposed them to the depredations of various indigenous groups, they had acquired a deserved reputation for treating their nonwhite dependents harshly. A long struggle with British humanitarian influences, experienced locally in the form of missionaries who complained to the authorities about how they

treated their slaves and servants, had intensified their racial consciousness. Fighting to preserve a white Christian identity in the midst of
black and brown heathens, whom they commonly described as *skep-
sels* (creatures) or progeny of Ham, they were enraged by any threat to
their somewhat precarious racial dominance. Such attitudes were why
many of them decided to join the Great Trek. It allowed them to opt
out of the new racial order by migrating into the interior, where they
were free to institutionalize their uncompromising racism.

The physical, economic, and social setting for emancipation and
its aftermath in the American South combined certain features reminiscent of the Jamaican or South African situations with some important elements of genuine uniqueness. The Old South had a plantation
economy, but most slaveholders were not planters. The forty-six thousand whites who had more than twenty slaves in 1860 may have resembled the plantocracy of Jamaica, but the 88 percent of all slaveholders owning less than twenty and the 72 percent owning less than ten
were comparable in their scale of operations with the general run of
masters of slaves and bonded servants in the Cape. In addition, 75 percent of the white population, mostly small farmers, owned no slaves at
all. Hence the South, like the Cape, had a substantial class of nonelite
slaveholders and was unique in having a white majority with no direct
economic connection with nonwhite servitude. The overall ratio of
white to black was also exceptional, since this is the only one of our
three cases in which whites actually outnumbered nonwhites—almost
two to one in all the slave states in 1860.

Like South Africa and unlike Jamaica, the colonial South had developed as an area of permanent white settlement where absenteeism
was rare. But like Jamaica and unlike South Africa, its economy from
the earliest times was dependent on raising staples for an external market. Its pattern of geographical expansion recalls the Cape rather than
insular Jamaica; but, if the extension of white settlement in South Africa led to the growth of a new economy based on livestock raising
rather than agriculture, the rise of the southwestern cotton kingdom
of the nineteenth century replicated the plantation-based economic
system that had arisen earlier on the eastern seaboard.

Race relations in the preemancipation era took on a character distinguishable from that of the other two societies. Except to a limited
and precarious extent in some parts of the lower South, no intermediate mulatto caste developed as in Jamaica. Cape society may also have
evolved toward a two-category system in the nineteenth century, but
in the South the line between the racial groups was more rigidly drawn
and less permeable. Although "passing" occurred, available evidence
suggests that it never did so on the scale and in the almost institutionalized way characteristic of the Cape Colony. Explaining adequately
these differences in fundamental race patterns would require another

essay as long as this one. But clearly important were the comparatively early balancing of the white sex ratio and the presence of a substantial class of nonelite whites, who could perform functions elsewhere assigned to mixed groups. Furthermore, these lower-class whites developed a caste pride that encouraged strict adherence to a "descent rule" under which whiteness was defined in terms of ancestry rather than appearance or culture.

As elsewhere, emancipation created a serious labor problem for former slaveholders. It was eventually resolved primarily through a system of share-cropping that evolved into a veiled form of peonage; for the Afro-American freedmen, like the emancipated coloreds of the Cape, were denied access to land of their own. Once Radical proposals for land confiscation had been rejected, blacks had no alternative but to enter into labor contracts with white planters under arrangements that became increasingly coercive as time went on. Not only was the good land in the plantation districts owned by whites, but the marginal land of the hill country and mountainous areas was, in contrast to Jamaica, already occupied by white farmers. Furthermore, blacks were sometimes inhibited from acquiring land by the terroristic tactics of white vigilante groups.

Yet the reaction of southern whites to the new racial order seems on the whole to have been less affected by purely economic concerns than that of the white Jamaicans or the majority of the Cape colonists. Emancipation presented itself to most southern whites preeminently as a racial or social challenge—a threat to the elaborate structure of caste privilege that had developed before the Civil War. In this they may have resembled the frontier Boers of South Africa, but unlike the dissident Afrikaners they had neither the inclination nor the opportunity to trek away. They had already tried their own mode of secession and had seen their efforts thwarted by the armies of Grant and Sherman.

The differing local settings in which white adaptation to the new order took place did not by itself predetermine the ultimate form of postemancipation race relations. It was rather the interplay of these local conditions with the political and ideological circumstances surrounding the attempted establishment of a new order by external authority that accounts for the divergent varieties of white supremacy that emerged.

In both Jamaica and the Cape Colony, the end of slavery came in the wake of a series of earlier measures to ameliorate slave conditions and improve the status of free people of color. In both areas virtual equality under the law for nonwhites who were not chattel slaves had been legislated before the abolition of slavery—in 1828 in the Cape and in 1830 in Jamaica. As colonial subjects of Great Britain, the local whites in both societies were vulnerable to pressure from the metropole in the 1820s and 1830s in a way that citizens of the "sovereign states" of the American South clearly were not in the 1850s. There was of course some resistance in both colonies to the campaign for humanitarian reform emanating from the Colonial Office and the philanthropic lobby in England. The Jamaican Assembly protested, delayed, and equivocated when called upon by the imperial government to improve the lot of slaves and free people of color. The most conspicuous local agents of British philanthropy, the Baptist missionaries led by the Reverend William Knibb, were threatened by mob violence and temporarily imprisoned after a slave rebellion in 1832; many of their chapels were subsequently burned by angry whites. In the Cape, where there were as yet no representative institutions to give vent to grievances of the white settlers, resistance took the form of petitions, protest meetings, and, at least once, mob action to enforce a boycott of new regulations requiring masters to make regular reports of the punishments given to their slaves. But in neither colony did abolition itself result in serious acts of resistance. Indeed, emancipation seems to have come as something of a relief after the difficulties associated with melioristic interference with the master-slave relationship. Furthermore, the British emancipators sweetened an otherwise bitter pill by providing partial compensation and a period of apprenticeship. Although the latter was designed to ease the transition to freedom, it in fact simply gave the masters four more years of slave labor.

The Great Trek can of course be seen as a dramatic act of resistance to the new order, but it was occasioned less by the abolition of slavery per se than by revulsion at the broader implications of the humanitarian policy. Also, the trekkers were a minority, even of the Dutch-speaking population, and were to some extent following a long-established pattern of frontier expansion, which was deflected in a new direction in the mid-1830s by the British government's refusal to conquer and displace the thickly settled African tribesmen on the eastern frontier.

A major postemancipation issue in both Jamaica and the Cape Colony, as in the United States, was the role of freedmen and other people of color in existing or proposed institutions of local self-government. In Jamaica, abolition automatically conferred the suffrage on former slaves who could meet a property qualification. But even the relatively low property requirement kept the mass of former slaves away from the polls, and a high qualification for office holding limited membership in the Assembly to the economic elite. But propertied mulattoes were routinely elected to the Assembly in the postemancipation years; by 1866 twelve of its forty-eight members were men of color. Between the 1830s and the 1850s there was in fact a strong tendency by whites to admit wealthy and prominent mulattoes into the ruling group; some even rose to positions of leadership and responsibility within the local establishment. But only rarely did colored politicians speak for the interests of the black freedmen. When a former slave was actually elected to the Assembly in 1846, he was refused admittance, and the intervention of the British government was required before he could be seated. By this time large numbers of black peasants had acquired enough property to qualify for the suffrage, but no one effectively mobilized them, and most chose not to register. Elite rule, which no longer meant strictly white rule, was therefore not seriously challenged in the 1840s and 1850s, although the growth of a potential black peasant electorate inspired further efforts to restrict the suffrage. But beginning in the middle fifties, a small group of dissidents emerged within the Assembly. Known to their enemies as the "demagogues," they began to articulate a rudimentary Jamaican nationalism premised on the inevitability of black and brown predominance. The rise of such views, accompanied by a continued decline in the white population and a rise in the black landowning peasantry, set the stage for the hysterical and brutal white response to the Morant Bay uprising of 1865 and the subsequent surrender of self-government.

In the Cape the nonwhite franchise had to await the granting of representative government. For a time the colonial authorities resisted settler demands for an elected assembly partly because of seemingly well-founded fears that the white minority would pass laws oppressing the nonwhite majority. When representative government was finally authorized in 1854, it was on the condition that the franchise be nonracial; the only real issue was whether the property qualification would be high or low. An unlikely coalition of English-speaking liberals, concerned with the protection of nonwhites, and of leading Afrikaners, who wished to include their poorer brethren within the franchise, carried the day for a low qualification.

The white colonists voluntarily accepted a political arrangement that gave former slaves and indigenes a potential voice in government not so much from egalitarian conviction as because they saw no threat to their social and political dominance from a color-blind franchise. By the 1850s, the colored classes of the colony were to a great extent locked once again into their traditional roles as farm laborers and servants. Since the relationship between white and nonwhite corresponded so closely to a European-type class division, the settlers found they could exercise effective control without recourse to legalized social discrimination. Technically color-blind master-servant laws giving the upper hand to employers could thus operate in a de facto racist fashion, and those farm laborers who could qualify to vote were under great pressure to support candidates favored by their masters. Furthermore, the franchise qualification was just high enough, given the substantial European population and the propertyless condition of most nonwhites, to ensure that whites remained a firm majority of the electorate.

By the 1880s, however, the low franchise came under increasing criticism, mainly from Afrikaners who had become aware that the British, a minority of the white settlers, were controlling most of the colored and African vote and using it to dominate the responsible parliamentary government that had existed since 1872. The growth of Afrikaner pressure for a larger share of political power coincided with an increase in the nonwhite vote resulting from the annexation of new African territories. Consequently there was a further restriction of the franchise in the late 1880s and early 1890s. But higher qualifications still left enough nonwhites on the rolls to give them a balance of power in several key districts. There were no more efforts to limit the franchise because, after a genuine two-party system developed in the 1890s, each party found that its hold on certain seats depended on African or Cape Colored votes. When the Cape participated in the deliberations that led to the founding of the Union of South Africa in 1910, its representatives defended almost to a man the principle of an impartial franchise with a property and literacy qualification against the northern Afrikaner or republican tradition of universal white manhood suffrage and nonwhite exclusion. The Cape's white leadership, both English and Afrikaner, had become convinced that their system of "equal rights for civilized men" constituted no threat to white supremacy but rather served as a useful "safety valve" for nonwhite discontent. The unsuccessful struggle to maintain and extend the "Cape liberal tradition" against the growing movement for political and social apartheid would constitute one of the major themes of twentieth-century South African history.

The political and ideological circumstances of emancipation and Reconstruction in the American South differed substantially from those in either the Cape or Jamaica. Of most obvious significance was that emancipation came suddenly and without compensation as the result of a bloody civil war, not gradually and with some adjustment to the desires and interests of local whites as in the British colonies. Furthermore, abolition was followed by the unique phenomenon of Radical Reconstruction involving the enfranchisement of the freedmen on the basis of universal manhood suffrage. Such an extension of full citizenship to a mass of propertyless and largely illiterate former slaves was, by nineteenth-century standards, an extraordinarily bold and radical innovation. Black suffrage, accompanied by the disfranchisement of leading Confederates, represented a far more serious threat to white supremacy than any actions of the British government in relation to its former slave colonies. In addition, the black vote made it possible for a northern-based political party—a party whose original rise to power had provoked southern secession and under whose auspices the military conquest of the Confederacy had been carried out—to achieve temporary dominance over the South. A use of the nonwhite vote for white partisan purposes had also occurred in the Cape, where the English-speaking minority created some ethnic hostility by relying on Cape Coloreds and Africans to outvote the Afrikaner majority. But the nonwhite vote was a relatively small addition to a substantial English settler electorate, not the major source of English political power as the blacks were for the Republicans in many parts of the Reconstruction South. The immense challenge to traditional white prerogatives and concepts of local self-determination that Radical Reconstruction, with all its limitations and deficiencies, actually represented can only be fully appreciated by comparison. From this perspective the currently fashionable assertion that Radical Reconstruction was "not radical enough" seems blatantly ahistorical, although it does call attention to the massive application of force that would have been required to complete the revolution that the Radicals initiated.

The intense and often violent white counterattack to Reconstruction stemmed not only from the magnitude of the provocation but also from the particularly strong racist tradition inherited from the antebellum period. The Herrenvolk ideology, as well as the racial fears that sustained it, had enabled the planter elite to line up most of the non-slaveholding whites behind a system of black servitude that offered them no economic benefits. As we have seen, nonelite whites in Jamaica tended to be directly involved in the plantation economy; those who were no longer needed after emancipation, such as sufficiency men and the slave-renting jobbers, presumably emigrated, helping to account for the continued decline in white population after 1831. In the Cape, on the other hand, those marginal whites most likely to view emancipation and equalization of legal status as a personal affront to their identity as white men tended to join the Great Trek, thereby ceasing to have a direct influence on colonial opinion. But, in the American South, the whites who derived their sense of status from racial pride rather than from real economic and social accomplishment, an element that had always been more significant here than elsewhere, remained in undiminished numbers and served as an apparently inexhaustible source of foot soldiers for collective action in behalf of white supremacy—whether in the form of antiblack rioting, Klan-type terrorism, open paramilitary activity to influence elections, lynching, or the forced removal of blacks from land they owned or rented. The continued need of the dominant group to use control, and accommodate a mass of less-privileged whites helped in complex ways to perpetuate and even strengthen the Herrenvolk tradition in the Reconstruction and post-Reconstruction years. It clearly inhibited the tendency to rely on class rather than race as the formal basis for social and political privilege, which was central to the white ideological response to the new order in both Jamaica and the Cape.

The differences found in 1900 by our mythical traveler would therefore have been primarily due to the contrasting ways in which the new orders had been originally imposed and to the differing ideologies and social situations influencing the local white response. Whether emancipation and formal equality had been perceived as legitimate or at least reconcilable with white attitude and interests, as generally the case in the British colonies, or as an intolerable imposition to be resisted at almost any cost, as in the South, had turned out to be of lasting significance. Because of peculiarities in the underlying demographic situation, the subjective legacy of the slave era, and the objective circumstances of emancipation and Reconstruction, white southerners had been less able than white Jamaicans or the majority of white settlers in the Cape to make even a limited and pro forma adjustment to color-blind principles of social and political organization. Thus the South went from being a testing ground for the most radical departure from white supremacy attempted anywhere in the nineteenth century to being a blatantly racist order that, in the comprehensiveness of its castelike distinctions, would not be exceeded until the triumph of rigorous apartheid in South Africa after 1948.

INDEX